Land of Amber Waters

The University of Minnesota Press gratefully acknowledges financial assistance provided for the publication of this book by Summit Brewing Company and August Schell Brewing Company.

Land of Amber Waters
The History of Brewing in Minnesota

Doug Hoverson

University of Minnesota Press

Minneapolis · London

Unless otherwise credited, all contemporary photography in this book, including objects from collections, is by Robert Fogt. The map on page 201 is by Parrot Graphics. Book design and production by Mighty Media, Inc.

Published by the University of Minnesota Press
111 Third Avenue South, Suite 290
Minneapolis, MN 55401-2520
http://www.upress.umn.edu

Library of Congress Cataloging-in-Publication Data

Hoverson, Doug, 1964–
    Land of amber waters : the history of brewing in Minnesota / Doug Hoverson.
       p.   cm.
    Includes bibliographical references and index.
    ISBN 978-0-8166-5273-0
    ISBN-10 0-8166-5273-2
    1. Brewing—Minnesota—History. 2. Brewing industry—Minnesota—History. I. Title.
    TP573.U5H68 2007
    663'.4209776—dc22

                                                          2006101172

Printed in China on acid-free paper

The University of Minnesota is an equal-opportunity educator and employer.

12 11 10 09 08 07   10 9 8 7 6 5 4 3 2 1

Contents

Preface   vii

Acknowledgments   xiii

From Barley to Bar Stool: The Art and Science of Brewing   1

Measuring Beer   5

1. **Pioneer Brewing**   13

Becoming a Brewer   26

2. **Fewer Ales, More Rails: Brewing Fills the State**   31

3. **Patronize Home Industry: The Glory Days of the Small-Town Brewer**   45

Collecting Breweriana   50

4. **Craft Becomes Industry**   65

Brewery Architecture   90

5. **From Temperance to Prohibition**   97

Malt Tonic   111

6. **New Jobs, New Containers, New Rules: Minnesota Beer Returns**   123

Brewery Jobs in the 1930s   132

7. **Sky Blue Waters, Bland Yellow Beer**   147

Brewery Advertising   153

"From the land of sky blue waters . . . wah-a-ters"   162

8. **The Waters Turn Dark Amber**   171

Brewery Preservation   180

Minnesota Breweries: From the Territorial Era to the Twenty-first Century   195

Minnesota Brewpubs: Pairing Beer and Food   311

Notes   317

Index   323

Preface

To a child growing up in Minnesota in the late 1960s and early 1970s, the beers of the state were part of the wallpaper of life. Their advertisements were placed prominently in the game programs and the home arenas of the Minnesota North Stars, Twins, and Vikings. The shouts of the vendors offering "Cold beer here! Schmidt beer here!" (or Hamm's or Grain Belt) built rhythm into the names. The advertising themes fostered regional pride: Hamm's was "from the land of sky blue waters," and Schmidt was "the brew that grew with the great Northwest." Grain Belt didn't need a slogan for regional identification since its name announced its Midwestern heritage. The breweries' point-of-sale merchandise and tap handles repeated the simple yet effective logos over and over, as did the beer cans left in parks and alongside roads in the days when environmental consciousness was just developing. Many youthful beer can collectors of my acquaintance were introduced to the hobby by attempting to get all the different scenes available in the Schmidt scenic, or "sportsman," cans. But little of this made any difference in what type of beer came home. In our household, beer was like bread: my dad bought whatever was on sale. The idea that the beer of the house would be something other than a local beer was inconceivable.

The only inkling I had that there was any variety to beer came at Christmas every year, when my uncle Jake brought my dad a case or two of Molson Export as a present. The stubby bottles were different (my dad usually bought cans), and the reverence with which the Export was consumed suggested that this beer might be different. Sure, my friend Jeff had several thousand beer cans, but the contents were irrelevant and the locations of the breweries never entered my mind.

The light finally dawned in college, when legality was no longer a factor and I found myself among companions who had traveled widely and knew of other beers. It was while I was a member of the University of Michigan Men's Glee Club that I was introduced to such exotic products as Old Style Dark, Stroh's Bock, and Beamish Irish Stout. The Village Corner had coolers full of exotic beer, including a few from small Michigan breweries, such as a porter from the Real Ale Company in Chelsea, Michigan, and Kalamazoo Stout (the latter from Larry Bell's Kalama-

Alexandria Brewing Co.'s Gopher Beer was sold in the mid-1930s. The University of Minnesota football team was domi-nant then, perhaps evoking more positive associations with a beer called Gopher. The link between beer and local culture enlivens the study of brewery history. FROM THE COLLECTION OF KEN MALZ.

zoo Brewing, which is flourishing at this writing as Bell's Brewery, Inc.). On a tour of the West Coast, my host in Seattle insisted that I try his favorite local beer, Rainier Ale. From that point on, my new motto was "Always try the local." Instead of returning from a trip with some empty cans in the trunk because I was trying to be like Jeff, now I filled my luggage on the way home with full six-packs of Kessler's beer from Montana, Catamount from Vermont, or Weltenburger Kloster from Bavaria.

But back in Minnesota, was there a local worth trying? In the mid-1980s it seemed like there wasn't much other than the brands my dad drank, which had taken up valuable space in the refrigerator that I wanted for storing Dr. Pepper. When I could afford good beer, I usually bought imports. There were a lot of those on the shelf in the liquor store that I hadn't seen before. And during bock season we'd usually try the various available Wisconsin bocks: Leinie's, of course, Huber Bock, and, as a rare treat, Point Bock.

By about 1987, though, there were a few new six-packs on the shelves at Sur-dyk's that caught my attention. One was Ulmer Braun, which was brewed in New Ulm. I had vaguely heard of Schell's brewery in New Ulm, but no one I knew ever drank Schell's—not because it was bad beer, but because we didn't think there was anything that set it apart. For an inexpensive honeymoon in 1987, my wife and I went to New Ulm and visited the brewery. Schell's had just introduced its Pilsner and Weizen. We were given only tiny samples of those after the tour, but they were good enough to encourage me to buy some when we got home. I have vague memories of going into Schell's gift shop and museum and seeing a map with pins stuck in it showing which cities in Minnesota used to have breweries. It didn't interest me much at the time. Little did I know that two decades later I would help update that map.

There were also some new brands that came in fully enclosed cardboard boxes. They looked kind of classy, so I tried Summit Great Northern Porter and James Page Private Stock. Other states had microbreweries, so I was glad to see Minnesota finally getting on board. In the early 1990s, Taps and Sherlock's Home opened, providing a glimpse of what the brewpub world could be. Now on those rare occasions when I went out with friends to have a beer, we went to Sherlock's almost exclusively. By this time I was a history teacher, specializing in American history and doing most of my serious research on Minnesota-related topics. But despite the fact that my motto in history was "Always study the local," it hadn't occurred to me yet to connect my two local interests. Sure, I learned there once was a brand of beer called Gluek's brewed in Minnesota, and while driving home from a friend's house on Marshall Avenue in Northeast Minneapolis I saw a huge building I'd never seen before, which turned out to be the Grain Belt brewery. But these findings sparked nothing other than a vague interest in what Gluek's Stite might have tasted like.

The pieces began to come together in the early 1990s, around the time my mom got me a James Page homebrewing kit for my birthday. It did not inspire historical research, but it got me more interested in the brewing process. More important was the summer class I was taking at the Minnesota Historical Society on Minnesota railroad history. While doing the research for our team project, I came across an ad in an 1882 Moorhead newspaper for John Erickson's Brewery. At first I was more interested in the fact that they had a telephone in a brewery in Moorhead only six years after it was invented, but eventually I became intrigued by the idea that there had once been a brewery in Moorhead. Who knew? Well, who did know? Around 1996 I decided to see if anything had been written about breweries in Minnesota. In the Minnesota Historical Society library I encountered the books that got me started: Bull, Friedrich, and Gottschalk's *American Breweries*, *Wing's Brewers Annual* of 1887, and Charles E. Dick's PhD thesis on the geography of Minnesota's brewing industry. At first it seemed like everything was pretty well settled. Dick's analysis was excellent and the lists contained far more breweries than I had ever imagined. But then I noticed that the lists contained discrepancies on the dates and proprietors of some of the breweries. I had a massive book on the history of nineteenth-century Dakota County, and the information it contained on the breweries of Hastings disagreed with that in *American Breweries* as well. For the first time I thought there might be something I could add to the literature on Minnesota's breweries.

With this vague possibility in mind, I wandered down the hill to a new brewpub, Great Waters Brewing Company, located in the Hamm Building. While enjoying a pint of cask-conditioned Mississippi Mild, a style of ale I'd never had before, I mentioned my idea to Mark van Wie, one of the cofounders of Great Waters. He was enthusiastic about the idea, but told me I should come over to the corner table and meet someone. Tod Fyten not only knew a lot about brewing in Minnesota, both past and present, but he also was a graduate of Saint Thomas Academy, my employer. Tod provided a number of suggestions, and his excitement made me believe that I really could write a book on Minnesota breweries. Someone should, so why not me?

To convince myself that it was worth the time, to convince my family that vacations should involve driving around Minnesota looking at vacant lots where breweries used to be, and to convince Saint Thomas Academy to give me a year off, I would have to answer the question, What's so important about Minnesota's brewing industry? Without making this sound like a research grant proposal, I think it is easy to demonstrate that the history of the brewing industry is important in understanding Minnesota's history and culture, and that Minnesota's brewing industry is important to the wider history of the brewing industry in general.

The history of Minnesota's brewing industry provides a cross-section of almost everything that happened in the brewing industry throughout the country. There were breweries of national importance such as Hamm's, Schmidt, and Grain

Fergus Breweries made Viking Lager from 1937 to 1948. The brand was one of many attempts to appeal to consumers by evoking local history. FROM THE COLLECTION OF KEN MALZ.

Belt, and there were breweries that rarely sent a barrel of beer outside a ten-mile radius. Some Minnesota brewers followed national trends, others were innovators: Gluek's invented malt liquor, Hamm's gave the world the Hamm's Bear. Some of Minnesota's breweries closed because of worldwide trends in the industry; others closed because the proprietor died and none of the heirs wanted to continue the business. Some breweries went out of business because their product was not worth buying; others survived because they made, or are still making, beers of great quality and distinction.

Studying the history of beer and the brewing industry in Minnesota also provides a window into the past to show how Minnesotans lived and what they valued. The stories of how Anthony Yoerg, John Orth, August Schell, and Jacob Schmahl struggled to succeed in business on the frontier are every bit as instructive as those of other settlers. The conflict between brewers and temperance advocates that resulted first in dry municipalities and ultimately in Prohibition shows how groups on all sides of an issue attempt to use government to their own ends. The treatment of German Americans, especially brewers, during World War I serves as reminder of the hysteria war brings on, while brewers' support of the war effort in World War II provides lessons in conservation measures.

Finally, studying the way in which beer is advertised, marketed, and sold helps illuminate many of the changes in American society. Beer was among the first food products to be sold with recognizable brand names, and in most cases the brand name was that of the proprietor of the company. Advertisements touted quality and consistency in an era when Americans were first becoming acquainted with mass-produced consumer goods. Brewers highlighted the purity and healthful nature of their products in response to the public concerns that led to federal food and drug legislation. In the 1930s, art deco ads focused on style. During World War II, the brewers' ads helped promote patriotism. In the 1950s, ads promoted community and good living. Since the 1960s, the dominant message in beer advertising has been enjoyment and fun. As America became more sensitive to racial justice, beer advertising consciously included minority characters in the ads.

As American life changed, brewing and drinking beer changed, too. The lack of social outlets for working-class men encouraged the saloon culture, and then the increasing political power of women helped close the saloons. The supermarket and the beer can made it much more convenient to drink beer at home than at the tavern. The gospel of efficiency elevated the massive breweries, and the increasing ease of highway transportation helped these large, efficient breweries push out their smaller, less-efficient counterparts. In recent years, a renewed love of craft and variety has helped the microbreweries and brewpubs thrive.

Beer is several thousand years old and was brought to America on the *Mayflower*. William Penn and Thomas Jefferson brewed beer on their estates, and George Washington was fond of porter. Minnesota's brewers also have a great sense of history and place. At the turn of the century, Hauenstein's produced Hermanbräu in honor of the Hermann Monument in New Ulm. Fergus Breweries launched a beer called Viking. Breweries and brewpubs throughout the state name their products after regional landmarks like the Witch Tree on the North Shore or after famous local characters such as Pig's Eye Parrant. Nearly two dozen brewery properties in Minnesota are on the National Register of Historic Places; community groups organized to preserve the Grain Belt, Hamm's, and Schmidt breweries from destruction; and the Hamm's Club erected a monument to the Hamm's Bear in downtown St. Paul. Minnesota history and Minnesota beer: I don't know why I didn't make the connection sooner.

Acknowledgments

"HEY, THAT'S A GREAT TOPIC! CAN I HELP WITH RESEARCH?" WELL, I DID need help, and sometimes it actually was the kind of help everyone was offering. But for every hour spent on a brewery tour, a hundred were spent squinting at a microfilm reader or unwrapping dusty tax records while wearing ill-fitting white gloves. Luckily, I did have lots of help. However, any errors in the book are not the fault of my helpers, and I will be happy to fix errors or omissions in the next edition.

The influence of Minnesota's breweries spread far beyond the boundaries of the state, even though Peoples Choice Old Style did not reach all the markets displayed on the label. Peoples Choice was brewed throughout the 1930s and 1940s. FROM THE AUTHOR'S COLLECTION.

Creating any book would be impossible without a talented production team. I am very grateful to senior acquisitions editor Todd Orjala, his assistant, Andrea Patch, and their colleagues at the University of Minnesota Press for making this dream become printed reality, and to Bob Fogt for his professional photography. Over the course of this project, Todd and Bob became valued friends as well as collaborators, and their guidance was essential in many ways.

Librarians and archivists throughout Minnesota and the Upper Midwest made my research possible and often enjoyable. Most important were the professionals at the Minnesota Historical Society—a few of them didn't think this could be done, but helped me do it anyway. Special thanks are due to Ruth Bauer Anderson, Debbie Miller, Hamp Smith, Duane Swanson, Adam Scher, Erik Holland, Craig Wright, Dan Cagley, and Eric Mortenson. The county historical societies of Minnesota are treasures, and the helpful people at the societies in Beltrami, Big Stone, Blue Earth, Brown, Carver, Clay, Dakota, Douglas, Fillmore, Goodhue, Hennepin, Jackson, Nicollet, Olmsted, Otter Tail (and East Otter Tail), Ramsey, Scott, Stearns, Wadena, Waseca, Washington, and Winona counties all made my visits profitable (and in a few cases, unnecessary).

Many scholars provided guidance and material assistance throughout the project. Professor George Green of the University of Minnesota was especially helpful in the early stages of my research. Sabine Meyer provided valuable assistance in interpreting the relation of the temperance movement to the brewing industry, and also passed along relevant items found in her research. I would also like to thank Professor Annette Atkins of St. John's University and the College of St. Benedict and an anonymous reviewer for helpful comments on early versions of the manuscript.

Two architectural historians helped put the history of the brewery buildings in context. Paul Clifford Larson got me interested in architectural history in the first place, and without him I probably never would have taken an interest in old brewery buildings or the history behind them. Professor Susan K. Appel of Illinois State University (Normal) offered assistance in identifying the architectural styles of breweries and provided information about the architects behind Minnesota's breweries. Architect Gary Raymond of RSP Architects gave me a tour of the restored Grain Belt Brewery and shared his research.

Without the help of breweriana collectors, this book would have been less visually appealing and less complete. Some allowed us to photograph their collections, and others provided important information about the breweries they have studied. Many provided hospitality during a long day of traveling. My heartfelt thanks go in no particular order to Pat Stambaugh, Bart Franta, Bob Hajicek, Mike Hajicek, Ken Malz, Brad Wilmes, Rei Ojala, Jim and Ruth Beaton, Herb and Helen Haydock, Bob Kay, Steve Ketchum, Ron Feldhaus, Dave Davis, Susan Ingeman, Dave and Joe Wendl, Bob Jackson, John and Paula Parker, Jeff Vick, Kirk Schnitker, Dave Craig, Lowell Peterson, and Pat Simon. Pete Clure lent me items from his archives, let me wear the Hamm's Bear head, and gave me my first-ever ride in a beer truck. Randy Carlson of Carlson Brewery Research graciously allowed me access to his extensive archives. Robert Rofidal shared research he had collected on several breweries. Members of breweriana organizations introduced me to people, provided research hints, and made me feel welcome. Other individuals who provided advice or resources include Tony Kennedy of the Minneapolis *Star Tribune*, Dick Kaye of Minnesota Revenue, James J. Jordan, MD, of the Hamm Clinic, and Heather Novak-Peterson of RSP Architects.

After completion of the manuscript, several talented professionals helped turn the pieces into a polished final product. Pam Price contributed expert copyediting, which removed errors and awkwardness but also retained my original intent and voice. Chris Long of Mighty Media did the layout work and managed to place more than three hundred illustrations where I had hoped they could be located. Daniel Ochsner, Rachel Moeller, and others on the University of Minnesota Press production team created key design elements and guided me through indexing and other production tasks. Lester Jones graciously provided access to the archives of the Beer Institute in Washington, DC, so I could do some final fact checking.

The owners, brewers, serving staff, and other employees of the breweries and brewpubs of Minnesota were very generous with their time and expertise. Thanks to Pete Rifakes, Mike Hoops, Jeff Williamson, and Kristin Whatton at Minneapolis Town Hall Brewery; Sean O'Byrne and Bob DuVernois (and before Bob, Jeff Martin and Joe Lanners) at Great Waters Brewing Company in St. Paul; Ron Flett of Mill Street Brewing Company in St. Paul; Dave Hartman and Chad Jamrozy at the Herkimer Pub & Brewery in Minneapolis; John Moore and Colin Mullen of Barley John's Brew Pub in New Brighton; Dave Johnson of Ambleside Brewing Company in Minneapolis; Bill Burdick of Sherlock's Home in Minnetonka and later of Granite City (various locations); Omar Ansari and Todd Haug at Surly Brewing Co. in Brooklyn Center; Bryon Tonnis, Todd's successor at Rock Bottom Restaurant & Brewery in Minneapolis; Matthew Tufto of Union Station First City Brewery in Bemidji; Dave Hoops of Fitger's Brewhouse in Duluth; Don Hoag and John Judd at Lake Superior Brewing Company; Dave Berg of the Bandana Brewery in Mankato; and Mike Kneip and DiAnn South of Gluek Brewing Company in Cold Spring. Gerri Kustelski of Summit Brewing Company allowed me to spend a morning in her laboratory, offering an unequaled look into the science of brewing. Gary Lee and Molly Bremer of Rahr Malting Co. let me look through the archive and lent artifacts for my research. Tod Fyten of Mantorville Brewing Company is a historian as well as a brewer and gave me information and suggestions about a variety of topics throughout my research.

Two brewers deserve special thanks: Ted Marti of August Schell Brewing Company in New Ulm and Mark Stutrud of Summit Brewing Company in St. Paul. Their material and financial support was critical to making this book a success.

Thanks to Al Boyce, Steve Piatz, Gera Exire LaTour, Jonathan Crist, John Longballa, Curt Stock, Kris England, Wayne Theuer, and everyone else in Minnesota's homebrewing community. They taught me brewing techniques and beer styles, and helped me prepare to become a certified beer judge.

I met many retired brewery employees who shared stories of their days in the breweries. I am grateful to Ron Tschida, Alf Martogon, Bob Carpenter, Sig Plagens, Frank Haselmann, Ruth Suttles, Mike Peck, Charlie Long, the Hamm's guys at the monument dedication, and everyone else who helped me understand what it meant to be a brewery worker. Thanks also to Pat Schwartz, who put me in touch with some of the Schmidt's guys in the first place.

Without the support of my employers and colleagues at Saint Thomas Academy I never could have finished this book. A grant of sabbatical leave allowed me a year to research, tour the state, go to Germany, and do the other work that couldn't be done while teaching. Thanks to past and present administrators Bob Slater, John Greving, Bob Oslund, Dr. Celeste Heidelberger, Dr. Tom Mich, and Jack Zahr for supporting my research. Thanks to my departmental colleagues who picked up some of my duties: Jamie Jurkovich, Dave Ziebarth, Josh Kaeppe, and Tom Klein. Special thanks to colleague Dean Simmons, who helped with German translation and Minnesota history; to Joel Koch, who taught my classes and coached the debate team during my absence; and to teaching partner Rebecca Benz, who was flexible enough to deal with schedule interruptions before, during, and after my sabbatical.

Several friends deserve special thanks. Jeff Helgemoe may have inspired this whole venture when he showed me his beer can collection (though at the time I was more impressed by the Coors waterfall sign). At the University of Michigan, Murray Scot Tanner entrusted me with one of his precious bottles of Beamish Irish Stout and broadened my understanding of what beer could be. Lance Boyd Jones and A. J. LoCicero are special friends who deserve to see their names in this book. Even though he doesn't drink, Nathan Wodarz accompanied me on many brewpub visits. Brian Ruhl offered friendship, encouragement, and marketing ideas. Judy Stinson read several chapters of an early draft. Over the years, Brad Peterson had many otherwise relaxing nights at a brewpub interrupted while I talked business with the brewer or proprietor. Many other friends gave support, encouragement, and advice along the way.

My family was very supportive during the course of the writing—from my brother Brian's well-chosen Christmas presents to cousin Alicia taking me to a brewpub when I was in San Francisco. Robert Garland inspired me with his own scholarship, and his work was a model of how to write readable history. My aunts Lossie and Jean Murray gave me everything from books on beer to editorial suggestions to reassurance that I could do this after all. My in-laws, Helen, Marty, and Pat Conway, have been supportive and a source of companionship to my family when I have been gone.

Both of my parents love history, and I hope they are proud of what their scholarship engendered in me. My mom, Connie Murray, went above and beyond the call of duty by taking a job at the Minnesota Historical Society (years before I conceived this book, but fortunate for me anyway). She introduced me to staff members, picked up photocopies, found sources, and visited me at my microfilm reader and brought me news of the world outside. My dad, Burt Hoverson, eventually managed to get beyond cheap beer and has been a great companion when exploring the worlds of beer and history (and, in Germany, both at once). His wife, Sandy, is one of the most tenacious breweriana collectors I have ever met; she can sense an unusual bottle cap on the ground at a range of fifty yards. Simply saying thank you and I love you really can't express my gratitude.

Our children, Claire and Alex, have been most patient during this process. Neither is old enough to remember when I wasn't working on this book. They came to terms with the fact that when we go out to eat, we are probably going to a brewpub (at least brewpubs usually have a good kids' menu). I love you both, and maybe next summer we'll go somewhere that you pick.

My very patient wife and friend, Kerry, and I have been together since before we could legally drink beer and before I became either a history major or a teacher, so I can't claim she knew what she was getting into. It will probably take me the rest of our lives to make up for the numerous times we drove out of our way to look at a hole in the ground that once held a beer keg, or the number of times that I left her with the kids so I could go research at a far-flung location, or the number of times (like right now) when I am writing in the office when I should be helping with dishes. I hope you think it was worth it, but at least it's done. Either way, I love you.

Minneapolis, Minnesota, 2007

From Barley to Bar Stool: The Art and Science of Brewing

BEER IS A MARVELOUS COMBINATION OF SIMPLICITY AND COMPLEXITY. IT is so simple that illiterate peasants were able to make it for centuries with whatever ingredients were at hand. It is so complex that some of the greatest minds of modern chemistry have devoted energy to solving the problems of producing it. In many places, from ancient Mesopotamia and Egypt to colonial America, governments and individuals have recorded their attempts to brew, tax, and drink a beverage fermented from local grains. And in a few cases, some scientifically minded brewers even left their recipes.[1]

Beer has a broad definition: it can be any fermented beverage made from a grain base. (The Japanese drink sake, often called rice wine, is actually a member of beer's extended family.) The terms *beer* and *ale* are nearly interchangeable, but not quite. An ale is a beer, but not all beers are ales. During the Middle Ages, the term *ale* was commonly used for traditional beverages and the term *beer* distinguished a new drink that was bittered with hops. Today, the term *ale* refers to beers made with top-fermenting yeast strains. (Ironically, most of the beer styles called ales today are much hoppier than other beers, in contrast to the ancient origin of the term.)

The Ingredients

Beer has four basic ingredients: water, grain, hops, and yeast. These ingredients can be combined in nearly infinite variations to create different styles of beer. The famous Bavarian purity law of 1516, the *Reinheitsgebot*, forbade the inclusion of any ingredient in beer other than pure barley malt, water, and hops (yeast had not been identified as a separate component of beer at that date). European regulations no longer allow Germany to enforce this law as a way of keeping out

This dramatic backlit illustration of Grain Belt Park was a part of a lighted sign first released in October 1963. The fountain was intended to be picturesque (the park hosted competitions for artists) and to draw attention to the importance of water in brewing. The park became a popular spot for recreation among residents of Northeast Minneapolis. FROM THE COLLECTION OF JIM AND RUTH BEATON.

Grain Belt...from perfect brewing water

imported beers, but many brewers still highlight their adherence to the Reinheitsgebot as a mark of quality. Brewers have developed new styles and flavors throughout history, sometimes by combinations of new ingredients and happy accident, sometimes by intentional experimentation and careful research.[2]

Water

Unlike wine, where water is not added during production, beer takes much of its character from the water used. The water of Pilsen (Plzeň) in the Czech Republic is low in minerals, and this soft water contributes to the clean flavor of the beer known as pilsner, or pilsener, variations of which have become the most common style of beer in the world. In contrast, the hard water of Burton-on-Trent in the English Midlands contains minerals that aid in extracting the bittering resins from the hops and thus contributes much to the hoppy character of English pale ales and India pale ales. Modern chemistry enables brewers from international breweries and even homebrewers to reproduce any water chemistry in the world and to brew styles from all over the world with local water. The biggest difficulty that multiplant breweries had to overcome in the mid-twentieth century was to make beer brewed at different plants taste the same. The success of the chemists allowed Anheuser-Busch, Molson, Falstaff, and other companies to make beer of remarkable consistency.

Several Minnesota brewers have featured the quality of their water in advertising campaigns, either directly or indirectly. Ads for Grain Belt claimed that "Perfect brewing water makes the perfect beer," and a large fountain in the park by the brewery emphasized the connection. The Schmidt Brewery in St. Paul has had a public water pump for many years, but it was converted to a coin-operated facility in the spring of 1998. The public pump at the Hamm Brewery was installed in 1979 to stop the public from simply using a tap on the side of the brewery, but it closed along with the (by then Stroh's) brewery in 1997.[3]

Grain

The color, sweetness, and much of the flavor and nutrient value in beer comes from the mix of grain in the recipe. While nearly any grain can be made to produce fermentable sugars, the traditional source of these sugars in beer is malted barley. Barley grows best in temperate regions; early English settlers in the warmer southern colonies complained that they could not grow suitable barley for brewing ale. Minnesota is in one of the most important barley-growing regions in the world, an area that stretches roughly from Lake Superior to the Canadian Rockies. There are many varieties of barley, but most are categorized as two-row or six-row, depending on the arrangement of the kernels.

To create fermentable sugars in the grain, it first must be malted. In malting, the grain is moistened and allowed to sprout. In this early germination period, the kernel produces starches to provide energy for the young plant as well as enzymes essential for their conversion. To retain the maximum amount of starch in each kernel, the maltster stops the germination by drying the grain. The malt then may be roasted or even smoked to give it unique color and flavor characteristics.

Of the 150 varieties of barley cultivated in North America, about a dozen make up most of the malting barley. COURTESY OF RAHR MALTING CO.

In the nineteenth century, most of Minnesota's brewers malted their own barley, laboriously rotating it with large wooden shovels to ensure even germination. Today automated machinery turns the moist grain in giant malting operations like that at Rahr Malting Co. in Shakopee. COURTESY OF RAHR MALTING CO.

Rahr Malting Co. was founded in Manitowoc, Wisconsin, in 1847 by William Rahr. He malted much more barley than his brewery could use, so he began selling malt to other breweries. Eventually the malting operation dwarfed the brewing side. Built just after the end of Prohibition, the Shakopee plant is the largest single-site malting facility in the world. Most of the breweries in Minnesota purchased at least some of their malt from Rahr. Today Rahr continues to supply malt to brewers ranging from Miller to homebrewers. COURTESY OF RAHR MALTING CO.

In the nineteenth century, breweries of all sizes malted their own barley. The local brewery was an important customer of farmers in the neighborhood. In modern times, only a handful of the very largest breweries still do their own malting. Other brewers purchase their malt from an independent maltster such as Rahr Malting of Shakopee, which is one of the largest such firms in the world.

Some beer styles contain grains other than barley. Adjuncts are ingredients other than barley or hops that impart certain flavors, colors, or other characteristics to the beer. Wheat beer (weizen or weiss beer, from the German word for both the grain and the color white) uses wheat for a large percentage of the grain bill. Wheat beers were granted an exception from the Reinheitsgebot as a separate product. Many of the world's most flavorful and best-selling beers (these are not the same) do not abide by the Reinheitsgebot. Many mass-market American beers include flaked corn (maize) or rice as an adjunct to lighten the color, provide certain flavor characteristics, and improve head retention. Many of the famous and flavorful beers of Belgium add whole fruit, candi sugar, and syrups. Holiday beers from many nations contain spices, and American microbrewers and brewpubs have become famous for their creative recipes.

To convert the starches in the malt to sugars that can be fermented by yeast, the grain must be mashed. The grain is first milled to separate the husk from the seed and to crack the seed just enough to expose the starches. The grain is then mixed with water to form a porridgelike mixture. By carefully controlling the temperature of the liquid in the mash kettle (or tun), the brewer can encourage different enzymes to work on the grains and break the large starch molecules into smaller sugar molecules that the yeast can digest. After the necessary sugars have been produced (usually requiring one to three hours), the sugars are rinsed from the grain in a process called sparging. This may be done in a separate vessel called a *lauter* tun, which has a strainer-like false bottom and rotating blades to help rinse the grain evenly. The liquid resulting from this process is called wort (pronounced "wert"). Before the twentieth century, it was a common practice to create two separate batches of wort from the first and second halves of the sparge. The "second runnings" were lower in fermentable sugars, and the resulting beer would therefore be lower in alcohol. (This is comparable to making a second pot of coffee from the same grounds.) This was then sold at a lower price as "table beer," "small beer," or "present-use beer."[4] A few homebrewers and brewpubs have experimented with reviving this tradition.

The wort is then boiled in the brew kettle; it is at this point that other fermentable sugars like fruit or syrups are added, as well as most of the hops or spices called for in the brew. The spent grains from the brewing process are often sold or given to local farmers, who consider it a high-quality livestock feed.

Hops

The wort resulting from the mashing process typically has a molasses-like consistency and a sticky sweetness. A beverage made simply by fermenting this would be virtually unpalatable, so some type of bittering agent must be added to balance the sweetness. In short, beer is supposed to have a bitter component to its taste; those who complain about the bitterness of beer are ignoring its essential role in the complex flavor of a well-made beer. Throughout the history of brewing, many different herbs have been employed for this purpose. During the early Middle Ages, the most common bittering agent was *gruit*, a mixture of herbs about which there is still much speculation, but the primary ingredient seems to have been bog myrtle. The nobility of the period controlled the distribution and cost of gruit and made this *gruitrecht* into one of their major sources of income. Historians have suggested that the adoption of hops as a bittering agent was partly because of their superior qualities but also because using hops enabled brewers to evade the tax on gruit. American colonists used spruce tips as a common bittering agent where hops were not available.

Measuring Beer

Brewery sizes are usually compared by measuring capacity, output, or actual sales. The most common standard unit in the brewing industry is the barrel, which is equal to 31 gallons. (Ironically, while brewery production is measured in barrels, the full barrel itself has not been used as a container in the industry for many years because of its awkward size and weight. The more-common half barrel contains 15 gallons, the quarter barrel contains eight gallons, and the eighth barrel, or pony keg, holds four gallons.) After bottled beer became common, production was sometimes measured in cases, which contain 24 bottles (or later, cans) of 12 ounces each. One barrel holds 3,968 ounces or 330 bottles, which converts to 13.8 cases per barrel. Consumption is also typically measured in barrels, at least in aggregate. Any modern American bar patron knows that the terms *glass*, *mug*, and *pitcher* have no legal meaning, and that *pint* is much more descriptive of a glass style than of its contents. Throughout this book, quantities are given in the units that were provided in the original source materials.

The mixing of fiscal years and calendar years in government and industry records complicates determining actual production of breweries, as does confusion between production and sales. The U.S. government measures beer for taxation purposes through tax-paid withdrawals, which is beer removed from the brewery cellar for shipment and sale. Even so, some revenue agents reported actual production on some occasions, tax-paid withdrawals at other times, and sometimes both. The term *production* is used in this book only when it is clear that the figure actually represents the amount made. For tax-paid withdrawals, the terms *output* and *sales* are used interchangeably. The capacity of a brewery is often a theoretical figure only—it represents what a brewery could make if it used all of its fermentation and storage vessels all the time and moved beer through the process as quickly as possible. Some breweries actually produced at full capacity for a brief period, but being at full capacity meant that there was potential to sell much more beer, and the brewery usually launched an expansion program to meet the demand. ❧

Chas. Ehlermann & Co. dealt in all sorts of brewing supplies, but it was a vignette of the hop harvest that the company featured on its invoices. These supplies were purchased by Adolph Remmler in 1886. COURTESY OF THE GOODHUE COUNTY HISTORICAL SOCIETY, RED WING, MN.

Hops are small conelike flowers that come from the female hop plant (*Humulus lupulus*). Like beer itself, hops are both simple and complex. These vining perennials grow wild in many areas and can be easily cultivated at home in most regions; in fact, they can be difficult to eliminate once established. On the other hand, a handful of universities around the world have hop culture programs, and new varieties are introduced with some frequency. Hop varieties are selected for resistance to disease and yield as well as for their brewing characteristics.

The tiny yellow particles at the base of the flower contain resins and essential oils that serve different functions in making beer. The resins are the source of the alpha acids that provide the bitterness in beer. Hops can vary widely in the amount of alpha acids that are available to be isomerized and dissolved into the beer during the boiling stage, which is measured as a percentage. The noble hops of Germany and the Czech Republic are typically low in available alpha acids (around 4 to 6 percent), whereas many hops grown in the Pacific Northwest can have more than 10 percent available alpha acids. Some high-alpha hops may have more than 16 percent available alpha acids. To impart bitterness to the beer, the hops must be boiled for at least sixty minutes. Hops may be added to the brew kettle either in their original whole-leaf form, as hop pellets, or (much less frequently) as liquid hop extract. The resulting hoppiness of the beer is commonly measured in International Bitterness Units (IBUs). Mass-market lagers are usually in the range of 8 to 25 IBUs, pale ales and stouts are often between 30 and 45 IBUs, and some craft brewers create exceptionally hoppy beers that exceed 100 IBUs.

The essential oils, on the other hand, primarily add flavor and aroma components to beer. These oils lose their potency if boiled or even if exposed to air for too long and therefore must be added to the brew very late in the brewing process so the flavor and aroma are not literally boiled away. Some brewers add hops to the fermenter or aging vats to retain the maximum amount of flavor and aroma in a process called dry-hopping. Unfortunately, one group of essential oils contains sulfur, which reacts with light to produce the undesirable aroma known as skunkiness. Brewers, retailers, and marketers are thus sometimes placed in a difficult position: the safest way to package and store beer is in dark bottles or cans in closed boxes away from strong sources of light, but sometimes the best way to draw attention to a brand is to package it in green or clear bottles in open carriers in a brightly lit display, which invites skunkiness.

Hops are added to the brew kettle at Summit Brewing Company. COURTESY OF SUMMIT BREWING COMPANY.

Yeast

Yeast converts sugars into alcohol through the process of fermentation. For centuries, the precise role of yeast in the brewing process was imperfectly understood. Monastic brewers in the Middle Ages are said to have called the fermentation process "God is Good," and brewers of the period observed semireligious rituals during fermentation. Wild yeasts present in the brewing environment were responsible for much of the fermentation in the premodern period; historians have speculated that some yeast was transferred from batch to batch on the surfaces of the brewing equipment. Not until after the development of the microscope and the fundamental chemistry research by Joseph Priestly of England and Antoine-Laurent Lavoisier of France were the tools and knowledge available to understand yeast. The work of Louis Pasteur and of Emil Christian Hansen of the Carlsberg Brewery in Copenhagen made it possible for brewers to isolate, breed, and maintain pure yeast strains. The purity of the yeast strain is critical to maintaining consistency of flavor, and modern brewers take great pains to protect their yeast from unwanted mutations.

While many different strains of yeast exist, most brewing yeasts can be divided into two classes (though some newly developed yeast strains blur the line between the two). Ale yeast, or top-fermenting yeast (*Saccharomyces cerevisiae*), generally ferments at higher temperatures, imparts more complex fruity aromas to the beer, and often remains on the top of the liquid after the process is complete. Lager yeast, or bottom-fermenting yeast, typically requires cooler conditions, imparts fewer fruity esters to the beer, and settles to the bottom at the end of fermentation. Some beer styles, such as the German hefeweizen (wheat beer with yeast), are served with the yeast still in suspension in the beer, giving it a cloudy, but not unattractive, appearance.

The fermentation process typically requires about a week. After fermentation is complete, what happens next depends on the type of beer. Cask-conditioned ales are moved directly into the vessels from which they will eventually be served and typically undergo some secondary fermentation while in the cask. Most beers are filtered and moved to aging tanks. At this stage the beer is carbonated either by the forced addition of carbon dioxide gas or through natural processes.

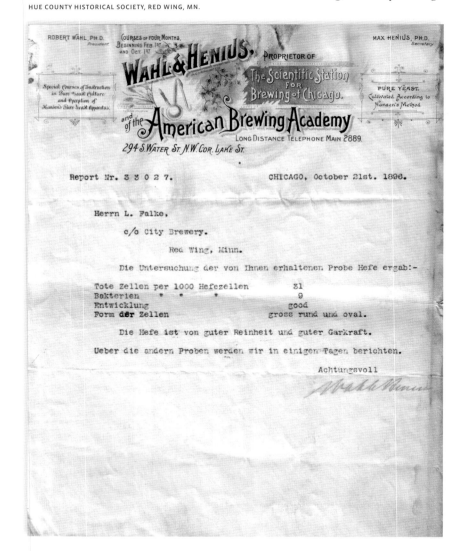

Remmler's City Brewery of Red Wing sought an analysis of its yeast from Wahl & Henius, which not only directed the American Brewing Academy but also propagated and analyzed yeast. According to the analysis, Remmler's yeast was of good purity and vigor. COURTESY OF THE GOODHUE COUNTY HISTORICAL SOCIETY, RED WING, MN.

In the case of lager beers (the word *lager* is from the German verb meaning "to store"), a longer period of aging is required to allow the beer to carbonate and to eliminate off-flavors from the finished product. Beer that has not aged long enough is called green beer; more than one American brewery has been doomed by attempting to shorten the lagering period. The most vivid example was Schlitz, which destroyed a century-old reputation in the late 1970s by attempting to do with chemistry what is best done with time.

After aging, the beer is ready for packaging in kegs, bottles, or cans and for shipping to the consumer. Brewers trust their distributors and retailers to ensure that beer is protected from damaging extremes in temperature and from other rough handling that could make the beer undrinkable or unsuited for display in stores. After this, the taste of beer is up to the drinker.

Enjoying Beer Properly

After taking into account that beer is best enjoyed safely and in moderation, a few simple steps will aid in appreciating the unique characteristics of each style.

Learn about the Different Styles of Beer

Broadly speaking, beer is divided into two main categories: ale and lager. Ales are made with top-fermenting yeast and are generally fermented at temperatures around 70°F. Ales tend to be fruitier in both aroma and taste than lagers. Lagers are brewed with bottom-fermenting yeast and require lower fermentation temperatures, around 50°F. There are also several varieties of hybrid beer, usually a beer using lager yeast fermented at ale temperatures or the other way around.

Within these main categories exist infinite variations. The 2004 Beer Judge Certification Program *Style Guidelines* lists twenty-three styles of beer, from "light lager" to "smoke-flavored and wood-aged beer." Within these styles there are a total of seventy-eight subcategories—and this doesn't even count the categories for fruit and specialty beer, for which any brew could be its own subcategory. For example, style twelve, porter, has three subcategories: brown porter, robust porter, and Baltic porter. Each subcategory has parameters for color, aroma, bitterness, flavor, and alcohol content. The style guidelines are useful, but should not be treated as a straitjacket. Many distinctive and flavorful beers do not fit clearly into any one category, and American craft brewers and homebrewers delight in pushing the boundaries of beer styles. The subcategory designation of "imperial" was borrowed from imperial stouts originally made by English brewers for the Russian market and is affixed to high-alcohol content examples from any style.

It is important to remember that color has no relation to strength whatsoever. A light-golden Belgian-style ale can have upwards of 10 percent alcohol by weight, whereas draught Guinness Stout, which is nearly black in color, is less than 4 percent alcohol by weight as served in Irish pubs.

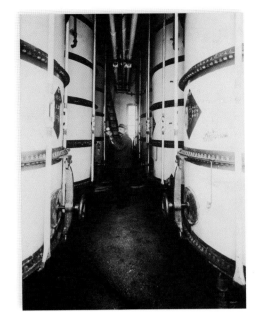

The glass-lined Pfaudler vacuum fermentation tanks at August Schell Brewing Company were the most advanced available at the turn of the twentieth century. FROM THE COLLECTION OF THE BROWN COUNTY HISTORICAL SOCIETY, NEW ULM, MINNESOTA.

Kristin of Town Hall Brewery pulls a pint of cask-conditioned SFO, a California common-style hybrid beer, in which lager yeast is allowed to ferment at warmer temperatures usually used for fermenting ale yeast. COURTESY OF TOWN HALL BREWERY, MINNEAPOLIS.

HIGH POINT DUNKEL

German for "dark," Dunkel is a rich, malty beer with hops present– but dominated by the sweetness of the roasted and toasted dark malts.

Color: Dark Brown
IBU: 29
Starting Plato: 14
Alcohol: 5.4%

HERHIMER
PUB & BREWERY

Because their customers have become more sophisticated, breweries and brewpubs offer more detailed information about their beers. IBUs (International Bitterness Units) provide an indication of how hoppy a beer is (this one is moderately hoppy). Starting degrees Plato measure what percentage of the wort is sugar and therefore available to be converted to alcohol. FROM THE AUTHOR'S COLLECTION.

Serve the Beer at the Proper Temperature

Most lager should be served cool but not ice-cold. Ales can be served at cellar temperatures (around 50°F to 55°F). The common American myth that the English drink warm beer is not true; a pint of bitter or stout is only warm in comparison to the near-freezing temperatures at which American mass-market lager is typically served. Don't ice the beer mug for anything other than a light American lager either. A rich and highly aromatic beer such as an old ale or a barleywine will be more enjoyable at room temperature or even warmed slightly by holding the glass in the palm.

Know the Alcohol Content of the Beer

Drinking a large quantity of an extremely smooth beer only to discover that it was nearly 10 percent alcohol can cause anything from a severe hangover to a serious safety hazard. There is a good reason that many strong beers come in small bottles and are served in small glasses. Most brewers around the world, like their counterparts in the wine industry, refer to alcohol by volume. In contrast, the U.S. government requires that alcohol in beer be measured by weight. The resulting percent by volume is about 125 percent of the figure computed by weight, which leads to the common myth that Canadian beer is stronger than American beer. A 5 percent beer in Canada has the same alcohol content as a 4 percent beer in the United States.

Learn Something about the Brewing Process

Even the largest modern breweries emphasize the history and tradition of their brands, and companies and want their patrons to know about it. Take a brewery tour, preferably at a small or a mid-sized brewery. Tours of the massive breweries are interesting, but are often presented by tour guides who have not actually worked in the brewery, and the tours tend to focus on quantity, efficiency, and packaging. At smaller breweries, the tour is more likely to be given by a veteran brewery employee, perhaps even the brewmaster, who is more likely to discuss the differences in beer styles and how they are made.

Whenever Possible, Pour Beer into a Glass

Pouring beer into a glass lets excess carbon dioxide escape and allows the aromas to work with the flavors. Often a feeling of excess gassiness results from drinking straight from the bottle or can, though sometimes it is unavoidable. Pour the first two-thirds of the beer down the side of the glass, but pour the rest into the middle to raise a good head on the beer. This releases carbon dioxide and simply makes the beer look better. European beer glasses are designed to contain a full legal measure of beer and still leave room for the type of head best suited for the beer (thick and creamy for a stout, big and frothy for a German hefeweizen). Pouring the entire beer down the side of a glass to minimize the head is primarily a North American habit designed to counter short-measure glasses or long lines at keg parties.

Among the most impressive features of a brewery tour is the automated bottling line. COURTESY OF SUMMIT BREWING COMPANY.

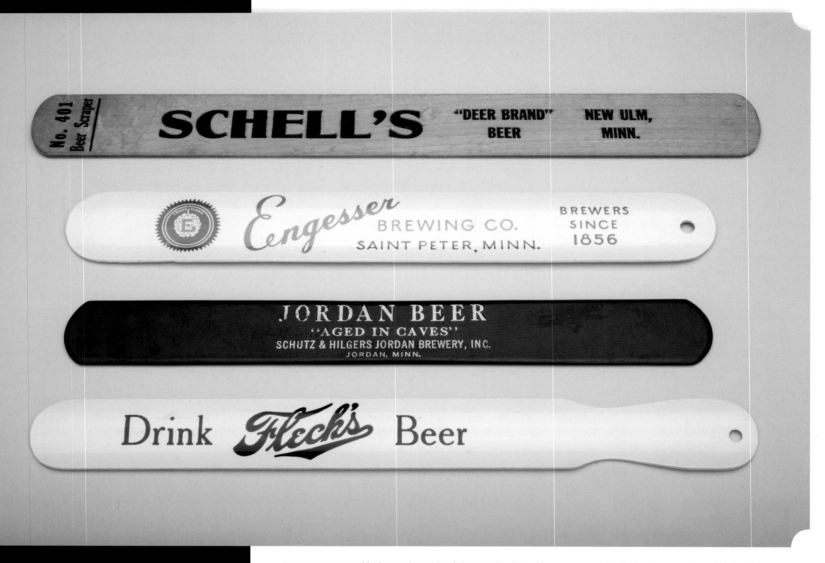

Foam scrapers, used by bartenders to level the top of a glass of beer, were popular during the years immediately after repeal. Concerns about sanitation led to their disappearance by the 1950s. Most of the Minnesota breweries that survived Prohibition were founded in the earliest years of settlement. Engesser and Fleckenstein claimed a founding date of 1856, Schell's was founded in 1860, and while Schutz & Hilgers Jordan brewery dated only to 1866, Jordan had a brewery prior to 1860. FROM THE COLLECTION OF PAT STAMBAUGH.

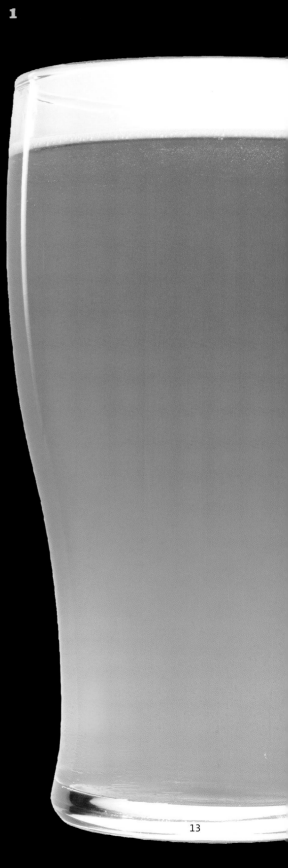

Pioneer Brewing

The full and perfect development of the grain which characterizes the cereal production of Minnesota, manifests itself, not only in the superior quality of the flour, but gives a recognized distinction to the malt and other liquors made from them. If we are indebted to the German element of the population for the general introduction of lager beer, it has now become an established American beverage, and whatever arguments may be urged on economical and moral grounds against the distillation of whiskey, beer may be justly reckoned among our most useful manufactures.

—*Minnesota: Its Progress and Capabilities*, Commissioner of Statistics, 1862

I N 1849 CONGRESS ESTABLISHED THE TERRITORY OF MINNESOTA, CREATED from land left out of the just-admitted state of Wisconsin. For many settlers and entrepreneurs, territorial status was an important mark of government sanction and stability that would make relocating to the area less risky. Minnesota Territory had only three settlements large enough to support any sort of commercial business: the territorial capital St. Paul and the two rival lumber towns of Stillwater on the St. Croix River and St. Anthony on the Mississippi River. All three possessed access to a river, access to raw materials, potential storage caves, and a population large enough to make a small brewery a possible source of profit.

A Changing Industry

When the first European Americans began to settle the area between the St. Croix and Mississippi rivers in the 1840s, the brewing industry was on the brink of the first major change in the nature of beer since the development of porter in the early 1700s. Up to this time, all of the beer produced in America contained top-fermenting yeast strains because they were widely available (wild yeast was generally used by households out of tradition and necessity) and less sensitive to change. Ale was easy to make. Top-fermenting yeast (*Saccharomyces cerevisiae*) tolerates warm temperatures, which was essential in the days before cold storage. If necessary, a variety of products that would produce a palatable beer could be

Steamboats were critical to the economic life of Minnesota in the days before railroads covered the state. During the summer navigation season, breweries imported raw materials and shipped barrels of beer as far away as Memphis, Tennessee. The *Red Wing Argus* reported in December 1869 that fourteen bales of hops weighing 3,015 pounds and nine kegs of beer had been shipped from Red Wing that year. (Undated photo.) COURTESY OF THE GOODHUE COUNTY HISTORICAL SOCIETY, RED WING, MN.

substituted for barley malt and hops. Breweries were common features on the estates of landed gentlemen such as William Penn, George Washington, and Thomas Jefferson, and people of all income levels brewed beer for their own consumption. Even though several hundred commercial breweries existed during the eighteenth and early nineteenth centuries, many taverns and households continued to make their own ale. Henry Sibley, a pioneer who was once a representative of the American Fur Company and was later the first governor of the state of Minnesota, is known to have purchased hops for making ale, and other pioneer families may have done so as well.[1] Homebrewing apparently continued long after Minnesota became a territory. The *Red Wing Argus* reported in 1871:

> A resident of the city whose business kept him in the country all through the holidays, reports that he was not deprived of his regular rations of beer, because most of the well-to-do Norwegian farmers brew for home use, and always have a large supply for the holidays. Some of them make as good clear beer as the brewers, and strong as the brewers' "Buck."[2]

Very few records were kept of such homebrewing, but it appears that many farmers engaged in all facets of the brewing operation, from harvest to packaging. A shed that once sheltered drying hops in Goodhue County is now at Vesterheim Norwegian-American Museum in Decorah, Iowa.

Toward Industrialization

Brewing historian Richard Unger has outlined six stages in the development of brewing. The homebrewing of Minnesota's preterritorial era represents the first stage, household production for domestic consumption. Minnesota skipped the second stage, that of household industry performed by specialists, largely because frontier life did not allow the sort of landed estates, such as those in Europe or on the Atlantic coast of North America, that could afford to keep a brewer among the domestic staff. The first commercial breweries in Minnesota represented the third stage, individual workshops with some commercial activity. Brewing moved from the home or tavern to the brewery largely because of a change in the way most beer would be brewed.[3]

The new development, scientific lager brewing, began in central Europe during the 1820s and spread quickly throughout the continent. The principal originators of the style were Gabriel Sedlmayr of Munich and Anton Dreher of Vienna. The beers of Munich were significantly darker than those of Vienna, but both were much clearer and mellower in taste than the beers that preceded them. During the 1840s, brewers in the Bohemian city of Pilsen (Plzeň) refined the style still further, using their extremely soft local water and distinctive Saaz hops to create an even lighter beer that soon was known worldwide as pilsner, or pilsener.

In 1840 John Wagner of Philadelphia brewed what most historians consider to be the first batch of lager beer in America. Unlike all previous American brews, this recipe featured a strain of yeast that sank to the bottom of the vessel as it fermented, a strain that Wagner appears to have brought with him from Bavaria. The new lager beer had a lighter, more refreshing taste than American ales of the time, and the fact that the yeast dropped to the bottom of the fermenter instead of rising to the top like ale yeast allowed for a very bright beer with a minimum of sediment. The increasing availability of mass-produced glassware made a beverage that looked good even more appealing. The new style had two major drawbacks for existing producers, however. The bottom-fermenting yeast strains require significantly cooler temperatures to work. (The Bavarian government decreed in the 1500s that lager could be brewed only from the Feast of St. Michael in late September until the Feast of St. George in late April because the temperatures would otherwise be too high and result in acidification of the beer.) Ales, however, did not require long periods of aging and were often drunk as soon as fermentation was over, especially when produced at home. For brewers, making lager required brewers to find or create sufficient cool cellar space to hold the beer while it aged. The need to dig caves, build cellars or, later, install expensive refrigeration equipment meant that the shift to lager would favor large commercial brewers over smaller operations.

The same year that Wagner started brewing lager in Philadelphia, the U.S. Army drove several dozen squatters off the Fort Snelling military reservation and forced them to settle what soon became St. Paul. The new town served not only as the seat of the government and of the Roman Catholic Church but also as the source of contraband goods for the soldiers at the fort. Pierre "Pig's Eye" Parrant was the most notorious of the liquor dealers who set up shop in St. Paul. Alcohol played an important part in St. Paul's early history, and as more settlers reached the area, it was not surprising that some would attempt to make a living from brewing beer.[4]

Stahlmann Brewing Co. was among the first Minnesota brewers to offer bottled beer, some of which is on display in this photograph taken in the 1880s. Large breweries offered steady employment to dozens of men, though the hours were long and the work was often physically demanding. COURTESY OF THE MINNESOTA HISTORICAL SOCIETY.

Commercial brewing began with lager beer in Minnesota because the land was opened for settlement at the beginning of a huge wave of German immigration. Had the area been settled a decade earlier, the first commercial brewer undoubtedly would have produced ale. But the introduction of lager yeast to America and its spread throughout the country coincided with a wave of new German immigrants coming to Minnesota and with Germans already in the United States moving west for greater opportunity. Some established brewers, especially in states farther east, were reluctant to try a new method and product. The biographies of brewers often reveal a pragmatic blend of the traditional and the technical. But ultimately, they chose to minimize risk and maximize profit just as any other business owner would. By the late 1840s, lager brewing was a tried and proven method, and there was a rapidly growing market for the refreshing new beverage. Iowa and Minnesota were the first two territories or states where the first brewery to be established (in 1845 and 1849 respectively) manufactured lager instead of ale.

The Pioneers

The first beer sold in Minnesota almost certainly did not come from a resident commercial brewer. The earliest documented beer sales were mentioned in testimony during a court martial in 1823. While attempting to clear himself of charges of encouraging desertion and neglect of duty, musician Cornelius Fuller reported that drum major Schillinsky was selling beer from his cellar in Fort St. Anthony (which would soon be renamed Fort Snelling).[5] It is likely that Schillinsky was making his own beer since ale was easy to make but difficult and expensive to ship, especially with the Army monitoring supply shipments.

In an account published in *One Hundred Years of Brewing*, Mathew Tschirgi of Dubuque, Iowa, claimed to have "sold the first beer in St. Paul" in 1848. Some have interpreted this to mean that Tschirgi built a brewery in St. Paul, but his own account stated that he could not leave Dubuque, the 1850 census locates him there, and Tschirgi himself notes that there was no brewery in St. Paul at the time.[6]

Given Bavaria's contributions to brewing science and culture, it is fitting that Minnesota's first commercial brewer was Bavarian native Anthony Yoerg. Born in 1816, he came to America at age 29. Like many immigrants of the period, he stayed for brief periods in different cities, first in Pittsburgh and later in Galena, Illinois. Galena was a major river port during the 1840s and 1850s. It served as a convenient place for overland travelers to connect with steamboats going upriver, and its industries, including its breweries, supplied less-developed towns such as St. Paul. Yoerg was trained as a brewer in Bavaria, but it is not clear whether he worked in breweries in Pittsburgh or Galena. Almost immediately after arriving in St. Paul in 1848, he began to build his brewery. In the spring of 1849 he became

Nineteenth-century breweries delivered kegs to local saloons with horse-drawn wagons. Initially, Yoerg's delivery range was limited by the primitive state of St. Paul's streets. When this photo was taken, around 1890, the streets were much better, and Yoerg's was delivering bottled beer to saloons, hotels, and private homes.
COURTESY OF THE MINNESOTA HISTORICAL SOCIETY.

When Anthony Yoerg moved his brewery to the east side of the Mississippi River in 1871, he selected a location where he was able to excavate the caves pictured here in the mid-1930s. A few breweries were forced to use caves more than a mile from the brewery. Yoerg's was one of the rare breweries to use its caves for lagering after Prohibition. COURTESY OF THE RAMSEY COUNTY HISTORICAL SOCIETY.

Ready for delivery.

the first person to sell beer that had been commercially brewed in Minnesota. The location of Yoerg's brewery, on south Washington street between Chestnut and Eagle streets, offered high bluffs into which caves could be carved for storage. While proximity to the river made shipping a possibility, it is likely that most of the product was consumed in the immediate area. In 1850, St. Paul's population was around 1,300 people (though, ironically, Yoerg's family was not included in the census for some reason). While records are incomplete, it appears that Yoerg did not begin shipping his beer beyond the immediate neighborhood until late 1851.

During the next few decades, the population of St. Paul exploded, with thirsty Germans among the most numerous of the new arrivals. Whereas Ramsey County had about two dozen Germans in the 1850 census, a decade later there were more than 16,000 German-born residents in the county. Yoerg remained at his first location until 1871, when increased demand encouraged him to build a new plant on the other side of the river at the corner of Ohio and Ethel streets. Even though demand had grown, Yoerg's remained a comparatively small brewery. Except during the first few years, when competition was almost nonexistent, it was never one of the largest in the state. Eleven years after the 1849 opening, the first set of reasonably accurate statewide production figures listed Yoerg's as tenth out of the twenty-some breweries listed. The records from the first full year of federal excise taxes in 1863 show Yoerg's as only the sixth-largest brewer in St. Paul.

It is not entirely clear who was Yoerg's first competitor. Two breweries claimed to have started in 1850, but solid documentary evidence exists only for John Orth's brewery in the town of St. Anthony. John Orth was born in 1821 in Alsace, a region under French control at the time but with an equally strong German cultural tradition that honored brewing. Orth and his young wife, Mary, settled in St.

Anthony and began to operate the brewery early in 1850. Like Yoerg, Orth picked a location near the Mississippi River and close to a likely market. His brewery, located at what would later be the corner of Marshall and Brewery, was 18 × 30 feet (but would become much larger over the next fifty years). The brewery had an artesian well for its water and nearby sandstone caves for storing the beer. Orth's first batches were brewed in a kettle that held two and one-half barrels of beer.[7] Unlike Yoerg, Orth featured ale and porter, though he offered lager as

John Orth's brewery, pictured here in 1880, was a busy place. At least four horse-drawn wagons are visible, along with employees and some of their children. The steep-roofed building behind the brewery is the malt house. COURTESY OF THE MINNESOTA HISTORICAL SOCIETY.

Frank Aiple fell from the roof of this house during construction and died of his injuries. The size and construction of the house suggest that Aiple's brewery was making a good profit. COURTESY OF THE MINNESOTA HISTORICAL SOCIETY.

well. This was probably because St. Anthony was a center of Yankee settlement and had very few German residents at the time. Orth placed the first known newspaper advertisement for a Minnesota brewery, which proclaimed that his ale and beer "would be found equal—yes superior—to that which is brought from below" (meaning farther down the river).[8] This ad recognized a situation that would challenge Minnesota's brewers from the very beginning to the present, competition from out-of-state breweries. Beer was generally expensive to ship, but it could be profitable in a market with little local competition. During this era, imported beer was advertised not by brewery but by city of origin. Taverns, billiard halls, and hotels advertised that they served the finest in St. Louis beer or, slightly later, as land transport improved, Milwaukee beer. While there were differences in water chemistry and other ingredients from city to city, only an expert would be able to tell the difference. The biggest advantage established brewing centers had over the frontier breweries was consistent quality. Even the most experienced frontier brewer could have difficulty adjusting to new water characteristics, different barley, or the bitterness of the local hops (if used). A single bad batch could be enough to doom a brewer's reputation.

Norbert Kimmick may have built a brewery on the corner of Third and Chestnut streets in Stillwater, a city with a large contingent of German settlers, in the same year Orth started business. Sources differ on the year Kimmick established the business and on whether the building on Third and Chestnut was a brewery or a distillery or possibly both. Even if Kimmick was not the second brewer in Minnesota, his claim on third place seems solid. In 1852, he moved to a location on South Main Street where a young brewer named Frank X. Aiple joined him two years later. Kimmick died in 1857, and his wife took over management of the brewery.

Susannah Burkhard and Other Brewsters

From ancient times to the beginning of commercial brewing, women made much of the world's beer. For most households, making ale was as much part of "women's work" as making bread. Brewsters, female brewers, probably became less common in America with the decline of ale, when brewing became a business rather than a household task. While it was rare for women to start commercial breweries, many women found themselves in possession of breweries upon the deaths of their husbands. While many brewers' widows quickly remarried the brewmaster (and some brewers' daughters' only apparent role was to marry the heir to the brewery), many women were critical to the survival and prosperity of the business. Christina Hoffman and Christina Heising both managed breweries in Red Wing after the deaths of their husbands and continued to expand the breweries even before remarrying. Mary Leslin was the proprietor of the Wabasha brewery even though her husband was alive and brewing. Louise Hamm was in charge of her husband's brewery beer garden and of operating the boardinghouse for single male employees. Once breweries began to incorporate, several women served as directors of their family firms.

Susannah Burkhard holds the record for being married to the most Minnesota brewers. She came to America from Germany with her family at age 22 and lived first in the large German community in Freeport, Illinois. There she met and married Norbert Kimmick, and in 1849 the couple moved to Stillwater. The couple found prosperity in Stillwater, expanded their original brewery to new quarters, and hired at least one additional employee, Frank X. Aiple, who soon was made a partner in the business. In 1857, after three years of this partnership, Norbert Kimmick died. Susannah took over management of the brewery while Aiple continued to supervise the brewing operations. The existing biographies make it clear that Susannah was running the brewery and Aiple was assisting her, at least until 1860, when the two were married and Aiple "assumed active management."[9] The couple had three children, Mary, Herman, and Frank Jr. The brewery was expanded in 1865 and was capable of producing more than 120 barrels per month, which made

Susannah Burkhard Kimmick Aiple Tepass, wife of three brewers, played an important role in managing the family brewery. This portrait was made around 1880. COURTESY OF THE MINNESOTA HISTORICAL SOCIETY.

it one of the largest breweries in the state outside of St. Paul. The brewery was destroyed by fire in May 1868, but rebuilding commenced immediately thereafter. Unfortunately, Frank Aiple was injured in a fall from the roof of his residence while doing some finishing work on the water pipes and died of his injuries in November. Susannah took over the brewery again and managed it herself until her marriage in December 1869 to Herman Tepass. After Tepass's death in 1887, Frank Aiple Jr. took over the brewery and managed it for about ten years.

Temperance Comes to Minnesota

The three pioneer breweries had little time to get established and build a market before a threat to their existence appeared in the form of temperance legislation. Many of the new settlers of Minnesota, especially its well-educated and wealthy inhabitants, were New England Protestants of various denominations, mostly Presbyterians.[10] They and other Protestants had been the primary advocates for the temperance movement that organized in reaction to the increased intake of spirits and to the increased influx of non-English immigrants who consumed them. Temperance advocates were cheered by the passage of legislation in Maine that prevented the sale of intoxicating beverages, and for the next decades, any such proposals were called Maine laws. The rough life and frequent drunken brawls of the frontier horrified many of the more-refined settlers such as school-teacher Harriet Bishop, who wrote:

> Alas! the demoralizing influence of ardent spirits. Nature had beautified our domain, but intemperance was laying waste its beauty, robbing the domestic circle of its charms, making paths of quicksand for the feet of young men, and more than brutalizing the poor ignorant native! The *bottle* was the unfailing attendant on *every* occasion and stood confessed the *life of every company*. . . . The beer soon created a thirst for something stronger: and not many months had elapsed, ere one and another had fallen never more to rise.[11]

When the territorial legislature met in January 1852, they were presented with several petitions requesting passage of a Maine law. Two of the petitions (one signed by men only and the other containing only women's signatures) claimed, "the use of alcoholic beverages is productive of evil only." The men's petition, signed by such community leaders as Norman Kittson, William Le Duc, Ard Godfrey, and Joseph Rolette, held that traffic in alcohol

> is attended with loss of time, character, health and life; that it renders the husband brutal—the father inhuman—the neighbor quarrelsome; that pauperism and crime are its inseparable adjuncts; and that it greatly increases the taxes for the support of paupers—the payment of costs in criminal prosecutions, and other public expenses . . .

The women's petition was less concerned with higher taxes than with higher nature. Signed by Harriet Bishop and by the wives, daughters, and sisters of several leading politicians or property owners, it stated that alcohol led to

> ... the indescribable suffering of our sex ... It deprives us of the affections and society of fathers, brothers, and husbands—it drags them from the high position among men, which their Creator intended for them to occupy, and subjects them to the contempt of others—it brings want and wretchedness to our once happy homes, and disgrace to our innocent children as the offspring of inebriates. And, too often, it brings us and our babes to premature and penniless widowhood and orphanage.

The temperance forces were much better organized than their opposition, and a Maine law referendum, introduced as House File 54, was quickly introduced. The referendum was sent to the voters, who approved it by a margin that surprised even its proponents. However, the state supreme court overturned the law on the grounds that the legislature had unconstitutionally delegated its lawmaking power to the people through the referendum. The next year, the forces opposing the Maine law were mobilized and submitted petitions of their own. The arguments were divided into categories that would become familiar for the next eight decades: "dry" forces emphasized the harmful influence of liquor in general and the saloon in particular on family and fortune, while "wets" emphasized liberty and urged regulation of the trade and prosecution of violators rather than banning liquor. There was also a dry petition signed by nine members of the Dakotah Nation, claiming that the laws prohibiting sale to Indians were routinely circumvented, and that the liquor trade led to "infamy."[12] The attempt to re-pass the law in 1853 failed, and while no further statewide prohibition was attempted, temperance and prohibition advocates continued to seek statewide legislation concerning the alcohol trade for the rest of the century.

Expanding Opportunity

The treaties of 1851 and 1855 opened vast tracts of land to settlement and development. The first brewer to take advantage of the newly opened lands was Jacob Schmahl, who is said to have built a hotel and brewery in "about 1852" in the newly formed town of Traverse des Sioux.[13] He maintained his brewery there until 1866. But by that time, neighboring St. Peter was overwhelming the once-thriving Traverse des Sioux and, to add to his predicament, Schmahl was one of three Nicollet County brewers to have their breweries seized in a tax dispute. Tax records show that the other two resumed operations, but Schmahl did not. He probably decided that the shrinking town and competition from three breweries in St. Peter made it unprofitable to continue there. Schmahl later operated short-lived breweries in Redwood Falls and Canby that were too far from beer-drinking

Jacob Schmahl's frontier brewery was not distinguishable from any other building unless one knew it was a brewery. The site of the building is marked at the Treaty Site History Center one mile north of St. Peter. COURTESY OF THE MINNESOTA HISTORICAL SOCIETY.

populations to make any significant profit. Schmahl was the Pa Ingalls of Minnesota brewers—moving west before others to profit by getting there first, but never quite realizing the potential, just like the father in the *Little House* books. (In an ironic twist, Jacob's son Julius would become a prominent state politician, and at the end of his term as secretary of state, he would be in charge of beginning the enforcement of Prohibition.)

Aside from Schmahl's jump into the wilderness, most new breweries were established along the rivers, relatively close to the areas already settled. Winona was the first new city to gain a brewery when the firm of Brentle, Scherer & Rath opened the Gilmore Valley Brewery in 1855. During the next two years, residents of Brownsville, Hastings, St. Peter, Mankato, Marine Mills, Red Wing, Rochester, Faribault, Belle Plaine, Sand Creek (today Jordan), and Shakopee all saw their first (and sometimes their second) brewery open. The 1857 Census, taken to confirm that Minnesota Territory had enough residents to become a

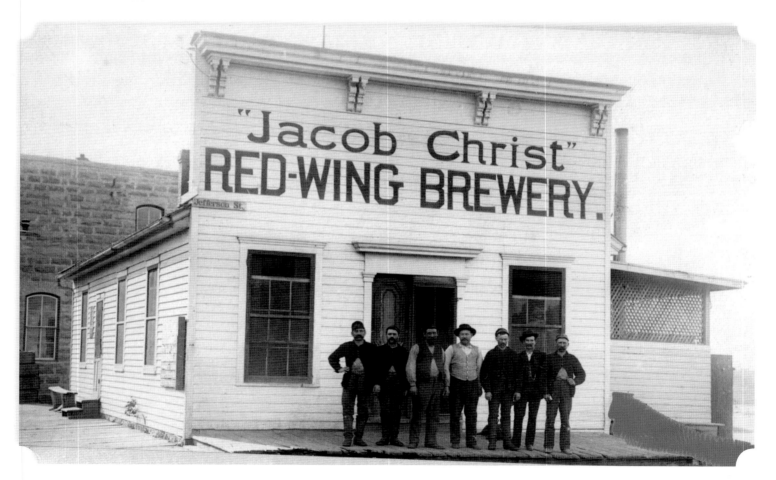

The office of Jacob Christ's Red-Wing Brewery appears in an undated photo. Christ was a popular saloonkeeper before marrying the widowed Christina Hoffman. It is likely that his contacts among saloon owners helped secure business for his new venture. COURTESY OF THE GOODHUE COUNTY HISTORICAL SOCIETY, RED WING, MN.

state, listed seventy men who identified their occupation as brewer (and excludes several others known to be present). While many were employed at breweries that had more than one employee, it is clear that when Minnesota was admitted to the Union in May 1858, there were at least thirty different breweries operating throughout the state.

Despite their role as pioneering industries in their respective towns, these breweries were not temporary frontier firms. Of the thirty-plus breweries found-ed before statehood, only five failed to make it through a decade, but sixteen lasted into the twentieth century and six survived to celebrate their hundredth anniversary in business. However, the financial soundness of these breweries was challenged immediately by the Panic of 1857. The resulting credit and currency shortages forced thousands of bankruptcies and business closures nationwide, but Minnesota's breweries survived unscathed. This may have been because few of the breweries had borrowed

Becoming a Brewer

Throughout the years, Minnesota's brewers have learned their craft through apprenticeships and experience, formal training, or a combination of the two. The proprietor of the brewery was not always the brewer. Theodore Hamm was the most prominent example of a non-brewing proprietor, but there were others throughout the state who hired trained "practical brewers" to make the beer. The term *brewmaster* is usually reserved for those who have completed the required training at an academy; head brewer is a more accurate title for brewery operators with less training.

Many of Minnesota's pioneer brewers were trained in their home countries—usually Germany, though Adam Stenger of Rochester was trained in London and others presumably studied or worked in their home countries. The biographies of these first Minnesota brewers are seldom clear on exactly what kind of training they had before arriving in the United States, though they occasionally mention previous

This diploma was awarded in 1900 by the Wahl-Henius American Brewing Academy to Henry Schmid, whose numerous positions would eventually include brewmaster at Duluth Brewing & Malting Co. The vignette displays many of the tools of the Brewer's art and, despite its medieval appearance, includes up-to-date microscopes and other instruments. FROM THE COLLECTION OF PETE CLURE.

work in a brewery. There were brewing academies in Europe, often connected with long-established breweries such as Weihenstephan near Munich. According to *One Hundred Years of Brewing*, schools devoted specifically to train-

In the mid-nineteenth century, brewers brought saccharometers into common use to determine the specific gravity of wort or beer. The Kaiser saccharometer pictured here includes a graduated scale indicating how many parts of sugar are present in 100 parts of wort or beer. Readings taken before and after fermentation show how much fermentable sugar has been converted to alcohol. This instrument also includes a thermometer so brewers could make adjustments for the temperature of the liquid. COURTESY OF THE MINNESOTA HISTORICAL SOCIETY.

ing brewers were not founded until the 1860s. Employees other than the brewmaster usually learned on the job rather than in an academy; tasks such as shoveling grain required little skill and could be learned quickly.

Upon arriving in the United States, brewers might find work in established brewing centers such as New York, Pittsburgh, Cincinnati, or Milwaukee to gain both experience and funds before moving west to seek their fortune in the business. After the Civil War, Minnesota cities such as Minneapolis, St. Paul, and Winona served as training centers for would-be brewery proprietors.

The sons and sons-in-law of the pioneer brewers were often sent to a brewing academy to prepare to take over the family business. (Families with more than one son might send one to a brewing academy and another to business school.) New York, Chicago, and Milwaukee all had prominent brewing academies, and the names of Minnesota's brewing families are found among the alumni of these schools. While a brewer in a small horse- or hand-powered brewery could brew for years without formal training, a brewer in a large modern brewery would have to be familiar with steam power, artificial refrigeration, yeast cultures, and many other aspects of the business. John Beerhalter's 1902 diploma from the American Brewing Academy in Chicago listed each of the courses a brewmaster studied over a four-month period: Principles and Practice of Brewing and Malting; Brewing Operations and Demonstrations in the Experimental Brewery; Elements of Chemistry; Physics; Mathematics—Brewing Materials; Micro-Organisms and Microscopy; Exercises in Microscopical and Chemical Laboratories; and Brewery Construction and Engineering. Beerhalter, who would later become brewmaster at Fitger Brewing Company in Duluth, earned an overall score of 99.2, among the highest ever at the academy. Practical brewers could expand their knowledge further by subscribing to one or more of the scientific brewing journals such as *Western Brewer* or *The Brewers' Journal*, which until 1894 was published in double column format with German and English language versions.

Brewers in Minnesota's modern breweries display the same range of experience and training as previous generations. Some have graduated from the Siebel Institute in Chicago or another academy—a few have graduated from homebrewing. ❧

Many of these nineteenth-century employees of August Schell Brewing Company in New Ulm hold distinctive tools that identify their occupations. The two men seated on the highest barrels used the large wooden shovels in the malt house to turn the grain so it soaked and dried evenly. The man in the center of the doorway holding a bugle may have been a foreman. The youth holding a wrench (far right) was probably a machinist in the steam plant. At far left, the man holding a whip was most likely a teamster, and the dapper man next to him may have been the sales manager. The man in the leather apron left of the kegs was most likely the cooper. The beer they are enjoying is quite dark and may have been bock beer. FROM THE COLLECTION OF THE BROWN COUNTY HISTORICAL SOCIETY, NEW ULM, MN.

any significant amounts of money to start their businesses, nor had they had time to go deeply into debt or to have extended their credit beyond what they could manage. However, the opening of new breweries slowed down as settlers waited until the economy stabilized to make major investments. At least ten new breweries first appeared in the records in 1857 alone—about twice as many as were started in 1858 and 1859 combined—most located in well-established cities. The frontier economy remained unsettled for several years and major bank failures continued into 1859.

By 1860 the economy had stabilized, Minnesota's population was increasing rapidly, and the brewing industry was growing at a brisk pace. In 1860, the Bureau of the Census took its first special count of manufacturing firms that transacted more than $500 of business in the previous year. Of the nearly fifty breweries in the state, twenty-six met that threshold. Seventeen different cities were represented, including six breweries in St. Paul and two breweries in the small but booming river town of Reads Landing. Jacob Schmahl's brewery at Traverse des Sioux reportedly produced the most beer—1,650 barrels—but this number is probably inaccurate since he was producing just ten barrels per month only five years later and 1,650 barrels was significantly more than was produced by major urban producers such as Christopher Stahlmann in St. Paul and John Orth in St. Anthony.

The census of 1860 contained other data that provide a good general picture of the brewing industry at the time. Most of these larger breweries employed two or three men, Yoerg employed four, and several other brewers were the sole employees of their firms. These workers earned on average between $20 and $30 per month, though Adolph Albachten in Shakopee paid his three employees a monthly total of $150. According to valuations provided in the census, the standard price of a barrel of beer was $4 in St. Anthony, $5 in St. Paul, and usually $6 or $7 in the outlying areas, though Charles Ginsberg in Mantorville valued his output at slightly over $2 per barrel and the firm of Sommers & Ibach in Preston valued theirs at $12 per barrel. (This estimate was $5 more than their advertised price a year earlier, when they were in a price war with Charles Deinhardt in nearby Chatfield.)[14]

This rapidly expanding industry required an equivalent expansion of raw materials. Minnesota's climate is ideally suited to growing barley, and cultivation of this crop expanded rapidly in the early years—from just over 1,000 bushels in 1849 to an estimated 300,000 bushels in 1860. The commissioner of statistics editorialized on the superiority of Minnesota barley and claimed, "This is beginning to be so generally recognized that it is already exported in considerable quantities to supply breweries in the Middle States." The incomplete statistics in these sources suggest that Minnesota breweries were using about 20 percent of the state's barley crop, and the rest was exported. The commissioner also noted that hops were grown in the state, but not in significant quantities.[15]

The pioneer brewers of Minnesota had become an important part of the new state's economy and culture. Many were accumulating wealth and influence that would confer high social standing. John Orth was on St. Anthony's first city council. By the beginning of the Civil War, breweries had been established along the Mississippi River from Brownsville near the Iowa border north to St. Cloud. Along the Minnesota River, breweries were a feature of most major settlements from Shakopee west to New Ulm. Since the business was profitable, competitors were encouraged to enter existing markets, and the continued westward movement of the frontier and the filling in of unsettled areas would allow many other brewers to start in areas free from immediate local competition. Many of the new companies would contribute to the economy and culture of Minnesota well into the next century.

By the 1880s, there were eleven coopers in Minneapolis. Many of them made flour barrels for the milling industry, but some also made beer kegs. (St. Paul, which produced more beer but little flour, had only five coopers listed in the city directory.) While many breweries employed a cooper to repair damaged barrels and perhaps make some as well, they often purchased new barrels from an independent cooper. Here, a wagon from John Orth's brewery is being loaded with kegs manufactured by the nearby Schon & Schnitzius' cooperage in 1882. COURTESY OF THE MINNESOTA HISTORICAL SOCIETY.

August Schell's brewery, pictured here in the late 1880s, shows how rapidly some of Minnesota's frontier breweries grew. Extensive stables lie in front of the brewery, and August and Teresa Schell's new mansion is visible at left. Of special interest is the icehouse at lower left. The ramp was used to haul blocks of ice from the Cottonwood River. COURTESY OF AUGUST SCHELL BREWING COMPANY.

CHAPTER 2

Fewer Ales, More Rails: Brewing Fills the State

We need a brewery in Alexandria. The Scandinavians and Germans of Douglas and Otter Tail counties are lovers of beer, and thousands of dollars go out of the country every year in payment of it. There is not reason why this beer should not be made here.
—*Alexandria Post*, 7 April 1869

MINNESOTANS GREETED THE OUTBREAK OF THE CIVIL WAR WITH A BURST of patriotic fervor. Governor Alexander Ramsey was the first governor to volunteer troops to defend the nation's capital, and Minnesotans literally knocked each other over to enlist. The first year of the war saw few major battles because both sides needed to assemble and equip their armies. The early battles demonstrated that many more men would be needed for a longer term than anticipated, and that supplies would need to be procured at a level never before imagined. Beer played a trivial role in recruiting troops but a major part in financing the war.

Death and Taxes

As the volunteers assembled at Fort Snelling, the initial enthusiasm was tempered by boredom and the realization that the rebels would not be whipped in a few weeks. The initial three-month term of enlistment proved too short, and commanders were under pressure to persuade their men to change their enlistments to three-year terms. In May 1861 the troops at Fort Snelling were treated to a party featuring numerous kegs of beer. Some claimed that the new enlistment papers were offered at the party and a number of soldiers signed while under the influence. Some members of the regiment as well as the general public expressed outrage at this tactic, and the validity of the enlistments was challenged.[1]

Alcohol use and abuse concerned troops and commanders throughout the war.

While some commanders believed an occasional drink had a positive effect on morale, most of the Army was concerned about alcohol's effect on troop readiness. Commanders in the field were often distracted by the need to discipline soldiers for drunkenness. Ironically, the Army seems to have had fewer problems with drunkenness during the War for Independence, when the soldiers had a daily ration of beer. The beer ration was replaced by a liquor ration early in the nineteenth century, probably because liquor was easier and cheaper to transport and because the Army was doing most of its fighting on the frontier rather than near urban brewing areas. Secretary of War Lewis Cass prohibited the consumption of liquor at any military installation in 1832.[2]

Raising Funds

To meet the desperate need for funds to conduct the war, Congress passed a sweeping excise tax law in the summer of 1862. Income was taxed, as were luxury goods such as pianos, carriages, and gold watches. Business owners were required annually to obtain a license at a rate dependent on the type and size of the business. In addition, excise taxes were placed on the production of many goods, including beer. The Internal Revenue Act passed on 1 July 1862 established a license fee of $25 for brewers making fewer than 500 barrels per year and a license fee of $50 for larger brewers.[3] Each barrel sold was subject to a $1 excise tax. With an average price of $5 to $7 per barrel before the tax, this amounted to a 15 to 20 percent increase in the cost per barrel to the customer.

Nationally, the new tax had some significant side effects in the short term. While the Germans tended to be strong Free Soil advocates and many served in the military during the war, the brewers still saw some parts of the law as unfair or impractical and wanted several changes made. A group of lager brewers in New York began to meet and later called for national involvement. These meetings led to what would soon become the United States Brewers Association. The USBA was successful in making the excise tax more efficient and even succeeded in getting the tax lowered to sixty cents per barrel for thirteen months. According to industry accounts, the close working relationship between the Internal Revenue Office and the USBA went both ways—the brewers claimed to be less prone to tax evasion than many other industries and they usually accepted regulations that were both necessary and unavoidable without much complaint.[4] However, the records of the collectors themselves indicate that most small and midsize breweries paid a tax penalty at least once, and some breweries tested the vigilance of the revenue agents on a regular basis. Numerous Minnesota breweries were seized by revenue agents for failure to comply with the law, and brewers were occasionally jailed for violations. (Many of these incidents are related in the histories of the individual breweries in the "Minnesota Breweries" section of this book.)

In his definitive book on American brewing history, Stanley Baron suggested that the other side effect of the new tax was to force small or less financially sound breweries out of business, leaving their markets to be consolidated by larger pro-

This quarter barrel revenue stamp featuring a vignette of Bacchus pouring wine was printed by American Bank Note Co., New York. Several brewers were arrested and fined for trying to reuse stamps that had been improperly cancelled. FROM THE AUTHOR'S COLLECTION.

ducers. This was not the case in Minnesota. For one thing, most of Minnesota's breweries were roughly the same small size, especially when viewed from a national perspective. When the tax was first implemented, only four brewers in the second collection district were assessed the higher fee for producing more than 500 barrels per year (Stahlmann, Jacob Bensberg, Drewry & Scotten of St. Paul, and Orth of St. Anthony) and none of these produced more than 1,000 barrels per year during the Civil War until Bensberg and Stahlmann both crossed this threshold in 1865. (By way of comparison, Moerlein & Windisch Brewery in Cincinnati produced 25,000 barrels in 1865, and Lill & Diversey Brewery in Chicago produced nearly 45,000 barrels a year just before the Civil War.)[5] Except for St. Paul, in towns and cities where there was more than one brewery, the breweries were fairly close in size, whatever size that was. The two breweries in Reads Landing, those of Charles Saile and Charles Leslin, both normally sold between 10 and 15 barrels per month during 1865, as did the two brewers in Chaska, George Ulmer and Gerhard Deuss. Likewise, the three brewers of St. Cloud in 1865—Lorenz Enderle, Frank Funk, and Peter Kramer—all averaged slightly fewer than 20 barrels per month. None of these breweries was likely to have had costs or other financial conditions that differed enough for the tax to have affected them differently.

The Civil War interrupted export sales for at least one Minnesota brewery. It appears that Christopher Stahlmann had been selling beer in Memphis before the outbreak of hostilities. The German-language newspaper *Minnesota Staats-Zeitung* reported in late June 1862 that the reopening of the Mississippi River for

Many of the breweries started in Minnesota's small cities during the Civil War survived into the twentieth century. Peter Ganser's brewery in Owatonna was founded by Adolph Knoblauch in 1861. It is unlikely that he was shipping his lager to the Deep South; Export was a common name for bottled beer, and this label from around 1910 appears to be a printing company's stock label designed for use by many breweries. William Schellhas Brewing Co. first started brewing as Neuffer & Becker in 1863. Even at this early date, it was the third (or possibly fourth) brewery to operate in Winona. This label dates from the mid-1890s. FROM THE COLLECTION OF KEN MALZ.

trade as far as Memphis would allow Stahlmann to resume the trade he had built up in that city before the war. Stahlmann's exports to Memphis appear to be the farthest any Minnesota brewer had shipped so far and were especially noteworthy as several cities with better-established breweries, including St. Louis, were much closer to Memphis.[6]

Of all the breweries for which records are available, only two that were open before the Civil War closed during it. One was the brewery of Barnhard Gloegglar in North Minneapolis, which disappeared from the records after August 1863. The brewery built in Faribault in 1857 by Norbert Paquin burned in 1865, but by that point both brewers who previously had leased it had their own breweries in town.

Not only did few breweries go out of business, more than thirty new breweries were mentioned for the first time in records dated from 1862 through 1865. Some were new breweries competing with existing businesses in the same town: five new breweries opened in St. Paul, the busy river ports of Winona and Red Wing each gained their third brewery, and Owatonna's first brewery had only about two years without a local rival. A few other new breweries were filling in territories between existing breweries such as those of Lake City and Waconia. Finally, some breweries sprang up on the fringes of settled areas to serve those who were pushing farther west, such as the brewery of Louis Brink in St. Joseph, west of St. Cloud.

The Dakota War

The brewery expansion to the southwest would be slowed somewhat by the events of August and September 1862, sometimes called the Dakota Conflict or the Sioux Uprising. Tired of waiting for their annuity payments and desperately hungry, several hundred Dakota warriors attacked the Indian Agency at Redwood and then turned their attention to the nearby settlements. The young settlement of New Ulm was the nearest town of consequence and was selected as a promising source of supplies and plunder. While the citizens of the area ultimately held the town and repulsed the Dakota, much of the surrounding area was set to the torch— some buildings were burned by the Dakota, but others were burned by the defenders to deny the attackers cover. While nearly 200 buildings were destroyed, one that survived was August Schell's brewery. Company histories credit this to his generally good treatment of the Dakota, in contrast to many other German settlers who considered the Dakota to be lazy and refused to help the hungry families. Many of the brewers (or future brewers) of the area served with the militia protecting the town. William Bierbauer of Mankato served as a captain in the force sent to relieve the siege, and John Hauenstein, Otto Vill, and Andreas Betz all helped defend their hometown. The settlement in New Ulm recovered relatively quickly, but expansion in the wider region would not regain its former pace until the arrival of the railroad in the 1870s.

Changing Tastes and Territories

Through the end of the Civil War, producers of ale continued to have a strong market in the major cities, especially where there was a large English, Scotch, or Irish community. Given that ale (including porter and stout) did not require long, cool storage (and often deteriorated after long storage), it was produced and sold at a more consistent volume throughout the year than lager, which was in greater demand as a thirst quencher during the hot months. For example, during 1865 the Drewry & Greig ale brewery of St. Paul sold 72 barrels of ale during their slowest month (February) and a high of 212 barrels during each of the winter months of November and December. Their ale output during the hot months of summer was about two-thirds of their high point. The other ale brewers of St. Paul had similarly flat output with pre-Christmas high points. By contrast, Christopher Stahlmann's lager brewery sold a low of 56 barrels in February, but a high of 504 barrels in August. Likewise, Anthony Yoerg's 1865 winter output averaged about 35 barrels per month, but jumped to the mid-60s in May and June and to more than 115 barrels per month in July and August. In the fall of 1869, the federal revenue agent recorded both production and sales for the breweries in Goodhue County. The four brewers who specialized in lager produced no beer at all during August but had resumed full production again by November. The ale brewers continued to make some beer throughout the summer.

Lager Pushes Out Ale

While ale was a steady business, it was not particularly widespread and was rare outside the largest cities. During the 1860s, St. Paul had two breweries that

The August Schell brewery in the mid-1860s. The building on the left was the family home and today is the brewery office. The horse treadmill used to provide power is clearly visible in front of the brewery. COURTESY OF AUGUST SCHELL BREWING COMPANY.

The Drewry Pale Ale label (c. 1907–1917) was similar in shape, color, and design to the labels for England's well-known Bass Ale, the most common of the imported pale ales. (The red triangle of Bass was Britain's first trademark.) FROM THE COLLECTION OF KEN MALZ.

produced only ale: the company operated by the Drewry family (with various partners under several different names) and Leip & Coffin (which became Coffin & Oakes in 1865). Coffin & Oakes shipped their ale to Hastings in the late 1860s (where it was featured on draught at the Tontine Billiard Room) and probably to other outlying cities as well.[7] John Orth produced an ale and a porter throughout his period as an independent brewer. After the merger that produced the Minneapolis Brewing Company, ale and porter continued to be part of the product line, with porter being advertised as the ideal companion to a man's evening pipe as late as 1897 in the Minneapolis city directory.

Outside the Twin Cities, there were very few breweries dedicated to ale, although several included ale or porter among their products for various reasons. Because he was trained in London, Adam Stenger, superintendent of City Brewery in Rochester, offered "English and Scotch Ales, Porter and Brown Stout" in addition to lager.[8] In 1865 William Heising of Red Wing made nearly twice as much ale as lager. J. G. Busch in Duluth, recognizing the number of Canadians living in Duluth, offered a range of several ales in addition to lager.[9] However, out-state breweries that exclusively offered English styles usually didn't last long. The Larkin brothers opened a brewery in the northwestern town of Moorhead in 1875, just four years after it was established along the Northern Pacific Railway. Having come from Canada, where English settlers were still in the vast majority and ale was still the preferred style, they elected to produce ale in Moorhead. Due to the probable combination of the lack of a market for ale and some quality control problems, their brewery survived less than a year.[10] In 1877, Gideon Smales arrived in Fairmont and joined an active group of English settlers in south-central Minnesota who maintained many of the upper-class customs of their homeland, from horse racing to boating. Smales had a natural local market for his ale and porter, which he claimed were "highly recommended by Physicians as containing strengthening and medicinal properties." He expanded his brewery rapidly, adding an ice house, a cellar, and a bottling house within the first year. His expansion may have been too rapid: records of the failure of the Bank of Fairmont in early 1879 show that Smales (a stockholder in the bank) had an overdraft against the bank of $1,693.26, which unfortunately was $400 more than his assets. The brewery property attracted the most active bidding at the sheriff's sale held to settle the bank's accounts.[11]

By the early 1880s, local breweries specializing in English or Irish ales, or indeed, making them at all, were nearly impossible to find outside the major cities. Even in the major cities, ale was a relatively minor sideline of the major breweries or was made for a limited market by a recent immigrant. Patrick J. Gilbride (sometimes spelled Gilbridge) was listed in the 1882 Minneapolis city directory as an ale brewer working and residing at 1420 South Third Street. The next year he is listed at the same address as a saloon owner, but is listed as a brewer again for three of the next four years, though his address kept changing. Gilbride appears to have found the ale business less lucrative than he hoped: in 1888 he is listed on

Based on the product listings, Drewry's two lines of business seemed to compete with each other. They both brewed and imported ale, stout, cider, and ginger ale. The firm also dealt in Milwaukee lager, though it is not known from which brewer. FROM THE COLLECTION OF STEVE KETCHUM.

the same block but as a confectioner. His story is representative of the difficulty in finding a sufficiently profitable market for ale. Though they were once among the largest breweries in the state, no ale producer would be the largest brewer in the Twin Cities until the end of the twentieth century. Even Drewry Brewing & Bottling Company eventually supplemented sales of its own product by becoming an importer of two brands of Irish stout, Guinness and Murphy's.

Railroads Fill in the Gaps

While much of the geographic expansion of population, agriculture, and industry was made possible by the extension of the railroads, this was less true for the brewing industry, except in the northwest portion of the state. Southeast of a line from Duluth through St. Cloud to the southwest corner of the state, most counties that would ever host a brewery had one before the railroad arrived in town. River transportation was well established in the southeast and east-central portions of the state and as far as New Ulm along the Minnesota River, and the local river often provided the advantages of plentiful water for brewing and topography suitable for lagering caves. But even where there were no major waterways, breweries often still predated the railroads. In the south-central part of the state, Charles Deinhardt established one brewery in Blue Earth before 1866 and another in Jackson in 1871, even though the Milwaukee Road spur would not reach the towns until 1873. The Minnesota Central line didn't reach Austin until 1869, but Frank Weinand's brewery had been there at least since 1865. In a few cases, though, the railroad may have provided the necessary conditions to introduce brewing to a locale in this region, such as at Albert Lea and Waseca. Local historians also credit the arrival of the Southern Minnesota Railroad in 1867 with the opening of two breweries in Rushford to serve the influx of new residents and businesses.[12]

For the most part, railroads had two effects on the distribution of breweries in the southeast portion of the state. For cities that became regional rail centers, the increase in business and industry (and thus population) that followed the railroads made it possible for these cities to support multiple breweries. After railroads reached Mankato in 1868, three (possibly four) new breweries were built in the next five years. While this is the most dramatic example, other cities such as

Austin's last brewery closed around 1880, but the city clearly did not have to go without beer. This photograph claims to show the amount of beer handled in one half-day in 1910 by the Wells, Fargo & Company Express service in Austin. The cases are loaded for distribution to brewery depots in and around the city. COURTESY OF THE MINNESOTA HISTORICAL SOCIETY.

Portion of beer business handled in one half day at Austin, Minn.

HAY CREEK BREWERY
JOHN HARTMAN, PROP.   GOODHUE CO., MINN.

Rochester, Red Wing, and St. Cloud experienced increases in production through a combination of new breweries and increased production from existing firms.

Another major effect of the railroads was to select winners and losers among cities, and therefore among the breweries located within them. Smaller cities and towns that were more than a half day's journey from the nearest large town were able to support a brewery, as shipping from the larger town was often difficult. With rail transport, large producers were no longer dependent on horse-drawn brewery wagons to deliver beer in the countryside. The production-cost advantage held by large producers was probably a contributing factor in the closure of breweries in towns like Le Roy that were not big enough to exploit their railroad connections. For the most part, though, the effect of shipping on small-town breweries would not be evident for many years.

On the other hand, the expansion of brewing to the northwest part of the state was much more closely tied to the railroads. In the southeast, many cities and towns were established ahead of the railroad, and while the railroad bypassed some isolated sites, for the most part the rails connected existing settlements. Northwest of St. Cloud, settlements were few and far between before the end of the Civil War, so the direction of the rail network determined where most towns would be located. Railroad companies tried to keep the exact routes of their proposed lines from becoming public knowledge to avoid having squatters claim land at the most desirable town sites. One such incident at Crow Wing (later Brainerd) forced the Northern Pacific Railway Company to pay twenty times the standard price per acre for land near the river crossing. In the northwest the railroads had a much more important role in selecting economic winners and losers. Georgetown was one of the very few settlements on the Red River before the Civil War; it was centered on a Hudson Bay Company trading post and was a key stop on the ox-cart trade route between St. Paul and the fur country to the north. When the Northern Pacific decided to cross the Red River fifteen miles south of Georgetown, the town lost any chance of becoming the major city of the region—a distinction that went to the two cities at the river crossing, Fargo and Moorhead. (The large number of cities and towns named after railroad company directors and investors, including Brainerd, Fargo, and Moorhead, demonstrates the influence of the railroads on the settlement of the region.)

Breweries located in the northwest had little choice but to locate near the railroads. Without the trains, they could not obtain raw materials or find a sufficient population to serve. Beyond this, prospective brewers still needed to meet a ma-

This photograph of Carl Volk's brewery in Alexandria shows clearly how Volk used the hillside location: storage caves could be accessed from inside the brewery. PHOTOGRAPH BY NEWTON J. TRENHAM; COURTESY OF THE MINNESOTA HISTORICAL SOCIETY.

jority of the necessary conditions for creating a viable brewery. A reliable supply of fresh water was essential, topography that would make caves easier to dig was highly desirable, and the population needed enough beer drinkers to support the business. These conditions, which were common in the southeast, were not as widespread in the northwest. The Great Plains begin in the western part of the state, which is notable for the flatness of the land. The small farm breweries that were common in Wisconsin and occasionally appeared in southeastern Minnesota were unknown in the northwest. Digging the necessary aging cellars required too much time and expense, and because the farms were generally larger than in the southeast, the neighboring population was too spread out to support part-time brewing. Finally, the population that settled the area had fewer Germans and more Scandinavians, who did not have the same beer-drinking tradition as the Germans. Many of the newer settlers were strong temperance advocates and sometimes established their settlements as dry right from the beginning.

With the relatively sparse beer-drinking population and less-than-ideal brewing circumstances, few cities north of St. Cloud were able to support more than one brewery. One exception was Alexandria, which for forty years had two breweries and offered three choices during the 1880s. In June 1869 the *Alexandria Post* offered encouragement to prospective brewers: "A brewery at Alexandria would meet with good home patronage. There is an abundance of barley growing, and Douglas and the neighboring counties are a beer drinking people. Who will secure the chance?" The question was answered in August when Charles Volk arrived from St. Joseph and purchased lots on the corner of Main Street and 4th Avenue for a brewery. An article announcing his purchase noted the importance of topography in his selection: "The steep bank on the lots he bought will admit a cellar some 30 or 40 feet deep." Volk's brewery began production in late 1870 and stayed in business for twenty years. (The cellar survived until 1943, when it was demolished to build a machinery business.) Volk was successful enough to have the resources to build a multipurpose block downtown, but also successful enough to draw competitors to his lucrative market. Rudolph Wegener, a young German brewer who had served as a corporal in the Franco-Prussian War, emigrated to America in 1870 and went to work in Milwaukee for the Phillip Best Brewing Company (soon to become Pabst). He moved to Alexandria and opened his brewery there in 1876. By 1880 Wegener was well established, but he and Volk were joined that year by Fred and Christ Aberle, who started the third brewery in town. One article from July of that year, praising Wegener's new brewery addition, landscaping, and "handsome picket fence," also noted with tongue in cheek that "One of the Alexandria brewers laments that last Saturday was a poor day for beer as he sold only 75 kegs."[13] Alexandria was a large enough brewing center to maintain two breweries (until enforcement of a long-ignored treaty made the entire region dry) and to be one of the rare out-state cities to host a brewery after the repeal of Prohibition.

With the exceptions of Alexandria and Fergus Falls, no city in the northwest

The two breweries in Reads Landing and those in nearby cities found a ready market for their products. At least three saloon signs are clearly visible in this photograph of Upper Main Street in Reads Landing. Several of the other buildings probably contain saloons as well. COURTESY OF THE MINNESOTA HISTORICAL SOCIETY.

supported more than one brewery at a time, though several breweries in the region experienced long periods of success and prosperity.

Minnesota is not as famous for ghost towns as the mining states farther west because most town sites offered some redeeming feature after the primary reason for founding played out. Still, there were many towns that grew quickly and became important in their region for a brief time—and grew large enough and busy enough to have a brewery. Unfortunately, many of these breweries were short lived, and the documentation for these breweries is extremely limited. A typical case is Otter Tail City, located between Wadena and Fergus Falls. Situated on the east shore of Otter Tail Lake, Otter Tail City was a boomtown hoping to profit from milling and railroad traffic. An article in the *Fergus Falls Daily Journal* looking back on the history of Otter Tail claimed that the boomtown had thirty-six saloons and a brewery. Sometime in early 1871, Joseph Barrett started a brewery in the rear of McArthur's City Hotel. It is clear that Barrett did not brew himself, given that his ads noted that he had "secured the services of a First Class Brewer." He offered beer "by the keg, barrel or load," and was shipping beer as far away as Fargo in Dakota Territory. In 1872 the new railroad was placed a mile to the east, the mill and the newspaper moved to other cities, and the original town site was abandoned in favor of one on the railroad. Barrett did not restart the brewery in the new town.

The story in Reads Landing (sometimes spelled Reed's or Read's) was quite different. Considered to be a den of iniquity by residents in nearby Lake City, the booming river town had enough saloons to keep two medium-sized breweries busy for decades. But the increasing importance of rail and the consequent drop in river freight resulted in most business forsaking Reads Landing for river cities that were also rail hubs, such as Wabasha and Red Wing. Despite the near disappearance of the town, the Upper Brewery remained in business until it was destroyed by fire in 1909.

By the end of the 1870s, the major railroad lines were established and new waves of immigrants were flooding the state to exploit the seemingly unlimited farming and business opportunities. The state had survived a massive economic crisis and a devastating grasshopper plague, making the promising future appear even brighter. Minnesota brewers of all sizes joined other residents in looking forward to a period of unprecedented growth.

This stunning corner sign, dating from around 1885, is the only one known to exist. Before its recovery and restoration, it had been used to catch leaks in a Brown County warehouse. COURTESY OF AUGUST SCHELL BREWING COMPANY.

Patronize Home Industry: The Glory Days of the Small-Town Brewer

Mr. Buselmeier makes a purer beer than any that is shipped in here and we are glad to know that the drinking public appreciate the fact. Every dollar that Mr. Buselmeier gets is expended in Pine City and those who patronize him are benefiting the village. The same can be said of every other home industry. . . . So when in need of a glass of beer, a glass of pop, a good cigar, a sack of flour, a newspaper, or in fact anything that is manufactured at home and will benefit home trade be sure and call for it. This is the way to build up a town.

—*Pine City Pioneer*, 29 August 1902

TECHNOLOGY, ECONOMICS, AND CULTURE COMBINED TO CREATE CIRCUM-stances that encouraged breweries to spring up in small cities and tiny farm towns and allowed them to survive for several generations between the Civil War and Prohibition. The main rail lines did not serve every town, and high freight rates made it prohibitively expensive for many brewers to ship by rail. Many breweries, therefore, depended on overland transportation of their goods and were limited in their deliveries by how far out a team of horses could go and return during a day. The roads of the period were slowly improving, but most were dirt roads in various states of repair, so the distance a team could travel carrying a heavy load of beer kegs was unlikely to be more than ten miles. Farmers (and others) could also pick up a keg at the brewery when they were in town, but they also were limited in how far they could travel during a day. The desire of saloon and hotel owners to have the freshest (and cheapest) beer possible for their customers encouraged the founding of breweries in almost every community that seemed able and willing to support a brewery, and even in several that

seemed much too small for a brewery to survive. While some brewers began to ship by rail immediately after the railroads were built, this was limited at first to a few adventurous breweries that could afford to both pay the shipping costs and establish depots along the rail lines to keep the beer cool until its final delivery. By the time many breweries overcame these obstacles, the small-town breweries were firmly entrenched.

With the exception of a few products, the era of national brands had not yet arrived for most consumer goods. Few goods that were brought in from the east were sold with a maker's name identified (with the notable exception of patent medicines), and most items were sold in bulk. Consumers placed their trust in the discretion of the local merchant to select the best goods rather than in the reputation of the faraway manufacturer. (This would remain true even with the advent of department stores and mail-order catalog houses—trust was placed in Sears, Roebuck and Co. or Montgomery Wards, not in a particular textile mill or toolmaker.) Consumers often assumed that any products that could be made locally would be made locally, and business owners expected to make a good living simply by supplying the local market.

Echoes of the Homeland Culture

Almost all of the brewing families that immigrated to Minnesota came from small cities or towns where one or more small breweries had provided a living to the family for hundreds of years and where very few brewers dreamed of a national market. Germany still supports scores of small, traditional breweries that serve a ten- or twenty-mile radius and are able to flourish and invest in new equipment based on income from their local markets. Residents of many towns in Franconia, the northern part of Bavaria, make regular trips to the brewery to buy beer and other bottled drinks at the *ausschank* (brewery outlet)—sometimes using wheelbarrows or homemade carts to return their empty bottles and to carry home their brewery-fresh beer. Many Franconian breweries offer kegs in sizes ranging from fifteen to fifty liters, and some breweries still provide home delivery service. Franconians are also fiercely loyal to their local producers. Even today in the cosmopolitan city of Nuremberg, almost every beer advertised is from Bavaria, and most are brewed within 75 kilometers of the city. It was this heritage of local dependence and loyalty that German (and later Czech) settlers brought with them to their new homes in America.

Most small cities and towns in Minnesota were founded primarily by one ethnic group, usually by happenstance but sometimes by specific planning. New Ulm, for example, was sponsored by a group of German immigrants in Chicago. While such planned settlements were not the norm, many new immigrants purchased land from a particular agent and would be likely located near fellow countrymen. Even those who followed diverse paths to Minnesota tended to settle near compatriots for support and fellowship. As a consequence, even a moderately

Along with many other small-town businesses, breweries sometimes offered credit or made payment in goods. Based on average beer prices of the era, this promissory note signed by John Hauenstein for fifty dollars' worth of beer could have been worth as many as four hundred gallons. FROM THE COLLECTION OF THE BROWN COUNTY HISTORICAL SOCIETY, NEW ULM, MINNESOTA.

skilled brewer could usually count on enough business from the immediate neighborhood to make a living and, quite frequently, become wealthy.

A Sine Qua Non in Western Civilization

For many settlers in Minnesota, a brewery was a logical part of the local agricultural and industrial landscape. This was true for the British as well as for the Germans and Czechs. In *The Wealth of Nations*, Adam Smith begins his classic explanation of the division of labor by proclaiming that "it is not from the benevolence of the butcher, the brewer, or the baker, that we expect our dinner, but from their regard to their own interest."[1] The brewer remained an example of fundamental agricultural industry throughout the era.

George E. Warner and Charles M. Foote note in *History of Dakota County, Minnesota* that "breweries, almost a *sine qua non* in western civilization, began to rise in this county in 1856, contemporaneously with wagon-making" and two years before the foundry was built.[2] Some cities, including Duluth, had a brewery before they had a commercial bakery. Though few historians are likely to go as far as Warner and Foote in claiming that the brewery was the single item without which Western civilization could not exist, most local newspaper editors were willing to include breweries and their proprietors among the great benefactors of the town. The frequent special editions and columns published to promote each city sang the praises of the brewers in terms that would seem hollow just a few decades later when Prohibition would turn these same benefactors into villains.

Many editors praised the brewing industry in general and singled out their fellow citizens for special praise. The *Alexandria Citizen* showered praise on both the city's breweries in 1900.

Brewery expansion was a lucrative source of jobs for local craftsmen and laborers. These men are building a boarding house at the John Hauenstein brewery in New Ulm around 1883. FROM THE COLLECTION OF THE BROWN COUNTY HISTORICAL SOCIETY, NEW ULM, MINNESOTA.

Nothing in the history of American enterprises is more remarkable than the perfection to which brewing has been brought, our leading breweries are now producing beer quite equal in purity, flavor and quality to the best brewers of the old countries. As proof of this statement we refer to the Northwestern Brewery, whose brewery has a remarkable and successful sale....

Alexandria Brewery. Established 1876. Alexandria is justly noted throughout the state for the beauty of its surroundings, elegant deep water lakes with a great abundance of fish, the enterprise of its business men, and for many other reasons as well, but there is one thing that has added no little to its industry and that is the above institution ...[3]

The idea that the brewery was a good corporate citizen was a common theme in references to breweries throughout this period and was often used by editors as proof that their town was an economic force to be reckoned with. In response to a dismissive article published in La Crosse, the *Freeborn County Standard* of Albert Lea listed all its businesses in 1871 and included "a brewery of considerable magnitude and which cannot be overlooked as an eliment [*sic*] of business in the place."[4] In addition to this general recognition of the brewery's position among the local manufacturers, newspapers called attention to building improvements and equipment upgrades at the local firm. Use of new technology was especially noteworthy. The Miksch Bros. brewery of Glenwood was celebrated for having the first ice plow (for cutting ice with horse power) in the area, and Bowman Bros. & Gerst of Albert Lea was recognized for adding telephone service at their brewery in 1885.[5] Even in cases where the brewery itself was not welcome, the economic boost was. The *Mower County Transcript* greeted the arrival in 1869 of the Huxhold & Wagner brewery by saying, "If people will drink beer we had rather see it bought of them than have the money go out of the town to bring it here from other breweries."[6]

Especially important for local boosters was the ability of local brewers to encourage other local industries and craftsmen. A mildly humorous item appeared in the *Rushford Journal* on 3 May 1872:

> We were somewhat startled on Tuesday last on seeing what we thought to be another phenomenon but upon nearer approach, we found it to be our fellow townsman, Carl Voorhees, striking through the street, encased in what we first took to be a mammoth set of Dolly Vardon hoops made of tin, there being a coil of tin pipes 170 feet long. The coil of pipes were manufactured by Carl for Messrs. Oechle & Shaupp [*sic*], proprietors of the Rushford Brewery, to be used in the process of beer cooling.

Purchases by local breweries could be small or large, but they were celebrated as long as business was transacted in the community. Union Brewery (later Schuster Brewing Co.) in Rochester got as much good press for commissioning a new harness for its delivery team from the local firm of Beardsley and Webber as it did for ordering 80,000 bricks from Whitcomb Bros. When the Schuster brothers invented a new portable bottle-draining cart, they contracted the manufacturing to Klinsmann Bros., their fellow townsmen. The *Rochester Post* took pride in noting that orders for this device came not just from other Minnesota breweries but from as far away as San Antonio and the brewing capital of St. Louis. Of equal importance was the fact that twenty men were employed to build the units. The creation of additional jobs was always worth celebrating.[7] The breweries benefited local farmers as well, by giving them a ready market for their grain, firewood, and hops. The *Chaska Valley Herald* reported that George Ulmer was building an addition to his brewery (presumably a malt house) in June 1865 and concluded that "we will

Collecting Breweriana

Breweriana is the term used by collectors to refer to any item produced by a brewery or bearing the name of a brewery or a beer brand. It includes everything from a slightly stained coaster picked up at a bar to a wall-sized lithograph of a brewery produced more than a hundred years ago. Some collectors even collect pieces of brewery equipment.

The reasons for collecting breweriana are as varied as the collections. Some collectors are members of the family that owned the brewery or are current or former brewery employees. Others specialize in the brewery or breweries of their hometowns to maintain a connection with their heritage. Beginning a collection of breweriana is easy and often inexpensive; many serious collectors started by saving colorful bottle caps or by taking home coasters from a night on the town. In contrast to these free items, some pieces of breweriana are works of art that fetch high prices at auctions or in private sales. Attending breweriana shows and viewing online auctions are the best ways to determine the value of any particular piece of breweriana. The value of an item depends on a combination of rarity, condition, and popularity of the brewery or item style.

As with any other hobby or field of study, brewerianists formed organizations to increase their knowledge and to facilitate transactions. There are four main national organizations for collectors of general breweriana, the youngest of which was founded more than a quarter century ago. They are:

- American Breweriana Association (ABA)
  www.americanbreweriana.org
- Brewery Collectibles Club of America (formerly the Beer Can Collectors of America, or BCCA) www.bcca.com
- East Coast Breweriana Association (ECBA)
  www.eastcoastbrew.com
- National Association Brewery Advertising (NABA)
  www.nababrew.com

Each of these groups publishes a journal containing articles about brewery history, breweriana types, and current prices. Each organization has an annual meeting featuring tours, presentations, and a public breweriana show. Within these organizations, chapters based on region or specialty provide collectors even more opportunities to meet. The North Star Chapter of the BCCA has members from all over the Upper Midwest and hosts several shows each year, the largest of which is "Guzzle 'n' Twirl," held every October in the St. Paul area. The Schell's Border Batch is made up primarily of collectors from southern Minnesota and northern Iowa, and the Nordlagers are mostly from northern Minnesota and Wisconsin. Information about these and other chapters can be found on the parent organizations' Web sites.

Numerous organizations and clubs specialize in a particular type of breweriana. Crowncap Collectors Society International (CCSI), Just for Openers (JFO), and many other groups publish newsletters and catalogs with detailed information on their specialties. Most of these organizations have Web sites, and most are linked through the sites of the four national organizations.

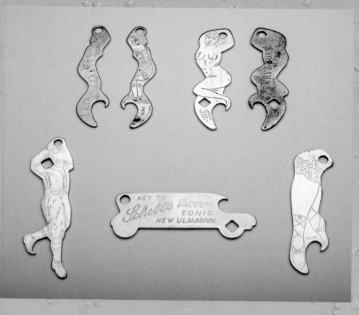

Flat figural openers were manufactured in dozens of shapes and varieties. One shape could be imprinted with different designs and brewery names. The modestly attired bathing girls (front and back, upper left) were patented in 1914 and used by the Math. Pitzl brewery of New Munich and Engesser Brewing Co. of St. Peter. The more risqué mermaid (back and front, upper right) was first used in 1913 by Cold Spring Brewing Company and by Drewry & Sons of St. Paul. Schell's capitalized on the rising popularity of baseball and the automobile, and Premier Brewing Co. of Fergus Falls offered an opener featuring a dancer's legs. The round holes were for attaching the opener to a key ring, and the square holes were for adjusting the gas headlamps on automobiles. FROM THE COLLECTION OF PAT STAMBAUGH.

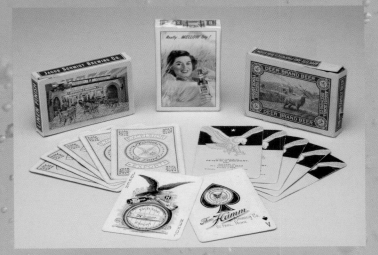

Playing cards while enjoying a beer dates at least to colonial times. The pack at upper left features a painting of the Schmidt Brewery rathskeller built in the 1930s. The pack in the center is also from Schmidt and portrays a young woman holding a bottle of City Club in a pose somewhat reminiscent of Grain Belt's *Girl in the Barley Field* poster. The pre-Prohibition Deer Brand deck uses the same vignette of a mighty buck overlooking the brewery that appeared on Schell's labels at the time. The Hamm Excelsior cards are from a very rare pre-Prohibition deck and feature brewery-specific artwork on the joker and ace of spades (at an extra cost that only a major brewery could afford). The Peter Bub All American cards were issued during World War II, probably right after the brewery changed the brand's name from Old German Style. FROM THE COLLECTION OF JIM AND RUTH BEATON.

The Hamm's Club (www.hammsclub.com) deserves special mention for all that the members have done to keep alive the memory of the Hamm's Bear and the story of the company. The Hamm's Club was responsible for conceiving and placing the Hamm's Bear monument on the Seventh Street Plaza (near the corner of St. Peter Street and West Seventh Place) next to the Hamm Building in St. Paul. The monument was designed by Bill Stein, one of the artists who drew the Hamm's Bear for advertisements.

Most of the significant collections of breweriana are held by private collectors and are seldom available for public viewing. Portions of their collections may be exhibited at breweriana shows. Some bars and restaurants—notably Fitger's Brewhouse in Duluth—include breweriana in their décor. A handful of national museums are in either the planning or the construction stage. The National Brewery Museum, located in the former brewery in Potosi, Wisconsin, is scheduled to have some portions open by the winter of 2007–2008. August Schell Brewing Company recently opened a new museum at the brewery featuring items from the second-oldest family-owned brewery in the country. ꙮ

One popular specialty of breweriana collectors is art deco pieces. The clamshell-style light advertising Duluth Brewing & Malting Company's Royal Bohemian was designed for display on a bar or a countertop. FROM THE COLLECTION OF PETE CLURE.

not be under the necessity of sending our barley to St. Paul to be manufactured." Farmers depended on breweries to purchase their barley, a crop that grew well in Minnesota's climate but was harder to process into food products than wheat or corn.

Even in cases where few new jobs were created, citizens took pride in the success of their brewers and in the increased visibility and importance they brought to their hometowns. Opening new markets for their beer was cause for both notice and celebration, especially if a small-town brewer found a market in a larger town. Emil Thiemer's short-lived brewery in Elysian was praised for "a superior article of beer that commands the trade of Waterville, Cleveland, and other towns in the county, beside meeting with a large sale in Faribault," which had three breweries of its own.[8]

In this photo from around 1908, Alfred Erlandson is shown collecting the spent grain from Minneapolis Brewing Company for use on a dairy farm near Lake Nokomis, several miles away. This practice continues during the twenty-first century: many of Minnesota's craft brewers allow farmers to collect spent grain at the brewery for feed. COURTESY OF THE MINNESOTA HISTORICAL SOCIETY.

Schroeder's Northern Pacific Brewery

A classic example of a successful small local brewery was Peter Schroeder's Northern Pacific Brewery, located in Perham in northwestern Minnesota. Sources disagree on exactly when the brewery started, but it is clear that Schroeder was in charge by 1878. He quickly built a reputation for quality and good business practices. He owned several saloons in Perham in full or in part, as well as establishments in Frazee, Vergas, Otter Tail, and other neighboring towns. He also owned the Globe Mill, for many years the largest building in Perham. But it was his brewery that became the most famous landmark, and it was for the brewery that his reputation spread throughout the countryside.

Schroeder was one of the rare brewers who was praised by newspapers in rival towns that had their own breweries. During the few years that Detroit Brewing Co. was operating in Detroit (later Detroit Lakes), the *Detroit Record* gave much more coverage to Schroeder's operations, and higher praise as well. In 1885 John H. Smith became the Detroit agent for what the *Record* called "the celebrated lager beer made by Peter Schroeder, of Perham." Smith provided kegs to local establishments and also bottled some of Schroeder's beer. Even though he had a reliable agent in town, Schroeder still made frequent trips to Detroit to check on his operations. A typical news item noted:

> P. Schroeder, the popular and enterprising brewer of Perham, called upon his Detroit friends last Monday. Notwithstanding the fact that Mr. Schroeder has enlarged his business during the past two years, until he now has one of the largest and best breweries in Minnesota, the reputation he has established for producing an "A No. 1" article has created such a demand for the product of his brewery that he is still at a loss to know how to fill orders as fast as they come in. He ships in large quantities to all points along the Northern Pacific and its branches, and in fact he is fast becoming the Jas. [*sic*] Schlitz of Minnesota.[9]

While Schroeder's brewery was hardly in the same league as Joseph Schlitz's brewery, he was shipping to points in Dakota Territory (soon to be North Dakota), and his beer was served on the famous North Coast Limited train. One correspondent observed, "Every day the trains going east and west throw off a lot of empty kegs and take on full ones, and from the regularity of this proceeding I conclude the beer is in brisk demand all along the Northern Pacific Line." The same writer had been impressed upon arriving at a hotel "kept by a cordial German who has a keg of beer just under the desk . . . and invites [the guests] to wash the dust of travel from their throats. This beer is a good honest, amber-colored fluid."[10] Northern Pacific's brewmaster, Andrew Fellerer, studied brewing in Milwaukee and was considered one of the finest brewers in the area.

With the addition of a bottling facility in 1905, Schroeder had created an enterprise that at its peak employed fourteen men. The brewery was a major buyer not just of grain (for which Schroeder was primary broker) but also of wood, as the plant used 150 cords per year. In addition to heat for brewing, wood was also burned to power the steam engine that pumped spring water into the vats and to drive other machinery in the building. The brewery's park was a popular gathering place for Perham residents and featured most of the usual amenities in addition to the standard 5¢ beer.[11]

Perhaps the Schlitz comparisons went to Schroeder's head, because he soon released a label for Schroeder's Beer that proclaimed it "The Beer that Makes Milwaukee Jealous." Schlitz promptly sued, and eventually won. According to local accounts, the excess labels were given away and were used by the town's children as play money.[12] While this loss was not fatal for Schroeder, it demonstrated that major national brewers were unwilling to take competition from any brewery lightly, no matter how small or remote. Schlitz had been one of the leading brands in the region since the 1880s, and increasing competition on the national level compelled them to fight to keep their territory.

Ultimately, a variety of circumstances combined to spell the end of the brewery in Perham. Increasing competition from outside brewers was undoubtedly a factor, but so was the death of Peter Schroeder in February 1912. The Fellerer family had been associated with the brewery since Andrew Fellerer became brewmaster in the mid-1880s and knew the brewing business, but Schroeder's thirty-year reputation as a salesman could not be replaced. The final blow to the brewery was the sudden enforcement in 1915 of an Indian treaty that declared virtually the entire sales area of the Northern Pacific Brewery to be dry territory, including the city of Perham itself. (The treaty issue is covered in chapter 5.) The Perham Holding Company took over the brewery, but denied the unique advantage of a regional marketplace and the ability to trade on its reputation, it was unable to keep the brewery alive. In November 1917 the *Fergus Falls Daily Journal* reported:

> Dismantling of the old Schroeder Brewery is under way and a considerable portion of the structure, which was gradually disintegrating, is being taken down. Such parts of the equipment as are saleable will be disposed of. The part of the brick structure that is in good condition will be left. The brewery is one of the landmarks of Perham, but its significance as a token of joy passed with the Indian Treaty enforcement.

The legend "the beer that makes Milwaukee jealous" provoked legal action from Joseph Schlitz Brewing Company of Milwaukee. Few of these labels exist today. BOB KAY COLLECTION.

The emotions that bind a city, a brewery, and its workers are not that easily broken, and the saga of the Perham brewery did not end in 1917. The Fellerer family bought the brewery from the holding company in 1919 and attempted to brew near beer for about a year, but gave up when the business proved unprofitable. After Prohibition, Joseph Fellerer, one of Andrew's four sons, took jobs brewing in Alexandria and in St. Cloud, "but his heart was back in Perham." He and his brothers, Frank, Ludwig, and Henry, took out a $69,000 mortgage, formed Perham Brewing Company in 1940, and printed stock certificates. They began restoration work on the building and sought out used brewing equipment

The ruins of Schroeder's brewery in 1974. Even in this condition, the building served as a reminder of how much the brewery once meant to Perham. COURTESY OF THE MINNESOTA HISTORICAL SOCIETY.

wherever they could find it. Joe bought a supply of kegs from his former employer in Alexandria when that brewery went out of business. Despite their effort, the project would never be completed. The stock sale met with little enthusiasm, and the Fellerers were unable to raise enough capital to complete restoration and begin brewing. As late as the 1970s, the remaining Fellerers and other brewing enthusiasts still dreamed of using the accumulated equipment to brew. At one point the boiler was actually fired up, but no beer was ever made. Joe Fellerer died in 1977, but the dream of brewing in Perham did not completely die until the building was finally pulled down in 1986—just over 100 years after being rebuilt following a fire.[13]

Celebrating Community

The local brewer frequently demonstrated community spirit by building a hall (or sometimes a *biergarten*) that served as a meeting place for the community. An early example was built in 1862 in Mantorville. According to the *Mantorville Express*:

Brewery Hall is in the the [*sic*] third story of a large and beautiful stone building, erected by Mr. C. Ginsberg of this place, and is now nearly completed. The build-

Ginsberg's brewery in Mantorville was shown more accurately in the 1874 *Atlas of Minnesota* than were many breweries during that era. FROM THE AUTHOR'S COLLECTION.

ing is 37 by 32 feet. The basement and second story is to be occupied as a brewery and residence, while the entire third story is to be finished off as a hall for dancing and other purposes. The whole building is substantially made and in good style, and shows remarkable enterprise and public spirit on the part of Mr. Ginsburg.[14]

Ginsburg's may have been the first brewery hall in the state, and Hamm's was probably the most famous of the biergartens, but similar facilities for public merrymaking were erected all across the state. Henry Schuster built a hall in Rochester that was used for everything from meetings of the German *männerchor* (choral society) to a group of German farmers seeking to form a mutual insurance company. At one point in 1872, a "personal liberty club" was formed there in an attempt to avoid the local Sunday consumption laws. It didn't work, and Schuster temporarily lost his retail license.[15] Just to the north, Adam Stenger of the Rochester City Brewery opened a beer garden in honor of the nation's centennial.

Last Wednesday being Mr. Stenger's 50th birthday he had made arrangements to properly honor the event by giving a public reception at his garden. The Rochester Cornet Band was engaged to furnish the music and in the afternoon quite a party of our citizens assembled at the charming spot and the time was spent in conviviality and festive enjoyment. A dance in the evening to music by Horton's string band was one of the pleasant features of the occasion, though this was somewhat interrupted by the rain. Quiet and good order are said to have prevailed throughout the festivities.[16]

Sometimes the opening of the brewery itself was the cause for celebration. The *Hastings Gazette* reported on the opening of the Smith & Latto brewery:

We are indebted to Messrs. LATTO & SMITH for a keg of their first run, received on Thursday last. It is very clear and nice, with a slight taste of the wood, as might be expected when the kettles, vats, tubs, kegs, etc. are all new. Of course it will be better after a time, but even now it is a great improvement over the beer we have been drinking for the past two or three years. The brewery was formally opened on Thursday evening, and good luck drank to the enterprising proprietors in many a sparkling glass. We hope they may find it as profitable as they anticipate, and that it may prove to be a paying investment.[17]

Many editors besides the *Gazette*'s had some extra incentive to praise the local brewery. The editor of Chaska's *Weekly Valley Herald* wrote of local brewer Bernard Leivermann: "Leivermann is furnishing his customers with a quality of Lager Beer, that cannot be excelled in the State. He left a sample keg with us last Tuesday and being somewhat of a judge, do not hesitate to pronounce it a No. 1 article,

Joseph Schmucker's Tivoli was a popular gathering place in New Ulm for many years. The building at 313 First Street North was razed in 1985. FROM THE COLLECTION OF THE BROWN COUNTY HISTORICAL SOCIETY, NEW ULM, MINNESOTA.

and see no reason for sending to St. Paul and Minneapoliss [*sic*] for an article every way inferior to our home manufacture."[18] Even editors who didn't sample the product praised the industry of the brewers. The *Sauk Rapids Sentinel* noted that "Momberg & Jochem are still engaged in carrying on improvements in their brewery and malt house buildings. We are not a judge in matters pertaining to the brewery business, but everything appears to be done in a first class manner about the premises."[19]

All Orders Promptly Filled

One way in which a local brewery could maintain customers in the face of outside competition was through superior service, especially home delivery. Two advertisements from Shakopee newspapers display this consistent feature of local service. Beginning in February 1862, Adolph Albachten advertised the lager beer made at his Lower Shakopee Brewery as "superior to that manufactured in St. Paul." He continued, "All orders will be promptly filled, and beer delivered to the purchaser if within a reasonable distance, or at the steamboat landing, or other shipping point, designated." Nearly fifty years later, the following ad appeared, conveying the same offer but new technology: "Patronize home industries. Try a case of quarts at $2.00 of the famous Shakopee Brewery's extra fine Lager beer, brewed and bottled by Hubert Nyssen, Shakopee, Minnesota. Wholesome and

The Jacob Schmidt rathskeller (pictured here in the mid-1920s) was a social center for employees and others from the neighborhood. A larger rathskeller was built under the new office building in the 1930s and used for a variety of events. Many who lived or worked in St. Paul knew a brewery employee who could get them a ticket or two for a beer. PHOTOGRAPH BY CHARLES P. GIBSON; COURTESY OF THE MINNESOTA HISTORICAL SOCIETY.

Founded prior to the Civil War by H. H. Strunk, Nyssen's Shakopee brewery survived until Prohibition. This label is from around 1900. FROM THE COLLECTION OF KEN MALZ.

refreshing every drop. Made of the best malted hops. Delivered free. Phone either line."[20] Many brewers made a special point of their willingness to deliver to farmers. Fred Troost, who in June 1860 became the new owner of City Brewery in Rochester, boasted, "I am prepared to supply every town in Southern Minnesota with LAGER, if required. Orders from the country solicited."[21]

Home delivery had its drawbacks for breweries, however. Retrieving empty kegs (and later bottles) was a serious problem for the brewers: if they ran short of containers, they could not continue to package beer and might have to stop brewing if no space was available in the storage vats. Many brewery ads contained calls for kegs to be returned. As late as 1899, Schuster Brewing Co. ads in the *Rochester Post and Record* urged farmers to "Please return empty beer kegs and cases you may have in your possession and greatly oblige SCHUSTER BREWING CO." Eventually some breweries moved beyond pleading for return of their property. In 1878, Peter Iltis advertised in the *Weekly Valley Herald*: "BEER KEGS! BEER KEGS!! All persons having beer kegs with my name marked thereon, or with the brand of the Union Brewry [sic] Chaska, are hereby notified to return the same at once, or I shall be compelled to put them to trouble and expense." A more creative approach was adopted by Rush City Brewery, which was in a hurry to retrieve kegs because the brewery was about to change hands, and kegs were an important part of each brewery's assets. An ad in 1894 offered "$15.00 Reward [:] To the person who will deliver at the Rush City Brewery the largest number

Breweries struggled constantly to retrieve their kegs. Branding served to identify kegs and may have reduced keg theft. This keg was property of Schuster Brewing Co. of Rochester. FROM THE COLLECTION OF PAT STAMBAUGH.

of beer kegs belonging to the brewery between the 12th of January and the first of July I will give $8; to the one bringing the next highest number $4; to the next $2 and to the fourth $1."

The Last Wave

New breweries were started at a much slower rate after the mid-1880s. As brewing evolved from craft to industry (covered in chapter 4), starting a brewery required much more capital than before. Most towns that were able to support a single brewery already had that firm. The railroad was approaching its maximum reach, and sites for new towns were few and far between. Many new towns were dominated by ethnic groups who did not share the vigorous brewing tradition of the Germans. Some of these settlements were actually hostile to the idea of alcoholic beverages and established themselves as dry towns or set such high saloon license fees that a brewer's potential market was limited.

The arrival of thousands of Bohemians in Minnesota was an exception to this trend. The Bohemians had developed a lager beer culture rivaling that of the Germans and produced beer that enjoyed a reputation for quality as high as that

This machine was used by August Schell Brewing Company to brand the heads of its kegs. The disc was heated and then brought in contact with the barrel by the levers. COURTESY OF AUGUST SCHELL BREWING COMPANY.

of their neighbors. The soft water around the city of Pilsen (Plzeň) and the local Saaz hops were the key ingredients in pilsner beer, the style of lager that became the model for most beers served in the post-Prohibition world. The Bohemians arrived in Minnesota along with other southern and eastern Europeans in the wave of immigration that lasted from the mid-1870s until the outbreak of World War I. Like the Germans before them, many of the Bohemians moved into rural Minnesota and established farm communities, especially in Rice, Le Sueur, Pine, and McLeod counties. Towns such as New Prague and Montgomery became centers of Bohemian culture and created demand for new breweries. Civic and ethnic loyalties as well as preference for the beer style of home allowed multiple breweries to survive in each of these cities despite their proximity to the Twin Cities and to the many established breweries in Shakopee, Jordan, Chaska, St. Peter, and Mankato.

Continuing the similarities with the Germans, some Bohemians set up breweries in tiny farming communities that to modern eyes seemed unable to support any significant industry at all. Veseli (spelled Wesley by English speakers who thought it was named for the founder of Methodism) in Rice County and Beroun in Pine County never had more than a few hundred residents, but each town managed to support a brewery. Joseph Pavek's brewery in Veseli lasted for at least twenty years. The Beroun Bohemian Brewing Co. was one of the last breweries founded before Prohibition and, despite being born in an atmosphere of intense competition and increasing anti-alcohol sentiments, managed to survive for five years. The brewery employed four men, and its opening was described as "a red letter day for Beroun." The *Pine Poker* reported, "it is expected that most of its brew will be shipped to St. Paul." This suggests that Beroun itself did not have enough of a market for beer to support a modern brewery and demonstrates a certain audacity in attempting to penetrate the most thoroughly saturated beer market in the state. Even though the brewery was not rebuilt following a disastrous fire in September 1908, it still indicated that recently landed immigrants had a strong desire to maintain their crafts and culture in their new land, and that the size of a community was no barrier to operating a brewery.

The Final Frontier

While most of these rare new breweries were in regions already served by Minnesota breweries, there was one attempt to open a new area for a local producer. The Roemer brothers started work in 1901 on a new brewery in Ellsworth, in the far southwest corner of the state. New Ulm and Mankato were more than one hundred miles away, but Sioux Falls was only about thirty miles away and the Iowa border was less than two miles from town. The potential for sales to Iowa customers was attractive because Iowa had been uniquely cruel to its brewers—establishing and repealing prohibition several times for varying intervals—discouraging sustained investment in breweries.[22] When Roemer Bros. started construction, Ellsworth was importing beer from Sioux Falls. In the same issue of the *Ellsworth News* that reported the Roemers' expenditure of $20,000 on the brewery, an ad appeared for the Blue Label Saloon (owned by the aptly named Matt Pint Jr.) announcing "Sioux Falls Beer always on tap."

As the brewery neared completion, enthusiasm over the possibilities grew. On 28 February 1902, the *Ellsworth News* reported:

> The new brewery got in the first consignment of kegs last Saturday. Brewing is being pushed rapidly, and the proprietors expect to have a fine grade of beer upon the market in a short time. It is a revelation to the uninitiated to see the work at the brewery. This is an Ellsworth enterprise that few of our people fully appreciate at the present time, but will later on when they see the amount of business this concern will transact.

Exactly a month later, the *Ellsworth News* exulted, "The brewery put out its first beer last Saturday and those competent to judge assert that it is equal to the best Milwaukee brands. With this grade of beer to go upon the market, the Ellsworth brewery cannot help making a success of its business." By the end of May, the Blue Label Saloon featured Ellsworth beer on tap. News items recorded the travels of John Roemer to Luverne, Jasper ("and points north"), and even to Sioux Falls in the interests of the brewery. By the end of the year, Ellsworth beer was being shipped to towns such as Rock Rapids and Lester across the Iowa border. The *Ellsworth News* continued to be a strong advocate for the young business and appealed to citizens in familiar terms: "The beer now being put out by the brewery is said to be as good as any on the market. This being true all our people who use beer should call for it, and 'boost' as much as possible at home and when away. The brewery is a home institution and every citizen should help it along."[23] While the brewery survived for only six years (ultimately succumbing to financial and legal problems), it provides an example of the desire of people to profit from the brewery business and the willingness of a small town to support a business (at least verbally) that would enhance its reputation and make the town an economic force to be reckoned with.

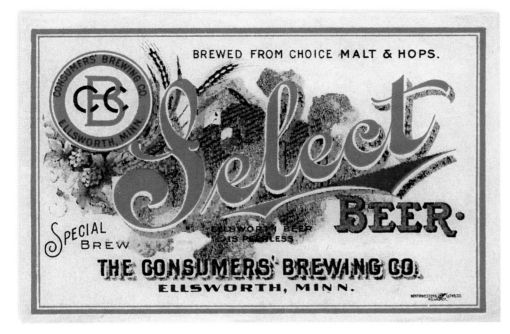

Consumers' Brewing Co. was the name used by the Ellsworth brewery during its last two years of existence (1906–1908). BOB KAY COLLECTION.

These are among the hundreds of bottles and dozens of cases left behind when Thomas Meighen closed his Forestville store in 1910. The bottles represent a cross-section of brands available in even the smallest towns. The Hamm Export and Excelsior bottles still have portions of the wire that held in the corks. The Excelsior bottle also has remnants of the lavender paper that padded the bottles in the case. The bottles at right are from the C. & J. Michel Brewing Co. of La Crosse, one of the first Wisconsin brewers to ship to southern Minnesota. The bottles in the center include (from left to right) a rare Miller Export bottling by Endres Bros. of Faribault, a bottle of Pabst before it was known as Blue Ribbon, Schuster's Malt Tonic, G. Heileman's Export beer (rear center), a bottle from the Preston Bottling Co., two different sizes of Gund's Peerless beer, and a bottle of Heileman's Old Style with a spectacular scenic label. All the bottles predate the 1907 label text requirements. COURTESY OF THE MINNESOTA HISTORICAL SOCIETY.

Craft Becomes Industry

The brewing of beer is an industry of importance in Minneapolis, where the conditions for efficient prosecution of brewing processes are well nigh perfect. Especially complete is the plant of The C. Birkhofer Brewing Co. . . . [Conrad Birkhofer] is a practical brewer, and by selection of the best qualities of malt and hop and the use of the best brewing process, maintains a high standard of merit for the production. . . . The plant is modern in every respect and supplied with every device and appliance for the prosecution of brewing operations, and a Linde ice machine of fifty tons daily capacity.
—Supplement to the *Minneapolis Journal*, 18 April 1900

B Y THE MID-1880S, ALL OF THE LARGE CITIES AND MANY OF THE MIDSIZE cities in Minnesota had more than one brewery. For brewers, this was a period of great expansion and profits. However, these profits indicated that the field was a lucrative one and drew in a constant stream of competitors. Success in this business, where profit margins were often thin, depended on a brewery's ability to stay solvent, to expand and invest in equipment, and to expand production and sales territory to take advantage of the economies of large-scale production that modern industrial developments encouraged. Technology and the beginning of brand name identification and mass advertising determined which brewers would become legends and which would become mere memories.

Economics and Expansion

As Minnesota's population grew and was connected by an ever-expanding web of transportation, the potential market for each brewery grew. At the same time, technological developments were making it possible for those brewers who were willing and able to invest in new labor-saving devices and quality-control tools to expand to fill these new markets. However, some of these developments forced brewers to plan their output according to what amount was cheapest to produce rather than how much could be sold in a known market. This spurred the race for markets that continues to the present.

Jordan Beer kept the "Aged in Caves" slogan even after the brewery itself closed. FROM THE AUTHOR'S COLLECTION.

Brewer's Cave was the name given to the line of Minnesota Brewing Company beers targeted to drinkers of craft beer. FROM THE AUTHOR'S COLLECTION.

IN 1855, BAVARIAN BREWER CHRISTOPHER STAHLMANN DISCOVERED PRISTINE NATURAL SPRINGS AND AN ABUNDANCE OF COOL, UNDERGROUND CAVES IN SAINT PAUL, MINNESOTA. STAHLMANN KNEW FROM EXPERIENCE THE CAVES WOULD BE IDEAL FOR BREWING HIS GERMAN STYLE LAGER, SO HE DEVELOPED A LARGE SYSTEM OF BREWING CAVES AND THE LEGENDARY CAVE BREWERY WAS BORN. TO ACHIEVE THE SUBTLE AND COMPLEX TASTE OF HIS BREWS, STAHLMANN HAND SELECTED THE FINEST MALT, BARLEY AND HOPS... ROASTING THEM IN SPECIAL OVENS, TRANSFORMING THEM INTO A VARIETY OF HANDCRAFTED ALES AND LAGERS.

TODAY, STAHLMANN'S BREWING CAVES STILL EXIST. ALTHOUGH WE NO LONGER USE THE CAVES, WE DO CARRY ON THE TIME-HONORED BREWING TRADITIONS CHRISTOPHER STAHLMANN ESTABLISHED OVER A CENTURY AGO. THE INTENSITY, PASSION AND EXPERTISE DEMANDED OF TRADITIONAL CAVE BREWERS IS BREWED INTO EVERY SMALL BATCH PRODUCED AT BREWER'S CAVE BREWERY.

Refrigeration Changes the Brewery

Mechanical refrigeration is probably second only to lager beer itself in the extent of the changes it caused in America's brewing industry. Before the 1880s, the ability to maintain the proper temperature for fermenting and lagering the beer was dependent on the climate and weather and on the availability of other natural controls. As noted in chapter 2, if possible, most early brewers located near a hill into which they could dig caves. Christopher Stahlmann's Cave Brewery was known throughout the region for the extent of its caves, which covered an area of more than a mile and went down several stories, "a perfect labyrinth of rooms and cellars and under cellars three deep."[1] The brewers often offered tours of their caves to gain publicity and to demonstrate the impressive assets of their firms. A representative of the *Rochester Post* was duly impressed by the caves of the Union Brewery:

By the kindness of Messrs. Schuster & Joest, of the Union Brewery, we were, a few days ago, shown through their establishment. A brewery is like a hill of potatoes; the best part of it is underground. So we thought, as we went through the immense vault built only a year ago, away down stairs and divided into a series of long, high, arched chambers, in which, we are told, there can be stored 1,200 barrels of beer at a time. It looks curious down there, among the immense hogsheads, each holding enough of the genial to wash down a ton or so of Switzer or Limburger.[2]

In addition to controlling the temperature of the stored beer, caves provided secure storage as well. Three years after the tour described above, the Union Brewery burned to the ground, but cellared beer worth $5,000 was saved. Likewise, when C. C. Beck's Gilmore Valley Brewery near Winona burned in September 1877, more than $12,000 in property and raw materials was lost, but no beer. The caves were so important to the mystique of the old family brewery that several breweries continued to advertise the "cave-aged" nature of their beer in the post-Prohibition era, including Yoerg, Fleckenstein, and Jordan. In the 1990s, Minnesota Brewing Company, located on the site of Stahlmann's old Cave Brewery, launched a line of craft beers called Brewer's Cave. (The label was revived late in 2006 by St. Paul's Frank Yarusso with hopes that it would appeal to craft beer fans with a sense of history.)[3]

Caves were not perfect, however. The labor involved in getting barrels of beer in and out of the cellars was bone-crushing work, sometimes literally. John Fetzner, at the time an employee of Huxhold & Wagner in Austin, "while carrying a keg of beer down celler [*sic*], lost his footing and fell down the stairway, the keg striking

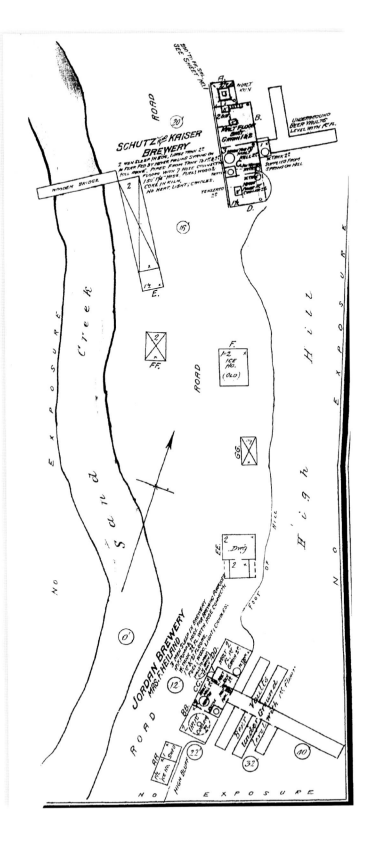

upon his right hand, smashing it badly."[4] In addition, caves grew warmer during the summer and therefore sometimes required ice, though not to the same extent as aboveground facilities.

Icehouses have left a small but important footprint on the American landscape since the early eighteenth century; many of the preserved estates of the nation's founders include icehouses. Ice cutting was a standard winter chore and sometimes a profitable business. Large blocks were cut from lakes by hand or horse-drawn cutters, hauled to ice sheds, and sometimes re-cut into smaller pieces according to the needs of individual customers. Because of the importance of the ice harvest to so many businesses, newspapers often kept track of the ice crop with the same attention given to agricultural commodities. Some breweries continued to cut and store large quantities of ice into the 1900s. In January 1905 the *Hastings Gazette* reported that "Gustav Kuenzel is putting up his supply of ice from the river, about twelve hundred tons. It is twenty inches in thickness, and of good quality." An account based on the recollections of Elizabeth Hjermstad, Kuenzel's daughter, described the large blocks as 36 inches long, 28 inches wide, and 18 to 20 inches deep. Cutting ice was both strenuous and dangerous—men sometimes slipped through holes in the ice or cut themselves with the sharp tools. It took Kuenzel's crew more than two weeks to harvest enough ice for Hastings Brewing Co., and it typically cost around $750, not counting the cost of tools dropped in the icy water (which Kuenzel insisted be retrieved at the worker's peril). Hastings Brewing Co. ordered carloads of sawdust from the mills in Stillwater to pack the ice—Kuenzel favored a ten-inch layer of pine sawdust.[5] While cutting and storing ice was not prohibitively expensive (during the 1870s and 1880s an icehouse cost only $100 to $200), it was a steady or increasing expense each year, and ice took up a lot of room—especially in caves that could have been used to store more beer. Despite the inefficiencies, some brewers continued to use ice. As late as 1915, the *Jordan Independent* reported that New Prague Brewing Co. had fifteen teams of horses and a large crew of men putting up ice for the summer.[6]

Switching to artificial refrigeration gave brewers advantages in efficiency, consistency, and publicity. Installation of the newest equipment was viewed as proof of prosperity and was testimony of the quality and sound management of the firm. When Schuster Brewing Co. of Rochester installed new equipment in 1899, the press produced several articles explaining the anhydrous ammonia process and describing a sample product of the ice machine:

> . . . a cake of ice 12 × 14 × 24 inches in size. . . . In the center of this cake is a bouquet of roses that looks as natural as though it stood in a quantity of water, and two bottles of the [malt] tonic. The cake is as clear as crystal, and was frozen in twenty-four hours. The machine has a capacity of twenty-five tons of ice in twenty-four hours, . . . The exhibit will be a most interesting one, and well worth the trouble of going to see.[7]

This stereograph shows men and horses cutting ice near Winona around 1880. The man in the background is standing on a tower of ice blocks. The width of the furrows can be seen in the foreground. PHOTOGRAPH BY HOARD & TENNEY; COURTESY OF THE MINNESOTA HISTORICAL SOCIETY.

Refrigeration equipment was one of the standards by which a brewery's modernity was judged. An April 1900 supplement to the *Minneapolis Journal* on local industry, but written for the average reader, made special mention of Minnesota Brewing Company's De La Vergne refrigeration systems and the Linde ice machines belonging to the Gluek and Birkhofer brewing companies. Brewing historian Stanley Baron neatly summarized the modernization of the brewery, stating that "the brewery superintendent, who at one time had been little more than a superior cook, had been transformed into a mechanic and an engineer."[8]

Bottled Only at the Brewery

The increasing reliability and popularity of bottled beer caused the consumption patterns of beer drinkers to shift somewhat during the late nineteenth century and laid the foundation for much greater shifts later.

Bottled beer, most often porter imported from England, was known during colonial times. Some early brewers bottled their beer: records exist of Thomas Jefferson's brewing and bottling efforts. However, the overwhelming majority of beer was drawn from a keg either at the saloon or at home. Breweries generally packaged beer in half barrel, quarter barrel, and eighth barrel (pony) kegs. The few existing brewery ledgers from the era show regular deliveries to households, saloons, billiard halls, and hotels, and sometimes to grocers and bottlers. Since most beer was intended to be drunk immediately, few homes kept a stock on

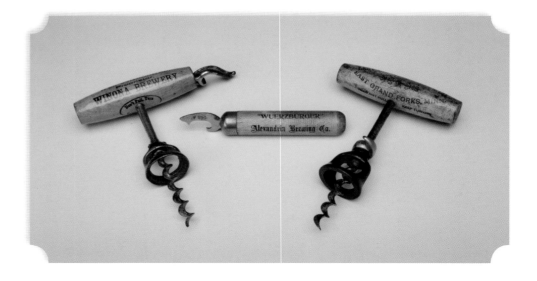

These openers mark the transition from corked bottles to capped bottles around the turn of the twentieth century. The corkscrew on the right features only one tool. The opener at left has both a corkscrew and a cap lifter. The style of opener in the center normally had a hole drilled in the wood for a small corkscrew; this rare example does not have this feature. FROM THE COLLECTION OF PAT STAMBAUGH.

hand. It was more common for farms than urban households to order kegs because farms often employed a number of hands who also lived on the premises. Most city residents brought home beer from the local saloon (or brewery if one was nearby) bottled or in a large jug or bucket called a growler. The common practice of sending a child to fetch the father's beer became one of the most potent symbols of the crusade against the saloon. Bottled ale and porter were more common than lager at first because they could be stored for longer periods without ice or refrigeration.

Early bottling was also limited by the nature of beer. Each time beer is handled after the wort is boiled, additional possibilities for oxidation and contamination—and thereby additional chances to ruin a brewer's reputation—are created. In addition, beer, particularly American lager, is highly carbonated and exerts great pressure on its container. Early glass and early closures could withstand the high pressure only with difficulty. Many early beer bottles were stoneware sealed with corks held in by a wire basket (much like champagne). By the 1870s glass technology had advanced to the point where glass bottles were strong enough to contain beer without being prohibitively thick (and therefore heavy).

While bottles were now suitable for the task, closures were lagging behind. Corks and their wire baskets had to be inserted and secured by hand, and while this was not an insurmountable obstacle, it was labor intensive. Numerous attempts at improving the process were made, but none were satisfactory until William S. Painter of Crown Cork and Seal Corporation developed the crown cap: the modern bottle cap. Besides being a reliable and inexpensive seal, the most important advance was the ability to apply the new cap quickly by machine. The new bottling machines quickly replaced the caves as the highlight of a brewery tour. (Much of the washing and filling process had been automated earlier, but corking, even when done by machines, tended to create a bottleneck in the process.) Established breweries added bottling lines as soon as they could afford to and many new breweries built after 1890 included a bottling facility in their original construction. In major national shipping breweries, women were often employed for jobs in the bottle house. In July 1903 the nine women labeling bottles at Minneapolis Brewing Company went on strike "because the company refuses to grant them an increase in wages of 1 cent an hour. The girls get 90 cents a day and ask

Developing a satisfactory closure was critical for brewers because it determined the speed at which beer could be bottled and how fresh the beer would taste when opened. From left: The Lightning stopper (c. 1875) featured a metal bail holding a rubber stopper in the mouth of the bottle and remained in use into the twentieth century. "Blob top" bottles provided a ridge to anchor a Lightning stopper, a Hutter stopper, or wire to hold a cork. The Yoerg bottle features a blob top adapted for the Baltimore loop seal, a rubber stopper that fit into a groove inside the blob and was pulled out with a small ring or loop. The Jacob Schmidt bottle features the Hutter stopper. Still in use today by many German and Dutch breweries, this example has a cork seal rather than the rubber or plastic seal common today. The Charles Mickus bottle was designed for the crown cap, introduced in 1892. Brewers that could not afford to adopt new closures continued to use earlier styles through Prohibition. FROM THE COLLECTION OF STEVE KETCHUM.

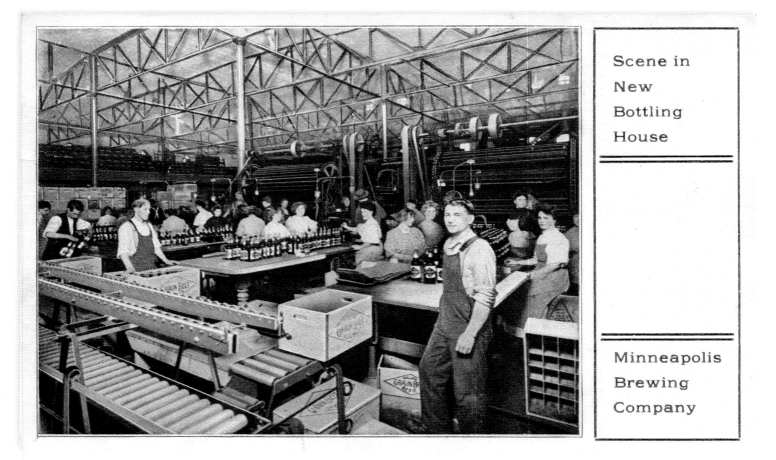

Scene in New Bottling House

Minneapolis Brewing Company

New bottling lines were showpieces of modern breweries. Women worked in the labeling department at Minneapolis Brewing Company and went on strike in 1903 to raise their pay to one dollar per day. This postcard is from about 1908. COURTESY OF THE MINNESOTA HISTORICAL SOCIETY.

$1 a day. They label 21,600 bottles of beer a day." (This works out to 900 cases each ten-hour day, or 36 bottles per minute.)[9]

A significant obstacle to cost-effective bottling was government rigidity. As noted in chapter 2, the federal government imposed an excise tax to help pay for the Civil War. This tax was levied on each barrel "removed for sale" and was marked by a tax stamp on the barrel. This system was logical enough before the advent of brewery-bottled beer, but it added several steps to the bottling process: All bottling had to be done in a building separate from the brewery, located across a public thoroughfare, and not capable of connection with the brewery. Stamped kegs were moved from the aging cellars to the bottle house and then hooked up to bottle fillers, since the government was not prepared to adapt the system to allow stamps on bottles or cases. Sometimes the government reduced the number of revenue agents and increased their territory, making fair enforcement much more difficult. In 1885 the government laid off one of the two agents serving the Twin Cities. The remaining agent had to work in Minneapolis in the morning and St. Paul in the afternoon, thereby limiting when these breweries could keg their beer.[10] Because of these rules, a large brewery had to fill several thousand barrels a year simply to take them across the street. In the case of A. Fitger &

Co. in Duluth, the bottling house was on the same side of Superior Street, so the kegs had to be rolled across the street, down the block, and back across the street again.[11] Not until 1890 was the rule changed (at the urging of Frederick Pabst of Milwaukee) so that beer could be transported from one building to another by a pipeline. Even then, a revenue officer needed to be present whenever the pipeline was used, the brewer still had to present the correct amount of canceled stamps, and the building separation requirements remained. The new Park Brewing Co. in Winona built its bottling house across the Chicago and North Western Railway tracks from the brewery, which required it to construct a bridge for the pipe with a clearance of twenty-two and a half feet over the tracks.[12] Despite some awkward plumbing, the pipeline method was a huge improvement and drastically reduced the need for barrels and labor.

Some breweries accommodated the bottling regulation by having their beer bottled by an independent contractor. Much of the early bottling was handled in this way, especially in markets distant from the brewery. Since all the beer had to be kegged anyway, it made little difference whether it was taken across the street, down the block, or to the railroad depot. Beer was shipped from the brewery to a local agent, who then bottled the beer with his own name on the bottle. Almost anyone could start a bottling business, since all it took was a supply of bottles and corks, some primitive bottling equipment, and a room in which to bottle. In some cases, bottlers used whatever bottles came to hand, perhaps even stealing them. Embossing beer bottles was not so much an issue of advertising as of ownership—bottles were expensive, and retrieving empties was a continuing concern. Some bottlers, such as Nic Petersen of Mankato and Rudolph Feigal of Minneapolis, became almost as well-known as the brewers themselves. Bottlers like

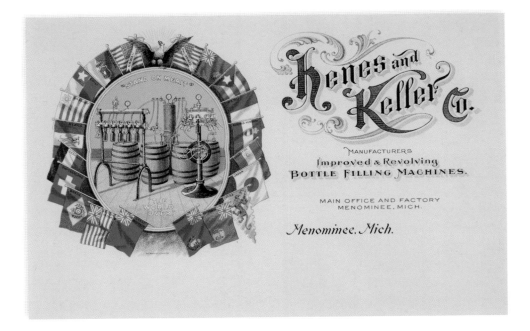

A variety of firms supplied the brewing industry with everything from pitch to sophisticated technical equipment. Very few of these firms were located in Minnesota; many were in New York, Philadelphia, or on the west shore of Lake Michigan. The machinery pictured on this Henes and Keller letterhead (c. 1899) was designed for smaller breweries that were still filling bottles from kegs rather than piping beer directly from storage tanks.
FROM THE COLLECTION OF STEVE KETCHUM.

The separation between brewers and bottlers is displayed clearly on this label from the mid-1880s. A. J.'s bottling works was just across the street from the brewery. Breweries often gave the name Export Beer to their standard bottled product. FROM THE COLLECTION OF KEN MALZ.

Petersen and Feigal relieved the brewers of some of their marketing duties as well as the need to keep a stock of bottles. Because early bottling was a low-tech, labor-intensive operation, it was easy to start with a minimum investment of capital. After the changes of the early 1890s, machinery became much more important, and the small independent bottlers began to disappear from city directories.

Klein & Pauntz and S. Alexander were Minneapolis saloonkeepers who also bottled beer. Bottles using Lightning stoppers such as these would have been easier and cheaper for saloons than investing in capping equipment. S. Alexander was at 34 & 36 South 6th Street from 1892 to 1903; Klein & Pauntz succeeded him in that location and remained until 1910. FROM THE COLLECTION OF STEVE KETCHUM.

Stabilizing the Brew

To survive in a time of increasing competition, not only did a modern brewmaster have to become a mechanic and an engineer but, again in Baron's words, "chemist and biologist as well." Two major biochemical developments prepared the way for the extensive shipping of bottled beer. French scientist Louis Pasteur discovered that many of the off flavors in beer were caused by bacteria and that heating the finished beer would kill any remaining bacteria or other unwanted microorganisms. It is not clear which Minnesota brewery was the first to pasteurize, or steam, its beer, but most new bottling works of the 1880s included the process. An account of the Schuster Brewery in Rochester described the process:

> Three hundred and sixty of these bottles are placed in another trough, that being filled with water to the height of the neck of the bottle, and steam is injected into the water, heating it to a temperature of 170 degrees. This extreme heat kills all germs and fermenting properties in the beer, and allows it to be kept from six months to a year without spoiling.

The steaming process adds confusion in interpreting the names of several breweries. In some cases, "steam" beer and "steam-brewing" seem to refer to pasteurization, but in others, "steam" probably referred to the power source of the brewery. It is less likely to refer to the beer style sometimes known as steam, or California common, where lager beer is fermented at ale temperatures and produces a large amount of carbon dioxide, or steam.

While invisible to a brewery visitor, the isolation and culturing of pure yeast strains by Emil Christian Hansen in 1883 at the Carlsberg brewery in Copenhagen was of vital importance in ensuring purity in the final product. This also had an effect on brewery appearance, because a sanitary brewing area was critical to avoid contaminating the pure yeast. Starting in the 1890s, new construction often featured tile, which was easier to clean than wood or stone, in the brewing areas.

All of these developments made brewing more consistent and made packaging and shipping the beer a more reasonable goal, provided the brewer could afford the new equipment. Those that could, generally breweries located in the largest cities, began to seek new markets both at home and farther abroad.

Milwaukee or St. Paul?

Beer was one of the first products to be advertised with recognizable brand names to mass audiences. Even so, when breweries first expanded into Midwest markets, the name of a brewer in a city hundreds of miles away was not expected to have much influence on consumer choice. However, certain cities had developed reputations as brewing centers, and these names were used commonly and almost assumed the role of brand names. The 1863 *St. Paul City Directory* contains an

This is essentially the same scene from the same era, but in two very different breweries. The Hamm brewhouse (*above*) is spacious and adorned with wrought iron staircases and railings. The Fergus Brewing Co. is much smaller and has exposed brick walls and much more utilitarian stairs and railings. The equipment is the same—only the size is different. The workers at Hamm are preparing to add hops to the brew kettle. HAMM PHOTOGRAPH COURTESY OF THE MINNESOTA HISTORICAL SOCIETY; FERGUS BREWING ILLUSTRATION FROM THE AUTHOR'S COLLECTION.

THE BREW ROOM

ad for M. Dorniden, who was a wholesale dealer in "Cincinnati, Philadelphia, Dayton & Pittsburgh Ale and Porter." The same edition also includes listings for two local breweries hoping to trade on the fame of others: William Leip's Chicago Ale Brewery and Andrew Keller's Pittsburg Brewery (Pittsburg was spelled without the final h at the time). Little is known of Leip's early career, but Keller was a brewer in the Pittsburgh area before he came to Minnesota. In both cases, they could have been attempting to enhance the prestige of the product or actually brewing a beer in the style of the city named. Adding to the confusion was the occasional use of the term *Milwaukee beer* to distinguish lager from ale. The tradition of naming beer styles after the city of origin goes back at least to the Middle Ages, and later, Munich, Vienna, and Pilsen each became famous for a distinct style of lager. The stylistic differences between Kulmbach, Würzburg, and Erlangen lagers are difficult for any but an expert to distinguish, but these cities also gave their names to dozens of American beers. (The most famous brand name derived from a city is, of course, Budweiser.) Whatever the case, the prestige of "imported brands" was often used by saloons or hotels as a mark of quality. Most towns had at least one establishment offering "fresh Milwaukee Beer always on tap." Prestige was also a way to neutralize the increased cost of providing imported beer. It was not a major issue in an establishment such as a hotel bar, where the cost could be made up elsewhere (or when the brewery owned the saloon, to be covered later), but in the case of a large beer garden where beer was the only product, the cost could make or break the enterprise. Planners of the temporary saloons at the Minnesota State Fair in 1885 estimated that "if Milwaukee beer is used, this will cost $8—a trifle over a cent a glass, or $576 for the 54,000 glasses. If, however, the purchaser of the privilege decides that he must figure close, St. Paul beer can be purchased at $6.50 per barrel, or thirteen-fifteenths of a cent per glass."[13] Serving only Minnesota beer at the State Fair to promote the state's agricultural products does not seem to have been an important consideration for the planners.

Importing beer was essential in the early years of Minnesota, before breweries were established or before they were able to produce enough to satisfy the thirst of the citizens. In 1859 the barroom of the Valley House in Henderson featured Dubuque lager (though Henderson would acquire a brewery later that year). The need was reduced as the home breweries multiplied and grew. However, the population of Minnesota grew even faster, and out-of-state breweries, especially those in Wisconsin, saw a golden opportunity to snatch some of this expanding market.

Wisconsin breweries had been shipping to Minnesota since territorial days, especially to markets across the river from La Crosse or otherwise accessible by water. Wholesalers such as Dorniden handled most of this beer and brought in whichever beer they could get at the best rates. But the expansion of imports began in earnest in the early 1880s. The filling in of the

Like many other breweries, Alexandria Brewing Co. named products after particular styles of lager, in this case, that of the Franconian city of Würzburg. It is impossible to determine whether the beer was actually in the Würzburger style or simply taking advantage of a famous name. The issue is confused even more by the image of the hooded child, since the *Münchner Kindl* is the symbol of Munich. Note the strange though reassuring recommendation at the top of the label, c. 1900. FROM THE COLLECTION OF KEN MALZ.

railroad network and the development of refrigerated rail cars made it possible to transport beer hundreds and even thousands of miles. Shipping brewers began to establish their own agents, branches, and depots in distant markets. A depot could be anything from a crude icehouse to a permanent refrigerated building. Agents were typically independent contractors, whereas branch offices were staffed by employees of the home brewery. Each method had advantages and drawbacks, but very large sales usually made a branch more profitable. As breweries shifted organizational systems, the bottles no longer bore the name of the local bottler but rather the name of the home brewery—though often with the branch location indicated. Pabst is generally credited with many of the early refinements of the branch method. It established its first Minnesota branch (and fourth overall) in 1881 in St. Paul.[14] However, most breweries remained with the agent system for a while, since it was easier to establish or abandon. The Charles and John Michel Brewery of La Crosse established an agent in Rochester in 1881, but this arrangement lasted only a few years. The Michels followed their fellow townsman John Gund into Minneapolis in 1882 and hired Charles Beuck as their local agent. Also appearing that year was an ad for the Milwaukee Bottling Company, which was the local agent for Blatz. A few years later, Blatz had a branch office in Minneapolis and became one of the most prominent advertisers in the city directory. By the end of the decade, Anheuser-Busch, Phillip Best, and Schlitz were also established in Minneapolis. By this time, the Michels had long since retreated from the Twin

During the early days of shipping, it was common for breweries to send kegs of beer to a bottler at the destination and have it bottled there to keep it fresh. These rare examples represent the few Wisconsin brewers that noted the bottling location on the bottles. From left: Waukesha Imperial Springs Brewing Co. made occasional appearances in the Minneapolis city directory—the first in 1897, the last in 1906. Milwaukee Bottling Co. was the agent for Val. Blatz Brewing Co. These bottles date to the earliest years of Blatz's Minnesota ventures, since the bottles were made by the Wisconsin Glass Co., which operated from 1882 to 1886. A. W. Doerr was the Minneapolis agent for Jos. Schlitz Brewing Co. This bottle was manufactured by Chase Valley Glass, which was in business only during 1880 and 1881. FROM THE COLLECTION OF STEVE KETCHUM.

The bottle-washing room of the Anheuser-Busch agency in St. Paul is easily identified by the wooden cases in the foreground. The business was located at 300–302 Chestnut from 1888 to 1898. FROM THE COLLECTION OF STEVE KETCHUM.

Cities market and focused their efforts on smaller cities in southern Minnesota with great success.

In 1897 two other Wisconsin firms entered the Minneapolis market, Miller Brewing Company (which had established depots in northern Minnesota a decade earlier and a century later would be one of the dominant brands in the state) and Waukesha Imperial Spring Brewing Co. (which would be a presence for only a few years). The last two invading Wisconsin breweries opened Minneapolis offices just after the turn of the century: Jung Brewery of Milwaukee and G. Heileman Brewing Company of La Crosse. This group of out-of-town breweries remained stable until Prohibition because the investment to open a new market had to be considered in light of the existing competition, which in Minneapolis was particularly fierce. The Pabst branch in Minneapolis had a lower rate of return to the brewery in 1886 than any other branch—a result of lower beer prices (less than $7 per barrel) and higher shipping costs than to other branches. (St. Paul's rate of return was more than a dollar higher, even though the price of beer was about fifty cents more per barrel.)[15]

Defending Their Territory

While no Minnesota breweries would approach the major Milwaukee or St. Louis shipping breweries in territory or volume, they put up a spirited fight to keep enough of the home market to stay profitable and even ventured into other states with some frequency. As with out-of-state brewers, the brewers in major cities were happy to meet the demand in areas with no breweries. John Lanvig's Refreshment Station in Granite Falls, about 125 miles west of the Twin Cities, advertised in 1877 that it kept "Miller & Heinrich's Minneapolis Beer always on hand." Similar ads in other cities touted their taps of fresh Minneapolis or St. Paul beer, and some watering holes in outlying areas featured beer from Winona or one of the other smaller brewing centers.

As business increased, the larger breweries began to set up their own depots in railroad towns. The local agent could pick up the beer and bottle it or deliver kegs to local customers as necessary. While a few depots were established in the 1880s, most were built between 1890 and 1905. Whether built by a nearby brewer or a national firm, small-town depots were usually simple wooden icehouses like the Schuster depot at Grand Meadow in Mower County, which was blown up by vandals with dynamite in 1894.[16] A depot or branch in a larger city was usually much more substantial, both to handle the larger volume and to enhance the reputation of the brewery. One firm moving into Rochester succeeded in impressing the local citizens:

> The plant of the Minneapolis Brewing and Malting Co. on North Prospect street is now completed and everything in shape for business. The storage room is large and capacious and is situated under an ice box of sufficient size to hold 140 tons of ice. The cold air is admitted through apertures in the ceiling in one end of the room, and the warmer air is given egress through holes in the other end. By an ingenious contrivance the temperature can be regulated to suit the needs. The sides of the storage room are in four thicknesses of boards, the interstices being filled with sawdust, thus preventing the temperature being affected by outside conditions. The building is solidly constructed, the pillars being of timbers 12 × 12 in size and the joists of timbers 12 × 14. The room adjoining the office is intended for the storage of case goods and is admirably suited to the purpose. The office contains all necessary appurtenances, including safe, desk, and other necessaries. A stable for the horses is in connection with the building. The team which will be used in delivering goods throughout the city, is a large black team, such as the company uses in Minneapolis and other large cities. As soon as the weather will permit the exterior of the building will be improved in appearance by painting and signs. There is on hand at the office a number of corner signs, intended for

customers. There are also on hand a number of large and handsomely framed lithographs of the brewing and malting plant at Minneapolis, on the corner of Marshall and 13th streets.[17]

While Minneapolis Brewing and Malting maintained a presence in Rochester until Prohibition, no other brewery established a branch there, most likely because of the strong hold Schuster Brewing Co. had on the local market.

For cities without a dominant local producer, the story was much different. Grand Rapids, a rail center near the lumbering and mining areas with no brewery of its own, hosted depots for Minneapolis Brewing Company, Pabst, and Blatz, as well as for nearby Fitger Brewing Company and Duluth Brewing & Malting Company. East Grand Forks, on the border of North Dakota, was the jumping-off point for brewers selling to a state that had declared itself dry in its constitution. By the late 1890s, nearly half the buildings pictured on the Sanborn insurance

Breweries took great pride in the quality of their horses. While the Clydesdales of Anheuser-Busch are the most famous in modern times, Minnesota's brewery horses were equally well-known within each brewery's sales territory. Minneapolis Brewing Company had nearly two hundred horses, all but two black. The single-horse delivery wagon pictured in front of Christ Church in Red Wing around 1900 could not have carried a full load of kegs and was more likely used for delivering cases of beer to households. COURTESY OF THE MINNESOTA HISTORICAL SOCIETY.

maps were beer warehouses. Eventually the city would host facilities for Minneapolis Brewing, Hamm, Miller, Blatz, Gund, Schlitz, and Duluth Brewing & Malting, which must have been intimidating for the local East Grand Forks Brewery, with its capacity of only 18,000 barrels.[18]

The presence of depots for Fitger's and Duluth Brewing & Malting—not to mention Schuster, Schellhas of Winona, and Bierbauer of Mankato—in other cities demonstrated a fact that the major brewers soon realized: the small brewers were not going to surrender their regional markets without a fight. American beer sales more than doubled from 1893 to 1914, but sales by the major Milwaukee and St. Louis shipping brewers did not keep up with the national rate of increase.[19] As mechanization became more common and more affordable, and as sales volume increased, more brewers could afford to update their plants and to expand their production to new markets. In Rochester, Schuster Brewing Co. undertook several expansions from 1897 to 1905 to increase capacity to 50,000 barrels at an expense of nearly $100,000. This output could not all be absorbed by Rochester, so the Schuster brothers attempted to expand to other markets in the upper Midwest, including Minneapolis and Kansas City. A large portion of Schuster's capacity was devoted to production of its malt tonic, which it shipped as far as the Hawaiian Islands and western Canada. (Malt tonic will be covered in more detail in chapter 5.)

One of the most remarkable ventures by a Minnesota brewery was the creation of a branch brewery in Ogden, Utah, by Becker & Schellhas of Winona. While Utah was not fertile territory for breweries because of Mormon restrictions on alcohol, Ogden had a strong gentile presence and elected a non-Mormon mayor in 1889. In October 1890, perhaps encouraged by an industrial fair sponsored by

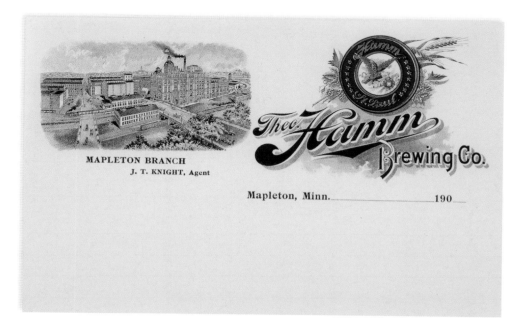

MAPLETON BRANCH
J. T. KNIGHT, Agent

Theo. Hamm Brewing Co.

Mapleton, Minn._____ 190__

To facilitate efficient shipping to customers in outlying regions, the major shipping brewers set up depots in cities large and small along the railroads. Mapleton is south of Mankato in Blue Earth County. FROM THE COLLECTION OF STEVE KETCHUM.

William Hope "Coin" Harvey, William Schellhas left for Ogden to supervise the construction of the brewery at the corner of 19th Street and Lincoln Avenue. By April 1891, Schellhas Brewing Co. released the first batch of Rocky Mountain Amber lager. Attempting to run the Ogden branch from Winona was cumbersome, and there were advantages in being a locally incorporated company, so Gustav L. Becker left Winona and became president of the new Becker Brewing & Malting Company in Ogden. Within the next few years, Becker expanded the product line with Export, Kulnbecher [sic], and Bohemian, and maintained the tradition of releasing a bock beer in the spring with great fanfare. The company, which eventually became Becker Brewing Company, survived until 1965 and sold beer in several western states.[20]

Minnesota's shipping breweries encountered legal roadblocks in addition to fierce competition. The agent of Minneapolis Brewing Company at Gladstone, in Michigan's Upper Peninsula, was at the center of a lawsuit in which the court ruled that all agents of out-of-state brewers had to purchase a $500 wholesale license, compared with the $65 manufacturing fee paid by Michigan brewers. (Michigan's Upper Peninsula was a particular target of Minnesota and Wisconsin brewers

PERFECTION GUARANTEED

DAKOTA BEER

Guaranteed to contain less than 2% Alcohol.

FITGER BREWING CO.
DULUTH. E. GRAND FORKS.

Fitger's Dakota Beer was designed for sale in North Dakota. This label is from the early 1900s. FROM THE COLLECTION OF KEN MALZ.

because they could reach it more easily than Detroit's brewers could.) Minnesota breweries were the logical suppliers for North Dakota, but no beer in excess of 2 percent alcohol could be sold there, so many northern breweries created special products for the North Dakota market.

City Brewery, Incorporated

While the number of new urban breweries established between the Panic of 1893 and the beginning of Prohibition was fairly small, the firms were usually relatively large and were never intended to be family businesses. A few small breweries were started in St. Paul, Minneapolis, and Duluth during these years, but they were quite short lived. Minneapolis seems to have been considered a more promising market than St. Paul by these entrepreneurs; J. L. Bausch & Son's one-year venture was the only new brewery in St. Paul between 1888 and 1986. In contrast, the Minneapolis city directories chronicle the comings and goings of Andrew Liden, Peterson & Matson, J. A. Swanson, Edward Hasle, John Carlson, Barrett & Barrett, the Youngstrom brothers, and others. Some of these brewers seem to have been trying brewing as one of several possible career choices—Andrew Liden (or Leden or Lideen) was listed in the directories variously as a brewer, a bottler, and a carpenter—others were just passing through town. Hasle appeared for the first time in the 1896 directory as a brewer at 2206 Riverside Avenue, but his listing in 1897 read "moved to Grafton, N.D."

The breweries that lasted were not able to start small and grow up along with the city, as had those of the previous generation. It was necessary to start as large as possible and to have significant financial resources available. While cellars were no longer necessary, and this allowed breweries to be built anywhere, the cost of refrigeration equipment added to the debt burden of the new firms. Conrad Birkhofer Brewing Co. was started in 1894 by a former officer of Minneapolis Brewing Company and boasted a capital stock of $150,000. The new brewery had the advantage of starting with all the most current equipment and thus would have efficiency and cost advantages over less-modern producers. This advantage was reduced by the lead other brewers had in finding outlets for their beer. However, there were enough new saloons, hotels, and gaming halls in the rapidly growing cities for a new brewery to claim a respectable market share.

An account of the spectacular Windom Building fire (26 February 1901) in Minneapolis reported that the fire started in the saloon of J. Cohen and that Birkhofer Brewing Co. (as owners of the saloon) lost two thousand dollars, which was fully covered by insurance. PHOTOGRAPH BY WINFRED C. PORTER; COURTESY OF THE MINNESOTA HISTORICAL SOCIETY.

The need for large amounts of start-up capital led many breweries to adopt the corporation structure for their businesses. Up to this point, most breweries, in fact, most businesses of any sort, had been sole proprietorships or partnerships, often with family members. These were easiest for most entrepreneurs to manage, but financial resources were limited to what the owners could raise themselves. Furthermore, if the owner died, the brewery could be tied up in probate court with the rest of the estate for several years. At least ten Minnesota breweries functioned for some period under the name of the estate of the late owner. The corporation, first commonly used in transportation enterprises but later in most sectors of industry, allowed firms to raise operating capital through stock sales. In addition, the corporation had an independent life that did not end with the life of any of its officers. Many of the small breweries in Minnesota incorporated themselves, but the motivation was often more to establish legal succession rather than to raise additional capital. Glencoe Brewing Co. incorporated in 1901, but its capital stock was only $27,000. (The brewery was expanding at this point, so money may have been a factor in the timing, but the directors were exclusively family members.)[21] In comparison, Gluek Brewing Company, another old family firm, incorporated in 1894 with a capital stock of $200,000, but again, only Gluek family members were directors.[22] Another typical case was Joseph Wolf Co. of Stillwater, which showed how little changed through incorporation. According to the January 1898 *Gazette Trade Review*, Joe Wolf ran the business himself

until March 1896, when feeling that a measure of the responsibility and much of the details of the fast accumulating business should be shifted to the shoulders of those younger than he, he suggested an incorporation which should include his three sons and two sons-in-law. . . . This infusion of young blood is bound to be of much advantage, as all the parties mentioned are by nature possessed of fine business qualifications, and had been in the employ of the original proprietor for many years, most of them occupying the identical positions they have filled since the new corporation came into existence.

Imperial Brewing Co. used the old Noerenberg brewery on Bluff Street to produce its Whale Brand products.
COURTESY OF THE MINNESOTA HISTORICAL SOCIETY.

For the new breweries, forming a corporation was a way to bring in a wide range of investors and to start fast in a business that was fiercely competitive but in which the profits were potentially great for those who succeeded. The lucrative Minnesota markets attracted some capitalists from outside the state, but not to the degree of some other brewing centers. Breweries in New York, Philadelphia, Baltimore, Milwaukee, Chicago, St. Louis, and elsewhere were the targets of British investors seeking to escape the industrial depression at home and take advantage of the expanding market. There is little evidence of British investors seeking to form enormous syndicates in Minnesota, though British parties put in a bid to buy A. Fitger & Co. in Duluth.[23] Out-of-state in-

STANDARD BREWING CO.

THE EXECUTION OF 38
SIOUX INDIANS AT MANKATO, DEC. 26TH 1862.
FOR HISTORY SEE OTHER SIDE.

MANKATO, MINN. U.S.A.

vestors coming to Minnesota more often were involved in starting new companies. When Imperial Brewing Co. was formed in 1901 in Minneapolis using the old Noerenberg brewery buildings, the financing capital came from investors in Minneapolis and Canada (and, according to some sources, Britain). Standard Brewing Co. of Mankato was formed in 1900 with financial backing from Chicago investors.[24] Both of these breweries were very aggressive in their attempts to establish themselves, but ultimately lasted only a few years. Standard Brewing Co. produced some of the most striking advertising pieces of any Minnesota brewery. Its "1776" label and the "Execution of 38 Sioux Indians" tray and sign are among the most sought-after pieces of Minnesota breweriana. The company advertised heavily in local publications and touted its modern equipment and expert management. However, by 1908 Standard had closed, unable to make an adequate profit in a market with a well-established local brewery and several shipping breweries.

Imperial Brewing Co. launched one of the riskiest expansion attempts of any new brewery, a planned branch brewery in Sandstone. The plans were announced

This tray issued by Standard Brewing Co. of Mankato is one of the most remarkable pieces of breweriana ever produced. Standard also issued a smaller, round tray showing just the execution scene, and other companies used similar copies of the illustration to advertise cigars and other items. While such a design would likely draw protests one hundred years later, at the time the image was commonplace and helped connect the product to a famous event in Mankato's history. The tray may have been issued to mark the 40th anniversary of the executions. The fact that neither these brands nor crown-capped bottles were available in 1862 was not important but urging large sales was: the three officers have apparently gone through most of two kegs and finished off two cases of 24-ounce bottles. FROM THE COLLECTION OF JIM AND RUTH BEATON.

Photographed in a rare quiet moment around the turn of the century, the Minneapolis Brewing Company's new brewery at the corner of 13th Avenue and Marshall Street NE was a masterpiece of Victorian architecture. Unlike many other breweries of the period, this structure maintained its original appearance through the twentieth century and did not suffer from additions or remodeling in different architectural styles. COURTESY OF THE MINNESOTA HISTORICAL SOCIETY.

in August 1904 with great fanfare, and the powerful name of railroad tycoon James J. Hill was mentioned as "interested in the enterprise," which was anticipated to pour $100,000 into Sandstone and create a minimum of fifty new jobs. Ultimately, the plans came to naught, and Imperial was out of business by 1905, leaving only large debts and one thousand barrels of spoiled beer. The firm left some legacy, however—the company's Whale Brand soft drinks had become popular and were acquired by William Massolt Bottling Co.[25]

The threat of foreign syndicates moving into the American beer market inspired brewers in many cities to form combinations of their own in defense. Large brewery groups formed in Baltimore, Pittsburgh, St. Louis, and elsewhere, but Minnesota did not follow this trend, with one major exception. In 1890 four of the five largest breweries in Minneapolis joined together and formed Minneapolis Brewing and Malting Co., which was reorganized three years later as Minneapolis Brewing Company. The Germania, Noerenberg, Heinrich, and Orth breweries all had been successful firms, but their competition had created price wars in Minneapolis that forced expensive expansion and reduced their profits. Mergers were common in all sectors of industry during this period, both horizontal mergers that reduced competition and vertical integration that assured sources of supply or outlets for finished goods. The merger of these four breweries reduced competition and pooled the saloons they owned together, guaranteeing a sizeable market for the new flagship brand, Grain Belt Beer. Taking advantage of its ability to use multiple facilities in the short term, the new company built a spectacular new brewery on the site of the old Orth Brewery at 13th Avenue and Marshall Street Northeast. The new combination and brand were instant successes, and the firm was highly profitable until the advent of Prohibition.

The Beer Barons

From the 1870s to the early 1900s, American society found its greatest heroes less among politicians and warriors than among the "captains of industry." The mythic self-made man who rose from poverty to great wealth by virtue of his hard work and honest dealing was held up as the model for American youth. While few of the railroad or manufacturing tycoons truly fit the description (most relied heavily on land grants or outside capital to build their much larger enterprises), many of Minnesota's leading brewers really had turned small family shops into famous brands. While some brewers struggled to make a living, there were a large number who prospered greatly and were considered among the leading citizens of their communities. No Minnesota brewer became as wealthy as rail baron James J. Hill, but Hill took larger risks than the often-conservative brewers and reaped greater rewards. Except for a few brewers such as the directors of Minnesota Brewing Company, the company providing the wealth often still carried the family name.

Numerous county and regional history books were compiled during and just after the Victorian period (in part to make money by selling copies to the citizens praised within their pages). While the literary excesses of the era and the desire not to offend purchasers may overstate the prestige of the brewers slightly, they were clearly held in high regard by the business-minded members of the community (if not always by the religiously inclined). A 1909 history of Blue Earth County offered high praise for the members of the Bierbauer family. According to this work, Albert was "as big of heart as he is big of body." He "has a large circle of warm friends and his splendid ability and integrity make him a prominent figure among the captains of Blue Earth county industries." The biography of Albert's uncle Jacob was even more flowery in its prose:

> A considerable portion of the pioneer population of Mankato consisted of men of German birth or parentage. Thus was given to the early development of the village the element of Teutonic thrift so indispensable to permanent prosperity. Conspicuous among the men who brought from Germany to Minnesota the sterling traits of character and keen energy associated with the primary growth of

Brewery Architecture

Pioneer breweries were sometimes indistinguishable from any other business or home in the area. But as the brewers became more prosperous, they built new plants that made the brewing process more efficient and showed off the proprietors' wealth.

Tall breweries exploited gravity to do much of the work in the brewing process. Once malt or other grains were at the top of the brewery, they could flow down into the mash tun, then into the brew kettle, farther down into the fermenters, and finally into storage tanks in the cellars. Artificial refrigeration and modern pumps have reduced the need to build upward, but some of the larger new breweries such as Summit Brewing Company in St. Paul still make use of gravity for some of the steps in the brewing process.

Most early breweries were constructed primarily of wood, though the foundations and cellars may have been stone. The combination of wood construction, combustible grain, and fire meant it was a rare brewery that did not have at least one significant fire. Those who could afford to rebuilt with brick, a statement of prosperity that was often remarked on in newspapers and industry publications. Except in the case of a catastrophic fire, few breweries started all over with a new building. Instead, they tended to add new buildings as needed or as possible. Adding larger brew kettles, new fermenters, or artificial refrigeration often entailed building large new structures.

By the 1880s, brewery architecture had become a subfield of its own as

The different parts of a typical 1880s brewery can be seen in this diagram of the Orth Brewery. COURTESY OF THE MINNESOTA HISTORICAL SOCIETY.

wealthy brewers were demanding efficient plants that would still be symbols of prosperity. Chicago, home of many famous architects, was a center of brewery architecture. Bernard Barthel, Louis Lehle, August Maritzen, Fred Wolf, and Wilhelm and Richard Griesser all undertook new brewery or brewery addition projects in Minnesota. The firm of Boehme & Cordella of Minneapolis designed some buildings for Gluek Brewing Company, but most recorded work was done by outside firms. The rare new breweries near the turn of the twentieth century afforded architects opportunities to build showpieces.

Minneapolis Brewing Company and Jacob Schmidt Brewing Company in St. Paul were the largest new breweries, but Park Brewing Co. in Winona and Virginia Brewing Co. were considered classic examples of small or midsize breweries. (The research of Professor Susan K. Appel forms the basis of most discussions of brewery architecture, and her assistance is greatly appreciated.) ❧

The Park Brewing facility in Winona was designed in 1904 by Richard Griesser of Chicago. Griesser also designed a later addition to the building. The designer of this tray followed the common practice of making the trains and other vehicles very small to make the brewery look much larger than it really was. FROM THE COLLECTION OF DAVE WENDL.

This spectacular lithograph-on-tin depiction of Jacob Schmidt Brewing Company in the early 1900s adds features to the brewery that were not there and takes great liberties with the buildings along West Seventh Street. Artists may never have seen the breweries they were depicting and usually based their work on breweries with which they were familiar. FROM THE COLLECTION OF DAVE DAVIS.

Intentionally or unintentionally, this photo captures the income disparity between capitalists and labor at the turn of the twentieth century. The vista is dominated by Theodore Hamm's gigantic brewery, but framed by the magnificent Hamm residence at 671 Cable Avenue on the right and by the tenements and shanties of Swede Hollow on the left and in the foreground. The brewery, designed by leading Chicago brewery architect August Maritzen and completed in 1894, expanded the firm's capacity and answered the new brewery of the Minneapolis Brewing Company. Theodore's son William built the twenty-room Queen Anne–style mansion while his father was in Europe and presented it as a gift upon his return. Poor laborers enjoyed no such luxury in Swede Hollow, a place where succeeding generations of new immigrants lived only until they could afford to move out. COURTESY OF THE MINNESOTA HISTORICAL SOCIETY.

the northwest, we mention the name of Jacob Bierbauer, who was born August 28, 1819, in Rhenish Bavaria, Germany, near the shores of the beautiful stream whose name was borne by the province and whose charm has formed the theme of countless songs and poems.

These biographies placed great importance on the civic activity of the brewers, so Albert's membership in the Elks lodge and the Sons of Herman and Jacob's involvement with the German Lutheran church and the Independent Order of Odd Fellows were mentioned prominently.[26] Many brewers ended up being involved in politics and becoming office holders, some reaching as high as mayor or state representative. While temperance activists often claimed that brewer-politicians were simply trying to gain favorable treatment for their degrading business—and no doubt many brewers were concerned with protecting their source of wealth—many held office out of genuine concern for their hometowns. Henry Schuster Sr. of Rochester, a two-term alderman, was particularly concerned with improving fire protection in the city and even donated equipment to the fire department. While his special concern with fire was no doubt a result of a catastrophic fire at his brewery, the benefit for the entire city was real and substantial. Local brewers were popular because their businesses were usually tied to the community by both supply and market, and the brewer could not move the business to gain a labor or price advantage. Brewers also had extraordinary name recognition since their names were not just on the business but also on kegs, bottles, and saloon signs all over town. A rare glass from Fred Busch's brewery in Hastings carries the slogan "The Workingman's Friend," which may well have been provided in connection with Busch's successful campaign for mayor rather than to describe the beer itself.

In common with other wealthy industrialists, brewers used their wealth to enjoy the good life. Many built opulent houses, dozens of which have survived into the twenty-first century. Theodore Hamm took his family for a grand tour of the Rhine valley and the Alps in 1886 (during which he embarrassed some family members by acting too much like an arrogant American capitalist).[27]

The most successful brewing firms often branched out into other businesses only tangentially related to brewing. The Hamm family, the Schmidt and Bremer families, the Schuster family, and others formed real estate or development companies. Real estate was a logical extension for large shipping brewers, as they had experience buying sites for saloons and depots and in managing large numbers of properties. A sizeable number of brewers also became involved with banking, at least in part because they brought their financial resources to the bank as directors. While Otto Bremer started as a bank

The beautiful Schell Mansion was built in 1885 for August and Teresa Schell. It combines features of several different architectural styles, a common practice in Victorian homes. The mansion is not open to the public, but visitors can wander through the gardens and look for the peacocks on the grounds. COURTESY OF AUGUST SCHELL BREWING COMPANY.

clerk, his share in the Schmidt brewery helped him build the resources and reputation to create a small banking empire. The large German-American Bank of St. Paul had several brewers serving as directors at various times. The term *captain of industry* could also be adjusted to reflect the size of the town. Although it was small, Mathias Pitzl's brewery in New Munich was one of the largest businesses in this small Stearns County farm town and helped Pitzl become vice president of the State Bank of New Munich.[28]

Unfortunately, the wealth and prominence of the great brewers made them more prominent targets of the temperance crusade, which came to a climax in the first two decades of the twentieth century.

Industrial Era Brewery Workers

As breweries grew larger, the proprietor and family members were no longer able to handle all the tasks themselves. As a consequence, they began to hire additional laborers to allow increased production. As with most growing industries, workers were generally hired for specific tasks. City directories of the era usually listed the occupations of each individual, and as early as the 1860s entries showed the

This is presumed to be a photograph of the Mathias Pitzl family near their home in New Munich. Note the man wearing overalls standing in the brewery wagon holding a pitcher of Pitzl's beer. FROM THE COLLECTION OF STEVE KETCHUM.

LAND of AMBER WATERS: *THE HISTORY of BREWING in MINNESOTA*

German immigrants were often among the most militant labor activists, but many brewery workers organized themselves along less adversarial lines. Many brewers encouraged a paternalistic system where workers were treated as dependents rather than employees, and indeed, many brewery workers boarded with the proprietor. As breweries grew larger and more mechanized, the unions of brewery workmen became more like those in other manufacturing industries. This local was undoubtedly organized at Minneapolis Brewing Company to coincide with the opening of the new brewery. The German banner proclaims God's blessing of the organization (*Grüß Gott* is a common Bavarian greeting) and bears a motto often found in breweries, *Hopfen und Malz, Gott erhalts*, "Hops and malt are blessed by God." FROM THE COLLECTION OF STEVE KETCHUM.

increasing specialization with occupations like brewer, maltster, foreman, laborer, and driver. Workers had opportunities to advance within the company, but others left to start their own breweries or for other jobs either in or out of the brewing industry.

DRINK *Schell's* CARBONATED MEAD

Schell's Bottling Department
NEW ULM, MINN.

Automobiling

N. Hyneman.

The automobile, shown here leaving the horse-drawn carriage far behind, was the ultimate symbol of technology and progress in the first decades of the twentieth century. Many who believed in progress—progressives—thought that human society was perfectible and that government could play a role in bringing this about. Prohibiting the consumption of alcohol was one of the most dramatic ways in which reformers sought to create an ideal society. COURTESY OF AUGUST SCHELL BREWING COMPANY.

From Temperance to Prohibition

Nearly two weeks ago was a Territorial Temperance Convention at St. Paul, and I can assure you St. Anthony Falls did herself credit on that occasion. The Temperance folks are wide awake and active—determined to get the unconditional enactment of that law this winter if possible. We have a Brass Band here, organized last summer. They went to the convention and played finely. The Glee Club sung admirably (so they say—I did not go). Over one hundred persons went in the procession from here—One four horse, nine two horse and six one horse teams. They had a beautiful banner. Mr. Nessen painted it. On one side was "St. Anthony Temperance Society—Try Again" on the other was a beautiful fountain playing in the midst of trees and shrubs with the motto over it "Drink from this fountain". O there is so much enthusiasm manifested—it would do your hearts good. I think the Legislature will not dare refuse to enact the law, if the House is ever organized.
—Ann Loomis North, 1853

A S SEEN IN CHAPTER 1, THE BREWING INDUSTRY IN MINNESOTA WAS NEARLY throttled in its infancy by the approval of a Maine law referendum prohibiting manufacture and sale of alcohol. Minnesota was a central battleground between the dry forces of prohibition and their wet opponents. To the east were the alcohol-producing and alcohol-consuming states of Wisconsin, Michigan, and Illinois. To the west were states that adopted statewide prohibition relatively early: Kansas, Nebraska, South Dakota, and North Dakota (which was dry from birth according to its state constitution). To the south was Iowa, which could not make up its mind and switched from wet to dry and back several times. In addition, Minnesota itself was split both statewide and at the local level. Southeast of a line drawn from Duluth through Stearns County and then down to Brown County, the largest non–English speaking immigrant group was beer-drinking Germans. West of this line, Scandinavians were more common, and many brought with them the belief that drinking was a problem, not a way to relax on Sunday afternoon. Finally,

because Minnesota was settled during the era when the primary countries of origin for immigrants were changing, most localities, including the major urban areas, had significant numbers of residents from dry and wet cultures. While part of St. Paul's political and economic elite were of Irish and German Catholic heritage, an equally important part were of Yankee Presbyterian stock—the same people responsible for the Maine law.[1]

The Growth of Temperance Ideals

Despite the modern connotations of the term *Puritan*, ale was an indispensable part of the diet of the earliest English settlers. From early settlement well into the nineteenth century, fresh water supplies were unreliable, and any drink where the liquid was boiled at some point was quite simply safer and more healthful. Ale and cider were common products of household manufacture in the colonies, and molasses and its distillate, rum, were among the most common imports to the colonies. Corn, rye, and other grain crops grew in importance as the settlers moved west, so the various members of the whiskey family became increasingly popular. As a side business, making whiskey was a lucrative way to use up excess farm production and to make some additional money. Distilled spirits had advantages over ale in addition to potency (if that is an advantage): they were less perishable and often improved with age. Transporting a barrel of whiskey to market rather than a barrel of ale would bring greater profits, and the whiskey would last longer at the saloon.

In the colonial period, the main target of reformers was drunkenness. While drinking alcohol was a part of everyday life for many, drunkenness was harshly punished by civil means such as fines, a term in the stocks, or social exclusion. In Massachusetts, a scarlet *D* served to mark a habitual drunkard and separate him from civil society. Ale was seldom mentioned as a cause of drunkenness—rather it was advocated as an alternative to hard liquor. James Oglethorpe banned spirits from his new colony of Georgia in the 1730s, but encouraged the use of sound English ale. This fit with the English belief (displayed in the famous engravings by Hogarth) that ale led to prosperity while liquor (specifically gin in Hogarth's example) would ruin civilization.

The foundation of the modern temperance movement was laid in the years immediately following the Revolution. Among the educated elites, the general spirit of the time emphasized civic virtue and a sense of collective order and stability. This idea of republicanism saw liberty more as something resting in the ordered community rather than in the individual. The drunkenness of the disorderly rabble in the tavern was at least as much a threat to civic virtue as it was a danger to bystanders. The single work that best set the tone for temperance reformers was *An Inquiry into the Effects of Ardent Spirits on the Human Mind and Body*, published in 1784 by Benjamin Rush. Rush was one of the heroes of the Revolutionary period—a signer of the Declaration of Independence, surgeon general to the Continental Army, and a famous politician and doctor—and therefore commanded attention. Rush's *Inquiry* was probably the first American work to treat drunkenness as a disease and to examine the effects of liquor on health. Rush believed that sound beer and wine had potential health benefits if consumed in limited quantities. He was among the first prominent Americans to call for a coordinated program of laws and treatment facilities to remedy drunkenness.

Despite Rush's position as a politician and a physician, most of the early leaders of the temperance movement were religious figures. Many Protestant denominations—Quakers, Methodists, Presbyterians, and some Baptists in particular—made sobriety an essential facet of the godly life and viewed drunkenness as a sin for which conversion was the best solution. The first national temperance organization, the American Society for the Promotion of Temperance, founded in 1826, was largely an extension of religious leaders already active in pursuing this cause. The society proposed abstaining from ardent spirits and held that use of non-distilled beverages would help prevent many of the evils associated with hard drink. However, during the 1830s, many organizations and societies shifted their focus from temperance to total abstinence. Because many of the pioneering ministers and teachers in Minnesota came from this Protestant tradition, they were able to ensure a solid following for temperance among the educated classes of the state.

Minnesota was one of the newest areas open to settlement when the huge migrations of Irish and Germans arrived in America in the late 1840s. These settlers had strong traditions of social drinking in their home countries. Irish immigrants sometimes resorted to drinking as a defense mechanism against a new society that was frequently hostile to them and in which they often struggled to succeed. The fact that many of these new immigrants were Catholic was a major cause of concern for the established Protestant elite, and the drinking habits of the newcomers only magnified the threat posed to the carefully structured republican order. While the peak period of anti-Irish violence in the 1840s occurred before Minnesota had enough settlers to be affected, many in the region brought the stereotype of the drunken Irishman with them. Because many Catholic parishes were organized along lines of nationality rather than geography, this made both the Celtic Irish and the Teutonic Germans appear unwilling to assimilate and adopt the American Protestant republican social order.

Beer Becomes a Target

For some temperance advocates, beer was a source of concern from the beginning. A Methodist report in 1832 worried that beer was being offered as a safe alternative and questioned whether "a man can indulge ... at all and be considered temperate."[2] Ironically, the fact that lager beer invigorated America's limited brewing industry increased the attention temperance advocates paid to beer. The high-volume public consumption by the new immigrants was used by social

German immigrants viewed Sunday as a day of relaxation. Sunday social gatherings, such as this one around 1885, often featured a keg of beer. COURTESY OF THE MINNESOTA HISTORICAL SOCIETY.

reformers as evidence of un-American behavior and began slowly to displace the idea that ale or lager used in moderation was healthful. A strained attempt at a pun in the *Houston County Journal* of Caledonia lamented: "Bottled beer is getting fashionable. It is a failure as a beverage, but is called a good tonic. In fact, it is rather teutonic."[3] For many workers in the industrial and service sectors, and to some degree in agriculture, Sunday was the only day of rest each week. The spread of biergartens across the state brought Germans, who viewed their day off as cause for celebration with song and drink, into conflict with many Protestants, who considered the Sabbath to be a day of sober worship. While antipathy to hard liquor was always present in the temperance movement, the increasing importance of lager beer and its German brewers, many of whom continued to conduct their business in the German language into the twentieth century, made beer a target in the eyes of reformers eager to form society according to their vision.

Early Temperance Sentiment in Minnesota

Quite aside from the factors present in the passage of the Maine law, temperance forces in Minnesota had some initial publicity advantages. The Protestant churches generally advanced a strong temperance line, and the Catholic Church condemned drunkenness even though clergy rarely advocated total prohibition at first. Newspapers of the era had a strong editorial slant (often reflected in titles such as *Democrat* or *Republican*) and generally reflected the established elite, regardless of party. Many more publishers and editors were transplanted New England Republicans than were recently landed German or Irish immigrants. Some did not accept advertisements from breweries or saloons despite the loss of potential revenue. Many adopted a strict temperance platform, featuring temperance articles prominently on their pages. The very first issue of the *Redwood Falls Mail* on 17 September 1869 featured an article on the evils of drink in the middle of the front page. The editor, V. C. Seward, covered the alcohol trade only in the case of a saloon fight or other negative circumstances. Believing that no one would want to be publicly identified as a saloon customer, he noted with glee after all bills were promptly paid to a local saloon owner who threatened to publish the names of all indebted to him in the paper that "no one desir[ed] such publicity."[4]

Some papers, often Democratic in sentiment, took a more balanced position. Many newspapers and civic groups that did not object to alcohol would provide a respectful audience for temperance writers and speakers, even though the favor was seldom granted in the other direction. The editor of the *Henderson Democrat* proclaimed: "We wish to have it distinctly understood that hereafter the Henderson Democrat will be on the side of temperance, but not in the spirit of fanaticism or proscription; it will not abuse those who drink or sell liquor; it will not advocate the Maine law chimera; but will occasionally, undertake to show the benefits resulting from temperance, and also the evil effects of intemperance."[5] The *Democrat* often published a temperance lecture or article on page one, but also carried ads for saloons. Concern for economic growth often acted as a counterbalance to a strict temperance position, which would drive not only thriving businesses out of town, but also those travelers who were unwilling to stay or do business in a dry town.

At the other end of the spectrum were Minnesota's several dozen German-language newspapers. These newspapers typically provided thorough coverage of developments at the local breweries and carried ads for breweries not always found in their English-language counterparts.

Fights between wet and dry forces often spilled over into other civic issues and magnified other conflicts. In 1877, a controversy erupted in Waseca when some members of the school board criticized teacher Lizzie Bierwalter over a grammar issue (in which she was apparently correct). The real issue seems to have been that she was the daughter of local brewer and liquor dealer John Bierwalter, which led some citizens to conclude that Lizzie was not a proper moral example for her students. Two Waseca newspapers, the *Leader* and the *Weekly News*, carried on a running battle throughout their joint existence, much of it related in some way to the alcohol issue.

A True Temperance Beverage

Some citizens were positive advocates of beer; this excerpt from the *Rochester Post* is typical of this sentiment:

> Lager beer seems to have been from the earliest antiquity the beverage that assimulated [*sic*] closest to the hygienic necessities of man, but the time when beer was first manufactured is wrapped in the dim chronology of the past. The great favor with which it has been received by the large majority of people has made its manufacture a business of immense proportions. And those who are so violently against its manufacture are, in our opinion, laboring under a misapprehension of the conditions. The history of mankind goes to show that with all people and in all ages, a stimulant of some kind has been invariably used and recognizing this necessity, it is, of course, desirable that such stimulant be as harmless and healthful as possible, and no objections can be reasonably made to pure lager beer on the ground that it is noxious, and no where in the country can beer be found of more uniform and healthy quality than that produced by the Union Brewery of our city.[6]

Beer was a common element of many celebrations, both public and private. While not often mentioned specifically, beer was made available at weekend outings and for national holidays. As noted in chapter 3, the brewery hall or park was often the site of major celebrations, or temporary saloons or biergartens were set up for the refreshment of the revelers. Local brewer and saloon owner Peter Ort was one of the coordinators for the 1880 July Fourth celebration in Brainerd, and provided for booths where the thirsty could get "harmless thirst quenching juicy beer."[7] Of course, some citizens objected to public consumption at such events. The *Sauk Rapids Sentinel* lamented on 9 August 1887, "It is said that beer was freely sold near the base ball grounds last Saturday at St. Cloud."

The original purpose of most temperance reformers was to focus on saving the individual drinker rather than prohibiting alcohol altogether. As a consequence, temperance organizations needed to be present in as many locations as possible to achieve their goal. Many temperance organi-

Members of the North Central Commercial Club enjoyed a glass in the beer tent at their fair sometime around 1910. COURTESY OF THE MINNESOTA HISTORICAL SOCIETY.

zations formed societies in Minnesota and often became social and political forces in their communities. The Good Templars, the Sons of Temperance, and the Woman's Christian Temperance Union (WCTU) became venues in which like-minded people could meet and work for reform outside of the sectarian limits of church-based organizations. The *Hastings Gazette* published a brief article in 1867 about a "most excellent temperance lecture" by the state lecturer of the Good Templars, a fraternal organization founded in Utica, New York, in the 1850s with a six-point platform of temperance activism. The *Gazette*, which was a supporter of the local breweries, nonetheless praised the Templars for "doing a most excellent work." The Templars were less threatening because they took pains to "assure us that the order relies on moral suasion for its success, and does not contemplate legal action for the suppression of intemperance" (though legal action was included in the Templars' platform).[8] Groups such as the WCTU became an important outlet for the political activity of women. Formed in Cleveland, Ohio, in 1874, chapters of the organization were founded throughout the state. The WCTU was the first women's organization of any kind in Freeborn County and probably elsewhere as well.[9] Eventually it was found in nearly every sizable community in the state. These organizations, focusing on individual behavior, soon found their work frustrated by the popularity of the saloon and began to shift their focus to eliminating the source of the problem rather than simply treating the symptom.

'Tis the Saloon!

For those who wanted to reduce the massive social ills associated with problem drinking, the saloon was the most obvious target. Attacks on the saloon also promised to increase law and order while avoiding total prohibition. There were numerous cases in which a municipality ceased granting licenses for saloons and revoked those that existed (called "no license") but allowed breweries to continue operation. In 1874, the entire county of Jackson went dry and revoked the retail license of brewer Evan Owens (though the county commissioners generously refunded his license fee). The *Jackson Republic* reported that Owens has "moved the stove out of his bar room, closed his bar, and henceforth will sell no more beer except as allowed by the U.S. revenue license." After noting that Owens would continue to sell kegs for customers to take home and share with their "wives and babies," the *Republic* editorialized: "This action is commendable in Mr. Owens, and all good citizens will earnestly hope he will maintain his resolve. If people have a taste for beer no one will object to their taking it home and quietly drinking it, and thus avoid bar room carousals or the still worse street broils."[10] Brewers often would remain in a dry town, sometimes because the location was too favorable to consider moving or because they could not get a good price for their property, but often because they believed that the area would overturn the no license ordinance or other laws shortly. Many cities and counties did, in fact, move back and forth between dry and wet, depending on the relative strength of the two voting blocs (Jackson County switched back and forth at least five times). On the other hand, Jacob Kiewel was not prepared to wait for Fergus Falls to revoke its (ultimately short-lived) dry ordinance, so he abandoned plans to rebuild his burned brewery there and purchased one in Little Falls instead.

For many prohibitionists, county option appeared to be the best way to get the most territory to go dry. The rural parts of many out-state counties could usually be counted on to vote dry in sufficient numbers to outweigh any wet majority in the principal towns. In such cases, wet activists countered with

Temperance advocates continued to enroll new dry counties even while state and national prohibition campaigns advanced. Opponents of county option distributed this card to illustrate the reality of a "bone dry" county. FROM THE COLLECTION OF PAT STAMBAUGH.

Do You Know What It Means if Blue Earth County Votes Dry?

You can't get a case of Beer
You can't buy it in the County
You can't have it shipped in
You can't carry it in yourself
You can't have it in your possession
You can't get it at all

Do You Want Blue Earth County

BONE DRY?

Do YOU want to be

BONE DRY?

Work No! Talk No and Vote NO

(FORM OF BALLOT)

Shall the Sale of Liquor be prohibited?	YES	
	NO	X

Mark Your Cross as Above Indicated; Vote NO

This is not the time to disturb present conditions. Constitutional prohibition will be voted on by the people at the coming November election.

Manufacturers and Dealers Committee

calls for local option, in which citizens voted by city or township rather than as an entire county. This allowed wet cities in the middle of dry counties and generally defeated the purposes of prohibitionists who wanted to make alcohol as hard to obtain as possible.

In the major urban areas, the saloon was in much less danger of being legislated out of business in the nineteenth century. Saloons were typically among the very first businesses established in frontier towns and as such became central locations to talk politics, hold court, hire workers, or even hold church services. Even after other institutions grew, the saloon retained an essential social purpose, especially in ethnic enclaves. The friendly neighborhood saloonkeeper was a source of information on local affairs and had connections with other businesses that might be hiring new arrivals.

The saloon deserved its reputation as a place for men to relax and find fellowship. Unfortunately, the saloon also deserved its reputation as a place where men could squander their hard-earned cash, get dangerously drunk, and find all

Saloons like this one appeared all over the state. Many municipalities banned furniture from saloons to make the environment less inviting. The requisite cuspidors stand ready to receive tobacco juice. At least three pieces of Schell's advertising are visible high on the wall, suggesting a location in southwest Minnesota. COURTESY OF AUGUST SCHELL BREWING COMPANY.

The bar of Schiek's Restaurant in Minneapolis was typical of the opulent bars in many clubs. This photograph is remarkable for the lack of items often present in a typical saloon: spittoons, paintings of nudes, and furniture. COURTESY OF THE MINNESOTA HISTORICAL SOCIETY.

manner of temptation. For every genteel hotel bar with elaborate decor there was at least one disreputable dive. The same saloonkeeper who knew how to find jobs would often insist that an unsuspecting worker's paycheck be cashed at the saloon—with a corresponding obligation to spend some of it there. The discussion of politics could turn to planning graft and herding noncitizens to vote in corrupt elections. Some men found their relaxation in the saloons with gamblers and prostitutes. Because of their decision to become directly involved with saloons, the major brewers surpassed the distillers as the major target of the anti-saloon forces.

Brewery ownership of saloons was nothing new. Nearly every brewery had some sort of bar attached to the brewery and most owned other properties as well. As the shipping breweries became larger and extended their reach ever farther, fierce battles arose between local and out-of-town companies to find reliable markets for their products. Throughout American industry, firms of all types were becoming vertically integrated—owning their own suppliers and outlets—and the brewers found owning saloons the answer to the question of how to dispose of their ever-growing capacity. Ownership of saloons also diminished the one form of leverage saloonkeepers had: the threat to change suppliers unless the brewer lowered the cost of beer. In municipalities where local laws prohibited breweries from owning saloons outright, such as Minneapolis, brewers often held the mortgages for the saloons or set up other types of shadow ownership. The saloon owner served at the pleasure of the brewing company and could be replaced if revenue did not meet expectations. However, the support provided by the brewery was essential for most small proprietors trying to get a start in business. The breweries provided the fixtures for the saloon, often including ornate artwork depicting the brewery as a modern industrial marvel, colorful signs, and even monogrammed chairs—all of which the saloon operator was required to make weekly payments for. The brewery provided a ready stock of beer and often the ice to keep it cold. Most important, the brewery advanced money for the license fee, which often ran as high as $1,000. As a consequence, a brewer's interest in a saloon owner was almost completely profit oriented. Whether a saloon owner respected law and order was usually less important than whether payments were made on time and in full. In a court case that otherwise went in favor of the brewers, a judge editorialized: "No doubt the pernicious practice of the defendant brewing company establishing impecunious and irresponsible persons in a business which at its best is a menace to society and difficult to control should be stopped. The evils resulting from keen competition of the brewing companies to plant saloons on every corner and every available spot within the patrol limits, are apparent. . . ."[11]

Despite the passage of more and more regulations, the brewers' hold over the saloons increased. According to an exposé in the *Minneapolis Journal*, by 1908 only 38 of 432 saloons in Minneapolis were actually run by their named individual owners. All others were controlled by breweries, including 131 run by Minneapolis

This saloon, believed to have been near Orinoco, advertised Schuster's Beer above the awning, on two corner signs, and on two rectangular signs below the windows. The postcard probably dates from around 1900. FROM THE COLLECTION OF PAT STAMBAUGH.

The F. A. Johnson Saloon, 35 Washington Avenue South, and the George McMahon Saloon, 37 Washington Avenue South, Minneapolis, were typical "tied house" saloons, which served the beer of only one brewery. It was common for rival breweries to have saloons next door to each other. COURTESY OF THE MINNESOTA HISTORICAL SOCIETY.

Brewing Company, 86 by Gluek Brewing Company, and 38 by Purity Brewing Co. (Blatz was the leading "foreign" owner, with 41 saloons.) The concentration of brewery-owned saloons in the Twin Cities was higher than in almost any other major American city. Despite an ordinance that allowed only individuals to be licensed to own saloons, the license register at city hall included a column for "holder of the license," in which the sponsoring brewing company was listed. Threatened with the loss of their charters as corporations, the local firms blamed competition from outsiders and made a few nominal reforms, but business continued much as usual.[12] One practice that continued to plague reformers was the creation of "pay check" saloons. Many saloons located near industries that paid by check on Saturday afternoons cashed the workers' paychecks using money advanced by the breweries. While this may have seemed convenient to the workers, there was an expectation that some of the money would be spent in the saloon—a convenience that many families preferred to avoid.[13]

As the competition grew more intense in the early 1900s, brewers bought more and more land to build more saloons to assure their market share. The first ward in northeast Minneapolis—home to Minneapolis Brewing Company, Gluek, and

Hennepin Brewing Co.—had forty saloons, but even more worrying to some civic leaders was the fact that brewing companies owned a total of 132 lots in the ward, including many prime corner locations and a number of vacant lots. The brewing companies were blamed for the reluctance of other businesses to move in because of the lack of prime corner lots, the lack of money to keep the neighborhood in good repair, and the general depreciation of property values in the ward.[14] However, many observers wondered if any effective action would ever be taken by the city, as the license fees paid by the brewers amounted to almost $400,000 annually for the city coffers. The loss of this revenue and the property taxes paid by the breweries would cause severe budgetary strain for the city.

The Movement Changes Method

During the nineteenth century, those who sought a major change in national politics, whether it was abolishing slavery, reforming currency, or opposing immigration, usually formed a new political party. The Prohibition Party was founded in 1869 and first ran a candidate for president in 1872. James Black received only about 5,000 votes, and subsequent candidates fared little better; the high water mark was in 1892 when they received just over 270,000 votes (2.3 percent of the total votes). The bulk of their strength came from conservative midwestern farmers, so it was not surprising that the party's first candidate elected to national office was Congressman Kittel Halvorson from northern Minnesota's 5th district. (He was also the candidate of the Farmers' Alliance, and this connection probably yielded more votes. He polled noticeably worse in Stearns and St. Louis counties where the breweries were concentrated.) Despite some local influence, the Prohibition Party was unable to defeat the existing parties, so new organizations such as the Anti-Saloon League began to support sympathetic candidates from the existing parties.

The Anti-Saloon League, under the direction of its general counsel, Wayne B. Wheeler, is considered by many scholars to have originated the high-pressure, big-money, single-issue lobbying tactics that have become standard operating procedure in modern politics. Founded in Ohio in 1893, the league avoided the pitfalls of seeking party status and thus gained the support of many churches that wished to support the cause but did not want to associate themselves with a specific political party. By 1908 only four states were without a state league organization, and the league was able to pressure politicians at all levels of government from every part of the country. Wheeler estimated in 1926 that the league had spent at least $35 million on efforts to influence public opinion.[15]

The increasing power of reformers pursuing pure food and drug laws also put pressure on the brewing industry. Brewers had been accused of adulterating beer for many years, though most of the claims were wild rumors, misunderstandings of the brewing process, or chemically impossible. In general, brewers worked with the agriculture department on legislation to maintain a good reputa-

The Anti-Saloon League built enthusiasm among its members and coordinated action through its national conventions. The delegate badge for the 1915 convention in Atlantic City proclaimed the organization's goals of "a stainless flag" and "a saloonless country." COURTESY OF THE MINNESOTA HISTORICAL SOCIETY.

Peoples Brewing Co. started production in 1907, just as the new labeling requirements went into effect. All labels had to bear the guarantee under the 1906 Food and Drugs Act, and all had to include an accurate measurement of the contents. Many breweries used their old labels with the new required texts squeezed into whatever open space was left in the design. FROM THE COLLECTION OF KEN MALZ.

tion with both regulators and the public. While the first actions toward pure food regulation took place before the turn of the century, the process was accelerated by the publication in 1906 of Upton Sinclair's novel *The Jungle*. Intended to advocate socialism, Sinclair's book became best known for its descriptions of conditions in the meatpacking industry. As part of the response to the public outcry, brewers were subject to new labeling rules, which required a statement of compliance with the 1906 Food and Drugs Act and an accurate volume measurement.[16]

Brewers countered the claims of adulteration by making strong (and in some cases ludicrous) claims for the health-giving properties of beer. As early as 1877, a Waseca grocer advertised "Bottled Milwaukee Beer, for the use of invalids."[17] To support their claim of purity, brewers in several states offered a reward of $1,000 to anyone who could document impurity in their beer. In 1907 the new owners of Conrad Birkhofer Brewing Co. changed the name to Purity Brewing Co. to emphasize this facet of quality. Brewers claimed that their product aided digestion, renewed strength, and at any rate was much better for health than coffee. One advertisement, presented in the guise of a news item about young women working in the U.S. Census Office, proclaimed:

It seems heartless to work girls until they must have a special room for those who break down; furthermore, it appears to be unnecessary. If they were nourished and strengthened with "Golden Grain Belt" beer, they would not break down. Those who drink it find they can stand a great deal more, for it is a powerful nerve tonic made from the purest barley malt and hops.[18]

Brewers and retailers alike made similar claims throughout the period. Anheuser-Busch contributed their national reputation to the campaign with a set of ads called the National Hero Series, which depicted great figures from Viking Leif Erickson to Hungarian revolutionary Lajos Kossuth and tied the use of malt beverages to achievement and the struggle for liberty.

While they were building toward national prohibition, reformers worked around the edges to try to increase the amount of dry territory in America by other methods. For many years, state and federal laws had prohibited the sale of alcohol to American Indians and had banned alcohol on reservation lands. Despite the fact that most treaty lands had since been sold to white settlers, in 1910 prohibition forces began to use the terms of several treaties to make large portions of northern and western Minnesota dry. Breweries were not prohibited from operating, but could not sell beer inside the affected territory. Brewers protested the ruling and gained some relief for a time. Bemidji Brewing Co. obtained a restraining order against federal agents in December 1914 in an attempt to sell the beer it had on hand at the time (it was able to sell two carloads). However, the restraining

The child in this postcard does not seem as sure of the benefits of Schell's Vacuum Tonic as his mother. The card bears the wishes of Otto Schell and family for a happy New Year in 1908. FROM THE COLLECTION OF PAT STAMBAUGH.

The depiction of the happy Victorian family on the Kiewel Cream of Malt Tonic label suggested the general contentment possible with regular use of a tonic. The fact that this product was produced by Kiewel's Crookston brewery shows that tonic production was not limited to large urban breweries. FROM THE COLLECTION OF KEN MALZ.

The label for Cold Spring Brewing Company's Red Star Tonic contained the usual claims that it improved digestion and sleep and was ideal for expectant mothers. The endorsement of its use by athletes was not common in Victorian times, but this was the 1930s, when even cigarettes were recommended for athletes in training. Cold Spring's tonic is one of the rare post-Prohibition examples of malt tonic. U-permit numbers were required on labels from 1933 to 1936. FROM THE COLLECTION OF KEN MALZ.

Malt Tonic

Malt tonics did not arise in response to Prohibition, but rather were an attempt by brewers to offer their own products in the crowded patent medicine market. The earliest versions appeared during the 1890s in distinctive, squat bottles with narrow necks and advanced an amazing array of health claims. While medical opinion on most treatments varies, there seems to be some evidence that malt products aid digestion. However, the health claims made on these and other brands were extraordinary. Malt tonics were a profitable way for breweries to use excess capacity—even more so since tonics did not have to be fermented or aged and so did not take up valuable storage space. Malt tonics did not do much to help breweries survive Prohibition. Their popularity declined along with many other patent medicines during the first decades of the twentieth century. 🍺

order was good for only one month, and in March 1915 Bemidji Brewing dumped 720 barrels of beer worth $4,500 through their drains into nearby Lake Irving, discoloring most of the ice on the lake. More than just the beer drinkers were upset: the *Bemidji Weekly Pioneer* reported soon after the closing that the city had lost $25,000 in license fees and personal property taxes and called the situation a "crisis."[19] Some breweries remained open, including the three in Duluth and two on the Iron Range that were covered under a different treaty, but other northern breweries were unable to find new outlets in the already fiercely competitive markets and joined Bemidji Brewing in closing.

The outbreak of war in Europe led to rising concern for military preparedness, so in 1914 Secretary of the Navy Josephus Daniels banned alcohol from all ships and naval installations. However, attempts to use the armed forces as a means to prohibition started even before hostilities began. During 1913 a bill was introduced in the Minnesota Legislature to limit the sale of intoxicating liquors within one mile of any U.S. military reservation in the state. However, as the United States Brewers Association (USBA) noted: "On its face the bill appears harmless, but there is a big woodchuck concealed within it. The term 'Military Reservation' covers a great many things. For instance, the Army Building located in St. Paul, on the corner of Second and Robert streets, is a military reservation, and so classified by the Federal Government. The bill in question would, therefore, wipe out more than half of the saloons in the city of St. Paul."[20] The bill did not pass, but the USBA worried that attempts might be made in other states more inclined to prohibition.

In general, the brewers' response to the rising tide of prohibition was too little and too late. The brewers were generally unable to match the organization and fervor of their opponents, and their ability to bribe or influence politicians was not an effective tool against county option votes. In 1910 the brewery interests organized the Loyal Liberty Protective League, which was incorporated to "protect the business interests of the state of Minnesota" by supporting politicians who would look after "the prosperity of the entire state." They may have had some effect, because a major debate in the gubernatorial election of 1914 between Republican William E. Lee and Democrat Winfield S. Hammond concerned the extent to which liquor interest money had dominated the state in the previous few years.[21] Brewers organized the Traveling Men's Liberty League to sign up supporters for their cause among merchants in each county and gave each member a booklet of statistics and arguments to use in debates with prohibitionists. While most of the large, urban brewers were members, nearly half the brewers in Minnesota did not sign up, and support from other merchants was not substantial.[22] County option votes continued in Minnesota, despite the efforts of the brewers.

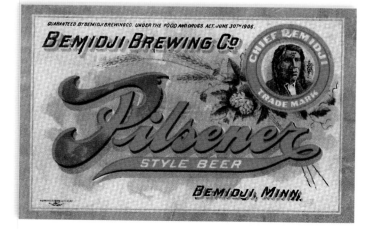

Bemidji Brewing Co. may have suffered the most from the "Indian Lid" (a term coined by the press at that time to describe prohibition achieved by enforcing treaties) since it was so far from other legal markets. It is perhaps ironic that a brewery closed in compliance with terms of a treaty with the Ojibwa used Chief Bemidji as a trademark. BOB KAY COLLECTION.

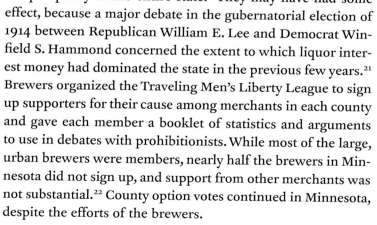

The Alien Industry

During the late 1800s, the Germans were widely considered to be one of the most successful immigrant groups in America. German music styles dominated classical music and were common in much popular and dance music, and German choral groups flourished across the nation. The German education model was being adopted everywhere from kindergartens to leading universities. The Turner gymnastic clubs became popular centers for recreation. Immigrants such as Carl Schurz became nationally known political figures. German advances in science and engineering helped develop fields from transportation to communications. Minnesota's new state capitol building, opened in 1905, featured a rathskeller-style restaurant and beer hall with German drinking mottoes painted on the ceiling. (The capitol rathskeller was restored to its original appearance in 1999, but beer did not return.) But the rising military threat of Kaiser Wilhelm II's empire eventually overshadowed these accomplishments and provided the impetus for the final moves toward national prohibition.

While there was some initial support among immigrants for Germany and the other central powers, the use of unrestricted submarine warfare turned most American citizens against the Kaiser and put German Americans on the defensive. After the revelation of the Zimmermann Telegram (containing a proposal for a German-Mexican alliance) and the declaration of war on Germany, the campaign against perceived German sympathizers was institutionalized. The Minnesota Commission of Public Safety took the lead in monitoring the activities of possible spies, slackers, and others who might inhibit the war effort. Common activities, such as choral societies, were viewed as conspiracies to prevent German American youth from becoming Americanized.[23] All Germans were assumed to be friends of the Kaiser unless they proved otherwise in a very public manner, despite the fact that many German families came to America to escape the monarchy. Some brewing families made notable contributions to the war effort. Among her several activities, Mrs. Fred Schuster of Rochester coordinated local efforts to collect binoculars and telescopes for the Eyes for the Navy program and was commended by Assistant Secretary of the Navy Franklin D. Roosevelt.[24] However, the fear of German spies and saboteurs added to the general suspicion of immigrants and caused many voters and politicians who were formerly unsympathetic to prohibition to support it to prove their "one-hundred percent Americanism."

Some legitimate wartime concerns led directly to the beginning of national prohibition. Grain was considered an essential war material, and its use for brewing purposes was severely limited by the Lever Food and Fuel Control Act of August 1917. Shortly thereafter, by executive order, President Woodrow Wilson limited the strength of malt beverages to 2.75 percent to conserve grain. Practically speaking, most brewing came to a halt before Prohibition became official because material shortages, high input prices, the shortage of labor, and patriotic fervor forced many breweries to close well before their product was banned outright.

Little is known about the Traveling Men's Liberty League, but its purpose was to enlist people engaged in allied businesses (e.g., tavern owners, cigar makers, distillers) to oppose prohibitory legislation. This booklet and card belonged to A. J. Noerenberg of Minneapolis Brewing Company, but do not appear to have been carried regularly. FROM THE AUTHOR'S COLLECTION.

The decoration of the Minnesota State Capitol rathskeller featured a mix of American eagles and German hops. German mottoes about the joys of beer and wine adorned the walls until they were painted over during Prohibition. PHOTOGRAPH BY CHARLES W. JEROME; COURTESY OF THE MINNESOTA HISTORICAL SOCIETY.

Volstead and the Vote

In December 1917 Congress passed the Eighteenth Amendment to the U.S. Constitution and sent it to the states for ratification. The actual wording of the Constitutional provision was short and simple, with most of the detail left to "appropriate" legislation: "After one year from the ratification of this article the manufacture, sale, or transportation of intoxicating liquors within, the importation thereof into, or the exportation thereof from the United States and all territory subject to the jurisdiction thereof for beverage purposes is hereby prohibited. The Congress and the several States shall have concurrent power to enforce this article by appropriate legislation."

Among the details to be worked out were enforcement and the definition of intoxicating liquors. The National Prohibition Act, written by Anti-Saloon League general counsel Wayne B. Wheeler, was sponsored in Congress by Representative Andrew Volstead of western Minnesota's 7th district. Volstead was first elected in 1902 and had risen to become the chairman of the powerful House Judiciary Committee. Volstead was not a renowned orator and was not among the most visible prohibitionists. He had a genuine belief in the ability of legislation to change behavior and probably would be remembered as an effective legislator had it not been for the ultimate inability to enforce his namesake legislation. The Volstead Act defined intoxicating liquor as having more than 0.5 percent alcohol, thus eliminating even the lightest of beers as possible alternatives. The Minnesota Legislature voted to ratify the Eighteenth Amendment on 22 January 1919, but the vote was meaningless because the required 75 percent of states had been reached a week earlier.

Preparing for a Dry Nation

During 1919 and early 1920, brewers and citizens alike began to prepare for a life without legal beer. Some individuals resorted to any means necessary to stock up

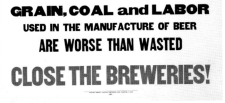

The WCTU distributed this poster during World War I to emphasize the danger of diverting vital resources to brewing beer. PHOTOGRAPH BY THE NATIONAL WOMAN'S CHRISTIAN TEMPERANCE UNION; COURTESY OF THE MINNESOTA HISTORICAL SOCIETY.

The employees of Remmler's Brewery in Red Wing made two appeals in this photograph: to purchase Remmler's Bock Beer and to vote Wet in the upcoming election. COURTESY OF THE GOODHUE COUNTY HISTORICAL SOCIETY.

While nowhere near as heart-rending as the appeals for prohibition, wet forces nonetheless attempted to sway votes through the use of promotional devices such as this match safe from the late 1910s. A large percentage of brewery workers were likely to lose their jobs if prohibition was enacted. FROM THE COLLECTION OF DAVE WENDL.

in advance of a long dry spell. The *Glencoe Enterprise* reported on 13 March 1919 that Glencoe Brewing Co. had been broken into and four cases of beer stolen. Others simply bought all they could afford and hid it away.

Despite the inevitable approach of Prohibition, many brewers with enough resources continued to brew, hoping that some form of beer might remain legal. The *Winona Weekly Leader* reported on 19 December 1919:

> Brewers in Minnesota and Wisconsin are anxiously awaiting the decision of the Supreme Court as to the status of beer under the wartime prohibition law. The decision is expected next Monday. If the court decides against the beer of 2.7 per cent alcoholic content, thousands of gallons may be run into the sewers, ultimately to swell the volume of the "father of waters." The Park Brewing Co. of Winona has about 2000 barrels of beer on hand. John Dietz, president of the brewing company, is reported to have said that the entire stock would be run into the sewer if the court decides that the manufacture of beer with 2.75 per cent alcohol is illegal. The manufactured stock cannot be converted into "near beer" without big loss. Not only the brewers, but millions of consumers are on the anxious seat, impatiently awaiting the final decree of the court. Five months of drouth [*sic*] have not reconciled them to the loss of their favorite beverage.

Ultimately, all beer was ruled intoxicating, and Park dumped more than 2,200 barrels of 4 percent beer, worth about $15,000. John Dietz's terse comment when asked about the future was, "The company is done."[25]

Other breweries, both large and small, began to look for alternative products to try to keep the companies alive and maintain the value of their investments. Minneapolis Brewing Company took the most common path by forming a company called the Golden Grain Juice Company and made near beer, marketing

In 1919, the C. M. Angle Saloon, 259 Sixth Avenue South, Minneapolis, was for rent on the eve of Prohibition. COURTESY OF THE MINNESOTA HISTORICAL SOCIETY.

non-intoxicating Minnehaha Pale Ale as "the entirely New and different drink."[26] Several brewers tried to market some sort of near beer, but the slow sales seemed to indicate that consumers placed little importance on the claims for digestive properties and found it a poor substitute for the intoxicating qualities and taste of real beer. At best, near beers served to keep experienced brewers employed and to keep equipment in operating condition. Some near beer was used as the base for "needle beer," which was injected with strong alcohol, but by and large, patrons seemed to prefer stronger spirits for their intoxication needs, both because of the higher alcohol content and because bootleg spirits tasted better when mixers were added. Even worse for the brewers, many Americans switched to soft drinks to satisfy refreshment needs that would previously have been met by a cold beer. The shift in American consumption patterns would make it difficult for brewers to regain significant portions of their old market once Prohibition ended.

The difficulties of remaining in business as a brewer of near beer were demonstrated by Schuster Brewing Co. of Rochester. Among the most successful and best managed of Minnesota's midsize breweries, it had produced a successful Malt Tonic since

Brewers who remained open after the start of Prohibition tried a variety of recipes to create a nonalcoholic substitute for beer. According to Schell's president Ted Marti, Schell's changed the name of its cereal beverage so many times because it was not well received. Of special interest is the temporary label for Forest Brew at upper right. COURTESY OF AUGUST SCHELL BREWING COMPANY.

Jacob Schmidt Brewing Company seems to have advertised its temperance beverages more aggressively than any other Minnesota brewery. Several striking examples of art deco advertising for City Club Special are in collections, and Schmidt used many of the same advertising formats for Malta as they did for beer. Vitrolite glass corner signs for any brewery are rare, and signs for malt beverages are seldom found. FROM THE COLLECTION OF PAT STAMBAUGH.

the 1890s and began manufacturing near beer during Prohibition. With its stable financial position and a well-established nonalcoholic product, Schuster Brewing appeared to be a strong candidate to survive the dry era. However, the effects of Prohibition caused the Schusters such frustration that they decided to close the brewery effective 1 January 1922. They had attempted to make near beer for two years but were unsuccessful in finding a market for the product. Fred Schuster blamed the "women of the country" and claimed that cereal beverage companies "making soft drinks containing a low alcoholic content, cannot compete with the 'kitchen' breweries manufacturing real beer containing from 4 to 10 per cent alcohol."[27] The Schuster family was able to make a successful transition into the real estate business (much like their larger St. Paul competitors Hamm and Schmidt), and the brewery was leased to a dairy cooperative.

Many brewers in small and midsize cities were able to survive by moving into businesses that didn't involve brewing. Red Wing Brewing Co. became Red Wing Food Products Co., Kiewel Brewing Co. became Kiewel Associated Products Co., and some, like Fitger Brewing Company, simply dropped *brewing* from their names. Duluth Brewing & Malting Company went furthest and became the Sobriety Company. Soft drinks were the easiest products for former breweries to produce since the equipment could be easily modified. The sanitary food preparation facilities and extensive refrigeration units also made production of other products possible. Furthermore, brewing companies were able to use familiar chains of distribution to stores and restaurants. The adaptations made by the Kiewel family in Little Falls exemplify the attempts made by midsize breweries to survive. The Kiewel brewery was modified in early 1920 to make ice cream, butter, condensed milk, and candy. Some of the old aging rooms were given extra insulation so they would maintain a subfreezing temperature more efficiently. The old malt house was modified to receive milk and cream instead of barley. The company offered a wide range of dairy products including vanilla, chocolate, and Palmer House ice cream and acted as the local agents for national brands such as Coca-Cola, Oh Henry candy bars, and Green Circle gum. The Kiewels maintained the capacity to brew and were ready to resume production "if the occasion presents itself." They also continued production of near beer, but since it did not need to age as long as lager, they were able to do so using much less space and did not need to sacrifice their other operations.[28]

Some brewers were unwilling to wait until public opinion shifted and beer became legal again. George Kiewel moved to St. Boniface, Manitoba, and built a new brewery there at a cost of $200,000. Gustav Kuenzel of Hastings Brewing Co. turned down a chance to make soft drinks and moved with his equipment to Kenora, Ontario.[29] Henry Schmid, who would return after Prohibition to become brewmaster at Duluth Brewing & Malting, took a job at Cervecería Cuauhtémoc in Monterrey, Mexico. Most, however, had a major financial stake in their breweries and stayed in town to realize as much as they could from their investments.

Some breweries managed to stay alive only by selling part of their assets during Prohibition. Minneapolis Brewing Company sold its Zumalweiss label to Theo. Hamm during the dry period, but even so they still were forced to stop all production at the beginning of 1929. Duluth Brewing & Malting Company (now the Sobriety Company), sold its popular Moose and Rex labels to crosstown rival Fitger. The sale seemed prudent during the mid-1920s, but the return of legal beer left Duluth Brewing & Malting Company without its flagship brands. The economic crisis that would soon become the Great Depression forced many brewers to cut their losses and made it much harder for them to come back after repeal.

The degree to which breweries continued to brew full-strength beer during Prohibition is unclear. A few brewers switched to making or selling liquor, but except for the occasional recorded arrest, most of the accounts are dimly remem-

A very rare example of one of Fitger's candy products from the 1920s: Chocolate Hash. It appears to have been shredded chocolate sold in bulk. The pencil-shaped object is hollow and may have been designed to hold the candy. FROM THE COLLECTION OF PETE CLURE.

The Fitger Company offered numerous bottled products during Prohibition. Silver Spray was a sparkling grape drink, and Pickwick was its near beer. The Isle Royal Ginger Ale extended the Lake Superior imagery farther out into the lake. FROM THE COLLECTION OF PETE CLURE.

bered or intentionally concealed family stories that are hard to document. Rumors concerning Schmidt Brewing Company brewing strong beer and shipping it out through a network of tunnels have been popular in St. Paul for many years, but no firm proof has been offered. An accident at the brewery in Mantorville caused 300 gallons of beer to spill from a tank in 1924. While the beer was said to have been six years old, it is inconceivable that Prohibition agents would have missed such a quantity when inspecting the breweries in 1920, so it is more likely that the beer was brewed more recently. In another Mantorville incident, William Schumann, the owner of the brewery, was arrested in 1927 for driving while drunk and for having bottles of home brew and grain alcohol in his car.[30]

In October 1923, federal agents raided the Pitzl brewery at New Munich and seized a large quantity of beer. The agents soon got word that a gang of men was stealing the beer, which had been left at the brewery until it could be transported to Minneapolis. A second raid of the brewery caught the thieves in the act, but a fight ensued in which Special Agent Albert E. Whitney suffered a fractured skull. Four men were arrested shortly after the raid, and three brewery employees, including Mathias Pitzl and his son Norberg, were later charged with violating the National Prohibition Act.[31]

Government agents and townspeople sometimes suspected that brewers were continuing to produce full-strength beer whether they were actually doing so or not. Some Hastings residents harassed Gustav Kuenzel's daughter Elizabeth by accusing her of peddling beer when in fact she was delivering milk to customers. When agents raided the home (and former brewery) of Joseph Hajicek, they put pressure on the family's children to give information about their father's liquor dealing. Winona may have been a special target because Prohibition Commissioner James M. Doran grew up there.[32] The raids and arrests, which appeared in nearly every day's newspapers, created a high level of tension in many communities. This tension was only made worse by the hypocrisy demonstrated by the drinking habits of many civic leaders and even some dry advocates.

By the late 1920s, it was clear to most Americans that Prohibition was failing. Civic groups organized to advocate repeal of the Eighteenth Amendment, and some states and municipalities allowed enforcement to lapse. Those brewers who had long believed that the country could not stay dry began to modernize their plants—sometimes well before repeal. The Peter Bub Brewing Co. in Winona hired Carlus Walter to be the new brewmaster in 1928. When the election of Democrat Franklin Roosevelt as president appeared certain, the state's brewers began to prepare in earnest for the new era.

As repeal sentiment began to rise, supporters of Prohibition reemphasized their position, claiming that "the eagle never flies backward." COURTESY OF THE MINNESOTA HISTORICAL SOCIETY.

Under strict guidelines, physicians were allowed to prescribe alcohol for patients. This prescription was written by Dr. Lewis K. Onsgard of Houston, Minnesota. COURTESY OF THE MINNESOTA HISTORICAL SOCIETY.

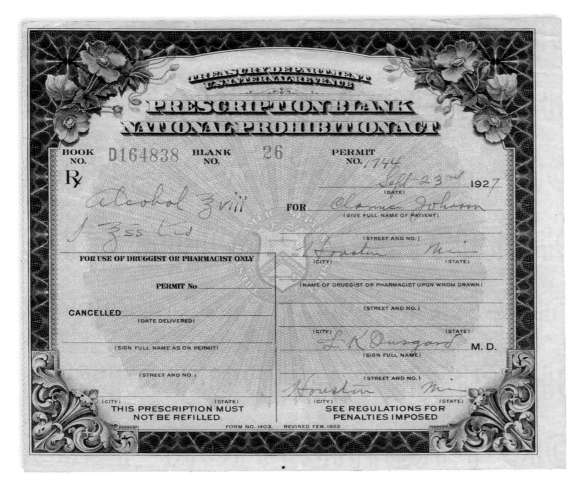

Art deco features were common in the first advertising pieces after beer was re-legalized. This is an artist's proof from a Schmidt campaign in the mid-1930s. FROM THE COLLECTION OF DAVE DAVIS.

New Jobs, New Containers, New Rules: Minnesota Beer Returns

"I'll take care of the beer bill," W. M. F. Miller, owner of the Peter Bub brewery at Sugar Loaf, today quoted Gov. Floyd B. Olson as saying yesterday when the local brewer called on him. Mr. Miller returned last night from a several days' stay in St. Paul attending sessions of the state senate. Edward Fleckenstein of the Fleckenstein brewery at Faribault and a number of brewers from New Ulm also were present, Mr. Miller said. The Winona brewer is a personal friend of Gov. Olson.
—*Winona Republican-Herald*, 22 March 1933

F OR NEW PRESIDENT FRANKLIN D. ROOSEVELT, THE RETURN OF BEER WAS not so much a return to a cultural tradition as a way to increase tax revenue and to eliminate the drain on the public purse from the cost of the ineffectual enforcement of Prohibition. While total repeal of the Eighteenth Amendment was in the uncertain future, the first steps to return legal beer were taken quickly. The Cullen Bill, passed almost immediately after Roosevelt's inauguration, modified the Volstead Act to define beer of 3.2 percent alcohol by weight as nonintoxicating and allowed its sale in any state that did not have conflicting prohibition laws. The 3.2 percent alcohol level was selected rather than the prewar 2.75 percent level because a higher level of alcohol was considered chemically necessary to make a better-tasting beer.[1] Minnesota brewers visited the state Capitol in force, but need not have worried: Minnesota was one of twenty states (plus the District of Columbia) that allowed the sale of 3.2 percent beer on the first possible date, 7 April 1933.[2]

Preparing for Production

For the few breweries that continued to make near beer throughout Prohibition, producing beer was as simple as eliminating the dealcoholizing step from the process of making near beer. These breweries, as well as several others that planned ahead for repeal, already had brewmasters employed and equipment in place. Hamm, Gluek, Bub, and Fitger were among the Minnesota breweries that had beer on sale the first day of legal sales.

One minute after midnight on Friday, April 7, gates opened and crowds swarmed the breweries, eager to get some of the first legal brew in thirteen years. Alvin Gluek, superintendent of the family brewery, dramatically announced that "police protection will be necessary if the lame and the halt are not to be trampled underfoot, and fenders and running boards of family cars are not to be squeezed and bumped."[3] Gluek Brewing Company planned to start delivery runs at midnight, but others abandoned such plans:

> The Peter Bub brewery in Sugar Loaf is swamped with orders for tonight, and will not undertake to make deliveries, but clubs, hotels and restaurants will be on hand to rush beer to customers at the earliest possible moment after midnight. Trucks and cars, it is expected at the brewery, will be at the loading platforms waiting for midnight. The beer cannot be sent off the brewery premises before 12:01 am, but will be loaded before that time. About 800 cases and 150 kegs of beer will leave the brewery soon after midnight. The price to dealers will be $2 a case and $15 a barrel, and $2.50 a case and $18 a barrel for home delivery.[4]

The options for individuals to pick up beer at the brewery and to receive direct home delivery later would be eliminated by the adoption of new legislation prohibiting direct sales by breweries and establishing the three-tier system (producer, distributor, retailer) in the alcohol industry.

While some parts of the country were forced to import beer from outside (several Minnesota breweries rushed to meet this need), Minnesota drinkers even had choices during the first heady days following legalization. The *Winona Republican-Herald* reported, "New brands from breweries not in the immediate vicinity were arriving today and many still thirsty beer drinkers were making the rounds sampling all kinds in search of that which best suited their taste."[5]

Other breweries were forced to delay reopening. While various reasons were given, lack of money for necessary repairs and modernizations was usually the root cause—not surprising considering the nation's economy had been mired in the Great Depression for several years. An ad for the local brewery in the *Mantorville Express* on 30 March 1933 lamented: "Since the election last fall we have been making repairs, improvements and generally prepairing [*sic*] our brewery for the anticipated return of brewed beer. The return, however, was quicker than we expected, we were caught short and are unable to supply the demand for the new malt drink." Most of these breweries attempted to make a virtue out of their delay.

Trucks and trains could be loaded before midnight but could not leave until 12:01 am. These trucks are waiting to leave the Gluek brewery grounds on Friday night, 6 April 1933. COURTESY OF THE MINNESOTA HISTORICAL SOCIETY.

The same Otto's Brewery ad proudly claimed, "We will not distribute an inferior brew in order to meet the large demand." Minneapolis Brewing Company advertised that it was "the first Brewery to prepare for manufacture in surroundings of snow white purity," and that "*We have not hurried*: Time has been taken so that our beer will attain a quality of mellow taste satisfaction which every experienced user instantly recognizes."[6] In fact, those breweries ready on April 7 had also aged their beer an appropriate length of time; there were no complaints about Minnesota breweries shipping "green" beer.

In a few cases, the breweries continued their Prohibition-era products, but this seldom lasted for long. In August 1933, Kiewel Brewing Co. announced it would continue to operate its creamery and Kiewel Associated Products Co. simultaneously with the brewery. However, the beer business was so profitable that by May of the next year they got out of the dairy product business to focus on brewing.[7]

In the years immediately after repeal, brewers made claims not only about health properties but also about strength. While 3.2 percent beer was legalized in Minnesota in April 1933, the Eighteenth Amendment was not repealed until the end of the year. By 1934 brewers offered higher alcohol beer such as Cold Spring Pep, which approached 6 percent alcohol by volume. The federal government quickly outlawed such claims. Ironically, the promotion of Hamm's brand as Hi-% is tempered by the fact that the beer was still no more than 4 percent alcohol by weight, and therefore the same strength as a typical American mass-market lager. FROM THE COLLECTION OF KEN MALZ.

This Otto's Lager label includes several significant elements: a waiter in formal attire (to show its distance from disreputable saloon consumption); a striking sketch of the Italianate-style brewery (to indicate tradition); and the claim that "It's Vitamized" (to take advantage of the trend to make health claims for beer in the years just after repeal). FROM THE COLLECTION OF DAVE WENDL.

Large breweries were complicated business enterprises, but could yield enormous profits. Minneapolis Brewing Company ordered new stock certificates during the process of reopening in 1933. Certificates for fewer than one hundred shares were orange, and certificates for fractional shares were brown. COURTESY OF THE MINNESOTA HISTORICAL SOCIETY.

Overenthusiasm and Failure

To the casual observer, the return of beer was an unqualified economic success. Brewing provided desperate farmers with a steady market for barley and other grains at good prices. Thousands of people returned to work: nationally almost 40,000 wage earners were directly on brewery payrolls, and thousands of others found work rebuilding breweries, producing equipment for the industry, or working in newly reopened taverns. The rebuilding of breweries was especially beneficial to the construction trades because other factory expansion and private sector construction slowed during the Depression. The $5 per barrel tax added more than half a billion desperately needed dollars to the federal treasury by the end of 1935, and millions more were collected by Minnesota and local governments.[8] The profits of some brewers attracted entirely unwanted attention: the infamous Barker-Karpis gang kidnapped William Hamm Jr. and Edward Bremer (banker and son of Jacob Schmidt Brewing Company's Adolf Bremer) in two of the most notorious crimes of the era. Minneapolis Brewing Company's directors avoided kidnappings, but on 6 June 1941 the office was the target of a dramatic armed robbery by gangsters with Chicago ties.[9]

The excitement generated by early sales and by the supposedly endless demand for beer attracted investors to Minnesota's small, historic brewing cities. Often from the Twin Cities, they did not always have brewery experience. In some cases, they became partners in existing brewing companies when the pre-Prohibition owner was having difficulty raising capital for necessary restorations or to market the beer successfully. In Montgomery, longtime partner Joseph Handsuch sold his interest in the local brewery to out-of-town investors in July 1933. Minneapolis investors purchased the Mantorville brewery in 1938, believing they could help the struggling plant make a profit. In most of these instances, the rapid failure of the brewing company happened not simply because outsiders did not understand the old family business but because the breweries either needed so much repair or were so deeply in debt that recouping the investment was impossible.

An unusual approach was adopted in the attempt to resurrect the Pitzl brewery in New Munich. At first a corporation was formed, including Mathias Pitzl's widow, Anna. However, a few months later, during the middle of remodeling, the directors reorganized and proposed the first cooperative brewery in the state. Its purpose, according to the articles of incorporation, was the following:

> To handle malt, and process grain with or for its members and others, individually and collectively, for mutual benefit and in a co-operative manner. The general nature of this business shall be to conduct on the co-operative plan among its members, stockholders and patrons the manufacture of beer, malt, and malt products, alcoholic or non-alcoholic beverages from agricultural products produced by its members, stockholders and patrons; and to sell and deal in such products upon the co-operative plan.

This plan was also unsuccessful, and the New Munich brewery never went into operation after Prohibition.[10]

In a few old brewing cities, enthusiasm ran so high that all-new breweries were constructed to meet the expected demand. The most noteworthy of these was Schatz-Brau of Melrose. Taking its name from an old German term for *sweetheart* used by John Heinrich, former Minneapolis brewer and grandfather of the president of the new company, the project was held up as an example of successful economic recovery. The *Melrose Beacon* exulted: "It is the day of the laying of the corner stone of the Schatz-Brau Brewery Co., the biggest building project in the state outside the big cities since President Roosevelt took command and said: 'This Nation asks for action, and action now. Our greatest primary task is to put people to work.'" The celebration of "Schatz-Brau Day" created "a spirit of festivity which made everybody happy and satisfied in the hope of better times to come.

This hope was accentuated at the sight of a large, modern factory under construction which will make it possible for this community to benefit directly from an industry which is in the front ranks in the march to national economic recovery." Congressman Harold Knutson, a Republican from the Sixth District and a strong advocate for the return of inexpensive "nickel beer," expressed his pleasure at the progress of the construction and lauded the project for providing a better market for grain and employment to many people. Ultimately, the striking castle-shaped building never produced any beer, but was occupied by various food-processing firms and was eventually converted into a cheese factory.[11] Schatz-Brau made it farther than several other proposed breweries, however. More than a dozen companies that formed and applied for federal brewing permits never brewed a barrel—some never even began construction.

One of the Finest Breweries Ever Seen

The only all-new brewery to go into production was the Alexandria Brewing Co. This firm was also unique in being the only brewery in Minnesota founded by

This photograph appears to show the dedication ceremony described by the *Melrose Beacon*. The brewery was not a new structure but a remodeled mill building. The reason the brewery never entered production may be visible in the foreground: Schmidt's City Club was a popular and well-established brand within a few months after beer was re-legalized, and many bar owners preferred to continue selling a profitable product rather than experiment with a new brand. FROM THE COLLECTION OF BOB JACKSON.

Greek immigrants. Sam Caldis and John Geanopolous, "inseparable partners in many business ventures," had backgrounds in the restaurant industry, including stints at exclusive clubs in Minneapolis. Caldis arrived in Alexandria before World War I and opened the Alexandria Candy Kitchen. While it is not clear exactly what made them go into the beer business, they unquestionably did so with gusto. Because the three previous breweries in Alexandria had been torn down or converted to other uses, they built an all-new brewery in Alexandria that was three stories high with a footprint of 50 by 104 feet. The plant was described by a local reporter as "well-equipped, well lighted and clean and sanitary looking." The reporter added the usual claim that the machinery "is of the very latest design to make the operation of the plant as near scientific as possible. . . ." (It appears that almost every brewery was "one of the most modern and up to date plants of its kind in the country," as was said of the Alexandria brewery.) When it first opened after considerable delays in June 1935, the brewery packaged beer only in kegs, but a few months later it added a bottling machine for its "Gold Seal" beer. When the first anniversary of production was celebrated in 1936, Caldis and Geanopolous claimed sales to "many retailers" and noted that several local restaurants were "handling Gold Seal beer exclusively."[12] All did not go well for the two, however, and they shut down production about a year later. In early 1939 Caldis and Geanopolous leased the brewery to a new version of the Alexandria Brewing Co., this time headed by a president with the equally unlikely brewer's name of Attilio Zadro, to produce the new Gopher Beer under longtime Minnesota brewmaster Joe Mickus. As with most other business openings, the *Park Region Echo* heralded the fact that twenty men would be employed and that "grain used in Gopher beer will be purchased around Alexandria," though the grain was sent to Minneapolis for malting.[13] Gopher Beer was not much more successful than Gold Seal, and by the early 1940s the brewery was offering Sam's Triple-A Premium Beer.

The Greek heritage of John Geanopolous and Sam Caldis, owners of Alexandria Brewing Co., is reflected in the unusual (for beer) Greek goddess image on the Gold Seal label (c. 1936). FROM THE COLLECTION OF KEN MALZ.

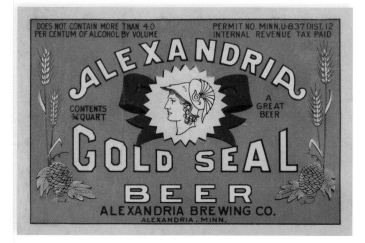

Employment for Local Men

Because the specter of Prohibition remained until after World War II, breweries were careful to stress their contributions to the community. The most important contribution, especially given the catastrophic unemployment during the Great Depression, was the number of jobs created directly and indirectly by the resumption of business. The *Mantorville Express* reported with pleasure that the soon-to-be-reopened Otto's Brewery "now gives employment to 17 people but in a short while, direct employment will be given to about 50, all of whom will be required to live in the village." This estimate was far too high, especially considering the firm would be in receivership in less than a year.[14] Kiewel Brewing Co. was much more realistic in its prediction that fifteen men would be employed

when the brewery was at full production, about 40,000 barrels per year. A larger brewery such as Mankato Brewing Company, with a capacity of around 100,000 barrels and a need to distribute the output, required about fifty workers including office staff and driver/salesmen. Its plans in late 1933 called for the brewery and packaging workers to be divided into four six-hour shifts, in accordance with the codes set for the industry by Roosevelt's National Recovery Administration.[15] While the NRA codes generally favored extremely large firms over small ones, even small brewing companies signed up and adopted the semivoluntary codes, in part to show their willingness to cooperate and to forestall moves to reinstate prohibition.[16]

Employment at the major Twin Cities breweries was much greater. Each of the four major breweries—Minneapolis Brewing Company, Gluek Brewing Company, Theo. Hamm Brewing Co., and Jacob Schmidt Brewing Company—employed several hundred men each. Yoerg Brewing Co. in St. Paul was much smaller, employing about 75 men after repeal. A list of brewery job descriptions compiled in the late 1930s (using two St. Paul breweries as the model) described more than three dozen distinct positions available at a large brewery, many of which, especially in the packaging and warehouse departments, required dozens of people each. Most of these jobs did not require previous experience and so were eagerly sought as entry-level jobs. In a large brewery, most positions offered opportunities for promotion, so most year-round employees expected to make a career out of their work in the brewery. A union history published in 1968 listed almost 150 employees who had been with either Hamm or Schmidt for more than thirty years, and several dozen who had been hired prior to repeal.[17]

Working conditions in the breweries were considered "as ideal as the work will allow." The breweries were "clean, well ventilated and well lighted." Hazards were considered "negligible," in comparison to many other industries, but breweries were not totally free of health or accident risks. The temperature in various departments ranged from more than 120°F in the malt kiln room down to 40°F in the racking (filling) room. Few workers moved directly from one room to the other, but frequent temperature changes sometimes led to health problems. The wet conditions in many areas created a danger of slipping and falling, but few severe injuries were reported.[18] Potentially dangerous chemicals often were

Brewery Jobs in the 1930s

A U.S. government–sponsored study of the brewing industry listed the following jobs available in a St. Paul brewery in 1939. This list does not include assistants to any of these positions. This brewery does not appear to have had a separate canning line and was still using wooden kegs (so it wasn't Hamm's).

- grain buyer
- grain elevator laborer (elevator man)
- grain elevator foreman (assistant grain buyer)
- machine maltster
- malthouse laborer (malthouse man)
- kiln/malthouse fireman
- brewmaster
- miller
- malt-crusher tender

- kettle man
- brewing equipment cleaner
- cellar man
- tank cleaner
- racker (keg filler)
- keg and barrel labeler
- racking room laborer
- shipping clerk
- checker (empty bottles)
- beer bottle sorter
- bottle conveyor feeder

- inspector (empty bottles)
- washer (empty bottles)
- beer bottle filler
- inspector (filled bottles)
- beer pasteurizer tender
- beer bottle labeler
- caser
- bear case sealer
- inspector (beer cases)
- hand trucker
- shipping clerk (bottled beer)
- inspector (kegs and barrels)
- checker (kegs and barrels)

- corker (kegs and barrels)
- pitchman (kegs and barrels)
- keg and barrel soaker
- branding machine operator
- cooper

From: Local Job Descriptions for Two Establishments in the Malt Liquor Manufacturing Industry. *Preliminary Job Study No. 5-113, Works Progress Administration and Minnesota Department of Education. (St. Paul: United States Employment Center, 1939).*

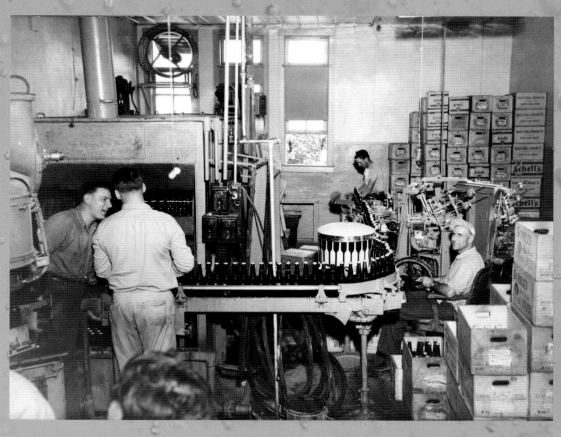

August Schell Brewing Company bottling-line workers are shown in this undated photograph. Notice the wooden cases in the front and the cardboard cases along the back wall. COURTESY OF AUGUST SCHELL BREWING COMPANY.

required for cleaning and maintaining the equipment, but again, few serious incidents occurred. (Though in one reported case, despite wearing a gas mask, a worker at Kiewel Brewing Co. died from poisonous fumes while varnishing a vat.)[19]

Working conditions for many were improved further by union membership. A single brewery often had to negotiate with several different unions representing different types of employees. St. Paul's bottlers earned wages of $25.50 per week in 1933 and received a raise to $27 the next year—excellent wages during the Depression. Wages rose steadily through the 1930s, and bottlers earned $35 per week on the eve of World War II. Brewers, whose positions required more skill and training, earned $3 more per week than bottlers.[20] Driver/salesmen were represented by a different union for many years and firemen (who operated the boilers or malt kilns) by yet another.

The brewery workforce was not diverse by modern standards. With the exception of a few office workers, the workforce was exclusively male. While some women were employed in bottling before Prohibition, social norms during the Depression reserved most jobs for the male breadwinner of the family. In addition, brewery workers were usually of German descent or from other nations with a brewing heritage. Many employees were hired based on recommendation from friends or neighbors, creating something of a closed society. The breweries in the Twin Cities had no African American employees, a situation that upset some members of that community. In 1935 Cecil Newman, editor of the *Minneapolis Spokesman*, led an eleven-month boycott of Twin Cities breweries. In edito-

As delivery trucks became more affordable, it became more convenient for small breweries to deliver throughout their regions. This Red Wing Brewing Co. truck was photographed in November 1934. PHOTOGRAPH BY LEE BROTHERS; COURTESY OF THE MINNESOTA HISTORICAL SOCIETY.

rials and cartoons, he asked how the companies could expect "Negro porters and waiters" to recommend the local beer when the breweries hired no "colored" help. Engesser Brewing Co. of St. Peter was able to gain some business from the Twin Cities African American community because it had an African American driver. Despite the boycott, the breweries did not hire any African American employees until after the end of World War II.[21]

A New Package

The beer industry in the 1930s faced a different world from that known before Prohibition. Many of the changes were due to technological advances made while the breweries were dormant. The increasing popularity of the automobile and the delivery truck, combined with the dramatic extension and improvement of roads, made distribution much more flexible for breweries that could afford their own fleets. The home refrigerator was changing the shopping and eating habits of the country—and the way in which beer was packaged and sold.

Immediately after repeal, packaged beer had a short-lived advantage over draught beer because of the shortage of kegs (and perhaps also because of the ease of shipping bottled beer to new markets). Shortly thereafter, the proportion of draught sales to packaged beer sales returned to the pre-Prohibition ratio of approximately three to one.[22] However, the advantages of packaged beer helped it overtake draught beer again almost immediately. More consumers were buying beer for consumption at home, both because refrigeration made it convenient and because many drinkers had lost the saloon habit during Prohibition. More taverns were serving bottled beer because it was easier to handle and allowed proprietors to offer more variety (often at a higher price and yielding a better profit). Brewers experimented with different bottle types as well. The stein, or steinie, introduced by Minneapolis Brewing Company in 1936, supposedly was easier to store and less prone to tip over, but it was popular for only a few years.[23] Glass manufacturers also introduced the nonreturnable, or "one way," bottle, but this would not become common until World War II.

The most important development of the 1930s was the introduction of canned beer. American Can Company had solved most of the technical problems involved with canning beer (mostly the lining of the can) and persuaded G. Krueger Brewing Company of Newark, New Jersey, to introduce the can in 1935. The "Keglined" flat-top can quickly convinced drinkers that there were no adverse taste effects, and the popularity of canned beer rose quickly: by 1940 canned beer represented almost 10 percent of packaged beer sales. Cans were unbreakable, shielded beer from the destructive effects of light better than glass, were lighter and easier to ship and handle, and were convenient for consumers since they didn't have to return them. Other companies, especially Continental Can Company and Crown Cork & Seal Company entered the market with their own unique styles, the cone-top and the Crowntainer. These two bottle styles had the advantage of being sealed with a cap, which meant that consumers didn't need a new type of opener to get at the contents and that breweries could fill them using existing bottling machinery. Gluek and Fitger were among the first dozen brewers in the nation to use Continental's cone-top style, though Gluek would eventually shift to Crowntainers and ultimately become one of only two Minnesota brewers to use all three major can styles (Schell was the other). Flat-tops were more expensive to begin with because of the new machinery, but they could be filled faster and yielded greater advantages in storage and stackability. It was easiest for Theo. Hamm, the largest and richest brewer in the state, to move immediately to American Can's flat-top style, and it thus became the only Minnesota canning brewer of that period never to use a cone-top or a Crowntainer can.[24]

Advertisements for canned beer, such as this one on the back of Minneapolis Brewing Company's in-house magazine, *The Friendly Faucet*, touted the advantages of the new package. COURTESY OF THE MINNESOTA HISTORICAL SOCIETY.

These six low-profile cone-top cans are among the earliest beer cans in Minnesota—indeed, in the world. The U-permit numbers visible on the Grain Belt and Kato cans date them to 1935. Most of these can labels simply duplicate the equivalent bottle labels, except that the Kato cans advertise "Cap Sealed Keg Flavor" and the Gluek can bears the legend "Brewed and Canned by . . ." Early cone-tops in excellent condition, like these used from 1935 to 1941, often command several hundred dollars at auctions. FROM THE COLLECTION OF DAVE WENDL.

A few brewers were able to install new canning equipment and reap the benefits of flat-top cans right away. The Hamm canning line is shown here in 1936, just after installation. COURTESY OF THE MINNESOTA HISTORICAL SOCIETY.

The Crowntainer was an early can made by the Crown Cork & Seal Company of Baltimore. Like the cone-top, it could be used on bottling lines and was therefore attractive to breweries with a limited equipment budget. It remained in use until the early 1950s. The Crowntainer was the only can style known to have been used by Yoerg's. The Jordan can is one of two known Minnesota examples of a Crowntainer with a paper label; the other was Gluek's Stite. Gluek's Silver Growler took its name from a common pre-Prohibition take-home package, but this growler was much more dignified than a simple pail of beer. FROM THE COLLECTION OF DAVE WENDL.

As package styles multiplied and markets expanded, large brewers were faced with a nearly impenetrable maze of labeling requirements. After Prohibition, federal and state governments tried to prevent brewers from engaging in their previous corrupt business practices through extensive regulation. Some of the federal regulations made little sense: Minneapolis

Early flat-top beer cans included instructions for consumers on how to open them (collectors refer to these cans as "opening instruction" or "OI" cans). The early instructions suggested making only one hole; later versions recommended two holes to allow the beer to flow more freely. These "Keglined" cans were made by American Can Company, one of the three major can producers. The can on the left is especially noteworthy: Hamm was forced to give up metallic gold paint during World War II and use this flat gold instead. FROM THE COLLECTION OF DAVE WENDL.

Brewing Company had a label rejected because it listed ¾ quart as 24 oz. (which are, of course, equal amounts). In 1941 the label for Minnehaha Ale was rejected because the brewery address and content information were not printed in easily readable type. The brewery successfully appealed to be allowed to deplete its stock of one million labels.

Federal regulations occasionally conflicted with state regulations, and state regulations themselves presented a nightmare of different requirements. Minnesota law required the word *strong* on beer stronger than 3.2 percent, but federal law prohibited advertising strength on the label. (The state law took precedence in this case.) Kansas City had different regulations from either Missouri or Kansas. When South Dakota proposed a label requirement change, the Minnesota Brewers Association appealed to South Dakota officials:

> It is sincerely hoped that these legends were held out merely as suggested forms subject to revision, to illustrate your meaning, and were not intended as arbitrary forms to be followed because expression in such form would make South Dakota another state requiring alcoholic content to be expressed in a form different from that used in any other state. The confusion and the expense in a brewery bottle house is indescribable where so many different varieties of labels must be used for the different states. Some of the breweries are now obliged to use 32 different labels and it is almost impossible to prevent mistakes and errors in the bottle houses of breweries which supply a number of states.

A chart created by Minneapolis Brewing Company in 1938 revealed that the maze of regulations required sixty different labels for a much smaller number of different products distributed in fourteen states from Illinois to Idaho.[25]

This Engesser sign was recovered from an old bar in the Frogtown section of St. Paul. It is almost certainly a remnant of the period in the mid-1930s when Engesser tried to capture the African American market in the Twin Cities. FROM THE COLLECTION OF JIM AND RUTH BEATON.

A Decade of Recovery

By the beginning of the 1940s, the brewing industry had made a major contribution to the economic recovery of the nation. About 600 U.S. breweries had survived the unsettled years following repeal, twenty of which were in Minnesota. The state usually ranked ninth or tenth nationally in production, and production increased from about 1.7 million barrels in 1934 to 2.7 million barrels in 1939. During that year, Minnesota's breweries employed 147 salaried employees and 1,654 wage earners, to which could be added more than 32,000 employees in wholesale and retail businesses. The State of Minnesota collected almost $1.7 million in excise taxes in 1940, and Minnesota brewers paid their share of the $268 million in federal tax collections. On 1 July 1940 the U.S. government raised the tax per barrel from $5 to $6, with the additional funds directed specifically to national defense.[26] The perception that the brewing industry was contributing even more than its just share would help the industry survive another wave of prohibitionist sentiment brought on by American entry into World War II.

Despite the overall recovery of the industry, individual firms continued to fail. Of the twenty-five breweries that began production after Prohibition, Otto's Brewery in Mantorville, St. Cloud Brewing Co., and Red Wing (later Midwest) Brewing Co. had closed by 1939, and several others were hanging on by a slender thread. Engesser Brewing Co., in business since 1856, suffered a major fire in 1940, and the economic strains of higher taxes and higher raw material costs forced it to close in 1941, leaving many of its workers unpaid for several months of work.[27] The economic constraints brought on by World War II would cause problems of some sort for all breweries, and would result in the closure of three more.

An Essential Industry

When the United States entered World War II following the Japanese attack on Pearl Harbor, the brewers had already laid the groundwork to make sure that legal brewing did not become a casualty of the war effort. Many months before Pearl Harbor, the three organizations representing breweries had combined to establish a Defense Liaison Committee. (The three organizations were the United States Brewers Association, the United Brewers Industrial Foundation, and the American Brewers Association.) In the meantime, dry forces began to introduce bills to limit sales to military personnel and near military posts. Most military leaders were strongly against such legislation and claimed that temperance would be reached better through controlled legal sales. Some also argued that establishing prohibition for the armed forces and not for the rest of the country would be unjust. Furthermore, beer was considered an essential item to maintain the morale of the fighting forces.[28] The dry advocates also made a fatal mistake in the days after Pearl Harbor when they blamed the disastrous results of the attack on excessive drunkenness among the sailors. Not only did investigations by a presidential commission refute this charge but the allegations also sounded too much like the enemy propaganda that blamed American decadence for the war.[29]

While the brewers of Minnesota were never really threatened by a return of wartime prohibition, they still made sure to contribute to the war effort in every way possible. Several brewers contributed to scrap-metal drives by contributing metal and by offering the use of their trucks or facilities. The brewing companies complied with the numerous government regulations restricting use of raw materials and transportation. In July 1943 the War Food Administration (WFA)

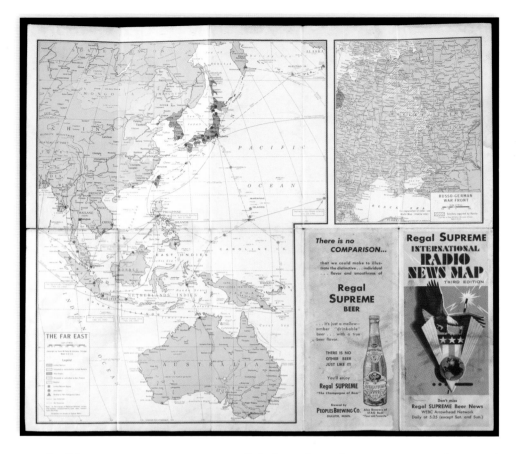

Like many other businesses, breweries contributed to the war effort in a variety of ways. This promotional map from mid-1942 was offered in conjunction with a local news broadcast sponsored by Peoples Brewing Co. FROM THE COLLECTION OF PETE CLURE.

Gluek was one of the four large Twin Cities breweries that had contracts to supply beer for the armed forces from 1942 to 1945. FROM THE COLLECTION OF KEN MALZ.

required brewers to use 15 percent of their grain to brew 3.2 percent beer and to reserve it for government purchases. The federal government established contracts with a few large Minnesota breweries for monthly purchases. Breweries also had employees serving in the armed forces, though some brewery employees were considered essential to the war effort and were exempted from service.

Breweries also supported various community efforts to conserve essential materials, support the troops, and keep morale up. Alexandria Brewing Co. was an active supporter of the local scrap-metal drive, helped sponsor several joint ads with other merchants that recognized men from the county in the armed forces and provided information on civil defense matters, and contributed two cases of beer to the Salvage for Victory Day event.[30]

In addition to their individual efforts, the largest (and most financially stable) brewing companies launched a major advertising campaign through the Minnesota Brewers Association. These ads, which appeared in newspapers throughout the state, combined appeals to maintain morale at home with proof of the brewers' contribution to the war effort through their tax payments. Minnesotans were urged to maintain a stable home life, invite the neighbors over, and sustain their faith in difficult times. Meanwhile, the proceeds of each day's taxes on beer production provided ten fighter planes, four B-17 bombers, nineteen tanks, or four

Kato PILSNER BEER

Tax paid at Rate Prescribed by Internal Revenue Law

This container has been put in use only as an emergency measure. Case material conservation makes the use of this case necessary.

This case contains 24-12 oz. Bottles

MANKATO BREWING COMPANY

BREWERS OF FINE BEERS

Kato Pilsner   *Kato Black Label Pilsner Strong*

MANKATO, MINNESOTA

This case label from Mankato Brewing Company reminded customers that during World War II all materials were subject to conservation. It may have been used on a damaged or improvised case. FROM THE COLLECTION OF KEN MALZ.

PT boats, depending on the ad. The Minnesota Brewers Association pushed both credibility and the government too far when it ran a series of ads that claimed beer was "comparable to or the equivalent of bread in nutritional value." The Federal Trade Commission stepped in and ruled officially that bread had greater nutritional value than beer, and the brewers agreed to discontinue the ads.[31]

Throughout the war, brewers were faced with the difficult task of trying to make a profit while contributing to the war effort and while trying to comply with a variety of often-conflicting wartime restrictions. Brewery advertising often asked for the cooperation of consumers: to buy quart bottles to help conserve bottle caps, to be patient through temporary shortages, and to recognize that any canned beer produced was destined for the forces at the front. Beer cans were the first casualty of wartime shortages. Leon Henderson, price administrator for the War Production Board, said in early 1942, "... we're giving up canning things like dog food, beer and caviar so we can whip Hitler and Hirohito and provide our families with the canned foods they really need."[32] Shortly after that, the use of tin plate for crown caps was strictly limited. Many brewers collected used bottle caps (sometimes in special containers with the brewery logo) and recycled them. Ultimately, the essential raw materials for beer were limited as well. To divert more malt to the production of industrial alcohol, small brewers could not exceed their 1942 malt usage in 1943, and large brewers had to make a 7 percent cut.

At the same time, brewers were expected to increase production to meet the government contracts and to relieve the nationwide beer shortage. The War Production Board made clear the government position in early 1942 by declaring, "Experience in other countries has indicated that [beer and wine] have a value in sustaining morale both to civilians and to the armed forces," and established that about two-thirds of the 1941 barrelage should be produced for civilian consumption (in addition to the government purchases) despite the shortages.[33]

Advertisements sponsored by the combined Minnesota breweries reminded citizens that beer could help maintain morale at home. The brewers' indirect contribution to the war effort through federal taxes was highlighted in each ad. COURTESY OF THE MINNESOTA HISTORICAL SOCIETY.

Entertaining at Home?
BEER IS APPROPRIATE

More Americans are playing host these days in their own living rooms. Simple entertaining, to ease the strain and tension of wartime, is both wholesome and necessary. Naturally the beverage you serve should be appropriate — mildly stimulating to promote good fellowship, refreshing, and, of course, economical. Beer is all of these, and is enjoyed for its own goodness by the majority of your friends. Remember it, too, as a nutritious beverage, carefully brewed from the rich grain harvests of Minnesota. True temperance, more important today than ever before, is best served by serving beer . . . . . . the beverage of moderation and true hospitality.

It's smart to serve beer

BUY U. S. WAR BONDS AND SAVINGS STAMPS

Published in behalf of the following Minnesota Breweries

FITGER · FLECKENSTEIN · GLUEK · GRAIN BELT
HAMM · HAUENSTEIN · JORDAN · KATO · KIEWEL
SCHELL · SCHMIDT

BEER ··· *a beverage of moderation*

Government restrictions on metal forced changes in packaging as bottle caps became scarce. Breweries such as Schmidt urged consumers to buy larger bottles such as Schmidt's "Victory Quart" or to drink draught beer. FROM THE COLLECTION OF DAVE DAVIS.

The restrictions on malt forced brewers to experiment with other grains in an attempt to keep production up while still creating a palatable beer. The substitute brewing materials included the common adjuncts yellow corn, unmalted barley, and wheat, but also ranged as far as "oats, rye, mandioca [cassava], and even potatoes." All of these "filled the gap between the demand for beer and the curtailment of malt."[34] Some of the new formulas were unmemorable and may have hastened the end of some breweries. However, Gluek developed a more successful brew that the company soon patented and marketed as Stite—generally considered the first-ever malt liquor. Stite's higher alcohol content not only helped mask the taste of the adjuncts but also created greater intoxication. After the war Stite became known as Green Lightning or Green Death, named for its signature green can and its ability to cause a hangover.[35]

Even more frustrating to shipping brewers were the transportation restrictions. In spring 1943, rail shipments of beer were limited to less than the previous year's amount, yet in the same announcement brewers were urged to try to gain transport savings without depriving any region of the country. A few months later, brewers were urged to make additional conservation plans and at the same time to find ways to meet the nationwide beer shortage. As the WFA noted, "Many brewers have already withdrawn from distant markets and are pushing sales in areas nearer their plants in order to save transportation."[36] Schmidt, Hamm, and Minneapolis Brewing were hit especially hard because they were among the major suppliers of some of the most sparsely populated areas of the country.

Finally, the draft left many brewers short of labor. During the war, women returned to the breweries for the first time since before Prohibition. But instead of being relegated to washing bottles as before, they often held some highly skilled positions, sometimes taking their husbands' places. Nationally, more than 7,000

Stite was one of the first products available in the small 8-ounce cans. Cans used during Gluek's last years in the 1960s abandoned the metallic green signature for the undistinguished design at right. When the Stite label was acquired by G. Heileman, the company changed the can to read "Since 1847," which applied to the Heileman company but not to Gluek's or to Stite. FROM THE COLLECTION OF DAVE WENDL.

members of the brewery workers union were in the armed forces, and more than 200 were killed in action.[37] A few lucky brewers were able to practice their craft in the service of their country. Frank E. Mathes of Minneapolis Brewing Company, serving as a corporal in the administrative department of the Air Force, was transferred to a special unit that reconditioned breweries in liberated areas to produce beer for American occupation forces. Almost sixty breweries in France, Germany, Italy, and even North Africa were repaired and pressed into service.[38]

A labor dispute involving the three St. Paul breweries forced the federal government to declare officially that beer was essential to the war effort. On 13 December 1944, members of brewery drivers Local 993 went on strike over a union jurisdictional struggle and a disputed bargaining unit election. The management of Hamm, Schmidt, and Yoerg argued, and the War Labor Board (WLB) agreed, that the walkout violated labor's no-strike pledge and threatened the war effort. Hamm and Schmidt had contracts to provide beer to the government totaling 500,000 cases per month, and the strike would prevent them from meeting this target. One month after the strike began, the WLB ruled that the striking workers had to return because beer was essential to the war effort and "necessary to civilian morale." The counsel for the AFL-affiliated local countered that beer was no more essential than music, referring to a strike by the Minneapolis musicians' union against KSTP radio in which the government did not intervene. When the drivers failed to return, the matter was referred to President Roosevelt, with the threat that he might order the breweries seized by the government. Roosevelt did not render an immediate decision, perhaps because he did not want to choose between two longtime supporters, Daniel Tobin of the International Union and Otto Bremer of Jacob Schmidt Brewing Company.[39] Beer finally flowed again two months after the strike began, but for many in the brewing industry, the most

Railroad cars were diverted to military use during the war, making it harder for breweries to ship their beer to distant markets. This Karlsbräu refrigerated rail car, or reefer, was photographed in August 1934, shortly after the brewery reopened. Reefers were necessary to supply distant markets with fresh beer. At various times, Duluth Brewing & Malting shipped beer as far as Alaska and Puerto Rico (though not to all points between). FROM THE COLLECTION OF PETE CLURE.

important outcome of the strike was that the government was forced to publicly recognize the importance of beer in American life.

At the end of the war, the brewing industry took several years to return to normal. Material restrictions were lifted only gradually: canned beer was not available for civilian purchase until the spring of 1947, and grain restrictions were lifted just in time to be reimposed for the Korean War. Just over a year after being idled by the strike, the three St. Paul breweries were again forced to shut down, this time for three weeks, because of a coal shortage.[40] Many of the wartime changes became permanent parts of the American beer scene: cardboard cases replaced wood, cans and one-way bottles continued to push out returnable bottles and draught beer, and the lighter, thinner beers of wartime remained even after malt restrictions were lifted.

Winning the War, Losing the Battle

While some of the large breweries emerged from the war ready to expand in the postwar world, many of the small breweries either closed during the war because of shortages or were mortally wounded and would be forced to shut down within a few years after the war ended. During the war, government purchasing agents found it easier to deal with large companies in all industries wherever possible, and despite some efforts to spread the orders around, small firms were often left out.[41] While Schmidt and Hamm had contracts for hundreds of thousands of cases per month, the much smaller Yoerg Brewing Co. had no contract. Alexandria Brewing Co. was forced to close in 1943 because of

Businesses of all types displayed posters reminding people to be cautious during wartime. Taverns were especially important places to remind people about refraining from loose talk that would disclose military information or lower morale. This was one of a series of eight posters issued by Theo Hamm Brewing Co. during World War II. FROM THE COLLECTION OF JIM AND RUTH BEATON.

wartime shortages, especially of bottle caps. Montgomery Brewing Co., already in shaky financial condition, also closed in 1943. Schutz & Hilgers Jordan Brewery was purchased in 1946 by Arizona Brewing Company (makers of A-1 beer), not for its brewery but for its grain allocation and other inputs. The idle Jordan Brewery was soon purchased by Mankato Brewing Company and put back into production for almost a year. Continued grain conservation measures forced the final closure of the Jordan branch in April 1948, though modernization of the plant continued for several months afterward. The purchase of the Jordan property was also the beginning of the end for Mankato Brewing Company, which never completely recovered from the large losses incurred.[42] When the United States went to war again in Korea, grain, metal, fuel, and transportation restrictions were reimposed, the excise tax was raised to $9 per barrel (though the original proposal was $12), and struggling breweries were again forced to the wall. Falls Breweries and Goodhue County Brewing Co. (which was on its third name in four years) both ceased to exist during the Korean War. But for the breweries that survived, the postwar prosperity held opportunities that would catapult a lucky few to regional and national fame.

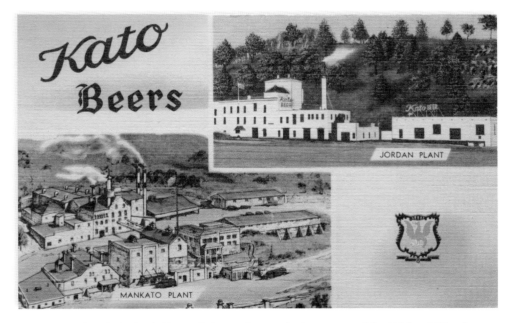

This postcard is from the brief period (1946–48) when Mankato Brewing Company owned the old Schutz & Hilgers brewery in Jordan. Ironically, while the Mankato brewery remained in production much longer, the Jordan structure outlived its Mankato counterpart. The Jordan building has been converted into shops and residences; the Mankato brewery was demolished in 1971. FROM THE COLLECTION OF DAVE WENDL.

The unlabeled tap handles of the pre-Prohibition period were replaced by ball-tap knobs that bore the name of the brewer (and usually the brand) in accordance with federal and state laws. The knobs were threaded to screw onto a tap handle and usually faced the bartender rather than the customer, as they were too small to be of much promotional value. By the 1960s these small knobs were replaced by the much showier tap handles that promote the beer as well as guide the bartender. The ball-tap knobs shown were used primarily from 1933 to 1957. FROM THE COLLECTION OF PAT STAMBAUGH.

Sky Blue Waters, Bland Yellow Beer

We must always emphasize the fact that our brews should be designed not to please ourselves nor even a few conventional connoisseurs but to satisfy the masses of consumers and potential consumers. . . . The general public today is looking for beer with a delicate flavor—not too pronounced a flavor. They want a beverage which they can enjoy and which will refresh them and which they can consume congenially and without unpleasant effects of any kind. Many drinkers who may even criticize lower strength or lighter beers which have appeared on the market will, nevertheless, drink them and possibly, in the long run, become more confirmed beer drinkers than they ever would have under other circumstances.
—*Brewers Digest* editorial, June 1946

A S MINNESOTA'S BREWERS EMERGED FROM THE RESTRICTIVE PERIOD OF World War II, they prepared to expand aggressively in many different ways. Years' worth of remodeling, expansion, product development, and territory extension that had been delayed by the war burst forth in an explosion of activity that was visible to almost everyone in the country. At the same time, this aggressive expansion led to struggles over market share that would see overall industry production increase dramatically but would also witness the loss of more than 80 percent of the nation's breweries and, eventually, all but four in Minnesota.

The New Beer Culture

Entering the 1950s, the brewing industry needed to adjust to operating under a new set of conditions, some of which had been developing since repeal, but all of which combined after World War II to make brewing significantly different from before. The most beneficial change for the brewing industry was that beer was beginning to reestablish the respected place it held in American social life around the turn of the century, before its reputation had been damaged. The restored position of beer in family life resulted from technological and commercial

147

developments. While home refrigeration first became affordable in the 1920s, it wasn't until the 1950s that a refrigerator could be found in nearly every home. The convenience of being able to simply go to the kitchen and grab a beer (or, as we might believe from popular depictions of the time, to have one's wife deliver a cold beer) made it less necessary to go down to the neighborhood tavern to have a beer. To a much greater extent than was possible before Prohibition, this made it possible for brewers to separate beer itself from the evils of the saloon and to present beer as a wholesome product to be enjoyed by everyone.

To cement this impression in the public mind, both the national and Minnesota brewing organizations began advertising campaigns with themes based on family life. The United States Brewers Foundation launched a series of national ads known as the Home Life in America series. By depicting beer as a harmless source of refreshment in the pages of *Life, Look, Collier's, McCall's,* and *Woman's Home Companion*, brewers were largely successful in positioning beer in the mainstream of American social life. They were so successful, in fact, that legislation targeting these ads was introduced in Congress by Representative Laurie Battle of Alabama. His unsuccessful bill proposed to ban all sorts of "misleading" advertising, including anything that suggested beer "would increase social or business prestige, or is traditional in American family life or a part of the atmosphere of the American home."[1] The Minnesota Brewers Association's campaign followed the national theme of Beer Belongs—Enjoy It! It, too, showed ordinary people enjoying beer in a variety of normal and wholesome circumstances.

Nearly every ad in the Beer Belongs series showed both men and women enjoying beer. The campaign sought to show beer as an integral part of home life and entertaining guests. This mirrored the trend toward increasing sales of take-home packages and decreasing sales of draught beer. COURTESY OF THE MINNESOTA HISTORICAL SOCIETY.

A Refreshing Glass of Beer Goes With YARD CLEANING

"Spring" spells yard cleaning. And it's pleasant, when you pause to enjoy a glass of refreshing Minnesota brewed beer.

Beer belongs enjoy it

PUBLISHED ON BEHALF OF THE FOLLOWING MINNESOTA BREWERIES:

BUB'S *Winona*   FITGER *Duluth*   FLECKENSTEIN *Faribault*   GLUEK *Minneapolis*   GRAIN BELT *Minneapolis*   HAMM *St. Paul*
HAUENSTEIN *New Ulm*   KIEWEL *Little Falls*   ROYAL BOHEMIAN *Duluth*   SCHELL *New Ulm*   SCHMIDT *St. Paul*

Beer advertising had, in fact, entered a new phase in the postwar period. As noted previously, brewers were very cautious in the immediate post-Prohibition period, sometimes because state laws forced them to be restrained. An article by Reginald Clough reprinted in *Brewers Digest* in April 1952 divided the development of beer advertising into four stages. Immediately after repeal, brewers were simply trying to establish their businesses and their names. In some states, beer advertising prohibited any product claims other than the fact that beer existed and that it was on sale in a certain location. In the second phase after repeal, brewers built their brands and emphasized the responsibility of (and economic benefits from) the industry. The phase during World War II promoted wartime morale while still keeping the brand name before the public. The final phase, reached at the end of wartime material shortages, emphasized the trend toward home consumption, and therefore the advertising focused largely on packaging and convenience.[2] A large portion of the advertising for beer in the late 1940s and 1950s focused on the fact that beer could be purchased at the local store and introduced a variety of convenient packages in which to bring it home. The six-pack, borrowed from the soft drink industry, was introduced in California in 1947 and spread quickly to the Midwest and throughout the country. Soon, innovation seemed to focus less on trying to make a better-tasting beer and more on making the most creative six-pack holder. In 1949 Jacob Schmidt Brewing Company introduced a new six-pack carrier with a pull-out handle, designed to make stacking easier and to take up less shelf space in the store or the refrigerator.[3]

The media through which beer was advertised were also undergoing a major shift in the early 1950s. The two major functions of advertising—building brand

Even small regional brewers were able to sponsor radio programs in their markets. Rance Valentine's signature song was "When You and I Were Young, Maggie." Peoples Brewing Co. sponsored *Yesterdays* during the 1930s. FROM THE COLLECTION OF PETE CLURE.

loyalty and encouraging a purchase at a particular moment—required different approaches. Building brand loyalty was pursued through newspaper ads, as it had been since the earliest days, and radio advertising of all sorts was continuing to expand. But the biggest change was the development of commercial television. Television ads had the potential to combine the strong visual effects of a large newspaper ad with radio's spoken text or jingles. Television also added attractive moving pictures to the mix: views of the brewing process, scenes of swiftly flowing streams of brewing water, or the irresistible image of a glass being filled from a tap, bottle, or can. Early television ads were not an art form, but beer commercials would help to change that. Some industry analysts saw television ads as a moving, talking point-of-sale promotion—just the thing to convince the bar patron watching the ball game to order another beer. Other observers believed that television advertising fit well with the general advertising approach of the breweries and with the shift of beer consumption to the home.[4] Spending on television spots by brewers was nonexistent at the end of World War II, but by 1951 it had exceeded $5.2 million and its rate of expansion would only increase. In less than a decade, the percentage of money spent on print advertising shrunk dramatically and television (and to a lesser extent, radio) spots came to dominate the overall industry expenditures. However, this change was not spread evenly throughout the industry. Network television and radio were expensive and only worthwhile for a handful of the largest national shipping brewers: Anheuser-Busch, Pabst, Blatz, Schlitz, and Ballantine. Regional brewers continued to advertise more heavily in newspapers and other local venues. Minnesota's breweries exemplified this trend. Throughout the early 1950s, Hamm's reduced its newspaper advertising expenditures and increased other forms in its attempt to be a true national brewer, while Minneapolis Brewing Company and Gluek, large but struggling regional producers, increased their newspaper presence. (Schmidt also decreased newspaper expenditures, but this seems to have been because of internal disagreements and personnel changes rather than part of a consistent strategy.)[5]

Unfortunately for many of Minnesota's breweries, they were just the wrong size to make the best use of significant advertising expenditures. While advertising showed a clear, positive effect on sales and profits, it was also expensive. The largest breweries were able to spread their advertising expenses over much greater production and spend much less per barrel than breweries producing between 100,000 and 250,000 barrels per year. (Breweries producing fewer than 100,000 barrels typically had much more localized advertising programs and were not competing for the same markets.) Only three Minnesota breweries were large enough to reap these economies of scale: Minneapolis Brewing, Schmidt, and Hamm.

Despite catchy slogans such as the one depicted on this coaster from the 1960s, Gluek Brewing Company was unable to overcome the restrictions imposed by its relatively small capacity and limited advertising budget. FROM THE AUTHOR'S COLLECTION.

Most at risk was Gluek, which, at a capacity of 250,000 barrels, was large enough to require a major regional advertising campaign but not large enough for it to be cost effective. Gluek was faced with the dilemma of needing to brew and sell more beer to make advertising pay, but needing to advertise more to sell enough beer to pay for the advertising. Gluek began to sell Stite in the Chicago area as well as other parts of Illinois and Wisconsin in the late 1940s, but needed to advertise even more heavily in these competitive markets. Unable to afford television, Gluek focused on newspaper advertisements to introduce the brand to Chicago, with only limited success.[6]

Another sector where brewery advertising literally dominated the landscape was outdoor advertising. Even a small brewery could rent space on a few billboards, and a large brewery could launch a major campaign or build spectacular permanent lighted signs. Such signs were not new: before World War I, Kiewel Brewing Co. had erected what was claimed to be "the largest electric sign in northern Minnesota," an advertisement for its White Rose beer that was 24 feet high and 36 feet long.[7] But with the increase in car travel and trucking that followed World War II and the development of the Interstate highway system, billboards reached more people than ever before. Billboards started to spread out from downtown areas, where they were often clustered around train stations and other transportation hubs, into the countryside, where they would stand out more from the surroundings. Some prominent brewery billboards and signs remained in downtown areas, including the large Grain Belt sign still extant on Nicollet Island in Minneapolis and the enormous Hamm's sign in downtown San Francisco. Minneapolis Brewing Company paid special tribute to the importance of outdoor advertising by giving its cartoon spokesmen, Stanley and Albert, the job of outdoor sign painters. Twin City Sign and Pictorial Painters Local 880 even presented the popular characters with union cards.[8]

Freed from the restraints of the early days after repeal, Minnesota's brewers joined other breweries across the nation in adopting much of the latest in advertising theory and were recognized throughout the industry as being among the most innovative in the field. Before the advent of the shipping breweries, few breweries gave much thought to producing a coordinated advertising campaign or even a trademark; many used a bewildering array of designs and items to promote their products. Labeling of bottles, wooden cases, and kegs was done more to ensure their return than to advertise the product. During the 1880s, major shipping and regional brewers began to standardize and register their images to capture more saloon accounts. Even then, the range of advertising media was

Card-carrying union sign painters Stanley and Albert are featured on this small point-of-sale display card, designed to be placed between six-packs in the mid-1960s. FROM THE AUTHOR'S COLLECTION.

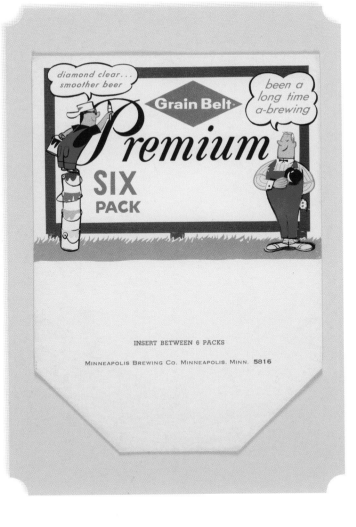

limited because most beer was consumed in the saloon and whatever beer was consumed in the home was either delivered by the brewery or purchased in stores where a clerk still fetched items for the customer from behind a counter. After the war, brewers began to seek images and slogans that could be used in as many different media as possible to present a simple, unified image to the consumer. In the early and mid-1950s, Hamm, Schmidt, and Grain Belt all made major redesigns of their flagship labels to create simpler logos that would be easier to identify and remember. In 1954, Minneapolis Brewing Company totally overhauled the Grain Belt label, retaining the signature red diamond but changing the shape of the label, the layout, and nearly everything else. Among the benefits of the new design was that stacked cases of the beer would create a repeating diamond effect. The label motif was also repeated on the sides of cans so the emblem would still be visible when viewed sideways. The Minneapolis School of Art hosted an exhibition that traced the development of the new design. This campaign showed recognition by Minneapolis Brewing of two major changes in beer cases: the final shift during World War II from wood to printable cardboard as the basic packaging material and the prominence of large displays in retail sales outlets.[9]

Brought to You By . . .

For many, the most evident proof that beer was fully established as a mainstream consumer product instead of an occasion of sin was the prominence of beer brands and breweries as sponsors of live events and radio and television broadcasts. The presence of brewers as advertisers at events ranging from baseball games to stage productions was nothing new, but the growing recognition that survival depended on advertising created a race among brewers to grab the most lucrative sponsorships. National brands began to sponsor broadcast television programs ranging from comedies to dramas to newscasts. Hamm was one of several brewers to

Like other manufacturers, brewers are susceptible to the idea that changing the packaging will improve sales. Minneapolis Brewing Company tinkered with its label design more than any other Minnesota brewery in the first two decades after repeal. From left to right, these cans represent the changes in design from 1935 to the 1950s. While the red diamond remained a consistent and recognizable feature, the text and background gradually became more repetitive. FROM THE COLLECTION OF DAVE WENDL.

Brewery Advertising

Even as radio and, later, television began to dominate brewery advertising expenditures, point-of-sale advertisements retained their importance in creating a brand image. Unlike a broadcast commercial, a painting, sculpture, or poster remained in place and could be viewed repeatedly and examined in detail—and with some of the art, repeated viewing reveals more depth. Some artists added subtle references to the product throughout the work; others added humor that became evident only upon second glance.

Brewery advertising also reflected the artistic trends of each era. The futuristic, streamlined look of the art deco style is evident in the new neon signs of the post-Prohibition period as well as in other signs and advertisements. Art deco pieces created a glamorous image for the product, making it attractive to upper- and lower-class consumers alike. In the 1930s, as colorful comic books and comic strips became popular with a public seeking relief from the Great Depression, brewing companies turned to humorous cartoons to catch the public's eye.

Advertising directors selected the characters portrayed in the ads carefully to reach a particular market and create a brand image. Many ads from the 1930s through the early 1960s featured middle-class Americans engaged in everyday activities as advertisers attempted to portray beer as an appropriate beverage for anyone at anytime. Characters in the ads enjoyed beer with a meal, as a refreshment after a task or game, and as a way to show hospitality in a variety of settings. 🐦

The use of humor in beer advertising did not begin with modern television commercials. Jacob Schmidt Brewing Company created a series of cartoons to promote its City Club brand in the 1940s. This example is displayed in its original frame. FROM THE COLLECTION OF DAVE DAVIS.

Diamond Clear - Grain Belt Beer - Since 1893

The *Girl in the Barley Field* poster took beer advertising beyond the point many members of the public were willing to go. According to the text on this reproduction created by Minnesota Brewing Company during the mid-1990s, Minneapolis Brewing Company created and began to distribute thousands of copies of the poster. Within days, complaints poured in that the poster was too suggestive and the brewery was forced to recall the posters still in the hands of the distributors. FROM THE AUTHOR'S COLLECTION.

Lawson Wood was a prominent illustrator during the post-Prohibition era, perhaps best known for his work for the St. Paul advertising firm Brown & Bigelow. In this ad for City Club, the chimpanzee (one of Wood's signature characters) is mocking a rooster whose mate has been hatching a duck. City Club was also advertised in a painting by Norman Rockwell, the most famous of America's midcentury illustrators. FROM THE COLLECTION OF DAVE DAVIS.

sponsor a news program, and the firm enjoyed the prestige conferred by association with one the most famous news reporters of all time, Edward R. Murrow. Hamm was making an aggressive move to be a truly national brewer, having recently expanded into the Texas and New York markets, and needed to advertise in the same formats as its primary rivals.[10]

The most certain method of building a national market, however, was by leveraging local connections to build a strong presence in many areas. The best way to encourage loyalty in the average beer drinker was to support the local sports teams. Professional baseball and college football had the largest national following after World War II, so brewing companies focused their efforts on these sports. The brewers of Minnesota were originally at a disadvantage relative to their national shipping counterparts, most of whom had several universities and at least one major league franchise in their home markets. Hamm solved this problem in several different ways. Starting in 1948, the company distributed "home schedule" cards for teams in nineteen major and minor baseball leagues. This campaign reached more than 140 cities, including each city in the American, National, American Association, Western International, Western Association, Wisconsin State, Arizona-Texas, Western, Three I, Central Association, Pioneer, Texas, Big State, Southern Association, Sooner State, and Northern leagues. The schedules were designed as point-of-sale items to be displayed wherever Hamm's beer was sold. Hamm also sponsored sportscasts and sports quiz shows in several major cities, including on KMBC in Kansas City, a major Hamm market. Hamm management credited these sponsorships with helping the brewery increase sales in Missouri by 37 percent in the year following their introduction. Hamm became a strong competitor in the Chicago market in the early 1950s by securing sponsorship in 1952 of the Chicago Cubs and White Sox television broadcasts, featuring legendary announcer Jack Brickhouse. Brickhouse would later announce other

Hamm's offered this metal and glass schedule holder to customers nationwide. The schedule for any local team could be placed in the frame and the holder could be used over and over, for any sport in any part of the country. FROM THE COLLECTION OF JIM AND RUTH BEATON.

sports shows for Hamm, including a wrestling show produced in Chicago that was broadcast on KVTV in Sioux City, Iowa.[11]

As major league sports moved into Minnesota in the 1960s, local brewers benefited from the exposure their brands gained on national television. Minneapolis Brewing Company had been a major advocate of bringing a baseball team to the Twin Cities and sponsored a float in the shape of the new Metropolitan Stadium in the 1957 Aquatennial parade. Photos and telecasts of the snow-covered stadium often showed the prominent Grain Belt and Gluek ads on the center field scoreboard. The Minnesota Vikings played their inaugural season in 1961, just as professional football was gaining a larger national audience and national telecasts were becoming part of America's regular Sunday afternoon schedule. As the local teams' fortunes rose, the breweries were able to bask in their reflected glory. The degree to which the stadiums were filled also influenced how many fans would hear the names of the beers hollered out by vendors. Brewers also used famous (and not-so-famous) athletes in various capacities. Minneapolis Brewing Company hired former University of Minnesota quarterback and kicker and eventual American Football League MVP Geno Cappelletti as a salesman; All-American guard and Heisman Trophy runner-up Tom Brown worked as a teamster during the summers; and Minnesota Twins utility infielder Billy Martin was a utility promotional and sales representative.[12]

Do Good to Do Well

Local breweries, both in the Twin Cities and in other locations, also sponsored local events of all types: sporting, cultural, and charitable. The guest rooms of the breweries hosted countless civic groups, and the facilities often had to be reserved well in advance. In an era when league bowling still commanded significant space in the sports section, brewery-sponsored teams were often among the league leaders. Retired drivers from the Schmidt (later Heileman) brewery in St. Paul recalled making sure that the local parishes and parochial schools always had a few kegs for their fund-raisers and some breweriana to use as prizes. Minneapolis Brewing became one of the major cultural anchors of "Nordeast" Minneapolis, starting in the late 1950s. The brewery undertook a major beautification campaign that included developing two parks and capped it off, literally, by placing on top of the brewhouse a reproduction of the Victorian-era weather vane that once adorned its peak. Grain Belt Park, featuring a fountain from the brewery's well of "perfect brewing water," was dedicated in the summer of 1963 and immediately became a focus of social life in the neighborhood. The park won the Men's Garden Club Award in 1964 (though it is tempting to wonder whether their votes were influenced by a cool drink at the Friendship Room). Many longtime residents still remember going to the park to see the tame deer on Sunday after Mass or on other special occasions. The Grain Belt deer were in the news much more often than deer should be. In October 1964 a couple of local residents killed two of the deer

Items such as this napkin advertised Hamm's sponsorship of Minnesota Twins baseball broadcasts. FROM THE AUTHOR'S COLLECTION.

WIN! TWINS!

Hamm's...
Your ticket to TWINS baseball on TV and Radio

From the land of sky blue waters.

Little League baseball was only one of the community activities sponsored by Schell's, which did everything from hosting festivals to donating broken wooden beer cases for homecoming bonfires. COURTESY OF AUGUST SCHELL BREWING COMPANY.

Jacob Schmidt Brewing Company sponsored a marching band that won the national marching band championship in 1939 and 1940. Their distinctive uniforms included beadwork created by members of the Ojibwa nation. After the group was disbanded in the 1950s, the uniforms were donated to a high school, where the sizes were altered to fit the younger musicians. Few uniforms are known to exist today, and the headdress pictured is one of perhaps two survivors. FROM THE COLLECTION OF DAVE DAVIS.

for their meat. (They were caught and prosecuted.) A year later, a farmer taking the (new) deer back to their home farm near Lake City had a fatal truck accident, and the deer escaped into the countryside.

The Grain Belt Concert Park hosted a series of concerts for several summers, beginning in 1965. Charitable contributions by the brewers even encompassed matters of life and death. Fitger Brewing Company of Duluth donated a super-centrifuge to the College of St. Scholastica for use in testing cancerous tissue.[13]

St. Paul's most prosperous brewing families set up foundations to offer long-term support to worthy causes in the community. The Hamm Foundation was founded in 1952 and started by creating a program of scholarships for the children of brewery employees. The Hamm Memorial Psychiatric Clinic was founded in 1954; its current goal is "improving the mental health of adults in the culturally diverse Twin Cities Metropolitan area, particularly those unable to afford the full cost of mental health care." The Communication Center, conceived in 1953, provides a variety of services for the blind, including recording Talking Books and transcribing texts into Braille. The Otto Bremer Foundation supports a variety of educational, medical, and charitable efforts in Minnesota, Wisconsin, North Dakota, and Montana.[14]

Cold Beer Here!

The switch from tavern to home consumption generally pleased the large breweries because it maximized their strengths and helped them to push out small and midsize breweries. Sales of canned beer, artificially slowed by material shortages and wartime restrictions, jumped from 15 percent of national sales in 1948 to 30 percent in 1954 and continued to grow steadily throughout the next two decades. While the popularity of one-way bottles grew more slowly at first, the growth was steady and increased sharply during the 1970s. (Today returnable bottles are virtually extinct in the United States.) The increasing popularity of cans and one-way bottles was an advantage to brewers with large and sparsely populated shipping areas because the empties did not have to be shipped back to the brewery at the expense of the consumer or distributor. (Nor did bar and restaurant owners need to use valuable space to store empties.)

Perhaps even more important, as more people bought their beer in stores, brewers were able to use what they had learned about pricing psychology. During the 1920s, when national brands and national chain stores were changing the way Americans shopped, merchandisers discovered that odd-numbered prices moved goods better than even-numbered prices, certain types of displays sold the product better, and various other consumer tendencies that could be used to increase sales. Beer sales in particular were extremely dependent on pricing practices.[15] Sales of six-packs or cases in a store allowed brewers to fine-tune their prices in a way that was impossible with sales by the glass in a bar. The American public had come to expect nickel beer after repeal, and brewers feared an attempt to increase the

Point-of-sale items often focused on price and convenience rather than flavor or quality. FROM THE COLLECTION OF PETE CLURE.

price of a glass of beer to ten cents in the early or mid-1950s would cost millions of dollars in sales. Nonetheless, brewers were facing ever-increasing material costs and taxes that were being raised with every federal or state revenue crisis. At one point, the brewing industry even joined with newspaper publishers, candy companies, soft drink manufacturers, and streetcar companies to advocate the creation of a seven-cent piece to allow for a needed price increase short of doubling the price to a dime.[16] A bar that changed the price of a glass of beer too often was sure to lose customers. In the store, however, brewers could adjust their price quickly and by a little at a time in order to meet a competitor's offer or to attempt to increase market share. Brewers recognized that beer was essentially an impulse purchase, so they introduced ever-more elaborate point-of-sale promotions to advertise the current price and to convince the shopper to take a six-pack (or two or four) home. Marketing research showed brewers that when shopping for the family, the wife purchased the beer more often than the husband (though the husband selected the brand three times as often).[17] As a consequence, brewers had to modify displays to appeal to women or, at a minimum, to not offend housewives.

A Feeling of Refreshment

One important aspect in which breweries were not competing in any serious way was flavor. The first decade after repeal saw minimal experimentation with recipes—some brewers simply approximated their pre-Prohibition recipes with adaptations as needed to meet the 3.2 percent requirement. The material shortages of World War II, however, led to experimentation with substitute brewing materials: brewers tried nearly anything that would yield a fermentable sugar, including potatoes. The most common and cheapest adjunct was yellow corn. American brewers had known for generations that a beer with some corn in the recipe would be more stable, lighter in taste and color, and yield a better head. Many brewers already utilized some corn, but the necessity of war helped change American tastes permanently. The eagerness with which industry spokesmen adapted to this new reality was philosophical and at times almost unseemly. At one point in 1946, *Brewers Digest* noted that "Comparatively few people want a satiating beer. Perhaps the food value idea in beer should be eliminated. A feeling of refreshment should follow a glass of beer, and not the full-feeling of a heavy meal." An editorial the same year opined:

> Let's be entirely practical about this question of the heaviness and strength of our product. Let's look squarely at the total market—not at just a small portion of it. To be frank many brewers have for a number of years been clinging to the conventional ideas of beer. But it must be pointed out and emphasized that for

every 1,000 beer drinkers we might lose or not fully satisfy among the so-called old-time beer consumers or even among people who are supposed to "know beer," we will probably stand to gain the favor and patronage of 2,000 new consumers from among the present untouched market potentials.[18]

Brewers looking for more customers and new markets were forced to make sure that their flagship beers would not offend anyone rather than seek to brew a unique product. While many breweries continued to release bock beer in the spring and sometimes included an "old-world style" product in their line, the homogenization of American beer was under way. Even the bocks and the so-called old-world brands became blander over time. Sometimes the bock was simply the flagship brand with food coloring added.[19]

Schmidt was the first major Minnesota brewer to publicize a concession to the new reality (Hamm's recipe was already a proven national winner). In the summer of 1949, Schmidt introduced a new "lighter, dryer beer" along with a new look for its labels and packaging. While the new product was generally well received, the company went through a period of rapidly changing management and as a consequence was inconsistent in promoting the product. The inability to jump to the next largest category of brewers made Schmidt a likely takeover target (see below). The next to take the plunge was the maker of Grain Belt. After rapid growth during the late 1930s, Minneapolis Brewing experienced a fifteen-year period of stagnation. A two-week strike in 1955 shocked the company into change. Frank D. Kiewel succeeded his father as president, Frank Mathes (of postwar European brewery rehabilitation fame) took over as brewmaster, and they made the decision to lighten the recipe. Evaluating the decision after twelve years of significant growth, the *Omaha World-Herald* reported:

Grain Belt has become a bland beer and Mr. Kiewel believes this is a major reason for the 12-year sales success. He commented: "The big successes among regional beers in the Western United States are Coors, Olympia, and Grain Belt. The big thing they have in common is that they are milder than competing beers. Young people, those between 21 and 35, represent the biggest consumers of beer by far." As they come of beer drinking age after a young lifetime of milkshakes, Cokes and candy bars, "there is a much easier transition to our type of product than to a bitter beer."[20]

As a result of these changes, and corresponding ones by breweries all over the country, beer became something that was distinguished by its image rather

While small breweries continued to brew bock beers, companies on limited budgets often could not afford to design unique labels. Instead, they had the brewery name overprinted on stock labels, as can be seen from these examples. The Altoona label is from before 1950; the "Internal Revenue Tax Paid" statement was not required after that year. The Kiewel label is from the 1950s but is noteworthy because Kiewel's bock was only 3.2 percent alcohol. FROM THE AUTHOR'S COLLECTION.

than by its taste. As Roy Kumm of G. Heileman Brewing Company (a major rival of Minnesota brewers in many markets) noted, "The industry has remarkable product control. I don't know of any bad beer."[21] This meant that the battle for supremacy would be fought with dollars and the media saturation they bought rather than with appeals to taste. As the *Minneapolis Tribune* put it, "The road to success is paved with advertising dollars."

Beating the Odds

There was no margin for error. The number of breweries had been nearly halved from 466 in 1948 to 240 in 1958. During the same time, the average net profits of the nation's breweries dropped from 7 percent to less than 1 percent per year.[22] No longer could the battle be won by buying saloons to guarantee the home market. The battle would have to be won through territorial expansion.

Hamm's

To survive in the post-war brewing world, a firm needed to expand markets and then expand capacity to spread costs (especially the dramatically higher taxes and advertising costs) over as many barrels as possible. The Minnesota brewery best positioned to make the necessary investments was Hamm's. Not only did it have solid cash flow and reserves, it had gained additional exposure through its government contracts during World War II. During the late 1940s, Hamm moved into Texas and New York, and increased its advertising in national magazines. As noted above, the company paid special attention to the Kansas City and Chicago markets, large urban areas that did not have their own major national breweries. But two states with rapidly increasing populations drew even more attention: Florida and California. Florida was an attractive market for northern brewers because Florida had few significant local breweries and because vacationers fleeing the snow and cold could be counted on to look for familiar brands from home. But the most important new market was California. Unlike Florida, California had several prominent existing breweries. But in 1953–1954, Hamm purchased the San Francisco plant of Rainier Brewing Company and became one of four national brewers to begin production in California. (Anheuser-Busch and Schlitz built new plants, and Pabst bought an existing facility at about the same time.) A few years later, in 1957, Hamm bought the former Rheingold plant in Los Angeles. Even before the fame of the Hamm's Bear had begun to spread (see page 162), Hamm had become one of the largest breweries in the country and ranked as high as fifth at the end of 1956.

Brewing science had advanced to where a brand brewed using local water in plants widely scattered around the country would taste virtually identical. This gave an advantage to multiplant brewing companies that could reduce shipping costs (and sometimes taxes) by producing near their markets. It was also possible to buy existing breweries and save millions in construction costs. Hamm's

Hamm's purchase of the Gunther brewery was not a financial success, but Hamm's was able to expand its sponsorship of major league sports to new markets. FROM THE AUTHOR'S COLLECTION.

purchase of the former Gunther Brewery in Baltimore and its lease of the Gulf Brewing plant in Houston seemed ideal choices based on geography and cost. However, these two expansions were as problematic as the California efforts were successful. While the Houston effort was simply a failure that ended after four years of indifferent sales and arguments with Hughes Tool (owner of Gulf Brewing), the Baltimore venture was a disaster. Despite saturation media coverage, Hamm's did not sell well in the Chesapeake region and the company was resented for eliminating the locally popular Gunther label. Hamm absorbed a $6 million loss that made the financial situation of the company shakier than it had been for decades.[23] Meanwhile, Hamm was losing ground in its home market to two companies that needed it to survive, Minneapolis Brewing and Schmidt.

Grain Belt

For people in small- and medium-sized cities from western Illinois to the Rocky Mountains, Grain Belt was a national brand. Perhaps fittingly, given the name of

"From the land of sky blue waters . . . wah-a-ters"

To Minnesotans of the baby boom generation, the radio and television jingle for Hamm's beer became something like a password—a true Minnesotan would always echo back "waters" in the manner of the jingle if someone else started the song. Though originally composed for radio ads, the jingle is linked to the immortal Hamm's Bear for many. Often included on lists of best or most memorable advertising campaigns, the bear became so popular that a Minneapolis newspaper printed a schedule of when the television ads were to be run so viewers wouldn't miss them. The oafish yet lovable Bear found himself in a number of capers where he was outwitted by smaller forest animals but remained cheerful in defeat nonetheless. Despite his clumsiness, he participated in nearly every sport and outdoor activity, often with disastrous consequences.

The Bear was the product of the Campbell-Mithun advertising agency of Minneapolis, but the precise creator of the idea is unknown. Different accounts variously credit Howard Swift, Cleo Hovel, or Albert Whitman with the original conception of the Bear around 1953. Whatever the case, by the end of the 1950s, the Bear appeared on television commercials, billboards, newspaper ads, sports schedules, placemats, and point-of-sale displays. The Bear also appeared on promotional giveaways such as key chains, cigarette lighters, banks, playing cards, and other items.

The Bear gradually became less important in advertising campaigns after the brewery changed hands in 1965. However, the Bear was brought "out of hibernation" in 1972 after company executives became convinced that dropping the Bear had been a mistake. But an attempt to recapture sales in established markets led to the creation in 1973 of a new style of Bear, Theodore H. Bear, who was no longer bumbling, but an eloquent corporate "spokescritter." This campaign lasted only a few months before Theodore H. Bear was replaced by a real bear, Sasha, and his trainer, Earl Hammond. The bumbling Bear returned in the late 1970s and was used in advertising by the latest owner, Pabst, into the 1990s.

By the mid-90s, however, Hamm's was no longer a major brand, and Pabst had become a "virtual" brewery that brewed under contract at other breweries and had little money to spend on advertising. The Hamm's Bear is kept alive today primarily by the Hamm's Club, a nationwide organization of collectors and enthusiasts that maintains a Web site, publishes a newsletter, sponsors events, and, perhaps most significantly, commissions and sells new commemorative Hamm's Bear items each year. This is an indication of the devotion the Bear inspired in his fans: few if any other advertising characters have been kept alive so vibrantly after the disappearance of the originating company.

The best single source of information on the Hamm's Bear and other Hamm's advertising is *The Paws of Refreshment: The Story of Hamm's Beer Advertising*, by Moira F. Harris (Pogo Press, 2000), from which this brief summary is drawn. 🐾

During its heyday, it seemed like the Hamm's Bear was everywhere. The Bear appeared on parade floats in local celebrations such as the Minneapolis Aquatennial and the St. Paul Winter Carnival, but also traveled as far as California for the Rose Parade. FROM THE COLLECTION OF JIM AND RUTH BEATON.

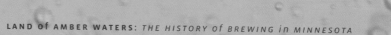

The Starry Skies sign is one of the classic pieces of post–World War II breweriana. It was distributed from about 1957 to 1963. The stars above the north woods lake scene twinkled and eventually formed two distinct constellations in turn: a line of four beer goblets and the Hamm's name. The version pictured here was used primarily in the Midwest. Another version with the legend "Refreshing as the Land of Sky Blue Waters" was used in the eastern market, and a variation that proclaimed "Western Prices" underneath Hamm's Beer was used on the West Coast. The legend "Born in the Land of Sky Blue Waters" was also used on the West Coast. FROM THE COLLECTION OF JIM AND RUTH BEATON.

its flagship beer, Minneapolis Brewing distributed its products from the Upper Peninsula of Michigan through the upper Midwest and even to the West Coast. A large portion of the market was a one-day truck drive from Minneapolis. One exception was the distributorship in Alaska, of which a 1957 article in the *Minneapolis Star* reported, "Salesmen often spend a month traveling to call on four accounts."[24] After the new management and brewery team took over in 1955, the company recorded twelve consecutive years of significant growth and nearly doubled production to almost 900,000 barrels. During the course of this ascent, Minneapolis Brewing focused on its local markets and local image. For many people, Grain Belt was the beer associated with their hunting and fishing expeditions to Minnesota. To build on this image, the company sponsored fishing contests during which distributors offered their warehouses as weigh-in stations.[25]

Despite this, in the mid-1960s, the management made a conscious decision to make a break with the company's local identification. In 1967 the company adopted the name of its flagship product and was renamed Grain Belt Breweries, Inc., bowing to the recognition that the public already used that name for the brewery. But Frank Kiewel gave another reason in *Brewer's Bulletin*:

> In 1967 we are beginning to reach out to new markets at the periphery of our previous major selling areas in Minnesota, North and

South Dakota, Iowa and Wisconsin. In areas outside those states, we are seeking new distributors. We, in turn, are being sought by distributors who want to handle our product. We believe that the old name (Minneapolis Brewing) is too suggestive of a long-ago local business. It does not identify with the name of our product nor does it suggest the widening area of our marketing opportunities. In possible future acquisitions by the company, the total identification of the corporate name with Minneapolis might prove a handicap.[26]

Other brewing observers agreed that the reputation of Minnesota brands was not as good as those from Wisconsin, and anything that blurred the distinction would probably help Minnesota breweries. Roy Kumm of Heileman said that it wouldn't be smart to be specific since "St. Paul has a Sioux City image."[27] (Hamm had eliminated the prominent St. Paul identifier from its label just before its major expansion at the beginning of the 1950s.)

Sure enough, the newly renamed Grain Belt Breweries had expansion plans in the works. Just a few months after the name change, the company announced its plans to lease the former Storz brewery in Omaha, Nebraska, and to brew Grain Belt there for distribution in Kansas, Oklahoma, Colorado, and Arizona. The new plant had a capacity (then substantially underused) of 750,000 barrels per year and 200 employees, nearly all of whom were kept on. Shortly after, Grain Belt exercised its option to buy Storz outright. For the first few years after the purchase, the move appeared brilliant. Growth was up 10 percent in 1967, which was much higher than the average of the rest of the top twenty-five brewers, a group that Grain Belt had just joined. In 1968 sales were up 25 percent, but this report was tempered by the note that earnings were limited, and the reason was a signal of things to come: "higher costs and unusual competitive pricing practices in certain markets by major breweries."[28] By 1970 growth and profits were flattening out. The purchase of the Hauenstein label from the recently defunct New Ulm brewery (see below) and the introduction of GBX malt liquor did little to increase sales but added to expenses. The Omaha plant was closed in 1972 as a cost-saving measure, but the company was still in trouble despite a popular flagship that was number one in the state.

Schmidt, or Introducing Johnny Pfeiffer

In contrast to Hamm and Grain Belt, Schmidt was purchased to be another brewery's extra capacity, but ended up outlasting its original buyer. As noted above, Schmidt had been through some rapid turnover in key positions and had invested a lot of money in improvements. The death of family patriarch Otto Bremer in 1951 also contributed to the directors' decision to seek a buyer. In the early 1950s, Detroit's Pfeiffer Brewing Company was one of the fastest growing breweries in the country

Along the right edge of this Storz label, the identification of the Omaha brewery has been overprinted and the Minneapolis location has been added. This enabled the company to save money by using existing label stock. FROM THE AUTHOR'S COLLECTION.

x

CONTENTS 12 FLUID OUNCES

Storz

Triumph.

BREWED & BOTTLED BY GRAIN BELT BREWERIES, INC., MINNEAPOLIS, MINN.

★ WORLD'S FINEST *Lager Beer* ★

and was looking for additional capacity. In 1954, Pfeiffer purchased Schmidt and used it to introduce its own flagship beer to the area in addition to continuing the Schmidt brands. The introduction of Pfeiffer was a flop, except among college students seeking the cheapest available case of beer, but the crew at the brewery on West Seventh Street began a period during which they routinely proved themselves to be the most efficient brewery in whatever company owned them. In 1962, Pfeiffer Brewing Company changed its name to Associated Brewing Company and purchased three other midsize breweries in the Great Lakes region. Four years later, Associated Brewing closed its home brewery in Detroit because it was not as cost-effective as the other plants, even though the company was making solid profits. Associated Brewing rose as high as tenth in the national rankings in 1969, with sales of almost four million barrels. Unfortunately, Associated Brewing did not have a strong national brand, simply a few good regional labels, and even the introduction of the "big mouth" bottle and Mickey's Malt Liquor were not enough to withstand the fierce advertising and price wars that resulted from Philip Morris's purchase of Miller and Anheuser-Busch's response. Ultimately, Associated Brewing sold the Schmidt plant to G. Heileman Brewing Company of La Crosse in 1972.[29] Again the plant became a leading producer in the far-flung Heileman empire, matching and sometimes beating the home brewery in La Crosse for production and efficiency. In addition to the Schmidt products, the brewery produced several other brands in the Heileman portfolio, including Blatz and Old Style. While Schmidt and Old Style were still brewed with their old recipes, most of what was ultimately shipped from the West Seventh brewery was Schmidt, no matter what the label read. Even though it was under out-of-state ownership, the Schmidt brewery remained a Minnesota institution and was a major sponsor of the state's sports teams, especially the new Minnesota North Stars professional hockey team. Brewery employees in all different positions praised Russell Cleary of Heileman for running the company well during his time as president. [30]

The Casualties

While the big three were expanding, most of the remaining breweries in Minnesota were unable to survive. The ultimate reason for closing was different in nearly every case, but for most the root cause was debt brought on by having to cut prices in times of rising expenses and by having to expand and advertise to compete. (For more about these breweries, see their respective entries in the "Minnesota Breweries" section of this book.)

One of the last nineteenth century–style breweries in the nation closed in 1955 when Fred Beyrer decided to retire. He had been brewing in Chaska for about three decades (not counting Prohibition) and ran the smallest brewery in the state. He did not bottle or can his beer—he only sold kegs to local taverns—and was the only officer (or employee) listed in brewing directories.

Falls Breweries, Goodhue County Brewing Co. of Red Wing, Yoerg Brewing Co. of St. Paul, Peoples Brewing Co. of Duluth, and Kiewel Brewing Co. of Little Falls were all casualties

When Peoples Brewing Co. of Duluth closed in 1957, it left behind a brand that survived into the twenty-first century. The malt liquor now named Olde English 800 was first brewed in Duluth under the name Olde English 600. It first appeared in 1948 as Ruff's Stout (left bottle), though it bore little resemblance to a true English or Irish stout. The early 1950s cone-top can at left is particularly rare. The flat-top at right was issued by Bohemian Breweries of Spokane, Washington. The brand later went to Henry Weinhard of Portland, Oregon, and then to Wisconsin, where it became part of the Pabst family of brands. FROM THE COLLECTION OF PETE CLURE.

of high costs and overwhelming competition during the 1950s. Some members of the Duluth brewing community suggested combining the operations of the three Duluth breweries to save money. The "three R" plan (Rex, Regal, and Royal brands) probably would not have saved Peoples, which closed in 1957.[31] The Kiewel plant would have a brief reprieve from 1959 to 1961, when it served as a branch of Minneapolis Brewing Company dedicated to producing the "cheap beer," White Label, but the brewery was too inefficient and was soon closed.

In 1964 two century-old, family-owned breweries closed within a few months of each other. Faribault's Ernst Fleckenstein Brewing, with a capacity of around 20,000 barrels per year, was believed to be the smallest brewery left in the nation when it closed in the spring. Its dwindling market was certainly not due to a lack of advertising—the Fleckenstein brewery created a collection of breweriana that was worthy of the major shipping brewers. Orpha Fleckenstein, the widow of a grandson of founder Ernst Fleckenstein, was the head of the company when it finally went bankrupt.[32]

The other brewery to close that year—Gluek of Minneapolis—drew much more attention on its way out. Gluek had been a major competitor in the region before Prohibition; it developed Stite, the first malt liquor; it was an active promoter of brewing research; and it had created popular and award-winning advertising campaigns. However, Gluek's capacity of 250,000 barrels made it just the wrong size to be efficient, and the brewery had neither the money nor the room to expand. Despite this, Gluek products were sold in twenty-seven states, and Stite had a well-developed reputation (though the reputation was not all good, considering its nickname, Green Death). The brewery had been struggling to adapt to changing technology and delayed adopting new can styles until the latest possible moment. In 1963, Gluek was unable to adopt the new snap-lid or zip-top cans because it would have been too expensive to make the change. Late in 1964, Gluek sold all its assets to an even older brewery, G. Heileman. Unlike the usual acquisitions in which the buyer offered public statements expressing hope to maintain the purchased facility, Heileman announced the plant would be razed "in the near future," though the staff would be retained. Charles Gluek, the sixth member of his family to head the brewery, said that it was "impossible for a small brewery to actively compete with the price cutting by the national breweries" and that they were unable to absorb "staggering production cost increases."[33]

The passing of Mankato Brewing Company was much more prolonged. After it incurred a large debt burden by buying the Jordan brewery (see previous chapter), it tried numerous approaches to stay afloat. It was one of about a dozen small brewers across the nation that joined a group in the late 1940s to produce and

A portion of the Gluek Brewing Company plant near Marshall Street and Twentieth Avenue Northeast during demolition in 1966. PHOTOGRAPH BY NORTON & PEEL; COURTESY OF THE MINNESOTA HISTORICAL SOCIETY.

market the Brewers' Best label—an attempt to create a national brand for small brewers that lasted less than five years. In 1951, Cold Spring Brewing Company bought Mankato Brewing Company and the Jordan brewery and eliminated the Kato flagship brand. Mankato Brewing Company regained its independence and got its brand back in 1954, but the company was never on solid financial footing. During the last few years, production was sporadic, and the brewery finally closed its doors in 1967, 110 years after the Bierbauer family began to brew on the site.[34]

The final casualty among the small breweries in the 1960s was Peter Bub Brewery of Winona. Despite being a twenty-minute drive from the massive Heileman brewery in La Crosse, Wisconsin, Bub's had survived since Prohibition by serving the local market and keeping prices low. However, a number of factors finally caught up with this small brewery at the end of the 1960s. According to brewmaster and president Carlus Walter, the combination of Congress eliminating the small brewer tax break, the cost of implementing new federal safety and health standards (OSHA), the inability to expand the brewery in its location against Sugar Loaf Bluff, and the flood of competitors that came in after the closing of the brewery in Fountain, Wisconsin, all made it too costly to continue.[35] (The ends of Duluth Brewing & Malting, Fitger, and Hauenstein are covered in the individual brewery histories.)

The Vanishing Giants

Minnesota's largest brewers were just as vulnerable to cost increases, price pressure, and changing legislation as their smaller cousins. In 1964, Hamm began to look for buyers. In January 1965, an agreement was announced between Hamm and Montreal's Molson Breweries. However, the U.S. Justice Department held that the merger would violate antitrust law and threatened a lawsuit if the deal went through. After another attempted purchase by a brewer failed, this time by Rheingold of New York, Hamm was sold in October to the drinks and food firm Heublein of Hartford, Connecticut. Hamm sales rose immediately after the sale, but soon declined and the company actually lost money in 1971. The next decades would see the once-mighty brewery bounced from company to company. A group of Hamm distributors bought the company from Heublein in 1971 but were undercapitalized and were forced to sell the brewery in 1975 to Olympia Brewing Company of Washington. In 1983 Pabst purchased the Olympia holdings, but then traded the St. Paul brewery to Stroh's as part of a complex deal to avoid antitrust action. As a strange result of this deal, the Hamm Brewery made Stroh's products while Hamm's brands were brewed in Milwaukee by Pabst and

The Brewers' Best experiment was intended to give small regional brewers a label with national market potential and to help them save money by using mass-produced advertising pieces. However, consumers may have been unwilling to develop loyalty to a generic-sounding product. FROM THE COLLECTION OF KEN MALZ.

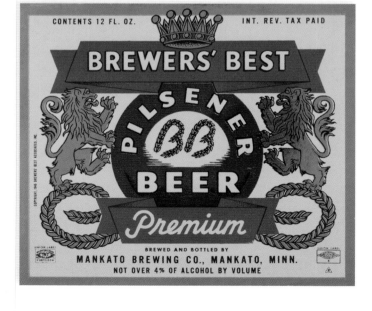

its successor holding companies.[36] While the brewery continued to operate until 1997, many Minnesotans thought that the special bond with Hamm disappeared when Heublein bought it and the subsequent string of out-of-town owners continued. The Hamm's Bear was phased out, and while he was eventually brought back, for most people it just wasn't the same. As beloved as the Bear was to many, Moira Harris has noted in *The Paws of Refreshment* that popular commercials didn't always lead to increased sales. Nor did the series create a crystal clear link to Minnesota: while researching for this book, I found otherwise well-informed Chicago residents who assumed Hamm's was a Wisconsin beer. Roy Kumm's statement on confusion between Wisconsin and Minnesota brands clearly had some merit.

For Grain Belt, the decline was not so protracted. In 1972, the company reported that sales were down for the first half of the year because of "unseasonable weather." However, more was wrong than just the weather. In November of that year, Grain Belt filed complaints against Anheuser-Busch and Schlitz for their pricing practices in Nebraska and Iowa. The cost cutting and the inflationary pressures of the mid-1970s combined to undermine the company's finances and forced the brewery to seek a buyer. In 1975 Minneapolis businessman Irwin Jacobs purchased Grain Belt. Less than a year later, the labels and some assets of the company had been sold to G. Heileman and the brewery was closed down. The Grain Belt label languished at Heileman, possibly because the people responsible for selling it were Grain Belt's former bitter rivals at the Schmidt brewery.[37]

By 1983 Minnesota was left with four breweries, and rival Wisconsin companies owned the three largest Minnesota brands. Somehow two small breweries, Schell and Cold Spring, had managed to survive the dance of the elephants and were poised to make a comeback. They would soon be joined by a host of new brewers who wanted to make distinctive beers as well as money.

When the last can of Royal 58 rolled off the line in 1966, an employee with a sense of history marked the can and saved it as a reminder of a business that had employed residents of Duluth since its founding seventy years earlier. The brewery was soon razed to make way for Interstate Highway 35. FROM THE COLLECTION OF PETE CLURE.

Since the 1930s, Minnesota's brewers have generally cooperated to encourage consumers to purchase local brands. This bumper sticker dates to between 1972 and 1975, after the closing of Fitger but before the closing of Grain Belt. COURTESY OF THE MINNESOTA HISTORICAL SOCIETY.

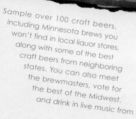

A FALL COLOR TOUR YOU CAN DRINK

Sample over 100 craft beers, including Minnesota brews you won't find in local liquor stores, along with some of the best craft beers from neighboring states. You can also meet the brewmasters, vote for the best of the Midwest, and drink in live music from

AUTUMN
BREW
REVIEW
2002

artists as colorful as the season. $20 advance admission ($25 at the door) includes beer, entertainment and a commemorative glass for the first 1,500 ticket buyers. call Ticket Works at 612-343-3390 or order at www.ticketworks.com.

SPONSORED BY THE MINNESOTA CRAFT BREWER'S GUILD (WWW.MNCRAFTBREW.ORG) AND THE MINNEAPOLIS DOWNTOWN COUNCIL

The Autumn Brew Review has become a popular event with beer lovers from around the region. Minnesota's breweries and brewpubs, along with breweries from other states, offer samples of their finest brews. FROM THE AUTHOR'S COLLECTION.

The Waters Turn Dark Amber

I think it can honestly be said that there has never been a better time to drink beer
in America than the present. And the future looks even brighter.
—Randy Mosher, *Radical Brewing*, 2004

I N THE LATE 1970S AND EARLY 1980S, THE BREWING INDUSTRY HAD SHRUNK
to about sixty breweries nationwide, about the same number in Minnesota
alone at the turn of the century. Schmidt, Grain Belt, and Hamm's continued
to be the three biggest sellers in the state, but Budweiser, Miller, and even Coors
were steadily eating away at their market share. The introduction of light beer
in the early 1970s put an additional burden on Minnesota's two large brewers,
because massive amounts of advertising were required to compete against the
major brewers' light beers and the cash-strapped owners were seldom able to
support their new line extensions. Hamm's Special Light, Grain Belt Light, and
Schmidt Light all appeared on the shelves, but none ever developed much of a
following. Some local drinkers considered the idea of Hamm's Light redundant
since the beer had such a light formula in the first place. Lite Beer from Miller
and later entries Bud Light and Coors Light dominated the draught beer accounts
and event sponsorships, effectively driving every other light beer to the fringes of
the market (along with many premium labels). However, another movement was
under way that would bring new opportunities for existing breweries and inspire
the first new breweries in Minnesota in half a century.

While not as dramatic or universal as the forces that shaped the price-conscious
bland lager culture of the 1950s, 1960s, and 1970s, social trends helped pave the
way for more expensive and distinctive beers. During the Reagan administration,
the relatively strong dollar made it cheaper for Americans to travel to Europe and
sample the historic beer styles of traditional brewing centers. Many American
beer lovers visiting Britain were inspired by the Campaign for Real Ale (CAMRA),
which was created in reaction to the consolidation of British breweries and the

As the craft beer movement looked back to historic brewing methods, a few attempts were made to bring back historic brands such as Fitger's. This attractive commemorative package sold by the Huber Brewing Company of Monroe, Wisconsin, in 1986 was not enough to make the brand successful. FROM THE COLLECTION OF PETE CLURE.

disappearance of cask-conditioned ales in favor of the cheaper force-carbonated "keg bitter." The strong dollar made European beers cheaper to import as well. The prosperity of the upper middle and upper classes during the Reagan years led to the yuppie, whose willingness to spend heavily on luxury items helped create the market for more expensive beers. This trend spread to a larger segment of the public through what one beer industry writer called the need for "badges." As Philip Van Munching (whose family's company imported Heineken) put it, the average person couldn't afford the BMW or the Armani wardrobe, but "imported beer is a badge, a status symbol. And it is an affordable one." Bottled beer was a better badge than draught beer because it was easier for everyone to see who had chosen the most expensive beer, and who therefore must have the best taste (or the most disposable income).[1]

Another trend inspired at least in part by the willingness to spend a little more, but more dependent on the environmental movement, was the return toward locally produced goods. For about a century after the Civil War, Americans had been conditioned by advertising to think that national brands were better, more consistent, and more prestigious. Anything imported from outside was considered better than the homemade article. After repeal, this rationale often applied to beer as well. Small-town breweries were often caught between the gratitude of the local population for jobs and the reluctance to buy their beer because "it isn't any good," or "it gives you gas," or any of the other complaints about the local product. (Most of the problems attributed to local beer were due to the quantities consumed rather than the product itself, especially because its lower price made it popular with youth and heavy drinkers.) But by the 1970s, Americans became concerned about the disappearance of the family farm, the corner drug store, the ma-and-pa grocery, and other institutions that were seen as an essential part of America's culture and heritage. At the same time, quality-control problems in the American auto industry and other fields made consumers reevaluate the relative value placed on efficiency compared to craftsmanship. One way in which people could "think globally but act locally" was to buy from local producers who produced small quantities using quality ingredients.

Some people with a sense of history sought to revive traditional methods and products that were disappearing as the secrets of their manufacture went to the grave with the passing generation. Bringing back seasonal and regional beer varieties echoed the goals of the Slow Food Movement, which seeks to stem the loss of traditional flavors and ingredients as tastes and production become more homogenized. The relatively small number of Americans who cherished distinctive beers began to create in America a veritable Noah's ark of vanishing beer styles.

As with so many reactions to mass-produced popular American culture, what has since come to be called the craft brewing movement started on the Pacific Coast. The craft brewing revolution was led by three different types of breweries: small community breweries that had survived the consolidation and developed different beer styles to create a unique selling point, new microbreweries, and brewpubs. In addition, some larger breweries, including St. Paul's two surviving plants, became "contract brewers," using some of their spare capacity to brew beer for other companies. Some of these contractors were restaurants that wanted a house beer, some were beer marketing companies that had no plants of their own, and some were microbrewers who needed packaging facilities or emergency extra capacity.

All four of Minnesota's surviving commercial breweries brewed beer for other companies: Stroh's brewed the Augsburger line of beer during the 1990s in the old Hamm brewery; Schell made the house beers for Sweeney's Saloon in St. Paul; and Minnesota Brewing brewed the Pete's Wicked products. Apollo Lager was produced at Minnesota Brewing and packaged in its award-winning blue bottle. The beer was much better than might have been expected from a product clearly intended to sell based on its packaging. FROM THE AUTHOR'S COLLECTION.

The Survivors

In 1965 Fritz Maytag (of the appliance family) learned that the brewer of his favorite beer, Anchor Steam, was about to close. Minnesota native Joe Allen had helped keep the brewery alive as a brewmaster and a partner in the business since just after repeal, but the same pressures that were forcing smaller breweries across the country to close were about to take their toll on Anchor. Maytag purchased a controlling interest in the brewery and by 1969 owned it outright. Not only did Maytag continue production of the brewery's signature steam beer, but by 1975 he had introduced other traditional styles such as porter, pale ale, barleywine, and an annual Christmas beer with different artistic labels every year.[2] Maytag's continued success at Anchor demonstrated to other brewers the potential in seeking new markets instead of trying to compete directly with the national brewers and their mainstream lagers.

Cold Spring/Gluek Brewing Company

During the late 1940s and the 1950s, Cold Spring Brewing Company was regarded by brewing industry analysts as one of the best models of how a small brewery could survive in the face of increasing industry consolidation. During World War II the brewery was insolvent, but within a few years, president Myron C. Johnson and his team had turned the brewery around, made it profitable, and begun an expansion program. By 1951 Cold Spring Brewing was in such a solid position that it was able to buy Mankato Brewing Company, a brewery of the same capacity as Cold Spring. Cold Spring divested itself of the Mankato branch a few years later, but without taking a substantial loss and only after reestablishing the Mankato brewery in its market. Johnson and Cold Spring were the subjects of several profiles in the brewing press, and Johnson was a popular speaker at industry meetings.

According to Johnson, the secret to Cold Spring's survival boiled down to being competent and efficient. The company hired experienced brewers to maintain quality, carefully calculated delivery routes to make the best use of time and vehicles, and insisted on cash payments (except from municipal liquor stores). Cold Spring emphasized its "Own Back Yard" and kept advertising to a minimum, using only point-of-sale pieces and local radio sports broadcasts.[3]

Throughout the 1960s and 1970s, little changed at Cold Spring. It continued to emphasize local sales and created special regional brands like Arrowhead and Western in an attempt to build local followings in other nearby regions. The brewery did contract brewing for the Amish community in Amana, Iowa, among several other clients. Cold Spring had some degree of protection from the woes of the typical small brewer because it had a profitable sideline with a bottled mineral water that scored high in national taste tests. Ironically, Cold Spring traded the rights to Cold Spring Mineral Water to Heileman in 1980 for the rights to the Gluek brands. Two decades later, this deal would give Cold Spring a recognizable flagship, but in the short term it created problems. When Heileman decided to

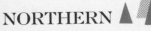

OTHER "REPUTATION BRANDS"
BREWED BY COLD SPRING . . . . ,

NORTHERN

The NORTHERN brand was for many years produced by a respected regional brewery in Wisconsin; it was acquired by Cold Spring Brewing Company to carry on the admirable NORTHERN reputation and to make it available over a broader market in a series of packages matched to current consumer preferences.

NORTHERN BEER is produced in coordinated packages of 6-packs of pull-top cans and twist-top one-way bottles, and in cases of 24 returnable bottles.

WESTERN

Cold Spring brews WESTERN BEER for a steadily-growing group of distributors and retailers who have found a favorable public response to its hearty flavor and attractive appearance. Each label is an unusual exhibit of cattle-brands symbolizing the Cold Spring family of beers.

WESTERN is packaged in cases of 24 returnable bottles, and in 6-packs of colorful cans.

To advertise its brands to distributors, Cold Spring produced this brochure showing the different packages available. FROM THE AUTHOR'S COLLECTION.

produce Cold Spring brand water at its La Crosse brewery, Cold Spring had to rename its water North Star. As the market for American lagers became ever more dominated by the big national brands, Cold Spring was forced to cut prices to maintain sales volume, and the brewery began to struggle. As a cost-cutting move, Cold Spring stopped brewing its own beer and instead brought in wort from the Schmidt brewery to be fermented and packaged.[4] By the mid 1990s, Cold Spring sold for $6.99 per case of twenty-four returnable bottles. Priced a dollar or two less than a case of Old Milwaukee, Cold Spring became a favorite of impoverished college students, but slow sales meant that a lot of old beer was on the shelves and the brand's reputation suffered even more. In 1994 Cold Spring, a plant with a capacity of 100,000 barrels, sold fewer than 3,000 barrels of its own brands. The brewery that a decade earlier provided jobs to eighty-five people was down to about thirty employees.

Even as craft brewing began to emerge in the marketplace, Cold Spring was not able to do much more than survive. The company acquired some much-needed exposure when Charles Finkel chose Cold Spring Export to be the standard American lager in his Merchant du Vin portfolio of nationally distributed brands, but this was not enough to pull the brewery out of its slump. Many of the contract beers that Cold Spring produced turned out to be dead ends as well. Instead of Pete's Wicked Ale or other beers that had a distinctive flavor and generated repeat business, Cold Spring ended up with a number of novelty beers like Elvira Beer (featuring the image of the briefly famous Mistress of the Dark character). Cold Spring was one of four brewers of the ultimate in novelty brands, Billy Beer, allegedly formulated according to the tastes of the brother of President Jimmy Carter.

Merchant du Vin introduced Cold Spring Export to a nationwide market in the 1980s. The need to include the bottle deposit amounts for nine different states, a bar code, and an explanation of what exactly this beer was resulted in a crowded label. FROM THE AUTHOR'S COLLECTION.

In 2005 Gluek Brewing Company of Cold Spring became one of the first breweries to use the Alum-A-Bottle. Like the old cone-top cans, it allows breweries to use existing bottling lines. This package chills faster than bottles and can be taken to places where glass containers are banned. As of this writing, the Alum-A-Bottle is used for the four products in the Stite family of beers: Light Lager, Amber Red Reserve, Black & Tan, and Golden Pilsner. COURTESY OF GLUEK BREWING COMPANY.

(Sorry, but that twelve-pack of Billy Beer cans with eleven still full isn't valuable—nearly everyone who bought a twelve-pack still has eleven full cans.) Even with the more distinctive beers, the name usually overshadowed the beer: Red Ass Ale, Bad Frog, Goat's Breath, and Naked Aspen. The management at Cold Spring was not responsible for many of these problems, since the marketers came to Cold Spring rather than the other way around. But a brewery makes less money from contract brewing than from selling its own brands, and though contract brewing helps a brewery pay the bills, it is seldom the road to growth.[5]

In 1995, following a 57 percent decline in sales of its own brands over four years, the brewery was sold to investors from Colorado. The group, known first as Pure Colorado and later as Beverage International, apparently hoped to cash in on the hunger for microbrewery stock offerings, but bought Cold Spring at the beginning of a downturn in the sector that made investors wary. In December 1996, Maurice Bryan, the brewery manager, called headquarters in Colorado only to discover that Beverage International had closed up shop and the chief officers had essentially disappeared. Beverage International left behind unpaid water and sewer bills, unpaid property taxes, and worthless paychecks. Payroll taxes had been deducted from the workers' checks but not paid to the government.

A little over a year later, a group of investors put together by Bryan purchased the brewery from the First National Bank of Cold Spring and discharged the unpaid obligations. As part of a move to emphasize the Gluek labels, the new owners renamed the brewery Gluek Brewing Company. At the heart of the revival was the resurrection of the Stite brand, a name that still evoked memories for older drinkers decades after it disappeared from the market.[6] By 2006 the Stite name was used on four beers: Golden Pilsner, Amber Red Reserve, Light Lager, and Black & Tan (none of which was the original malt liquor recipe). These

brands were offered in the new Alum-A-Bottle, a package that re-created the cooling and packaging advantages of the old cone-top can with a more streamlined shape. On the strength of its new flagship brands, Gluek improved the ratio of brewing its own brands to contract brewing and began to show a profit again after years of financial instability. In the past few years, increased contracts for soda and energy drinks have resulted in significant growth and the need to construct new warehouses. Beer is only about 15 percent of Gluek's production volume as of this writing.[7]

August Schell Brewing Company

With the closing of crosstown competitor Hauenstein in 1969, August Schell Brewing Company became the only brewery in southwestern Minnesota. Because the company did not have much outstanding debt, it was free from some of the pressures that affected other breweries, but it still had to sell beer to survive. There was a small, loyal market for Schell's Deer Brand in southern Minnesota, but not enough to run efficiently. So Schell took advantage of the hobby that was verging on a craze in the 1970s: beer can collecting. Schell began to produce commemorative cans from A to X: from the Algona, Iowa, quasquicentennial (125th) anniversary to Xmas Brew, with scores of festival, contract, and collectors' items in between. In many cases, the collectors would open the cans from the bottom and let the beer drain out, so the quality of the beer in the can was not particularly important. (While Schell and other brewers produced some air-filled cans, many collectors do not consider a beer can to be authentic unless there was once beer in it.) At this point, Schell's contract brewing business was based on the container, not the beer.[8]

The growing interest in new specialty beers provided an opportunity for Schell to use some of its excess capacity for something other than can filler. It served as the brewer of the house beers for Sweeney's Saloon in St. Paul, of Whiskey River beer for the St. Peter bar of that name, and of the Ulmer and Hauenstein labels for Arneson Distributing of Sleepy Eye.[9] Schell's contract brewing business did more than simply use excess capacity; it helped establish the brewing team as one of the most capable in the country. The Pete's Wicked line was the most famous of the Schell contract lines, but Schell has at various times brewed the bottled versions of the James Page beers, the Three Floyds brand from Indiana, the Schlafly beers from St. Louis, and beers from other growing and well-regarded microbreweries. Some of these contracts were for as many as 30,000 barrels, a significant portion of the brewery's capacity.[10]

Schell's commemorative cans varied from simple to colorful. The only festival beer that actually bore the Schell's brand was Farmfest, which was held in Schell's home territory. FROM THE AUTHOR'S COLLECTION.

PRECISION GERMAN ENGINEERING

August Schell

Octoberfest BEER

By 1986 Schell was ready to bring out craft beers under its own name. The Pils and Weizen earned rave reviews and immediately gained a following in Minnesota. Because of their price and quality, a number of liquor stores and restaurants listed these beers as imports, and in some cases actually thought they were from Germany. (This was partially because they were distributed nationally by Charles Finkel's importing company, Merchant du Vin.) Beer expert Michael Jackson called the Pils "the best example of the style brewed in America," and the Weizen won awards at numerous competitions.[11] Schell had continued to brew a bock beer throughout the postwar years, but the brewers reformulated it with a more traditional recipe and took advantage of the renewed interest in dark beer. By 1992 the craft beer movement was well established, and the brewery began to extend its line. The first new recipe was Schmaltz's Alt, based on a German amber style. Eventually Schell featured several year-round beers and a rotating selection of seasonal beers including a Christmas beer, a double bock, and a Mai bock.[12]

In 1999 the brewery undertook a major upgrade of the brewhouse to improve reliability and replace some components that were a century old. Some industry analysts considered this a gamble, but it paid off in 2002 after Schell won the auction for the Grain Belt label, which was sold in the liquidation of Minnesota Brewing Company's assets. The brewery launched an ad campaign called Here's to Local Heroes, which focused on Minnesota's heritage and featured such local icons as former pro wrestler Baron von Raschke, famed stadium vendor Wally the Beerman, and the Juicy Lucy hamburger from Matt's Bar in Minneapolis. Within the next few years, Schell's annual production doubled, mostly on the strength of Grain Belt sales. Schell appears well positioned to survive as an independent brewery with both a line of well-regarded craft beers and a solid mass-market beer to keep production volume high.[13]

Minnesota Brewing Co.

By 1990 G. Heileman Brewing Company of La Crosse, Wisconsin, was in the midst of a major financial crisis. Heileman had been purchased in October 1987 by Alan Bond, an Australian corporate raider. Increased competition and mismanagement caused Heileman's sales to slip badly, though some products were still doing well. Unfortunately, Bond was in the middle of a financial meltdown that would feature the largest one-year loss in the history of Australia (US$1.86 billion) and end with Bond serving prison time for several counts of fraud. The former Schmidt brewery on West Seventh Street in St. Paul and the Grain Belt, Hauenstein, and Stag brands were put up for sale. Despite the attempts of then St. Paul Mayor Jim Scheibel, City Council member Dave Thune, and others, no buyer was found for the brewery by the 23 June 1990 deadline. According to the brewery logbook, the boiler fires were shut off at 9:00 P.M. on June 29, and the conditioning tanks full of fermenting beer were being dumped. A tradition spanning 135 years appeared to be at an end, and the company's workers were out of a job and without benefits.[14]

For more than a year, the brewery remained idle. But in the fall of 1991, a group led by Twin Cities investor Bruce Hendry purchased the brewery, formed Minnesota Brewing Company, and called 150 employees back to work. In December a keg-tapping ceremony was held for the new brewery's inaugural product, Landmark Premium Beer. The initial reaction to Landmark and Landmark Light was lukewarm at best, but the reception was much more positive for the next product, Pig's Eye Pilsner, introduced in May 1992. Pilsner, soon joined by Amber, Ice, Non-Alcoholic, and the cleverly named Lean Pig's Eye light beer, was a low-price beer that featured a roguish character on the label and took its name from the legendary bootlegger who settled at the site of St. Paul. By mid-June, the brewery was completely sold out of Pig's Eye, much to the relief of the company, which had a backlog of more than 100,000 cases of Landmark on hand.[15]

Minnesota Brewing Company also began a major effort to revitalize the Grain Belt brands, which had been purchased along with the brewery. By the end of 1993, Grain Belt made a significant comeback, and in 1994 it won the Gold Medal in the American Lager category at the Great American Beer Festival in Denver. Grain Belt replaced Landmark as the brewery's flagship brand, and Landmark was licensed to a Chinese brewery.[16]

Despite the popularity of the Pig's Eye products, the brewery was not selling enough of its own brands to allow the two million barrel capacity brewery to operate at peak efficiency. Minnesota Brewing became one of the largest contract brewers in the country, brewing labels ranging from Pete's Wicked Ale to Rhino Chasers to 90s Choice, a beer marketed to homosexual drinkers and named after a popular bar in Minneapolis. Clients interested in marketing a new brand of beer came to the brewery, described the type of beer they wanted to brewmaster Sig Plagens (or brought in a sample of what they wanted the beer to taste like), and the brewing crew created a recipe to match. At one point in 1994, the brewery added a second shift of workers to meet the demand for bottling contracts and exhausted the hiring list of those put out of work by the closing of Heileman four years before. The brewery did the job well: Coyote Amber, marketed by Black Moon Brewing Company, won a gold medal at the 1996 Great American Beer Festival, and brewing publications speculated that other Minnesota Brewing

Brewery Preservation

Of the 250-odd historic breweries known to have operated in Minnesota, about two dozen still stand to some extent. Of these, August Schell and Gluek are the only functioning commercial breweries, though the Fitger brewery briefly hosted Lake Superior Brewing Company and today contains Fitger's Brewhouse. Several breweries have been converted to residences and appear to be in little danger of being torn down. These include the breweries in Glencoe, Preston, and Sleepy Eye; Hauenstein in New Ulm; and Schutz & Hilgers in Jordan. Others, such as Park Brewing Co. and Peter Bub Brewing Co. in Winona, have been used for commercial purposes. The restoration of the Minneapolis Brewing Company brewhouse by RSP Architects was a triumph, but took a quarter of a century to bring about.

The two largest breweries in St. Paul, Hamm and Schmidt, present challenges for the preservationist. Both are extremely large properties that would require either a very large development or splitting the property into sections. Parts of both breweries have been used for industrial purposes since they closed. However, parts of both also have been burglarized and vandalized since they closed, and one of the oldest sections of the Hamm plant suffered a fire in 2005. Ten Minnesota breweries, including Schell, have buildings on the National Register of Historic Places, though Hamm and Schmidt are not among them as of this writing. Groups of citizens have worked to preserve much of both breweries, though a viable solution may still be in the future. 🦢

The Jacob Schmidt Brewery on West Seventh Street in St. Paul awaits renovation. PHOTOGRAPH BY ROBERT FOGT.

Company products had earned medals under other names. However, the clients were not always reliable; they sometimes switched breweries, ordered insufficient cans, bottles, or labels, or simply went bankrupt. The brewery was often left with tanks full of beer they could not package or sell.[17]

The next several years were filled with ups and downs for Minnesota Brewing Company as the firm struggled to make a steady profit. In August 1997, a day after announcing a record loss, the company signed a deal to sponsor sporting events at the University of Minnesota and even won a battle with Miller over exclusive rights, but the deal was later shortened to address concerns about sending inappropriate messages to students about drinking. Minnesota Brewing stood to benefit from a contract between Northwest Airlines and James Page Brewing Company to serve Page's beer on flights, but Northwest forced Page to replace Minnesota Brewing Company as contractor in retaliation for Hendry's earlier criticism of Minnesota's financial assistance to the airline. A strike by brewers and bottlers slowed production in the spring of 1999. However, by mid-2000, the brewery was operating three shifts, employing 218 people, and had reported the best quarterly profits since reopening. A plan to manufacture industrial ethanol at the plant promised to share operating costs and bring in additional revenue.[18]

But less than two years later, financial problems caught up with the brewery again. A new bottling line caused the company major problems, and the ethanol plant was the subject of a lawsuit by the city of St. Paul, which was responding to complaints by neighbors concerning odors given off by the manufacturing process. In February 2002 the company filed for bankruptcy, and at the end of June the brewery shut down operations for good. The ethanol plant continued operations until May 2004, and ultimately closed because of financial troubles.[19] As of this writing, the future of the historic buildings is uncertain.

Microbreweries

The first microbrewery was started in 1976 by Jack McAuliffe in Sonoma, California. His New Albion Brewery (after the name Sir Francis Drake gave to California) brewed beers similar to those McAuliffe enjoyed while traveling in Europe. Consistency problems plagued the brewery and it closed after a few years, but New Albion had shown that it was possible for a small brewery to make and, more important, to sell European-style beer. Shortly after New Albion closed, Boulder Brewing Company was started in Colorado and Sierra Nevada Brewing Company was founded in Chico, California, both of which recently celebrated their silver anniversaries and proved that small breweries could stand the test of time.

Industry experts disagree on how big a brewery can be and still be a microbrewery; the line has been drawn anywhere from 2,000 to 35,000 barrels. Some of the original microbreweries are now so large that a new category was created: regional craft brewers. Many brewers prefer not to be forced into categories, but legislatures and revenue departments have created categories for taxation

Summit's Winter Ale is made with a slightly different recipe each year. Despite its spicy aroma and flavor, it is still made according to the Bavarian Reinheitsgebot, which forbids the use of ingredients other than water, malt, hops, and yeast. COURTESY OF SUMMIT BREWING COMPANY.

The packaging for the earliest James Page products emphasized local symbols. The Stone Arch railroad bridge of Minneapolis was depicted in the Private Stock label, and the loon and the bear lent north woods character to the Boundary Waters wild rice beers. FROM THE AUTHOR'S COLLECTION.

purposes. As of 2006, the Minnesota Department of Revenue defines a microbrewery as a brewery producing fewer than 2,000 barrels per year.[20]

The Pioneers

Minnesota's first new brewery since World War II began production in a converted auto parts warehouse on University Avenue in St. Paul. Summit Brewing Company was conceived by Mark Stutrud, a former clinical social worker who was inspired by the idea of brewing the flavorful beers of previous eras. After four years of researching, finding equipment, and cajoling investors, the brewery shipped its first keg across the street to Johnny's Bar on 25 September 1986. The next year, bottled Extra Pale Ale and Great Northern Porter appeared, offering true choices for Minnesotans who wished to support local breweries but wanted to move beyond mass-produced lagers. During the first year, the brewery had three employees and produced 1,300 barrels of beer (compared with the million-plus barrel capacities across town at Hamm and Schmidt). At first the brewery did its own distribution, but after the two labels proved popular, local distributors were willing to take a chance on the newcomers. After five years, production had increased to 8,000 barrels, 70 percent of which was the flagship Extra Pale Ale. By this point, Summit had introduced two seasonal beers, the summertime Sparkling Ale and the stronger, richer Winter Ale. (Sparkling Ale lasted only a few years as the summer seasonal, but Winter Ale gained a substantial following among craft beer fans, some of whom purchase it by the case to guarantee a stock for the long Minnesota winter.)[21]

Meanwhile, in Minneapolis, James Page was refurbishing another former industrial site on Quincy Street Northeast, about a mile east of the vacant Grain Belt brewery. Brewing began in spring 1987, and the first beer was available on draught in October. The first brand was called Saint Anthony Lager, but this pilsner style failed to stand out from the mass-market beers. It was soon replaced by James Page Private Stock, an Oktoberfest-style beer that proved much more distinctive and popular and became the flagship of the Page product line. The brewery also was responsible for the first truly "Minnesotan" beer, a brew made with wild rice called Boundary Waters. A bock version of Boundary Waters was also offered for a few years. James Page also began to brew beers for two Minneapolis restaurants, Palomino and Shelly's Wood Roast. (Ironically, Shelly's Wood Roast was owned by Sheldon Jacobs, brother of Irwin Jacobs, the last owner of Grain Belt Brewing.)[22] The Quincy Street brewery did not have a bottling line, so Page was forced to use Schell and Minnesota Brewing Company facilities for bottled beer.

Summit and James Page had the Minnesota microbrew market to themselves for several years, but they were not without competition from outside. One problem in selling to consumers who are always interested in trying new beers is that they will continue to try new beers without developing strong loyalty to local brands. As liquor stores and distributors noticed the increase in sales of craft and imported beers, they began to increase their selection to facilitate this brand hopping. Beer drinkers who had become fans of a particular beer on a trip to Europe or California or Colorado might now be able to find that beer at large liquor stores in the Twin Cities area. Wisconsin's surviving small breweries, such as Leinenkugel of Chippewa Falls, Huber of Monroe, and Stevens Point Brewery, began to increase distribution of their bock beers in Minnesota during the late winter and early spring. Because most bars would accept only one draught line for a bock, there had always been a struggle to be first, but Leinenkugel pushed the release earlier to catch the lucrative Minnesota market.[23] But the biggest threat came from Jim Koch, who founded the Boston Beer Company in 1985. The beers in his Samuel Adams line were full of flavor, had great patriotic imagery, were available almost everywhere, and were priced high enough to have snob appeal but low enough to compete directly with the local craft products.[24] Right behind Koch was Pete Slosberg, creator of Pete's Wicked Ale. This brand was the first widely distributed American Brown Ale, which was darker and maltier than Summit's Extra Pale Ale or Sam Adams Boston Ale. Pete's was easy to distribute in Minnesota because he brought his homebrew recipe to Schell to be brewed. Both Sam Adams and Pete's had a cost advantage over Summit and Page because they were contract brewers and did not have investments in brewery space and equipment to pay off, as the latter two did. Pete's Wicked products grew so quickly that the company was forced to move its contract from Schell to Minnesota Brewing in St. Paul to accommodate the demand.[25] At the same time, Schell's products were gaining acclaim and competing well in the craft brew segment. Because of the political and regulatory climate, opening a brewery in Minnesota was not as easy as in some nearby states. As a consequence, no new microbreweries opened in Minnesota for almost a decade after Page and Summit. Another source of competition came from imported beers. Several of Minnesota's beer distributors became adept at locating hard-to-find foreign specialties and bringing them to retailers in the larger cities.

Minnesota did have a few brewing companies that contracted their actual production to other breweries, usually to Schell. Stillwater homebrewer Karl Bremer founded St. Croix Brewing Company in 1994 to brew his St. Croix Maple Ale and later his Serrano Pepper Ale. Serrano Pepper Ale won *Chile Pepper* magazine's 1998 Fiery Food Challenge, and Maple Ale claimed to be the first nationally distributed beer incorporating pure maple sugar. Because these two products were unique, they were able to move outside the Minnesota market more quickly than products that had local competitors. Maple Ale was introduced in 1995 and by the end of 1996 was available in twelve states. St. Croix sought distribution arrangements for Serrano Pepper Ale in Colorado, California, and Japan.

Many microbrewers offered their beer in 22-ounce "bomber" bottles, hoping that customers would be more willing to try a new product if they did not have to purchase a six-pack. The larger bottles also saved packaging expenses because no six-pack holders and fewer bottles and caps were required. This St. Croix Maple Ale bottle dates from the mid-1990s. FROM THE AUTHOR'S COLLECTION.

Saloon Brewing Co. was formed in 1986 by Leo Gadbois to create and market house beers for his popular St. Paul watering hole, Sweeney's Saloon. In addition to the several year-round and seasonal beers produced for the saloon, three varieties were bottled: Summer Lager, Kilkenny Lager, and Auburn Dark Lager. These brands were shipped to Florida, Colorado, and Illinois, where the flamingo-themed packaging caught some attention.[26]

The Second Wave

The steady and sometimes spectacular growth in the craft brewing segment encouraged other Minnesotans to start microbreweries in the late 1990s. Most entrepreneurs had done their research during a period of unrestrained expansion but entered production as the growth was beginning to level off. The spurt of openings in the last half of the decade came at a time when some industry analysts believed that craft brewing was a fad whose time had passed. This made financial backers more hesitant and distributors less likely to invest energy in a brand that might not survive, which often became a self-fulfilling prophecy.

Lake Superior Brewing Company was started in 1994, just ahead of the second wave. Located at first in a 400-square-foot room of the old Fitger brewery, it started by serving a small number of local restaurants. By the end of 1998, its production had reached 1,000 barrels, and it needed to expand and install bottling equipment. That winter the brewery moved to new quarters at 2711 West Superior Street, where it remains today. By 2005 production was approaching 2,000 barrels, and the brewery stood to benefit when Duluth mayor Herb Bergson announced in the spring of 2005 that he intended to enforce a little-known law requiring Minnesota beers to be available whenever beer is sold in publicly owned or operated buildings.[27]

The most unusual of the new breweries was Mantorville Brewing Company, formed in 1996 in sight of the caves of the old Ginsberg brewery. The founders were a group of seven homebrewers who decided to go professional, using converted dairy equipment and advice from the staff of Lake Superior Brewing Company. After about a

Some beers are the product of beer marketing companies, which brew under contract at a commercial brewery but handle distribution and promotion themselves. Finnegans Irish Amber was the idea of Jacquie Bergland, who created the concept along with pub owner Kieran Folliard. A portion of the profits go to the Finnegans Community Fund (formerly the Spud Society), which provides grants to organizations helping the working poor. FROM THE AUTHOR'S COLLECTION.

BLARNEY IS NOT AN IRISH DINOSAUR.

FINNEGANS

IRISH AMBER

AS IRISH AS IT GETS.

year of delays, their draught-only Stagecoach Ale was available in fourteen locations in the greater Rochester area. Tod Fyten bought a share of the Mantorville operation in 1999 and has kept the company going with various partners as of this writing.[28]

In contrast to the Mantorville operation, Ambleside Brewing Company of Minneapolis began production with all new equipment in the spring of 1997. Owner David Johnson, a former wine manager at Surdyk's Liquor Store in Minneapolis, started the new brewery in an industrial park near the University of Minnesota with an investment of almost $800,000. Unlike the other microbreweries in the state, Ambleside had its own bottling capability right away. Johnson was the only full-time employee, but he employed four part-time workers to bottle and package the beer. The beers originally offered were Ambleside Pale Ale, Lakeside Cream Ale, and St. Cloud Wheat. (A limited quantity of the test-run brew was made available in bottles under the name Calibration Ale.) Ambleside also brewed Lake Superior Inland Seas Pale Ale under contract. Johnson was well aware of the predictions of microbrewing's imminent demise, but he pointed out that even with the numerous closings, the craft brewing industry was nowhere near as crowded as the craft wine segment. However, cost overruns during construction put the company in financial trouble right from the beginning, and production never reached the goals Johnson set (which some industry observers thought were too high—it took James Page a decade to reach the volume Johnson wanted to reach in the first year). As a consequence, Ambleside closed just over a year after it opened. The equipment was purchased by the Tyranena Brewing Company in Lake Mills, Wisconsin, where it is still in use.[29]

Ambleside's short-lived product line included Pale Ale (not pictured), Lakeside Cream Ale, and St. Cloud Wheat. Lake Superior Inland Seas Pale Ale was brewed under contract for another company. All the products used twist-off caps and came in cardboard cartons to present a premium appearance. A very limited release of the first batch produced by the new brewery was called Calibration Ale because it was brewed to make sure the brewhouse was functioning properly. FROM THE AUTHOR'S COLLECTION.

The only microbrewery to open far from a major urban market was Glacial Lakes Brewing Company of New York Mills. Founded in 1997 by Sandy Waldon and Mark Hoffman, Glacial Lakes occupied a former drug store in the small Otter Tail County town. As with most microbreweries, it started with draught-only operations, but began to sell 22-ounce bottles in 1998. Waldon noted, "These [bottles] are great if someone wants to try a beer they've never had before. They don't have to buy a whole six-pack to have a taste." Her business partner, Hoffman, added, "It can be a challenge to get an establishment to give us more than one or two taps. The bottles allow us to market smaller batches of specialty beers."[30] While not facing the same overhead problems as Ambleside, Glacial Lakes still had trouble selling enough beer to make the enterprise profitable, and was forced to close after about five years.

Meanwhile, the original two craft breweries were launching major expansions in 1997. James Page Brewing Company, which maintained the name even after James Page sold his interest in the brewing operations in 1995, began work to double the size of its Quincy Street facility. The goal of the first phase was to increase capacity to 10,000 to 12,000 barrels per year. Under the second phase, a bottling line would be added so that Page would not be dependent on Minnesota Brewing Company or Schell for bottled beer, nor would they have to use the yeast strains required by the contract brewers. To raise the more than $800,000 required to install the bottler and pay off existing debt, Page became one of the first companies to take advantage of Minnesota's Small Corporate Offering Registration program, which allowed small companies to sell stock directly to the public. Information about the stock offer was included in six-packs, and later information about the offering was mailed to local residents. The goal was met with the help of a $200,000 investment by David Gilson of Bloomington. For a brief time, the future of the company looked very good. Page beers were featured on Northwest Airlines flights, and the brewery won both a gold and a bronze medal at the 1999 Great American Beer Festival. But the proposed bottling line was never built and the company was in debt again only a year after the stock offering was completed. Despite increasing sales and a strong local following, the brewery could never

Minneapolis residents received an offer by mail to buy stock in James Page Brewing Company. FROM THE AUTHOR'S COLLECTION.

quite get past the debt or upgrade its patchwork of old dairy and champagne equipment used at the Quincy Street facility. At the end of 2002 the company closed the original brewery and moved all production to New Ulm. The most recent change occurred in March 2005 when the Stevens Point Brewery in Wisconsin purchased the brands from the James Page company.[31]

Meanwhile, back in St. Paul, Summit was breaking ground for the first new complex to be built specifically as a brewery since the Alexandria Brewing Company was built in the mid-1930s. The new building was designed to immediately increase the brewery's capacity from 35,000 barrels to 65,000 barrels, with space for future expansions that could expand output to more

Summit Brewing Company opened its new brewery in 1998. COURTESY OF SUMMIT BREWING COMPANY.

than 300,000 barrels. As with the first brewery, a used brewing system was purchased in Germany and shipped over. The control unit was badly damaged during shipping, but this gave the brewery a chance to build an all-new control system (though at considerable expense). Opened in 1998, the facility allowed both for expanded production and for increased experimentation. Starting in 2004 the brewery began to release occasional draught-only specialties. The inaugural release was a style that had been requested by local beer fans for a long time, a Summit oatmeal stout. The brewers also began to create special cask-conditioned beers to showcase at beer festivals. Summit's success has enabled the company to become an active sponsor of everything from music festivals to sporting events to public radio and television. Summit's story to date is a rare one in the brewing industry: steady growth that is consistently ahead of the rest of the industry combined with critical acclaim from beer experts and the public alike.

The newest microbrewery in Minneapolis opened in January 2006 when Surly Brewing Co. began brewing in Brooklyn Center. President Omar Ansari bought a used brewing system from a defunct brewery in the Dominican Republic and installed it in a building owned by his family in a north-suburban industrial park. He hired his old schoolmate Todd Haug away from the Rock Bottom Restaurant & Brewery in Minneapolis, and they began a quest to brew styles of beer not already being made commercially in Minnesota. Surly's first two offerings were Furious (an extremely hoppy pale ale) and Bender (a brown ale).[32] In October 2006 Surly became the first craft brewer to offer beer in cans when it introduced Furious and Bender in 16-ounce cans. In January 2007, Jeff Williamson started production at Flat Earth Brewing Company in St. Paul, making it the most recent addition to the list of Minnesota's creative breweries.

Surly Brewing Co. elected to package Bender and Furious in one-pint cans rather than bottles because cans protect beer from light better than bottles, and because cans allow customers to enjoy a quality craft beer in situations where bottles are inconvenient or prohibited. FROM THE AUTHOR'S COLLECTION.

Introducing the Brewpub

In 1982 Washington brewer Bert Grant cut through the bureaucratic tangle of federal and state laws and founded Yakima Brewing and Malting Co., which brewed and served its own beers in a restaurant/bar on the premises. While breweries usually had a saloon on the premises prior to Prohibition, the practice was outlawed after repeal (though breweries could give away samples in a tasting room). Grant's concept, soon to be called a brewpub, seemed to slide between the cracks of the laws as it straddled the line between brewery and restaurant. Ultimately, most states adjusted their laws to allow brewpubs to operate, but usually only after several years of work. In Minnesota, Bill Burdick was the entrepreneur who did the most to slice through the tangle of laws and policies to make brewpubs possible. By working carefully with state Senator Phyllis McQuaid (R-St. Louis Park) and legislative staff, he was able to create a narrowly written bill that would pass the legislature without drawing active opposition from the beer wholesalers or the licensed beverage organizations.[33]

Brewpubs combine the pressures of the brewing industry with all the risks and rewards of the restaurant business. Single establishments close if the proprietor retires or goes into another business. Many restaurants also operate at the pleasure of their landlords, and in some cases, brewpubs have had their buildings sold or demolished from around them. If the location is undesirable or the service is poor or the kitchen has problems, a brewpub may end up closing no matter how good the beer is. After four brewpubs closed in 2003, Minnesota beer writer James Lee Ellingson noted with regret that "Brewpubs live and die on their restaurant management. Great beer can't change this fact." While not always true, there have been more brewpubs with mediocre beer saved by a popular restaurant than there have been mediocre restaurants saved by great beer. In enough cases, however, the management's respect for the beer carries over to the food and creates a restaurant with a menu good enough that people who don't like craft beer will still go there regularly.[34]

The Two Meanings of Taps

Taps Waterfront Brewery and Comedy Club became the first brewpub in Minnesota when it opened in 1989 in a former warehouse along the Mississippi River in Old Saint Anthony. Taps featured a mix of ale and lager styles that ranged from a standard pilsner to a strong doppelbock. Under the direction of Tom Netolesky and Bill Grones, the brewpub built something of a cult following among the small but growing group of Twin Cities beer lovers. Unfortunately, they suffered from some inconsistency and from being innovators in the field, and their location was famous for killing off businesses. It was located in an area where streets and parking were confusing to people not familiar with the area, and for many patrons their first trip to Taps was a frustrating one. In 1991 the state's pioneer brewpub closed and the brewing equipment was sold to buyers from Yugoslavia.[35]

Taps was the first brewpub to open in Minnesota—and the first to close. FROM THE AUTHOR'S COLLECTION.

When Bill Burdick was living in Britain, he developed a taste for the real ale served at cellar temperature (not warm, as many Americans conditioned to ice-cold beer claim). When he returned to America, Burdick decided to re-create the feel of a British hotel pub at Sherlock's Home in Minnetonka. With an elaborate bar that was a replica of the Dover Castle Hotel pub in London and a dining room with white linen tablecloths and English fare, Burdick preferred to call his establishment "a four-star restaurant that brews" instead of a brewpub. The bar also featured an impressive lineup of several dozen single malt Scotches, many not readily available in Minnesota. The Sherlock Holmes theme was carried through the logo, the names of the two halves of the restaurant, and even the street on which it was located, Red Circle Drive. ("The Adventure of the Red Circle" was a short story that featured Holmes tracking a hit man from an Italian crime syndicate.)

The most important aspect of Sherlock's was the introduction of real ale to Minnesota. To qualify as real ale, beer must be naturally carbonated and drawn, or pulled, from casks using a spigot or a beer engine and must not contain any preservatives. Sherlock's offered four pulled cask ales: Stag's Head Stout, Palace Porter, Piper's Pride Scotch Ale, and Bishop's Bitter. In addition, it served three other brews kept under pressure, or pushed: Star of India IPA, Gold Crown lager, and Queen Anne Light. (Queen Anne herself was actually quite large, so there was a bit of a pun involved.) Another technique new to the state was serving seasonal beers from firkins: small kegs kept on the bar with beer drawn through

Bill Burdick of Sherlock's Home at work in the brewhouse of his Minnetonka brewpub. COURTESY OF WILLIAM E. BURDICK.

Brewpubs throughout the state offer growlers in which patrons may take home a half gallon of their favorite beer. The BrauHaus growler (used for its Belgian Dubbel) proclaims Lucan's population of 220 in Flemish and superimposes an outline of Belgium inside that of Minnesota. The brewpub at O'Hara's in St. Cloud was founded in 1996, though the establishment itself dates to 1945. The Rock Bottom Restaurant & Brewery in downtown Minneapolis is part of a nationwide chain. FROM THE AUTHOR'S COLLECTION.

a spigot. Eventually, the range of seasonals included two German styles—an alt and a wheat beer—and traditional English styles like its Winter Warmer.

In a short time, Sherlock's became the center of the Twin Cities brewing community. It sponsored or hosted homebrew competitions, beer and Scotch tastings, and local appearances by renowned English beer writer Michael Jackson, "The Beer Hunter." Sherlock's remained a very popular establishment for fourteen years, until Burdick closed it in late 2002 to focus attention on his new Granite City chain of brewpub restaurants.[36]

Several years elapsed between the opening of Sherlock's and the opening of the next brewpubs in the state. Because of the legal complexities involved, it was harder to start a brewpub than a restaurant or bar, and city regulations often created limits above and beyond those of state or federal law. Two brewpubs that opened in 1994 would ultimately close at least in part because business was disrupted by construction. Rochester's Clubhaus was located in a former bank building downtown, but it was not connected to the city's skyway system and its diminishing business was hastened by major road construction in that part of town. Shannon Kelly's, in downtown St. Paul, was the victim of urban renewal, in this case the construction of the Lawson Software building on its site. The 1994 arrival that survived, Rock Bottom Restaurant & Brewery, was established in downtown Minneapolis in an area that was becoming the center of the downtown theater district and in a new complex that was in no danger of being demolished. This, combined with the new Target Center arena just a few blocks away, helped Rock Bottom develop a regular clientele for the restaurant independent of its brewpub status. The corporate management of Rock Bottom gives its brewers considerable freedom to create their own recipes in addition to the purchasing power and financial resources of a large operation. Rock Bottom has offered a range of creative seasonal beers in addition to a solid line of regular beers that helped expand the restaurant's following beyond the after-show crowd.[37]

Other brewpub chains have had mixed results in the Twin Cities area. The Brunswick Corporation (best known for bowling lanes and equipment) started what it planned to be a chain of brewpubs tied to bowling alleys with a location in Eden Prairie. A Brunswick executive said, "Our company has been tracking the trend in specialty brews from brewpubs and decided that Eden Prairie, because of its economic strength and solid sense of community, is a great location for this business."[38] While the evaluation of Eden Prairie's attributes was accurate, Water Tower Brewery did not perform as expected, and it closed in 2003. The Florida-based Hops chain opened two locations adjacent to major shopping centers: in Maple Grove just off Interstate 94, and in Eden Prairie about a mile from Water Tower Brewing. While much more dependent on corporate-designed recipes than the brewers at Rock Bottom, both Ryan Walker at the Maple Grove location and Bob DuVernois at Eden Prairie managed to create some memorable beers. However, both operations were the victims of circumstances and corporate retrenching. Hops, a largely southern chain, decided in 2004 to close some of its more distant locations and concentrate efforts in the south to save distribution costs. (All brewing supplies were sent from a central warehouse in West Virginia, so malt purchased in Wisconsin was first shipped south and then back to the Twin Cities.) In addition, the Eden Prairie location was extremely difficult to find, even with a map, and the Maple Grove location, though easy to reach, faced competition less than a mile away from the newest chain of brewpubs, Granite City.

Granite City started as a joint effort between Bill Burdick and Steve Wagenheim of the Champps Americana restaurant chain. The first establishment was located in St. Cloud, long known as the Granite City. The company's strategy is to make the running of brewpubs as efficient as possible, and to then expand into parts of the Midwest where brewpubs were much less common, such as Iowa, Nebraska, and the Dakotas. The restaurants are located in suburban mall settings rather than downtown areas. The chain has expanded rapidly and as of this writing is pursuing a plan to open at least eighteen new restaurants in three years.

A few brewpubs create a local tavern atmosphere along with their beer. The

St. Ansgar's Oatmeal Stout

Dark full-bodied, a rich brew combining six different malts and rolled oats. The rolled oats add to the richness, producing a creamy texture. The depth of character is enhanced with Cascade hops.

(Low Hops OG 1.058)
Color code **gold** on your taster board

First Street Wheat

A crisp clean lightly hopped ale with just a hint of clover honey. Brewed using American 2-row malt and 25% malted wheat. Willamette hops produce a lightly hopped flavor.

(Low Hops OG 1.048)
Color code **yellow** on your taster board

Seasonal Express Ale

Our seasonal beers are made in 4 barrel (8 keg) batches which we will brew as needed. Ask your server about our seasonal selection on tap.

Color code **light brown** on your taster board

Coal Train Porter

This London Style Porter has a full maltiness that grows into espresso coffee and caramel flavors. Four different malts are used to create this dark ruby red colored ale. Willamette hops balance out this rich brew.

(Medium Hops OG 1.057)
Color code **black** on your taster board

Cannon Ball Red Ale

This beers rich eye pleasing deep red color. Is produced by adding crystal malt, Munich malt and roasted barley in small amounts to a base malt of Midwestern 2-row malted barley. Willamette hops are used to balance the caramel flavor of this ale.

(Medium Hops OG 1.050)
Color code **red** on your taster board

Orient Express India Pale Ale

A stronger, more aggressively hopped ale than our others. This style of beer was originally brewed strong to survive shipboard passage from England to the tropical colonies. Imported Kent Goldings hops are added to the kegs to give it the full floral nose.

(High Hops OG 1.060)
Color code **blue** on your taster board

Many brewpubs offer samplers of beers to patrons looking to find the style that best fits their tastes. Menus or cards such as this one (c. 2005) from the defunct First City Brewery in Bemidji provide detailed information about each beer. FROM THE AUTHOR'S COLLECTION.

Bandana Brewery in Mankato was located in the old Elks club and attracted many of the same patrons who enjoyed its pool tables, pull-tab gambling, sports bar atmosphere, and affordable food. Despite a number of distinctive seasonal spe-

A barrel of Rosie's Ale ages in the cellar at Barley John's Brew Pub. Based on the restaurant's Wild Brunette wild rice brown ale, the aged version typically reaches an alcohol content around 20 percent and is served in appropriately small glasses. COURTESY OF BARLEY JOHN'S BREW PUB.

Carol Rifakes, mother of Town Hall's operator, Pete Rifakes, quilts an elaborate banner for each medal earned by Town Hall's entries in the Great American Beer Festival. Czar Jack, a Russian Imperial Stout brewed by head brewer Mike Hoops, won a gold medal in 2001. COURTESY OF TOWN HALL BREWERY.

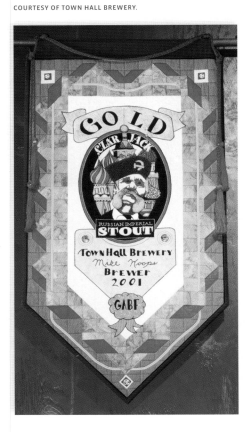

cialties made by brewer Dave Berg, many customers still ordered national mass-market lagers. Bandana stopped brewing in 2006, though the restaurant remained open. The BrauHaus in tiny Lucan (population 220 in 2005) was in many ways a microscopic replica of the Bandana Brewery—one pool table, televisions set to either a sporting event or Country Music Television, and several flavorful beers. Growlers of Dustin Brau's beers were sold in coolers right next to six-packs of Anheuser-Busch and Miller products. In fall 2006, Brau converted his operation from a brewpub into the Brau Brothers Brewing Co.

A handful of independent brewpubs in Minnesota have gained national reputations for the quality and creativity of their beers. Fitger's Brewhouse in Duluth has become a destination for beer lovers from the Twin Cities and all over the region because of the consistently high quality of its beer, first under Mike Hoops and then (and currently) under his brother Dave. Established in 1995 in the old Fitger Brewing Company complex and decorated with many advertising items from the old Fitger's brewery, the Brewhouse has become a center for local music and for outdoor sports enthusiasts. In 2005 they also opened a separate bar across the hall called Red Star, which features martinis but also includes several Brewhouse beers created especially for that establishment. Town Hall Brewery, located in the Seven Corners area of Minneapolis near the University of Minnesota, has won medals at the Great American Beer Festival for its Scotch Ale and for stronger experimental products such as Czar Jack Russian Imperial Stout and Snowstorm Ale. Great Waters Brewing Company is located, appropriately enough, in the Hamm Building in downtown St. Paul. It typically features four pulled cask-conditioned ales and four or five pushed beers. The selection of cask ales is in harmony with the goals of the British Campaign for Real Ale (CAMRA), which seeks to keep the tradition of cask conditioning alive and to fight the encroachment of mass-produced beers. Great Waters built up enough of a clientele to survive the National Hockey League strike of 2004-05, which eliminated the post-game crowds from the nearby Xcel Energy Center arena. In the northern suburb of New Brighton, John Moore and Laura Subak started Barley John's Brew Pub. According to Moore, his brewery has the smallest system capable of performing the traditional German decoction mashing method in the country. His small batch size allows him to be quite creative, and he is probably best known for Rosie's Ale, which has an alcohol content "in excess of 20 percent."

SERIES OF 1893.

50

DOLLARS PER YEAR

Stub for
Special Tax Stamp.

No. 5521

Issued by W Bickel — Collector:

Peter Oehlschlager

Brewer of less
than 500 barrels annually.

at Fergus Falls

On the 13 day of Nov 1883

Form 11, filed 13 day of Nov 1883

For period commencing
Nov 1st 1883

ending April 30th 1884.

AMOUNT OF TAX $ 25

Coupon for BREWER'S of less than 500 Bbls. per Year. SPECIAL TAX for May 1883.

Coupon for BREWER'S of less than 500 Bbls. per Year. SPECIAL TAX for June 1883.

Coupon for BREWER'S of less than 500 Bbls. per Year. SPECIAL TAX for July 1883.

Coupon for BREWER'S of less than 500 Bbls. per Year. SPECIAL TAX for Aug. 1883.

Coupon for BREWER'S of less than 500 Bbls. per Year. SPECIAL TAX for Sep. 1883.

Coupon for BREWER'S of less than 500 Bbls. per Year. SPECIAL TAX for Oct. 1883.

This very rare example of an original special tax stamp was issued by collector William Bickel to Peter Oehlschlager of Fergus Falls in November 1883 for the remaining half of the tax year. Brewers commonly registered as small producers even when their production was likely to be more than five hundred barrels. Brewers were often fined for exceeding the limit. No records exist of penalties for Oehlschlager. FROM THE COLLECTION OF PAT STAMBAUGH.

Minnesota Breweries: From the Territorial Era to the Twenty-first Century

A NTHONY YOERG BEGAN PRODUCTION AT HIS BREWERY—MINNESOTA'S first—in 1849, the same year that Minnesota became a territory. Since then, approximately 290 breweries and brewpubs have opened in Minnesota, and about 270 breweries and brewpubs have gone out of business. Some closed within a few years of opening (in one case, only a few months after opening); others survived for more than a century before falling to competitive pressures or internal weaknesses. At least some portion of the history of each Minnesota brewery is included in the pages that follow.

Why Almost 300?

The difference between the number of breweries throughout Minnesota's history and the number of breweries in the history of neighboring states represents differences in geography and settlement. Minnesota had far fewer breweries than its eastern neighbor, Wisconsin, which, with nearly 600 total breweries, had more than any other state except Pennsylvania and New York—both of which had a head start of many decades. Minnesota's brewery total was similar to its fellow Mississippi River states to the south, Iowa and Missouri (though Iowa's total was built mostly on short-lived pre-Prohibition companies, whereas Missouri became home to the largest brewing company in the world). In contrast, Minnesota had more breweries than the Dakotas, Nebraska, Kansas, and Montana combined. Part of this can be attributed to the favorable brewing geography of the Mississippi River valley, which offered ready access to brewing water and a rugged terrain that made it possible to dig caves for cooling. The Great Plains were much more

arid, and the flatness of the land made it much more difficult to dig lagering caves. The states along the Mississippi were well settled before the Civil War, and the existence of many isolated towns encouraged the founding of many small breweries. A large percentage of the new settlers were Germans, who brought their beer-drinking culture with them to their new homes. The Plains states were sparsely settled until after the Civil War, by which time railroads determined where most towns would be located, which meant that regional and national brewers could dominate the market before local breweries could be established. While there were Germans in these states, many of the new immigrants came from cultures where beer was less important. This division runs through Minnesota—of the state's 87 counties, the 57 that hosted breweries were primarily in the southeast of the state.

Of Minnesota's 290 breweries, 250 were founded before Prohibition. Only a few of the 40 breweries started after 1933 were commercial breweries—most were brewpubs that brewed beer for sale in the restaurant on the premises. The high watermark for brewery population was 1875, when 123 breweries were recorded in a combination of sources. The number of breweries in Minnesota remained at over one hundred throughout the 1870s and 1880s, but began a slow decline in the late 1880s that accelerated as Prohibition approached. Two dozen breweries responded to the re-legalization of beer in the 1930s, but attrition began almost immediately, until the state was left with four breweries from 1975 to 1985. Not until the brewpub boom of 1997 did the number of brewing operations in the state pass the number that existed during the Great Depression. The rank of Minnesota as a brewing state remained fairly constant throughout the periods when accurate records exist. The state was usually ninth or tenth in total production and somewhere between fifth and eighth in the number of breweries.

This set of histories is limited to those breweries that produced beer on their own premises. Many businesses marketed beer made under contract at an existing commercial brewery, but maintained their own company names. A casual glace at a collection of beer cans from the late 1970s may suggest that New Ulm had many breweries, but all the beer was brewed and packaged at Schell's. Some of Minnesota's landmark breweries merit their own books; the accounts that follow are merely an introduction to their history. Some of Minnesota's breweries had been lost to history and are documented here for the first time. A few of the breweries listed are included based on one or two references in reliable contemporary sources. It is possible that some of them never produced a barrel of beer, but they are included here partially in the hope that readers with information about the breweries or the families will be encouraged to add it to what is known about the history of Minnesota's brewing industry.

In Search of Lost Breweries

Researching the histories of individual breweries can be both exhilarating and frustrating. In cases where the brewery was a leading industry in the community, where the editor of the local newspaper was well disposed toward brewing, and where owners and employees or their descendants are alive and available for interviews, a researcher can paint a very detailed picture of a brewery's history. In many cases, however, the story must be pieced together from fragmentary and sometimes conflicting accounts. The sketches of individual breweries that follow are the result of comparing dozens of national, regional, and local sources.

The starting point for any brewery research is *American Breweries II*, edited by Dale Van Wieren and published in 1995 by the Eastern Coast Breweriana Association (ECBA). This is an updated version of the original *American Breweries*, compiled by Donald Bull, Manfred Friedrich, and Robert Gottschalk in 1984. These works list nearly every brewery in the United States, along with years of operation and addresses where known. They can be considered definitive in most cases, especially since 1932, where their source was the government listing of breweries authorized to operate. However, since the majority of the information was taken from secondary sources, such as brewing publications, the information is not always complete, especially before 1876 when *The Western Brewer* began publication. The information contained in brewery listings in these journals was usually provided by the brewers themselves, but was sometimes out-of-date by the time of publication. Nevertheless, the dates and ownership changes noted in *American Breweries II* have been retained unless there was specific contrary evidence available from a reliable source. A number of breweries that closed before being listed in an industry journal are listed here for the first time, and many breweries included in *American Breweries II* are now known to have started earlier than listed.

A work of similar importance with a Minnesota focus is *The Bottles, Breweriana, and Advertising Jugs of Minnesota, 1850–1920*, vol. 1, *Beer, Soda, Household*, edited by Ron Feldhaus and the members of two Minnesota bottle-collecting groups. This 1986 publication includes a list of breweries, with some corrections to *American Breweries*, and adds illustrations of breweriana and short histories of the principal breweries.

Schade's Brewers Handbook contains a directory of brewers along with their stated sales in 1874 and 1875, and Frederick W. Salem's 1880 book, *Beer, its History and its Economic Value as a National Beverage*, includes a record of every brewery in the nation that responded to his survey of production. These lists provide vital statistics on 109 breweries operating in 1874 and 1875 and 114 breweries operating in 1878 and 1879, including several for which no other specific records exist. The book *One Hundred Years of Brewing*, published in 1903 as a supplement to *The Western Brewer*, has short sketches of several dozen Minnesota breweries operating at the time. These vary in quality, and some contain significant errors. In some cases, however, these are still a good source for information on some breweries.

The most precise government sources are the assessment lists for the Minnesota collection districts for the federal excise taxes, first imposed in 1862 (Internal Revenue Service record group 58.5.23, held by National Archives Regional

Depositories in Kansas City and Chicago). These can be considered definitive for time periods where they exist, since all brewers were required to have a license, and monthly production was recorded for the first several years of the tax. However, records are extremely thin after 1870, since the switch from monthly collection to prepaid stamps was complete, and many individual records have disappeared. These excise tax records often pinpoint when a brewery began production or when ownership changed hands. However, there were situations in which the brewery was simply leased and not sold, and the operator of the brewery listed in a brewery directory is different from the person responsible for the tax. Production records other than those for 1874–1875 or 1878–1879 are taken from excise records.

Federal census records provide a useful snapshot of who was living in a particular location every ten years and reveal a number of brewers previously lost to history. Minnesota also had a special census taken in 1857 in preparation for statehood. The 1850, 1857, 1860, and 1870 census records were examined on microfilm page by page for this book. The 1880 census can be searched by occupation on Ancestry.com. Most of the 1890 census was destroyed by fire. Searches for individuals can also be carried out on Ancestry.com, which was the method used to locate brewers in the 1900 and 1910 records. In 1860, 1870, and 1880, the government also included a separate Census of Industry (also called the Census of Manufactures in 1880), which provided detail on capital invested, employment, inputs, and outputs. Census records have their own flaws, and these were taken into consideration. While Minneapolis and St. Paul are known to have padded their census totals in 1880, in the case of small-town brewers it is safe to assume that a person listed was actually present. Of course, some people known to have been present in a locale were occasionally omitted from the census. It is possible that some persons listed as brewers were not actually pursuing that occupation at the time of the census. These instances are identified within the histories. Minnesota conducted its own census during the pre-Prohibition period in years ending in five, but these records did not include occupation and so are only useful for determining whether a person lived in a given place.

When they exist, city directories and state business directories and gazetteers provide listings of businesses in a given area. These are often not complete, since brewers had to respond to the survey, and sometimes pay, to be included in a listing of businesses or breweries. While many of these directories should be considered more reflective of the situation in the year before publication, presence of a brewery in such a listing can usually be considered positive proof of its existence.

County and city histories are often useful sources for detailed records on business history. In some cases, however, they are based on memories of interview subjects rather than detailed records and sometimes conflict with facts given elsewhere. The massive county histories published between 1880 and 1920 emphasized businesses open at the time of publication, and sometimes ignored breweries altogether if the local editors were prohibitionists. These histories were treated as reliable unless evidence to the contrary was found in a contemporary source.

The most definitive sources were local newspapers. This book is the result of several hundred hours of research examining uncountable thousands of newspapers on microfilm. These provided weekly or even daily records of brewery construction, destruction, and production. Since the writer of these accounts was present and may have spoken personally to those involved, the dates given in local newspapers for the beginning or end of production replace those found in any other source. Newspapers have their own limitations as sources, however. In some towns, the opening of the brewery predated the founding of a newspaper. In other cases, the local editor was hostile to alcohol and did not cover events of the local brewery, in some cases ignoring it even when it burned to the ground. Major metropolitan daily papers seldom covered the opening or closing of any but the very largest breweries, and indexes for the pre-Prohibition area are incomplete or nonexistent. The newspaper collection of the Minnesota Historical Society, housed in the Minnesota History Center in St. Paul, is by far the most extensive in the state and contains microfilmed versions of nearly every newspaper ever published in Minnesota. The Olmsted County Historical Society has made the WPA newspaper index available online, and the Winona State University Winona Newspaper Project has provided fully searchable versions of Winona newspapers from 1859 to 1946 (so far) on its Web site.

Brewery histories are a common feature in the journals published by breweriana collecting organizations, brewing industry publications, and other periodicals intended for beer enthusiasts. Currently, there is no central location where the general public may use these for research, but by 2008 the American Breweriana Association plans to have a library operating in the National Brewery Museum in Potosi, Wisconsin. The breweriana organizations have lending libraries through which members may borrow copies. Finally, a number of collectors and independent historians have extensive files of records concerning various breweries. Some of these contain interviews with brewers or family members, family records, and other artifacts. These generous people are listed individually in the acknowledgments.

Breweries and Brewpubs in Minnesota

Breweries

1. Albert Lea, Weile/Thoreson/Bowman & Gerst (1870–1886)
2. Alexandria, Carl Volk (1870–1890)
3. Alexandria, Rudolph Wegener (1876–1919)
4. Alexandria, Aberle/Towgood/Alexandria Brewing Company (1878–1917)
5. Alexandria, Alexandria Brewing Company, Inc. (1935–1943)
6. Alton, Leiferman & Ploog (1868–1869)
7. Appleton, Ginsberg/Pulkrabek/Appleton Brewing Company (1884–1915)
8. Austin, Frank Weinand (1865–1876)
9. Austin, Huxhold & Wagner/Weisel (1869–1880)
10. Beaver, O.P. Ramsey (1873–1873)
11. Beaver Falls, Lumpp/Betz (1868–1888)
12. Belle Plaine, Swingler/Schmitt (1860–1916)
13. Belle Plaine, Frank/Stradcutter (1865–1871)
14. Bemidji, Bemidji Brewing Company (1904–1915)
15. Berne, Dilesby (1857–1860)
16. Berne, Hirschi/Closner (1857–1868)
17. Beroun, Beroun Bohemian Brewing Company (1904–1908)
18. Blue Earth, Faunce (1860–1860)
19. Blue Earth, Fleckenstein (Paul) (1863–1906)
20. Blue Earth, Deinhardt/McNeal & Toliver (1866–1871)
21. Braham, Kallberg (1907–1907)
22. Brainerd, Hoffman (1872–1875)
23. Brainerd, Ort/Brainerd Brewing Company (1881–1915)
24. Brooklyn Center, Surly Brewing Company (2006–)
25. Browerville, Minars (1892–1918)
26. Brownsville, Knoblauch (1855–1858)
27. Brownsville, Schwarzhoff (1865–1877)
28. Brownsville, Brownsville Bluff Brewery (1871–1910)
29. Caledonia, Schwebach & Wagner/Arnoldy (1873–1884)
30. Canby, Schmahl (1877–1880)
31. Cannon Falls, Mellin/Brisman/Kowitz (1868–1888)
32. Carver, Keller/Hertz (1864–1889)
33. Chaska, Ulmer/Leivermann (1862–1920)
34. Chaska, Duess/Windolf/Nagel/Leivermann (1864–1875)
35. Chaska, Fritz & Rouch (1866–1867)
36. Chaska, Young/Iltis/Karcher/Beyrer (1866–1955)
37. Chatfield, Deinhardt/Ellinson/Collins (1857–1873)
38. Chatfield, Schewing (1859–1865)
39. Cold Spring, Sargl/Cold Spring Brewing Company/Gluek Brewing Company (1874–)
40. Courtland, Koke (1858–1859)
41. Crookston, Walter/Burkhardt/Schnagl/Kiewel (1875–1915)
42. Detroit Lakes, Detroit Brewing Company (1886–1888)
43. Duluth, Luce/Busch/Decker/Fink/Fitger Brewing Company (1857–1972)
44. Duluth, Klein & Kiichli (1859–1861)
45. Duluth, Kiene (1869–1876)
46. Duluth, Kreimer/Camahl & Busse (1871–1875)
47. Duluth, Decker/Franke (1882–1885)
48. Duluth, Duluth Brewing & Malting Company (1896–1966)
49. Duluth, Johnson/West End Malt Ale Company (1901–1914)
50. Duluth, Burg (1907–1907)
51. Duluth, Peoples Brewing Company (1907–1957)
52. Duluth, Lake Superior Brewing Company (1994–)
53. East Grand Forks, Mundigel/Hoffman/East Grand Forks Brewing Company (1886–1917)
54. Elizabeth, Koehnlein (1871–1872)
55. Ellsworth, Consumers Brewing Company (1902–1908)
56. Elysian, Theimer (1874–1877)
57. Evansville, Schwartz (1882–1901)
58. Fairmont, Smales (1877–1879)
59. Faribault, Fleckenstein (Gottfried), (1857–1907)
60. Faribault, Paquin (1857–1863)
61. Faribault, Fleckenstein (Ernst), (1860–1964)
62. Faribault, Brandt & Gerdes/Mueller (1862–1884)
63. Faribault, Ahles (1875–1875)
64. Fergus Falls, Zaiser & Lumpp/Lohmeier/Oehlschlager (1875–1884)
65. Fergus Falls, Brown (1878–1884)
66. Fergus Falls, Aberle/Fergus Brewing Company (1882–1951)
67. Fergus Falls, Kiewel (1881–1892)
68. Forestville, Douglas, Odell & Meighen (1856–1860)
69. Frazee, Frazee City Brewery (1874–1879)
70. Frontenac, Minges (1862–1863)
71. Glencoe, Lemmel/Eickman/Glencoe Brewing Company (1874–1919)
72. Glenwood, Miksch/Thompson (1884–1887)
73. Granger, Hasse/Engelhorn (1874–1901)
74. Hastings, Schaller/Ulmer (1856–1867)
75. Hastings, Hastings City Brewery (1866–1893)
76. Hastings, Saile/Yaeger & Borser (1867–1870)
77. Hastings, Keffler & Boser/Busch (1869–1902)
78. Hastings, Norrish (1875–1878)
79. Hastings, Steffen/Hastings Brewing Company (1885–1918)
80. Henderson, Ritter/Enes (1859–1918)
81. Hokah, Root River Brewery (1858–1887)
82. Hutchinson, Abel/Plotzer & Wetzig/Kleinmann/Hajicek (1870–1920)
83. Jackson, Deinhardt/Owens (1871–1880)
84. Jackson, Gilmore (1891–1895)
85. Jordan, Brabender/Nicolin/Heiland/Jordan Brewing Company (1857–1916)
86. Jordan, Nicolin & Gehring/Schutz & Kaiser/Schutz & Hilgers/Mankato Brewing Company (1866–1948)
87. Kensington, Bisek (1888–1893)
88. Lake City, Reidinger/Fitzsimmons/Beck (1862–1884)
89. Lake City, Minges/Wise/Schmidt (1864–1901)
90. Lanesboro, Kimber/Frietschel (1873–1881)
91. Le Roy, Inward (1869–1873)
92. Le Sueur, Kinzel/Veith (1869–1880)
93. Le Sueur, Arbes/Vollbrecht (1878–1899)
94. Litchfield, Lenhardt/Litchfield Brewing Company (1875–1916)
95. Little Falls, Brick/Medved/Koch/Kiewel Brewing Company (1880–1961)
96. Long Prairie, Rohner/Beyrer/Long Prairie Brewing Company (1874–1918)
97. Lucan, Brau Brothers Brewing Company (2006–)
98. Madelia, Brennis (1878–1897)
99. Mankato, Bierbauer/Mankato Brewing Company (1857–1966)
100. Mankato, Welch/Ibach/Graeber (1867–1884)
101. Mankato, Wolf & Trout/Leiferman/Gassler (1868–1883)
102. Mankato, Blatt & Boeckler/Jacoby/Ibach (1873–1887)
103. Mankato, Haas & Schmidt/Lamm/Ibach (1873–1875)
104. Mankato, Standard Brewing Company (1900–1908)
105. Mantorville, Hirchi/Ginsberg/Naegli/Schnagl/Otto's/Mantorville Brewing Company (1858–1939)
106. Mantorville, Mantorville Brewing Company (1996–)
107. Marine on St. Croix, Kaufmann/Graf/Wichman (1856–1882)
108. Marion, Kennedy (1865–1866)
109. Mazeppa, Trausch/Hilger/Rother & Manske (1878–1899)
110. Melrose, Schnitz/Kuhn/Hemmisch/Melrose Brewing Company (1882–1914)
111. Millville, Behrns (1879–1881)
112. Minneapolis, Orth/Minneapolis Brewing Company/Grain Belt Brewing Company (1850–1975)
113. Minneapolis, Bofferding (1857–1860)
114. Minneapolis, Gluek Brewing Company (1857–1964)
115. Minneapolis, Hofflin (1859–1860)
116. Minneapolis, Gloeggler (1861–1863)
117. Minneapolis, Hein & Koehnlein/Lohff (1866–1874)
118. Minneapolis, Kranzlein/Mueller/Heinrich (1866–1897)
119. Minneapolis, Kreitz (1867–1872)
120. Minneapolis, Ort (1867–1867)
121. Minneapolis, Zahler/Nohrenberg (1874–1890)
122. Minneapolis, Olson & Johnson (1877–1877)
123. Minneapolis, Gilbride (1882–1887)
124. Minneapolis, Westphal & Mueller/Germania Brewing Company (1884–1890)
125. Minneapolis, Liden/Sundbeck (1891–1911)
126. Minneapolis, Monahan Bottling Company (1891–1896)
127. Minneapolis, Birkhofer Brewing Company/Purity Brewing Company (1894–1920)
128. Minneapolis, William Massolt Bottling Company (1894–1897)
129. Minneapolis, Peterson & Matson (1894–1895)
130. Minneapolis, Swanson (1894–1896)
131. Minneapolis, Karlson & Lundquist (1895–1899)
132. Minneapolis, Hasle (1896–1896)
133. Minneapolis, Olsen & Andersen (1896–1896)
134. Minneapolis, Barrett (1900–1900)
135. Minneapolis, Imperial Brewing Company (1901–1905)
136. Minneapolis, Lauritzen Malt Company/Hennepin Brewing Company (1903–1920)
137. Minneapolis, Tjerneld (1903–1905)
138. Minneapolis, Youngstrom (1905–1906)
139. Minneapolis, Edelweiss (1916–1916)
140. Minneapolis, James Page Brewing Company (1986–2005)
141. Minneapolis, Ambleside Brewing Company (1997–1998)
142. Minneiska, Parker/Mead/Phillips (1871–1877)
143. Minnesota City, Vill (1869–1918)
144. Montgomery, Chalupsky/Handsuch & Pexa/Montgomery Brewing Company (1882–1943)
145. Montgomery, Richter/Pepin Lake Brewery (1892–1905)
146. Montgomery, Choudek/Perchal & Brazil/Hug, Pagel & Sparr (1893–1899)
147. Moorhead, Larkin/Erickson/Aslesen (1875–1901)
148. New Munich, Froehler/Pitzl (1868–1920)
149. New Prague, Radly & Chalupsky/Roemer/Mickus (1877–1906)
150. New Prague, Menars/Kokes/Piemeisel/Rybak/New Prague Brewing Company (1884–1920)
151. New Ulm, Betz/Friton/Schmucker/New Ulm Brewing & Malting (1858–1917)
152. New Ulm, August Schell Brewing Company (1861–)
153. New Ulm, John Hauenstein Brewing Company (1864–1969)
154. New Ulm, Karl/Holl/Piemeisel (1865–1871)
155. New Ulm, Bender/New Ulm Brewing Company (1866–1911)
156. New York Mills, Glacial Lakes Brewing (1997–2001)
157. Northfield, Keller/Maes/Grafmueller/Wenner (1866–1920)
158. Ortonville, Geiger & Eberman/Fey/Lemmel/Lakeside Brewing Company (1882–1912)
159. Oshawa, Vieth (1877–1881)
160. Otter Tail City, Otter Tail City Brewery (1870–1872)
161. Owatonna, Knoblauch/Mannheim/Ganser/Fuermann (1861–1920)
162. Owatonna, Maes/Bion (1865–1891)
163. Perham, Schroeder/Northern Pacific Brewing Company (1878–1915)
164. Pine City, Brandes (1870–1876)
165. Pine City, Buselmeier /Blass (1882–1915)
166. Pine Island, Ferber/Geil (1869–1893)
167. Preston, Somers/Ibach/Smith/Yager/Riedel/Knapp (1859–1919)
168. Princeton, Roos (1886–1890)
169. Read's Landing, Leslin/Burkhardt (Upper Brewery) (1858–1909)
170. Read's Landing, Saile/Ruckhaber/Voelke (Pepin Brewery) (1858–1880)
171. Red Lake Falls, Red Lake Falls Brewing Company/Walter (1884–1890)
172. Red Wing, Hoffman (Philip)/Christ/Zimmerman & Featherston/Red Wing Brewing Company (1857–1937)
173. Red Wing, Heising/Remmler/Goodhue County Brewing Company (1861–1951)
174. Red Wing, Hoffmann (Lorenz) (1865–1882)
175. Red Wing, Hay Creek Brewery (1866–1880)
176. Red Wing, Melander/Bombach (1866–1878)
177. Red Wing, Berg (1867–1867)
178. Redwood Falls, Schmahl (1870–1876)
179. Redwood Falls, Weiss/Dietrich & Drischel (1871–1888)
180. Richmond, Weber (1866–1884)
181. Rochester, Drescher/Schuster Brewing Company (1857–1920)
182. Rochester, Heising/Smith/Cascade Brewery (1857–1881)
183. Rochester, Troost/Rappold/City Brewery (1860–1882)
184. Rush City, Vietor/Fahrenholz/Schnagl/Weid/Rush City Brewing Company (1872–1904)
185. Rushford, Larson & Nelson/Gjernes/Oechsle/Pfeiffer (1865–1907)
186. Rushford, Erickson/Ibach/Oleson (1867–1873)
187. St. Charles, Mueller/Waltham/Pfister & Waller (1875–1890)
188. St. Cloud, Kramer & Seberger/Schaeffer (1857–1871)
189. St. Cloud, Enderle/Schindler/Merz/Udermann (1864–1916)
190. St. Cloud, Funk/Thiery/Balder/Zertler (1864–1897)
191. St. Cloud, Herberger/Brick/Preiss & Wimmer/St. Cloud Brewing Company (1867–1939)
192. St. Joseph, Brink (1862–1875)
193. St. Michael, Zahler/Weiss/Dick (1862–1891)
194. St. Paul, Yoerg Brewing Company (1849–1952)
195. St. Paul, Bruggemann/Aiple (1853–1905)
196. St. Paul, North Mississippi Brewery (1853–1898)
197. St. Paul, Fleckenstein (Gottfried) (1855–1857)
198. St. Paul, Stahlmann/Schmidt/Pfeiffer/Heileman/Minnesota Brewing Company (1855–2002)
199. St. Paul, Troyer/Schweitzer/Emmert (1855–1901)
200. St. Paul, Arnold (1859–1860)
201. St. Paul, Keller/Hamm/Olympia/Stroh (1859–1997)
202. St. Paul, Wurm & Winker (1859–1860)
203. St. Paul, Drewry/Holland/Constans/North Star Brewing Company (1860–1900)
204. St. Paul, Leip (1861–1865)
205. St. Paul, Nessel (1863–1864)
206. St. Paul, Wurm (1863–1889)
207. St. Paul, Fetsch (1864–1865)
208. St. Paul, Kranzlein & Schmidt/Kranzlein, Smith & Miller (1864–1867)
209. St. Paul, Coffin & Oakes/Drewry (1865–1917)
210. St. Paul, Funk (1865–1902)
211. St. Paul, Kreitz (1865–1866)
212. St. Paul, Putnam & Dexter (1867–1867)
213. St. Paul, St. Paul Malt & Ale Company (1868–1872)
214. St. Paul, McFarland/Upham/Hornung (1874–1881)
215. St. Paul, Roelke (1874–1875)
216. St. Paul, Minnesota Weiss Beer Brewery (1884–1884)
217. St. Paul, Hamm & Reimer (1885–1891)
218. St. Paul, Setzer & Reichow (1885–1887)
219. St. Paul, Schlenk (1888–1889)
220. St. Paul, Bausch (1895–1895)
221. St. Paul, Summit Brewing Company (1986–)
222. St. Paul, Flat Earth Brewing Company (2007–)
223. St. Peter, Engesser Brewing Company (1856–1942)
224. St. Peter, Veith (1865–1873)
225. St. Peter, Keoke & Kuhl/Stelzer (1866–1891)
226. St. Peter, Hohmann (1867–1883)
227. St. Vincent, Raywood (1879–1880)
228. Sauk Centre, Gruber/Diehl/Ahrentz/Minette (1865–1891)
229. Sauk Rapids, Momberg & Jochem/Sauk Rapids Brewing Company (1884–1895)
230. Shakopee, Strunk/Winker/Nyssen (1856–1920)
231. Shakopee, Albachten/Husmann/Heller/Engelhorn (1857–1908)
232. Silver Lake, Chalupsky/Silver Lake Brewing Company (1887–1919)
233. Sleepy Eye, Kramer/Burginger/Steffen/Schueller (1873–1920)
234. Spring Grove, Myhre (1866–1873)
235. Stillwater, Kimmick/Aiple/Tepass (1851–1896)
236. Stillwater, Knips (1858–1877)
237. Stillwater, Wolf (1869–1919)
238. Stillwater, Hasse & Hermann (1875–1875)
239. Taylor's Falls, Schottmuller/Beyer/Zigner (1856–1890)
240. Tower, Fink/Iron Range Brewing (1892–1919)
241. Traverse des Sioux, Schmahl (1852–1866)
242. Veseli, Rapham & Pavek (1887–1907)
243. Virginia, Virginia Brewing Company (1906–1918)
244. Wabasha, Leslin/Ginther/Anderman/Grass (1872–1919)
245. Waconia, Zahler/Karcher (1865–1888)
246. Wadena, Carl & Roller/Wermerskirchen (1881–1885)
247. Wadena, King & Ebner/Wadena Brewing Company (1886–1916)
248. Waseca, Ginsberg/Kraft (1869–1880)
249. Waseca, Bierwalter/Ramsdale/Guyer/Wenner/Reichel (1879–1912)
250. Watertown, Dietz/Becker/Lueders (1865–1884)
251. Waverly, Brown (1868–1868)
252. West Albany, Hook (1870–1871)
253. West Newton, Eckert & Feeder (1870–1871)
254. Willmar, Gilger (1878–1898)
255. Winona, Gilmore Valley Brewery/Beck (1855–1877)
256. Winona, Weisbrod/Bub/Sugar Loaf Brewery (1856–1969)
257. Winona, Comersburgh (1860–1860)
258. Winona, Becker/Schellhas (1863–1920)
259. Winona, Park Brewing Company (1904–1919)
260. Young America, Krahnschnable/Schmasse (1866–1879)

Brewpubs

A. Albert Lea, Green Mill Brewing Company (2003–2004)
B. Bemidji, 1st City Brewery & Grill (1999–2006)
C. Duluth, Fitger's Brewhouse (1995–)
D. Eagan, Granite City Food & Brewery (2005–)
E. Eden Prairie, Water Tower Brewing Company (1997–2003)
F. Eden Prairie, Hops (2001–2004)
G. Lucan, BrauHaus (2004–2006)
H. Mankato, Bandana Brewery (2003–2006)
I. Maple Grove, Hops (1999–2005)
J. Maple Grove, Granite City Food & Brewery (2004–)
K. Minneapolis, Taps Waterfront Brewery (1989–1991)
L. Minneapolis, Rock Bottom Brewery (1994–)
M. Minneapolis, District Warehouse Brewing (1996–1999)
N. Minneapolis, Town Hall Brewery (1997–)
O. Minneapolis, The Herkimer (1999–)
P. Minnetonka, Sherlock's Home (1989–2002)
Q. Moorhead, Trader & Trapper (1996–2001)
R. New Brighton, Barley John's Brew Pub (2000–)
S. Rochester, Clubhaus (1994–1999)
T. Roseville, Granite City Food and Brewery (2006–)
U. St. Cloud, O'Hara's Brew Pub (1996–)
V. St. Cloud, Granite City Food and Brewery (1999–)
W. St. Louis Park, Granite City Food and Brewery (2006–)
X. St. Paul, Mill Street Brewery (1995–)
Y. St. Paul, Shannon Kelly's (1995–1998)
Z. St. Paul, O'Gara's (1996–)
AA. St. Paul, Great Waters Brewing Company (1997–)
BB. St. Paul, Vine Park (1997–2003)
CC. Shakopee, Brew Station/Harwell's (1999–2003)
DD. Stillwater, Vittorio's (1997–2001)
EE. Winona, Backwater Brewing Company (1995–)

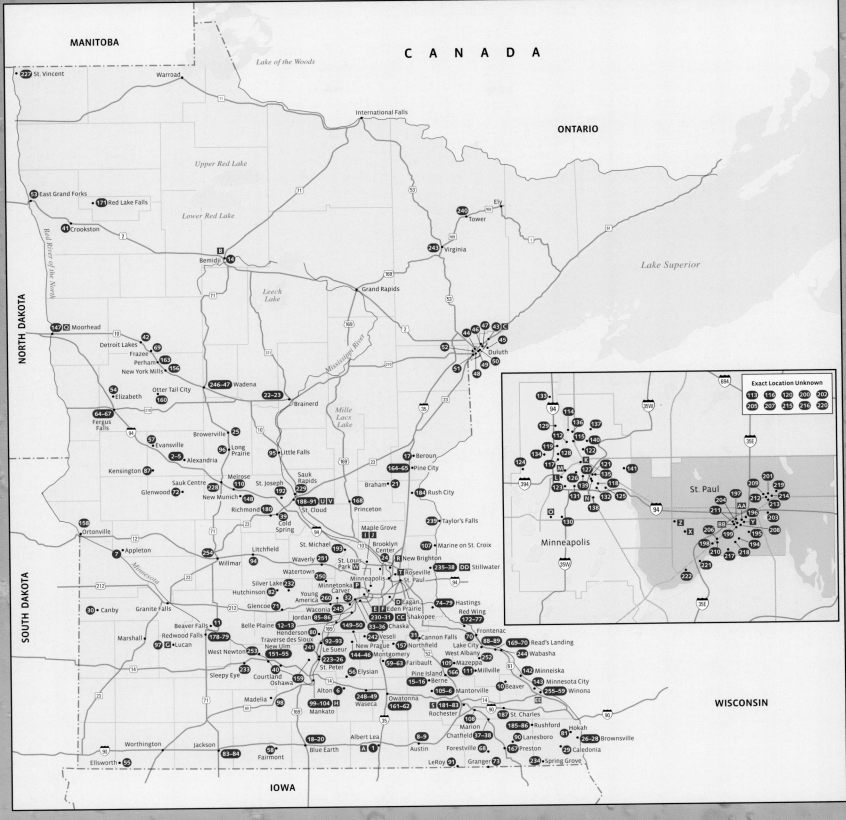

MANITOBA

CANADA

Lake of the Woods

ONTARIO

227 St. Vincent

Warroad

International Falls

NORTH DAKOTA

Upper Red Lake

53 East Grand Forks

171 Red Lake Falls

Lower Red Lake

41 Crookston

Red River of the North

240 Tower   Ely

243 Virginia

147 Q Moorhead

B Bemidji 14

Leech Lake

Lake Superior

42 Detroit Lakes

69 Frazee

Perham

163

156 New York Mills

Mississippi River

52   44 46 47 43 C
51   48 49 50 45
Duluth

54 Elizabeth

160

Otter Tail City

246-47 Wadena

22-23

Brainerd

64-67 Fergus Falls

Mille Lacs Lake

35

57 Evansville

25 Browerville

96 Long Prairie

95 Little Falls

17 Beroun

164-65 Pine City

2-5 Alexandria

87 Kensington

228 Sauk Centre

110 Melrose

St. Joseph

229

Sauk Rapids

21 Braham

72 Glenwood

148 New Munich

192

188-91 U V

St. Cloud

168 Princeton

184 Rush City

158 Ortonville

180 Richmond

39 Cold Spring

7 Appleton

254 Willmar

Litchfield

94

St. Michael 193

Maple Grove   10   I J

Brooklyn Center

24 New Brighton

239 Taylor's Falls

107 Marine on St. Croix

30 Canby   Granite Falls

Waverly 251

250

Silver Lake 232

Hutchinson 82

Watertown

St. Louis Park W

Minneapolis
St. Paul

Roseville T

235-38 DD Stillwater

R

11 Beaver Falls

Marshall

178-79 Redwood Falls

97 G Lucan

West Newton 253

Young America

260 32 P Minnetonka Carver

71 Glencoe

Waconia 245

85-86 Jordan

Belle Plaine 12-13

Henderson 80

Traverse des Sioux

New Ulm

151-55

241 Le Sueur

92-93

223-26 St. Peter

149-50 E F Eden Prairie

230-31 CC Shakopee

33-36 Chaska

242 Veseli

31 Cannon Falls

New Prague 157 Northfield

144-46 Montgomery

59-63 Faribault

109 Mazeppa

74-79 Hastings

Red Wing

172-77

70 Frontenac

88-89 169-70 Read's Landing

244 Wabasha

252

111 Millville

142 Minneiska

143 Minnesota City

255-59 Winona

D Eagan

233

40 Courtland Oshawa

159

56 Elysian

15-16 Berne

105-6 Mantorville

10 Beaver

Madelia

98

99-104 H Waseca

248-49

Owatonna

161-62

S 181-83 Rochester

166 Pine Island

187 St. Charles

185-86 Rushford

90 Lanesboro

81 Hokah

26-28 Brownsville

Sleepy Eye

Courtland

St. Peter

Alton 6

Mankato

108 Marion

Chatfield

37-38

167 Preston

29 Caledonia

SOUTH DAKOTA

18-20

Albert Lea

8-9 Austin

A 1

Forestville

69

234 Spring Grove

Worthington   Jackson

83-84

58 Fairmont

Blue Earth

LeRoy 91   Granger 73

Ellsworth 55

IOWA

WISCONSIN

EE

St. Charles

Exact Location Unknown

113 116 120 200 202
205 207 215 216 220

St. Paul

Minneapolis

133
129 114
136 137
112 115
119 134 128 140
117 M 122
124 K 121
123 L 126 135 141
131 N 139 118
138 132 125
O 130

694

35W

35E

94

197
204 209 201 219
211 AA 212 214
196 213
BB 203
198 199 195 208
206 Y
210 217 218 194
221

222

35E

35W

Albert Lea [Freeborn County]

Weile & Co. (1870–1880?)
John Thoreson (1880?–1884?)
Bowman Bros. & Gerst (1884–1887)
Location: Unknown

Rudolph Weile (a native of Poland) and Jens Christenson (from Denmark) probably started their brewery in late 1870. (Existing documents from early 1870 do not mention them, but records from 1871 list improvements to the brewery rather than the original construction.) Some residents were probably brewing at home before this, since the *Freeborn County Standard* contained advertisements for hops, including "some that were grown in the county." During the next several years, the firm added on to the brewery several times, including a major addition in 1874 that cost almost as much as the new Congregational church. The brewery had a barn for its horses and several other outbuildings. The brewery needed the business of the surrounding countryside since Albert Lea had a strong temperance community and many of the existing saloons continued to feature Wisconsin beers. Still, Weile sold 238 barrels in 1874 and 352 the next year.

Some sources suggest that Weile leased the brewery to local saloon owner John Thoreson for a few years during the early 1880s, but few records of this period exist. In 1884 Weile leased the brewery to Bowman Bros. and Gerst, formerly of Marshalltown, Iowa. Chased out of Iowa by one of that state's frequent episodes of prohibition, they hoped to use Albert Lea as a base from which to keep supplying thirsty Iowans with beer. The company shipped 10,000 kegs up from its Iowa facility and proved (as the *Standard* noted) that the company "undoubtedly means business." In May 1885 Bowman Bros. and Gerst purchased the brewery and an additional parcel of land just north of the mill for a proposed new building. In the meantime, the company made more than $2,000 worth of improvements on its property in the third ward. The brewery hosted several groups of Germans who came up from Iowa on Sunday excursions to continue their customary afternoons in the beer garden, though the brewery soon stopped allowing the groups to use its property and simply supplied the beer. The brewery continued to advertise heavily and made a special point of the fact that its Salvator Beer and National Export bottled beer were made entirely of Minnesota barley.

The heavy expenditures on expansion seem to have been more than the firm could support, because in 1887 the company and property were sold at a sheriff's auction to meet creditors' demands. The *Freeborn County Standard* reported that "the business has been mismanaged here, and the firm has lost, it hardly knows how, seven or eight thousand dollars." Apparently neither Weile nor Thoreson wanted to return to brewing, so the business was discontinued.

Alexandria [Douglas County]

Carl Volk (1870–1890)
Location: Fourth Avenue and G Street (now Broadway)

Carl Volk moved from St. Joseph to start his Alexandria brewery in 1869. It was in production by November 1870 and remained open until 1890. In the mid-1870s Volk was producing just over 100 barrels per year, but by 1879 was up to 450 barrels. The Volk brewery closed in 1890.

Rudolph Wegener & Oscar Gutheil (1876–1877)
Rudolph Wegener (1877–1901)
Estate of Rudolph Wegener (1901–1902)
Rudolph Wegener Brewing Co. (1902–1919)
Location: Northwest corner of Eighth Avenue and G Street (now Broadway). The city directory of 1911–12 lists the address as 224 Main Street (now Broadway).

Rudolph Wegener and Oscar Gutheil started the second brewery in Alexandria. Within a year Wegener became the sole proprietor. He began to expand the brewery, and by the mid-1890s, he had filled much of the block with barns and stables, a grain house, and an icehouse. His bottling house was built before 1889. The brewery itself was 160 × 72 feet. As early as 1880 he had two men working with him in the brewery. By the time he died in 1901, he was one of the leading businessmen of the area—a stockholder in several local businesses and a major property owner.

After Wegener's death, the brewery was sold. Alexandria resident Hans Birkhofer, along with family members Conrad and Sophia Birkhofer of Minneapolis, incorporated Rudolph Wegener Brewing Co. with $25,000 of capital stock. The corporation apparently did well for

This Rudolph Wegener Brewing Co. label was in use from 1902 to 1906. It touts "The Beer That Never Fails." BOB KAY COLLECTION.

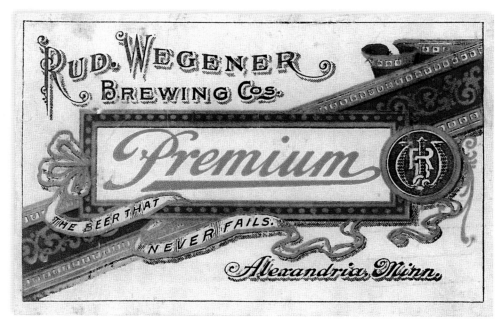

the next several years, but Alexandria went dry in 1915. Hans Birkhofer tried to keep the brewery alive by opening a depot in Albany to sell beer, but this was a short-term solution at best, and in 1919 Birkhofer had the brewery refitted as a flour mill and continued in that capacity into the 1920s. By 1929 the former brewery was the Kiger Feed Mill. No buildings from the brewery remain today.

Aberle Bros. (1878–1884)
Christian Aberle (Northwestern Brewery)
   (1884–1895)
Walter A. Towgood (1895–1904)
Kathleen A. Towgood (1902–1904)
Christian Aberle (1904–1905)
Alexandria Brewing Co. (1905–1916)
Alexandria Brewing Association (1916–1917)
Location: Southwest corner of H Street (now Hawthorne) and Third Avenue

In 1878, Christian and Fred Aberle started brewing on a limited scale in Alexandria. They are listed in several ads and the 1880 census as grocers and saloon owners, but an 1878 list of businesses includes three breweries, and a 1908 account claims Alexandria Brewing Co. was 30 years old. The brothers built a new brewery in 1882 and continued to enlarge it over the next decade, eventually replacing horsepower with steam in 1891. (Census data does not show whether these Aberles were related to Andreas Aberle of Fergus Falls.)

In 1895 Christian Aberle sold the brewery to recently arrived Englishman Walter Towgood, who expanded it and ran it for nearly ten years, manufacturing both beer and other drinks. Kathleen Towgood appears in the records as the proprietor for several years late in this period. Since Walter was still alive, it is not clear why the enterprise was placed in Kathleen's name. Towgood was apparently delinquent in his payments, and Aberle regained control of the company in 1904. Although Aberle kept the staff in place, he did not want to return to the beer business and sold the brewery the next year to a group of Milwaukee investors led by August and Henry Nagel, who incorporated Alexandria Brewing Co. The *Alexandria Post News* credited the Nagels with expanding the brewery and its business and restoring the firm's financial health.

The Breckinridge, Minnesota, syndicate of John Heatherington and Edward and W. B.

Sam's Premium beer represented the last attempt to save Alexandria Brewery. The label is from around 1941. FROM THE COLLECTION OF KEN MALZ.

Plaisted purchased the company in 1908 for $55,000. Within the next two years, Heatherington was no longer listed in connection with the firm and had become a saloonkeeper in town. The 1914 Sanborn map lists P. L. Peterson as the proprietor. In 1915 the city of Alexandria went dry and the advance of Prohibition made it impossible for the business to stay afloat. The brewery closed in 1917.

Alexandria Brewing Co. (1935–1942?)
Alexandria Brewery, Inc. (1942?–1943)
Location: Fillmore Street and Third Avenue

Unconnected with the pre-Prohibition Alexandria Brewing Co., this Alexandria Brewing Co. was opened in an all-new brewery in 1935 by local entrepreneurs Sam Caldis and John Geanopolous. Their Gold Seal Beer was offered first in kegs, but they began to bottle beer a few months after production began. Despite newspaper reports that the brewery had signed several large contracts, the business had difficulty competing against larger out-of-town breweries. Gopher Beer replaced Gold Seal,

and Sam's Premium succeeded Gopher, but changes in labels and management did little to change the fortunes of the business. Alexandria Brewery, Inc., the successor firm, was in a precarious financial position and unable to survive any external shock; it closed in 1943 due to wartime material shortages. The building was converted to a poultry and egg processing plant in 1951. Additional information on the brewery and the Gold Seal label may be found in chapter 6; the Gopher Beer label appears in the preface.

Alton [Waseca County]

Leiferman & Ploog (1868–1869)
Location: Unknown

This brewery appears only in the excise records. According to the 1868 records, Laiferman and Plack [*sic*] received their small-brewery license in October 1868 with the address of Peddler [*sic*] Grove. The same firm, though spelled differently, is listed in the 1869 excise annual but as being located in Alton Township, just south of Janesville in Waseca County. There was a Henry Leuferman listed in the 1870 census as a laborer living in Alton, but no Ploog.

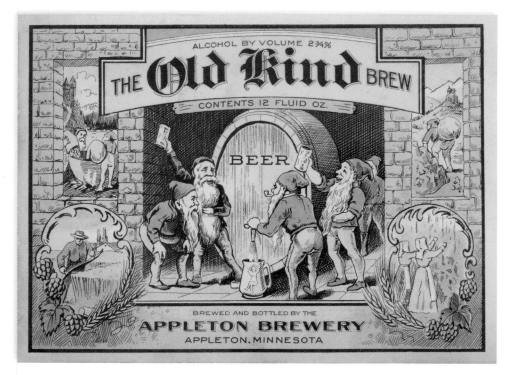

Appleton [Swift County]

Ginsberg Bros. (1884–1887)
Strauch & Ginsberg (1887–1888)
Edwin Ginsberg (1888–1894)
Solomon Ginsberg (1894–1904)
Charles Pulkrabek, Appleton Brewing Co.
   (1904–1917?)
Location: South of the river, north of Dakota Avenue between First and Second streets

In late May 1884, the *Appleton Press* reported, "The brewery is a sure thing. A piece of ground has been purchased by Messrs. Ginsberg just west of the Reinsmith building on Dakota Avenue, and work will begin next week." When Charles Ginsburg returned to Mantorville, his brother Edwin took on Adolph Strauch as a partner and the firm was known as Strauch and Ginsberg until 1888. Late that year Ginsberg bought out Strauch's share and continued the business on his own. The brewery, built at a cost of $7,000, was a popular place—it hosted a "hop" (dance) even before it was finished. As with many breweries of the period, it suffered from construction delays and production interruptions but was generally successful. Ginsberg advertised that he would supply beer to saloons and families

This rare label from the Appleton Brewery dates to around 1900. FROM THE COLLECTION OF KEN MALZ.

at such "low prices that Eastern breweries cannot compete." Another brother, Solomon Ginsberg, took over the brewery in 1894 after Edwin's death the previous year, and continued its modest but steady business.

In 1904 the brewery was sold to Charles Pulkrabek, who operated it until it closed before Prohibition. The 1915 Sanborn insurance map includes a note that the brewery was no longer in operation, but the excise tax records from December 1917 include a listing for Pulkrabek Brewing Co. of Appleton. The brewery may have moved in and out of production during the last few years before Prohibition. By the mid-1920s none of the brewery structures remained.

Austin [Mower County]

Frank Weinand (1865?–1876?)
Location: Unknown

Frank Weinand was brewing in Austin in 1865, and possibly earlier. During 1866 he sold an average of sixteen barrels of beer in the winter

months and as many as thirty in midsummer. Mower county histories include him in lists as late as 1876, but he does not appear in *Schade's Brewers Handbook*.

Huxhold & Wagner (1869–1877)
Jacob Weisel (1877–1881)
Location: Unknown

C. H. Huxhold and Wagner (first name unknown) began production in November 1869. They offered free delivery of beer in town and shipped to stations along the railroad. During the first year of operations, the company suffered even more misfortune than usual for a beginning brewery. In March John Fetzner (later of V. & J. Fetzner of Brownsville) fell down the stairs to the beer cellar and had his hand smashed by the keg he was carrying. Two months later, a lot more fell into the cellar when spring floods caused the cellar vault to cave in, plunging all the brewing vessels and part of the icehouse through the floor. The resulting damage was about $3,000—about as much as it cost to build a brewery from the ground up. Despite the rough start, the brewery was producing more than 600 barrels per year by the mid-1870s.

In 1877 the operation of the brewery passed to Jacob Weisel. Weisel increased production dramatically, from a mere 241 barrels in 1878 to 969 in the next year. (It is possible that he may not have been in operation for all of 1878.) The brewery was destroyed by fire in April 1881, and though the $7,000 loss was insured, Weisel did not rebuild.

Beaver [Winona County]

O. P. Ramsey (1873?)
Location: Northwestern Winona County

A tantalizing reference to a brewery in Beaver, Winona County, appears in the 1873 *Minnesota Business Directory*. Research has produced no further information on this brewery. Excise records for Collection District One from 1871 through 1875 are no longer in existence, and no other independent confirmation has been discovered.

Beaver Falls [Renville County]

H. A. Lumpp (1868–1869)
Andreas Betz (1869–1888)
Location: West side of Main Street, near the churches (northeast of Redwood Falls)

Andreas Betz began his Minnesota brewing career in New Ulm in the brewery of August Friton. In 1864 he went into partnership with John Hauenstein, and they opened their own brewery near the August Schell brewery. Five years later, Betz moved away from brewery-filled New Ulm to take over a brewery started in late 1868 by H. A. Lumpp. Details about the life of the brewery are scarce, but production remained very small. Betz's production averaged about twenty-five barrels per year, with a high of thirty-nine barrels in 1874, the lowest recorded production of any brewery that was in operation during the last half of the decade.

Belle Plaine [Scott County]

Anton Swingler (1860?–1866)
Swingler & Stradcutter (1866–1867)
Anton Swingler (1867–1869?)
B. Osterfeldt (1870)
Christian Schmitt (also Birk and Schmitt)
    (1871–1904)
Estate of Christian Schmitt (also Matt Schmitt)
    (1904–1917)
Location: Near Brewery Creek

Brewing may have begun near Belle Plaine as early as 1857, when a recent English immigrant, Edward C. Townsend, was listed in the territorial census as a brewer. No further information has been found on Townsend or his brewery. The first confirmed brewery was built sometime around 1860 by Anton Swingler at a cost of $500. According to Harold Albrecht's *This is Our Town: Belle Plaine, MN*, this brewery burned in 1866, and a new one was built nearby, giving the town two new breweries. By June 1866, Bernard Stradcutter had left his partnership at the other brewery and joined with Swingler, possibly to help with rebuilding. Stradcutter is listed in tax records only through the beginning of the next year. Swingler ran the brewery at least through 1868, but does not appear in tax records in 1869. The excise records for 1870 list B. Osterfeldt (about whom no other information has been found)

as the owner of this brewery, which for the first time is registered as a brewery of more than 500 barrels per year.

In 1871 Christian Schmitt purchased the brewery and operated it until it was destroyed by fire in 1877. Schmitt rebuilt immediately and began to increase his business. In the first two years after the fire, Schmitt produced 235 and 399 barrels, but by 1881 he was again producing more than 500 barrels per year. Schmitt continued to expand the business and added a bottling line. He advertised regularly in the local newspaper, where he called his beer "a beverage that helps sustain the system" and made other claims for its health-giving properties.

Christian Schmitt died in 1904, and his family continued to run the brewery. Even before he died, Schmitt had turned over management of the company to his son Mathias. The Belle Plaine brewery suffered from competition from larger breweries in the area and closed before Prohibition arrived.

Images of a bell and a wood plane on this rare and attractive glass (c. 1890s) symbolize the location of Chris. Schmitt's brewery (note the alternate spelling of his name). FROM THE COLLECTION OF PAT STAMBAUGH.

Hartland & Stradcutter (?–1866)
Neiman & Frank (1866)
Schmitt & Frank (1866–1867)
John Frank (1867–1870)
Frank & Stradcutter (1870–1871)
Location: Northeast of town on the Neiman/Ische/ Stradcutter farm

For several years, there were two competing breweries in Belle Plaine. Sometime before 1866, Hartland (first name unknown) and Bernard Stradcutter built a brewery just northeast of town. During the summer of 1866, Stradcutter moved to join Anton Swingler at Belle Plaine's other brewery, and this brewery lay idle for several months. (Summertime closures were not uncommon for small breweries, since brewing conditions were less than ideal and beer sold during the hot summer season had been brewed months earlier. Little money would be lost during this period.) In October, two new owners, John Frank (sometimes listed as Frink) and Neimer (first name unknown) reopened the brewery. By December, Neimer was gone, replaced for a short time by Christian Schmitt. Excise records at the end of the year show Frank on his own again, and he remained sole proprietor through most of 1870. Late in 1870, Stradcutter joined the firm again, which turned out to be fortunate because John Frank drowned in 1871, and Stradcutter was able to continue the firm. However, he stopped brewing beer and focused on soft drinks. Harold Albrecht's *This is Our Town: Belle Plaine, MN* was the source for the brewery location and the fate of John Frank.

Bemidji [Beltrami County]

Bemidji Brewing Co. (1904–1915)
Location: North shore of Lake Irving, east side of Mississippi Avenue

Bemidji Brewing was started in 1904 under the direction of Fred Eberlein. This was an ambitious undertaking, as several outside breweries had well-established markets in the city. According to local accounts, Eberlein was a good brewer and businessman as well as a patriotic booster of Bemidji. The brewery built up a large regional following for its Golden Belt and Pilsner brands, and added a bottling line in the summer of 1909 to bottle its Pilsner. By the time treaty enforcement closed the brewery in 1915 (covered in chapter 5), it was shipping between 6,000 and 7,000 barrels each year in addition to its substantial bottled-beer business. Portions of the brewery remained standing until the 1980s. A label from Bemidji Brewing Co. appears in chapter 5.

Berne [Dodge County]

John Dillesby (1857?–1860?)
Location: West of the parsonage

In 1856 Swiss immigrants platted a town in Milton Township and named it Buchanan after the newly elected president. Since the name was already in use elsewhere, they changed it to Berne in honor of the Swiss canton where many residents were born. A book on the history of the local Zwingli church, written by Mary E. Zeller, mentions a brewery "west of the present parsonage," which is a different location from the Hirschi-Closner brewery (described below). This brewery maintained a bowery on the grounds, which apparently was a popular gathering place at one time. This brewery may have been operated by John Dillesby, who is listed as a brewer in that township in the 1857 territorial census. (It is possible that Dillesby is just a very inaccurate rendering of Hirschi, but Dillesby was from Germany rather than Switzerland so he was probably a different person.)

John Hirschi (1857–1860)
Closner Bros. (Christian and David) (1860–1868)
Location: South of the Andrist store, northwest of the bridge

John Hirschi started a brewery a year after the township was founded and operated it for three years. (According to local accounts, he also started a brewery in Mantorville. The two locations are far enough apart so it is unlikely that these references are to the same brewery.) In 1860 he sold the brewery to the Closner brothers (sometimes spelled Klossner or Clossner), though only Christian is listed as a brewer in the 1860 census. Detailed information about the brewery is scarce, though local accounts state that the Closner family lived in the brewery, and the 1866 excise records indicate that David Closner sold as many as fifteen barrels of beer during summer months. (The excise records list Closner as being from Pine Island, but that is likely to have been a mailing address, since there was not yet a brewery in Pine Island.) Closner's last appearance in the

excise records is in 1868, which agrees with the local accounts.

Mary Zeller's account also includes the tantalizing statement that "breweries were built at various locations around Berne," suggesting that there may have been more than two. Some farmers may have had small breweries on their properties, and newspaper accounts from Red Wing have confirmed that some of the farmers southwest of that city were brewing around that time.

Beroun [Pine County]

Beroun Bohemian Brewing Co. (1904–1908)
Location: Unknown

In 1903, Joseph Chalupsky, J. Kubesh, and the Horejs brothers began construction on a brewery in Beroun, one of the smallest Minnesota communities to host a brewery. The *Pine Poker* printed frequent updates on the construction, reporting in January 1904, "The brewery ice house is now filled. Now for the article that needs the ice." Production began in July, and by September the Horejs brothers were planning to ship some of the beer to their hometown of St. Paul. A fire that started in the chimney spread throughout the plant and burned it to the ground in 1908, with a loss of $10,000, only $2,400 of which was insured. Joseph Chalupsky, by now the sole proprietor, planned to rebuild immediately and even began preparing the site, but eventually abandoned the idea.

Blue Earth [Faribault County]

Horrace Faunce (1860?)
Location: Unknown

There appears to have been a brewery in Blue Earth as early as 1860, when the U.S. census lists Horrace A. Faunce as a brewer (both names are difficult to read and may not be correct). This 23-year-old native of Maine lived alone and owned property in Blue Earth, but no other information about him or the brewery is known.

Joseph Shimek (1863–1868)
Paul Fleckenstein (1868–1904)
Theodore Fleckenstein (1905–1906)
Location: South side of Tenth Street (formerly both Douglas and Harris) between Nicollet and Linton

According to an account by Fleckenstein descendant Jean Paschke in *American Breweri-*

ana Journal, May-June 1995, Joseph Shimek began a brewery in Blue Earth in 1863. If so, the Treasury Department was unaware of it, because no such brewer appears in the excise records. In 1865 Paul Fleckenstein, brother of Ernst and Gottlieb Fleckenstein of Faribault, married Theresa Shimek and was placed in charge of the brewery.

In 1868 Paul Fleckenstein took control of the brewery (a development of which the Treasury Department was aware). The brewery was a small one and does not appear to have produced more than 500 barrels per year until 1888. According to the 1870 Census of Industry, Fleckenstein was the only employee and produced just over 312 barrels in the previous twelve months. During the mid-1870s, Fleckenstein maintained a production of more than 300 barrels a year, but this dropped to just over 200 barrels by the end of the decade. This may have been a consequence of the increased presence of the railroads in southern Minnesota and the competition the railroads brought. The brewery closed in June 1904 because of Paul Fleckenstein's failing health. He died three months later. *American Breweries II* lists Theodore Fleckenstein as taking over the firm for the next two years, but local accounts do not record any production. Theodore may have continued membership in brewing organizations or maintained the license for that period.

Charles Deinhardt (1866?–1869)
McNeil & Tolliver (1869–1871?)
Location: Unknown

Sometime before 1866 Charles Deinhardt moved from Chatfield to Blue Earth and began to brew again in his new home. He sold more than 140 barrels in 1866, with a high of 21.75 barrels in July. Deinhardt continued to brew in Blue Earth until October 1869, when Westwood Tolliver took over the brewery. According to the census, Tolliver, who was born in Mexico, was a farm laborer, and management of the brewery was left to his son Charles and to Alexander McNeil. The 1870 Census of Industry shows the pair had $1,000 invested in the business and had produced one hundred barrels of beer, at a total value of $900, in the year ending June 30. Deinhardt moved west to Jackson to start a brewery there. McNeil and

Tolliver (also spelled McNeal and Toliver) disappear from the records after 1870.

Braham (Isanti County)

Anders Kallberg (1907)
Location: Unknown

In early 1907, Anders Peter Kallberg (sometimes spelled Chellberg) started what may have been the shortest-lived brewery in Minnesota's history. Braham was a risky place to start a brewery since both the village and Isanti County as a whole were strongly prohibitionist. A victory by the saloonkeepers in one election on the license question would be met with redoubled efforts by dry forces the next year. Kallberg managed to sell nine barrels of beer in April, May, and June 1907 before the town voted dry for good. Even though the village at first allowed medicinal malt beverages to remain on sale, it banned these as well after raiding a saloon that was selling Digesto, which was alleged to have 4 percent alcohol content. Kallberg did not attempt to continue his business. By the time notice of his brewery appeared in *Brewers' Journal*, it was closed.

Brainerd (Crow Wing County)

John Hoffman (1872–?)
Location: Unknown

John Hoffman established the first brewery in Brainerd in 1872. It appears to have been a short-lived enterprise, and outside of excise records for that year, nothing else is known about Hoffman's operations. It is possible that the brewery was still operating as late as August 1875, because the *Fergus Falls Weekly Journal* reported that "John Zaiser has been influential in inducing H. Lumpp, of Brainerd, to start a brewery in Fergus."

Peter Ort (1881–1887)
Brainerd Brewing Co. (1887–1915)
Location: East side of Boom Lake (listed in city directories as the south end of Fourth Street at Pennsylvania Avenue)

Brainerd Brewing Co. began in 1881 when local saloonkeeper Peter Ort began to supply his own beer. Ort expanded his business quickly and by late 1883 registered as a brewer of more than 500 barrels. A local history by Carl Zapffe suggests that Ort was in business for only a year or two and that in 1882 or 1883 the brewery was owned by George Donant.

The same account states that around 1884 Fred Hoffman purchased the brewery and began to expand it. However, articles in the *Brainerd Dispatch* from 1884 indicate that Ort still owned the brewery and was refurbishing the brewery saloon and adding a bottling department, and *Wing's Brewers Handbook* of 1887 still lists Ort as proprietor. By the late 1880s, the brewery was doing business as Brainerd Brewing Co., so Ort probably sold out to Donant in 1887 or shortly thereafter. Ownership may have changed several times, since an ad in the *People's Gazette* (St. Paul) of 20 October 1894 listed Tac Dobmeier, Joseph Kerner, and Frank Stumpp as principals in the firm. The same ad also noted that the brewery offered lager and export beer.

Brainerd Brewing Co. entered the twentieth century under the management of Fred Hoffman and Edward Boppel. The brewery was expanded until it had a capacity of between 6,000 and 10,000 barrels per year (sources differ on the brewery's size). According to the 1903 city directory, the brewery had at least four employees and two drivers working under foreman Theodore Skreypek. The company was incorporated in 1906, headed by Boppel and Werner Hemstead. Competition was fierce, since Brainerd was home to agencies for Duluth Brewing & Malting Company, A. Fitger & Co., Gund Brewing Co. of La Crosse, and Minneapolis Brewing Company. The 1907 city directory contained an unusual contradictory advertisement by the Brainerd Brewing Company: "Patronize Home Industry. Beer that is absolutely pure—Brewed in the City of the Pines. We fill orders for Miller's Milwaukee Bottled Beer." The local firm may have felt a need to offer a Milwaukee product to its customers to keep their business, but in the next year's directory, Miller was no longer advertised as part of its product line. Brainerd Brewing Co. continued to operate until it was closed by federal treaty enforcement in 1915. Two employees of Brainerd Brewing Co. tried to reenter the brewing industry in 1933. Arthur Boppel, son of Edward, and brewer John Hoerner were both involved in the unsuccessful attempt to start a brewery in Shakopee after repeal.

This Brainerd Brewing Co. Old Pilsener Style Lager Beer label was in use 1894–1906. FROM THE COLLECTION OF KEN MALZ.

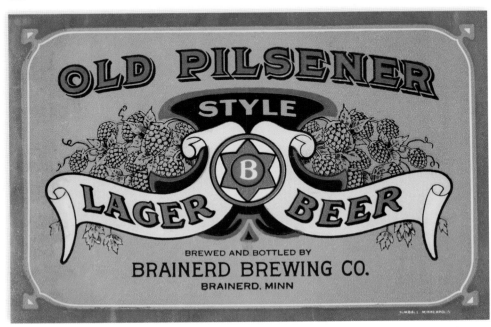

Brooklyn Center [Hennepin County]

Surly Brewing Co. (2006–present)
Location: 4811 Dusharme Drive

Omar Ansari named Surly for the attitude a beer lover could develop if he or she couldn't find a beer that was flavorful enough. Ansari found a space in a warehouse owned by his family, recruited Todd Haug to be the brewer, and spent much of the summer of 2005 waiting for brewing equipment to arrive from the Dominican Republic. Surly's first two beers were released at the Minnesota Craft Brewer's Guild's 2006 Winterfest: a brown ale called Bender and an extremely hoppy pale ale named Furious. By the time of the brewery's open house in May, two more styles were available: a Belgian-style ale called Cynic, and a limited edition of Bender brewed with coffee. Since then Surly has continued to offer new styles including a Russian imperial stout called Darkness and an Oktoberfest-style beer labeled Surlyfest. In October 2006, with the release of Bender and Furious in 16-ounce cans filled at the brewery, Surly became the first Minnesota microbrewery to offer beer in cans.

Browerville [Todd County]

(Albert) Minars Brewing Co. (1892–1918)
Location: On Town Road, just west of the Catholic cemetery

Excise tax records indicate that Albert Minars started brewing near Browerville in Hartford Township in November 1892, and that he incurred a tax penalty within six months of opening. By 1896, Minars had increased production to more than 1,000 barrels and was classified as a large brewer for taxation purposes. It remained a largely one-man operation, though the 1900 census listed John Kullick as a brewery laborer. *The Western Brewer* reported in 1918 that the brewery had closed, but the precise date is not known.

Brownsville [Houston County]

Adolph Knoblauch (1855–1858)
Location: Unknown

Among the new buildings erected in Brownsville in 1855 was a brewery. Adolph Knoblauch apparently did not make it large enough, since the *Southern Minnesota Herald* proclaimed in early 1856:

Mr. Knoblough [*sic*], Brewer, is unable to supply the demand for beer created by the consumption here in town. For this reason, he is unwilling to advertise, until his establishment is enlarged, which will be done immediately. It is a significant fact to us that, as the consumption of beer increases, the drunken rows in our streets are less frequent.

Knoblauch had previously brewed in Hannibal, Missouri, and ended up in Brownsville by way of St. Paul. Knoblauch continued to brew in Brownsville for three years, but his brewery burned in 1858. The 1860 census, while listing him as a brewer, claims he owned no real estate and only $60 of personal property. In 1861 Knoblauch moved to Owatonna and started the first brewery in that city.

Adolf Schwartzhoff (or Schwarzhoff) (1865–1877?)
Schwartzhoff & Gluck (1866)
Location: Corner of Main and Seventh

In late 1865, Adolf Schwartzhoff placed an ad announcing that he had "erected a large and spacious BREWERY in Brownsville ...

This drawing of Schwarzhoff's Brownsville Brewery dates from the early 1870s. As with many other breweries of the era, the proprietor lived in a house adjacent to the brewery. COURTESY OF THE MINNESOTA HISTORICAL SOCIETY.

Where he believes he can furnish the public with a good article of Beer." Schwartzhoff took local hotel owner Fred Gluck as a partner for a while during the summer of 1866, during which the brewery sold as many as thirty-six barrels in some months. The brewery burned in November 1866, but was rebuilt immediately. Schwartzhoff became sole proprietor after the fire and ran the brewery for several more years. He is listed in the 1872 Minnesota Business Directory, and a drawing of his brewery is included in the 1874 Andreas *Atlas of Minnesota*. Schwartzhoff appears in the excise records as having produced beer in September of 1877. However, he disappears from the records after this point, and the brewing business of the town was taken over by the Fetzner brothers' Brownsville Bluff Brewery.

Brownsville Bluff Brewery (1871–1910)
Location: One and one-half miles west of town on County Highway 3

According to *The History of Houston County*, the Brownsville Bluff Brewery was a new brewery built in 1871 by brothers John and Valentine Fetzner. The original brewery was a two-story building, 40 × 24 feet, but the brothers added to it later that year and again in 1873.

Under the Fetzners, the brewery maintained a steady business despite competition from several large breweries in nearby La Crosse. In the late 1890s, the Bluff brewery even maintained a depot in Caledonia. After

Even very small breweries sought to increase business through advertising. This rare glass from the Brownsville Bluff Brewery dates to between 1896 and 1900 when Valentine Fetzner was sole proprietor. Because these delicate glasses were most likely intended for homes rather than saloons, it suggests that Fetzner made frequent deliveries to households. FROM THE COLLECTION OF JIM AND RUTH BEATON.

a nearly thirty-year career as brewers, both Fetzners retired and became farmers in the township (Val kept bees on his farm), but John's son Herman Fetzner went to work for Miller Brewing in Milwaukee. The brewery was advertised for sale in *Brewers' Journal:*

> For Sale: My brewery, in good repair. Capacity about 5000 bbls, good local trade, located 1½ miles from RR depot in picturesque valley with an abundance of fine spring water, will sell cheap. A good chance for a practical brewer with limited means to get established in a paying business.

The Brownsville Bluff Brewery went through several different owners in its last decade. Fackler and Landowski operated the brewery for about five years. In 1906 Land-

owski took over the brewery on his own. Excise tax records show its output was still less than 500 barrels. Landowski made improvements in the brewery, but financial problems, including delays by customers in paying their accounts, put limits on the amount he was able to expand. Ultimately, Landowski sold the brewery in September 1906 to August Sinderman, formerly of Appleton, Wisconsin. Sinderman brought the brewery back into production, and by the beginning of 1907, he was offering bottled beer as well as kegged product. He delivered beer to several surrounding communities; in March 1907 he and his wagon apparently got stuck on a slough in the Mississippi River on the way to Stoddard, Wisconsin, and he "had trouble bringing his load to land." After this harrowing incident, he chose to ship by rail. Despite its small size, the Bluff Brewery under Sinderman offered a bock beer in May 1907, which was on tap at several saloons. Ultimately, Sinderman went out of business and sometime in 1908 John H. Smith came into possession of the brewery property. He soon sold it to Philip Klenk, who refurbished the buildings with equipment purchased from the defunct brewery in Willmar. By March he had resumed delivery of beer and advertised "Good wholesome beer for family use." The *Brownsville News* was a strong advocate of Klenk's beer, suggesting it both as an ideal tonic and as the best refreshment after threshing. Sometime during the fall, Klenk sold the brewery to F. W. Lademan and R. Kraatz, both from Milwaukee, who not only continued brewing but captained the south side and north side baseball teams, respectively. Unfortunately, the brewery burned just before Christmas and was not rebuilt, even though Lademan and Kraatz renewed their license for 1910. The *Brewers' Journal* reported that Bluff Brewing Co. was closed just a few months after the company was formed.

Caledonia [Houston County]

Philip Wagner (1874?–1876)
Schwebach & Wagner (1876–1880)
Peter Arnoldy (1880–1884)
Location: Kingston Street

While sources differ on the date, Philip Wagner apparently began brewing in Caledonia sometime between 1873 and 1875. In July 1875, the

Houston County Journal featured an advertisement for what was still being called the new Caledonia brewery. In addition to beer, Wagner also offered ice and malt for sale and was prepared to pay "the Highest Price" for barley. *Schade's Brewers Handbook* reported production of 317 barrels during the first year of operation (whatever it actually was). Two years later, a new ad, this time listing Philip Schwebach and Wagner as proprietors, claimed that the brewery had been "retrofitted and improved" and that they also dealt in "choice Wines, Liquors, & Cigars." Different sources list Wagner or Schwebach or both as owners, but they may simply have been imprecise in reporting ownership. By 1880 the brewery appears to have been comparatively large, since three people in addition to Schwebach are listed in that year's census as working in the brewery. The brewery produced 739 barrels in 1878, but reported no production in 1879.

Edward D. Neill's *History of Houston County* reported that Peter Arnoldy purchased the brewery in 1880 (presumably late in the year, since he is listed as a machinery agent in the 1880 census) and produced about 400 barrels of lager during his first year. No local information about the brewery after this point has been found.

Canby [Yellow Medicine County]

Jacob Schmahl (1877–1880?)
Location: Unknown

Schmahl's third and last brewery in Minnesota was his shortest lived as well. Canby was not a good location for a successful brewery, both because of its relative isolation and because of the strong temperance sentiment that dominated the county. One county history cites the *Granite Falls Journal* welcoming the new business in September 1877, "Peter Erickson and J. Schmall [*sic*] are building a brewery, and in about two months we will have fresh lager beer." The *Journal* later noted that he was bringing equipment from Redwood Falls, so it seems that he simply moved his equipment from site to site. One later account states that "early settlers of the Minnesota Valley between Redwood Falls and Lac Qui Parle will recall him bringing beer to the farm houses and towns along the way, and referring to it as 'Schmahl's Best.'" Schmahl was a very small producer—he produced only sixty-seven and fifty-nine barrels in 1878 and 1879 respectively. Precisely when Schmahl stopped brewing is not recorded.

Cannon Falls [Goodhue County]

Carl G. Mellin (1868–1869?)
Gerhard Brisman (1869–1871)
Ferdinand Kowitz (1876–1888)

Location: North bank of the Cannon River, just below the Goodhue mills

Carl G. Mellin started a brewery in Cannon Falls in fall 1868. Excise tax records suggest that he ran this brewery for about a year. No brewers are listed in the 1870 population census, but Gerhard Brisman was reported as having produced fifty-five barrels of beer in the fiscal year ending 1 September 1871. Brisman disappears from the records after 1871, and it is possible that no brewing was done in Cannon Falls for several years. The Minnesota state business directories of 1872 and 1873 do not list a brewery in Cannon Falls, though other breweries known to have been in operation were not included.

Ferdinand Kowitz was born on 4 July 1842 in Prussia. According to Connie Brickman's history *Roots & Wings . . . a Scrapbook of Time: Cannon Falls, Minnesota,* Kowitz learned the brewery business in Berlin and later moved with his new wife, Caroline, to La Crosse, Wisconsin. He found a position in G. Heileman's brewery and remained there for about fifteen years. Seeking a brewery of his own, he moved to Red Wing, where he and a partner started a new brewery (records are not clear which brewery it was, but the description seems to fit the short-lived Bombach and Koke [Kowitz?] brewery). Kowitz probably recognized that Red Wing was overcrowded with breweries and moved in 1876 to nearby Cannon Falls to open a brewery there. (Records do not indicate whether he restarted the existing Mellin/Brisman brewery or built a new structure.) He harvested ice on the Cannon River near his brewery property and raised pigs to help feed his brewery workers. The 1880 Census of Industry suggests that Kowitz was making a good profit on the brewery. That year he paid $1,500 in wages to his three employees, used

$1,700 of inputs, and sold $6,000 worth of beer. Kowitz owned a number of buildings in the downtown area, ran a saloon and a liquor store, and eventually built a fortune worth well over half a million dollars.

As of 1886, Kowitz's brewery consisted of a 32 × 36 foot brewery, a 24 × 36 foot malt house, and a 22 × 42 foot icehouse. Like many other breweries, Kowitz's brewery succumbed to fire several times, as did several of his other properties. He rebuilt the brewery after the first two fires, but following the third fire in January 1888, he decided to leave the brewing business. He supplied his saloon with beer from Remmler's Brewery in Red Wing, and continued as a leader of the community until his death in 1897.

Carver [Carver County]

Hall & Keller (1864)
Keller & Gebhardt (1864–1867)
Keller & Hertz (1867–1868)
Berthold Hertz (1868–1886)
Annie Hertz (1886–1889)

Location: South of town on the river

The firm of Hall and Keller was established in time to be included in the May 1864 excise tax list of brewers. The first notice in the press was the account in the Chaska *Weekly Valley Herald* that reported Mich. Hall was building the first underground beer cellar in the county. Hall left the firm shortly thereafter, and Keller (first name unknown) took on Gebhardt (first name unknown) as a partner. This partnership lasted for nearly three years, when Gebhardt was replaced by the man who would operate the brewery for nearly two decades, Berthold Hertz. By spring 1868, Hertz had become sole proprietor.

Hertz's brewery appears to have maintained a small but steady business throughout its existence. All excise tax records indicate that it brewed fewer than 500 barrels per year (or exactly 500 in the 1870 tax year). Production in 1878 and 1879 was 348 and 360 barrels, respectively, making Hertz's brewery about half the size of its Carver County neighbors. After Berthold died of stomach cancer in 1886, his widow, Annie, took over the business briefly, but then leased the brewery to Loe (first name unknown). The brewery burned down in April 1889, forcing Loe and his family to escape the

brewery in their nightclothes. Mrs. Hertz's mortgage interest was insured, but Loe had an uninsured loss of $4,500.

Chaska [Carver County]

Fritz & Ulmer (1862)
George Ulmer (1863–1875)
Bernard Leivermann (1875–1904) (Some sources list Mrs. B. Leivermann as proprietress at various times during this period.)
August Leivermann (Leivermann Bros.) (1904–1920)

Location: West of the current intersection of Pine Street and U.S. Highway 212

Joseph Fritz and George Ulmer built the first brewery in Chaska in 1862 on a bluff northwest of town. This partnership did not last long, since Ulmer appears by himself in the excise records of 1863 and the Chaska *Weekly Valley Herald* reported in October 1863 that Fritz was building a new brewery. Ulmer's brewery did a small but steady business, like all of Chaska's breweries during the late 1860s. Ulmer typically sold five to ten barrels in the winter months but sometimes sold almost fifty barrels per month in the summer. Ulmer operated a malt house and purchased barley from local farmers.

The story of the next decades of the brewery are summarized by Jim Faber in "Eine Geschechta doe Brauerei," in the *Chaska Herald* on 14 April 1994 and in LaVonne Barac's *Chaska: A Minnesota River City* (though their accounts are sometimes contradicted by contemporary reports). In 1875 Bernard Leivermann (also spelled Leiverman), a former employee of Martin Bruggemann in St. Paul and more recently owner of the Nagel brewery in Chaska, purchased the brewery and began to increase production. (Some sources list a brief partnership in 1875 with C. H. Lienau, sometimes spelled Leman.) By 1878 his production was nearly 900 barrels per year. The brewery experienced a close call in 1884 when Leivermann's barn burned down and the fire spread to the roof of the brewery itself. The fire department was able to limit damage to the brewery even though the pumping engine did not work because the water was too muddy.

Leivermann added a bottling plant in 1887 and began deliveries to local residents. A disastrous fire in 1897 interrupted the growth of the company, but Leivermann responded by immediately rebuilding and expanding the facility. Leivermann's eldest son, Augustus (Gus), left the saloon business and helped manage operations in the new brewery. Leivermann recognized the risks in launching a rebuilding program during a period when national brewers were increasing their presence throughout the region. He had to compete not only with Milwaukee and La Crosse breweries, but Hamm had a depot in Chaska and Schutz and Kaiser of Jordan had accounts in Carver County. He wrote a letter to the *Weekly Valley Herald* that encouraged local residents to trade with him since his prices were lower and the profits stayed in the community.

Bernard Leivermann died in 1904, and his sons Gus and Albert took over the brewery. They made nearly $3,000 of improvements in 1907, including a new engine, boiler, and bottling machine as well as a new 28 × 28 foot brick building. The brewery remained in operation until it was closed by Prohibition. When State Highway 12 (now U.S. Highway 212) was expanded in the early 1920s, the brewery was torn down.

Joseph Fritz & Co. (1863–1864)
Gerhard Deuss (1864–1867)
Anton Windolph (1867–1869)
Otto Nagel (1869–1873)
Bernard Leivermann (1873–1875)
Location: Unknown

The second brewery built in Chaska was started by Joseph Fritz during the summer of 1863. Apparently this enterprise lasted no longer than his earlier brewery with George Ulmer, since Gerhard (or Gebhard) Deuss had replaced him in the excise records by September 1864. Deuss maintained steady sales of between five and ten barrels per month until Anton Windolph took over in late fall 1867. In 1869 Otto Nagel took over the brewery and increased output to the point where it was the leader of the three Chaska breweries. Bernard Leivermann moved to Chaska in 1873 and purchased the Nagel brewery, but it burned in June 1875. In a peculiar move, the cellars of this brewery were sold to Peter Iltis in 1874. No records of digging new cellars have been found, and it is possible that one of the owners was trying to eliminate an inconvenient property. Leivermann then purchased the Ulmer

brewery and operated that firm for almost thirty years.

Fritz & Rouch (1866–?)
Location: Unknown

What appears to have been Chaska's third brewery was built in 1866, again by Joseph Fritz. Its construction is mentioned in the *Weekly Valley Herald* on 21 July 1866 along with that of the Young and May brewery. The article refers to these two new firms as joining "those already in full blast," seeming to indicate that there were at least two then in operation. The firm of Fritz and Rouch appears in the excise records in 1866 but then disappears. It is possible that Windolph took over this brewery instead of that of Deuss, but the size of the brewery and Fritz's prior record of unstable business relationships suggest that Windolph owned a larger, more established business. All four Chaska breweries appear at the same time in the excise records of 1866, so it appears there really were four breweries in town at one point.

Young and May (1866–1867)
Henry Young (1867–1873) (with lessees John Ketterer [1869] and Joseph Heimberger [1871–1873])
Peter Iltis (1873–1878)
George Karcher (1878–1883)
Peter Iltis (Iltis & John Sheavy) (1883–1885) (with lessees Norbeck, Krotsch, and Karl, 1884)
Gottlieb Beurlen (1885–1894)
Fred Beyrer (1906–1920)
Fred Beyrer (1934–1955)
Location: 597 Stoughton Avenue (corner of Beech and Stoughton)

Henry Young and Charles May began work on Chaska's fourth brewery in spring 1866. (The excise records of 1866 list a Young and Sauerbrey, which is possibly just a singularly poor rendition of Charles May.) Young carried on the business by himself for a few years, though by the early 1870s he was devoting more time to his other pursuits and leased the brewery to others. In 1873, he sold the brewery to Peter Iltis, one of Chaska's most important businessmen. Iltis retained Joseph Heimberger as his brewer and proceeded to expand the business. Iltis increased output of the brewery, sometimes called the Union Brewery to distinguish it from Ulmer's Chaska Brewery, to more than 800 barrels by 1878. He made plans in 1874

to dig a cellar in the bluffs near the junction of the Laketown, Waconia, and Chaska roads, but apparently decided to buy the cellar of the burned-down Leivermann brewery instead.

Iltis decided that he, too, wished to spend more time on his other enterprises and sold his brewery to George Karcher in August 1878. The remaining inventory of the brewery was apparently not included in the deal, since one of a series of notices published in the August 8 Chaska *Weekly Valley Herald* announced that he was selling 400 eighth barrels for 75¢ each. Karcher ran the brewery until 1883, when he retired from the business. (His retirement was quite short, since that October he was reported as working in a brewery in St. Cloud and he took over the Waconia brewery in 1886.)

Following Karcher's retirement, Iltis again took possession of the brewery until a suitable buyer could be found. In 1885 Gottlieb Beurlen purchased the brewery and operated it until his retirement in 1894. The brewery was out of operation for more than a decade, until Fred Beyrer moved from Long Prairie

Beyrer's Chaska brewery supplied local taverns with kegs like this half barrel. FROM THE COLLECTION OF PAT STAMBAUGH.

to take over the brewery in 1906. Beyrer had originally considered a site in Waconia, but found the asking price too high. Beyrer continued operating the brewery with the help of his son, also named Fred. The younger Beyrer took time out to attend business school in Stuttgart, Germany, in the early 1910s and also worked at a brewery outside Stuttgart. He also served in the U.S. Army during World War I, including eleven months of active duty in France.

After Prohibition ended, Beyrer returned to Chaska from Northfield (where he had been operating a soft drink factory) and reopened the family brewery. The Beyrer brewery was unique among post-Prohibition Minnesota breweries in that it never bottled or canned any beer. Beyrer provided kegs to local businesses from 1934 until 1955, when he retired. Beyrer died in 1976. The brewery no longer stands.

Chatfield [Fillmore County]

Charles Deinhardt (1857–1860?)
Mannheim & Lacy (1860–1865?)
Eugene Ellinson (1865?–1866)
Conrad Ellinson (1866–1868)
Thomas Collins (1868–1873?)
Collins and O'Connell (1870)
Preiser & Codletz (1873?–1877)
Location: Elmira Township

Unraveling the brewing history of Chatfield is complicated by the fact that Chatfield lies in two counties and three townships. The first brewery was built in the part that lies in Elmira Township (occasionally spelled Almira) on the northeast side of town. Here Charles Deinhardt started the first of his three breweries in Minnesota. His first advertisement, in the 23 December 1857 *Chatfield Democrat*, announced that he was prepared to furnish both lager and ale for $8 per barrel, or in casks of 5, 10, or 20 gallons. Deinhardt's advertisements continued through 1859, but then disappeared. The 1860 census lists his occupation as brewer, but does not include any real estate, which suggests he had sold the brewery, probably to John Mannheim (a saloon owner) and John Lacy. According to the 1860 Census of Industry, the brewery had produced 1,000 barrels of beer in the previous year, though at a price of only $6 per barrel. This had to be the former Deinhardt brewery, since the other

brewery in Chatfield was not in production for the entire tax year.

The period from 1860 through 1865 is largely a mystery. In October 1865 the *Democrat* reported that the Chatfield Brewery had been sold three months earlier to "parties from La Crosse" for $800 and then resold shortly thereafter for $1,850. The latest purchasers were the Ellinson family (sometimes spelled Ellenson or Ellerson). Conrad is listed as proprietor most often, though the name Eugene occasionally appears. In 1866 they sold between ten and twenty barrels per month. The identity and location of this brewery are clarified in the 1867 excise records when Conrad's brewery is listed alternately in Chatfield and in Elmira township. In August 1868 the brewery was taken over by Thomas Collins, one of the rare Irish immigrant brewers in Minnesota. He continued to operate the brewery through at least 1873, as recorded in state business directories. For at least some of this time he had a partner, Michael O'Connell. The Chatfield brewery burned to the ground on 23 July 1877, at which time it was owned by Preiser and Codletz. The brewery was a total loss except for a few barrels of beer in the back cellar, and the uninsured loss was estimated at $3,000.

George Schewing (1859–1865?)
Miller & Ackerman (?–1870?)
Location: Farrington's Addition

For a few years, Chatfield had two breweries. The *Chatfield Democrat* announced on 6 August 1859 that a new brewery was to be built on Farrington's Addition by George Scheining [*sic*], formerly of Milwaukee. The 1860 census lists George Shening [*sic*] as a brewer living in Orion Township, Olmsted county, which includes Farrington's Addition in the northwest corner of Chatfield. The editor of the *Democrat* thanked Schewing for two kegs of beer in April 1864, and he was listed in an 1865 Minnesota business directory. Later excise tax records leave open the possibility that two breweries were still operating in Chatfield as late as 1870. The excise records of that year show a brewery registered in October under the name of Miller and Ackerman as well as that of Collins and O'Connell. Since the Collins brewery was licensed in May and remained in the records for several more years, this listing is unlikely to have represented a change in ownership.

The importance of water in beer is indicated on this label not just by the fountain image but also by the claims that the product is by the "bottlers of the famous Cold Spring mineral water" and "Spring water used exclusively." Despite its pre-Prohibition appearance, this bottle was labeled in 1935–36. FROM THE COLLECTION OF DAVE WENDL.

Cold Spring [Stearns County]

Michael Sargl (1874–1881)
Ladner & Sargl (1881–188?)
John Ladner (188?–1886)
Ladner & Haemen (1886–1888)
Jacob Haemen (1888–1890)
Haemen & Oster (1890–1895) (Haemen, Oster & Roedel for three months in 1891)
Oster & Hilt (1895–1899)
Oster & Peters (1899)
Cold Spring Brewing Company (1899–1920, 1933–1996)
Gluek Brewing Company (1997–present)
Location: 219 North Red River Street

According to most sources, Michael Sargl (sometimes spelled Sargel) began brewing beer in Cold Spring in 1874. Based on its history in the nineteenth century, few would have bet that it would be one of only three breweries started in that century still operating in the twenty-first century. Sargl's site, with its supply of pure spring water, was ideal, but Stearns County already had six other breweries and the St. Cloud area was large enough to draw attention from major shipping breweries. In its early years, Sargl's brewery was among the smallest in the county, behind Gruber's Sauk Centre brewery and frequently behind Weber's brewery in Richmond.

The Cold Spring brewery also went through a greater than average number of ownership changes. Local histories differ on precisely when one partner replaced another, but none lasted a decade at the brewery until John Oster joined the firm in 1890. According to an article by Duane Kuss in the *Record-Journal-Patriot 2005 Area Guide*, Oster was not a brewer, but he owned a steam engine that was mounted on wheels and used to power threshing machines. The engine was used throughout the brewery, making it more efficient and profitable.

This Kegle Brau can from the mid-1960s was the only gallon beer can ever made by a Minnesota brewery. As with the first beer cans, opening it required new equipment and instructions. CAN FROM THE COLLECTION OF DAVE WENDL; INSTRUCTIONS FROM THE AUTHOR'S COLLECTION.

Henry Hilt's hay fever was so severe that he was forced to move from the area in 1898, but he sold his share in the brewery to a relative, Ferdinand Peters, who had been the agent for the Minneapolis Brewing Company in Brainerd. Oster and Peters hired Eugene Hermanutz as their brewmaster in 1900 and offered him part ownership in the company. Hermanutz had previously worked as a brewmaster in Wadena for two years and for another year in Walla Walla, Washington. The three incorporated the firm as Cold Spring Brewing Company in 1900, though the name had been used in 1899. They built a malt house in 1902 and expanded their sales area throughout the region and into the Twin Cities. The company was extremely successful in the decades before Prohibition, and the three partners built luxurious homes for their families near the brewery. Peters is credited with the idea of bottling the water from the brewery's spring and selling it as Red Star water. The company claimed that the water was sold up to one thousand miles from the brewery. By 1914 production was up to 16,000 barrels and the brewery was the twelfth largest in Minnesota.

In July 1919 federal agents arrived at Cold Spring Brewing Company to enforce the Prohibition laws and dump the remaining stock of the brewery into the nearby creek. According to local accounts, Hermanutz was unable

to watch his beer being destroyed and had to leave the scene. Despite this loss, Cold Spring was better prepared to survive Prohibition than most other breweries. Cold Spring Mineral Water Company had been incorporated in 1906, and the combination of mineral water, spring water, Red Star tonic, and some near beer led to the company doing more business in June 1921 than in any previous June. Unfortunately, neither Oster nor Hermanutz lived to see the brewery reopen in 1933.

At midnight on 7 April 1933, a federal marshal unlocked the brewery gates and the first of what would be more than 400 vehicles left the brewery grounds to deliver the first legal beer since Prohibition. Cold Spring beer was the first to reach St. Cloud, arriving in taverns there at 12:35 am. The brewery continued to thrive for the next several decades and eventually expanded distribution into nine states. Under Myron C. Johnson, the brewery was considered a model of regional breweries. Cold Spring purchased and operated Mankato Brewing Company for a few years during the early 1950s, but later sold it again to focus on its own brewery and brands.

Cold Spring Brewing Company attempted to survive the period of brewery closure and consolidation by concentrating on the local market and creating low-cost regional brands like Arrowhead and Western. It also brewed

beer for other companies on a contract basis—most notably Gemeinde Brau for the Amana Amish colony and the infamous Billy Beer. However, the flagship, Cold Spring Export, became a victim of cost-cutting wars and gained a reputation as a cheap beer. The brewery tried to reposition Export as a craft beer during the 1980s but without much success.

A group of Colorado investors purchased the struggling brewery in 1995, but this arrangement fell apart the next year and left behind unpaid bills and unpaid workers. Maurice Bryan led a group of local investors who purchased the property and renamed the company Gluek Brewing Company. Cold Spring had acquired the Gluek brands from G. Heileman of La Crosse almost two decades earlier in a trade for the Cold Spring mineral water brand and now used the Gluek name to revitalize the business. The brewery introduced a number of new products under the Gluek name, including Honey Bock and Red Bock, and, using the old Stite name, brought out four products in the Alum-A-Bottle package.

(Cold Spring Brewing Company's decline and the rise of Gluek Brewing Company in its place are covered in more detail in chapter 8. Additional Cold Spring artifacts are pictured in chapters 5, 6, and 8.)

Courtland [Nicollet County]

Koke & Heydrich (1858?)
Koke & Friton (1858)
Koke's Brewery (1858–1859)
Koke's Brewery (Ludwig Krauch, lessee) (1859–?)
Location: On the Nicollet County side of the Minnesota River, about a mile and a half east of downtown New Ulm

Sometime before March 1858, Koke and Heydrich started a brewery in the Minnesota River valley, about a mile and a half east of New Ulm on the Nicollet County side of the river. The *Neu-Ulm Pioneer* of 4 March 1858 commented on the scenic location of the brewery and described a walk through spring flowers to reach it. Koke may have been difficult to work with, since this partnership with Heydrich ended less than a month after they began to advertise. Koke then had a short-term partnership with August Friton, who shortly left to start his own brewery in New Ulm proper. Koke leased the brewery to Ludwig Krauch in 1859, but it

is not known how long he ran the brewery or how long it remained in production.

Crookston [Polk County]

August Walter (?–1879)
Burkhardt & Co. (1879–1884)
August Walter (1884–1893)
Julia Walter (1893–1894)
Koch, Seamen & Schnagl (1894)
Rausch, Schnagl & Reidesel (1894–1898)
Kiewel Brewing Co. (1899–1915)
Location: Between Front Street and the railroad tracks, between Fourth and Fifth streets

The Crookston Brewery was started sometime before 1879, perhaps as early as 1875, by August Walter (or Walters). The brewery was listed in the 1880 Census of Industry, and though no production figures were given, it was recorded that the brewery employed four workers. Local records are scarce during the early years of this brewery, and many of the existing national records are incomplete or contradictory. Burkhardt and Co. is listed in a business directory for 1880, but no Burkhardts appear in the 1880 census of Crookston. August Walter is listed as a brewer in Crookston, though he may have been an employee of the Burkhardts. To further complicate matters, Burkhardt and Co. continues to appear in excise records as late as 1887. August Walters was also involved with the brewery in Red Lake Falls, but may have been an investor rather than a brewer.

The history of the Crookston Brewery is better known starting with the arrival of Ferdinand Schnagl in 1894. Schnagl came to Crookston from Rush City, where he had been proprietor of the brewery. Schnagl went into business with two local partners, but left four years later to take over the brewery in Mantorville. The Crookston Brewery was purchased in January of 1899 by Jacob Kiewel, who already owned a brewery in Little Falls. The Kiewels began to improve and expand the plant and eventually built the capacity to more than 20,000 barrels per year. Charles Kiewel took over management of the Crookston branch and brought Eugene Buehl from Little Falls to be the new brewmaster. The new Kiewel brand, White Seal, was a companion to the Little Falls brewery's White Rose brand. The brewery also made a malt tonic and lower-strength beer for sale in North Dakota. The "red demon" contin-

ued to follow the Kiewel family, however. The Crookston branch suffered a fire in the cooper shop in 1905 and another fire in the brewery in 1910 that did $4,000 of damage.

During Prohibition, the Crookston facility served as the local branch of Kiewel Associated Products Co. However, Charles E. Kiewel went to St. Boniface, Manitoba, and opened Kiewel Brewing Co. there in 1925. The flagship White Seal brand was based on the Crookston beer of the same name. The Crookston brewery closed along with the other breweries forced to shut down because of treaty enforcement.

Besides White Seal, Kiewel's Crookston Brewery also made Red Ribbon. FROM THE COLLECTION OF KEN MALZ.

The Crookston branch's White Seal brand was advertised on this small pocketknife. FROM THE COLLECTION OF PAT STAMBAUGH.

Detroit Lakes (Becker County)

Detroit Brewing Co. (1886–1888?)

Location: On the west side of the Little Pelican River near the Northern Pacific (now BNSF) tracks

The pending establishment of a brewery in Detroit (now Detroit Lakes) was first announced in the *Detroit Record* in late June 1885. Within a week, "a large force of men" was at work on the brewery, located near the old Tyler Hotel on the west side of the Little Pelican River near the Northern Pacific tracks. It appears that construction stalled shortly thereafter, and the first (unnamed) owners sold the property to Ole Estad and Christian Anderson. Bearing out the *Record*'s favorable opinion of the new firm's prospects, the work was completed in time to release the first batch in mid-April 1886.

The company advertised that it was "producing an article unsurpassed by any brewery in the Northwest, and believe that a trial order will secure for us at least a portion of your patronage." It was unusual for a brewer to make a moderate request, but in light of the state of the market, it reflected reality. During the previous year, Arthur Blanding had established a company to bottle Schlitz beer, and John H. Smith was preparing to bottle for Peter Schroeder of Perham, less than twenty miles away. Schroeder's competition was more of a threat to the Detroit brewery since he was a very active salesman and had an excellent reputation along the Northern Pacific line. His visits to Detroit were noted in the paper about every two months. *Wing's Brewers Handbook* of 1887 contains a listing for Faeder and Arnold, a small lager brewery in Detroit, which probably represents another change in ownership. The brewery appears to have closed sometime in 1888, though nothing is known about the circumstances.

Duluth (St. Louis County)

Luce/J. G. Busch Brewery (1857–1866)

Nicholas Decker (1866–1877)

Michael Fink (M. Fink & Co.) (1877–1885)

A. Fitger & Co. (1885–1903)

Fitger Brewing Company (1903–1972) (operated during Prohibition as the Fitger Co.)

Location: On Superior Street between Sixth and Seventh avenues east

Sidney Luce was a speculator who arrived in Duluth in 1857, during the middle of the finan-cial panic of that year. Duluth was slow to recover, so Luce provided some encouragement by allowing H. S. Burke, Gilbert Falconer, Harry Fargo, and J. Gottlieb Busch to start a brewery on his land near First Street and Washington Avenue. The small stream that trickled into Lake Superior at Seventh Street East near that point was named Brewery Creek. None of the four men is listed in the 1860 census as a brewer, but their absence is not conclusive. Busch seems to have been the dominant partner, since J. G. Busch and Co. appears on the tax records from 1862 to 1866. An ad in the *Superior Chronicle* (WI) in October 1864 emphasized that the brewery was situated on "a pure mountain stream" and offered an unusually wide range of beers including Cream Ale, Stock Ale, Wheat Ale, and "Present-use Ale" ("small beer") in addition to lager. Luce sold the property and the brewery to Nicholas Decker in 1866, but Busch remained for a few years as the "practical brewer."

By the 1870s, Decker was well established as a businessman and politician, and he decided to leave the actual brewing to others after an unsuccessful attempt at brewing himself in the late 1860s. Even so, the editor of the *Duluth Minnesotian* at first suggested throwing the new brewer (probably Christian Spier) into the lake, or at least into a vat of his "watery beer." (The editor warmed up after the keg was finished.) Decker's hotel and saloon profits enabled him to buy out a neighboring brewery and use its equipment to enlarge his own brewery. Decker also undertook a multiyear search for a suitable partner for the business. After several unsatisfactory combinations, including a brief period in 1872 when he was out of brewing altogether, Decker finally sold a share in the brewery to Michael Fink. Fink had arrived in Duluth after spending a few years brewing in Stillwater and was well prepared to take over the brewery in 1877, when the Decker family sold him the brewery following the death of Nicholas two years earlier.

Like Decker and Luce before him, Fink combined business and politics, but business would prove more frustrating. Shortly after he took control of the brewery, it was seriously damaged when the creek undermined the foundation and caused a partial collapse. While operations continued, it was clear that a new building was needed. In fall 1881, Fink began construction of a new brewery on Superior Street between Sixth and Seventh avenues east. M. Fink and Company's Lake Superior Brewery sold its first beer in 1882, beginning a ninety-year run at that location. In November of that year, August Fitger was hired as the new brewmaster. He purchased half of the brewery from Fink six months later, and Fink devoted his efforts to expanding the brewery's market. In April 1885, Fink sold his remaining half of the brewery to Percy S. Anneke, formerly of Milwaukee. (Fink tried several ventures after leaving the brewery, including another brewery in Tower, but never achieved much success and died in poverty in 1899.)

The new partners, operating under the name of A. Fitger & Co., moved quickly to modernize the brewery and increase production and quality. They built a bottling plant and introduced their first bottled beer in November 1885. They constructed new storage buildings and in 1890 became one of the first breweries in Minnesota to install artificial refrigeration. The building projects, which were designed by several of the most successful brewery architects from Chicago, continued for two decades and eventually occupied more than a block along Superior Street. The additional

This rare Fitger's miniature stein (about two inches tall) was made before 1903 because it still bears the name of A. Fitger & Co. It advertises the Bohemian and Bavarian beer styles. FROM THE COLLECTION OF PETE CLURE.

production allowed Fitger Brewing to expand its market throughout northern Minnesota, with the beer shipped from a railroad spur that was built to the brewery in 1904. Fitger established tied houses and depots all the way to the North Dakota border. Business was so profitable that the partners were able to expand into real estate, hotels, mining, and other ventures (though August Fitger turned down an opportunity to invest in a struggling abrasives company that would later become 3M). By 1910 the brewery was producing 78,000 barrels a year and was one of the largest breweries in the state outside the Twin Cities.

St. Louis County and the surrounding counties voted to go dry well before national Prohibition took effect, but Fitger still had some sales in Wisconsin, which had not yet gone dry. Some Duluth customers took advantage of a loophole to buy beer from the Fitger agency in Superior, but when delivery was stopped, customers lost their brand loyalty. Fitger survived Prohibition by making soft drinks and candy and also distributed cigars made by other manufacturers. Its most successful product was Silver Spray, a sparkling mixer that was eventually distributed in thirty-one states, including some on the West Coast. Part of the old brewery was converted into the Silver Spray Gym, a highly regarded training facility for up-and-coming boxers. Fitger purchased the business property of The Sobriety Company (formerly Duluth Brewing & Malting Company) in 1930 and gained several popular labels, but still never made a profit during any year of Prohibition.

In 1933 Victor Anneke (Percy's son) and brewmaster John Beerhalter saw their decisions vindicated when Prohibition was repealed and beer returned to Duluth. Because it remained in operation during Prohibition, Fitger was one of the handful of breweries to ship beer on April 7, the first day of legal sales. Fitger was one of the first breweries in the country to offer beer in cans and also offered unpasteurized beer in 64-ounce picnic bottles. In 1937 Victor Anneke's failing health forced him to delegate all brewing management to Beerhalter and transfer management to his longtime friend Arnold Fitger. That year Fitger introduced a new label, Nordlager, and launched a series of outdoor-themed advertis-

This extremely rare coaster dates from the period immediately after beer was re-legalized in 1933. FROM THE COLLECTION OF PETE CLURE.

ing efforts. (The outdoor theme would be used with great effect by Fitger and would result in some of the most distinctive pieces of Minnesota breweriana, if not necessarily increased sales.)

The creativity shown in advertising and sponsorships could not make up for problems with distribution and brewing, which would start the company on a long slide. In 1937 Fitger began to lose draft accounts to larger breweries that could afford to provide taverns with draft equipment that Fitger could no

In the mid-1950s Fitger considered offering a special can at Christmastime but was advised that this would be undesirable since it would clearly indicate that beer left on the shelves after Christmas was old. This can blank and an alternate version without the red trim are all that remain of that idea. FROM THE COLLECTION OF PETE CLURE.

longer give for free. To make matters worse, the taste of Fitger's Beer was becoming a liability. Fitger used a substantial amount of malt extract in the brewing, which can produce a metallic tang and/or additional sweetness, depending on the brewing process. Everyone from bar patrons to friends of Arnold Fitger voiced the complaint that Fitger's was too "sweet." The company's response was, "Our beer is not a sweet, but a Mild and Mellow Beer." Duluth Brewing & Malting Company emphasized in ads that they malted their own barley—a lightly disguised swipe at their cross-town rivals. Despite a strong identification with the Great Lakes and the north woods, Fitger sales continued to slip. The company was hurt even more by increased price competition from national brewers. In a 1966 letter to stockholders that announced a paltry profit of $1,605.99, John S. Beerhalter Jr. blamed much of the dollar and volume loss in Wisconsin on price cuts and special deals made by Schlitz on the Old Milwaukee brand that Fitger was unable to meet.

In 1969 John Ferris became president of the company and purchased much of the stock from the Beerhalter heirs. Despite his attempts to put the company on a firm financial footing, sales continued to plummet and the brewery lost more money. The stock dropped in value from $20 in mid-1969, when Ferris began his purchases, to 49¢ a share less than a year later. Some stockholders alleged that the company had been mismanaged and that officers were raiding the assets by selling off the land and by closing the Pop Shop without selling the brands. Matters were made worse by the state of Minnesota, which was considering routing an extension of Interstate 35 through the brewery property and was also requiring the company to install expensive pollution abatement equipment to stay in operation. Ultimately, the state forced the brewery to refrain from installing the equipment since it would simply make the brewery more expensive to purchase for demolition. The brewery finally closed in September 1972. Fitger Brewing Company later sued the state of Minnesota for damages relating to the forced closing and won a partial settlement in 1986. Eventually, pressure by Duluth residents and the Minnesota State Historic Preservation Office resulted in selection of a highway route that avoided the brewery complex. Most of the brewery still stands and serves as a restaurant, hotel, shopping complex, and Fitger's Brewhouse brewpub.

(The next stage in the history of the Fitger complex is covered in the Brewpubs section.)

Klein & Kiichli (1859–1861?)
Location: Seventh Avenue West and Fourth Street

Louis Kiichli is the only person to be listed as a brewer in Duluth's 1860 population census. According to the few available sources, Klein and Kiichli moved their brewery from Superior, Wisconsin, to Duluth in 1859. They do not appear in any tax records from 1862 through 1872, so it is unlikely that they survived more than a couple of years. While some accounts have this brewery being absorbed into the Decker and Fink company, it is more likely that the firm of Kreimer Bros. was the brewery acquired. It is possible that Kreimer Bros. occupied the old Klein and Kiichli site, but no documentation confirms this.

Gustav Kiene (1869–1876?)
Location: Minnesota Point, about a mile from Franklin Square

Gustav Kiene's brewery appears in tax records for the first time in November 1869. The 1870 census lists the 22-year-old's brewery as being next door to two saloons that doubled as brothels. The *Duluth Minnesotian*, which understood the different beer types, wrote that Kiene was producing "Lake Superior Ale." One source indicates that Kiene's brewery burned down in 1871—and tax records do not list him in 1872—but the same records indicate he sold some beer in November 1874, and he is listed in *Schade's Brewers Handbook* as producing 54 and 143 barrels in 1874 and 1875 respectively.

Kreimer Bros. (1871–1872)
Camahl & Busse (1874–1875)
Location: Unknown

The Kreimer Bros. brewery seems to have resulted from the breakup of the Kreimer and Decker partnership that lasted from mid-1871 to mid-1872. Little else is known about the firm except that it produced fewer than 500 barrels a year for its short existence. This firm may have been taken over later by Camahl and Busse, another partnership about which little is known. *Schade's Brewers Handbook* includes the brewery in the listing, but with no production given.

Benjamin Decker (1882–1884?)
W. Franke & Co. (1884–1885?)
Location: Washington Avenue between First and Second streets

The 1884–85 *Duluth City Directory* listed W. Franke and Co. as operating a brewery on the west side of Washington Avenue between First and Second streets. Franke was still listed as a brewer in the next year's directory, but his partners, Charles Unden and Louis Eichstadt, were no longer listed with him. *American Breweries II* includes a listing for Benjamin Dickler, who operated a brewery from 1882 through 1884. This is probably Benjamin Decker, eldest son of Nicholas, who was returning to the family business, apparently on the family's old Washington Street property. Decker was listed in tax records as starting a brewery with a capacity of more than 500 barrels in January 1882. It is possible that Franke and Co. was the successor firm to Decker, but no conclusive evidence has been uncovered.

Duluth Brewing & Malting Company (1896–1920, 1934–1966)
The Sobriety Company (1920–1934)
Location: 231 S. Twenty-ninth Avenue West

For a firm that became so well-known, Duluth Brewing & Malting Company was a relative latecomer to the Minnesota brewing scene, though the industry was slower to develop in northern Minnesota than elsewhere in the state. The A. Fitger & Co. brewery had been without local competition for more than a decade when Reiner Hoch founded Duluth Brewing & Malting in 1896. According to an article by Pete Clure and Doug Davis in *American Breweriana Journal* (January–February 1999), Hoch had moved to Duluth from Negaunee in Michigan's Upper Peninsula, where he had operated a brewery with business partner Charles Meeske. Hoch expanded the brewery rapidly, adding a bottling department and bringing the capacity of the plant up to 45,000 barrels per year. The company's Moose brand lager became popular and the company was able to expand its distribution throughout northern Minnesota. By 1910 Duluth Brewing & Malting operated depots in cities from Chisholm on the Iron Range to East Grand Forks on the North Dakota border. The company also brewed a special low-alcohol product called Our

Tame Moose for sale in North Dakota, where strong beer was prohibited by the state constitution. Hoch also built a malt house with a capacity much larger than needed for the company's own production so the excess could be sold to other breweries. When Michigan's early move to prohibition forced Charles Meeske's Marquette, Michigan, brewery out of business, Hoch invited Meeske to join him in Duluth and renew their partnership.

The company remained profitable up through Prohibition due to the success of its Moose and Rex beer brands and the Lovit line of soft drinks. However, Fitger Brewing purchased the Lovit brand in an agreement that included a provision transferring the rights to all of Duluth Brewing & Malting's labels to Fitger. Fitger would later produce both Moose and Rex—the latter becoming one of Fitger Brewing's flagship brands in the mid-twentieth century.

During Prohibition, Duluth Brewing & Malting went further than any other brewing company to emphasize the changed nature of its products by renaming the new beverage firm The Sobriety Company. Its advertising touted the quality of Lake Superior water and its contributions to the company's healthful beverages. As with many other breweries that attempted to stay alive by producing near beer and soft drinks, the temperance products did not bring in enough revenue to cover expenses,

Our Tame Moose was a low-alcohol brand introduced well before Prohibition. Several northern breweries made low-alcohol beers for sale in North Dakota, though this label (c. 1900) does not include a North Dakota permit number. FROM THE COLLECTION OF KEN MALZ.

and the additional financial hardship that followed the stock market crash in 1929 forced the company to suspend operations.

Upon repeal, Charles Meeske's son Carl began to prepare the brewery for reopening. He purchased equipment from Germany and had a 450-barrel brew kettle that was believed to be one of the largest in the country. The brewery was one of only two in the Great Lakes region to have its own malting plant. (Theo. Hamm in St. Paul was the other.) Meeske hired a new brewmaster, Henry Schmid. Schmid had 44 years of experience in brewing, including a stint at Cervecería Cuauhtémoc in Monterrey, Mexico, during Prohibition. The need to upgrade the brewery delayed reopening, and Fitger and Peoples beat Meeske to the punch. But by 1934, Duluth Brewing & Malting was ready to introduce its new flagship beer, Karlsbrau, to the region's beer lovers. The Karlsbrau brand name was chosen in a contest sponsored by Meeske, and it is probably no coincidence that the winning beer was named after him. Karlsbrau was produced in Duluth until 1966, and its popularity led to the label's survival with other brewers. G. Heileman acquired the brand after the Duluth brewery closed and later sold Karlsbrau to Cold Spring, where it was brewed into the 1980s.

In addition to Karlsbrau, Duluth Brewing & Malting introduced several other brands in the years immediately after repeal. Castle Brew was a low-priced brand that survived only a few years. Gold Shield later became Royal Bohemian Gold Shield Beer and ultimately Royal Bohemian. Despite being listed in brewing publications as one of the company's flag-

Of these five brands, only Royal 58 had any extended success. Royal 57 had a short run during 1951, and Castle Brew (in the steinie bottle), Royal Brau (quart-size bottle), and Gold Shield were offered briefly in the late 1930s. The Royal 58 bottle shown here dates from 1966, when it was brewed by G. Heileman. FROM THE COLLECTION OF PETE CLURE.

ship beers, Royal Bohemian suffered from a poor reputation and the brand was eventually dropped. Royal Brew was a short-lived brand, probably since adopting the name of an unpopular label was not good marketing. In 1951 the Royal name reappeared as Royal 57—a beer named for its 5.7 percent alcohol content. It had an extremely short life due to stories that 57 was being referred to as "the ketchup beer." While some accounts claimed that Heinz had threatened to sue, Clure's interviews with company personnel showed the truth was that Duluth Brewing & Malting simply did not want its beer marked with that unappetizing comparison. The beer was reintroduced in December as Royal 58, with the alcohol content changed to reflect the new name. The slogan "Make a date with 58" had much more appeal

This very rare reverse-on-glass and neon sign dates from the 1930s. Reverse-on-glass pieces are painted on the back side of the glass to protect the art from damage. FROM THE COLLECTION OF PETE CLURE.

and carried the brand through the next several years.

During World War II, Duluth Brewing & Malting was challenged by the same issues as every other brewer in the country—particularly the need to keep production up while using ever more limited amounts of barley. The malting division of the company was enlisted to make distillers malt for the government, which was used both to make industrial alcohol and a by-product that was used in the manufacture of smokeless powder for munitions.

After the war, Duluth Brewing & Malting continued to expand its market. Its brands were sold throughout the upper Midwest and some product was shipped as far away as Alaska. While the company continued to turn a profit and enjoyed a solid reputation, finances were always tight. It did not have as large an advertising budget as its competitors, so display pieces for the brewery are much more scarce than for crosstown rival Fitger. In the early 1960s, the company sold the malting plant, the bottling line, and everything but the brewhouse itself to G. Heileman Brewing Company of La Crosse, Wisconsin. The final blow to Duluth Brewing & Malting was the extension of Interstate Highway 35 to Duluth. The route ran directly through the brewery, and the brewery ceased production in 1966. The brewery was demolished shortly thereafter, and the freeway took its place. Some stock buildings remain and are used today as warehouses.

C. J. Johnson/Scandia Bottling (1901–1906)
West End Malt Ale Co. (1910–1914)
Location: 1909 W. First

C. J. (Charles J.) Johnson appears in 1905 excise records as a producer of beer, but no other records exist other than listings in the Duluth city directories and *Brewers' Journal*. This firm, operating under various names from 1901 through 1914, had a product called Swedish Malt Ale, but this may not have been a beer brewed at this address. C. J. Johnson was an officer of the West End Malt Ale Co., providing a link between firms with different names at the same address.

E. F. Burg (1907)
Location: 2234 W. Michigan

The 1907 *Duluth City Directory* lists Edward F. Burg as a brewer. This was the only year he ap-

pears as a brewer; the next year he was listed as a dealer in bar supplies. The address was the former location of Geyser Bottling Works, which is sometimes listed as a brewer, though it is unlikely it did any actual brewing on the premises. (Geyser also had an office downtown at 218 East Third.)

Peoples Brewing Co. (1907–1920)
Peoples Bottling Co. (1920–1933)
Peoples Brewing Co. (1933–1957)
Location 4230 W. Second Street

Some of the eastern European immigrants who arrived in northern Minnesota to work in the rapidly expanding mining industry brought with them the socialist ideals that were growing in appeal in the industrialized economies. While many times the socialist and communist organizations encouraged temperance activities, in a few cases the desire to resist the evils of capitalism affected the brewing industry directly. One such case was Peoples Brewing of Duluth.

Martin Smith, F. G. Sandstedt, and M. J. Gleeson were saloon owners in Duluth who were looking for a way to obtain beer without having to submit to the terms of the Duluth breweries or out-of-state brewers. In 1907 they

started Peoples Brewing Co., which began operations in an office in the Burrows Building, downtown at 301–303 West Superior Street. By the next year, they had opened their brewery at Forty-second Avenue West and Second Street and begun to brew. The member saloons guaranteed the brewery a market for draught beer, but labels exist that show the company bottled beer as well. Peoples remained profitable until Prohibition, and survived through the dry years as a bottler for various products, including 7UP.

Because of its bottling business, Peoples was ready to reopen in mid-1933, the second of Duluth's three breweries to resume brewing beer. Carl O. Hanson led the reorganization of the firm after Prohibition. The basic brand was first named Peoples, then Peoples Choice, and finally, Stag. The brewery's premium brand, which was much more heavily advertised, was Regal Supreme. After World War II, Peoples followed the lead of Gluek Brewing in Minneapolis and produced a malt liquor. It was first marketed under the name Ruff's Stout, but this name was dropped in favor of Olde English 600. Olde English was shipped to the Pacific Northwest and even as far as Puerto Rico.

This corner sign from the 1930s highlights the brewery's use of Lake Superior water. FROM THE COLLECTION OF PETE CLURE.

Olde English 600 was shipped to Puerto Rico, as this rare crown cap from the mid-1950s demonstrates. FROM THE COLLECTION OF PAT STAMBAUGH.

Despite its popular brands, Peoples was by far the smallest of Duluth's three breweries (by the mid-1950s, Duluth was the only city in the state to have three breweries). Its capacity of 75,000 barrels per year was half that of Fitger, and only slightly more than half that of Duluth Brewing & Malting. By 1957 Peoples was unable to keep up with the local or national competition, and the firm was liquidated.

Much of the brewery still stands and is used as a warehouse.

Lake Superior Brewing Company's Seven Bridges Brown Ale celebrates the bridges that are a prominent feature of Duluth's cityscape. This label style was used in the early 2000s. FROM THE AUTHOR'S COLLECTION.

Lake Superior Brewing Company (1994–present)
Location: 2711 W. Superior Street

Lake Superior Brewing Company started out in a small room in the Fitger complex. In the winter of 1998–1999, the company moved to larger quarters that would hold a bottling line.

Lake Superior Brewing produces four year-round beers: Special Ale, Kayak Kölsch, Sir Duluth Oatmeal Stout, and Mesabi Red. Six different seasonal beers are offered in rotation, and the brewery produces house beers for the Hacienda del Sol restaurant. (Additional information may be found in chapter 8.)

While later audiences might read this advertisement as accusing Sieur du Luth of brutality, during the 1950s this incident was intended as praise of his resolute character. ADVERTISEMENT PROOF FROM THE COLLECTION OF PETE CLURE.

East Grand Forks
[Polk County]

Mundigel, Zingel & Co. (1886–1890)
Mundigel & Hoffman (1890–1893)
Nicholas Hoffman (1893–1896)
White & Jarvis (1897–1899)
East Grand Forks Brewing Co. (1899–1917)
Location: Washington Avenue at the southwest corner of Dakota

Mundigel, Zingel, and Co. began to brew in East Grand Forks sometime in 1886. The company was dependent on the financial backing of Nicholas Hoffman, a wealthy local farmer. The brewery was a modern and relatively large facility located in an important railroad center on the border of a dry state. Despite its advantages, the first few years of the brewery were troubled. An article by Robert Hajicek in *The Breweriana Collector* (Summer 1997) showed that Hoffman was gradually forced to take over the business himself, first in partnership with John Mundigel and then as sole proprietor. Hoffman appeared to be having trouble paying his tax bills, since excise records include a penalty assessed in February 1896. Later that year, a Boston company foreclosed on the brewery and placed it in receivership. In the course of the negotiations on his property, Hoffman died of a self-inflicted gunshot wound.

Thomas White became the new owner of the brewery

and began to expand its operations despite the hostile environment. North Dakota, like many of the Great Plains states, was a temperance stronghold, but individual Dakotans still patronized White's brewery and the agents of the numerous urban breweries who set up shop in the border region. Polk County itself went dry in 1915, though loopholes remained. At first, nonintoxicating malt beverages could still be sold at soft drink parlors (of which there were about twenty in East Grand Forks), but these were often used as a front for the sale of liquor, and all malt beverages were prohibited in April 1916. The brewery was raided multiple times on suspicion of violating the law, but continued to bounce back.

North Dakota's prohibition clause permitted residents to make beer for their own use, so John McInerny, White's son-in-law, devised a plan to create a cooperative brewery. North Dakotans signed contracts to purchase the raw ingredients and the brewery turned their ingredients into beer. The brewery functioned as usual, except that the labels on the bottles bore the name of the individual contractor, not the brewery. This made the brewery one of the most profitable businesses in the city, but drew unwanted attention from North Dakota's newly elected attorney general, "Wild Bill" Langer. In July 1917 he and local law enforcement officers staged a

raid on the brewery, arrested McInerny, and charged him with bootlegging. Despite having company records with the names of 5,000 members of the cooperative, McInerny was found not guilty.

In early October 1917, the excise tax on beer was doubled from $1.50 to $3.00 to raise revenue for the war (and to discourage brewing and consumption). The brewery would not have been able to make back on sales what it would have paid in tax, especially with the more vigorous law enforcement in North Dakota. The *St. Cloud Times Weekly* described the final event in the brewery's history:

> Stretching back through 36 cellars a foam bedecked stream trickled its way behind the East Grand Forks brewery to the Red Lake river, where it was lost to view. It started as a slender thread of brown, smelling of ripened hop fields, slowly moving down a runway and then out into a culvert, where it found its way to the river.
>
> Presently a man waded up the stream and threw open the doors to the cellars, and the slowly moving thread became a rushing, tumbling mountain of foam, dashing along rapidly to the river, where it changed a narrow strip of the Red Lake river to a moving field of white. . . .
>
> As nonchalantly as though he were draining a cup of tea, Deputy Revenue Collector G. A. Aubol of St. Paul ordered the vats opened so the beer could flow into the river.

The brewery never reopened. Much of the building was torn down and the land was used to grow potatoes.

Elizabeth [Ottertail County]

John Koehnlein (1871–1872?)
Location: Unknown

In 1870 John Koehnlein's brewery and house in Minneapolis was destroyed by fire. In the fall of 1871, Koehnlein began brewing in Elizabeth (sometimes called Elizabethtown), a town about five miles north of Fergus Falls. He brewed for at least a year, but is not mentioned in local records. The equipment from the Elizabeth brewery eventually was purchased in

White's Old Style Beer was approved for sale in North Dakota. This label, which is a bit vague about the exact amount of beer in the bottle, predates the 1906 label regulations. FROM THE COLLECTION OF KEN MALZ.

THIS BEER GUARANTEED PURE
White's
OLD STYLE BEER
CONTENTS ABOUT 12 OZ. N.D SERIAL NO. 7.
BREWED, BOTTLED & SOLD EXCLUSIVELY BY THE
EAST GRAND FORKS BREWING CO.
EAST GRAND FORKS, MINN.

1878 by Charles Brown and Co. of Fergus Falls to equip its new brewery.

Ellsworth [Nobles County]

Frank Roemer & Sons (1902)
Roemer Bros. (1903)
Consumers Brewing Co. (1903–1906)
Eagle Brewing Co. (1907–1908)
Location: North side of town, north of W. Sherman Avenue

The brewery in Ellsworth was started by Frank Roemer of New Prague, along with his sons John and Jim. The next year Frank turned the brewery over to his sons, who expanded the business as far as nearby South Dakota and Iowa. They changed the name to Consumers Brewing Co. later in 1903 and continued to operate the brewery until financial problems forced them to close in 1906. A group of local investors incorporated the brewery under the name Eagle Brewing Co. in November 1907 and remodeled the brewery to begin production the next year. It was still unable to make a profit, and the brewery was forced to close again in 1908. The legal difficulties of the corporation continued for several years as creditors sought payment of debts.

Additional information on this brewery and a label from Consumers Brewing is included in chapter 3.

Elysian [Le Sueur County]

Emil Theimer (1874–1877)
Location: Unknown

This small town gained a brewery in 1874 when Emil Theimer began to make beer that summer. An article in the 23 July 1874 *Le Sueur Sentinel* claimed that Theimer made "a superior article of beer that commands the trade of Waterville, Cleveland, and other towns in the county, beside meeting with a large sale in Faribault." It was referred to by locals as a "large brewery" and was proclaimed "one of the best in this part of the state."

Little is known of the middle years of this brewery, but it met a spectacular end. The *Sentinel* reported on 3 May 1877 that the brewery "was discovered to be on fire on Wednesday morning of last week ... and was wholly consumed." The editor of the *Sentinel* asserted that the fire was the work of "an incendiary," because "there was little or no fire in the stove

when the brewery was left the previous night." Theimer had somewhat more insurance coverage than the average brewery of the time, so about $3,000 of his $4,000 loss was covered. Nonetheless, Theimer did not rebuild after the fire.

Evansville [Douglas County]

John Schwartz & Bro. (1882–1890)
Peter Schwartz (1890–1900)
Albertina Schwartz (1900–1901)
Location: South of State Street on the east side of First Street

The 1886 Douglas County plat book lists John and Peter Schwartz as the proprietors of the Evansville brewery. This firm was probably started around 1882, but reliable local records do not exist. In 1890 John sold his interest in the brewery to his brother, who continued it on his own. Peter died in 1900, and his widow, Albertina, continued the business for several months with her two oldest sons, John and Joseph, who were listed as brewers in the 1900 census. A 1912 county atlas shows no structures at the brewery location.

Fairmont [Martin County]

Gideon Smales Smales (1877–1879)
Location: At the foot of Main Street

Fairmont was a temperance stronghold in the early 1870s, and the few mentions of beer in the local press referred to imports from Jackson, about 25 miles to the west. But the presence of an active "English Club" that came to dominate the local economy created an attractive environment for an ale brewer. In June 1877, Gideon Smales Smales came to join his older brother in town and shortly afterward purchased the Fairmont brewery (wording from the newspaper seems to indicate that one existed before his arrival, though no other references to it have been found). In November, an ad appeared offering "the highest market price" for oats and corn, suggesting that Smales may have produced an oatmeal stout. By the end of 1877, Smales had invested $1,700 in brewery improvements and new outbuildings, including a bottling house.

Early in 1878, Smales began to advertise in the *Martin County Sentinal* [*sic*], offering "Pure English Ales, Porter &c" in kegs or bottles at "reasonable rates." By August, Smales believed

he had enough business to justify building a new brewery at the foot of Main Street. The new facility featured a large cellar, which was referred to as "an eighteen hundred dollar hole." A large piece of petrified wood was found during the excavation of the cellar. Unfortunately, the "eighteen hundred dollar hole" was financial as well as physical. Smales's over-extension was a contributing cause to the failure of the Bank of Fairmont in January 1879. The brewery and other assets were sold to satisfy creditors and did not operate again.

Faribault [Rice County]

Fleckenstein Bros. (1857–1860)
Gottfried Fleckenstein (1860–1896)
G. Fleckenstein & Son (1896–1904)
Louis Fleckenstein (1904–1907)
Location: Corner of Oak and Third streets

Gottfried (Godfrey) Fleckenstein arrived in America in 1853, about three years after his parents. He quickly left New York and headed for Cincinnati, where he found a job in one of the breweries in that important brewing center. Gottfried ran a brewery in St. Paul for a short time, but by 1857 he and his brother Ernst decided to establish a brewery in the fast-growing town of Faribault.

The Fleckenstein Bros. brewery was built at a cost of about $2,000 and held equipment brought from St. Paul. The brothers also began what would be the first in an extensive series of aging caves in the sandstone bluffs. In 1859 the brothers added a still to the facility, but this part of the business was discontinued when the excise tax was established in 1862. A local history claims that it was used to make whiskey, which is possible, but distilling a flawed batch of beer into beer brandy was an old Bavarian tradition, and the distillery may have been used for this product. According to an article by Fleckenstein descendant Jean Paschke in *American Breweriana Journal* (May–June 1995), Gottfried and Ernst did not get along, so Ernst left in 1860 to start his own brewery. Gottfried remained at the original location. The first brewery had a capacity of about five barrels per day and was operated without the aid of any machinery. In the mid-1860s, Gottfried added horse-driven machinery and was able to increase efficiency and production. In 1866 his brewery sold 665 barrels and was classi-

This Sheeran & Filler label for Gottfried Fleckenstein's beer may be the earliest known Minnesota beer bottle label. Sheeran & Filler did business under that name from 1877 to 1880. BOB KAY COLLECTION.

fied as a large brewery. His brewery stayed relatively free of calamity during its early decades (unlike his brother's) and steadily increased production. In 1872 he tore down the brewery and rebuilt it on a much larger scale at a cost of $20,000. By 1879 he was producing more than 1,300 barrels and owned the twenty-fifth largest brewery in the state.

In 1877 Gottfried contracted to have his beer bottled by the firm of Sheeran and Filler. An 1882 history of Rice County reported that in 1880 Sheeran and Filler moved its facility to a location across the street from Fleckenstein's brewery, since this portion of its trade brought in about $16,000 per year.

The Gottfried Fleckenstein brewery continued to prosper throughout the rest of the nineteenth century, even though the brewery was severely damaged by fire in 1892. The loss of $30,000 to $40,000 was at least partially insured. When the brewery was rebuilt and expanded the next year, the family took advantage of the opportunity to install modern brewing equipment. In 1896 Gottfried brought his son Louis into the firm to prepare him to take over the business. Louis became the proprietor in 1904, following the death of his father, and continued to operate the brewery until 1907. During the later years, the brewery's flagship brand was called Salva-

tor, but the product line also included a malt tonic and a temperance beer.

In 1936 Felix Frederickson purchased the caves and started Treasure Cave, Inc., which became the first commercial producer of blue cheese in the United States. Seventy years later, the Faribault Dairy Company used the caves to produce award-winning blue cheeses. Additional information may be found on the company's Web site at www.faribaultdairy. com/cheesecaves.html.

Norbert Paquin (1857–1863)
Location: Willow Street between Eighth and Ninth avenues

Norbert Paquin arrived in Faribault with the intent of building a hotel but changed his mind and built a brewery instead. The building also contained facilities for distilling whiskey. Paquin soon tired of brewing and turned to other interests: the 1860 census lists him as a real estate dealer and his brother Felix as the brewer. According to an 1882 history of Rice County, Ernst Fleckenstein leased Paquin's brewery for a few months in 1860 while waiting for his own brewery to be built. The liquor dealers Brandt and Gerdes were the next to lease the brewery, which they operated for about two years until they built their own brewery on Willow Street. After Brandt and Gerdes vacated the brewery, Edward Kelley op-

erated the distillery until the building burned in 1865. It was not rebuilt.

Ernst Fleckenstein (1860–1901)
Ernst Fleckenstein Brewing Co. (1901–1920)
Ernst Fleckenstein Beverage Co. (1920–1933)
Ernst Fleckenstein Brewing Co. (1933–1964)
Location: East bank of the Straight River, across from the end of Eighth Street NW

Ernst Fleckenstein Brewing Co. was one of only a very few Minnesota breweries to survive for more than a century. While many accounts speak of its 108-year history, the first four years should be credited to the brewery of his brother Gottfried.

According to Jean Paschke's 1995 article in *American Breweriana Journal*, Ernst learned the brewery business in Bavaria at the family brewery, which had been started in 1577. His parents, Johannis and Anna, came to America around 1850 and began sending money back to the homeland to buy their sons out of the army. Most accounts have Ernst and his brother Gottfried arriving in America and moving together from New York to Cincinnati to St. Paul to Faribault. However, the 1900 census gives different years of immigration (1853 for Gottfried and 1854 for Ernst), the 1855–56 *St. Paul City Directory* does not list Ernst, and only Gottfried is mentioned by name in Cincinnati brewing histories. None of these sources is conclusive, but it is possible that Johannis and Anna were able get only one son out of the army at a time and that the brothers may not have traveled together across the country but met up from time to time. Ernst may have left St. Paul early to examine the prospects in Faribault, since some accounts have him arriving there in 1856 and beginning work on the caves.

Whatever the path, by 1857 both Gottfried and Ernst were in Faribault and constructing a brewery. Local histories say that Ernst "retired from the firm" in 1860, but this phrase simply concealed the disagreements between the brothers. Ernst leased the Norbert Paquin brewery for a few months and began production in his own brewery on the east bank of the Straight River, just downstream from his brother, near the bridge that crossed the river at Eighth Street. Just as he had at Gottfried's brewery, Ernst began what would eventually be a massive complex of lagering caves—one of the few caves still in use after Prohibition.

By 1866 Ernst had to change his status from small brewer to large brewer since his production topped 500 barrels.

In 1869 an apparently deranged brewery employee set fire to the brewery and was later found dead near the river. Fleckenstein incurred an uninsured loss of between $2,000 and $3,000, but immediately he began to re-

Tin signs with simulated wood grain and paintings of good fellowship were made for many different breweries around the turn of the twentieth century by the Meyercord company. FROM THE COLLECTION OF DAVE WENDL.

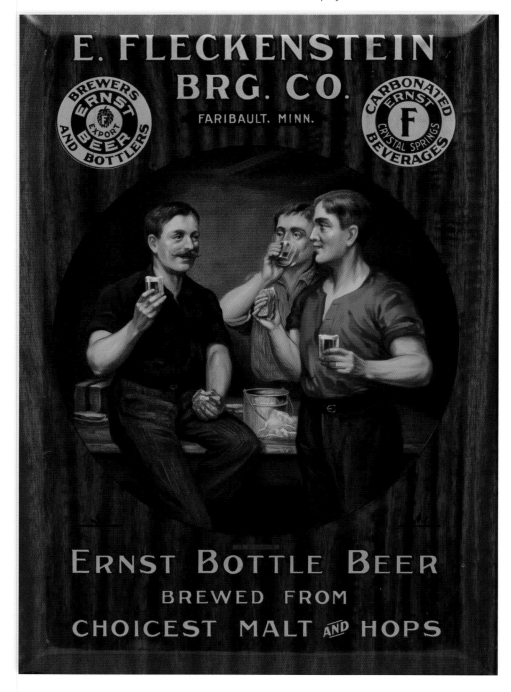

build and enlarge the brewery. The new brewery opened in 1872 (a date that is inaccurately used by *100 Years of Brewing* and some other sources as the starting date for the company). By the end of the decade, Ernst's brewery was still the smallest of the three Faribault breweries, doing less than half the business of his brother's brewery and slightly more than one-fourth as much as Brandt and Sheffield. Despite this, the brewery continued to grow steadily and eventually began to bottle Ernst Beer. Ernst Fleckenstein died in 1901, but his four sons took over the brewery and expanded the product line. In 1902 the company installed a new bottling line and began to produce drinks like Choco-Malt and Golden Dew under the Crystal Springs label.

A series of misfortunes struck the company as the United States was entering World War I. In October 1917 the brewery suffered another fire that gutted the interior of the

Part of the reason the Ernst Fleckenstein Brewing Co. survived against all odds for more than a century was the variety of beverages and souvenirs it offered. Mini-bottles were popular in the 1940s and 1950s: the bottle opener version at left includes tax payment text that dates from the 1940s, and the salt/pepper shaker to the right has a replica of the 1950s label. The bock bottle is from the late 1940s. The root beer bottle is from the brewery's last years. FROM THE COLLECTION OF DAVE WENDL.

building, but rebuilding began the next day. However, the long-term crisis of Prohibition forced the company to change its focus. Since it was already in the soft drink business, it was easier for Fleckenstein to survive on sodas and other drinks than it was for many other breweries. The company began to produce popular brands such as Orange Crush and Hires Root Beer in addition to its own brands. The company also held Minnesota permit L-21 to brew nonintoxicating cereal beverages (near beer) during the dry years.

Because Fleckenstein had continued to operate throughout Prohibition, it was one of the handful of Minnesota breweries that was ready to go on 7 April 1933, the first day real beer could be sold. A series of articles in the *Faribault Daily News* fifty years later recalled the scene. Three trucks left the brewery grounds at 12:01 A.M. to begin deliveries, avoiding the long lines of cars and trucks waiting outside the brewery. Customers came from as far away as Austin, Mankato, Rochester, and the Twin Cities. The new flagship beer had a similar logo to the old Ernst Beer but was now called Fleck's Beer. The brewery also produced Felsenkeller Brau, which emphasized the tradition of aging lager in caves, and bock beer in the spring. It also continued to manufacture soft drinks. Fleckenstein managed to recover and retain its local market and expanded into the countryside. Fleck's survived the years of World War II and was able to succeed for a time in a market increasingly dominated by giant breweries. Stanley Baron, in his classic 1962 study, *Brewed in America*, stated that Fleckenstein, with its capacity of only 20,000 barrels per year, was the smallest remaining brewery in the country.

Unfortunately, the brewery could not keep up with the industry giants, and Ernst Fleckenstein Brewing was forced into bankruptcy in 1964. Fleckenstein left behind a legacy of breweriana that a multimillion-barrel brewery might envy: glasses, bottles, coasters, signs, tap knobs, openers, tape measures, and nearly every other item that could be made with a brewery name on it. However, only one neon sign is known to exist and is in the possession of a Minnesota collector. The brewery itself lay abandoned after closing and was eventually demolished to eliminate a safety hazard. The

Promotional items from Ernst Fleckenstein Brewing Co. included everything from an egg timer to the tape measure shown here. FROM THE COLLECTION OF JIM AND RUTH BEATON.

Eighth Street bridge was removed in 1979, and what was once one of the busiest areas of Faribault now shows little trace of its history.

Brandt & Gerdes (1862–1869)
Brandt & Co. (1869–1881) (also known as Brandt & Sheffield or S. A. Sheffield)
A. W. Mueller & Co. (1881–1884)
Location: Willow Street, 1,000 feet south of Front Street

The firm of Brandt and Gerdes began in Faribault in the late 1850s as dealers in wine and liquors. An 1859 newspaper advertisement also listed Milwaukee lager and bock beer for sale. The company began brewing in Faribault in Norbert Paquin's brewery in 1862, and the firm was listed in a state business directory of 1865. By 1866 Brandt and Gerdes was by far the largest of the three breweries in Faribault, selling just under 200 barrels in July alone. The original 24 × 40 foot, two-story stone building was enhanced in 1870 with an addition that included a 25-horsepower steam engine. In 1878 Brandt and Sheffield announced production of nearly 2,400 barrels, making it the eighth largest of the 114 breweries that reported their output. However, production decreased by almost 500 barrels the next year, dropping Brandt and Sheffield into fourteenth place. This was the beginning of a decline that would not be reversed.

A rare ledger book from 1880–1881 lists both the purchases and sales of the company. Records for October and November 1880 show that most of its sales were of quarter- and eighth-barrel kegs, though half barrels appear

occasionally. This ledger was the last under the name of Brandt; Mueller and Co. took over the brewery in February 1881. The fortunes of the firm diminished quickly, and the October 1884 Sanborn fire insurance map lists Mueller and Company's Brandt Brewery as "not in operation." *American Breweries II* lists a George M. Baxter as owner of the brewery from 1882 through 1884, but since he was a local lawyer, he may have been the receiver of the bankrupt firm rather than the proprietor.

John Ahles (1875–?)
Location: Unknown

Little is known about John Ahles's career in Faribault. *Schade's Brewers Handbook* includes Ahles and his production of ninety-nine barrels in 1875. Ahles was in Minnesota from 1874 to 1875, because a six-year-old daughter born in Minnesota was listed in the 1880 census, but her two younger siblings were born in Iowa. In 1880 Ahles was listed as a brewer in Belle Plaine, where he was probably working for Christian Schmitt.

Fergus Falls [Otter Tail County]

Zaiser & Lumpp (1875–?) (on the creek near Lee Morrill's)
Lohmeier (?–1878)
Peter Oehlschlager (1878–1884)
Location: Northwest corner of E. Mt. Faith Avenue and N. Ann Street

John Zaiser first announced his plans for a brewery in September 1871, when he opened his restaurant on Lincoln Avenue, but it would be several years before they were realized. Finally, Zaiser hired Henry Lumpp from Brainerd to be his brewer, and construction was completed in the fall and winter of 1875. The next few years of this brewery's life are not clear. It is likely that this brewery passed into the hands of Mr. Lohmeier, since no accounts of building a new brewery have been found. Likewise, Lohmeier's career as a brewer is also a mystery. The first clear information is that he leased the brewery in the fall of 1878 to Peter Oehlschlager.

Oehlschlager came to Fergus Falls from Lake City, where he was a brewer in Edward Wise's brewery. His new operation suffered misfortune almost immediately. Almost a year to the day after he announced its opening, the brewery suffered a fire that cost Oehlschlager several hundred dollars in equipment and Lohmeier part of his building. However, the brewery was rebuilt, and advertisements for Oehlschlager's City Brewery appeared in the *Fergus Falls Advocate* in January 1880. The ads continued to run until April 1881, after which they disappear. While the only brewery included in a business list of 1882 is that of T. Judnitch, this is not proof that Oehlschlager's brewery ceased operations. The 1884 Sanborn insurance map lists Oehlschlager's City Brewery as operational, and the 1896 map shows the building still present, though no longer in operation. (The location is on a creek, so it could be the same as the Zaiser and Lumpp brewery.) Oehlschlager left brewing and retired to farming. He was an active farmer until his death, at age 80, from an accident while harvesting hay.

A special tax stamp issued to Peter Oehlschlager is pictured on the opening page of this section.

Charles Brown & Co. (1878?–1884?)

Locations: First location unknown; second location was southwest of town on J. A. Gray's land

Charles Brown was already brewing in Fergus Falls in 1878 when advertisements in the *Fergus Falls Advocate* proclaimed he had "Fresh Lager Beer and Family Ale always on hand." Brown offered bock beer at his brewery on May 1 of that year to celebrate spring. That summer, Brown brought J. A. Gray into the company, apparently to obtain a good parcel of land to use for a new brewery. Gray's property offered a grove of trees for use as a beer garden and well borers discovered good water at a depth of eighty-six feet. The brewery was fitted with the equipment of the defunct Elizabeth brewery and was ready to produce a sample keg for the approval of the *Advocate*'s editor by December. Brown may also have had some of his beer bottled by James O'Brien, since O'Brien offered Fergus Falls beer at $1.60 per dozen (in contrast to $2.75 for Milwaukee beer and $2.50 for St. Paul beer). In 1878 Brown and Company brewed 100 barrels; the next year it nearly doubled this amount to 180 barrels.

It is possible that Brown's brewery was a forerunner of either the Kiewel or the Aberle brewery of Fergus Falls, but the evidence suggests the other firms were new breweries.

Aberle & Ahrentz (1882–1884)
Andreas Aberle (1884–1893)
C. J. Bender (1893–1896)
Andreas Aberle (1896–1900)
Anton Meyer (1901)
John Bauer (1901–1903)
Theodore Hubner (1903–1907)
Fergus Falls Brewing Co. (1907–1908)
Fergus (Falls) Brewing Co., Inc. (1908–1920?)
Premier Brewing Co., Inc. (1933–1935)
Fergus Brewing Co., Inc. (1935–1937)
Fergus Breweries, Inc. (1937–1948)
Falls Breweries (1948–1951)
Location: 121 N. Peck Street

In 1883 Aberle and Ahrentz built a new brewery in Fergus Falls at a cost of $6,000. A year after construction, Andreas Aberle became the sole proprietor. Aberle's career as a brewer appears to have been relatively uneventful, especially compared with the setbacks suffered by crosstown rival Jacob Kiewel. In 1893 Aberle sold the brewery to Charles Bender, who operated it for three years before returning it to Aberle. After Aberle retired, the company went through a series of ownership changes. In 1908 Theodore Hubner sold the brewery

to the partnership of Feinstein, Kimball, and Maas, who incorporated Fergus Falls Brewing that year. Fred Meyer was hired to be the brewmaster, and the new company began working to increase its market in the area. Eventually, Philip Maas became the lead partner and was the person most associated with the brewery. Fergus Falls Brewing was among the many northern breweries that had their market restricted by the enforcement of treaty provisions against selling alcohol on former tribal lands, and its business decreased even before Prohibition arrived.

During Prohibition, the brewery was converted into a sausage factory, but the building was maintained largely intact. An article in the 7 November 1929 *Fergus Falls Daily Journal* recalled the old days: "Many old timers remember every nook and crook in this building, and how the strains of 'Sweet Adeline' drifted away on the balmy atmosphere of a spring evening when a trip was made to or from this institution, and particularly from."

The re-legalization of beer offered the opportunity to convert the factory back to beer, and Premier Brewing Co. was formed to bring

Fergus Brewing Co.'s Export Pilsener was "Bottled Expressly for Family Use" in 24-ounce bottles. This label dates to 1907–1919. FROM THE COLLECTION OF KEN MALZ.

brewing back to Fergus Falls. Premier was not ready to begin brewing right away, and did not brew its first batch of one hundred barrels until August 1933. Like many other small breweries in the 1930s, the struggle to regain markets and the costs of restarting the brewery put Premier in financial difficulties almost immediately. The company was reorganized in July 1934, but articles about the firm's financial condition appeared in the local newspapers every few months throughout the next two years. Premier may have been limited by the lack of a strong tie to Fergus Falls—president L. F. McCarthy was from Winnipeg, vice president W. W. Pritchard Jr. was from Thief River Falls, and secretary-treasurer Theo. Christenson was from Fargo.

At the end of 1935, the company was reorganized as Fergus Brewing Co. This version of the firm fared little better and was reorganized again as Fergus Breweries in 1937. While most of the officers and stockholders were from the Twin Cities, former owner Philip Maas was on the board as vice president. While the name of the company stayed the same for the next decade, the brewery's fortunes did not immediately improve. The brewery was closed for several months in 1938 and 1939, and was finally reopened in May 1939 with a new German-trained brewmaster, Alfred Holz, who had been hired away from Anheuser-Busch.

Another common symptom of a brewery in trouble, in addition to changes in company names and changing directors, is frequent changes in flagship beer brands. In the 18 years it was open after Prohibition, the brewery offered half a dozen main brands and several other brews. The Premier Brewing flagship brand was simply Premier, but the main brand of Fergus Brewing was Heinie's Lager. Under Fergus Breweries, this was changed slightly to Heinrich's—one of the few Minnesota beers to retain such a German name during World War II. Fergus Breweries also launched several other labels: Six Horse, Staat's, and Lord Chumley's Ale. Fergus Breweries had some contracts with the U.S. armed forces; a Fergus Falls native who was in the Philippines discovered that the cases of beer stored in his ship's hold were from his hometown brewery.

In 1948 the brewery was reorganized yet again, this time as Falls Breweries. The product

This can includes the legend "Brewed and Bottled by Falls Breweries." The appearance of "Brother Joe" on the can suggested this was a companion package to the brewery's 7-ounce Little Joe bottle. FROM THE COLLECTION OF DAVE WENDL.

line was simplified with Falls and Falls Velvet beers, as well as a near beer called International Club. However, the packaging choices were expanded as Falls Premium Pilsner was offered in 7-ounce bottles called Little Joe and cone-top cans named Brother Joe. Falls Breweries attempted to expand its market as far west as Montana, but continued financial instability and increasing competition finally forced the brewery to close its doors for good in 1951.

F. Juditsch or J. K. O'Brien (1882)
Kiewel & Miksche (1882–1883)
Kiewel & Haas (1883–1884)
Jacob Kiewel (1884–1892)
Location: St. Andrews Street at W. Bismarck Avenue (Bismarck Avenue no longer exists. It was one block south of West Stanton Avenue.)

The origins of the Fergus Falls brewery that became Kiewel's are confusing. *American Breweries II* claims Frank Juditsch started the firm in 1882. While T. Judnitch [*sic*] was listed as a brewer in a December 1882 issue of the *Weekly Journal*, *Western Brewer* affirms Kiewel & Mischke [*sic*] took over from J. K. O'Brien. However, the excise records for 1882 indicate that the firm of Kuewel (presumably Kiewel) and Miksche began operation as a brewer of fewer than 500 barrels in April 1882. After a few years working with business partners, Kiewel became sole proprietor in 1884.

Kiewel met with several difficulties while in Fergus Falls. In July 1883 his brewery burned down, though he rebuilt immediately with a new capacity of 800 barrels per year. In 1887 he was arrested for selling a keg of beer on Sunday and was sentenced to a fine of $30 plus time in jail. Most of the brewery roof was blown off in May 1889, and he was forced to borrow a large tent from Company F to protect the inside of the brewery. The final straw for Kiewel was when the brewery burned again in fall 1892. Though he considered rebuilding, the city of Fergus Falls voted in April 1893 to deny all saloon licenses. Even though the city would not remain dry for long, Kiewel did not want to take a chance on rebuilding in this unfriendly environment. He purchased the struggling Little Falls brewery in May and moved his family there to continue his brewing career.

Forestville (Fillmore County)

Douglas, Odell & Meighen (1856?–1860)
Location: Forestville State Park (The location is indicated by an historic marker on the bridle path.)

One tantalizing yet poorly documented pioneer brewery is the one that may have been run by Robert Douglas, Reuben Odell, and Felix Meighen just outside Forestville. According to the historic marker at the site of the distillery, an 1860 deed of transfer listed brewing equipment among Meighen's property. No other references to such a brewery have been found, but it was certainly possible that they operated a small brewery on this property for personal use and limited sales.

Frazee (Becker County)

Frazee City Brewery (1874?–1879)
Location: Unknown

Frazee City Brewery probably was built during 1874 by Louis Brink, formerly of St. Joseph. It appears in a list of Frazee businesses published in the *Perham News* in February 1875, but with no proprietor named. In December of that year, Brink began to advertise in the *News*, claiming that he offered "the best" beer at "St. Paul prices." His ads continued for several months. By August 1876 the brewery was run by John Smraker who incurred a tax penalty in October of that year for having purchased insufficient stamps for the amount of beer he produced. The brewery did not produce any beer during 1878, and in 1879, now under the proprietorship of George Carl, it produced a mere fifty-six barrels. The last mention of it appears in Polk's 1880 state gazetteer, though it is listed under Joseph Carl. There was no such person in the 1880 census, and George Carl was listed as selling trees rather than beer, so the brewery was probably out of operation by this point.

Frontenac (Goodhue County)

John Minges (?–1863)
Location: Unknown

The excise records of 1862 and 1863 list John Minges as a brewer in Frontenac, located on the Mississippi River several miles north of Lake City. While it is possible that this is simply his Lake City brewery under another name, that brewery was in the middle of the city and is unlikely to have been listed as Frontenac for any reason. In addition, there was a gap in the excise records, which may represent the time during which he was moving from one brewery to the other. Conclusive evidence supporting either scenario has not yet been located.

Glencoe (McLeod County)

Edward Lemmel (1874–1896)
Peter Eickmann (1896–1901)
Glencoe Brewing Co. (1901–1919)
Location: Southeast corner Hennepin Avenue S and First Street E

Edward Lemmel (also Lammel) began brewing beer in Glencoe sometime in 1874. According to an article by Robert Hajicek in *The Breweriana Collector* (Winter 1993), the main brewery building was constructed in 1877. Little is known about the first two decades of the brewery, but Lemmel built a solid reputation and may have experimented with different styles of beer since he offered an extra Christmas beer in 1894. In 1896, Lemmel sold the brewery to Peter Eickmann and moved west to take over the brewery in Ortonville.

Eickmann had been involved in several previous manufacturing businesses, including a cigar factory, in Glencoe before purchasing the brewery. In 1901 he and two partners incorporated Glencoe Brewing Co. and immediately began a major expansion program. A large, new brick brewhouse was built, and the old building was converted into a bottling house and icehouse. Eickmann brought new brewing equipment from Chicago and hired additional employees to help increase

production. According to one local account, there was a bedroom at the brewery for the drivers to sleep between trips with their beer wagons. In 1903 Fred Jumer joined the firm, trading a farm in North Dakota to Eickmann for brewing company stock. He and his brother Max eventually purchased Eickmann's shares and took control of the brewery. They replaced the existing brewers with Jacob Herman and charged him with improving the consistency of the beer. One of the previous brewers, Peter's brother Frank, went to Ft. Wayne, Indiana, to take a job with Berghoff Brewing Company but by 1910 was vice president of Preiss and Wimmer Brewing Co. in St. Cloud.

Consistency was important to the survival of the company, because Glencoe was located on a major railway and was large enough for outside brewers like G. Heileman and Minneapolis Brewing to establish depots in town, and Theo. Hamm had at least one tied saloon in town. Jumer's attempts to establish the business were severely undermined when a large fire gutted the brewery in 1907, causing about $13,000 of damage, only about half of which was insured. However, Jumer and Herman appear to have been equal to their tasks, since by 1915 the *History of McLeod County* claimed that the business of the brewery

This label probably dates from 1906 since it lists the volume but not the text required by the 1906 Food and Drugs Act. The unusual volume reflects the relative lack of standardization in bottle sizes during the period. FROM THE COLLECTION OF KEN MALZ.

increased from 4,500 barrels before the fire to 13,000 barrels. Uncle Sam New Style Lager Beer (later just Uncle Sam Beer) became popular throughout the county and was available on tap even in cities that had their own breweries, like Silver Lake.

Even as Prohibition approached, the brewery remained a center of attention in Glencoe, for reasons both positive and otherwise. In March 1919 burglars broke into the brewery and stole four cases of beer (suggesting that they got away on foot). A month later, the first airplane to land in Glencoe touched down on the pasture of Glencoe Brewing. However, the brewery would soon become dormant and lay vacant for several years. In 1922 Fred Jumer started a poultry-processing plant in the building and continued it until his retirement in 1926. When beer was re-legalized in 1933, a company under the name of Glencoe Brewing Co. received a permit to manufacture beer, but never went into production. The plant was then turned into a mink farm and used for that purpose for about twenty years. At this time, much of the brewery building still remains and is used for apartments.

Glenwood [Pope County]

Miksch Bros. (1884–?)
George Thompson (1887?)
Location: Unknown

Very little is known about the brewery in Glenwood. The Miksch (or Mitsch) brothers are mentioned in the *Pope County Press* only a few times, once praising their new ice plow, the other times when they were being sued by John Finstad, who won a judgment against them for $42.94.

George Thompson is included in the list of brewers in *Wing's Brewers Handbook*, but is not mentioned in any other source. Neither proprietor is listed in the existing excise records.

Granger [Fillmore County]

Henry Hasse (1874–1884)
Reinhart Hasse (1884–1895)
Mrs. Bina Engelhorn (1895–1897)
Granger Brewing Co. (J. M. Engelhorn) (1897–1902?)
Location: West of town at the point where the Upper Iowa River bends closest to County Highway 30

The brewery in Granger has the distinction of being the southernmost brewery ever to operate in Minnesota, being only four blocks from the Iowa border. Granger was also one of the smallest towns ever to host a brewery.

Henry Hasse began brewing in the summer of 1874 on the north bank of the Upper Iowa River. His brewery was one of the first businesses of any type in Granger. According to Orel Felland's book, *Memoirs and History of Granger*, the brewery was popular with young people who could not obtain beer elsewhere and who could buy a pony keg (eighth barrel) there for 75 cents. Hasse's operation was about the right size for a very small town—he typically produced just over 300 barrels, but had a high of 536 in 1878. He dropped back under 300 barrels in 1879, but part of the reason for the drop in production may have been trouble with the law. In May 1879 Hasse was arrested and charged with transferring beer from keg to keg in order to use revenue stamps multiple times.

Henry ran the brewery until 1884, when his son Reinhart took over. Until 1895 all seemed well. But in March 1895, Reinhart Hasse was standing in the brewery paying one of his workers. According to the account in the *Preston Times*:

> He counted out the amount and laid it on the table, the hired man in the meantime signing a receipt. Instead of turning over the money he put it back into the drawer. This operation he performed twice. Finally the hired man said he would go to breakfast and come back and get his money. In opening the door upon his return, he smelled powder and commenced looking around for the cause when he discovered Hasse lying in an adjacent room dead. . . . The theory is that he stood before a large mirror, and taking deliberate aim, sent the bullet crashing through the center of his forehead. The cause of Hasse's rash act is thought to be despondency.

After Hasse's death, the brewery passed to the Engelhorn family. It was first operated under the name of Mrs. Bina Engelhorn, but J. M. Engelhorn changed the name to Granger Brewing Co in 1897. Excise records show that the brewery was in production at least until 22 May 1900.

Hastings [Dakota County]

Michael Schaller (1856–1864)
Jacob Schaller (1865–1866)
M. Ulmer (1867)
Location: Barker's Addition

The 1881 *History of Dakota County* by Warner and Foote proclaims that the county's first brewery was built in 1856 in Barker's Addition. The proprietor was Michael Schaller, who had just moved with his family from Chicago. The 1857 census also lists Charles Gaeto and Christopher Schoepf as brewers residing in Hastings, but no record of other breweries exists, so they were probably employed by Schaller. By 1860, Michael's brother Jacob joined the firm. The size of the brewery is unclear because of conflicting records: it supposedly made 400 barrels of beer in 1860 but the excise records of 1863 and 1864 suggest that the brewery's capacity was no more than fifteen barrels per month. Warner and Foote indicate that the brewery burned at some point, and it may have been sometime between 1860 and 1863. By 1865 Jacob Schaller is listed as the proprietor, and the sales of the brewery were nearly fifty barrels during the summer months.

The Schallers disappear from the excise records at this point, and there are conflicting accounts of the last year of the brewery. Warner and Foote claim that the brewery was taken over by Yeager and Borser, but contemporary newspaper accounts indicate that Yeager bought Charles Saile's brewery. The construction of this brewery was described by the *Hastings Gazette* as "near the old site of Schaller's brewery," which seems to indicate that the Schaller brewery no longer existed, and may have been the source of confusion in the Warner and Foote account. The *Hastings Conserver* reported in October 1866, "Schaller's brewery has been sold to parties near Milwaukee, including residence, for eleven thousand five hundred dollars." It is likely that this new owner was M. Ulmer, whose career as a brewer in Hastings was very brief. A fire broke out in the brewery in March 1867, which forced Ulmer and his employees to jump from a second-floor window. The brewery was gutted, and though the cellar was unharmed, Ulmer's uninsured loss was approximately $7,000.

Latto & Smith (Schmidt) (1866–1868)
Smith & Grauss (1868–1872)
Schmidt & Kelnhofer (1872–1874)
Ficker & Kelnhofer (1874–1875)
Ficker & Doffing (1875–1878)
Ficker & Donndelinger (1878–1884)
Anthony Kelnhofer (1884–1893)
Hoffman & Grubb (1893)
Location: South side of Lake Isabel at Sixth and Lea

The firm sometimes called the Hastings City Brewery began operations with great fanfare just before Christmas in 1866. Rudolph Latto and Peter Smith had a grand opening celebration to mark the opening of their new brewery on the south shore of Lake Isabel. The brewery, which had two levels of cellars, was built for approximately $16,000, according to the *Hastings Gazette*. The brewery was designed primarily to make lager, but excise records show that in 1870 Smith and a new partner, Wendell Grauss, were producing both ale and lager. By that year the brewery had become the largest in Hastings, employing four men to produce more than 700 barrels per year. In December 1870, the *Gazette* reported that Schmith [*sic*] and Grauss were excavating a cellar ten feet wide and one hundred feet long in Nininger, about two miles northwest of the brewery. Apparently the cellars at the brewery were not maintaining temperature properly, since the *Gazette* noted "although it will necessitate a vast amount of teaming, it is expected to yield a fair return in the extra quality of the beverage."

The city brewery's frequent partnership changes did not seem to affect the growth of the business. By 1880 the brewery ranked in the top third of Minnesota's breweries, with a production of nearly 1,200 barrels per year. Less is known about the later years of the brewery. The brewery closed in 1893 and remained vacant for more than a decade. The building was torn down in January 1907, and the building materials were used for other projects.

Charles Saile (1867–1870)
Yeager & Borser (also Boser or Boeser) (1870)
Location: Third Street

Charles Saile left his Pepin Brewery in 1867 and moved to Hastings. Apparently he planned to start brewing earlier than he actually did, since his April and May entries in the 1867 excise tax records are crossed out. A note in the 3 August 1867 *Hastings Gazette* about the construction of a new brewery in Barker's Addition seems to match with the appearance of Saile in the 1868 excise records. Tax records from 1868 and 1869 suggest that the capacity of Saile's brewery was about twenty barrels per month. His production in October 1869 was about one-third that of the other two breweries in Hastings, those of Smith and Grauss and Keffler and Borser. By January 1870, it had dropped even further as he sold only seven kegs of beer that month. The *Dakota County Union* reported in February 1870 that: "Mr. Chas. Yeager, proprietor of the American Hotel, has purchased the dwelling, brewery, and fixtures of Charles Siely [*sic*]." Saile moved to Rice Lake, Wisconsin, where he operated a brewery for most of the next decade. The 1870 Census of Industry shows that the Yeager and Borser brewery was operated by horsepower and had a machine mill and water and beer pumps. It produced 650 barrels in the tax year, which was a substantial increase over the production under Saile's administration. Warner and Foote report in their 1881 *History of Dakota County* that the brewery of Yeager and Borser was destroyed by fire, but it is most likely that it was the former Saile brewery, not the former Schaller brewery that cost Yeager his loss.

Warner and Foote also claim that Fred Busch purchased the Saile brewery in 1867, but this was somewhat unlikely since Busch would have been only 18 at the time. Busch does not appear in the excise records until 1870.

Keffler & Borser (1869–1870)
Fred Busch (1870–1891)
J. L. Busch & Sons (Teutonia Brewery) (1891–1901)
Laurent & Murphy (1901)
Minnesota Brewing Co. (1901–1902)
Location: North shore of Lake Isabel at Adams Street

The origins of Busch's Brewery, sometimes called the Lake Brewery, are blurred by conflicting accounts. Edward F. W. (Fred) Busch (sometimes spelled Bush) was born in Saxony in 1849, came to America with his family in 1852, and was definitely operating a brewery in Hastings by 1870. Excise tax records and production figures suggest he started in 1870, though some local accounts claim he started by purchasing the old Saile brewery in 1867. While it is possible he owned a brewery by age 18, this would make him perhaps the youngest brewery proprietor in state history. He may have obtained the brewery with the financial help of his father, but John Lorenz Busch did not move to Hastings until 1871. Finally, Saile probably didn't have a brewery to sell in March, when some sources claim Busch made his purchase.

The most likely origin of the brewery was in the short-lived partnership of Keffler and Borser. The *Hastings Gazette* reported in October 1869, "Pozer [*sic*] & Co.'s new brewery is nearly completed. This will make the third brewery for Hastings." Excise tax records show that about one-third of Keffler and Borser's output was ale, with the rest being lager. While not conclusive, the 1870 census suggests Busch lived three houses away from Borser (Pozer) and may have started working in the brewery and subsequently purchased it.

Whatever the precise origins of the firm, Busch invested heavily to build up the business. The 1870 Census of Industry reported that Busch had invested $7,000 in the horse-powered brewery, but the improvements apparently forced him to close the brewery for some time because the same report lists his output at only fifty-one barrels in four months of operation. According to the detailed 1870 excise tax records, Busch produced both lager and ale, though during the hottest months of the summer he made only ale. In 1873 Henry Gleim, one of three employees, was grinding malt when a chain broke. The chain struck his legs so hard that they were permanently damaged.

By 1879 the Busch brewery was established as a midsize brewery by Minnesota standards, though it was one of the smaller firms in the crowded Mississippi and St. Croix river valleys. Production in 1878 and 1879 was around 700 barrels per year, and the 1880 Census of Industry shows that the brewery employed four men. Warner and Foote reported in their 1881 *History of Dakota County* that the main building was 40 × 40 feet and included a thirty-barrel mash kettle, plus an addition to the brewhouse of 26 × 40 feet and a two-story icehouse.

Several members of the Busch family were involved in the brewery, most importantly Fred and his father, John. Both were listed as brewers in the census records and as proprietor at different stages. When John died in 1894, Fred took over the brewery again. By the turn of the century Busch had a variety of interests other than the brewery—he was mayor of Hastings and owned a farm in Ipswich, South Dakota, where he spent much of the summer. The 1900 census lists John Haas as a brewer for the company, and he probably assisted Busch with management as well.

The firm of Laurent and Murphy took over the brewery in 1901, but held it for only a few months. In the summer of 1901, a group of Minneapolis investors formed Minnesota Brewing Co. with a capital stock of $50,000 and purchased the former Busch brewery. The *Brewers' Journal* reported in September that "the stockholders of the newly organized Minnesota Brewing Co. expect to enlarge their present brewery, which is now in operation, to three times its present capacity." Financial problems dogged the firm, however, and it was reincorporated in 1903, this time with $70,000 behind it. The grand plans went nowhere, and the brewery remained closed.

Samuel Norrish (1875?–1878?)
Location: Unknown

American Breweries II includes an entry for the brewery of Samuel Murisch. It is likely that this is actually the short-lived brewery of Samuel Norrish. Little is known about its operations; the only positive evidence comes from the excise tax records from 1877 indicating that Norrish paid his license fee for the three-year period from April 1875 to April 1878. *Schade's Brewers Handbook* lists the brewery, but with no production in either 1874 or 1875. Salem does not include Norrish in his list of producing breweries in 1878 or 1879, and Norrish is listed as a druggist in the 1880 census.

Balthazar (Bat) Steffen (1885–1902)
Hastings Brewing Co. (1902–1918)
Location: Between Ramsey and Tyler streets on the south side of the levee

Balthazar Steffen was one of two brewers in his family (his brother Anton was for a time proprietor of the brewery in Sleepy Eye). Balthazar Steffen moved to Hastings in 1869 and was involved in a variety of businesses before entering the brewing industry. In 1885 he began construction of a new brewery in Hastings along the levee. He began brewing in October of that year and made his first deliveries in late November. At first he purchased his malt from Hastings Malting Co., but in December 1885 be rebuilt an old stone building east of his brewery as a malt house. The brewery was damaged by fire in November 1886 but was quickly rebuilt. Over the next several years, the brewery was expanded regularly to keep up with demand for its product. Steffen served as an alderman for fifteen years and was a respected leader of the community.

In 1902 Adolph Gustav Kuenzel left the Stevens Point, Wisconsin, brewery of which he had been proprietor for five years and moved to Hastings. At first he was a partner of Bat Steffen, but in October of that year Kuenzel bought out his partner's shares and became sole proprietor. Kuenzel changed the name of the firm to Hastings Brewing Co. and

immediately expanded both the brewery and the company's presence in the community. Kuenzel finished the improvements begun by Steffen and added more of his own. The 1904 Sanborn fire insurance map listed the capacity of the brewery as 8,000 barrels. Between 1910 and 1911, Kuenzel added a bottling plant to the brewery complex, which also included the family home built in 1902. Despite the modernity of so much of the brewery, Kuenzel continued to cool his brewery with ice cut by his employees from the Mississippi River.

Kuenzel also took an active role in supporting community affairs. He was a talented and enthusiastic musician and helped form the German American Band in Hastings. (Unfortunately, he lost a finger in an accident at the

Emblazoned "Compliments of Fred Busch," this glass is one of the most elaborate of the late-nineteenth-century etched glasses (other than those featuring views of the brewery). FROM THE COLLECTION OF PAT STAMBAUGH.

Bat Steffen's brewery offered this glass as a premium to customers during the 1890s. Few artifacts from Steffen's era are known. FROM THE COLLECTION OF PAT STAMBAUGH.

brewery, which prevented him from playing his beloved zither.) He sponsored a baseball team called the Kuenzel Brewers and purchased new uniforms for the team's inaugural game in 1903 (which they lost to Ellsworth, Wisconsin, 6–2).

When Prohibition arrived, Kuenzel closed the brewery rather than attempt to make other products. The family tried to get by on income from their farm in Vermillion, but Kuenzel missed brewing. He moved to Canada to take a position in Kenora, Ontario. During Prohibition, Hastings residents did their best to forget that the town ever had a brewery. Kuenzel's family was harassed, and when Bat Steffen died in 1925, the lengthy obituary made no mention at all of his nearly two decades as proprietor of a significant brewery. After Prohibition ended, Kuenzel returned to the United States and worked at several breweries, but made no attempt to restart the family business. The buildings remained for several years, but

by the 1970s only a few ruined walls and the brewmaster's house remained. In 2002 developers proposed a hotel, shopping, and restaurant complex named Bailly's Landing on the site of the former brewery that would include a brewpub operated by Ted Marti of New Ulm's August Schell Brewing Co. As of this writing, nothing has come of these plans.

Henderson (Sibley County)

Joseph Ritter (1859?–1879)
Christian Klinkert (1879)
Milwaukee Brewery, Christian Enes & Co.
   (1879–1885)
John Enes and John Groetsch (1885–1887)
John Enes Brewing Co. (1887–1895)
Hans Enes (1895–1918)
Location: South of town on Fifth Street

Sometime in 1859 or 1860, Joseph Ritter established a brewery in the town of Henderson, near the Minnesota River. Excise tax records from 1866 show that he usually sold between thirty and forty barrels of beer during the summer and about half that amount during the winter. In late 1879, a financial crisis precipitated by the burning of the family home a few years earlier came to a head. The town granted the family an allowance for temporary relief, and Ritter sold the brewery to raise cash. Articles in the *Sibley County Independent* and the production figures in Frederick W. Salem's 1880 book, *Beer, its History and its Economic Value as a National Beverage,* suggest that the brewery was out of production for part of 1878 and all of 1879. Christian Klinkert, the buyer (who is sometimes erroneously listed as a brewer in Arlington), quickly sold the property to John Enes, who had been a brewer in Milwaukee since at least 1860 and was proprietor of the Prairie Street brewery there in 1862 and 1863. Enes apparently purchased the brewery for his 25-year-old son Christian, who moved to Henderson to take over the business. (Ritter was still listed as a brewer in the 1880 census, but probably was no longer active in the business.)

Enes arrived in Henderson and soon brought the rest of his family, including his father, who was somewhat involved with the brewery but who also ran a saloon in town with his wife, Sophie. A boarder with

the family, Albert Miller, also worked in the brewery. News items in the *Independent* show that Enes constructed a new brick brewery immediately after taking possession of the property. According to the book *Henderson, Then and Now,* Enes went into partnership with his brother-in-law John Groetsch. The new firm was called the Milwaukee Brewery, Enes and Company, following a once-common tradition of naming a brewery after a famous brewing center in which the proprietor once worked. In 1885 Christian sold his shares in the brewery to his mother, and she and John sold their saloon and moved into the brewery. John Enes joined John Groetsch in the partnership. The firm became a local institution by, among other things, offering free glasses of beer to those who came to the brewery to pick up a keg. The brewery advertised that bottled beer, which was packaged by an independent bottler, was available. In 1888 John Grassinger came to Henderson and began the first of his twenty-three years as brewmaster at the Enes brewery. In 1887 Groetsch left the partnership, and John Enes became sole proprietor. John's son Hans went to New York to study brewing. He joined his father in partnership upon return and purchased the brewery in 1895. (The brewery was still in John's name on the 1900 Sanborn fire insurance map.) Under Hans's direction, the brewery added a new patent icehouse in 1895 and a new waterworks system in 1901. The 1910 census lists Christian Enes as the proprietor of a malting business in Henderson, which was presumably the malting business that belonged to the brewery.

The brewery continued to operate through 1918, when the supposedly temporary wartime prohibition rules forced the brewery to shut down. As the supply of beer ran short, the *Independent* reported in May: "The 'growler' days are over in Henderson, we learn. In order to conserve beer the saloonkeepers got together and agreed to discontinue the selling of that beverage by the 'can.'" Despite the anti-brewer sentiment prevalent at the time, Hans Enes was elected to the school board in the July 1918 election. The brewery property was purchased in 1920, and despite attempts to start another business in the building, it was eventually torn down in 1925. Rumors of buried vats of abandoned beer persisted in the area

A graceful tray such as this one was probably designed as a premium for home customers of Hastings Brewing Co. rather than for saloon use. FROM THE COLLECTION OF STEVE KETCHUM.

for several years, but no evidence of such a cache was ever found.

Hokah [Houston County]

Root River Brewery (1858–1887?)
Location: North bank of the Root River near the point where State Highway 16 crosses the river, about two miles east of Hokah

Joseph Pfeffer's Root River Brewery began operations in 1858 and rapidly grew into a very large brewery, considering its isolated location. Lowell M. Peterson, in an article in *Breweriana Collector* (Fall 2004), points out that the brewery and the adjacent livery stable were a regular stop on the stagecoach route from La Crosse, Wisconsin, to Caledonia, and this provided Pfeffer with a steady stream of customers. The 1860 Census of Industry reported that in the previous twelve months, Pfeffer had made 200 barrels of beer, which sold for $6 per barrel. By 1866 Pfeffer sold more than 200 barrels in July and August alone, and for the year sold more beer than all but a handful of breweries in the state. Outside of the Twin Cities, only the two breweries in Winona, Brandt and Gerdes in Faribault and Schell and Bernhard in New Ulm exceeded Pfeffer's total. The excise tax records show that Pfeffer also had $400 of income for that year and owned a gold watch.

Pfeffer took advantage of his profits to build a new $10,000 brewery in 1867. The 1882 *History of Houston County* claims that the brewery had a capacity of about thirty gallons per day, but this should probably have been barrels, not gallons, since the brewery was licensed as a producer of more than 500 barrels per year. Since a barrel equals thirty-one gallons, thirty gallons a day would have been a substantial decrease in production. Pfeffer operated the brewery for only two years after the expansion, and the brewery went through a series of ownership changes, although, as Peterson points out, the brewery stayed in the extended family when it was taken over by the Langens, who were relatives by marriage. John Striegel took over the brewery in 1877, but Pfeffer is still listed as a brewer in the 1880 census. However, at age 70, he may have been only a part-time worker. Peterson's article, which is based on interviews with Langen family descendants, indicates that some bottled

beer was sold, though bottling may have been limited to the annual bock beer.

Unfortunately for the family, the importance of the stagecoach stop diminished during the 1870s as the railroad network was extended throughout the state. The rail lines that connected La Crosse to Caledonia went well around Hokah, and the efficiency of rail travel made the stagecoach largely irrelevant. Hokah's proximity to La Crosse likely hurt the business as well, since major brewers such as Michel and Gund were establishing depots throughout southern Minnesota. Production dropped to 236 barrels in 1878 and 140 barrels in 1879. The *History of Houston County* stated that the brewery property was the subject of litigation in 1882, and the brewery probably closed down within a few years. Peterson estimates that Striegel probably operated the brewery for about ten years.

Hutchinson [McLeod County]

Herman Abel, Hutchinson Brewery (1870–1873)
(Michael) Plotzer & (Robert) Wetzig (1873–1876)
Kleinmann Brothers Brewery (1876–1905)
Joseph Hajicek Brewing Co. (1905–1918)
Location: North bank of the Crow River at approximately Third Avenue NW and Glen Street

Hutchinson was perhaps the most unlikely city in Minnesota to host a brewery. The town was founded by the Hutchinson family, a troupe of singers famous for advocating temperance and abolition of slavery. Despite the founders' strong stance against alcohol, Herman Abel built a brewery and began production during the summer of 1870. In his first year of brewing, he sold eighty barrels of beer, which was one of the smallest totals in the state but probably eighty barrels more than the Hutchinson family ever anticipated. In 1873 Abel sold the brewery to Michael Plotzer, who soon added Robert Wetzig as a partner. According to the history of the brewery published by Michael and Robert Hajicek in the Spring 1997 issue of *The Breweriana Collector*, the brewery partners encountered financial difficulties, and the property was foreclosed and sold to John Kleinmann in 1876. The excise records of 1879 still list Plotzer and Wetzig as proprietors of the brewery, but it is not clear why. Salem's list of Minnesota breweries includes Engelhorn and Co. of Hutchinson, producers of just over

This Kleinmann Bros. glass, featuring a frothy goblet of beer, was probably made in the early 1890s. FROM THE COLLECTION OF PAT STAMBAUGH.

200 barrels in 1879. This is presumably Max Engelhorn, who, along with John Kleinmann, was listed as a brewer in the 1880 census.

After this period of management turmoil, John and Charles Kleinmann settled down and operated the brewery until 1905, when they traded the brewery for the 500-acre farm of Joseph Hajicek, who lived about ten miles south of town. According to family histories related by Michael Hajicek, Joseph's wife, Anastasia, cried for several days when she saw the small brewery that was to become the home for their nine children. Joseph Hajicek began making modest changes and expansions to the brewery, hired William Frank of Chicago as brewer, and began production.

Hutchinson voted to go dry in 1908, and while Hajicek was allowed to remain in operation, he could not sell beer in the city or within one-half mile of the city limits. Brewery records cited by the Hajiceks in their article show that the Hutchinson brewery sold 1,200 barrels in 1907 and only 900 in 1909, a year after the restrictions were imposed. To export beer more effectively, Hajicek added a small bottling facility in 1909 and shipped Bohemian Style Beer by the case. The brewery was charged several times with selling beer illegally, but the family managed to keep the brewery open through the turmoil.

Joseph Hajicek died in 1914, and his sons Ben and John took over operations, along with their brother-in-law John Hoerner, who had been brewmaster at the Litchfield brewery for almost four years. In 1918, the Hutchinson brewery closed due to the combination of prohibitionist sentiment and wartime emergencies that affected brewers large and small. Closing the brewery did not end the family's brushes with the law—they were investigated several times on suspicion of bootlegging during Prohibition. After Prohibition ended, Ben became a salesman first for Theo. Hamm and then for Minneapolis Brewing Company, but no attempt was made to restart the Hutchinson brewery. The buildings were torn down in the 1940s.

Jackson (Jackson County)

Charles Deinhardt (1871–1872)
Owens and Davis (1872–1873)
Evan Owens (1873–1880)
Location: North bank of the Des Moines River, northwest of the center of town

Charles Deinhardt sold his brewery in Blue Earth city in 1871 and moved to Jackson to build a brewery there. Deinhardt purchased a former hotel property and began work excavating a cellar and erecting the walls for his new business. By December 1871 Carl (as he was known locally) began to supply beer to his thirsty customers.

At the time, Jackson was the farthest southwest that a brewery had been established in Minnesota. The terrain in southwestern Minnesota is less favorable to digging cellars than that in the eastern part of the state, especially the area around Chatfield where Deinhardt had his first brewery in Minnesota. Jackson, however, had several hills near the river which made it an acceptable brewery location. The settlers in southwestern Minnesota were also more likely to support temperance than residents in the eastern half—the 1872 Fourth of July celebration in nearby Worthington

featured the destruction and burial of a beer keg. However, there was still a market in the region. The *Fairmont Sentinel* had occasional articles about travel parties that went to Jackson to purchase beer.

In 1872 Deinhardt died of complications from a hunting accident suffered in August 1871. The brewery was purchased by Evan Owens and Levi Davis, who prepared "to supply this and other markets with the Teutonic beverage." The *Jackson Republic* described them as "wide awake gentlemen [who] no doubt will push things." Davis sold his share of the brewery to Owens in 1873, after which Owens remained sole proprietor for the next several years. Owens quickly built a good reputation in Jackson, and Owens' Hall was the host of the Christmas ball and oyster supper on Christmas night in 1873.

Jackson voted to close all saloons in 1874, the first of several times it would do so. The city council revoked Owens's liquor license but allowed him to continue selling beer by the keg to residents for consumption in their own homes. Owens remained open until at least 1880, though his production was extremely low. Salem's record of Minnesota breweries lists Owens as having produced just eighty-five barrels in 1878 and sixty-seven barrels in 1879, the fifth-lowest total of any established brewery in the state for those years.

Schade's Brewers Handbook lists Mary Winker as a brewer in Jackson from 1874 through 1875. There is no Mary Winker in Jackson in the 1875 Minnesota state census, and an exhaustive search of Jackson newspapers turned up no mention of any person by that name. Schade lists her production in 1874, the year the city went dry, as more than 900 barrels—ten times Owens's production. It is much more likely that this was Mary Winker of Shakopee.

C. J. Gilmore (1891–1892)
Krejci & Gilmore (1892)
Gilmore & Peschak (1892–1893)
William Gilger? (1894–1895)
Location: Southeast corner of White and Fifth streets

A second fleeting attempt to maintain a brewery in the general region in and around Jackson was made by C. J. Gilmore and his partners during the early 1890s. The only appearance

of the brewery in the *Jackson County Pilot* was when the proprietors, Krejci and Gilmore at that point, were arrested for selling beer illegally to an undercover detective. The two each paid a $300 fine plus court fees. The hostile climate must have persuaded the partners to give up the effort, since the 1894 Sanborn fire insurance map shows the Joe Peschak brewery as "not running."

Information about William Gilger operating the brewery during 1895 has not been found to date. The excise records for June 1898 indicate that L. Kiesel produced forty barrels of beer in Jackson, but no other references to Kiesel or another brewery in Jackson have been found.

Jordan (Scott County)

Henry Brabender (1857?–1869)
Frank Nicolin (1869–1870?)
Fred Heiland (1870?–1881)
Jordan City Brewery, Catherine Heiland (1881–1902)
Koschel & Mesenbrink (1902–1905)
Jordan Brewing Company (1905–1912)
Jordan Brewing Association (1912–1916)
Location: Just south of the Schutz & Hilgers brewery on Minnesota Highway 21

The 1857 Minnesota census lists recent German immigrant Henrick [sic] Brabender as a brewer living in Jordan precinct with his wife, Maria, and three children. By 1860 his brewery was producing about 150 barrels per year, which made it one of the smallest in the state and substantially smaller than the two breweries just downriver in Shakopee. Brabender continued to operate the brewery until 1869, when it was purchased by Frank Nicolin, perhaps the most important businessman in the early decades of the city and former owner of the Sand Creek brewery next door. According to the 1870 census, two Swedish brewery employees, Henry Gusting and George Black, boarded with Nicolin.

In 1870, Fred Heiland (sometimes listed as Heil) and his wife, Catherine (Kate), were farming in Derrynane Township, south of Jordan in Le Sueur County. Sometime soon after the census was taken, they moved up and purchased Nicolin's brewery. The constant competition not only from Gehring and Paier next door but from the numerous other breweries in the Minnesota River valley, forced the Heilands to expand production and maintain high quality. By 1880, the Heilands' brewery was just a few hundred barrels behind Gehring and Paier and the Shakopee breweries, which were the largest on the Minnesota River outside the Twin Cities.

When Fred Heiland died in 1881, Kate Heiland took over management of the brewery. She continued to operate the brewery with the help of skilled brewers—first John Piemeisel, who would later brew in New Ulm and New Prague, and later William Koschel, who had previously worked for Jacob Schmidt in St. Paul. Heiland's son John eventually became active in the management of the brewery as well. By the turn of the century, the brewery featured an extensive network of lagering caves excavated from the bluff behind the brewery, evidence of the expanding business of the firm.

Gail Andersen's book *The Jordan Independent: A Newspaper Looks at a Town* includes many clippings that chronicle both the major developments and the day-to-day operations at Jordan's two breweries. For example, in February 1891 a horse went out of control while making a delivery of Heiland's beer, scattering kegs all over the street. In 1900 John Heiland traveled to Le Sueur Center (today Le Center) in an attempt to open accounts in that town.

Koschel and Mesenbrink purchased the brewery from Kate Heiland in 1902 and spent the next three years modernizing the buildings. A new water supply was constructed in 1903, and the building was wired for electricity in 1905. By this time, the firm was known as Jordan Brewing Company. One more name change occurred in 1912, with the firm now becoming known as Jordan Brewing Association. The brewery was heavily in debt and was forced to closed in February 1916. In 1918 the brewery was converted to make sorghum syrup. The oldest brewery in Jordan was torn down in 1924 when the state highway was widened.

Nicolin & Gehring (1866–1867)
Gehring & Paier aka Sebastian Gehring, Sand
    Creek Brewery (1867–1885)
Schutz & Kaiser (1885–1903)
Schutz & Hilgers City Brewery (1902–1918)
Schutz & Hilgers Jordan Brewery (1934–1946)
Lancer Brewing Co. (1946)
Mankato Brewing Co. (1946–1954)
Location: S. Broadway Street (MN Hwy 21), south of Mill Street

In 1866 Frank Nicolin decided to add brewing to his business interests and entered a partnership with Sebastian Gehring. They first appear in the federal excise records as a large brewery in December 1866, and sold fifty-two barrels that month. Their sales the next month totaled seventy-five barrels—an amount that outpaced the available revenue stamps. In August 1867 Nicolin left the brewing industry again, and Gehring took 33-year-old Baden native Frank Paier on as his new partner. Census records from 1870 indicate that the two men owned equal $5,000 shares in the brewery. By 1879 the brewery was producing more than 1,800 barrels per year, which made it the largest brewery between August Schell's brewery in New Ulm and the Twin Cities.

Peter Schutz and William Kaiser purchased the brewery in 1885 and made several improvements during their partnership. Some of the upgrades were made in the ordinary course of business; some were forced by factors beyond their control, such as the new barn built in 1888 to replace one swept away by a flood. The owners continued to expand the network of cellars in the bluff behind the brewery, and in 1895 they added a bottling department. An 1892 ad also mentioned that Schutz and Kaiser were dealers in barley and malt and offered the "highest cash price paid for barley."

While it was most likely a coincidence, both of Jordan's breweries experienced ownership changes in 1902. William Kaiser was in poor health, and he sold his shares to Peter Hilgers, who brought renewed vitality to the enterprise. The brewery took the lead in developing a park and pavilion across the high-

An unidentified worker is pitching a barrel in Jordan's Schutz & Hilgers Brewing Co. Hot pitch was injected into the barrels until the entire inside was coated. This sealed the barrel and helped preserve the beer. High-quality pitch did not impart any taste to the beer. Pitching was uncomfortable and dangerous work because of the heat, open flame, and hot liquids. In at least one case, an overheated pitch stove caused a fire that burned down part of a brewery (the Schellhas brewery in Winona). Photograph c. 1910. FROM THE COLLECTION OF KEN MALZ.

way from the brewery, wired the brewery for electricity, and increased business through the force of Hilgers's salesmanship. Newspapers in towns throughout the region made mention of Hilgers's visits to check on local accounts. The brewery had a horse-drawn beer sleigh that Hilgers sometimes used on his routes. Ironically, according to an article by Gail Andersen in the 7 April 1975 *Jordan Independent*, Hilgers himself did not drink and discouraged the use of beer by his family. This may have been at least in part due to his ten years as Scott County sheriff, where he undoubtedly saw the dark side of overindulgence firsthand.

The Schutz and Hilgers brewery continued to flourish until American entry into World War I began to restrict brewery operations. In January 1918 brewers were forced to reduce the alcohol content, and finally, at the end of November, Schutz and Hilgers shut down the brewery with the onset of Prohibition. An article in *American Breweriana Journal* by Kevin Busse in 1997 reported that the brewery was converted into a chicken hatchery with the installation of a giant incubator able to hold 47,000 eggs.

Because the brewery had not even made near beer during Prohibition, the plant needed significant retooling, but by January 1934, the Schutz and Hilgers Jordan Brewery was ready to host an open house to celebrate the return of locally brewed beer to Jordan. The new product was advertised as being lower in hops than the pre-Prohibition brew, and it quickly became popular. The Cedar Lawn Hatchery still controlled the bottle house, so the company built a new bottling house and quickly introduced the nonreturnable bottle to customers. At the high point, Jordan Beer, Natural Product Beer, and Old Style Brew were distributed in seven states in addition to Minnesota.

After World War II, J. F. Lancer of Arizona purchased the Jordan Brewery not for its brands but to obtain its share of the government-regulated grain allocation. Dan Bruzek, a former Schutz and Hilgers employee now working for Mankato Brewing Company, purchased the Jordan Brewery from Lancer to help Mankato Brewing increase production. New equipment was installed to increase capacity, and the brands produced were limited to Jordan and Kato beers. Mankato Brewing

This rare opener contained no metal because of wartime shortages. The text urges the user to return the caps along with the bottles and promotes war bonds as well. FROM THE COLLECTION OF PAT STAMBAUGH.

Company encountered severe financial difficulties, in large part because of the Jordan purchase, and the Jordan plant was closed in 1949. Jordan Beer was still brewed for a few more years in Mankato, and even appeared in a now-rare Crowntainer can with a paper label. Atlas Brewing Co. of Chicago later acquired the Jordan brand name and offered the beer in 12-ounce flat-top cans from 1957 to 1962. The building itself was reconverted to the egg business in 1954 and used as a warehouse until the brewery was damaged by fire. The building remained vacant until the mid-1990s, when Gail Andersen converted the old brewery into apartments and retail space.

Kensington [Douglas County]

Joseph Bisek (1888?–1893?)
Location: Unknown

According to *American Breweries II*, Joseph Bisek operated a brewery in Kensington for about five years. No local information on this brewery has been found to this date.

Lake City [Wabasha County]

Charles Reidinger & Co. (1862?–1873)
James Fitzsimmons (1874–1877)
Peter Beck & Co. (1877–1884)
Location: One and one-half miles west of Lake City on the Rochester road (U.S. Highway 63)

Sometime before the introduction of the excise tax in September 1862, Charles Reidinger established a brewery west of Lake City. According to their early records, Reidinger and his partner, James Fitzsimmons, had a very limited business—not until the summer of 1866 did they sell more than ten barrels in a month. Part of this may have been due to the strong temperance sentiment in Lake City. During that era, the local newspapers frequently published articles proclaiming that a saloon-free Lake City could be a beacon of morality for the region and holding in special contempt saloon-ridden Reads Landing just down river. By 1870, Reidinger and Fitzsimmons had increased production of their horse-powered brewery to around 500 barrels a year.

Late in 1871 Reidinger advertised the brewery for sale "at a bargain." He claimed that "it does a good business, and has a capacity for manufacturing 15 barrels of beer per day." Despite these advantages, and "one of the best stone cellars in the state," Reidinger found no takers. Three years later, he sold his shares to Fitzsimmons, who became sole proprietor for a few years. By 1877 the brewery was in the hands of Peter Beck. He continued to operate the brewery for several years, though by 1879 production had dropped below 400 barrels. Details about the last years of Beck's brewery have not been located so far.

John Minges (& Co.) (1864–1869)
Wise Bros. (1869–1879)
J. C. Schmidt, City Brewery (1879–1901)
Location: Northwest corner of Center and Garden streets

In 1864 John Minges moved his brewing business from Frontenac to the middle of Lake

City. He appears to have gradually expanded sales from an average of about ten barrels per month in 1864 to nearly twenty-five barrels per month in 1866. The *Lake City Weekly Journal* in September 1865 contained a dissolution of co-partnership notice concerning the firm of Minges and Bush, though this may have been a business other than the brewery, since the notice said that John L. Bush was in charge of clearing all accounts.

In September 1869, Minges sold the brewery to the Wise brothers, Charles and Edward. Living with Edward Wise in 1870 was one of his employees, Peter Oehlschlager, who would eventually purchase a brewery of his own in Fergus Falls. The Wise brothers made several improvements to their brewery, ranging from a few hundred dollars of repairs in 1872 to a $5,500 stone addition and a new icehouse in 1873. In 1876 Charles bought his brother's shares and became sole proprietor. The *Winona Daily Republican* reported in April 1876 that John C. Schmidt had purchased a share in the brewery for $60,500 (which is likely to have been a misprint of $6,500). Sometime in late 1878 or early 1879, Wise sold the brewery to Schmidt, who conducted it as sole proprietor for several years, and eventually took his son John E. Schmidt into partnership. The father and son partnership made no major expansions of the brewery during their ownership. The Schmidts must also have owned a saloon, since they are listed as saloonkeeper and bartender respectively in the 1900 census. In January 1901 City Brewery suffered a catastrophic fire that did more than $12,000 worth of damage and destroyed the brewing equipment. The family elected not to rebuild.

Information about the breweries of Lake City is more difficult to find than for many other cities of similar size, since many of the civic leaders and opinion shapers of the city were strong temperance advocates and unwilling to mention even a well-run business if it concerned alcohol. The 1920 *History of Wabasha County* provides substantial biographies of both Schmidts, but never mentions brewing. It only says that John E. returned to Lake City in 1896 and "established the business here which he successfully conducted."

Lanesboro [Fillmore County]

Kimber Bros. (1873–1878)
M. Frietschel (1878–1879)
Kimber Bros. (1879?–1881)
Location: Holt Township

In March 1873 the *Lanesboro Clarion* announced, "The Lanesboro Brewery will soon be ready to furnish as good lager beer as can be got anywhere." The Kimber brothers, Emmet and Isaac, appear to have started the brewery in that year. Few details are known about the operation of the brewery, but it appears to have been leased to M. Frietschel at least part of the time, since Salem lists Frietschel as having produced 207 barrels in 1878. *Schade's Brewers Handbook* does not contain a listing for a brewery in Lanesboro. The brewery apparently was not in operation during 1879. The name Samuel Marke was also listed in connection with the brewery at one point, but no other information has been found.

In late 1879 or early 1880, the Kimber brothers resumed control of the brewery, but only operated it for a short time, if at all. Isaac is listed as a brewer in the 1880 census and Kimber Bros. is included in the Polk *Gazetteer*'s list of Lanesboro businesses for that year. The *Winona Daily Republican* noted in passing in April 1881 that "the brewery at Lanesboro is to be converted into a creamery. Is the product to be cream ale?"

American Breweries II includes Radly and Chalupsky in the listing for Lanesboro, but their brewery should be listed under Lanesburg Township (New Prague). The number of names associated with the Lanesboro brewery offers the possibility that there may have been multiple breweries in the town, but all local accounts refer to the brewery in the singular.

Le Roy [Mower County]

Charles Inward (1869–1873?)
Location: Unknown

Charles Inward (Wanner in some records) began brewing in the railroad town of Le Roy in fall 1869. Little is known about the brewery since very few newspapers from the area at that time remain, but Inward remained in business until 1873.

Le Sueur [Le Sueur County]

George Kinzel (1869–1873?)
A. F. (Fred) Veith (1874?–1877?)
Location: Unknown

In March 1868 the *Le Sueur Courier* claimed that a brewery is "one of the most pressing wants" of the town. In February of the next year, George Kinzel began brewing in Le Sueur. Little is known about Kinzel's brewery. In fact, it is possible that Kinzel's brewery was the predecessor of Peter Arbes's Le Sueur brewery rather than of Fred Veith's brewery. Kinzel is listed in the existing excise records until 1871 and appears in a Minnesota business directory in 1873.

While several addresses exist for Fred Veith's breweries, it appears that he operated a brewery in Le Sueur from approximately 1874 to 1877, dates that seem to indicate he purchased the Kinzel brewery. An ad in the *Le Sueur Sentinel* encouraged hotels, saloons, and restaurants to contact A. F. Veith, Le Sueur, Minnesota. Veith advertised "prices down to bed-rock figures, and every keg warranted No. 1.," and specifically solicited the trade of the area farmers. He also offered ale and porter in bottles, which also was promoted as "the celebrated Veith make."

The year 1877 was filled with misfortune for Veith's Le Sueur brewery. Veith was the victim of vandalism in January. Rumors accused the local Good Templars of the acts, but the *Sentinel*'s editor absolved them of blame. In May two brewery workers suffered severe accidents: a worker named Sweiger "had the misfortune to crash his hand" and had several of his fingers amputated, and a cooper had his face badly burned by hot pitch while preparing the barrels. Finally, in July, a local resident drowned in the river near the brewery. In late 1877 Veith appears to have moved his operation across the Minnesota river to Oshawa township.

Peter Arbes (1878–1895)
Emil Vollbrecht (1895–1899)
Location: South of Le Sueur on County Highway 36

While it is possible that Peter Arbes purchased Veith's brewery, the latter's brewery was listed in Le Sueur Township in 1870, and Arbes's brewery is technically in Ottawa Township. In addition, the book *Le Sueur, Town on the River* claims that Arbes was the first to operate his brewery. A search of contemporary local newspapers has revealed nothing that clears up the confusion.

Peter Arbes began brewing just south of the city in 1878. He produced just under 300 barrels in his first year and nearly 700 the next year. Excise records list the brewery as Arbes and Seifert, but the partnership seems to have been brief, since Seifert is not listed as a brewer in Le Sueur in the 1880 census. Arbes's brewery remained a fairly small operation throughout its existence—its reported capacity was approximately 1,000 barrels per year. In the mid-1890s Emil Vollbrecht took over the brewery and operated it until just before the turn of the century.

Litchfield [Meeker County]

Lenhardt & Roetger (1875–1882)
Erhardt Lenhardt (1882–1905)
Litchfield Brewing Co. (1905–1916)
Location: On the north shore of Lake Ripley

The *Meeker County News* reported in April 1874 that "material for the brewery which is to be built near the Lake, are being taken out, and work will go on without delay." The brewery, built at a cost of $1,500 by local contractor N. W. Hawkenson, was operated by Lenhardt and Roetger, and produced just a few hundred barrels of lager each year. The largest capacity ever listed for the brewery was 1,500 barrels.

Very little is known about the history of the Litchfield brewery. The 1900 census indicates that Lenhardt's son Edmund was also working in the brewery. In 1905 the Lenhardts sold the brewery to William Schulz, who renamed it Litchfield Brewing Co. A series of events in 1916 resulted in the demise of the brewery. In January brewmaster John Hoerner left to work at Joseph Hajicek's brewery in Hutchinson. Two months later, William Shultz (spelled Shoultz by the *Litchfield New Ledger*) leased his share in the brewery to his partner, Rudolph Hoefs, and retired to his farm. Finally, in August, there was a fire in the living quarters at the brewery. While a bucket brigade from the lake managed to save surrounding buildings despite the wind, the damage, combined with the threat of prohibition, caused Hoefs to shut down the brewery.

Kiewel brewed Security beer in addition to White Rose at his Little Falls brewery. The Little Falls are pictured on this label from around 1900, though with some artistic license. FROM THE COLLECTION OF KEN MALZ.

Little Falls [Morrison County]

Leo P. Brick (1880–1884)
Little Falls Brewing Co. (1884–1888)
Marin & Medved (1888–1891)
Peter Medved (1891–1892)
R. J. Koch (1892–1893)
Jacob Kiewel (1893–1899)
Jacob Kiewel Brewing Co. (1899–1920)
Kiewel Products Co. (1920–1933)
Kiewel Brewing Co. (1933–1959)
Kiewel Brewing Co./Branch of Minneapolis Brewing Co. (1959–1961)
Location: 512 NE Seventh Street

The brewery in Little Falls appears to have been started in 1880 by Leo P. Brick. Information about the early years is scarce, but it is known that the brewery burned down in February 1884 and was rebuilt a few months later. Later that year the firm was renamed Little Falls Brewing Co. and kept that name until 1888, when Marin and Medved took over. Peter Medved ran the brewery on his own for a year and advertised that he had improved the brewery and increased its capacity. Rudolph (sometimes Reinhold) J. "John" Koch purchased the brewery in 1892, but sold it the next year and moved to Sandusky, Ohio, intending to continue in the brewing business there.

In 1893 the period of turnover ended when Jacob Kiewel purchased the brewery for either $13,000 or $15,000 (newspaper accounts disagree). Frustrated by Fergus Falls' brief flirtation with prohibition, Kiewel abandoned his recently burned property there and purchased Koch's business in Little Falls. Kiewel immediately began to improve the facility by digging a new well, increasing storage capacity, and building a new three-story malt house. In 1900 he added a bottling plant to the complex and began to ship his White Rose brand throughout the region. Over the next two decades, the extent of his improvements made good his claim that the brewery would be "second to none in Northern Minnesota."

By 1899 the Kiewel family was doing well enough that they were able to purchase the brewery in Crookston, and Charles and Ben Kiewel took over management there. (See the separate account of the Crookston brewery.) The White Rose brand brewed in Little Falls proved to be quite popular. White Rose advertising, unlike the advertising of many other brands from small or midsize breweries, was directed toward women. During Prohibition the company carried on as Kiewel Associated Products (see chapter 5), but two family members left for Canada to continue making real beer during Prohibition. Charles built a new brewery in St. Boniface, Manitoba, which brewed a White Seal beer based on the Crookston product. He also introduced a dark Bavarian-style beer called Buffalo Beer, which was very uncommon in the Canadian market. George went to General Breweries of Prince Albert, Saskatchewan, and guided it through a merger with the Red Wing brewery of the same city. The family became even more important in the Midwest brewing industry when Charles returned from Canada to become president of Minneapolis Brewing Company after Prohibition and other family members joined him in that firm.

Kiewel Brewing returned to production in August 1933 and had beer on sale by October. The Little Falls brewery used the old Crookston label, White Seal, as its 3.2 percent product, eventually adding Strong and, in 1943, Super White Seal. In 1936 Kiewel expanded and began offering White Seal in cone-top cans. World War II forced ingredient changes, and some consistency problems led to decreased popularity of the brand. While White Seal still had some following in Minnesota's lake country, increasing competition from larger brewers squeezed the brewery hard. Kiewel Brewing was leased in 1959 by Minneapolis Brewing Company and used to brew White Seal as a cheap beer for Minnesota markets, as requested by distributors. (White Seal had already been brewed and marketed outside Minnesota, especially in Kansas City.) At the end of the two-year lease period, operations were discontinued because the Little Falls brewery was inefficient and too small to be worth updating. The building was used for light industrial shops and storage for several years, but by the mid-1970s it had fallen into disrepair and was considered a safety hazard. While rehabilitation and reuse might have been possible in some places, it was not considered practical in Little Falls. The brewery was razed in 1982 with little objection, with some of the distinctive yellow brick salvaged for other uses.

Long Prairie [Todd County]

Gebhardt Rohner (1874–?)
John Meiner (1882–1890?)
Gebhardt Rohner (1890–1899?)
Joseph Slaby (1901–1902)
Fred Beyrer (1902–1906)
Long Prairie Brewing Co. (1906–1918)
Location: On Venewitz Creek

According to *Todd County Then and Now*, Long Prairie Brewing Company began when Gebhardt Rohner started brewing in 1874. *Schade's Brewers Handbook* records no production in 1874 but forty-five barrels the next year. The brewery seems to have gone in and out of production with some frequency. Rohner himself was in Perham in 1880 working for Peter Schroeder, though his family was still in Long Prairie. The Polk *Gazetteer* and Salem's list of breweries do not include an entry for Long Prairie. The dates given above are from *American Breweries II*, but the 1900 census lists Rohner as a farmer, so the brewery may have been idle again.

The brewery began a period of stability when Fred Beyrer left his brewing position in Rice Lake, Wisconsin, to revive the Long Prairie brewery. When he sold the brewery to Charles F. Hirth and Joseph Niedermair in 1906, it had been turned into a going concern. *Todd County Then and Now* noted that the brew-

These two "high-profile" cone-top cans from Kiewel Brewing are scarce Minnesota cans. Both of these cans are for 3.2 percent brews. White Seal came in three varieties: 3.2 percent, strong (4 percent), and Super White Seal (5 percent). FROM THE COLLECTION OF DAVE WENDL.

ery "was equipped with many of the modern improvements necessary for the sanitary brewing of pure wholesome beer," and that it served patrons in a twenty-mile radius.

Long Prairie was a hostile environment for brewers during the years before Prohibition. The *Long Prairie Leader* carried frequent attacks on the brewers and the politicians aligned with them. By 1918 the brewery was closed for good.

Lucan [Redwood County]

Brau Brothers Brewing Co. (2006–present)
Location: 201 First Street

The Brau family ceased brewing at the Brau-Haus brewpub in early 2006 and began work on a new microbrewery. The new brewery, which released its first beer in October 2006, produces several of the favorites from the BrauHaus, including Scotch Ale and Strawberry Wheat. Five beers are regularly available in bottles and on tap in southwest Minnesota, and a series of rotating seasonal beers is planned.

Madelia [Watonwan County]

Peter A. Brennis (Brennes) (1878–1897)
Location: Southwest corner of Broadway and Walker

Peter Brennis's brewery in Madelia appears to have been a typical small-town brewery. In the first two years of operation he produced only a few hundred barrels each year, but by the mid-1890s he was licensed as a producer of more than 500 barrels and was listed in one brewing directory as having a capacity of 1,000 barrels. The 1880 census lists Brennis's 21-year-old stepson, John Hoffman, as the only other employee of the brewery. The 1894 Sanborn fire insurance map does not show a bottling house. There are no Madelia newspapers extant that cover the period of Brennis's brewing, and the brewery does not appear in industry periodicals, so details about the brewery's history are minimal.

Mankato [Blue Earth County]

William & Jacob Bierbauer (1857–1862)
William Bierbauer (1863–1894)
William Bierbauer Estate (1894–1903)
Louisa Bierbauer (1903–1905)
Wm. Bierbauer Brewing Co. (1905–1920)
Mankato Brewing Co. (1933–1951)
Cold Spring Brewing Co. (Mankato Branch)
  (1951–1954)
Mankato Brewing Company (1954–1967)
Location: Seventh and Rock streets

The first and longest-lived of Mankato's breweries was started by German immigrant William Bierbauer. He and his wife, Louisa, were among the pioneering families of Mankato. Bierbauer started in the brewing business at Seneca Falls, New York, and later was employed by Phillip Best in Milwaukee. He and his brother Jacob started a brewery on North Front Street and, according to Mankato brewery historian and collector Gail Palmer, brewed their first batch in April 1857. (The brewery later claimed a starting date of 1856, but this may have been an attempt to boost sales by celebrating the centennial early.) The 1860 Census of Industry recorded production of 190 barrels in the previous twelve months. During the Dakota War of 1862, William served as captain of a volunteer regiment that went to relieve the siege of New Ulm.

In the same year, Jacob sold his share of the brewery to William and pursued a variety of other business interests. William began constructing a larger brewery on a hillside southeast of his original site. By 1866 his sales averaged about eighty barrels per month,

This tin-on-cardboard sign advertising Bierbauer's Export Beer is from near the turn of the century. FROM THE COLLECTION OF PAT STAMBAUGH.

making his brewery the second largest in the southwest part of the state, behind only Schell and Bernhard. By 1870 his total was more than 1,000 barrels, and by 1879 he was approaching 1,500 barrels. An 1868 *Mankato Union* article enthused that Bierbauer could make one hundred barrels a day if necessary.

Others observed the potential of the Mankato beer market, and Bierbauer had a parade of competitors from 1867 to the mid-1880s. To maintain his position of leadership, Bierbauer made continual additions to his brewery until he had a sprawling complex that extended for several blocks. He began bottling his own beer in 1886, though Mankato had several independent bottlers who may have had contracts with Bierbauer before that year.

When William Bierbauer died in 1893, he left a thriving business to his family. His sons, Albert and Rudolph, built large Victorian mansions across the street from each other on North Sixth Street, and their mother, Louisa, continued to live in the large home on East Rock Street. While the name changed slightly, the Bierbauer family brewery survived until Prohibition with very few of the problems that beset many other breweries. The Bierbauer brewery held off all local competitors and eventually became the only brewery in the largest city in the southwest part of the state.

Bierbauer Brewing did not adopt other lines of business during Prohibition, so the

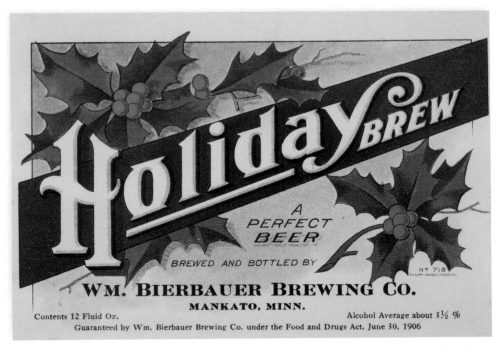

Many breweries offered a Christmas beer, and a stock label saved money. This label could be ordered from the Philipp-Schulz Litho Co. of Milwaukee and was then overprinted with the brewery's name and other data. Unlike the high-alcohol holiday brews of many modern craft brewers, Bierbauer's was the same strength as a standard lager. (label c. 1907–20). FROM THE COLLECTION OF KEN MALZ.

brewing equipment was allowed to deteriorate. But Gerald R. Martin of Minneapolis believed that the re-legalization of beer could make a brewery in Mankato a paying proposition, so in May 1933 he completed a deal to purchase the Bierbauer brewery. A team of eighty men began work, cleaning and refurbishing the plant now known as Mankato Brewing. The brewery, which had a capacity of 25,000 barrels a year before Prohibition, was expanded to 90,000 barrels to meet the assumed need of the public for real beer. The account in the *Mankato Free Press* on September 22 noted that the new brewmaster, George Volkert, had 30 years of experience, including at Wolf's brewery in Stillwater and in Canada during Prohibition. The first batch of Kato Lager Beer went on sale almost exactly five months after the brewery was purchased. Initial demand for the beer was high, and the company was com-

pelled to install ten new storage tanks to keep up with the demand.

Mankato Brewing used a variety of packages to get the beer to its customers. The same 24 May 1934 *Free Press* article that described the new storage tanks also announced that the brewery would soon be selling unpasteurized "keg beer" in 64-ounce bottles. Kato Lager and Kato Gold Label brands also appeared in cone-top beer cans before the end of 1936. The brands had a modest following in the Twin Cities but were also shipped to Iowa and other points south and west.

Despite its early promise, Mankato Brewing soon found itself in significant financial trouble. The purchase of the former Schutz and Hilgers brewery in Jordan was "a tragic mistake" according to the last brewmaster, James Schorn, and the attempt to update and expand it required more financial resources than Mankato Brewing had. In 1951 Cold Spring Brewing Company purchased Mankato Brewing and used the brewery for expanded capacity. By 1954 Mankato investors were able to buy the brewery back, and three years later they attempted to expand their market by acquiring two popular brands from the defunct Peoples Brewing of Duluth, Regal Supreme and Stag. These efforts were to no avail, and

the brewery ran out of money in 1960. The brewery was mortgaged for $40,000, and a group of twelve investors and twelve brewery employees came up with enough money to reopen the brewery.

Several factors caused Mankato Brewing to shut down for good in April 1967. An article in the *Free Press* on July 19 summed up the problems: poor management, inability to pay off the mortgage or to pay city utilities, high tax payments, and a lack of local support. Only 10 percent of Mankato Brewing's four brands (Kato, Jordan, Regal Supreme, and Stag) were sold in the Mankato area. One investor bemoaned the "complete lack of civic pride" and the "lack of cooperation within Mankato to back a local product," and contrasted the situation with New Ulm, which, while smaller, was still supporting two breweries. The brewery remained vacant for about a decade, but was finally torn down as a safety hazard. The houses of Albert and Rudolph still flank Sixth Street, but only a portion of the brewery gate remains of what was once one of Mankato's largest businesses.

Welch & Wolf (1867–1868)
Peter Welch (1868–1875)
Joseph Ibach (1876–1879)
Graeber & Co. (Graeber & Son) (1880–1882?)
Nicholas Graeber (1882–1884)
Location: West Mankato near the county bridge

The *Mankato Record* reported on 2 March 1867 that "Mr. Welsh [*sic*], a gentleman lately of Goodhue County, last year purchased several acres of ground bordering on the Blue Earth river, near where the old government bridge across that stream was constructed, and is engaged in erecting a brewery. The location is said to be a good one, the high sand rock bluffs offering excellent opportunities for excavating cellars."

The brewery's earliest appearances in the excise records indicate a brief partnership with George Wolf, but the latter left to start another brewery with Conrad Trout, leaving Welch (often spelled Welsh) as the sole proprietor. C. J. Klein also took advantage of the location to establish the Union beer garden on the hill near the brewery and built a dance hall on the premises.

The west end of Mankato was a fine location for breweries and beer gardens, which sometimes makes it difficult to untangle the lineage of the breweries located there. Gail Palmer's research into the bottlers of Mankato (included in a self-published monograph and a series of articles in Blue Earth County Historical Society newsletters) solved many of the brewery ownership transition problems, though some remain. The Welch brewery is probably the best documented of the smaller breweries of Mankato. By 1868 Welch was listed in excise records as a producer of more than 500 barrels, and his reported production in 1874 was 907 barrels. At the end of 1875 he leased the brewery to Joseph Ibach, who was looking for a more productive brewery than the one he was then operating. Ibach advertised lager and bock beer while operating Welch's brewery, but after three years moved on to his next brewery.

Welch sold his brewery to Nicholas Graeber of Red Wing early in 1880. Graeber operated the brewery with the assistance of his son John and a boarder, R. C. Boeckler, formerly of Blatt and Boeckler. The Graebers are listed in the 1880 Polk *Gazetteer* and excise records. The brewery burned in April 1882, destroying the brewery and all the equipment. While the company continues to appear in directories through 1884, it appears that the brewery was never rebuilt.

Wolf & Trout (1868)
Gerdts & Wolf (1868–1869)
Clemens Leiferman (1869–1873?)
George Wolf (1873–1874?)
Gassler & Co. (Naegli & Gassler) (1874–1883)
Location: South end of Front Street, west end of Mankato, near the Blue Earth River bridge

George Wolf left his partnership with Peter Welch to start his own brewery with local saloonkeeper Conrad Trout. Building began in the late fall of 1867 on two acres of land purchased from Judge Branson and included excavating a 50-foot-long cellar into the sandstone bluff. The brewery opened in March 1868, and the *Mankato Record* reported that the first samples gave "pretty general satisfaction." Trout sold his interest in the brewery to Mr. E. Gerdts, who recently had moved to Mankato.

Though no specific record of the sale exists, it appears that Clemens Leiferman (George or Carl in some records) acquired the brewery

from Wolf in October 1869. It is possible that Leiferman started a new brewery, but no record of any such construction has been discovered. His first appearance in the excise records is as a large brewer, and he produced well over 400 barrels in the 1869–1870 tax year, so it is more likely that Leiferman took over Wolf's established brewery. Wolf is still listed as a brewer in the 1870 census, but could have been working for another brewery (he lived right next to Welch's brewery) or may have been between jobs. An article on the brewing industry published in the *Mankato Review* stated that as of October 1869 there were three breweries in Mankato—a number supported by excise records. The Leiferman brewery is still listed in the 1873–1874 *Mankato City Directory*, but the *Minnesota State Business Directory* of 1873 lists G. Wolf instead of Leiferman. (Excise records of 1873 through 1875 for the First Collection District, which includes Mankato, no longer exist to help clear up the discrepancy.) Leiferman may have leased the brewery from Wolf, who took it over again before selling.

The period of rapid ownership changes came to an end sometime in 1874 when William Gassler (or Gessler) purchased the brewery. Gassler and his partner, John Naegli, increased the brewery's production from 326 barrels in 1875 to 1,112 barrels in 1879. However, in March 1883 the company suffered a double stroke of misfortune. Gassler and Naegli were arrested and taken to St. Paul for what the *Mankato Review* described as a trivial revenue violation on the same day the brewery was gutted by fire. The coincidence of events suggests that the brewery had made some vindictive enemies. While the brewery remained in city and brewers' directories for a few years, there is no evidence that the brewery was rebuilt.

Blatt & Boeckler (1873–1875)
Anton Jacoby (1876–1878)
Joseph Ibach (1878–1880)
Margaret Ibach (1880–1884)
Joseph Ibach (1884–1887)
Location: Tincom's Addition

The early history of what eventually became Joseph Ibach's third brewery in Mankato is shrouded in conjecture. The standard account given in Neill's *History of the Minnesota Valley* is that Ibach purchased the brewery from

Anton Jacoby, who purchased it from its original owner, Conrad Boeckle [*sic*], who, according to Gail Palmer's research, originally built the brewery in 1868. This creates difficulties with both dates and names, since there were only three breweries in Mankato from 1868 to 1870, and all are accounted for. Further, there is no one in the 1870 census who appears to match the description of Boeckle.

On the other hand, the firm of Blatt and Boeckler, established sometime in 1873, seems to fit the description. Philip Blatt was listed as a retail liquor dealer in the 1870 census, and his partner appears to have been R. C. Boeckler, who does not appear in the 1870 census but is listed as a brewer at age 29 ten years later. The company is listed as Blatt and Blockler in the *Minnesota State Business Directory* of 1873, and is included in *Schade's Brewers Handbook* as Blatt and Boehler with production totals of 530 barrels in 1874 and 744 barrels the next year. It is not clear what happened to the business, though it is likely that growing so big so quickly may have put Blatt and Boeckler in debt. It is probably this brewery that Ibach bought from Jacoby, since it would have been big enough to represent a move up for Ibach, and it was probably sold for a relatively low price to raise cash.

Ibach's brewery did not appear in the newspaper often, but local accounts exist that suggest that the brewery and neighboring beer gardens were still popular resorts for Mankato's residents. It is not clear why the business was conducted in the name of his wife, Margaret, for four years, but her name appears both in brewers' directories and excise records during the early 1880s. The brewery was destroyed by fire in 1887, and Joseph Ibach decided to retire rather than rebuild.

Haas & Schmidt (1873–1874)
Stephen Lamm (1874)
Joseph Ibach (1874–1875)
Location: West Mankato

The biographical sketch of Joseph Ibach in Thomas Hughes's 1909 *History of Blue Earth County* provides a clear chronology of Ibach's brewing career in Mankato, but in so doing raises other questions that remain unanswered. Hughes reports that when Ibach arrived from Preston, he purchased the brewery of Stephen Lamm. This is the only known reference to

The Standard Brewing Co. brewery was an impressive structure, but drawings that advertised it looked much grander than this. A personal message from "Gertrude" at the bottom admonishes the recipient, "Now don't get dry." FROM THE COLLECTION OF DAVE WENDL.

Lamm's brewery—it does not appear in excise records, business directories, or brewing handbooks. The 1873–1874 *Mankato City Directory* includes the brewery of Haas & Schmidt in West Mankato, but no other information exists on this brewery. Stephen Lamm owned a large tract of land in western Mankato and was one of the city's important business leaders, so it is possible that he either purchased the Haas & Schmidt brewery or foreclosed it and disposed of it to Ibach.

Standard Brewing Co. (1900–1908)

Location: N. Fourth Street, southeast corner of Elm

Few of Minnesota's early-twentieth-century breweries were launched with as much fanfare as Standard Brewing Co. of Mankato. Started by several local businessmen, with help from Chicago capitalists, Standard was designed to be a modern and efficient brewery. The *Mankato Free Press* published an account of a tour of the new facility in June 1900, covering everything from the brew kettles to the whitewashing machine and freight elevator. The plant was valued at $200,000 and began with a capacity of 25,000 barrels. Apparently

this was not enough; within the next two years *Brewers' Journal* carried notices of significant new additions and expansions that ultimately brought capacity to 40,000 per year.

Despite an advertising blitz carried out in newspapers, city directories, saloons, and promotional items, Standard was unable to make

a profit. While Mankato may have seemed a logical place for a new brewery, the Bierbauer brewery was well established and so were several nearby competitors. Out-of-state brewers were also represented in Mankato, a fact that was well-known to one of the organizers of the company, Nic Petersen, since he had spent a significant portion of his business life bottling Milwaukee beer. Poor planning may have played a role, since the original syndicate was formed to start an electric street railway—the brewery was developed as a substitute enterprise when the railway plans fell through. Some brewerianists have even speculated that the brewery was cursed because it capitalized on the execution of thirty-eight Dakota after the 1862 conflict. The brewery issued a small round tray with a reprint of the famous engraving of the execution as well as the large tray (pictured in chapter 4) with Army officers sitting on a porch calmly drinking Standard Beer. Whatever the reason, in 1906 the struggling company was bailed out by a syndicate

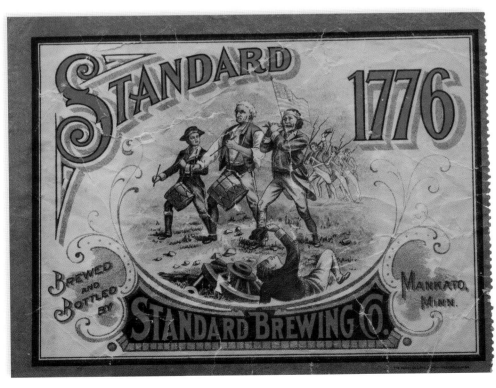

The 1776 label is highly sought-after by collectors of Minnesota breweriana. FROM THE COLLECTION OF DAVE WENDL.

of "Eastern capitalists" (though their homes ranged from Schenectady to St. Louis). This group controlled the brewery for a little more than a year, after which it was sold to Stephen Lamm of Mankato. He died shortly afterward, and his executors took over the brewery to protect his estate and not, as John H. Hohmann said "because we were desirous of engaging in the manufacture of beers." The *Free Press* article that documented the closing on 10 December 1908 also quoted Hohmann's statement on the distribution of the other brewery properties:

> We have sold all our leases and properties in South Dakota and western Minnesota to the C. & J. Michel Brewing company of La Crosse, and all our local trade, including the Wells agency, to the William Bierbauer Brewing company of this city. The Michel company was very desirous of gaining control of our Mankato business, but we did not feel that it would be proper to sell this business to an outside brewery.

The brewery was torn down shortly after it closed, and the land was used for houses. Because of their visual and historical appeal as well as their scarcity, breweriana items from Standard Brewing Co. are prized by collectors.

Mantorville [Dodge County]

John Hirchi (1858–1859)
Henry Naegli & Charles Ginsberg (1859–1860)
Charles Ginsberg (1860–1878)
Anna Ginsberg (1878–1885)
Henry Naegli (1885–1899)
Ferdinand Schnagl (1899–1906)
Ferdinand Schnagl Estate (1906–1907)
Anna Schnagl (1907–1910)
Anna Schnagl Estate (1911)
John George Schnagl (1911–1917)
Otto's Brewery, Inc. (Otto Schumann) (1934–1937)
Mantorville Brewing Company (1937–1939)
Location: 6 Bluff Street

According to the booklet "Mantorville Today" (written sometime in the 1890s), the first brewery in Mantorville was built in 1858 on Fifth Street by John Hirchi (sometimes spelled Hirschi), who also brewed in nearby Berne. In 1859 he sold the Mantorville brewery to Henry Naegli and Charles Ginsberg, who was married to Henry's sister Anna. A year later, Ginsberg bought his brother-in-law's share and became sole proprietor. Ginsberg's business quickly outgrew the existing brewery, so he built a new brewery just to the east, though local accounts offer the years from 1861 to 1863 as the date when the new building was completed. The early date is most likely, since Ginsberg held a Fourth of July ball in his brewery hall in 1862, with seventy couples in attendance.

Ginsberg apparently met with success in the new brewery. His production in 1866 was less than that of the large Rochester, Winona, and Red Wing breweries, but greater than that of almost every other brewery in the southeastern part of the state. The excise tax records of that year also show Ginsberg being taxed for owning a carriage—a luxury item that was relatively rare at the time.

Ginsberg's profits enabled him to embark on a building program that resulted in one of the finest breweries in the region. Built entirely out of stone quarried from the bluff into which it was built, the four-story brewery featured a twenty-horsepower boiler and engine, making it one of the first breweries in Minnesota to convert to steam power. A twenty-five-barrel brew kettle, made of copper and iron and weighing more than 500 pounds, was manufactured in St. Paul and installed in the brewery. The complex included four different cellars: a small one from the previous brewery and three large new ones to hold fermenting and aging beer. Although many brewery illustrations of the day embellished reality, the real Ginsberg brewery was every bit as impressive as the sketches suggested. (A fine depiction of the brewery is included in chapter 3.) The Dodge County Brewery, as it was sometimes called, employed three men, including Ginsberg's brother-in-law Henry Naegli, who was back from his service with the 8th Kansas Volunteers. The brewery was now producing more than 500 barrels per year, making it a large brewery for tax purposes.

It was fortunate that Naegli was back in town, because a series of family tragedies befell the Ginsberg family in 1877 and 1878. In addition to brother Edwin's medical troubles (covered under the entry for his Waseca brewery), Anna Ginsberg, mother of three brewers, died at the asylum in St. Peter in January 1878.

New Style Lager was one of the first brews made by Otto's Brewery after it reopened. BOB KAY COLLECTION.

Four months later, Charles went missing just before he was due to travel to Waseca to visit his brothers. A search of the brewery grounds revealed his body in a pool near the dam. The coroner ruled it death by suicide. The *Dodge County Republican* speculated that his plight may have been caused either by his deep financial trouble or by a severe bruise on the head suffered when he fell into a cistern the week before—no accounts made any connection with the recent death of his mother. Following this tragedy, Henry Naegli assumed management of the brewery and operated it for the next twenty years, though for the first several years Anna Ginsberg (Charles's widow) remained the proprietress.

The next two decades were largely uneventful. The brewery was spared major fires or other disasters, and Naegli continued to expand the brewery until its capacity reached 7,000 barrels (though it is unlikely it produced at capacity during this time). In 1899 Naegli sold the brewery to Ferdinand Schnagl, who had previously brewed at Rush City and Crookston. The brewery's market was primarily in the Dodge County area, though there are accounts of Mantorville beer being on draught as far away as Pine Island. The Schnagl family continued to operate the brewery until 1917, when it closed with Prohibition on the horizon.

During Prohibition, the brewery sat idle for a few years, then in 1924 was converted to a creamery and pop factory. Apparently the brewery was not entirely idle, for during the conversion a vat of strong beer was accidentally punctured by workers. The proprietor, William Schumann, was also arrested for drunken driving in 1927 and was found to have bottles of homebrewed beer and grain alcohol in his car.

When beer became legal again in 1933, the building was reconverted to produce beer, with the preliminary name of Schumann Brewing Co. By the time the brewery was ready in the spring of 1934, the company's name was changed to Otto's Brewery, after the brewmaster, Otto Schumann. The first kegs of New Style Lager Beer left the brewery in May 1934, but whatever claims the *Mantorville Express* made for the quality of the beer, the company was in financial trouble almost immediately.

By November the brewery was in receivership with more than one hundred creditors claiming more than $400,000. After a few years of uncertainty, the brewery was reorganized as Mantorville Brewing Company and, under brewmaster Walter Swistowisz, began to sell Man's Beer on draught and in bottles. However, the brewery's debt was too high and competition from out-of-town breweries made it impossible for the brewery to recover. Moreover, the *Claremont News* also suggested that "the product did not meet the approval of the buying public." The brewery closed its doors for good in 1939. Most of the building was torn down in April 1942, and some of the scrap metal from the brewery was used for the war effort.

Mantorville Brewing Company (1996–present)
Location: 501 N. Main Street

Mantorville Brewing Company was formed in 1996 in sight of the caves of the old Ginsberg brewery. The founders were a group of seven homebrewers who decided to go professional. Their draught-only Stagecoach Ale is available in the greater Rochester area. Tod Fyten bought a share of the Mantorville operation in 1999 and has kept the company going with various partners. Additional information may be found in chapter 8.

Marine-on-St. Croix [Washington County]

John Kaufmann (1856–1857)
J. J. Graf (1857–1866)
J. J. Graf & Son (1867–1870)
Wichman and Gartner (1870–1880)
John Wichman (1880–1882)
Location: By the river bluff, just south of the mill-stream (where the mill site historic marker is today)

John Kaufmann founded a brewery in the town of Marine, just north of Stillwater, in 1856. A year later he sold it to John Jacob Graf (sometimes spelled Graff), who operated it for eight years, but later built a new brewery following a fire. The original business appears to have been quite small—not until July 1865 did he sell ten barrels in a month. Graf's new brewery doubled his output, but his operation was still dwarfed by the three breweries just to his south in Stillwater. It is likely that beer from the Marine brewery was provided only to saloons in the town itself.

In fall 1870, the partnership of Wichman and Gartner (with various spellings) took control of the brewery. This team continued a small but steady production for the next decade, until Wichman took over upon the death of Gartner. Edward D. Neill's 1881 *History of Washington County and the St. Croix Valley* claimed that Wichman had an annual production of 300 barrels, though this is probably an exaggeration. No recorded annual production was over 200 barrels, and by 1879 output dropped to 98 barrels. Wichman also operated a saloon in conjunction with the brewery.

The brewery burned down in 1882 in a fire that threatened the nearby sawmill and inspired the town council to investigate buying a fire engine and five hundred feet of hose. Wichman rebuilt his saloon, but it is likely that competition from the larger breweries that surrounded Marine made it cheaper and easier for Wichman to buy beer for his saloon than to make it.

Marion [Olmsted County]

D. Kennedy (?–1866)
Location: Unknown

Sometime before 1866, D. Kennedy began brewing in Marion, southeast of Rochester. He sold slightly fewer than thirty barrels of beer in 1866, with a peak of seven and a half barrels in June. The incomplete records suggest that Kennedy was in business before 1866, but no conclusive proof has been found. Kennedy does not appear in excise tax records after 1866.

Mazeppa [Wabasha County]

Joseph Trausch (1878–1882)
John Hilger (1882–1884)
Joseph Trausch (1884–1897)
Rother & Manske (1898–1899)
Location: Corner of Oak and Second streets

Joseph Trausch's first year of brewing in Mazeppa very nearly ended in tragedy. The *St. Paul Daily Globe* reported on 17 October 1878 that Trausch's father-in-law, Peter Lippert, fell through a hatchway in the brewery and struck his head on the floor ten feet below. Mr. Lippert survived the fall, and Trausch managed to brew just over one hundred barrels in his first year of operation.

Little is known about the brewery's operations, except that its largest listed capacity was about 500 barrels. Trausch appears to have leased the brewery twice, first to John Hilger and later to Rother and Manske. The brewery was torn down in 1905.

Melrose [Stearns County]

John P. Schnitz (1882–1883)
Kuhn & Hess (1883–1884)
Kuhn & Mayer (1884–1885)
J. M. Hemmisch (1886–1897)
Melrose Brewing Co. (Weisner & Wrede)
 (1897–1899)
Melrose Brewery (various owners) 1899–1909
Melrose Brewing Co. (1909–1914)
Location: North side of Mill Pond at the end of High Street (today approximately at the east end of East River Heights Drive)

Located in a heavily Germanic section of the state, the brewery in Melrose grew quickly and was licensed as a large producer by 1885. J. M. "Mat" Hemmisch ran the brewery with a few interruptions for nearly two decades. The *St. Cloud Times* reported in May 1884 that Kuhn and Mayer's brewery manufactured about 3,000 gallons of beer a week, which if true was nearly 5,000 barrels a year. (It seems unlikely since this would be equal to the production of all of St. Cloud's breweries just three years earlier.)

The management team of Weisner and Wrede (who apparently leased the plant from Hemmisch) built a new brewery, which the *Times* reported cost $12,000 and went into production in July 1897. Weisner and Wrede advertised regularly in the German-language *Melrose Anzeiger*. After Hemmisch's death, the Melrose Brewery changed management several times. Hilt, Molitor, and Rossmeisel were succeeded by Hilt and Molitor, and finally, Anton Molitor became sole proprietor in 1904. Under Molitor, the brewery was seldom mentioned in the brewing industry trade journals, which can be good and bad: while it meant the brewery had not burned down, it also indicated a lack of expansion and improvement.

In 1909, however, *Brewers' Journal* announced that Melrose Brewing Company had been formed and was planning a new brewery. Over the next four years, output jumped from just over 1,000 barrels per year to more than 3,000. A bottling plant was added in 1910, and Old Bohemian Style beer was made available to customers in the area. Tragically, this promising start was abruptly halted when a massive fire destroyed the brewery in September 1914, resulting in a loss of $50,000. The stockholders chose not to reopen the brewery.

The Schatz-Brau brewery, sometimes listed as a post-repeal successor to Melrose Brewing even though it never went into production, was a completely different company and plant and is discussed in chapter 6.

At first glance it appears impossible that this elaborate die-cut paper piece is an advertisement for a brewery, but it encourages patrons to call "Double Two" and order a case of Melrose Brewing Co.'s Old Bohemian. Clearly not intended for a saloon, this piece from the early 1910s was designed to encourage women to order from the local brewery instead of giving their patronage to out-of-town brands. FROM THE COLLECTION OF JIM AND RUTH BEATON.

Millville [Wabasha County]

William (Claus) Behrns (1879–1881)
Location: South of town

The History of Wabasha County, published in 1884, reported, "From about 1879 to 1881 Claus Behrns run [*sic*] the Midland brewery, but it was accidentally burned, and its ruins still remain." Behrns was listed as a brewer in the 1880 census and the 1880 Polk *Gazetteer* of that year. No production figures have been found for this brewery in Oakwood Township.

Minneapolis [Hennepin County]

John Orth (1850–1883)
John Orth Brewing Co. (1883–1890)
Minneapolis Brewing & Malting Co. (1890–1893)
Minneapolis Brewing Co. (1893–1920)
Golden Grain Juice Co. (1920–1929)
Minneapolis Brewing Company (1933–1967)
Grain Belt Breweries, Inc. (1967–1975)
Location: Thirteenth Avenue and Marshall Street NE

John Orth and his wife, Mary, are sometimes considered the first German settlers in St. Anthony, even though Orth's home in Alsace was part of France at the time. Orth's brewery was the second brewery in Minnesota, and while the first wooden brewery was only 18 × 30 feet, it grew quickly. By 1860 he was producing more than 1,000 barrels a year, and ten years later he and his six employees produced almost double that amount. Competition from upstarts Mueller and Heinrich on the other side of the river forced Orth to increase his capacity, and by the late 1870s, although he was still behind Mueller and Heinrich (and Stahlmann in St. Paul), he was now turning out nearly 7,000 barrels per year. The brewery utilized the latest in technology and was one of the first in Minnesota to switch from caves to "ice cellars" (specially built, aboveground buildings) for lagering the beer. The brew kettle used in 1880 held 120 barrels, compared with the 2.5-barrel kettle Orth started with in 1850.

By the time the firm changed its name to John Orth Brewing Co. in 1883, the business was well established and Orth's sons, John W., Alfred, and Edward, were brought into the business. After the founder died in 1887, the sons carried on the business.

This rare label is from the 1880s, before John Orth Brewing became part of Minneapolis Brewing & Malting Co. BOB KAY COLLECTION.

Starting in the late 1880s, British syndicates sought to take over American breweries for their investment value. This coincided with a general trend in American business for companies to band together in trusts or other combinations to reduce competition and increase profits. To resist takeover by foreigners and to reduce the cutthroat competition prevalent in Minneapolis, representatives of the city's breweries met to consider a merger. In July 1890, Minneapolis Brewing & Malting Co. was formed from the Orth, Heinrich, Noerenberg, and Germania breweries. (Early accounts suggested Gluek was to join as well, but elected to remain independent.) All of the breweries except Noerenberg's remained in use while the company planned and built its massive new 150,000-barrel brewery. The site of Orth's brewery was chosen at least in part because it was not hemmed in by bluffs and had more room to expand. The new brewery, designed by August Maritzen of Chicago, was and is one of the landmarks of Northeast Minneapolis. As the new brewery opened in 1893, the company dropped *Malting* from the firm's name and adopted a new brand for its flagship beer—Grain Belt. While XXX London Porter and Gilt Edge Beer kept their names for a few years, by 1897 all the company's beers bore the Grain Belt name.

The new company very nearly lost its new brewery the very year it opened. A fire that destroyed several city blocks in August 1893 burned the stables and some storage buildings but spared the brewery itself. The firm took the opportunity to expand during the rebuilding, since it was clear that Martizen's original brewery was not big enough for the rapidly expanding business. Nearly every year, a notice appeared in *Brewers' Journal* that Minneapolis Brewing Co. was building a new brewhouse, bottling facility, warehouse, or stable. The brewery owned 186 horses, all black except for one team of bays, and these were a familiar sight making deliveries to the scores of tied saloons controlled by the company.

By the turn of the century, the brewery had a published capacity of 500,000 barrels, and though it controlled almost one-third of the saloons in Minneapolis, the company needed to expand its market to remain competitive. Saloons serving Golden Grain Belt beers appeared from Michigan to Montana, and the company built depots to serve its customers. Entries from *Brewers' Journal* and excise records show depots from Albert Lea to International Falls in Minnesota, and from Michigan's

This early Grain Belt label is from between 1896, when all the Minneapolis Brewing Co. brands took the Grain Belt name, and 1906, when Food and Drugs Act label requirements were enacted. FROM THE COLLECTION OF KEN MALZ.

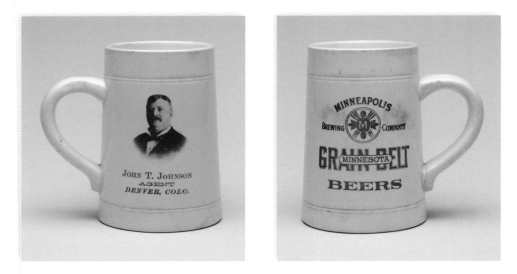

John T. Johnson was the Grain Belt agent in Denver, Colorado, proving how far Minneapolis Brewing Co. expanded its market in the years before World War I. FROM THE COLLECTION OF STEVE KETCHUM.

after repeal and entered the 1940s with its market secure.

The late 1940s and early 1950s were a period of stagnation for the brewery. Frank D. Kiewel, in an article in the *Minneapolis Tribune* in July 1960, blamed the drift on a lack of young drinkers caused by low birth rates during the Depression years and on over-expansion during the 1940s. In 1955 Kiewel promoted Frank Mathes to brewmaster, and under the new management team, the brewery's growth continued into the late 1960s. In 1967 the name of the company was changed to Grain Belt Breweries to move away from a geographically identified name that might limit future expansion. Shortly thereafter, Grain Belt purchased the struggling Storz brewery in Omaha, Nebraska, and bought the recipe and label from the defunct Hauenstein brewery in New Ulm.

An article in *Greater Minneapolis Magazine* in 1974 featured an interview with Gerald Meyer, the company's president, in which he noted that Grain Belt was still the number one beer in Minnesota and that Grain Belt was

Upper Peninsula to Judith Gap, Montana. In 1915 Grain Belt moved southwest as the company was incorporated in Nebraska and opened an office in Kansas City.

Two variations on the Minnehaha theme: at left is the Minnehaha label pasted onto a bottle from the Leisy Brewing Co. of Peoria, Illinois. FROM THE COLLECTION OF DAVE WENDL.

As Prohibition approached, Minneapolis Brewing prepared for the inevitable by transferring all its assets to a new corporation, Golden Grain Juice Company. Minneapolis Brewing owned 5,993 of the 6,000 shares of Golden Grain Juice stock, with one each held by individual directors. The company introduced Minnehaha Pale Ale and a variety of other different beverages, but these were not sufficient to keep the company profitable, so it shut down the brewery in 1929 and awaited the return of beer.

When beer returned in April 1933, Grain Belt was not among the labels greeting the thirsty drinkers. Minneapolis Brewing undertook a massive modernization project and did not begin to sell beer until several months later. Despite the slow start, the company moved quickly to recapture its old territory. Because each state had its own regulations, the brewery was forced to seek approval for sixty different labels to be used on different-sized packages of various products for sale in fourteen states. Grain Belt was the first beer to appear in the short "steinie" bottles, and Minneapolis Brewing was among the most enthusiastic early adopters of canned beer. While the brewery suffered from occasional strikes and even a daring daylight robbery, Minneapolis Brewing survived the initial shakeout period

The half-gallon bottle allowed Minneapolis Brewing Co. to create a large label with a field of barley and the brewery in the background. This label was approved in 1935. FROM THE COLLECTION OF DAVE WENDL.

"here to stay for a long time." Even though the brewery and its beers were local institutions, financial problems exacerbated by price wars on the national level forced the brewery to seek a buyer in 1975. Local investor Irwin Jacobs purchased the brewery, and just a year after Meyer's prediction, the brewery was closed and the brands sold. G. Heileman Brewing of La Crosse purchased the Grain Belt label, but it lost ground relative to Heileman's own labels and to Miller and Anheuser-Busch, whose presence in Minnesota was growing rapidly.

While the fates of both the brewery and the beer were in limbo for a quarter of a century, both were saved shortly into the new millennium. RSP Architects purchased and renovated the main brewery and converted two smaller brewery buildings into the Pierre Bottineau Community Library. Other buildings in the brewery complex still stand and are used for a variety of purposes, including studios and storage. August Schell Brewing Company of New Ulm bought the Grain Belt recipe and label in 2002 and began to reinvigorate the brand.

More information on Orth and Minneapolis Brewing Company can be found throughout this book.

Nicholas Bofferding, Minneapolis Brewery
(1857?–1860)

Location: North Minneapolis

Nicholas Bofferding and his brother John began brewing sometime before the territorial census of 1857. Their operation may have been a fairly large one since Ferd. Isenbach and Louis Smidt, a brewer and maltster respectively, lived nearby. Nicholas and his brewery were listed in the business section of the 1859–1860 *Minneapolis City Directory*, but he was listed as a farmer in the 1860 census. It is possible that he brewed on his farm, but he may have stopped brewing by the time of the census. His status in 1860 and thereafter is difficult to verify because of the lack of existing city directories from 1860 to 1865.

Mississippi Brewery, Gluek & Rank (1857–1862)
Gottlieb Gluek (1862–1880)
G. Gluek & Sons (1880–1893)
Gluek Brewing Co. (1894–1964)

Location: Twentieth Avenue and Marshall Street NE

After spending two years working for John Orth, Gottlieb Gluek teamed up with John

Collectors now believe that these small promotional glasses (this example is called a shell glass) were not used in saloons but were designed for the home. A few examples of serving trays with a handle and etched glass bottoms exist; these were most likely designed to hold a set of four glasses. Etched glasses ranged from very simple designs to complex factory scenes, such as this one (c. 1890s) from Gluek's Brewing Co. in Minneapolis. FROM THE COLLECTION OF PAT STAMBAUGH.

Rank to open the Mississippi Brewery about a mile north of Orth's brewery. According to the 1860 Census of Industry, the brewery had one employee (probably in addition to the proprietors) and produced approximately 1,000 barrels of beer. (In his article on the brewery for *Hennepin County History* [Winter 1998–1999], Roland C. Amundson gives Gluek and Rank's first-year production as nearly 4,000 barrels. This figure is more likely to be the dollar value of the output or 4,000 small kegs, since 4,000 barrels was more than three times the output of any other brewery in the state and is inconsistent with other known totals.) Near the end of 1862, Rank left to become a liquor dealer and Gluek carried on the firm by himself. His sales averaged about thirty barrels a month until the middle of 1865, when a 50 percent jump in output suggests he probably expanded the brewery. Gluek's steady growth

continued throughout the 1870s as production approached 4,000 barrels annually.

According to Amundson, Gluek used caves on Nicollet Island to age and store the beer. This turned out to be fortunate, for in March 1880 a fire gutted the brewery. Four workers were forced to jump from the brewery, but there was no loss of life. Gluek immediately began to rebuild the brewery, but the strain may have been too much for him; he died in October.

Gluek's sons, Louis, Charles, and John, took over the newly rebuilt brewery and named it G. Gluek and Sons. The new plant featured a two-story brewhouse and had a capacity of forty-five barrels per day. The brothers made additions regularly until about 1888 and invested in another expansion program about a decade later. A supplement to the *Minneapolis Journal* in 1900 reported that the brewery's output at that time was 50,000 barrels per year, but that expansion plans were under way to raise the capacity to 125,000 barrels.

The brothers felt confident enough about the stability of their family business to decline the offer to join the Minneapolis Brewing Company merger. Early reports in *Brewers' Journal* included the Gluek brewery among the firms comprising the new company, but the Glueks remained independent and instead incorporated as Gluek Brewing Co. in the last week of 1893.

Charles had studied to be a banker and took over financial management of the firm. His financial skills proved to be especially important as Gluek Brewing prepared to defend its market against competitors from near and far. The company had built a solid local market for its product and concentrated its efforts on the Minneapolis trade. Existing records show a distinct lack of depots or advertisements for Gluek's beer outside Minneapolis, in stark contrast to the expanding reach of Minneapolis Brewing, Hamm, or the Milwaukee breweries. A survey of *Brewers' Journal* from 1893 to 1917 yields eighteen announcements of new depots for Minneapolis Brewing and one for Gluek (in Foley). Even A. Fitger & Co. and Duluth Brewing & Malting had more depots spread throughout the state. On the other hand, Gluek had 86 tied saloons in Minneapolis alone by 1908, fewer than Minneapolis

Brewing's 130, but more than twice as many as any other brewer. The present-day Gluek's Restaurant and Bar on North Sixth Street in Minneapolis is in a building that was once a tied saloon. Gluek Brewing paid much less attention to bottled beer than many of its competitors. The 1885 Sanborn fire insurance map does not show a bottling house associated with the brewery, and the first mention of a bottling house in *Brewers' Journal* does not appear until 1898. Though the company improved its bottling facilities several times during the 1900s, it appears that most of its bottle trade was in the local area. The relative scarcity of pre-Prohibition Gluek labels compared to other breweries of similar importance is circumstantial evidence that Gluek concentrated on draught beer sales in its saloons.

The advent of Prohibition brought difficulties for the Gluek family. They now had scores of saloon properties that had decreased in value. The brewery converted to make non-intoxicating beverages such as Indian Maid Ginger Ale, but these products did not sustain the company and it suspended production a few years before Prohibition ended. The Gluek family had other sources of income, including farms on which they raised prize-winning live-

Advertising is quick to capitalize on current celebrities, and the heart-warming story of Seabiscuit captured the public's imagination during the late 1930s. This two-piece cardboard sign produced a three-dimensional effect. FROM THE COLLECTION OF JIM AND RUTH BEATON.

SEABISCUIT

Gluek's Beer

GLUEK BREWING CO., MINNEAPOLIS, MINN.

PURE and TRUE IN FLAVOR
... PROTECTED BY OUR
"KILLING-RAY" STERILAMPS

G

stock and Belgian horses, so they were able to wait for the eventual re-legalization of beer.

Since the brewery had been maintained in running order throughout the 1920s, the brewery was in an advantageous position to be ready to sell beer on 7 April 1933. Like other breweries open that day, Gluek Brewing Company was the site of traffic jams as brewery trucks going out met customers trying to get in. The company capitalized on its head start and rebuilt a solid local following. No longer able to rely on tied saloons, Gluek Brewing became an innovator in packaging and began to expand its distribution area. Gluek was one of the first brewers to adopt the beer can, and eventually used all major styles of can. (Photographs of the cans may be found in chapter 6.) It also used nearly every style and size of bottle and continued to maintain as many draught accounts as possible within the limitations of the new system. Gluek's Beer, Pilsener Pale, and Gluek's Bock made the company one of the success stories of the first years after repeal. The officers of the company, Alvin, Arthur, Eugene, and Louis Gluek, had managed to navigate their brewery through the changing conditions that caused hundreds of breweries to fail during the 1930s.

Gluek Brewing continued to innovate throughout the 1940s. During World War II, grain shortages forced breweries to do the best they could with what grains were available. Alvin Gluek patented a new recipe for a brew called malt liquor, which was marketed under the name Stite. Higher alcohol content helped to compensate for the change in taste, and the new product became known as Green

Sterilamps may well have been effective, but the short life of this neck label suggests that customers did not find a process called "killing-ray" appetizing. FROM THE COLLECTION OF KEN MALZ.

Death for its ability to induce headaches. Despite this, the product retained a following for several decades and was the brand used to spearhead the company's move into Illinois in the late 1940s. *Brewers Digest* praised Gluek in 1947 for being one of the first breweries to install "sterilamps," which helped protect wort from infection when it was being chilled before the addition of yeast. Barley Field Day, a collaboration between the University of Minnesota agricultural program and Minnesota brewers designed to create better barley varieties, was hosted in 1951 at Gluek Farm number two. When Alvin Gluek died in 1952, the brewery was recognized nationally as an industry leader.

Unfortunately, Gluek Brewing was just the wrong size of brewery to survive in an increasingly competitive environment. With a capacity of about 200,000 barrels and no room to expand the plant, it was too small to compete on a national level. Gluek's primary territory included Minnesota, Iowa, the Dakotas, and Nebraska, along with some careful expansion into Wisconsin and Illinois. However, to break into new markets, the company would have to advertise extensively, and Gluek could not spread the advertising costs out over as many barrels as Hamm or Minneapolis Brewing. On the other hand, the brewery was too big to be a local producer, and had to be run as near capacity as possible to produce at the lowest cost. Increasing financial pressures and competition from national brands in traditional Gluek strongholds forced the family to sell the company to G. Heileman Brewing Company of La Crosse in 1964. Heileman continued to brew Stite until the Gluek labels were sold to Cold Spring Brewing Company. The brewery was demolished in 1966 to make way for expansion by Northwestern Corrugated Box Company. A small city park remains on the site of the brewery. (Information about the post-1996 Gluek Brewing Company may be found in chapter 8 and in the Cold Spring Brewing Company entry. Additional illustrations are in chapters 1, 5, 6, and 7.)

Joseph Hofflin (1859?–1860?)

Location: Near the corner of Third and Prairie Street (near today's Twelfth Avenue NE and Third Street NE)

Joseph Hofflin is listed as a brewer in both the 1859 *Minneapolis City Directory* and the 1860 census. His production was not large enough to meet the $500 threshold required to be listed in the 1860 Census of Industry, and no other information about his brewery has been discovered.

Barnhard Gloeggler (1861?–1863)

Location: North Minneapolis

Excise tax records clearly prove that Barnhard Gloeggler brewed in Minneapolis, but nothing else is known about him or his brewery. It is possible that he took over Nicholas Bofferding's Minneapolis Brewery in North Minneapolis, but he may have occupied other premises. He is listed in the first assessment of license fees in September 1862, so it is likely he was in business before that time. A note in the excise records indicates that he brewed lager, but he may have brewed ale as well. In June 1863 he sold thirteen and one-half barrels of beer, making his one of the smallest breweries in the Twin Cities. His last appearance in the excise lists is in August 1863. A survey of Minneapolis newspapers revealed no information about the brewery closing.

Hein & Koehnlein (1866–1868?)
Koehnlein & Lohff (1869–1871)
Henry Lohff (1871–1874)

Location: 807 N. Third

Henry Hein and John Koehnlein (also listed as Kochenlein and Heil) were part of a brief boom in brewery building in Minneapolis that followed the Civil War. Koehnlein (sometimes spelled Keinlein) appears to have been the brewer, since he lived next to the brewery and Hein lived elsewhere. Henry Lohff replaced Hein sometime between 1867 and 1869. When Koehnlein left to start a brewery in Elizabeth, Lohff moved into the house next to the brewery. This was unfortunate, since in October 1870 both the brewery and Lohff's dwelling burned. Lohff rebuilt the brewery and reappeared in the excise records in December 1871. He also appears in both the 1873 and 1874 city directories (after being absent from the 1871 directory) and is also in the 1873 *Minnesota State Business Directory*. Lohff probably left the business sometime in 1874, since he does not appear in any of the brewing industry publications after that year.

The former Heinrich brewery (which was a branch of Minneapolis Brewing & Malting at the time this photograph was taken in 1895) was located on the Mississippi River and featured a ramp on which barrels could be rolled to boats docked at the levee. COURTESY OF THE MINNESOTA HISTORICAL SOCIETY.

Kranzlein & Miller (1866–1871)
John G. Kranzlein (1871–1874)
Mueller & Heinrich (1874–1884)
Heinrich Brewing Association (1884–1890)
Minneapolis Brewing & Malting Co., Heinrich Branch (1890–1893)
Minneapolis Brewing Co., Heinrich Branch (1893–1897)

Location: Lower Levee, Fourth Street and Twenty-second Avenue

The firm of John G. Kranzlein and John B. Miller began operations during the fall of 1866, though Neill's *History of Hennepin County* puts it at 1860 and *Bottles, Breweriana and Advertising Jugs of Minnesota* claims it began as early as 1857. If so, neither the census takers nor the revenue agents knew about it, since neither of the two are listed in the 1860 census and their first appearance in the excise records is in 1866. The brewery's initial output rivaled that of Gottlieb Gluek's decade-old brewery in St. Anthony. The brewery's location at the steamboat landing placed it at the center of transportation and made shipping easy. After five years, Miller left the firm and Kranzlein

carried on the business. Around 1874 Kranzlein sold the business back to Miller (now usually spelled Mueller in the documents) and his new partner, Adolph Heinrich. These two began a significant building program, erecting a new brew house in 1875 and a new malt house, machinery house, and new icehouses the next year. The system of caves dug into the bluff behind the brewery eventually reached a total length of about half a mile. In 1880 the original thirty-horsepower boiler was supplemented with another one twice that power. Throughout the decade, Mueller and Heinrich dueled with Christopher Stahlmann in St. Paul for the title of Minnesota's largest brewer as both closed in on 10,000 barrels per year.

Mueller and Heinrich were shipping beer as far west as Granite Falls by 1877, and around 1881 they contracted with Rudolph Feigal, who located at the brewery and began to bottle "Mueller & Heinrich's celebrated Export Beer!"

Heinrich bought Mueller's share in the brewery in 1884, and he and his three sons formed the Heinrich Brewing Association. The next year they tore down most of the previous frame brewery and built a large stone addition. In 1887, just before the Heinrich Brewing Association was merged into Minneapolis Brewing & Malting, its listed capacity was about 25,000 barrels, making it the fourth-largest brewery in the state and the second largest of the partners in the new mega brewery.

The Heinrich plant was used for three years after the merger, but was retired after the new brewery on Marshall Street was completed. The building was torn down in December 1903 and the materials sold for other uses. A note in the January 1905 *Brewers' Journal* reported that Julius Heinrich, one of Adolph's sons, was considering starting a new brewery in North Minneapolis, but nothing ever came of this idea.

Herman Kreitz (1867–1868)
Kreitz & Bernds (1872?)
Location: First Street N. by Douglas (now Eighteenth Avenue N.) and Buchanan

While there is little specific information on Kreitz's brewery, he is mentioned in enough different sources that he probably did exist and brew around this time. He is listed in both a city directory and a gazetteer in 1867. The most conclusive evidence is that he was licensed as a small brewer in January 1867. In the 1867 annual list, compiled in May, he was taxed as a large producer. The 1868 excise records list him as a distiller rather than a brewer. Since he had been listed as a distiller, or rectifier, before, it is possible that brewing was a temporary experiment. The brewery may have been a cover operation, for in March 1868 customs agents seized his brewery for illicit distillation of whiskey. Kreitz did not return to the brewing business immediately, but there is an entry for the firm Kreitz and Bernds in the 1872 excise records, which may have represented Kreitz's second attempt to brew. No other documentation on Kreitz and Bernds is known.

C. Ort (1867?)
Location: Unknown

C. Ort's brewery is mentioned only in a gazetteer of 1867. This is not a duplication of John Orth, because he is listed separately in the gazetteer, and C. Ort's address was in Minneapolis rather than St. Anthony. While the gazetteers of the period may have occasionally included businesses that closed before publication, they were unlikely to include a business that had not yet begun. Ort does not appear in the incomplete excise records or city directories, so independent confirmation is not possible.

Anton Zahler (1874–1877)
Zahler & Noerenberg (1877–1880)
F. D. Noerenberg (1880–1890)
Minneapolis Brewing & Malting Co. (1890)
Location: Bluff Street and Twentieth Avenue S.

Anton Zahler was employed as a foreman at Christopher Stahlmann's brewery in St. Paul before starting his own brewery in Minneapolis. As an experienced brewery manager, Zahler was able to increase business quickly—production jumped from 319 barrels in 1874 to more than 1,500 the next year. Frederich Noerenberg joined Zahler in 1877 and the pair continued to push production close to 2,000 barrels per year. (Some sources have held that Noerenberg and Zahler's City Brewery was the second largest in Minnesota at this point, but data in Salem's list show that they were still the smallest of the four breweries in Minneapolis and St. Anthony.) Neill's *History of Hennepin County* reported that the brewery employed eight men and had a payroll of $85 per week. Zahler died shortly after the partnership began (some sources say he died in 1880 but the 1878 city directory lists Wilhelmina as Anton's widow), and Noerenberg took over the brewery.

During the 1880s, Noerenberg supplied draught beer to saloons and other accounts, and his brother August started a bottling works near the brewery and bottled the company's "celebrated Export beer." The brewery continued its steady growth until it became part of Minneapolis Brewing & Malting in 1890. The brewery itself was not useful to the new company and was eventually sold to Imperial Brewing Co.

The Noerenberg family's estate, Wilkommen, spanned 73 acres, contained nearly 8,500 feet of shoreline on Lake Minnetonka, and featured a spectacular Queen Anne–style home with eight bedrooms and many other features. The home was razed in the early 1970s in accordance with the will of Lora Noerenberg Hoppe, the last resident of the home, who bequeathed the land to the Three Rivers Park District. The estate is now a formal park and gardens.

Olson & Johnson (1877?)
Location: Corner of Jefferson and Spring

It seems only fitting that Minneapolis, with such a strong Scandinavian heritage, once had a brewery called Olson and Johnson. Thomas Johnson and William Olson are included in the business section of the 1877–1878 city directory as weiss beer brewers. Some contemporary sources categorize this product made with a high percentage of wheat as a nonintoxicating beverage more like a carbonated soft drink. A claim made during the late nineteenth century that a beverage was nonintoxicating should not be taken to mean it was nonalcoholic. While weiss beer was typically low in alcohol, it was (and is) still definitely beer. Olson and Johnson disappear from the city directory the next year and do not appear in any other records.

Patrick J. Gilbride (1882–1887)
Location: 1420 (and 1422) S. Third Avenue

Patrick J. Gilbride (or Gilbridge) brewed ale in Minneapolis on and off during the mid-1880s. He was listed among the brewers in the business listings of the city directory only in 1882, but appeared as an ale brewer in the individual listings several other times. According to the

1883 city directory, he was operating a saloon at the same address, so it is likely that his brewing was limited to supplying his own and a few neighboring saloons. While Gilbride was not listed as a brewer in the 1883 city directory, excise records indicate that he had started brewing again that year, and his occupation in the 1884 city directory was again given as ale brewer. He was last listed as a brewer in the 1887–1888 directory; the next year he was still at the same address but working as a confectioner.

H. A. Westphal & J. B. Mueller (1884–1885)

H. A. Westphal (1885–1888)

Germania Brewing Association (Germania Brewing Co.) (1888–1890)

Minneapolis Brewing & Malting Co. (1890)

Location: Glenwood Avenue near Wirth Lake (then Keegan's Lake), between Western and Sixth

Herman Westphal was a successful ice dealer in the mid-1880s, and in 1884 he joined with J. B. Mueller, formerly of Mueller and Heinrich, to build a brewery near his icehouse on Keegan's Lake. The account of the brewery given in *Bottles, Breweriana and Advertising*

The label for Muenchener Beer featured an image of the goddess Germania. A sculpture similar to this was removed from the Germania Building in St. Paul during the anti-German hysteria of World War I. BOB KAY COLLECTION.

Jugs of Minnesota reports that a dance hall and a bowling alley were additional attractions on the brewery property.

Westphal retired to the ice business around 1888, and the new Germania Brewing Association began to offer its specialty Muenchener Beer. The use of the word *association* in the name and the presence of local saloon owner Jacob Barge as treasurer suggests that this company may have been designed to give Minneapolis saloon owners leverage against larger breweries to keep beer prices down. Rather than beating the large brewers, however, Germania joined them in 1890 when it became part of the giant Minneapolis Brewing & Malting Co. Tragically, Mueller did not live to see two of his former companies become part of one of the largest breweries in the region since he took his own life earlier that year.

Andrew Liden (also Leden or Lideen) (1891–1909)

Arvid Sundbeck (1910–1911?)

Locations: 2210 Sverdrup, 2118 Riverside

Andrew Liden (to use the most common spelling) moved in and out of the brewing business for almost two decades. His first appearance in the business listings is in the 1891 city directory at 2210 Sverdrup (today occupied by a park and Riverside Hospital), though in the individual listings his occupation was given as carpenter and he was living next door at 2208. The next year he is absent from the business

listings, but is still listed as a carpenter. In the 1894 directory he has returned and is included as a brewer in both listings. This time it was for real, since excise records indicated that he started brewing in July 1894 and made 120 barrels in the next twelve months. *Brewers' Journal* includes Liden in the list of new brewers in August 1895. By 1897 Liden was back to carpentry again, but the excise records show he obtained his brewing license again in August 1898. After a few years of absence from the directory, Liden reappeared in 1901, this time as a bottler at 2118 Riverside. He was listed again with the brewers in 1903 and appeared on and off for the next five years as either a brewer or bottler. He may have capitalized on the interest in Swedish malt products since one known bottle embossing reads "A. Liden Malt Ale." He disappears from the directory altogether in 1909, and in October *Brewers' Journal* noted that his firm had been succeeded by Arvid Sundbeck. Sundbeck never appears in the city directory, and *Brewers' Journal* reported early in 1911 that the brewery had closed.

Monahan Bottling Co. (1891?–1896)

Location: 419 Washington Avenue S.

Monahan Bottling Co. was included in the 1891 excise records as a brewer and was listed at least once in a brewing journal. It is likely that they brewed only weiss beer.

Conrad Birkhofer Brewing Co. (1894–1906)

Purity Brewing Co. (1907–1920)

Location: 211 Fourteenth Avenue S.

Unlike many of the large new breweries that were founded in the two decades around 1900, Conrad Birkhofer Brewing Co. had an experienced brewer and administrator in charge. Conrad Birkhofer worked at several breweries in the Midwest before taking the position of brewmaster at John Orth's brewery. After the merger, Birkhofer served as superintendent, but left to start his own brewery just as the new brewery was finished. The new brewery was designed by renowned Chicago brewery architect Louis Lehle and built at a cost of approximately $100,000. Soon the brewery's lager beer, extra pale lager, export, Kaiser, and Wiener beers, along with London Porter, were offered in saloons, restaurants, and homes in Minneapolis.

Selling beer was more important to a brewery's survival around the turn of the cen-

GERMANIA BREWING Co. MINNEAPOLIS, MINN. EXPORT MUENCHENER BEER MADE EXPRESSLY FOR FAMILY USE FROM SELECTED HOPS AND MALT.

In the 1890s breweries that bottled their own beer often called special attention to this on their labels. Brewery-bottled beer was supposed to be higher quality than beer bottled by an independent bottler. Some independent bottlers acquired empty bottles of respected brands and sold them refilled with any available inexpensive beer. FROM THE COLLECTION OF KEN MALZ.

tury than having sufficient capacity to brew it. Birkhofer's connections in the industry probably helped him here as well. The company's red triangle logo began to appear on saloon walls throughout Minneapolis. When Birkhofer sold the brewery, the property included approximately three dozen saloons in Minneapolis alone, as well as depots as far away as Cass Lake.

The Birkhofer brewery was sold to a group of investors headed by Dr. Peter Lauritzen who used the plant to expand production of their own products. (Lauritzen is covered in more detail in the Lauritzen/Hennepin Brewing Co. entry.) To emphasize the healthful qualities of Lauritzen's malt products, and to counter attacks made on beer ingredients during the lobbying for the 1906 Food and Drugs Act, the new firm was named Purity Brewing. (The corporation was called Purity Malt Brewing Co. for a few months, but never produced under that name.) The *B* in the logo was changed to a *P*, but beyond that, the history of the brewery seems to have been generally uneventful. It suffered no major fires or calamities, and it owned enough saloons to stay in business profitably until the onset of

Prohibition. The saloons were perhaps the biggest problem for the brewery, since a series of attacks on tied houses and political corruption related to saloon licensing erupted in 1908. Purity was ideally placed to produce alternative products since it was such products that gave Lauritzen his start in Minnesota. Purity launched its Carmo brand drink, which was described as a nonintoxicating malt-free beverage. Nonetheless, Purity did not operate after the beginning of Prohibition. The competition in other product lines was so great that even Minneapolis giants Gluek and Minneapolis Brewing Co. closed during the late 1920s. After beer became legal again, P. J. Kelley of Kelley Breweries purchased the Purity brewery and prepared to brew again. According to the November 1933 issue of *The Western Brewer,* "a large sum is being spent for new machinery and equipment." These plans fell through, and P. J. Kelley went to Fergus Falls to try to rejuvenate the brewery there.

Purity's attractive Hochsteiner label was designed for both 24-ounce (pictured here) and 12-ounce bottles. The label claimed the beer was brewed "expressly for Hotel and Family Trade." FROM THE COLLECTION OF DAVE WENDL.

William Massolt Bottling Co. (1894–1897?)
Location: 126–128 Plymouth Avenue

William Massolt Bottling Co. advertised in the 1895 city directory that its "celebrated Weiss Beer cannot be beaten." The company probably brewed it only a few years. In 1905 it purchased the Whale Brand soft drinks from the bankrupt Imperial Brewing Co. and continued them for several decades.

J. O. Peterson (1894)
Peterson & Matson (1895)
Location: 3033 Washington Avenue N.

John O. Peterson appears as a brewer on his own in the business section of the 1894 *Minneapolis City Directory* and with Andrew Matson the next year. According to the excise tax report of June 1895, the firm started production in October 1894, though no information on output was recorded. The individual listings in the city directories show that both Peterson and Matson lived on the premises of the brewery. Neither of them was listed in either the business or individual listings of the 1896 city directory, so it is likely that they moved away from Minneapolis.

J. A. Swanson (1894–1896)
Location: 2923 Nicollet Avenue

J. A. Swanson was listed in the business section of the 1895 and 1896 city directories as an ale brewer. According to excise records, he made fifty barrels of ale in the year starting July 1894. The individual listings in the city directories show that Swanson lived at the location where he brewed. He is not present in either section of the 1897 directory.

More & Carlson (1895)
John A. Carlson (1897)
Karlson & Lundquist (1899?)
Location: 1017 South Eighth (rear)

The brewers More and Carlson appear in the excise records in June 1895, indicating production of eight barrels since May 15. There is no entry in the Minneapolis city directory corresponding to this firm.

Excise records indicate John Karlson began brewing in July 1896. No production figures are given. The city directory of 1897 lists Carlson among the brewers and as a brewer in the individual listings (but as Carlson with a *C* rather than a *K*). The entry in the city directory adjacent to his was another John A. Carlson, who was a driver for Conrad Birkhofer Brewing.

Karlson and Lundquist was included in a list of new breweries in *Brewers' Journal* in late summer 1899, but no local directory listing or census record confirms this. Karlson and Lundgren is listed in the excise records of August 1899 as having produced one barrel of beer, and this is probably the same firm.

Edward Hasle (1896)
Location: 2206 Riverside Avenue

Edward Hasle was listed with the brewers in the business section of the 1896 city directory. Though his business was on Riverside Avenue, he boarded at 1811 Washington Avenue South.

The individual listings in the 1897 city directory contained a note that he had moved to Grafton, North Dakota. There is no evidence that he continued to brew in his new home.

Olson & Anderson (1896)
Location: 4215 Lyndale Avenue N.

Olson and Anderson were included in a list of new brewers in *Brewers' Journal* in 1896, but no one matching their description was listed in the city directory. This brewery may have been proposed but never completed.

Barrett & Barrett (1900)
Location: 1028 Plymouth Avenue

The firm of Barrett and Barrett was included with the brewers in the business listings in the 1900 city directory. However, none of the Barretts in the individual listings had the occupation of brewer, and no other source provides any additional information about their operations.

Imperial Brewing Co. (1901–1905)
Location: 21–23 Twenty-first Avenue S.

Imperial Brewing was formed by a combination of local, Canadian, and English investors to locate an English-style ale brewery in the former Noerenberg Brewery. The foreigners behind the project believed that an ale brewery would find a ready market in Minneapolis and to that end, imported a brewing team from England and offered a complete line of pale ale, porter, and stout under the Whale Brand label. The company also produced a variety of sodas and other products under the same brand. Imperial's ad in the 1902 city directory proclaimed boldly that "these goods are superior to anything manufactured in the United States."

In 1904 the press in Pine County was excited by the news that Imperial Brewing was planning to build a "monster plant" on the west side of the city of Sandstone. The *Pine Poker* claimed that "four or five buildings will be needed and these will be built of native stone." Rumor also had it that "J. J. Hill is interested in the venture." Throughout the fall and into the winter, managers from Imperial visited the proposed site with architects from Chicago and contractors from Minneapolis. However, the plans fell through, and Imperial's problems became evident. The investors had misjudged the demand for authentic English ales and the company apparently had quality

This rare bottle of Whale Brand Pale Ale has several features much more common in Britain than in the United States at the time. The bottle was sealed with a cork when most American brewers had already switched to crown caps or other types of stoppers. Separate front and back labels were much less common in the States than in Britain. The neck label contains instructions to decant carefully without shaking, indicating that this ale was bottle-conditioned and still had some yeast in the bottle. The perforations on the label indicate this bottle was filled 25 June 1905. A century later, craft beer enthusiasts would welcome a Minnesota-made bottle-conditioned ale, but at the time it did not satisfy local tastes. FROM THE COLLECTION OF DAVE WENDL.

intoxicating, but many brewers claimed that beer was nonintoxicating. Lauritzen Malt was licensed as a brewer and the product was sold in beer bottles instead of malt tonic bottles, so it is likely that the Gold Foam brand was beer and not tonic. (Since it was not carbonated, tonic would not foam either.) Confusion over the alcoholic content of Lauritzen beer persisted even after Lauritzen himself had moved on to Purity Brewing. According to *Bottles, Breweriana and Advertising Jugs of Minnesota*, an illegal saloon, or "blind pig," was raided and charged with selling Lauritzen's North Star brand, which was in excess of 2 percent alcohol, on draught. The claims of the owner that the product was nonintoxicating and not subject to the regulations were viewed with suspicion since health tonics were seldom if ever sold on draught. The rare advertising pieces for North Star also advertise it like a beer rather than a digestive aid.

Bad publicity from the incident was probably a factor in the decision to change the name of the company to Hennepin Brewing Co. in 1910. The new firm expanded its plant and shipped its product into Iowa and the Dakotas. But since these states went dry before Minnesota, the firm found itself in financial difficulty. Hampered by loss of markets and constantly changing management, Hennepin Brewing went into receivership in 1917. *Brewers' Journal* reported plans to convert the plant to manufacture other beverages, but the business closed for good in 1918.

control problems as well. According to *Bottles, Breweriana and Advertising Jugs of Minnesota*, when the brewery closed, 32,000 gallons of soured ale and porter were dumped into the Mississippi River, with the unintended result that poultry kept on the nearby Bohemian Flats became intoxicated.

Whale Brand Ginger Ale was the one notable success from the enterprise, so William Massolt Bottling acquired the Whale Brand soft drinks and continued to produce them for many years.

Lauritzen Malt Co. (1903–1909)
Hennepin Brewing Co. (1910–1920)
Location: 1900 Third Street NE

Dr. Peter Lauritzen was the founder of the Swedish Movement Cure Institute, a Minneapolis facility that advocated a health program based on exercise and controlled diet. It was common in late Victorian times to tout beer and malt products for their digestive properties, and it was therefore a logical extension of his business to start Lauritzen Malt Co. in a converted building in Northeast Minneapolis. Lauritzen advertised his products as non-

Brewers continued to offer corkscrews as premiums well after the crown cap became popular. This attractive knife from Hennepin Brewing Co. was distributed during the 1910s. FROM THE COLLECTION OF PAT STAMBAUGH.

John Tjerneld (1903–1905)
Location: 2014 Central Avenue

Brewers' Journal listed John Tjerneld among the new breweries in the summer of 1903. He was listed in the 1904 city directory as a Manufacturer of Swedish Malt Drinks. Less than two years after it opened, *Brewers' Journal* listed the brewery among the recently closed breweries.

Youngstrom Bros. (1905–1906)
Location: 2119 Snelling Avenue

The Youngstrom brothers, John and Alfred, made a very brief appearance on the Minneapolis brewing stage. They apparently started brewing in 1905, though *Brewers' Journal* did not announce the opening of their brewery until the next year. A few months later, the same column contained news of their closing. The 1907 city directory lists John as a laborer at the old brewery address and Alfred as a teamster boarding downtown.

Edelweiss Brewing Co. (1916)
Location: 919 Washington Avenue S.

Edelweiss Brewing Co., under G. W. Wilhelm, manager, was listed in the 1916 city directory as the maker of Edelweiss Beer. Wilhelm was still living at 3604 Park Avenue South according to the individual listings in the 1917 directory, but no occupation was given. The existing excise records for this period are incomplete at best, and no other documentation has been found. It is possible that Edelweiss was an early example of a beer marketing company—a business that did not actually brew beer itself but rather sold beer made under contract at another brewery.

James Page Brewing Company (1986–2005)
Location: 1300 Quincy Street NE

James Page founded the first microbrewery in Minneapolis in 1986. His first bottled offering, James Page Private Stock, was an Oktoberfest-style amber lager. His Boundary Waters wild rice beers were the first commercial beers to use wild rice.

The Page brands were popular, but the patchwork brewhouse was an expensive liability. A public stock offering to raise money to install a bottling line met the goal, but the funds raised were used for other concerns. In 2005 the company was liquidated and the labels were purchased by Stevens Point Brewery.

In the late 1990s, the company's artwork was redesigned to create an image of James Page as a rugged explorer while still emphasizing the brewery's home in Northeast Minneapolis. FROM THE AUTHOR'S COLLECTION.

More of the history of James Page Brewing can be found in chapter 8.

Ambleside Brewing Company (1997–1998)
Location: 727 Kasota Avenue

David Johnson left the wine business to start Ambleside Brewing Company in 1997. The name was taken from a village in England's lake country. The brewery's product line included Pale Ale and St. Cloud Wheat. Ambleside also brewed Inland Seas Lake Superior Pale Ale under contract. Construction cost overruns and slow sales caused cash flow problems that could not be overcome. The brewery closed sixteen months after opening. The brewhouse equipment was purchased by Tyranena Brewing Company of Lake Mills, Wisconsin.

Minneiska [Wabasha County]

William Parker (1871–1874)
Parker & Mead (Meade) (1874–1875)
Mead & Phillips (1876)
John C. Phillips (1876–1877)
Location: Next to railroad station

Local merchant William Parker started a brewery in Minneiska in December 1871. The brewery is listed in excise records and business directories under his name until sometime in 1874, when H. W. Mead became a partner in the firm. (*Schade's Brewers Handbook* includes a separate listing for Mead in 1874, but this is likely to be duplication of entries rather than a separate brewery, since the 1875 production figure of 324 barrels was the same for both breweries.)

By April 1876 John C. Phillips of Chicago had replaced Parker as Mead's partner. The new team apparently had great expectations, since during the summer of 1876 they placed ads in the *Winona Daily Republican* offering ales, porter, and lager in both kegs and bottles. It was unusual for a brewery of only 300 barrels to offer bottled beer, and it is not clear whether they had a small bottling operation of their own or contracted the work to an independent bottler.

Unfortunately for Phillips, Mead was in trouble with the Treasury Department. He apparently applied for a license as a small brewer, exceeded his 500-barrel limit, and hoped to pay the increased assessment later, on the premise that it is cheaper to ask forgiveness than permission. The new bottled beer business may have left him short on cash. In August Mead left the business, and Phillips carried on alone. Phillips continued to advertise in the *Daily Republican* throughout the summer under his own name and appears in the excise records for 1877, but the brewery probably closed shortly thereafter. In 1885 the brewery was purchased by Gentzker Bros. and used as a boat store.

Minnesota City [Winona County]

Vill & Rothenberger (1869–1870)
Otto Vill, Minnesota City Brewery (1870?–1915)
Hardke & Karow (lessees) (1897)
Otto Vill Brewery (1915–1918)
Location: On Rollingstone Creek at the end of Lake Street

Otto Vill came to Minnesota in 1857 as part of the Turners' settlement in New Ulm. During the Dakota War of 1862, Vill served in the New Ulm Company (alongside Andreas Betz, a brewer in that city). According to Vill's obituary in the *Winona Republican-Herald* of May 6, 1914, two of Vill's children died during the war, which may have lead him to leave New Ulm and start over in Minnesota City in Rollingstone Township. For several years Vill operated a brickyard. He also invented something he called the Improved Railway Tie, which he featured on his letterhead years later.

The *Winona Daily Republican* reported in July 1868 that the cellar for Vill's new brewery along Rollingstone Creek was completed. Vill probably began to brew in 1869, though the first appearance of the brewery in excise records was not until 1870, under the name of Vill and Rothenberger. Vill's brewery started out as a large brewer; the first known figures list his production as more than 800 barrels in both 1874 and 1875. He used ice from the nearby mill pond to cool his storage cellars and quickly gained a reputation in the area for his fine beer. An article entitled "I am the Oaks" at the Winona County Historical Society claims that in 1888 Vill's beer was awarded first prize at a St. Louis exposition for being the purest beer. Vill also produced bock beer in the spring and advertised it with a colorful poster.

This bock poster is among the most colorful pre-Prohibition advertising pieces from Minnesota. Relatively small breweries in small towns could afford to advertise in this way since the artwork was usually a stock design. This was number 470 from Donaldson Litho Co. of Newport, Kentucky. FROM THE COLLECTION OF PAT STAMBAUGH.

Vill's brewery managed to avoid the fires common to breweries, though the brewery property was subject to flooding and in 1882 one of his horses fell through a trapdoor thirty-five feet into the brewery vault and died. In 1897 Vill leased the brewery for a short time to Otto Hardke of Bethany and Ernst Karow of DeForest, Wisconsin. This arrangement, planned as a five-year lease, seems to have lasted less than a year, and Vill returned to active brewing shortly thereafter. When Otto Vill died in 1914, his son Oswald took over the brewery and managed it until Prohibition. The Sanborn fire insurance map of 1917 shows a small bottling house attached to the brewery, so Vill must have bottled some beer during the last years of the brewery. The brewery was converted into a hotel and soft drink parlor called The Oaks, which was in business until 1927 and burned in 1935.

Vill's brewery appears under two addresses, Minnesota City and Rollingstone. This had led to claims that Vill had two breweries, and that the one in the city of Rollingstone was leased to Hardke and Karow. However, there is no evidence of a brewery in Rollingstone either in excise records or in local newspapers, and Minnesota City is located in Rollingstone Township along Rollingstone Creek. Local newspapers and family accounts always refer to Vill's brewery in the singular, and since it was very unusual for a small brewer to operate two plants at the same time, this certainly would have merited comment. Absent other evidence, the Rollingstone and Minnesota City breweries should be interpreted as different addresses for the same location.

Montgomery
[Le Sueur County]

Matthias Chalupsky (1882–1884)
John Chalupsky (1884–1891)
Montgomery Brewing Co. (1891–1893)
Handsuch & Pexa (1893–1898)
Montgomery Brewery (Handsuch's Brewery)
   (1898–1905)
City Brewery (1905–1913)
Montgomery Brewing Co. (1913–1919)
Montgomery Brewing Co. (1933–1943)
Location: 201 Boulevard Avenue W.

Ross Mattson's definitive unpublished history of Montgomery Brewing Co. states that the

Montgomery brewery was founded in 1882 when Matthias Chalupsky purchased land and began to build his brewery. Excise tax records show that Chalupsky was producing beer by April 1883 and that he was licensed as a large brewer. In 1884 John Chalupsky purchased the brewery with help from his brother James. Their new brewmaster was Joseph Handsuch, who presumably knew John Chalupsky from the New Prague brewery. The stated capacity of this brewery in 1887 was between 1,500 and 2,000 barrels per year.

The Chalupskys sold out to local businessmen J. L. Murphy, John Sheehy, and C. L. Merz in 1891, but Handsuch stayed on as brewmaster. These three were less interested in the brewery than their other business interests and sold the brewery to Handsuch and his partner, Frank Pexa, for $10,000. They continued to call it the Montgomery Brewing Co. or the City Brewery for a short while, but they eventually changed the name to reflect the new partnership. Pexa sold his shares to Handsuch in 1898, and the latter became the sole proprietor for the next seven years. Handsuch continued to expand the brewery, though the 1899 Sanborn map shows that the brewery had no bottling house at this time.

In 1905 Handsuch entered a partnership with Edward Richter, and the two merged Richter's Pepin Lake Brewery into City Brewery. Richter also owned the nearby barrel-heading mill. Handsuch's son Joseph M. attended the Siebel Brewing Academy in Chicago and returned in the fall of 1905 to take over as brewmaster. (Joseph M. also changed the spelling of his last name to Handschuh.) He became a partner in 1907, and the new firm spent the next several years enlarging the brewery and building a bottling house. After many delays, Chief Beer was introduced in 1913. Like its rivals in New Prague, Montgomery Brewing used ice to cool its storage areas until Prohibition, making the harvesting of ice a constant task in the winter. According to Mattson, by the time the brewery closed in 1919, its production of the popular Chief Beer was between 8,000 and 10,000 barrels per year.

In 1933 Richter began to prepare the brewery, which was idle throughout Prohibition, to produce Chief Beer again. The Handsuchs sold their shares of the brewery, and Richter

Montgomery Brewing Co. offered sewing kits featuring four different female portraits to encourage women to order Chief Beer for their homes. This 1914 version is noteworthy for the misspelling of *Nourishing* on the inside. FROM THE COLLECTION OF JIM AND RUTH BEATON.

brought in Harry Cokins of St. Paul and Ralph Maertz of New Prague to provide financial support. The *Montgomery Messenger* reported on the progress of the brewery with great enthusiasm and noted with pride that most of the estimated $75,000 spent on upgrading the plant would be spent locally. The new capacity of the brewery was given as 40,000 barrels, and the owners planned to distribute Chief Beer in the local area and in northern Iowa. Chief was released to great fanfare two days before Christmas in 1933, with ads suggesting that Santa Claus himself would be drinking Chief Beer.

In 1934 Joseph M. Handschuh left the company and was replaced as brewmaster by Alphonse Walz. Mattson suggested that it was at this point that Chief was replaced with Bohemian Club. This product became popular in Montgomery—the local basketball team was even named after it. The brewery also offered a brand called Heinie's to appeal to the German

market. Unfortunately, success in a relatively small local market was not enough to pay off the debt incurred to modernize the brewery. By 1943 the financial problems of the firm, probably exacerbated by wartime shortages, forced the dissolution of Montgomery Brewing.

Most of the brewery building remains today, though it has been vacant for many years and is in poor condition.

The Handsuch & Pexa brewery comes alive in this photo from the mid-1890s. Above the proprietors' names, a painting of a nobleman raising a glass (perhaps a Czech version of King Gambrinus, the patron saint of brewers) proclaims the nature of the business. The man on the horse at lower left has a keg (presumably empty) on his shoulders, and the other employees give the appearance of pausing only briefly for a photo before returning to work. COURTESY OF THE MINNESOTA HISTORICAL SOCIETY.

Pepin Lake Brewing Co. (1892?–1900)
Richter Bros. & Hug (1900–1901?)
Richter Bros. (1901?–1902)
Richter-Washa Brewing Co. (1902–1904)
Pepin Lake Brewery (1904–1905)
Location: On Pepin Lake, north of Montgomery

The *Montgomery Messenger* reported in June 1891 that the Pepin Lake brewery was almost completed. According to family descendant and brewery historian Bart Franta, August Richter, the proprietor of the Lake Pepin brewery, had paid for a substitute to take his place during the Civil War and this, along with other dealings, acquired for the family a reputation as draft dodgers and bootleggers. Richter also reportedly spoke Czech, German, and some American Indian dialects as well as English.

The brewery seems to have gone through several ownership changes in the mid-1890s, and one article in the *Messenger* associates Soulek and Bazil of the Rice Lake brewery with this business. It was purchased in 1898 by Augst and Hong of Faribault (Hong may be another interpretation of Hug).

By 1900 operation of the brewery had passed to George Richter, who ran it with Louis Hug, with other Richters owning shares. Brother George Richter sold his share in the brewery to John Washa and Ben Richter in 1902 and emigrated to the Alaskan gold fields. In 1905 the remaining partners sold their interests to Edward Richter. He formed a partnership with Joseph Handsuch of the Montgomery brewery. Later that year, the two companies were merged and the Pepin Lake Brewery was shut down.

Soulek Brothers (1893–1894)
Perchal & Bazil (1894–1896?)
Hug, Pagel & Spar (1899–?)
Location: About three miles northeast of Montgomery, probably on Rice Lake

The Soulek (or Choudek) brewery adds confusion to the story of brewing in Montgomery. The *Montgomery Messenger* contains a handful of references to Choudek's brewery beginning in May 1891. In October of that year, there is a reference to machinery arriving in town for the new breweries (with emphasis on the plural), one of which was clearly the Richter brewery on Pepin Lake; the other was probably Choudek's, which was probably on or near Rice Lake. A news item on 30 December 1892 noted that Choudek's brewery was nearing completion and *Brewers' Journal* included the Soulek Brothers in the list of new breweries in May 1893. It appears that one of the Souleks was in a partnership with Mr. Bazil, since the *Journal* had already reported that the partnership of Soulek Brothers had succeeded the firm of Soulek and Bazil. (One local source has Soulek and Bazil connected with the Pepin Lake Brewery). In late 1894 Mr. Bazil rejoined the firm (though this time the *Journal* spelled it Brazil). In 1899 a brewery with the name Hug, Pagel and Spar (or Spass) appears in excise records with a Montgomery address, and in *Brewers' Journal* with a Lanesburg address. Since Lanesburg Township stretches from northern Montgomery to southern New Prague, it is likely that Hug, Pagel, and Spar were the new operators of the old Soulek brewery. No further references to this brewery have been found, but there is enough evidence to list this firm as a separate brewery—the dates, location, and owners are inconsistent with this simply being another incarnation of either the Montgomery brewery in the city or the Pepin Lake Brewery.

Moorhead [Clay County]

Larkin Bros. (1875–1876)
Erickson & Larkin (1876)
John Erickson (1877–1895)
Ole Aslesen (1897–1901)
Location: Fourth Street (in what is now Riverfront Park)

Mark Peihl, in his article "Moorhead's Brewery" (*Clay County Historical Society Newsletter*, January–February 1992), stated that the Larkin brothers, George and Joseph, arrived in Moorhead from Winnipeg in spring 1875 and began work on a 56 × 24 foot brewery just north of the Northern Pacific Railway tracks. As Canadians, the Larkin brothers made ale rather than lager, and Peihl noted that they had arrived in town too late to make lager during their first year anyway. Not only was the beer not to the tastes of American drinkers, but it appeared to have had quality problems as well. (*Schade's Brewers Handbook* includes an entry for Larkin Bros., but lists the production as zero.) The brewery was foreclosed by its creditors and ended up in the hands of local entrepreneur and politician John Erickson.

Erickson was mayor of Moorhead from 1886 through 1889 and was a prominent hotelier who owned the Erickson House and Jay Cooke House, purchased for $80,000 in 1881. Under Erickson's management, production grew from 379 barrels in 1878 to 1,835 in 1882. Erickson and his brewmaster, Fred Wachsmuth, took advantage of the small number of breweries to their west. Erickson's newspaper ads in 1882 announced that they would ship to any point on the Northern Pacific line. Having a ready market did not translate into steady growth and profit, however. Erickson was frequently overextended and in financial trouble because of his business deals—Peihl reported that the brewery was sold at sheriff's sales at least twice. The business was also hurt by the frequent turnover in brewmasters. Wachsmuth committed suicide in 1884 after being laid off; he was replaced with Joe Jennister. The 1891 *Moorhead City Directory* lists Rudolph Blatz as the brewer. Sanborn fire insurance maps of the building show no bottling house, and the brewery was still powered by horse through the 1890s. The First National Bank of Moorhead foreclosed the brewery in 1895 and evicted Erickson for good.

After remaining idle for two years, the brewery was purchased by Ole Aslesen, who had operated a brewery in Fargo until state prohibition chased him to the Minnesota side of the river. Aslesen had the brewery in operation again by August 1897 and ran it successfully for four years. Unfortunately, the brewery burned to the ground on 30 August 1901. The *Moorhead Weekly News* reported that "the buildings were entirely consumed and portions of the brick wall which were left standing were pulled down to prevent accident from toppling the walls." Only about $3,000 of Aslesen's $10,000 loss was covered by insurance, and the devastated Aslesen elected not to rebuild.

New Munich (Stearns County)

John Froehler (1868?–1875)
John Froehler & Son (1875–1877?)
Schmidt & Miksch (1878–1879)
Schmidt & Co. (1879–1882)
Froehler Bros. (1882–1883)
Wimmer & Froehler (1883–1884)
Victoria Froehler (1884–1889)
Mathias Pitzl (1889–1905)
Pitzl & Schweiberg (1905–1909)
Mathias Pitzl Brewing Co. (1909–1920)
Location: East side of Main Street, north of town

It is only fitting that a city named New Munich host a brewery. Sometime during the 1860s John Froehler built a brewery in the town named after one of the world's great brewing centers, though it did not appear in excise records until 1872. William Bell Mitchell's 1915 *History of Stearns County* claims that Froehler came from Ohio in 1861 and started his brewery. It is unlikely that the brewery was operating as early as 1861, but it may well have been in operation without the knowledge of the Treasury Department before 1872. The 1870 census lists Froehler as a brewer in Oak Township (which includes New Munich). An article in the *St. Cloud Journal-Press* from 21 August 1933 reporting on the possible reopening of the brewery claimed that the brewery dated back to 1868.

For most of the first two decades, ownership changed frequently and production fluctuated but remained small. In 1876 production was only eighty-eight barrels, perhaps because Froehler was preparing to leave the business. In Nicholas Schmidt's first year of operation, he produced 476 barrels, but by 1882 the brewery was back in the Froehler family, this time with brother Michael involved.

The source of future stability arrived at the brewery in the mid-1880s in the person of Mathias Pitzl. He started as a driver, went to work at a brewery in St. Paul to learn the brewer's art, and returned in 1889 to take over management of the brewery. From the mid-1890s throughout the next decade, he completely rebuilt the brewery with iron and cement construction, adding modern machinery and increased capacity. According to Mitchell's *History of Stearns County*, Pitzl increased the capacity from 18 to 800 barrels per month. The brief partnership of Pitzl and Schweiberg

was most likely made to gain access to additional funds for expansion. Pitzl bottled some beer, and his Wiener lager was said to have a good reputation throughout the county.

When Prohibition arrived, the brewery continued to operate. Unlike most other breweries, which switched to producing other products, the New Munich brewery apparently continued to make real beer. It was the site of a 1923 raid by Prohibition agents during which one of the raiding agents was badly wounded by a blow to the head. This contrasts dramatically with the calm account of the *St. Cloud Sentinel* ten years later that "malt was made in the New Munich plant for a short time after beer was prohibited."

After beer made its legal return to Stearns County, the Pitzl brewery became the subject of speculative brewing ventures. In August 1933 several investors, including Mathias's widow, Anna, formed a corporation to remodel and reactivate the old brewery. A brewmaster residing in Canada named A. Walz was hired to operate the proposed brewery. By February 1934 the plans had changed and the Pitzl brewery was to be reorganized as a cooperative brewery. However, none of these ideas came to fruition and the brewery remained dormant.

New Prague (Le Sueur/Scott Counties)

Radly & Chalupsky (1877–1886?)
Frank Radly (1887?–1892?)
Schulz & Kaiser (1891–1892)
New Prague Brewing Co. (1892–1895?)
Roemer & Peshek (1895?–1896)
Frank Roemer (1896–1899)
Frank Roemer & Son (1899–1900)
Roemer & Kodoek (1900)
Roemer & Mickus (1900–1901)
Charles Mickus (1901–1904)
Mickus & Rybak (1904–1906)
Location: First Avenue SE, three-quarters of a mile south of Main Street

The brewery owned by Radly and Chalupsky, often listed as being in Lanesburg (or sometimes Lanesboro), should be considered the first brewery in New Prague: Lanesburg Township includes the Le Sueur County part of New Prague, and it was here that Frank Radly and Matthias Chalupsky began brewing in 1877. Their production was nearly 700 bar-

rels by 1879, but this brewery soon fell prey to the rapid ownership changes that also bedeviled their rivals across the county line. Tracing the history of this and the next brewery listed is complicated by the fact that they were both called New Prague Brewing Co., though at different times. In addition, Rybak moves back and forth between the two breweries. Frank Roemer divided his time between New Prague and helping his sons get started in Ellsworth. To confuse matters further, Charles Mickus is listed in the 1910 census as manager of the brewing company and his son Joseph as a driver for the brewery. Joe would later be a brewmaster for several breweries after Prohibition.

Menars (Menaks) & Kokes (1884–1887?)
Albert Menaks (1887?–1891)
Kokes & Maruska (1891–1893)
Kokes & Piemeisel (1895–1898)
Piemeisel & Rybak (1898–1904)
New Prague Brewing Co. (Kokes' Brewery)
    (1905–1920)
Location: Second Avenue NW and Fifth Street N.

Thomas Kokes and Albert Menars (Menaks) started brewing on the Scott County (north) side of New Prague in 1884. The rapid changes in ownership suggest that Kokes leased his brewery to Menaks or that he was in need of financial backing. His need for financial help was at its greatest in 1894, when the brewery was destroyed by fire. After rebuilding, Kokes remained in the firm for three years, after which John Piemeisel and Mathias Rybak laid the groundwork for its transition to New Prague Brewing Co., which, according to Gresham's *History of Nicollet and Le Sueur Counties,* was again owned by Thomas Kokes. The company remained in operation until Prohibition, after which it converted to cereal beverage and soft drink production under the name of Rybak and Heimen (Hemen).

New Ulm (Brown County)

Andreas Betz & August Friton (1858–1862)
August Friton, City Brewery (1864–1869)
George Wiedemann (1869–1870)
Joseph Schmucker (1870–1904)
Joseph Schmucker Brewing Co. (1904–1910)
New Ulm Brewing & Malting Co. (1910–1917)

Location: Center Street and German Avenue

The first brewery in Brown County was started by August Friton and Andreas Betz in 1858. Friton had been involved in another brewery just across the river from New Ulm in Nicollet County (see Courtland), but he left that partnership and joined with Andreas Betz in creating the first brewery in beer-crazy New Ulm. The German-language *Neu-Ulm Pionier* rejoiced in late December 1858 that in the previous several months, the need to import beer from St. Peter, Traverse des Sioux, and Mankato had been eliminated and that the money spent on beer would henceforth remain in the community. Friton's brewery was one of many build-

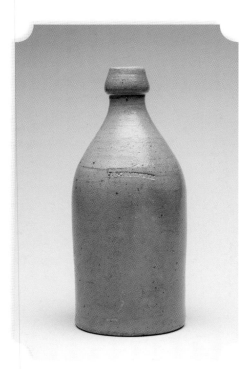

New Ulm was a center for stoneware production as well as for beer. John Stoeckert was a prominent potter from 1867 to 1900 and probably made this bottle for Joseph Schmucker's brewery. FROM THE COLLECTION OF STEVE KETCHUM.

ings burned during the Dakota War of 1862, but he began rebuilding almost immediately. Local accounts record that the new City Brewery on Center Street was completed in 1864, but excise records suggest Friton might have started producing as early as September of the previous year.

In 1866 Friton's brewery was the second largest of the four in New Ulm, well behind August Schell but just ahead of fellow newcomers Hauenstein & Betz. In April 1866 Friton considered the possibility of turning his brewery into an "Actien Brauerei," a German form of company that falls somewhere between a corporation and a cooperative. The results appeared to be unsatisfactory, because in August an advertisement appeared in the *Neu Ulm Post* offering the brewery for sale. This worked no better, and Friton remained in charge until 1869. Finally, in November 1869, he leased the brewery to George Wiedemann, who ran it for slightly less than a year. The snapshot of the brewery provided by the 1870 Census of Industry showed that 1,200 bushels of malt and 640 pounds of hops went into the 250 barrels of beer produced—worth $2,000 at the prevailing New Ulm price of $8 per barrel.

Friton's search for a long-term solution to the ownership problem ended in 1870 when Joseph Schmucker, one of Friton's former employees, returned from a two-year stay in Minneapolis to lease the brewery. Schmucker bought the brewery outright in 1872 and began a 32-year run as proprietor of a successful brewery. For the first year, Schmucker worked in partnership with Heinrich Frenzel, but that arrangement was dissolved in August 1873.

With four other breweries in New Ulm, competition was vigorous. In 1879 Schmucker added a malt house to his operations, but an article in the *New Ulm Review* noted that every other brewer in town was making significant improvements as well. Production figures for 1878 and 1879 show Schmucker's brewery to have been the fourth largest in size with production of just over 200 barrels per year, down dramatically from the more than 900 barrels reported in 1874. While the Schmucker brewery was badly damaged in the great cyclone of July 1881, the family's most heartbreaking loss was indirectly caused by the storm. Their son

Otto, aged seven, died a few weeks after the storm. The boy apparently had been scared badly by the storm, and it was believed that he had died of a sudden fright.

After rebuilding following the cyclone, Schmucker's next important expansion was on the retail side of the business. In September 1885, he opened the Tivoli, an opulent indoor-outdoor biergarten located at 313 First Avenue North. The *Review* described the building as "one of the strongest and at the same time handsomest brick structures in the city," and indeed it was—it survived for exactly a century until it was razed in November 1985. (A photo of the Tivoli appears in chapter 3.)

Schmucker continued to expand his operations over the next several years. In 1890 he built a new, larger malt house, and in 1891 he built an expanded icehouse, but with the idea that this would be a temporary measure until he could afford a new brewery with artificial refrigeration. The new brewery building was started in 1897, but artificial refrigeration was not installed until 1902. After these modernizations were completed, the Schmucker brewery, which forty years earlier brewed just over 100 barrels a year, could now brew 100 barrels a day.

As Joseph Schmucker grew older, managing the brewery became more of a strain, and in June 1904 the firm was incorporated as Joseph Schmucker Brewing Co. It seems that Schmucker's leadership was more important than anyone realized, because the brewery began to suffer financial difficulties, and by the fall of 1908, just after Schmucker's death, the new company went bankrupt. The $60,000 cement-and-iron brewery and malt house was sold to the Brown County Bank for one-fifth of that amount.

In 1910 a new firm took over the plant. New Ulm Brewing & Malting Co., under the leadership of manager Joseph Groebner and brewmaster Karl Brunner, tried to revive the business. The first few years went well, but by the beginning of World War I the company was losing money again, and the firm was dissolved in March 1917. In September 1919 the brewery plant was sold to Johnson and Co. of St. Peter, a manufacturer of overalls, which used it to expand its factory.

Schmucker's trademark depicting a gopher drinking a beer must be considered a Minnesota classic. The quality, purity, and health claims in the four corners were common at the turn of the twentieth century. FROM THE COLLECTION OF KEN MALZ.

August Schell (1860–1864)

Schell & Bernhard (1864–1866)

August Schell (1866–1902)

August Schell Brewing Co. (1902–1920)

August Schell Co. (1920–1932)

August Schell Brewing Company (1933–present)

Location: 1860 Schell Drive

August Schell Brewing Company is one of the great success stories of the brewing industry, not just in Minnesota, but in all of North America. It is the second-oldest continuously operating family brewery in the United States and one of the oldest breweries of any type.

Schell's ability to survive wars, Prohibition, and several changes in American taste point not just to luck, but to several generations of careful management and cautious risk taking.

August Schell was born in 1828 in Durbach, Germany. He arrived in the young settlement of New Ulm in 1856 as part of a group from Cincinnati and found a job at the Globe flour mill as a machinist and supervisor. The German-language *Neu-Ulm Pionier* reported in January 1861 that August Schell was building a brewery on a site in the Cottonwood River valley near "a good strong spring" that would provide easy access to brewing water. The ar-

Pre-Prohibition Vitrolite corner signs are prized by collectors, and this Schell Beer example is among the most visually appealing examples known. COURTESY OF AUGUST SCHELL BREWING COMPANY.

ticle predicted it would be completed by September, but it was not until late October that the *Pionier* was able to report that the roof was in place and operations were ready to begin. By this time, Schell had taken on a partner—Jacob Bernhard (or Bernhardt), a former brewmaster at Jacob Bensberg's North Mississippi Brewery in St. Paul. The company's official history lists production of 200 barrels during the first year of operation, among the smallest in the state at the time, but not bad for the first year. Schell's was not the first brewery in this distinctively German city, but in less than two years, it would be the only one. During the Dakota War of 1862, more than one hundred buildings in the city and surrounding area were burnt to the ground—many by the attacking Dakota, but some by the defenders to eliminate hiding places for the attackers. Schell's brewery was one of the few structures to survive, partially because it was well away from the city center, and partially, according to family accounts, because the Schell family was more generous to the starving Dakota than many of the other German settlers, who simply saw them as lazy. Whatever the case, Schell's business survived even if many of his customers were dead or scattered throughout the countryside. This would be just the first of many times that

Schell and his successors avoided calamities that struck other area brewers. The end of the war and the increasing settlement of southwestern Minnesota did wonders for Schell's business. From the beginning of excise tax collection in October 1862 (just after the Dakota War) until April 1866, Schell sold 575 barrels of beer. In the remaining eight months of 1866, Schell sold more than 600 barrels.

Progress did not come without some drama, however. In August 1866 Bernhard's health had deteriorated to the point that he was forced to leave the business. On Saturday, August 11, a crowd of area residents gathered on the grounds of the brewery to bid on the brick brewery building, house, stables, garden, and brewery equipment. The German-language *Post* reported that the "lucky" winning bidder was in fact the original partner, August Schell, with a bid of $12,000—a relatively high price for a rural brewery at the time. In spite of the opening of four competing breweries in New Ulm from 1864 to 1866, Schell more than doubled his sales by 1870. The 1870 Census of Industry showed that Schell had invested $13,000 in a brewery that paid three workers $1,900 per year and used 4,000 bushels of barley and 1,400 pounds of hops to make 1,300 barrels of beer worth $11,700 at local prices. Among these workers was August Schmasse, who would move on to start his own brewery in Young America a few years later.

The constant competition among the city's brewers forced August Schell to expand his brewery on a regular basis. The *New Ulm Review* lauded Schell in 1879: "Although this gentleman already is the proprietor of one of the largest and most extensive breweries in the State, he allows no year to pass by without adding new buildings, machinery, etc., and his place begins to assume the appearance of a little village of itself." In 1878 Schell built a bottling facility, making him among the first Minnesota brewers to bottle his own beer. The 1879 improvements praised by the *Review* included a new three-story malt house, expanded ice cellars, and a twenty-horsepower boiler and engine to convert the brewery's operation to steam. With the change to steam came a change in management. August was stricken by arthritis at age 50 and turned over management of the brewery to his eldest son, Adolph.

August Schell is seated on the balcony in this group photograph from 1885. As is common in photographs of brewery employees, many are holding the tools of their trade. What is much less common is Schell's pet crane in the left foreground (which did not stand still for the photograph). Both the crane and the horse show traces of being touched up after the photograph was taken.
COURTESY OF AUGUST SCHELL BREWING COMPANY.

A few years later, Adolph moved to California and the next-eldest son, Otto, added management duties to his existing brewmaster position. In 1879 August's daughter Emma married George Marti, who would spend several years working in the pharmacy business but would later come back to join the family firm.

August's family took over a brewery and business in sound shape—with production of more than 2,500 barrels, Schell was the ninth-largest brewer in the state and in a virtual tie for second in breweries located outside the Twin Cities. The 1880s were a decade of steady growth for the Schells, in contrast to the catastrophic losses suffered by rivals Hauenstein and Schmucker in the cyclone of 1881. The family displayed its prosperity with the construction of a distinctive family mansion on the brewery grounds. The beautiful Victorian house featured an aviary highlighted by August's pet crane. August was able to enjoy his retirement for six years, but died in September 1891 at the age of 63. It appears that the family decided the best way to cope with its grief and honor the patriarch was by doubling the brewery's capacity. The Chicago firm of Wolf and Lehle drafted plans to increase the brewery's capacity to 20,000 barrels—small compared with the one million barrels produced by Pabst or even with the 150,000-barrel brewery being planned by the newly formed Minneapolis Brewing & Malting Co., but still a noticeable percentage of the roughly 360,000 barrels brewed in Minnesota that year.

Throughout the next two decades, Otto Schell continued to expand the brewery. New packaging and storage facilities were added in 1900, and a new brewhouse, malt house, and keg-washing house were added in 1902. Not only was the brewery enlarged, so was the name. In 1902 the business was incorporated as August Schell Brewing Company. Otto was the first president, August's widow, Theresa, was vice president, and George Marti became secretary-treasurer. But in 1911, when Otto died suddenly on January 14, and Theresa died four months later, sixty years of having someone named Schell in charge of the brewery came to an end. George Marti took control of the brewery and not only kept the brewery in the Schell extended family, but began the period of Marti family management that continues to the present.

Peacocks freely wander the brewery grounds today, a century after this advertisement for Schell's Malt Tonic was created. COURTESY OF AUGUST SCHELL BREWING COMPANY.

August Schell Brewing Company arrived at the eve of World War I with a solid market in southern Minnesota and Iowa as well as what the 1916 *History of Brown County* called "an excellent mail order business." According to the same work, Schell's employed "32 men and 12 deer," a reference to the deer park that not only served as a local attraction but also provided the name of the brewery's flagship product. A mighty buck, pictured on top of a hill overlooking the Cottonwood valley with the brewery in the distance, adorned labels of Schell's Export Beer, display signs, and the back of playing cards. However, the brewery would need all the strength and agility of the official state animal to survive the next several decades.

Schell was better prepared to survive Prohibition than many breweries. It had offered diverse products for many years, including a successful malt tonic and even a mead made from fermented honey. However, the arrival of World War I brought not just increasing calls for prohibition, but increasing anti-German sentiment. As one of the most traditionally German settlements in the state, New Ulm was a particular target of disloyalty charges—Governor J. A. A. Burnquist removed the mayor and city attorney from office for their participation in an antidraft rally in New Ulm, which was attended by more than 5,000 people. The Martis were able to weather this particular storm, but still had to contend with Prohibition. The company switched to making near beer and soft drinks, and distributed candy and whatever other products would help pay the bills. Prohibition agents raided the brewery during the 1920s, as they did most breweries, but Schell avoided major problems with the law. More important, continued production enabled the Schell brewery to keep a brewmaster employed and the equipment in working order, which would make the transition back to making beer quick and smooth.

August Schell Brewing was among the nine Minnesota breweries that had received permits and were ready to begin sales on 7 April 1933. Ironically, the city of New Ulm was not among the many that hurried to license taverns to sell beer at the first possible moment. In fact, New Ulm would not issue beer licenses for weeks after 3.2 percent beer became legal, so Schell

Brewing was forced to concentrate on building up markets in outlying areas and making up for beer shortages elsewhere. George Marti lived long enough to see Prohibition repealed, but died in 1934. The presidency of the company went to his widow, Emma, and their son Alfred took over management duties.

Alfred Marti guided the brewery in a rapidly changing industry for the next thirty-five years. Beer consumption increased as the economy recovered and Schell's was able to rebuild its regional market. Current president Ted Marti referred to his grandfather's era as the heyday of the small brewer. According to Ted Marti, Minnesota's small brewers generally respected each other's home markets during this period. Schell did not challenge Fleckenstein in Faribault, and Fleckenstein stayed out of New Ulm. For the most part, each brewery's salesmen competed for accounts on the edges of their territory. Of course, Schell had a rival just down the road in Hauenstein. Marti recalled his grandfather's stories about the competition to get their annual bock beer into local taverns. Alfred Marti and the Hauensteins would agree on a date in mid- to late February to release the bock, but, according to Marti, Hauenstein would release its bock a few days early, and Schell would lose a draught account it had been counting on. Schell Brewing had more success expanding to the south and west than to the north and east. The brewery's salesmen did business the old-fashioned way:

The colorful painting on this drum from the Hobo Band's early days reminded audiences of Deer Brand Beer. COURTESY OF AUGUST SCHELL BREWING COMPANY.

traveling to bars and taverns, buying a round for the house, and winning and maintaining accounts through personality and persuasion. Al Marti also started Schell's Hobo Band—still famous in the area for its circus-style music and humorous antics.

Schell was relatively late in embracing a new packaging method that would ultimately gain it a national reputation: the beer can. This transition was not without problems, however. After they were filled, an entire load of early cans was discovered to have leaky seams and had to be dumped. Nevertheless, Schell continued to experiment with new types of packaging. At some point or another, Schell has used nearly every size and shape of package, from "steinie" bottles to 16-ounce cans, from Crowntainers to giant picnic bottles.

In the later years of Alfred Marti's administration, the brewing industry became much less friendly to small breweries. As smaller, often family-owned distributors went out of business, they were replaced by larger companies that focused on national brands. Schell's distributor in the Mankato area was Wesley Bros. of Eagle Lake, which handled only Schell's beer. When Wesley Bros. sold the business, it was taken over by State Distributing, which replaced many of the Schell accounts with Schlitz. As national brands continue to expand into regional markets they had previously ignored, Schell faced challenges from Schlitz, then Pabst, then Budweiser. Since nearly every beer on the market was basically the same pale, lightly hopped lager, making distinctions on taste was nearly impossible. One of Schell's responses, in common with most other regional brewers, was to cut prices. However, as Ted Marti noted, customers do not respond to a lower price for beer the way they do to a lower price for soft drinks. When customers find a low price on cola, it's a bargain, but a low price for beer is considered an indicator of inferior quality. The same year that Alfred Marti retired, Hauenstein closed its doors for good because of the pressure from national brands.

New president Warren Marti was faced with the task of helping the brewery survive the new realities. He introduced a new five-color can with the slogan "It's a Grand Old Beer" and began to diversify into other prod-

uct lines. Perhaps the most successful was 1919 Root Beer. Available only on draught, it is based on a traditional root beer recipe (though not one actually used by Schell's during Prohibition). More unusual was the plan to grow hydroponic tomatoes on some empty land near the brewery. The project was mildly successful, but was dropped after a few years.

The most visible way that Schell kept its volume high enough to be profitable was through filling collectible beer cans. During the late 1970s, a variety of local festivals capitalized on a rapidly growing hobby by issuing commemorative cans. Schell's facility was the right size for marketers seeking to produce a relatively small batch (though the minimum can order was 1,200 cases), so events ranging from small rural celebrations to beer can collector conventions to the St. Paul Winter Carnival had their commemorative cans filled in New Ulm. For the first of these, Farmfest 1976, the Schell's brand was prominently displayed on the can, but after that the brand was not attached to beer that was likely to be poured out anyway. During the 1970s, Schell began to introduce new brands. Deer Brand was joined by Schell's Export Beer and, in a nod to national trends, Schell's Light. Even though Export was brewed as a premium beer, it still wasn't priced that way, and the brewery risked being trapped in the "cheap beer" segment.

The renewal of August Schell Brewing Company as "A Brewery of Substance" (as it now advertises itself) began in the 1980s when, working with Charles Finkel of Seattle-based Merchant du Vin importers, the brewery introduced Schell's Pilsner and Schell's Weizen. These labels, along with Ulmer and Ulmer Braun, gave Schell's a place on the premium and import shelves and gave the brewery credibility with the growing number of consumers looking for more flavorful beers. Under new president and brewmaster Ted Marti, who took over when his father, Warren, retired in 1985, Schell began to expand the variety of styles it offered. Most of the new varieties were in the German tradition, such as Doppelbock and Oktoberfest, but Schell's Pale Ale is closer to an English India Pale Ale in style and ingredients.

Firmly established in the craft beer market, Schell invested in a major upgrade of the brewhouse in 1999 by adding four new brew kettles to improve efficiency. At the time, the brewery was producing just over 40,000 barrels per year—an amount that would have impressed August Schell, but was still less than two-thirds of the brewery's capacity. In 2002 the company won the bidding for the Grain Belt brand name. The traditional Grain Belt recipe was placed in a keg in a ceremony at the old Grain Belt brewery building and transported to its new home in New Ulm. In the years following the acquisition of Grain Belt, Schell roughly doubled its production and rebuilt the reputation of Grain Belt in the region.

Today the brewery makes nearly forty different beers, about a third of which are brewed under contract for other companies and not sold under the Schell name. The company completed a new museum and visitor center in 2006 to better display the heritage of Minnesota's oldest brewery.

Hauenstein & Betz (1864–1869)

Hauenstein & Toberer (1869–1871)

John Hauenstein (1869–1900)

John Hauenstein Brewing Co. (1900–1920)

John Hauenstein Co. (1933–1969)

Location: 1601 S. Jefferson Street

The Hauenstein brewery was one of the handful of family-owned breweries to last for more than a century. It was built in the aftermath of the Dakota War of 1862 and was one of the last local breweries to succumb to the pressures of national competition. Given the catastrophes that have befallen it, the survival of Hauenstein's was perhaps more noteworthy than the survival of any other Minnesota brewery.

John Hauenstein came to New Ulm with a group from the Cincinnati Land Society in 1857 and found a job in a distillery. After the Dakota War, during which he assisted in the defense of New Ulm, Hauenstein joined with August Friton's former partner, Andreas Betz, to start a new brewery south of town, just on the other side of a hill from August Schell's brewery. They took advantage of natural springs for a ready supply of pure brewing water. Betz remained with Hauenstein for five years, but then left for Beaver Falls to take over

a brewery there. Local jeweler John C. Toberer purchased Betz's shares early in January of 1869, but in 1871 Hauenstein bought out Toberer's shares and became sole proprietor.

Hauenstein gradually built up his market throughout the 1870s and sold his share of the hundreds of barrels of New Ulm beer that were being exported along the line of the Chicago & Northwestern railroad. To keep up with his expanding neighbors, Hauenstein launched a series of major improvements at the end of the decade. According to articles from 1879 and 1880 in the *New Ulm Review*, Hauenstein added two stories to his original brewhouse, making it a four-story building. He built a two-story malt house and in 1880 added new machinery to power the brewery entirely by steam. Unfortunately, a massive cyclone struck the town in July 1881, and Hauenstein suffered the greatest financial loss in the area—damage to his new brewery was estimated to be from $12,000 to $30,000. Stereoscopic views of the devastation of the brewery were available just over a week after the storm—quick work given the photographic duplication technology of the era. The rebuilding project included a boarding house for the ever-increasing number of employees. Tragedy struck the brewery again

in 1884 when Herman Wykowski, a foreman at the plant, fell headfirst into a vat of hot beer and was scalded to death. Despite these setbacks, Hauenstein regrouped after each tragedy and continued to improve his business.

By 1890 Hauenstein's beer was bottled by Fred Behnke, who operated a bottling works in the old J. B. Karl brewery building. During that year Behnke bottled fifty barrels per month, equivalent to more than 40,000 bottles. Hauenstein's rebuilt brewery had a capacity of around 7,500 barrels per year, but even this proved inadequate as southwestern Minnesota's population increased and Hauenstein's reputation grew. In 1891 he embarked on another major remodeling in which he doubled the capacity of the brewery by adding new equipment for almost every stage of the brewing process. The *Review* took special note of a carload of cedar from Washington for fermenting and aging vessels, the first load of such wood ever shipped to New Ulm. This $25,000 project apparently paid dividends, since in 1897 the brewery bought the New Ulm Bottling Works, Fred Behnke's new and expanded company, though Behnke remained with the company to superintend bottling operations.

Hauenstein's new rock cutter logo is featured on this label from the company's last years. FROM THE AUTHOR'S COLLECTION.

The company prospered through the turn of the century, and was incorporated in 1900. A brand named Hermann Brau was introduced to commemorate the Hermann Monument in New Ulm. (No bottles or labels from Hermann Brau have been located; the brand is known mostly from images on trays.) John's son Charles was the president and John Jr., a graduate of the American Brewing Academy in Chicago, was the brewmaster. By 1907 business had expanded so that a new bottling house and storage building were needed. Rebuilding was required again in 1910, but for a much more dramatic reason. In September 1910, just after the workers went outside for their lunch break, there was a massive explosion and the storage building and part of the three-story brewhouse collapsed. The cave-in destroyed about 2,000 barrels of beer then in the aging tanks, buried several delivery trucks with rubble, and ruptured the refrigeration system, sending clouds of ammonia into the air. The cause of the collapse was attributed to a weakening in the foundation caused by frequent blasting in the stone quarries about two miles away. The damage to the buildings and other property was estimated at $15,000 to $20,000, not including about $12,000 worth of beer that flooded the brewery grounds. Yet again the Hauensteins rebuilt, commissioning brewery architect Richard Griesser of Chicago to direct the work. In 1914, at age 82, John Hauenstein Sr. died of complications from kidney and bladder ailments. The founder of the company had been in the brewing industry in New Ulm for fifty years.

While in retrospect it seems extremely risky to rebuild with prohibitionist sentiment rising, New Ulm and its German heritage continued to provide a strong market for brewers. Hauenstein Brewing Co. continued to operate right up until the breweries were closed by wartime restrictions. The 1916 *History of Brown County* reported that the company had a capacity of 20,000 barrels (just greater than the capacity of Schell), consumed 35,000 bushels of grain, and sold its product in Minnesota, Iowa, and the Dakotas and by mail order. In a tongue-in-cheek reference to the entry in the same book for the August Schell Brewing Company, it was also reported that Hauenstein employed forty men and zero

Among the most striking Minnesota can designs from the period is Hauenstein's bright red high-profile cone-top can. The logo proclaimed that the beer was pure, palatable, and delicious. FROM THE COLLECTION OF DAVE WENDL.

deer. The company continued to exist during the Prohibition years, but rather than making substitute products, it became a retail distributor for near beer and other products.

After beer became legal again, Hauenstein had to refurbish the brewery, and therefore was not ready to sell beer in April 1933. The company made up for lost time, however, and rebuilt its capacity to 25,000 barrels by 1939 under the leadership of Hans P. Hauenstein, the third member of the family to head the firm. An article in the *New Ulm Journal* celebrating the company's seventy-fifth anniversary described the company's activity in 1939:

Brewery operations begin at 4 o'clock in the morning and by 5 a. m. the trucks are pulling out for New Ulm and at 7 o'clock the trucks leave with their loads of beer for Southern and Central

Minnesota and South Dakota. At the height of the season the brewery gives employment to 70 and 75 people [*sic*] and their yearly payroll totals $45,000 a year.

By the mid-1950s, Hauenstein reached a capacity of 40,000 barrels per year—large enough to compete well in the local area, but not so large that it needed to compete against major national brewers for advertising spots. Hauenstein Brewing sold canned beer, but financial limitations prevented the company from investing in a new canning line capable of filling flat-top cans, so it offered only cone-tops. The company adopted a new logo of a German cartoon character chiseling a rock (a play on the German name Hauenstein: *hauen* meaning to hew or cut, *stein* meaning stone) and it appeared on labels and crown caps. Hauenstein's New Ulm beer remained the flagship brand, though the company continued to release a bock beer in the spring.

As the ability of small brewers to compete against national brewers declined, Hauenstein's less-automated equipment made it much less efficient than its Twin Cities and out-of-state competitors. In November 1969 John Hauenstein Co. finally bowed to the inevitable and closed. The *New Ulm Review Journal* eulogized the company:

The tavern regulars will miss a tradition of the brewing trade when the representative of Hauenstein came around and bought a round for everyone in the house. The blood donors at the bloodmobile will no longer have to make a choice for Hauenstein or Schell. When loyal, local beer drinkers are asked their choice at a bar or club, they won't have to look up and down to see if Hauenstein's Roger is near or Schell's Al before calling their brand.

Two dozen men lost their jobs when the brewery closed its doors for good.

But the Hauenstein story did not end here. Grain Belt Breweries of Minneapolis purchased the formula and the trademark (as well as some bottles and other supplies) and began bottling the beer in spring 1970. Eventually, it added cans to the lineup as well. Company officials claimed that they would try to duplicate the formula, though they did not rule out attempts at "improvement." But Hauenstein's stay in Minneapolis would be short, since the Grain Belt brands were acquired by G. Heileman of La Crosse, Wisconsin, in 1975. Hauenstein was brewed at Heileman's St. Paul brewery for several years, but that plant closed in 1990. Several years later, Brown County residents Al and Rae Ann Arneson bought the Hauenstein label and had it brewed under contract at Minnesota Brewing Company in St. Paul, in the same brewery where it had been brewed as part of the Heileman stable. Currently, Hauenstein is being brewed by its old crosstown rival, August Schell Brewing Company. The brewery itself has also survived—owner David Harmening has converted it to a private residence.

Johann Baptist Karl (1865–1871)
August Holl (lessee) (1878–1879)
John Piemeisel (1887–?)
Location: 522 S. Minnesota Street

Johann Baptist Karl (sometimes anglicized to John Carl) established a brewery in his New Ulm saloon sometime in late 1865. The first existing tax assessment for him, in January 1866, was for selling twelve barrels, but since his largest summer sale in 1866 was five and a half barrels, this was probably for several previous months. Karl continued to brew until at least 1871, though he put the brewery up for sale in September 1871. He appears to have been unsuccessful in the attempt, because an article in the *New Ulm Review* from 18 August 1880 mentioned that "Mr. Karl is renovating his brewery into a malt house." A description of New Ulm in the 1880 Polk *Gazetteer of Minnesota* mentioned five breweries in operation, and Salem reported that August Holl brewed 35 and 173 barrels in 1878 and 1879 respectively, so it appears that Holl had leased Karl's brewery, probably late in 1878.

The brewery lay idle for several years until John Piemeisel purchased it in 1887 and began renovations. Piemeisel did not remain long and moved to New Prague, where the brew-

ing business was much less crowded. In 1890 Fred Behnke leased the building to bottle Hauenstein's beer until his new building was finished.

American Breweries II includes a listing for John Piemeisel in New Ulm for 1879–1884, but these dates conflict with local reports of the conversion of the brewery into a malt house and its subsequent idleness, and according to the census, Piemeisel was in Jordan working at Fred Heiland's brewery in 1880.

The building still exists, though it has been significantly altered and converted to apartments.

Jacob Bender (1866–1888)
New Ulm Brewing Co. (1888–1893)
Jacob Bender (1893–1911)
Location: Southwest corner of East Front Street and Second Street S.

Less is known about the Jacob Bender brewery than about its New Ulm counterparts. Jacob Bender, the fifth brewer to open shop in New Ulm during the 1860s, began brewing in fall 1866. His output was small compared with that of his rapidly expanding rivals Schell and Hauenstein, but by 1879 he was producing nearly 300 barrels per year. He suffered a fire in December 1869, but he rebuilt and was in

Photographs of brewery saloons are very rare. The brewery and saloon of Johann Baptist Karl was once an impressive brick structure. FROM THE COLLECTION OF THE BROWN COUNTY HISTORICAL SOCIETY, NEW ULM, MINNESOTA.

This bottle from Bender's brewery dates to the last few years of the brewery, since the manufacturer, American Bottle Co., started business under that name in 1906. The use of blob top–style bottles more than a decade after the crown cap was introduced suggests that Bender may not have been able to afford new bottling equipment. FROM THE COLLECTION OF STEVE KETCHUM.

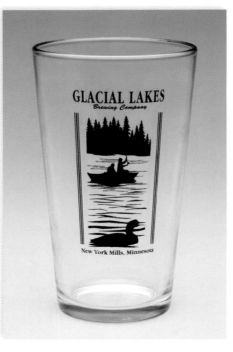

Like many Minnesota businesses, Glacial Lakes Brewing Company of New York Mills used outdoor imagery to promote its brand. FROM THE COLLECTION OF WAYNE THEUER.

operation by the next December. Bender suffered another crisis in December 1885 when a former employee was killed during a fight at the brewery, and his license was temporarily revoked.

The Sanborn fire insurance map of 1899 shows a bottling house at the brewery, and known artifacts indicate Bender continued to bottle until the brewery closed in 1911.

New York Mills [Otter Tail County]

Glacial Lakes Brewing Company (1997–2001)
Location: 17 Main Avenue N.

Sandy Waldon and Mark Hoffman began brewing in a former drug store in New York Mills in 1997. Two brews were offered in 22-ounce bottles: White Tail Pale Ale and Sunset Wheat Beer. The brewery went out of business in late 2001.

Northfield [Rice County]

A. F. Keller (1866–1869)
Maes Brothers (1870–1872)
Maes & Grafmueller (1873–1877)
Adolph Grafmueller (1877–1896)
Herman Wenner, Northfield Brewery (1896–1920)
Location: Greenvale Avenue (near the soccer fields at the base of the bluff below St. Olaf College)

A. F. Keller appears in the excise records for the first time in October 1866. During his first few months of brewing, he averaged sales of only five barrels a month. The Maes brothers, Henry and Dominick, came over from Owatonna to take over the brewery and operated it until it burned in December 1872. Dominick Maes and Adolph Grafmueller rebuilt the brewery in 1873, though *Schade's Brewers Handbook* lists no production in 1874 or 1875. *Western Brewer* reported in March 1878 that "a brewery in Northfield, Minn. has a colored

man for foreman." The name of this pioneer has not yet been discovered.

When Herman Wenner took over the brewery near the turn of the century, it was a modern steam-powered brewery, but had no bottling plant on the premises. Wenner's location was in a difficult market—while Northfield was and is a college town, the city and schools had a strong temperance and reform orientation. In addition, Wenner was surrounded by brewers in Red Wing, Rochester, Faribault, Owatonna, and even tiny Veseli—not to mention the major shipping breweries from the Twin Cities and Milwaukee. Nonetheless, Wenner survived until Prohibition, when the brewery was converted to producing cereal beverages for a few years.

Ortonville [Big Stone County]

Geiger & Ebermann (1882?–1885)
John Fey (and Son) (1885–1895)
Ortonville Brewing Co. (Hochmuth & Glander) (1895–1897)
Eahtonka (Lemmel) Brewery (1897–1904)
Lakeside Brewing Co. (Bauer & Foell) (1905–1912?)
Location: Along the east shore of Big Stone Lake, about six blocks north of city hall

The first newspaper reference to the Ortonville brewery is in the *Big Stone County Herald* of 19 October 1882, where it is noted that "Geiger and Ebermann are building an addition to their brewery, for an ice house 18 by 50 feet." Since this was an addition, the main structure must have been completed before then, though possibly only earlier that year. Geiger seems to have been the majority partner, since he was later mentioned in connection with a falling beer keg that broke his arm as "the gentleman who runs the Ortonville brewery." The brewery was able to take advantage of the lack of local competition to expand its market to other towns in far west central Minnesota as well as to Milbank, South Dakota. The brewery drew its water from a spring just north of the plant.

In late 1884 or early 1885, Geiger sold the brewery to John Fey. Fey had ten years of experience in brewing but left his brewery in West Mitchell, Iowa, when that state imposed prohibition. Fey brought his son Frank into the firm and continued to build the brewery's business and reputation over the next decade but sold it on the twentieth anniversary of his

One of the Ortonville brewery's South Dakota accounts is chronicled on this invoice. FROM THE BOB KAY COLLECTION.

start in the brewery business to concentrate on his saloon. He later became the local agent for Theo. Hamm Brewing Co.

Mr. Hochmuth and Charles Glander, the successors to John Fey, operated under the name Ortonville Brewing Co. In late 1897 the brewery was sold again, this time to Edward Lemmel (spelled Lammel by the *Herald*), who arrived with his family, property, and a brewery mechanic, August Liebtrau. Apparently Hochmuth and Glander had allowed the brewery to decay, since the announcement of Lemmel's arrival notes that "the work of completely overhauling the brewery" was under way. The new name of the brewery was to be Eahtonka Brewery, but in practice it was usually called the Lemmel Brewery or the Ortonville Brewery. Lemmel, who had operated the brewery in Glencoe for more than twenty years, brought in an experienced brewer from Milwaukee and began to expand the capacity and market of the plant. One local estimate put its production at 150 cases of beer per day.

Little is known about the last few years of the brewery: the Lakeside Brewing years. In 1910 the company was in the hands of Joseph Bauer and Jacob Foell, but few other details exist. The Ortonville brewery was caught up in the attempts to enforce the alcohol sales provisions in Indian treaties, in this case the Treaty of Traverse des Sioux of 1851. President Taft initially delayed making a ruling from early 1911 until later that year, but by 1912 Ortonville had gone dry. The precise date on which the brewery ceased production is not known. Part of the old brewery remains as a private residence.

Oshawa [Nicollet County]

Fred Veith (1877–1881?)
Location: Unknown

After meeting with misfortune in Le Sueur, Fred Veith built a new brewery in Oshawa township. Veith operated the brewery with his son Fritz for a few years, though the exact closing date is not documented. According to the 1930 booklet *Lower Oshawa* by Amelia and Florence Turner, the brewery had a flat roof on which beer was cooled in large flat pans (called *kuhlschiffe* by the Germans). The beer was lagered in caves in which ice blocks helped maintain a temperature of 42 degrees.

One of Veith's young grandsons had the job of crawling into the kettles to wash them with a broom after each brewing. The brewery was never very large—Salem reports Veith's production as 311 barrels in 1878 and 145 barrels the next year.

There is some confusion concerning the dates and locations of Veith's breweries. *Schade's Brewers Handbook* lists Veith's address as Oshawa in 1874 and 1875, when the brewery is known to have been in Le Sueur. Veith had a farm in Oshawa township and may have dug caves there to cool beer from his Le Sueur brewery.

Otter Tail City [Otter Tail County]

Otter Tail City Brewery (Miner & Barrett)
(1870–1872)
H. Winters & Co. (1872)
Location: The corner of state highways 78 and 108

Located on the east shore of Otter Tail Lake, Otter Tail City was a boomtown hoping to profit from anticipated milling and railroad traffic. Sometime in late 1870 or early 1871, Joseph Barrett started a brewery in the rear of McArthur's City Hotel. Barrett did not brew himself, since his ads noted that he had "secured the services of a First Class Brewer." He offered beer "by the keg, barrel or load," and was shipping beer as far away as Fargo in Dakota Territory. It is unlikely that he actually shipped many "loads," since his output in the year ending 1 September 1871 was only forty-one barrels.

Though beautifully situated, the town site was an unfortunate choice for business purposes, because in 1872 the railroad was routed a mile east of the lakeshore. The mill and the newspaper moved to other cities, and the original town site was abandoned. A new Otter Tail City was started inland on the rail line, but the brewery was not restarted in the new town. The firm of H. Winters and Co. renewed the brewery's license in 1872, but no production is recorded. Some remnants of the City Hotel still exist.

Phoenix rising from the ashes was an all-too-common allegory for fire-prone breweries. The unusual yellow color on this glass (c. 1895–1901) comes from a pebbled glass surface application rather than etching. FROM THE COLLECTION OF PAT STAMBAUGH.

Owatonna [Steele County]

Adolph Knoblauch (1861?–1865?)
Knoblauch & Mannheim (1865?–1866)
Mannheim & Ganser (1866–1867)
Ganser & Engles (1867–1868)
Ganser & Brother (1868–1872)
Peter Ganser (1872–1894)
Charles Fuermann (1894–1900)
Peter Ganser (1900–1916)
Peter Ganser Estate (1916–1920)
Location: S. Oak Street, south of School Street

After his brewery in Brownsville burned, Adolph Knoblauch moved to Owatonna and opened a new brewery in his new home. There are no records of the earliest years; by the time of the first extant excise records, Knoblauch is in partnership with Mr. Mannheim, most likely John Mannheim, formerly of Mannheim and Lacy in Chatfield. In 1866 Knoblauch sold his share in the brewery to Peter Ganser. After a brief transition period, Ganser entered a five-year partnership with his brother Adam, which ended with Adam's death in 1872.

Ganser spent the next two decades as sole proprietor of the brewery, but they were not calm years. The brewery burned to the ground in 1878 with a loss of about $12,000. Ganser rebuilt immediately, only to have the new brewery burn in 1884. The new brewery lasted, but

The Ganser Bräu label uses an old German street scene to emphasize brewing traditions, although this label was for Ganser's near beer product. FROM THE COLLECTION OF DAVE WENDL.

in 1894 Ganser sold it to Charles Fuermann. Fuermann sold the brewery back to Ganser in 1900, and Ganser operated it until his death in 1916. The brewery continued to brew beer for the next three years and produced near beer and soft drinks for the first three years of Prohibition. In 1923 the brewery was sold to the Owatonna Medicine and Cabinet Co. for use as patent medicine warehouses.

Henry Maes (1865?–1866)
Maes & Knoblauch (1866–1867)
Henry Maes (1867–1870)
Louis Bion (1870–1884)
Marie Bion (1884–1888)
Christian Bion & Son (1888–1890)
Location: Bridge and Oak streets

Sometime during the Civil War, Henry Maes came to Owatonna and started the second brewery in the city. Adolph Knoblauch joined

Maes for about a year after he sold his share in his original brewery to Peter Ganser. Maes sold the brewery in 1870 to Louis Bion, who had been a brewery foreman in Winona for the previous six years. Bion increased the brewery's production from just over 500 barrels in 1875 to more than 1,100 in 1878, making his brewery the larger of the two in Owatonna and among the largest in the region.

Unfortunately, the brewery ran into financial trouble, as did Bion. The brewery burned in 1884, and Bion incurred substantial costs trying to rebuild. In 1885 he was sentenced to ten years in the penitentiary for what a newspaper account called a "criminal assault on a married woman." His case was given a rehearing later that year, but Bion died in 1886. The probate hearings revealed that there were more than $10,000 in claims on the brewery. The building was mortgaged to First National Bank for $3,500 and the land was mortgaged to Phillip Best Brewing Company of Milwaukee. Bion had been acting as Best's agent in the region, and Best also had a suit against Bion for $1,800 worth of empty kegs and bottles that had not been returned.

Louis's widow, Marie, kept the brewery running for a few years and then turned it over to Christian Bion, who was probably Louis's brother. But the tragedies had not yet ended. The brewery burned again in May 1890, with an uninsured loss of nearly $5,000. Finally, in 1892, Theodore Bion suddenly fell dead while standing in Jahrless's saloon near his family's old brewery.

Perham [Otter Tail County]

Peter Schroeder (1878?–1905)
Northern Pacific Brewing Co. (1905–1909)
Peter Schroeder Brewing Co. (1909–1912)
Perham Holding Co. (1912–1915)
Location: 540–560 Oak Street, east of Perham

Peter Schroeder started brewing in Perham in the late 1870s. Some sources claim that there was a brewery in Perham before 1878 and suggest that Schroeder purchased the older firm, but this claim is not supported by excise records, local newspapers, or Schade's list of brewers. While Schroeder produced only a few hundred barrels during his first years, he built a large business in northwestern Minnesota with his energy and a reputation for fine lager.

Newspapers in towns along the Northern Pacific line reported with pleasure that Peter Schroeder was in town on brewery business. Schroeder's lager was served on the North Coast Limited train and shipped throughout the Dakota Territory.

Schroeder added a bottling line in 1905 and began to offer beer by the case. One of his earliest labels proclaimed that his was "The Beer That Made Milwaukee Jealous." Joseph Schlitz Brewing Company sued Schroeder over the use of this label, and Schroeder was forced to discontinue it. Peter Schroeder's death in 1912 was a great blow to the business because his reputation and goodwill throughout the region were impossible to replace, no matter how good the beer was. The business began to decline and the closing of the brewery was unavoidable when enforcement of an Indian treaty banned alcohol throughout much of northern Minnesota.

After Prohibition, the Fellerer family made several attempts to reopen the brewery with which they had been associated since Andrew Fellerer became brewmaster in the 1880s. Ultimately, the project was abandoned and the brewery was torn down in 1986. Illustrations and additional detail about the brewery may be found in chapter 3.

Pine City [Pine County]

Brandes & Tag (1870–1872)
Henry Brandes (1872–1876)
Location: Unknown

The firm of Brandes and Tag appeared first in the census records late in 1870 and brewed its first beer in 1871. In its first year, the company brewed forty barrels. The 1872 excise records lists the brewery under the name of Henry Brandes. While Brandes was not listed in any subsequent excise records or in *Schade's Brewers Handbook*, the *Taylor's Falls Journal* of 6 March 1876 reported that the Pine City brewery owned by Brandes had been destroyed by fire.

Rudolph Buselmeier (1882–1884)
Amalie Buselmeier (1885–1910)
John Blass (1910–1913)
Amalie Buselmeier (1913–1915)
Location: On Cross Lake, south of Fifth Street

After a lawsuit over the Rush City brewery (see that brewery's entry), Rudolph Buselmeier (or

Busselmeyer) moved to nearby Pine City to start his own brewery. After Rudolph's death, his widow ran the brewery for many years. Like most breweries, the Buselmeier brewery suffered a number of misfortunes in addition to Rudolph Buselmeier's untimely death: part of the brewery's cellar washed out in 1896, and the brewery burned to the ground in June 1899 for a loss of $6,000. Amalie Buselmeier rebuilt the brewery with a capacity of about 4,000 barrels per year. In 1910 John Blass took over the brewery for a few years, but Amalie Buselmeier ran the brewery for the last few years until it closed.

Pine Island [Goodhue County]

John Ferber (1869–1871)
John H. Geil (1871–1874)
John Ferber (1874–1893)
Location: West side of Main Street between Walnut and White (former street names), just south of the Zumbro River

In 1869 John Ferber began making beer in Pine Island. Excise records suggest that his capacity was just under ten barrels per month. Ferber produced both lager and ale—as late as 1882 he advertised ale, porter, and "good lager beer." After two years he apparently traded his brewery for John H. Geil's (or Gill's) farm and took up farming. (In 1872 the *Red Wing Argus* reported that a dog pup with six legs had been born on his farm.)

In 1874 Ferber returned to brewing—though given his production, he might have been doing it part time. He brewed only forty barrels in 1875, and his largest recorded production was not much more than one hundred barrels. Part of the reason for this may have been that Pine Island voted to go dry several times during Ferber's career. On 30 March 1883 the *Pine Island Journal* carried the following article:

> On Wednesday of last week John Ferber was arraigned before the court and his case was continued until Monday. On Monday he plead guilty to the charge of selling beer and was fined $25 and costs or twenty days in jail. Immediately following this case he was arrested upon another case, plead guilty, and was fined $50 or sixty days in jail. He will board at Red Wing.

Ferber continued to brew on a small scale for the next ten years, but finally retired in 1893 and returned to farming.

(The brewery of David Clossner, sometimes listed as being in Pine Island, was actually in Berne, and its story is told under that location.)

Preston [Fillmore County]

Somers & Lint (1859–1860)

Somers & Ibach (1860–?)

Joseph Ibach (?–1874)

Smith (1874–1878)

Fred Yager (1883)

Yager & Luhmann (1887–1900)

George Riedel (1900–1908)

Preiss & Eickmann (1910–1912)

Albert Meyer (1912)

August Knapp (1912–1919)

Location: On the Root River, beyond the corner of Bluff and Spring streets

Most accounts claim that the Preston brewery was started in 1859 by Somers and Lint. Nothing is known of Somers, but Lint may have been Jacob Lint, a cooper. By 1860, the Census of Industry lists the brewery under the name of Somers and Ibach. Joseph Ibach had been a fireman on a Mississippi riverboat until he decided to settle down at Preston and try his hand at brewing. (The J. Hach listed in some accounts is clearly a misreading of Ibach.) Ibach remained at Preston until 1874, when he moved to Mankato to operate three breweries in turn.

The next decade of the brewery's history is not clear. Ibach apparently sold the brewery to Mr. Smith. Upon his death, sometime before 1878, the brewery passed into the hands of his widow. The brewery was still in operation in 1878, but an event that year probably led to its closing. The *Winona Daily Republican* reported that a fight took place at the brewery and was called "the most terrible affair that ever happened in that town." The brewer was badly injured, and this may have caused Smith's widow to close the brewery. Most accounts report that Yager and Luhmann restarted the brewery in 1887, but Fred Yager (or Yeager) appears in the excise records in 1883. This may have been a false start, but all sources agree that by 1887 Yager and Peter Luhmann were operating the brewery and restoring its repu-

tation. Late in 1900 they sold out to George Riedel, who operated the brewery until his death in 1908. The brewery was closed again in 1909 and went through a rapid sequence of ownership changes until it was purchased by August Knapp in 1912 (though some local accounts say Knapp came into possession of the brewery in 1911). According to an interview with Knapp's son Rupe, related in an article by Vienna Drake in Preston's 125th anniversary album *Coming Home*, Knapp began to bottle and sell beer under the name Peerless, bringing him into conflict with Gund Brewing of La Crosse, which had already registered Peerless as a trademark. The name was then changed to Forget-Me-Not, with a label featuring intertwined leaves and flowers. Preston beer was delivered to all parts of the county by horse, and the brewery shipped to some more-distant locales by rail.

Ironically, Knapp's beer could not be sold in Preston. The town had voted itself dry, and though the brewery was allowed to stay in business, all the product was shipped out of town. A unique incident happened in May 1914 when a fire broke out at the brewery. A group of temperance advocates was picnicking near the brewery and when the call of fire went up, the picnickers all left their festivities and helped the fire department save the brewery. But there was no saving the brewery from the flames that were the prohibition movement. In 1919 the sheriff dumped the remaining inventory, and Preston became totally dry. The brewery produced soft drinks for a brief time, but this venture ended after just a few years. The brewery was converted into a residence and still stands.

Princeton [Mille Lacs County]

Roos Brothers (1886?–1890)

Location: Main Street

Little is known about the Roos Brothers' brewery. Jacob and George may have begun brewing in Princeton before 1886, but the first known ad is from March 1887. They advertised "First Class Beer by Wholesale or Retail at Less than Half what Down River Beer Costs." By 1890 their ads also included their position as local agents for Val. Blatz of Milwaukee. It was probably more profitable for the brothers to act as agents for Blatz than to brew their own beer,

and closing their brewery would leave more time for their ice business. There is no record of the Princeton brewery after July 1890.

Reads Landing [Wabasha County]

Charles Leslin, Upper Brewery (1858?–1865)

H. & J. Burkhardt (1865–1866)

Henry Burkhardt (1867–1869?)

Burkhardt & Leslin (1871–1872)

H. Burkhardt & Co. (1872–1874?)

G. Burkhardt & Co. (1874–1877)

Samuel Burkhardt (1877–1880)

Gottfried Burkhardt (1880–1884)

Burkhardt Bros. (1884–1894)

Gottlieb Burkhardt (1894–1909)

Location: On Brewery Creek

Upper Brewery was one of two breweries started near Reads Landing in the years between the 1857 territorial census and the 1860 census. Charles Leslin produced about 350 barrels of beer during the 1860 tax year, almost twice as much as the Pepin Brewery, but by the end of the Civil War, both breweries were selling about the same amount, fifteen to twenty barrels per month.

In 1865 Leslin sold the brewery to Henry and Jacob Burkhardt. The Burkhardt family controlled the brewery through the next two generations. Different members of the family were associated with this brewery at different times, since the family also had interests in breweries in Crookston and Menominee, Wisconsin. The family was apparently out of the brewing business for a few years since Henry Burkhardt is listed as a butcher in the excise records for 1869 and 1870 and in the 1870 census and Jacob was not in the state. (Jacob may have left because of the shooting incident at the Pepin Brewery, listed below.)

The excise records tell a confusing tale of the partnership between the Burkhardts and the Leslins in 1871 and 1872. The records suggest that Mary Leslin was sole proprietor of the brewery for a few months during 1872, when Mary and Charles were building their own brewery in Wabasha. In November, when Henry resumed control of the brewery, he bought the remaining stock of fifty barrels of beer from Mary, but these were among the eighty-three barrels destroyed in a fire shortly thereafter.

The Burkhardt family built a steady trade in the area and had a published capacity of approximately 1,500 barrels. (They may have switched breweries in 1880—see the Pepin Brewery listing below.) At one point, according to the Sanborn fire insurance maps, the brewery featured an attached bowling alley. The location near Brewery Creek provided convenient caves (remnants of which still exist) but also made the brewery vulnerable to floods, the worst of which washed out the brewery's cellars and the nearby bridge in 1883.

The brewery survived into the twentieth century without significant modernization. As late as 1902, the Sanborn maps show that the brewery was still operated by horse power and lighted by candles. The brewery burned in January 1909 and was not rebuilt.

Charles Saile & Co., Pepin Brewery (1858?–1866)
Ruckhaber & Walty (1866–1874?)
Ruckhaber & Grams (1875–1876)
J. Voelke (1877–1880)
Location: Unknown

Charles Saile started the Pepin Brewery sometime before 1860. The 1860 Census of Industry lists production of 200 barrels during the 1859–1860 tax year. Saile and his partner, Michael Ulmer, built a new brewery in 1862; during the mid-1860s Saile and Co. sold between fifteen and twenty barrels of lager each month. In fall 1866 Saile sold his brewery to Gottlieb Walty and moved to Hastings. Walty brought Benjamin Ruckhaber on as a partner, and the new owners increased production. By 1870 Ruckhaber and Walty were selling as many as seventy barrels per month. Excise records indicate that this brewery produced both lager and ale, but lager outsold ale by a three to two margin in months where figures are available.

Competition between the breweries in Reads Landing was fierce and, once, even toxic. The *Lake City Leader* in April 1867 reported that Jacob Burkhardt was shot at the Reads Landing brewery under "circumstances not yet fully known." But the *Winona Daily Republican* had the rest of the story:

A brewer in Wabashaw [*sic*] named Wealthy [*sic*] detected one Burkhart [*sic*] in the act of throwing poison (phosphorus) into the cooler of the brewery. Wealthy fired twice at him with a shot-gun loaded with buckshot, wounding him severely. The poisoning had been repeated two or three times, when a watch was kept with the above result.

According to available figures, production suffered a steady decline through the 1870s, dropping from 1,000 barrels in 1871 to 180 in 1879. The brewery may have been closed by the time of the 1880 census, since there are no brewers in the records unconnected with the other known breweries.

However, an article in the 16 January 1909 *Winona Daily Republican* raises another possibility. It claims that the recently burned Burkhardt brewery had been built in 1862 by Saile and Ulmer and purchased by the Burkhardts in 1880. While the Burkhardts clearly did not purchase the Saile and Ulmer brewery when those two moved to Hastings, they may have purchased it from Voelke in 1880 and continued to operate it, perhaps moving their operations here from their other property.

Red Lake Falls [Red Lake County]

Red Lake Falls Brewing Co. (1884–1887)
Terry & Walter (1887–1888)
August Walter & Co. (1888–1890)
Location: Unknown

Aside from appearances in brewing industry lists and excise records, little is known about the Red Lake Falls brewery. *Wing's Brewers Handbook* and the 1887 excise records both put the brewery's capacity at less than 500 barrels per year. The editor of the *Red Lake Falls Gazette* apparently didn't think much of Terry and Walter, since the 26 August 1887 issue included an invitation: "To any practical brewer who has the capital, a better point can not be found for the establishing of a good brewery. A large business can be worked up—a large amount of country can be made to yield a paying patronage." *Brewers' Journal* reported in 1906 that Louis Borchers was considering a brewery in Red Lake Falls, but no brewery was built.

Red Wing [Goodhue County]

Philip Hoffman (1857–1868)
Philip Hoffman Estate (1868)
Mrs. Philip (Christina) Hoffman (1868–1871)
Christina Christ (1871–1872)
Jacob Christ (1872–1890)
Christina Christ (1890–1893)
Red Wing Brewing Co. (1893–1904)
Zimmerman & Featherston (1904–1909)
Red Wing Brewing Co. (1909–1920)
Red Wing Brewing Co. (1934–1935)
Midwest Brewing Co., Inc. (1935–1937)
Location: 1610–1636 W. Main Street

Philip Hoffman was the pioneer brewer in Red Wing, establishing his brewery in a year that saw many other long-lived Minnesota breweries established. From 1860 to 1863 his sales averaged about fifteen barrels per month, but the fact that sales doubled the next two years suggests that Hoffman expanded his brewery. Hoffman advertised his lager beer, but excise records indicate that he also made ale, like many of his counterparts in the area.

Hoffman died in late 1868, but his widow, Christina, took over the business and ran it quite capably for the next three years. In 1871 she married respected local saloonkeeper Jacob Christ, a veteran of three years in the Seventh Minnesota Volunteer Infantry. Eventually, the Christ name went on the brewery, and Jacob used his connections and energy to expand the business—sales increased from nearly 500 barrels in 1870 to more than 1,400 barrels by 1878. In that year the brewery was rebuilt of stone and its capacity increased yet again. Unlike some of his fellow Red Wing brewers, Christ managed to stay out of the newspapers except for routine announcements, and the couple's brewery continued to grow. Local histories suggest that Christina's knowledge and skill were critical to the smooth operation of the brewery, which was proven again when Jacob died and Christina assumed control of the brewery once more.

In 1893 Christina Christ decided to retire and sold the brewery to the newly formed Red Wing Brewing Co., which was under the direction of Franz Sommer, J. F. Oliva, and Dan Metzler. This firm operated the brewery for a decade, when it was sold to Zimmerman and Featherston. Even when the brewery's name was later changed back to Red Wing Brewing

This label features the Minnesota state seal but does not indicate what type of beer is in the bottle. BOB KAY COLLECTION.

Co., the company continued to advertise "Good Old Zimmie's" beer until Prohibition.

During Prohibition the brewery became Red Wing Products Co. and made other beverages and ice, though ice was later dropped in favor of vinegar and cider. While this should have given Red Wing a head start in bringing beer to market after re-legalization, significant modernizations were needed, and Red Wing Brewing did not have beer for sale until 1934. The Red Wing and Cokin's labels were not profitable enough to pay the remodeling debts, so after a year the company was reorganized as Midwest Brewing. The Red Wing label was retained, and Otto's Own replaced Cokin's. The brewery closed down in 1937, unable to compete against the national brands in a changed environment.

The red wing is the central feature of this Pilsener label from Zimmermann & Featherston.
FROM THE COLLECTION OF KEN MALZ.

William Heising, City Brewery (1861–1873)
Christina Heising (1873–1877)
Remmler's Brewery, Adolph Remmler (1877–1908)
Remmler's Brewery (also A. Remmler Estate)
   (1909–1920)
Remmler Brewing Co. (1934–1948)
Goodhue County Brewing Co. (1948–1951)
Location: 405 W. Fifth Street

William Heising moved from Rochester to Red Wing in late 1860 or early 1861 and started Red Wing's second brewery in what had been the Old Minnesota House at the corner of Bush and Fifth streets. Heising brewed both ale and lager and sold beer wholesale and retail at the brewery.

For the first several years, production at Heising's City Brewery was about two-thirds of the output at Philip Hoffman's Red Wing Brewery, but in 1869 Heising began a $6,000 expansion. He built a new three-story, 40 × 80 foot brick brewhouse and installed new brewing equipment to more than double capacity. The *Red Wing Argus* enthused that "Heising's new brewery building is a model for permanent structures. Its firm foundation and thick walls ensure its standing for a century." By

These glasses probably date to the 1890s. Unlike standard golden-colored lagers, Wiener (Vienna-style lager) was caramel-colored and was based on the style first brewed by Anton Dreher in Vienna to compete with Bohemian Pilsner. FROM THE COLLECTION OF PAT STAMBAUGH.

1871 the brewery was the largest in Red Wing and was producing over 600 barrels a year.

Heising experienced setbacks in 1869 as well. In August he was arrested for violating revenue regulations, apparently using improper procedures involving tax stamps. In September the storehouse behind his brewery was set on fire and he lost malt, hops, and equipment worth about $3,000. Heising also had trouble with his cellars flooding and in 1871 was forced to dig an 800-foot-long sewer to drain the cellars.

Despite the setbacks, Heising continued to be one of the leading brewers of the area. The *Argus* of 2 May 1872 proclaimed that "Heising's Buck [Bock] Beer is extra good this season. We are sorry for those who are away and all others who cannot enjoy it. As for the *Argus* folk, they know how it is, for Mr. Heising's May-Day compliments were accompanied by a keg."

William Heising died in December 1873, and his widow, Christina, carried on the business and continued to expand the facility, including a large icehouse and a 180-foot-long

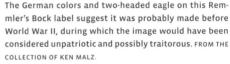

The well-dressed man at left is probably Adolph Remmler. The horses appear to be very closely matched; matched teams were commonly mentioned as a point of pride for breweries. Note also the elevated wooden sidewalks in front of the brewery buildings. COURTESY OF THE GOODHUE COUNTY HISTORICAL SOCIETY.

cellar. In January 1877 Mrs. Heising married Adolph Remmler, who had come to Red Wing in 1875 to manage brewing operations. He renamed the brewery and took over as proprietor, though Christina continued to play an active role in managing the company. Among the improvements Remmler made was the installation of bottling facilities during the

The German colors and two-headed eagle on this Remmler's Bock label suggest it was probably made before World War II, during which the image would have been considered unpatriotic and possibly traitorous. FROM THE COLLECTION OF KEN MALZ.

summer of 1877. Remmler offered a dozen bottles of lager for $1.50 to consumers and $1.25 to dealers. He claimed it "will keep any length of time in any climate," and was recommended for "invalids, families, and shipping." This move had increased urgency since tavern owner Hokan Lindberg was offering bottles of Chris Stahlmann's St. Paul lager for $1.60 per dozen.

By the 1890s Remmler's Brewery had a capacity of approximately 6,000 barrels per year and was serving much of the surrounding countryside. A ledger in the collection of the Goodhue County Historical Society listing Remmler's accounts during the years 1891 through 1896 includes customers throughout Goodhue County and in Hammond, Ellsworth, and Plum City, Wisconsin. In 1893 Remmler even shipped six half barrels to an account in Minneapolis. By this point, prices had dropped so that bottled beer was $1.10 per dozen and

kegs of beer in three sizes (half-barrel, quarter-barrel, and pony kegs) were sold at prices pro-rated from the $8 per barrel base price. Adolph Remmler died in 1908, but his son Otto took over the business and ran it until Prohibition.

Unlike rival Red Wing Brewing, Remmler Brewing did not produce alternative products during Prohibition but maintained the buildings until repeal. While the basic structure was present, Remmler's brewing plant needed significant improvements to be brought back into production when brewing resumed. Nonetheless, the improvements were made and Remmler Brewing went back into production in 1934. Although it outlasted Red Wing Brewing, Remmler Brewing struggled from the start. Its capacity was never more than 20,000 barrels per year, which made it one of the three smallest breweries in Minnesota and among the smallest in the country. The brewery tried several different brands, including Remmler's, Royal Brew, Security White Cross, and Six Horse, none of which was able to take a significant share of the market away from the giant Twin Cities breweries slightly over an hour away or from the Wisconsin breweries just across the river. In the mid-1940s Remmler's hired a new brewmaster, Joe Mickus, who had held the same position at the now-defunct Alexandria Brewing Co. Despite his best efforts,

Struggling breweries did whatever they could to save money, including using secondhand supplies. Goodhue County Brewing pasted a Red Wing Premium case label (c. 1949–51) over a Brewers' Best case from National Brewers in Great Falls, Montana. Here, the 84-cent deposit on the case was more than the cost of the beer. FROM THE COLLECTION OF PAT STAMBAUGH.

by the beginning of 1948 Remmler Brewing was no longer in operation.

A group of investors tried to resurrect the company later in 1948 under the name Goodhue County Brewing Co. Mickus' new brand, Minnesota Club, featured an unusual label printed on both sides—on the reverse was a sketch of Mickus and his personal endorsement of the beer. The new firm was no more able to make a profit than its predecessor, and the brewery closed for good in 1951.

Lorenz Hoffman (1865–1882)
Location: Bush Street, north of Third

In late 1865 Lorenz Hoffman went into business for himself in the former Norquist Building on the corner of Third and Bush. According to the description of "Hoffman's Steam Brewery" in the 1878 *History of Goodhue County*, the brewery itself measured 23 × 70 feet and was supplemented by a dry kiln, an engine room, and an icehouse (built in 1870). Hoffman aged his lager in caves dug into Barn Bluff, the scenic landmark on Red Wing's east side. Just five years after opening, Hoffman surpassed the production of his late brother's brewery and was one of the two Red Wing breweries to be classified as large by the federal government. Production statistics from the early 1870s suggest that Hoffman may have sold slightly more beer to large accounts than other Red Wing brewers since he usually led the list in number of quarter-barrels sold, but seldom led in eighth-barrels, which were more likely to be sold to individuals. Hoffman's production seems to have topped out at just over 600 barrels per year, which put him behind the expanding breweries of Jacob Christ and Adolph Remmler. Hoffman employed as many as three hands at the brewery by 1880. Hoffman's brewery had disappeared from the records by 1882, and no evidence of his brewery is depicted on the 1884 Sanborn fire insurance map.

Hay Creek Brewery, John Hartman (1866–1880?)
Location: Hay Creek Township, on the west end of Featherstone Road

John Hartman began brewing (and apparently distilling) south of Red Wing along Hay Creek at Featherstone Road in the summer of 1866. Hartman produced both ale and lager, as did several of his rivals, and his production typically ranked in the middle of Red Wing's brew-

ers. In 1871 he produced 373 barrels, but this figure dropped to 167 barrels by 1879. Hartman made $250 worth of improvements to his brewery in 1870, but he seldom appeared in lists of building expenses.

Hartman's local fame was perhaps not so much for the quality of his product as for his brushes with the law. In August 1869 he was arrested for distilling without a license. Though he was at first found guilty, the *Red Wing Argus* reported he was soon granted a new trial "upon such grounds as ensures his being cleared of the charge. His friends here will be glad to hear this, knowing as they do that he has not deserved the severe penalties which might have been imposed if the first trial had stood." In May 1871 a boy who had gone missing from Pine Island turned up alive and well and working for Hartman. While Hartman was not accused of wrongdoing, it was clear that some found Hartman's establishment to be of dubious reputation. In the 1878 *History of Goodhue County*, the editors wrote, "In the Southwest part of the city, John Hartman runs a brewery. It is one of the manufacturing industries, but the proprietor is one of those unaccountable characters from whom we could obtain no information that would be of use in this volume." Sometime in 1880 the 64-year-old Hartman appears to have retired from the brewery business. (A contemporary drawing of the Hay Creek Brewery appears in chapter 2.)

National Brewery, John Melander (1866–1876?)
Bohmbach & Koke (1876?–1877)
Henry Bombach (1877–1878?)
Location: North side of Main, east of Jefferson

John Melander, one of the few natives of Sweden to own a brewery in Minnesota, took out a license to be a small brewer in November 1866. Excise tax records suggest that his capacity was not much more than twenty barrels per month. During the 1870–71 tax year he produced 158 barrels, 130 barrels behind the next-smallest producer and less than one-quarter of William Heising's production. The 1870 Census of Industry lists Melander as having one employee, but the population census shows two men boarding with him, both listed as brewery workers.

Records indicate that Melander typically took at least one month off from brewing during the summer—a common practice among smaller brewers, many of whom were either out of cellar space or ice necessary to keep lager beer cool during the aging process. Melander brewed both ale and lager, though lager was a more popular product.

While no direct connections between the proprietors have been found, it is more likely that the firm of Bohmbach and Koke acquired Melander's brewery than that they built a new one of their own in the already crowded Red Wing market. Nothing is known about Bohmbach and Koke's brewing record, except that in June 1877, the partnership between Henry Bohmbach and Koke was dissolved, and Bohmbach applied for a federal license on his own. The dissolution notice announced that Bombach would "continue the business at the old stand," but it is unclear how long he stayed in business. By 1880 there are no records of this business either in the census or in any of the published business directories.

Gustaf Berg (1867)

Location: Unknown

Gustaf Berg filed for his brewery license in February 1867. The Red Wing market was already crowded, and nothing is known about Berg's brewing. Excise tax records for 1868 show he was licensed as a photographer instead of a brewer.

Redwood Falls [Redwood County]

Jacob Schmahl (1870–1876)

Location: Southwest corner of East Bridge and Washington avenues

In 1870 Jacob Schmahl arrived with his family at Redwood Falls and built a brewery and a saloon at the southwest corner of East Bridge and Washington avenues (at the time called First Avenue). The brewery was a two and one-half story building measuring 30 × 50 feet. In 1871 he added a one-story 18 × 40 foot stone vault. The saloon must have included a large hall since it hosted everything from Thanksgiving balls to Methodist church meetings. In 1874 and 1875 Schmahl produced fifty-one and thirty-six barrels of beer, respectively. Neither the brewery nor the saloon proved to be particularly successful, but he continued with them until after his house burned in March 1876 (though he remained long enough

to host the local Centennial Ball at Schmahl's Hall). The brewery was pulled down in early 1877, and the material was used for the new owner's house.

John Weiss (1871–1880)

Dietrich & Drischel (1880?–1888)

Location: Unknown

The list of new buildings and improvements in Redwood Falls for 1871 includes two one-story structures built by J. Weis [sic], a frame brewery measuring 21 × 32 with a basement and a small malt house measuring 12 × 14 feet. The brewery cost $800 and the malt house cost $100. His first advertisements appeared in February 1872, claiming that his "Ale and Beer is pronounced by competent judges, fully equal to the best Chicago or Milwaukee manufacture." During the four years for which production figures exist, Weiss never sold more than sixty barrels.

Little is known about the operations of Dietrich and Drischel. They appear in the 1886 excise records because they paid a $135.95 tax penalty. They had regular ads in the *Redwood Falls Reveille* until mid-February 1888. There is then a three-month gap in the microfilmed issues, after which the ad no longer appears and there are no other references to the brewery.

Richmond [Stearns County]

Claudius Weber (1866–1884)

Location: East bank of the Sauk River, west of Richmond

Claudius Weber began brewing with his father-in-law, John Meyer, in fall 1866. (Some sources suggest 1864, but he is not included in the tax records, and no independent confirmation has yet been found.) Weber bought out Meyer's share of the brewery sometime in 1868, had a partner named Klouser for less than a year, and was in business on his own by 1870. Weber's business was never large—his largest known annual production was 220 barrels in 1870, and most years he produced fewer than 200 barrels. Weber was listed in the 1880 census as "brewer and farmer," which suggests that brewing had ceased to be a full-time occupation. Excise tax records list William Heinsath as the operator of the brewery for a period in 1877 to 1878, but no additional information is known. The Richmond brewery disappears

from the records after 1884; the reason for closing is not known.

Rochester [Olmsted County]

Adam Drescher (1857?–1865?)

Henry Schuster, Union Brewery (1865–1885)

Estate of Henry Schuster, Union Brewery (1885–1897)

Schuster Brewing Co. (1897–1920)

Location: Corner of Main and College (now First Avenue SW and Fourth Street SW)

As is often the case with frontier breweries, the precise date of the brewery's opening is not clear. Because the brewery predated local newspapers, data must be pieced together from sources not always equal to the task. Most sources claim that the origin of Schuster Brewing Co. lay in a brewery started by Adam Drescher in 1857 or 1858, though one source places it as early as 1854. Drescher does not appear in the 1857 territorial census or the 1860 census, but this absence is not conclusive. It is certain that any brewery in Rochester was very small, since none reached the $500 of production necessary for inclusion in the 1860 Census of Industry. The brewery may have lain idle for several years.

According to a family history, Henry Schuster Sr. moved with his wife, Josephine, and their son Henry Jr. from Wisconsin to Minnesota in late 1862. Henry Sr. had been trained as a blacksmith and established a shop on the corner of Broadway and Center streets. In 1865 Schuster purchased an interest in the brewery and became part of the firm of Schuster and Joest. Apparently he continued at least some of his work in manufacturing since the federal excise tax records for 1866 record him as having produced eleven wagons. The same records show Schuster and Joest producing just under 500 barrels of lager in 1866, making it the largest of the three breweries operating in Rochester.

Schuster's success as a blacksmith allowed him to accumulate enough capital to provide for his family in style and to expand his new business. In its list of building improvements for 1867, the *Rochester Post* reported that Schuster had spent $3,000 to "put up a neat two story brick residence on his lots on Main street," and had made $1,000 worth of improvements to his brewery. In early 1870

Schuster bought out Joest's interest in the brewery. Joest remained in town and opened a cooperage. The new ads proclaimed that the Union Brewery had "Ale and Lager Beer, of the best kinds, kept constantly on hand."

Schuster had only a little more than a year to enjoy the fruits of his new status. In late April 1871, the one-story frame building burned down, probably due to a fire in the malt kiln located near the center of the plant. The fire department was able to save neighboring buildings (including the county jail), but the brewery was leveled, causing Schuster a loss of about $8,000 and the family dog, Hector. The beer in the cellars, worth an estimated $5,000, was salvaged. As was typical of most brewery owners of the time, Schuster had insurance on only about one-half to two-thirds of the value of the property. However, only two weeks later, the *Post* reported that Schuster had built a shed on the property and was making plans to re-build. The new brewery had a main building three stories tall and forty feet square. The top floor was the malt loft, the second floor was for drying the malt, and the ground floor for the brewing operations. Perhaps having learned from the fire, Schuster built a separate one-story building with solid brick walls to house the furnaces and heating plant. The rebuild-ing was a boon to local contractors and sup-pliers—Schuster spent more than $5,000 on the facility and one local brick maker supplied 80,000 bricks for the walls.

The next several years brought continued expansion and success to Schuster and the Union Brewery. He built a two-story brick building measuring 44 × 70 feet behind the brewery in 1877 for $5,000, and during most years the lists of building improvements in-cluded at least $1,000 worth of additions or new fixtures for the brewery. The new build-ing included a hall in which community groups could meet. Schuster was involved with many fraternal societies and German cultural organizations, and Schuster's Hall was the site of meetings ranging from the German *Män-nerchor* (men's chorus) to a group of German farmers seeking to organize an insurance com-pany. Schuster's civic involvement was recog-nized in the late 1870s when he was elected to the first of his terms as city alderman. Throughout his time in office (during which

he served alongside W. W. Mayo), Schuster took particular interest in matters pertaining to the fire department—unsurprising given the flammability of the breweries in town—to the point of purchasing additional hose for the company. Schuster's devotion to his adopted home was evident in other ways as well. One sketch of his life approvingly quoted a news-paper item from May 1865 that referred to Schuster as "the man who knocked down the traitor for exulting over the death of the presi-dent . . ." Henry Schuster's untimely death in 1885 at the age of 54 was an occasion of grief for the entire city. His funeral procession in-cluded citizens from every walk of life.

Henry Schuster Jr. and Frederick W. Schuster were in their early twenties when they took over management of their father's estate and business, but they were prepared for the task. Henry had already been working in the Schuster office as a clerk and took over the business end of the operation. Fred began work in the brewing operations of the family firm and later went to work for Franz Falk Brewing Co. in Milwaukee. Upon his father's death, he returned to manage the brewing de-partment in Rochester. The brothers continued to develop their home market throughout the 1880s. Union Brewery became the only brew-ery in Rochester in 1882 and enjoyed several years without serious competition. As with most other brewers in small Minnesota cities during this period, they did a large keg trade with farmers in the outlying areas. (Getting the kegs back from the farmers was another matter entirely, as the newspaper ads of the period in-dicate.) The Schusters maintained the German tradition of brewing a bock beer for release in the spring. The 1887 bock beer was celebrated with a small but colorful parade described by the *Rochester Post* as featuring "their delivery wagon fitted up in good style with a patriotic platform draped with the national colors on which Caprus Ægagrus, Esq., better known by his every day name, Mr. William Goat, stood, the admiration of all beholders. The equipage was drawn by four black horses driven by Charley Jackson, resplendent in a stove pipe hat and ample shirt front. It was a parade to delight the heart of the thirsty." Throughout this period, capacity was typically listed as about 2,000 barrels per year, but this would

change dramatically in the years before Prohi-bition as the Schuster brothers embarked on a campaign of steady expansion.

The ascent of Union Brewery into the ranks of the leading breweries of the upper Midwest began with the construction of a bottling department in 1888. One of the local papers noted in typical style that "a visit to the Schuster Bros'. Bottling Works of Export Wiener Beer is not devoid of interest. This branch of their brewing business has been added but recently, but regardless of the short period in which it has been in operation, the works are crowded to keep up with the orders for their celebrated beverage." The article de-scribes each step: bottle rinsing, filling, pas-teurization, and packing. Of special interest to collectors is the note that "very handsome labels are pasted onto the body and lower part of the neck. The top of the neck is wound with tin foil . . . ," thus indicating that Schuster labels could be as old as 1888 and that neck labels were used at this early date. The initial bottling runs were about forty-five cases per

An invoice from the Union Brewery advertises bottled and keg beer. COURTESY OF THE OLMSTED COUNTY HISTORICAL SOCIETY.

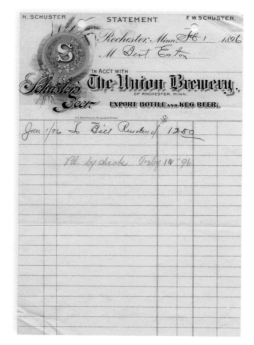

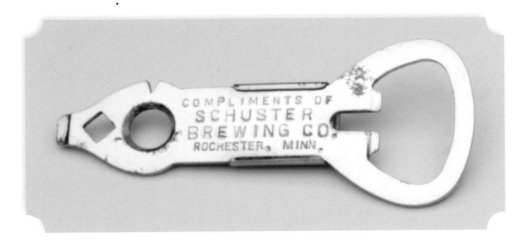

Schuster Brewing Co. is the only Minnesota brewery known to have offered this unusual opener: type N-8 in the *Handbook of United States Beer Advertising Openers and Corkscrews*. In addition to a cap lifter, it also claimed to be a sliding cigar cutter, a cigar box opener, a nail puller, a screwdriver, and a gas auto headlamp key (the square hole). The design was patented in 1909. FROM THE COLLECTION OF PAT STAMBAUGH.

day, but with additional temporary help, it was possible to fill and pack fifteen cases of quart bottles per hour.

The optimistic projections of the local press were justified—within a decade the newly renamed Schuster Brewing Company was forced to build not only a larger bottling house but also a new cold-storage facility and to make plans for the imminent remodeling and expansion of the brewhouse. The expanded bottling house was necessitated by the introduction of a new product, Schuster's Pure Malt & Hop Tonic. Fred may have been inspired to introduce the tonic during his course with the American Brewing Academy of Chicago in 1896. Whatever the case, the growth of this product was rapid. By 1898 Schuster Brewing Company claimed that its tonic was on sale at 2,000 drug stores throughout Minnesota, Wisconsin, Iowa, the Dakotas, and Montana. Just over 10 years later, the company reported sales of ten million bottles and announced, "This product is shipped to all points, particularly to the Pacific coast, the Hawaiian Islands, the South, and western Canada." In much of the company's publicity from this period, the malt tonic was given top billing over the beer.

With sales of the malt tonic expanding rapidly, the Schuster brothers took advantage of this favorable position to modernize and expand the brewery yet again. During the winter of 1898–99, the company contracted with Pfaudler Vacuum Fermentation Company to install their "vacuum system" in the brewery. Schuster celebrated the new system in May 1899 with the release of "Vacuum Brau," available on tap in the area. To increase capacity, the Schusters added ten hundred-barrel finishing casks, made of white oak by F. Ketler Cooperage of Milwaukee. The efficiency of the plant was improved in early 1899 by the installation of a twenty-ton ice machine and refrigeration system made by Vilter Manufacturing Co., also of Milwaukee.

The Schuster brothers were not totally dependent on the innovations of others to make their brewery more efficient. Among their improvements was a device known as "Schuster's Patent Bottle Truck and Drainer." Orders for this bottle truck came from nearby breweries such as August Schell Brewing Company in New Ulm and from as far away as San Antonio and St. Louis. A local manufacturing firm made and shipped more than two dozen bottle trucks in the first two months after being awarded the contract. In the context of this prosperity, another fire at the brewery (set by what the *Post* called "the Small Boy Match Fiend") and even the destruction of a small-town depot were relatively minor annoyances.

The final chapter in the expansion was the construction in 1905 of an all-new five-story brewhouse along with additional storage, coo-

perage, and mechanical facilities. The building, designed by renowned brewery architect Richard Griesser of Chicago, followed the gravity plan in which the raw materials began on the top floor and descended from malting to boiling and finally to fermenting. An interesting blend of new and old technology was represented in the new outbuildings—one was a coal storage room capable of storing ten railcars of coal for the boilers, another was an extensive new barn for the Schusters' prize teams of horses. The new additions represented an investment of more than $50,000 and resulted in an imposing structure that would be one of the main features of the Rochester skyline for several decades.

Schuster Brewing experienced continued prosperity until Prohibition, despite being a relatively small brewery in the center of the brewing heartland. Numerous other breweries attempted to crack this potentially lucrative market. Schuster Brewing was able to use its strong reputation to hold competitors at bay and even to expand beyond its home market. Schuster had agents listed in the Minneapolis city directories for a few years before Prohibition, and even penetrated markets as far southwest as Kansas City, Missouri.

With its stable financial position and a well-established nonalcoholic product, Schuster Brewing might have appeared to be a strong candidate to survive Prohibition. However, the advent of Prohibition caused the Schusters such frustration that they decided to close the brewery effective 1 January 1922. While they had attempted to make near beer for two years, they were unsuccessful in finding a market for this product. Fred Schuster blamed the "women of the country" and claimed that cereal beverage companies, "making soft drinks containing a low alcoholic content, cannot compete with the 'kitchen' breweries manufacturing real beer containing from 4 to 10 per cent alcohol." It is possible that the diversification of the Schuster family into real estate made it easier for them to walk away from brewing than for a family that had all of their assets in the brewery property. At any rate, Schuster Brewing made no attempt to recommence production when beer was re-legalized in 1933. The monumental brewery buildings were converted to dairy produc-

The Schuster Brewing Company facility as it appeared in 1937, when it was a dairy. The date is found on the Ford dealership in the foreground. COURTESY OF THE OLMSTED COUNTY HISTORICAL SOCIETY.

tion and served in this capacity until the late 1950s.

William Heising? (1857?–1861?)
R. Smith and Bro. (?–1869?)
Cascade Brewery (1869?–1881)
Location: South bank of Cascade Creek on Horton Avenue (now Ninth Avenue NW) between W. Seventh and Eighth streets (now Second and Third streets)

The origins of the Cascade Brewery are less clear than those of either of the other two major breweries in Rochester. While the *Rochester Post* gives a founding date of 1857 in an article describing a fire at the brewery, confirmation is elusive. William Heising appears as a brewer in the 1857 territorial census and the 1860 census and may have been the first proprietor of this brewery. (Heising started his brewery in Red Wing in 1861.) The firm of R. Smith and Bro. appears in the excise tax records and in the 1864 city directory; since it was slightly larger than City Brewery (see next listing), it is likely that Smith's operation was the precursor of the Cascade Brewery.

The first known mention of the Cascade Brewery by that name appears in 1869, when it was owned by J. F. Neuffer. The *Rochester Post* in 1871 noted that Neuffer "has been getting out a superior article of lager beer, and favored us with a sample keg of it that we found very refreshing, one of the hot days of this week." Mr. Neuffer died in the early 1870s, and his wife took over the business and ran it until around 1879. Her son-in-law, Joseph Bang, became the brewmaster and was eventually listed as the proprietor in 1880.

In 1875 Cascade Brewery became the second Rochester brewery to be reduced to ashes. Early on a Sunday morning in late September, the family awakened to find the brewery ablaze and was forced to flee without even pausing to take a change of clothes. The all-wood structure, built in several stages, burned rapidly, and the fire department was unable to save it. (Part of the reason was that the brewery was too far out of town, but another was that too few of the engine company members responded to pull the hand-drawn fire engine.) The loss amounted to several thousand dollars, and most of the insurance was on objects that were saved—the barn, horses, and wagons.

Mrs. Neuffer immediately began to rebuild both the residence and the brewery. The new $4,000 plant was a considerable improvement on the old one. The brewhouse was two stories high, with an additional elevation for the malt drying facility. A new cellar was dug, and the final touch was a 20 × 40 foot beer hall on the main floor. By 9 February 1876 the brewery was ready to host a grand opening celebration with a free lunch and a dance in the evening. (Notice of this event appeared in the newspaper immediately below an advertisement for a temperance lecture occurring the day before.) The building was not completed until two years later, when the brick exterior and ornamental stonework were finished.

While Joseph Bang continued to improve the brewery over the next two years, the beer business must have become less attractive to him. In late 1881 Marvin and Cammack leased the building and converted it into the Crescent Creamery. This change was probably a net benefit to Rochester, since by April 1882 the creamery was already employing 30 workers. Crescent Creamery was the predecessor of Marigold Foods, the producer of Kemps brand dairy products, which are found throughout the upper Midwest and in the Gulf Coast states.

City Brewery (?–1860)
Fred Troost (1860–1865?)
Chris Rappold (1866–1867)
Mrs. C. Rappold (1867–1869)
City Brewery (1869–1878?)
Neusuess & Troost (1878?–1882)
Location: Foot of Zumbro Street

Sometime before the outbreak of the Civil War, Fred Troost began brewing in Rochester. He is listed as a brewer in the 1860 census, and ads for his "Rochester Brewery" appeared in the *City Post* beginning in June 1860. The brewery may have started before Troost's era, since the advertisements say he had purchased the brewery. While the Troost family would be involved with the brewery in some way for much of its history, Civil War excise tax records of the mid-1860s list Chris Rappold as the proprietor. Rappold's brewery produced 286 barrels of beer during 1866, making it the smallest of the three Rochester breweries. Rappold made $1,500 worth of improvements during 1867, but he died shortly thereafter and did not see the fruit of his work. His widow carried on in his absence and apparently ran the brewery by herself until the end of 1869. Even after she hired Adam Stenger to be the superintendent, she remained the owner of the brewery for several years.

Adam Stenger came to City Brewery with several years of experience in London and St. Paul. His early advertisements, in which he offered "English and Scotch Ales, Porter and Brown Stout" in addition to lager, demonstrated his dedication to the English brewing tradition. He did not neglect lager, however. In 1871 he built a large beer cellar to age and store his increased production of this hot-weather favorite.

In December 1872, City Brewery provided a strange news item. Rochester had been hit by an epidemic that weakened half the horses in town. The *Rochester Post* reported, "A cow harnessed in a sled is the oddest advertisement on our streets of the horse disease. It is driven by young Troost in delivering beer from the City Brewery."

Animal maladies aside, City Brewery prospered over the next several years. Stenger added a malting facility in 1875, along with additional storage space. The next year, to honor the nation's centennial and his fiftieth birthday, he built a beer garden just inside the city limits and hosted numerous events there. The prosperity was not to last, however. City Brewery ended in the same way as too many other breweries. On 17 May 1882 the brewery caught fire. The building and the contents, valued between $4,000 and $5,000, were a total loss and were not insured. The *Rochester Post* claimed that this fire and another the same night "were the works of incendiaries," and editorialized the next week that the fires might have been set by "working class anarchists." The owners, Mrs. Neususess and Henry Troost, and their superintendent, Louis Schroeder, decided not to rebuild.

Rush City [Pine County]

Gustav Vietor (1872–1879)
Louis Fahrenholz (lessee) (1880–1881)
Rudolph Busselmeyer (1881)
Louis Fahrenholz (1881–1884)
Christensen (lessee) (1882)
Ferdinand Schnagl (1884–1894)
Nicolas Weid (1894–1898)
Rush City Brewing Co. (1898–1904)
Location: S. Grey Avenue between W. Fourth and W. Fifth streets

Gustav Vietor began brewing in Rush City in October 1872. He gained a good local reputation for quality and his business grew steadily. Tragedy struck in 1879 when Vietor died of typhoid fever at age 41. His wife, who was also stricken, recovered and leased the brewery to Louis Fahrenholz. Fahrenholz eventually bought the brewery and in turn leased it to Rudolph Busselmeyer. Fahrenholz and Busselmeyer had a dispute over a loan that ended up in court, and Busselmeyer was also charged with selling beer without a license. Busselmeyer left for Pine City (where his name was usually spelled Buselmeier) to start a brewery there, and according to the *Pine County Record* of 2 July 1881, "Fahrenholz is happy." Fahrenholz rented the brewery in April 1882 to Mr. Christensen, who appears to have operated the business for a short time.

Ferdinand Schnagl took over the brewery for ten years, then left for Crookston to run the brewery there, and finally ended up at Mantorville. The *Rush City Post* reported upon one of Schangl's return visits to Rush City that "the gentleman has grown more corpulent since he left this city, but his grip is just as warm." The brewery survived a fire during the first year of Nicholas Weid's tenure and stayed in business under different names until 1904. The telephone directory published in the *Post* in February 1903 includes two breweries, one under the name D. McGuire and the other under J. McLaughlin, who also owned a saloon. The *Post* offered no other evidence to prove whether Rush City actually had two breweries for a time.

The *Post* also reported in 1903 that Gustav Vietor Jr. was attending brewing school in Chicago, and thereby keeping both his father's memory and his business alive.

Rushford [Fillmore County]

Larson & Nelson (1865?)
S. Thompson (1866?–1867)
Gjernes & Reidy (1867–1868)
Gjernes & Pfaffin (1868)
Ochsele & Gjernes (1868–1873)
Oechsle & Schaupp (1873–1875)
Jacob Pfeiffer (1875–1901)
John Pfeiffer (1901–1905)
Estate of John Pfeiffer (1905–1907)
Location: 303 N. Elm Street

Alden O. Droivold's *History of Rushford: Whiskey, Wheat and Wagons* states that the Rushford brewery was built in 1867 by Gjernes and Reidy. However, excise records indicate that a brewery operated by Larson and Nelson sold eight and a half barrels of beer in June 1866. The *Southern Minnesotian's* listing of Rushford's new buildings in 1867 includes a $6,500 brewery built by S. Thompson, which only confuses the matter more. Gjernes and Reidy are in the excise records of 1867, but for the next several years the proprietor listed in the tax records changed frequently.

Jacob Pfeiffer purchased the brewery in 1875 and operated it for the next twenty-six years. The brewery was powered by horse and had a capacity at this point of ten barrels per day. Pfeiffer gradually expanded output despite occasional bouts of local prohibition. Sometimes advertised as the Sand Hill Brewery, the brewery was still allowed to operate during the dry periods, provided Pfeiffer did not sell beer in town. In 1889 Pfeiffer went on trial for selling beer at smaller quantities than his wholesale license allowed—in other words, for selling beer by the glass at the brewery. Ironically, the trial was held after the dry ordinance was lifted. The *Winona Daily Republican* reported that Pfeiffer sold 7,000 kegs of beer in 1885, but it is unlikely these were full barrels.

Jacob Pfeiffer retired in 1901 after the death of his wife, Anna, and their son John took over the brewery. Unfortunately, John fell into a vat of boiling water in June 1905 and died of his burns. Jacob attempted to operate the brewery himself, but he died in 1906 of complications from a gallstone operation. The brewery passed to John's widow, but she sold it to Peter Schief of Milwaukee. He was unable to complete the deal, so the brewery

This rare label from Pfeiffer's Rushford brewery appears to be a stock label with the name of the city and brewer printed in the available spaces. The metallic copper-colored background makes an otherwise simple label much more attractive. FROM THE COLLECTION OF DAVE WENDL.

was sold twice more and eventually torn down in 1909.

Erickson & Ibach (1867)
Ibach & Oleson (1867–1868?)
Oleson & Ackerman (1869?–1870)
Erick Oleson (1870–1873?)
Location: South of Rushford

A brewery sometimes called the South Rushford Brewery is mentioned in a few newspaper accounts and appears in excise records from 1867 to 1870. It was built during 1867 at a cost of $4,000, which suggests it was somewhat smaller than its competitor in Rushford proper. Joseph Ibach also had a brewery in Preston at this time, and while he may have split his time between the two breweries, it is also possible he was merely an investor in the Rushford enterprise. Local historian Alden O. Droivold speculated that the brewery ran into financial trouble during the Panic of 1873 and was unable to compete with the larger brewery in Rushford.

St. Charles [Winona County]

F. W. Mueller (1875–1879)
Henius & Co. (1879–1880)
John Waltham (1881–1884)
Pfister & Waller (1884–1890)
Location: North end of Whitewater Avenue, on the west side near Second Street

The *Winona Daily Republican* reported in 1874 that "it is rumored that Winona parties are to build a brewery at St. Charles." However, William Mueller, the proprietor, was actually from Rochester. The brewery was in operation by the end of the year, and Mueller produced almost 250 barrels in his first year. By 1878 production was more than 900 barrels. The brewery underwent several ownership changes during the next five years, until it was purchased by "parties from Iowa."

Pfister and Waller took over the brewery in 1884, but had two major misfortunes during their tenure as proprietors. In 1887 a fifty-barrel tank of malt broke through the brewery floor and the contents spilled into the cellar. In July 1890 brewery worker John Schurt, who slept in the brewery, discovered the building was on fire. He was able to escape and give the alarm, but the fire company did not arrive until it was too late. The brewery was destroyed, but the stables, icehouse, and cellar were saved.

Pfister and Waller tried to make the best of the situation by selling the remaining kegs of beer before they spoiled at fifty cents each. They elected not to rebuild the brewery.

St. Cloud [Stearns County]

Kramer & Seberger (1857?–1863)
Peter Kramer (1863–1866)
Kramer & Schaefer (1866–1867)
Schaefer & Meyers (1868–1869)
George Schaefer (1869–1871)
Location: Near Lake George (caves on the riverbank between Third and Fourth streets)

Kramer and Seberger began brewing in St. Cloud sometime between 1857 and 1859. Neither is listed in the 1857 territorial census, but the firm is listed in the 1860 Census of Industry, with production of 500 barrels in the previous year. The partners continued to expand production, selling an average of fifty barrels per week in 1863 and 1864. The arrival of Frank Funk and Lorenz Enderle in St. Cloud cut into business dramatically, and for the next few years the three (and later four) breweries in the city all sold about twenty barrels per month.

Kramer left brewing in 1867, and the firm quickly lost ground to the other breweries in St. Cloud. Schaefer sold only 317 barrels in the 1870–71 tax year, by far the fewest in the city. In August 1871, the excise collector noted that Scheffer [*sic*] had stopped production and had petitioned to be exempted from tax on the last forty barrels of his stock, which had soured.

Enderle & Hoffman (1864–1865)
Lorenz Enderle (1865–1882)
Schindler & Co. (1882–1891)
Wendelin Merz (1891–1893)
Caroline Merz (1893–1896)
Valentine Udermann (1896–1909)
Val. Udermann Brewing Co. (1909–1916)
Location: Sixth Avenue N. between Sixth and Seventh streets

Lorenz Enderle built a brewery near a creek in 1864 with Mr. Hoffman, but by the next year Enderle was sole proprietor. Enderle, described by the *St. Cloud Democrat* as "lately of New Ulm" joined a nearly even race with the other two St. Cloud breweries. In 1865 all three breweries averaged sales of about twenty barrels per month. By 1879 Enderle had expanded sales to nearly 1,600 barrels per year, though this was still well below the capacity of 15,000 barrels he quoted when offering the brewery for sale in 1882.

Wendelin Merz, M. Schindler, and J. H. Eich purchased the brewery from Enderle for $10,000 and continued to expand the business. The *St. Cloud Journal Press* reported in 1888 that Schindler and Co. employed six men and made 2,400 barrels of beer during the previous year.

In 1891 Wendelin Merz purchased Schindler's share in the brewery (Eich sold his some years previously) and moved from St. Joseph to take the lead in managing the brewery. In 1893 Merz completely rebuilt the brewery at a cost of $30,000, but tragically died later that year. His widow, Caroline, took over management of the brewery and kept it going for the next few years.

Valentine Udermann purchased the brewery in 1896. Sometimes known as the Empire Brewery during this time, it had a capacity of 5,000 barrels per year. In 1909 a group of

This unusual blue design (c. 1900) was produced by the same process as for the Fuermann Brewing Co. glass pictured in this section. Udermann's name is spelled here with only one n; in other sources it has two. FROM THE COLLECTION OF PAT STAMBAUGH.

saloon owners purchased the brewery and incorporated it as Val. Udermann Brewing Co. Newspaper articles claimed that thirty-five saloons were ready to do business with the new company. The brewery remained in business until 1916.

Frank Funk (1864–1870)
Funk & Thiery (1870–1876)
Remelly & Thiery, City Brewery (1876–1880)
Balder & Weber (1881–1886)
Frank Balder (1886–1895)
Fred Zertler (1895–1897)
Location: 518 Eighth Avenue between Fifth and Sixth streets

Frank Funk became the second brewer in St. Cloud when he produced seven barrels of beer in November 1864, one month before Enderle and Hoffman began making beer. Business continued to grow to the point where the brewery sold almost 1,200 barrels of beer per year in the late 1870s. The horse-powered brewery burned down in a spectacular fire in 1878, though the hops, beer, and company safe were all saved.

Nick Weber and Frank Balder purchased the brewery in 1881. In 1886 they raised the tower on the malt house to 65 feet, making it one of the tallest structures in the neighborhood. Weber retired in 1886 and moved to Montana, leaving Balder as sole proprietor. In 1887 Balder employed thirteen men who produced 6,000 barrels of beer. According to the 1888–89 city directory, the brewery had its own cooperage and bottling house and got its water from a nearby spring. Fred Zertler operated the brewery for two years before it closed. The structure remained vacant for several years but was eventually converted to the St. Cloud Woolen Mills.

Herberger Bros. (1867–1872?)
Herberger & Schmidt (1872?–1876)
John Brick (1876–1882)
Brick and Legler (1882–1884)
Preiss & Wimmer (1884–1900)
Preiss & Wimmer Brewing Co. (1900–1912)
Preiss Brewing Co. (1912–1920)
St. Cloud Brewing Co. (1933–1939)
Location: Ninth Avenue between Sixth and Seventh streets

According to *One Hundred Years of Brewing*, Fritz Herberger began brewing in St. Cloud in 1857. Neither the 1857 territorial census nor

the 1860 census lists Herberger as a brewer, and the Herberger brewery does not appear in the excise records until 1867, and then under Carl Herberger. On 11 June 1864, the *St. Cloud Times* reported that Herberger was starting a wagon shop on Washington Street, so it seems likely that the *One Hundred Years* account is off by ten years (or confused Herberger with Seberger). The brewery remained in the Herberger family until 1876, when it was purchased by John Brick, recently arrived from Canada.

Brick was only 25 years old when he took over the brewery, but quickly became a popular figure in St. Cloud. He maintained the brewery's position as the largest in St. Cloud and advertised heavily in the German-language *Nordstern*. He had a saloon and a hotel connected with the brewery and actively sought the patronage of families. In May 1879 he published a long poem touting the virtues of his bock beer. Sources differ on when Brick left brewing, but he died in May 1886. He had been in poor health for several months, and his condition was exacerbated by the cyclone of 1886, which he survived only by clinging to the lightning rod of his house. His funeral was said to have been the largest ever in St. Cloud.

The firm of Preiss and Wimmer steadily expanded what came to be known as the St. Cloud Steam Brewery over the next two decades. Before 1888 they installed a thirty-two-horsepower steam engine to power the brewery and produced twenty-five barrels a day with ten employees. For the next several years, the *St. Cloud Journal-Times* announced new building projects at the brewery. The company was incorporated in 1900, and over the next several years added a new bottling house, enlarged it soon after, built a new ice plant, and prepared to double the capacity of the brewery. It appears that the expansion took a financial toll on the company, since it filed for bankruptcy in 1909. The firm went into receivership, but continued to operate until Prohibition.

During Prohibition the brewery was converted to the Nicolin Beverage Co. J. H. Nicolin, who had been the manager of Jacob Schmidt Brewing Company since it began in 1900, began to produce soft drinks in the plant. The brewery was raided and seized in 1920 and

1921 by federal agents who found real beer being brewed for shipment to the Twin Cities.

When beer was legalized again in 1933, Nicolin began converting the plant back into a brewery. St. Cloud Brewing was not ready for the first day of legal beer, but did have Old Heidelberg beer in bars by July and in bottles by November. Despite obtaining the services of experienced brewmaster Ernst Weiss, St. Cloud Brewing was not able to make a sufficient profit and was forced to close in spring 1939. Civic leaders met to see if they could create a plan to keep the brewery open and retain the forty jobs it provided, but to no avail.

St. Joseph (Stearns County)

Louis Brink (1862–1875?)
Location: Near County Road 138 and Seventy-fourth Avenue S.

Sometime before fall 1862, Louis Brink began brewing in St. Joseph, a town about six miles west of St. Cloud (though today the sense of separation has diminished with the expansion of St. Cloud). One map locates the brewery on the Section 13 township line near the Waite Park to Rockville Road and the creek. The same map declares that Brink's was the first brewery in Stearns County, though no date is given. By the time the federal excise tax was implemented in 1862, Brink (sometimes spelled Brenk) was producing at least four barrels per month, and he continued to brew similarly modest amounts for the next several years. In some months, the excise records specifically note that Brink did no business. It appears that he tried to supplement his brewing income by distilling, since an article in the *St. Cloud Journal-Press* in November 1872 reported that Brink had been arrested for making liquor, which he claimed was "only vinegar." The paper also noted that it was Brink's second offense and predicted that the trial "might go hard with him."

In 1875 the St. Joseph brewery changed hands as the Maurin brothers of Cold Spring took over the operation. Brink moved northwest to Frazee (perhaps feeling that the revenue agents were less likely to bother him further out in the countryside) and started the Frazee City Brewery there (see the Frazee entry). No records exist of the Maurin brothers operating the St. Joseph brewery. The building was later converted to a dwelling, which burned to the ground in March 1881.

St. Michael (Wright County)

Zahler Bros. (1862–1869)
Zahler & Weiss (1869–1871)
George Weiss (1871–1888)
Dick Bros. (1888–1891)
Location: Near the Crow River

According to Curtiss-Wedge's *History of Wright County,* the Zahler brothers built the first brewery in Wright County in 1862, though they do not appear in the excise records until 1864. The brewery burned in 1867, and Joseph Zahler rebuilt it with the help of George Weiss, since his brother Michael had moved to Waconia to start his own brewery.

In 1871 George Weiss became sole proprietor, but was even less fortunate with fire than the Zahlers. The brewery burned shortly after Weiss took over, and then again in 1877. Weiss rebuilt the brewery in a more substantial manner, but it burned again in 1884. Weiss took a couple of years to rebuild this time, but was back in production by 1887. Excise records suggest that Weiss leased the brewery to Frey and Zahler for at least a year in the early 1880s. The Dick brothers operated the brewery briefly before it closed for good.

The frequent changes of proprietor and address (sometimes caused by changes in municipal boundaries) have led some researchers to conclude that there was more than one brewery in the township. Some lists include a brewery in Frankfort Township or in Hanover, but no evidence has been found that conclusively shows a second brewery in the area, and the site was part of Frankfort and Hanover at different times. Weiss was listed as a brewer in all three locations, but local sources do not mention him operating three different breweries.

St. Paul (Ramsey County)

Anthony Yoerg (1849–1896)
Yoerg Brewing Co. (1896–1920)
Yoerg Brewing Co. (1933–1952)

Locations: S. Washington Street between Chestnut and Eagle (1849–1871); 229 Ohio Street (1871–1952)

Anthony Yoerg established Minnesota's first commercial brewery in 1849. Some sources suggest that the brewery began operations a year earlier, but the earliest accounts agree on the later year. Within a few years, other breweries entered the St. Paul market, and their rapid growth relegated the pioneer brewery to a position as a midsize brewery after about fifteen years. Yoerg's location near the levee in St. Paul offered access to water transportation and allowed for caves to be excavated into the nearby bluffs, so other breweries were established nearby.

Yoerg eventually outgrew the cramped space on the east bank of the Mississippi and moved to a new location on the West Side in 1871. By 1880 he had installed steam power, excavated cellars into the bluff behind his brewery, and expanded his capacity to approximately 20,000 barrels per year. It appears that much of this capacity was unused since production figures for 1879 list his output at just under 3,000 barrels. The family remodeled the brewery again in 1885 to make the brewery more efficient.

Yoerg never expanded his business to the same degree as rivals Hamm and Stahlmann, though his son Louis established a separate brewery in Hudson, Wisconsin, in 1870. The St. Paul brewery had depots and agencies in scattered locations throughout the state, including one in Moorhead that opened in 1888. During this period, the brewery employed between fifteen and twenty men annually, including brewmaster Joseph Slappi, who earned $50 each month. Employees were also compensated with free beer—Internal Revenue forms filed in 1883 recorded that fifteen barrels were consumed in the brewery each month. If this consumption was limited to employees, this would be a gallon of beer per day per man.

During the 1890s the brewery offered Pilsner, Culmbacher, and Export beers in addition to its lager, or Standard beer. A trade leaflet in the collections of the Ramsey County Historical Society emphasized that Yoerg's beers were made with Minnesota barley and Washington hops, since "we think it our duty to patronize our American industries, and do not intend to deceive the public by stating to them that we only use the best Imported Hops and Barely."

Yoerg's brewery seems to have avoided most of the calamities to which breweries were prone and was seldom mentioned in the news. It suffered few major fires or natural disasters, though one young employee of the brewery cracked his skull in 1878 while attempting to kick a thief (the man survived the fall). When Anthony Yoerg died in July 1896, he had presided over almost fifty years of brewing in Minnesota and had built a business that had a steady market in the region, even if it did not compare to the local or out-of-town giants. Yoerg's five sons all ended up taking leadership positions in the family business and helped the company avoid the problems that other breweries experienced with ownership changes. Anthony's grandson Alfred Yoerg was the president when the company finally went out of business in 1952.

During Prohibition Yoerg Brewing went into the dairy business to survive the dry years, but according to an article by James B. Bell in *Ramsey County History* (Summer 1996), Yoerg Milk Company was unable to compete against the four large dairies already established in the city. When beer was legalized again in 1933, Yoerg returned to brewing, with some initial success. The company offered a few promotions, such as a deal in which customers who collected eight coupons from cases of beer could redeem them for a deck of

In contrast to the more common masculine imagery used to sell beer, Yoerg's proclaimed its Royal Export "the Queen of Beers." The label is probably from the 1890s. The source of the handwriting is unknown. FROM THE COLLECTION OF KEN MALZ.

cards. However, the small size of the brewery made it extremely difficult to compete with gigantic neighbors Hamm and Schmidt. The brewery was in financial hardship for several years before it finally closed in 1952, though it survived long enough to become one of the handful of Minnesota breweries to celebrate a century of business.

Martin Bruggemann (1853–1855?)

Bruggemann & Schweitzer (1855?–1864)

Martin Bruggemann (1864–1897)

Estate of Martin Bruggemann (1897–1900)

Aiple Brewing Co. (1900–1905)

Locations: Corner of Sixth and Pleasant (now Smith and Kellogg) (1853–1872); corner of Channel and Edward (south of Wabasha Street) (1872–1905)

According to St. Paul historian Gary Brueggemann (no relation), Martin Bruggemann started his brewing career in a house near the corner of Smith and Kellogg. His first brewery burned, so he built a new one near Assumption Church.

Bruggemann started small, but by 1866 was selling as many as 175 barrels of beer during hot summer months. His brewery could not keep up with demand, so he followed the lead of Anthony Yoerg and moved across the Mississippi River to a location at the foot of the sandstone caves west of Wabasha Street. This new brewery enabled him to approach a production level of 2,000 barrels by 1879.

Martin Bruggemann continued to brew until his death in 1897, at which point his sons John and Frank took over the brewery. The sons ran the brewery for three years until they sold it to Aiple Brewing of Stillwater, which operated the plant for five years.

North Mississippi Brewery, unknown founder
    (1853–1856)

Mr. Rowe (1856–1859)

Charles Rausch (1859–1862?)

Jacob Bensberg (1862?–1866)

F. A. Renz (1867)

Frederick & William Banholzer (1871–1879)

William Banholzer (1879–1897)

William Banholzer Estate (1897–1898)

Locations: Corner of Robert and Seventh (1853–1867); above Shepherd Road near Drake Street and Stewart Avenue (1871–1898)

The early years of the North Mississippi Brewery are confused by incomplete and conflicting accounts. Neill's *History of Ramsey County* pro-

The Banholzer family and the brewery employees posed for this picture in 1889. Unlike many photographs of brewery employees, this one does not picture the employees with the tools of their trade nor does it show a full range of bottled and kegged beer or any signs with the brewery's name. Even if names were not written on the photograph, William Banholzer could be identified by his appearance, especially by the watch chain draped across his vest. COURTESY OF THE MINNESOTA HISTORICAL SOCIETY.

vides the dates of founding and of the transfers to Rowe and Bensberg. Charles Rausch's term is known only for an event reported in the German-language *Minnesota National Demokrat* in April 1859 and embellished in Newson's *Pen Pictures of St. Paul*. Brewmaster Karl Katzenberger fell into the mash tun and was scalded by the hot, sticky mash. Rumors spread throughout the city that the beer was contaminated and Rausch had to sell at a sizeable loss.

Jacob Bensberg is listed in the excise records from 1863 to 1866, though he may have taken over from Rausch earlier. According to excise records, Bensberg's brewery was quite large—in some of the hot summer months he sold more than 200 barrels of beer, and during 1863 and 1864 he sold more beer than Chris Stahlmann. Apparently Bensberg had been able to restore confidence in the brewery. However, F. A. Renz suffered a fire soon after he bought the brewery and was forced to abandon the enterprise.

The brewery was reconstructed in 1871 by Frederick and William Banholzer, a father-and-son team that increased the size of the brewery and restored its reputation. Capacity was increased to 12,000 barrels by 1881, even though production in 1879 was just over 600 barrels. William Banholzer was able to build

a stone mansion on Stewart Avenue with the profits from his business. William died in 1897, and Frederick was unwilling to return to the brewery business, so the brewery was closed as soon as the company's affairs could be settled.

Gottfried Fleckenstein, St. Paul Brewery and
    Lager Beer (1855–1857)

Location: Corner of Main and Exchange

The accounts of Gottfried Fleckenstein's brewing career report that he spent approximately two years operating a brewery in St. Paul. This is confirmed by his presence in the 1856–57 city directory. Many of the same accounts suggest that his brother Ernst was also involved in the St. Paul operation, but he does not appear in the city directory. Little is known about the history of this brewery since it operated before the imposition of excise tax and newspaper coverage of small businesses was very limited.

Christopher Stahlmann, Cave Brewery (1855–1882)

Christopher Stahlmann Brewing Co. (1882–1898)

St. Paul Brewing Co. (1898–1900)

Jacob Schmidt Brewing Company (1900–1954)

Pfeiffer Brewing Co. (Jacob Schmidt Brewing
    Company) (1954–1962)

Associated Brewing Company (Pfeiffer, Schmidt)
    (1962–1972)

G. Heileman Brewing Company (1972–1990)

Minnesota Brewing Company (1991–2002)

Location: 882 W. Seventh Street

While Christopher Stahlmann was not the first brewer in St. Paul (nor the second or even the third), his brewery quickly became the largest in the state. By 1860 production had reached 1,200 barrels per year and Stahlmann was exporting lager as far south as Memphis, Tennessee. In 1879 Stahlmann became the first Minnesota brewer to sell more than 10,000 barrels in a year. According to *Wing's Brewers Handbook* of 1887, capacity of the brewery was almost 25,000 barrels per year. Stahlmann was one of the first brewers in Minnesota to bottle his own beer, and newspaper advertisements from around the state during the late 1870s suggest that it enjoyed wide distribution.

Unfortunately, Stahlmann died of tuberculosis in 1883, and the business was not nearly as successful without him. According to St. Paul historian Gary Brueggemann, each of Christopher's three sons also succumbed to tuberculosis over the next decade, and these experienced men who had been trained in the family business were replaced by George Mitsch, who was not equal to the task. In 1897 the brewery was sold to St. Paul Brewing Company, but this company only lasted for three years before selling the brewery property to Jacob Schmidt Brewing Company.

Jacob Schmidt started his Minnesota career as Theodore Hamm's brewmaster, but William Constans lured him away to rejuvenate the struggling North Star Brewing Co. The company recovered and prospered, and in 1899 Schmidt turned over a large portion of his share of the brewery to a new corporation led by his son-in-law Adolph Bremer and Adolph's brother Otto. A disastrous fire in 1900 left Schmidt and the new management team without a brewery, but St. Paul Brewing had a brewery in need of vigorous new leadership. Jacob Schmidt Brewing Company bought

Early in the twentieth century, prohibitionists, prompted in part by a case in 1900 of arsenic contamination in Manchester, England, claimed that brewers adulterated their beer with poisonous chemicals. Many brewers countered these charges by offering a $1,000 reward to anyone who could prove the beer was impure. By the time this label appeared in 1914, the offer was so common on labels that there was no need to explain what the reward was for. By the next year, the label simply advertised "$1000 Natural Process Beer" with no reference to the reward. FROM THE COLLECTION OF DAVE WENDL.

the former Stahlmann brewery site and immediately began building an all-new brewery and many other structures. Jacob Schmidt died in 1911, but the Bremers were skilled businessmen, and the firm continued to grow. The company brewed a range of products including Export Beer (later replaced with Natural

Process Beer) and Salvator (a dark beer that was replaced by Dunkelbrau).

On 1 July 1919 a dramatic change appeared in the company's shipping records as wartime prohibition took effect and beer sales were banned. Schmidt's Malta, a near beer, now became the best-selling product. Though the brewery made a wide range of products, including eight different soft drinks, Jacob Schmidt Brewing Company was one of the few breweries in the nation to experience any real success with its "temperance beer." Malta and City Club Select were both supported with advertising campaigns equal to those launched on behalf of the company's beers. The brewery even introduced Easter Special, which appears to have been an attempt to offer a bock-style near beer during the spring. Of course, rumors flew that the brewery was continuing to produce real beer, though no documentary proof has ever been found.

When beer was re-legalized in April 1933, Schmidt was ready with City Club on the first day. Supported by a large advertising campaign, City Club quickly became one of the best-selling beers in the upper Midwest. In 1936 Schmidt was the seventh-largest brewery in America, and though other breweries passed it in size, the company continued to grow. The Bremers recognized the potential benefits of offering City Club in cans and Jacob Schmidt Brewing became one of the first Minnesota breweries to offer beer in cans. Like Hamm's, Schmidt's first cans were flat-tops, which required new equipment but yielded greater cost savings than cone-top cans. However, Schmidt was one of the rare breweries that changed from flat-tops to cone-tops. When the familiar oval City Club logo first appeared on cans, it was in the cone-top container.

City Club was proclaimed "Tops . . . in any town" and was indeed one of the best-selling brands in the upper Midwest. Jacob Schmidt Brewing had a contract to supply City Club to the U.S. government during World War II, and Otto Bremer's long friendship with Franklin D. Roosevelt may have helped end the brewery truckers' strike in favor of the brewers in 1945. (The full story of the strike is presented in chapter 6.)

After Otto Bremer died in 1951, the brewery went through a series of management changes, and in 1954 the brewery was sold to Pfeiffer Brewing Company of Detroit. A change of equal significance was made in the early 1950s when the City Club brand was phased out in favor of Schmidt Beer. Acceptance of the new brand was helped greatly by the introduction of the scenic can series—one of the most attractive sets of cans produced by any brewery. This long-running series was continued despite ownership and name changes, so many variations of these cans exist. Ironically, the St. Paul branch of Pfeiffer outlasted the original Detroit brewery, which was not efficient enough to be competitive in the national market.

After eighteen years with Pfeiffer and its successor, Associated Brewing Company, the brewery was sold to G. Heileman Brewing Company of La Crosse, Wisconsin. As under Pfeiffer, the former Schmidt brewery was just one of several plants in a large corporate empire, but the St. Paul branch consistently rivaled the La Crosse branch in efficiency and production. In addition to Schmidt Beer and other Schmidt products, many of the Heileman brands were produced in St. Paul, including Old Style and Blatz. Grain Belt and Hauenstein were added to the brewery's lineup when Heileman purchased the brands from the defunct Grain Belt Brewing Company. While Old Style and Schmidt were brewed to the original recipes, retired brewery employees report that many of the other labels packaged by the brewery were just Schmidt Beer in different cans or bottles.

Under the management of Roy Kumm, and later Russell Cleary, G. Heileman pursued a strategy in which the company purchased struggling regional breweries throughout the country. Heileman continued to produce those local brands that maintained a loyal following and used the excess capacity to produce the company's other brands. While this plan made Heileman the fourth-largest brewing company in the country by 1981, the company was still vulnerable to competitive and financial pressures. Australian corporate raider Alan Bond purchased the company in 1987, which caused Heileman to become part of the largest financial collapse in Australian history. Heileman closed the brewery in 1990, despite the efforts of St. Paul city leaders to preserve the business and the hundreds of jobs that would be lost.

The plant remained idle for more than a year until it was reopened as Minnesota Brewing Company in 1991 by a group of local investors. Minnesota Brewing Company tapped the first keg of Landmark beer in December 1991, but its first real success was Pig's Eye Pilsner, first released in 1992. Minnesota Brewing began to revitalize the Grain Belt brand and won a gold medal at the Great American Beer Festival in 1994. The brewery also brewed and packaged dozens of different brands for other beer companies, including the Pete's Wicked line of beers. However, the brewery faced numerous problems with old or inadequate equipment and was stuck in a position where the brewery was not large enough to compete

The spectacular City Club sign on top of the Marigold Ballroom at 1336 Nicollet Avenue was a worthy rival to the Grain Belt sign on Nicollet Island at the other end of downtown Minneapolis. While City Club may have been "Tops in Any Town" (including rival Minneapolis), Grain Belt was not as successful in St. Paul. This photograph was taken in May 1953, in the last days of the famous target logo and shortly before the sale of Jacob Schmidt Brewing Company to Pfeiffer. PHOTOGRAPH BY NORTON & PEEL; COURTESY OF THE MINNESOTA HISTORICAL SOCIETY.

CONTENTS 12 FL. OZS.

صانع شمت سينت بال الامريكيه

شراب الغلال الممتاز

الخالي من الكحول

صنع حصيصا

عبد الهادي بن عبد الله التطاني واولاده بالدمام

PRODUCT OF J. SCHMIDT BREWING CO.
ST. PAUL, MINN., U.S.A.
NON-TAXABLE UNDER SECTION 5051 I.R.C.

Schmidt SELECT

America's Most Famous Cereal Beverage

NON-ALCOHOLIC

This unusual can from the early 1950s represents an attempt by Schmidt to market near beer in Saudi Arabia. The plan was discarded when Saudi authorities decided that one-half of 1 percent was still too much alcohol, and a shipment of thousands of cases had to be dumped in the desert. FROM THE COLLECTION OF DAVE WENDL.

The brewery was relatively small by St. Paul standards in the mid-1860s, but it was growing. The most barrels sold in a month in 1864 was forty; two years later, Frederick Emmert and Schweitzer sold nearly 200 barrels in each of the summer months. Emmert's brewery boasted a capacity of 6,000 barrels by 1880, and throughout the 1870s it usually produced close to 3,000 barrels each year.

Emmert died in 1889, and his sons took over City Brewery and renamed it in honor of their late father. The sons sold the brewery to Theo. Hamm Brewing, which used it for a storage facility.

J. B. Arnold (1859?–1860?)
Location: Reserve Township, on the east bank of the river, south of Iglehart Avenue (now Desnoyer Park)

One of the bigger mysteries in St. Paul's brewing history concerns what happened to J. B. Arnold. He is recorded as having produced 1,000 barrels of beer in 1860, second in the state behind only Chris Stahlmann. He had two employees listed in the population census: John Bernard and Sebastian Gehring, who would later become a partner in a brewery in Jordan. Aside from the 1860 census, Arnold appears nowhere else.

This envelope from Frederick Emmert Brewing Company bears instructions to return the letter if it is not claimed, recalling a time when many postal customers had to pick up their mail at the post office. FROM THE AUTHOR'S COLLECTION.

with the major national brands but was too large to produce small amounts of craft beer efficiently. Financial problems forced the brewery to close for good in 2002, though an industrial ethanol plant remained open for two more years.

The history of this brewery is covered in more detail throughout the book, especially in chapters 1, 6, 7, and 8. Other photographs of artifacts can be found throughout these chapters as well.

Dominick Troyer, City Brewery (1855–1860)
Funk & Schweitzer (1860–1866)
Emmert & Schweitzer (1866–1871)
Frederick Emmert (1871–1889)
Fred. Emmert Brewing Co. (1889–1901)
Location: 168–170 Exchange Street

Dominick Troyer started City Brewery in 1855. He decided to return to Europe, so he sold the brewery to William Funk and Ullrich Schweitzer (sometimes spelled Switzer).

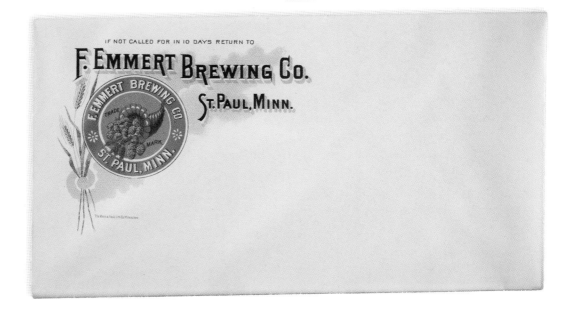

IF NOT CALLED FOR IN 10 DAYS RETURN TO

F. EMMERT BREWING CO.
ST. PAUL, MINN.

F. EMMERT BREWING CO.
TRADE MARK
ST. PAUL, MINN.

Andrew Keller, Pittsburg Brewery, Excelsior
    Brewery (1859?–1864)
Theodore Hamm (1864–1896)
Theodore Hamm Brewing Co. (1896–1920)
Theo. Hamm Brewing Co. (1933–1975)
Olympia Brewing Company (1975–1983)
Stroh Brewing Company (1983–1997)
Location: East Minnehaha and Payne Avenue

Andrew Keller probably started Pittsburg Brewery before 1860 (the date given in some sources), since in the year before the 1860 Census of Industry he had produced 850 barrels of beer, an unlikely total for an infant brewery to produce in just half a year. To expand his renamed Excelsior Brewery, Keller sought help from Theodore Hamm, a St. Paul hotel and saloonkeeper, who took out a mortgage on the property. Keller was unable to pay back the loan, and Hamm, somewhat by accident, found himself the proprietor of a brewery. When Hamm's brewery first appeared in the excise records in 1865, it was only the fifth largest in St. Paul. Two decades later it would be the largest in the state.

The brewery was located near Phalen Creek, which provided water for brewing, cleaning, and putting out any fires that might break out. The property also had room in which the brewery could expand, as it indeed did. Under the management of brewmasters Jacob Schmidt and Charles Fritschle, the brewery expanded output to more than 8,000 barrels by 1879 and nearly tripled this figure a few years later. The increasing production required additional labor, so Hamm hired additional employees. The single men lived near the brewery in dormitories managed by Hamm's wife, Louise. Louise also managed the beer garden, which became known for its family atmosphere and fine food. But according to historian and Hamm family descendant John T. Flanagan, Theodore Hamm preferred raising livestock and managing the operations of the nearby Brainard Flouring Mills, in which he was a partner.

Hamm's brewery expanded rapidly and eventually occupied several city blocks. The brewery's trade extended throughout Minnesota and into Dakota Territory. To meet the growing demand, a massive new brewery was built in 1894, making Hamm's one of the largest breweries northwest of Chicago. The brew-

ery was among the first in the state to bottle beer, and its products were shipped throughout the upper Midwest through an extensive network of depots and agencies. In small towns and cities throughout the state, Hamm placed regular ads in weekly newspapers to compete against out-of-state brewers, and did so with a large degree of success. (Photographs and artifacts from this era appear in chapter 4.)

Theodore Hamm died in 1903, and his son William took over the family firm. (Theodore's wife, Louise, had died seven years earlier.)

Company events such as the Drivers' Picnic were a way in which even giant brewing companies like Theo. Hamm could maintain a paternalistic family atmosphere and discourage strikes. COURTESY OF THE MINNESOTA HISTORICAL SOCIETY.

An early example of contract brewing, Prince of Pilsen was probably brewed by Hamm's for St. Croix Mercantile Co. around 1900. Note the unusual volume of 1 pint 7 ounces. FROM THE COLLECTION OF DAVE WENDL.

William was trained as a manager rather than a brewmaster, but the brewing side of operations was in the capable hands of Chris Figge. By 1915 the brewery was capable of producing 600,000 barrels of beer annually—not in the same category as the million-barrel producers Pabst, Schlitz, and Anheuser-Busch, but still among the largest in the Midwest. As nearby states began to go dry, the brewery began to lose business, and the adoption of wartime prohibition in 1919 forced the company to cease brewing beer. The brewery remained open during Prohibition, producing Excelso near beer and a variety of soft drinks. The economic consequences to the family were cushioned by the business of Hamm Realty Company (today known as United Properties), which included

The appearance of a camel and a desert on a cherry soda label may have been related to the Rudolph Valentino craze during the 1920s. It also could be symbolic of this product being a way for Hamm's to make it through a long dry period. FROM THE COLLECTION OF DAVE WENDL.

the opening of the graceful Hamm Building on St. Peter Street in downtown St. Paul in 1919.

When legal beer returned, the Hamm brewery quickly returned to regional prominence under the leadership of William Hamm Jr. and William Figge. Hamm was the victim of a dramatic kidnapping by the Barker-Karpis gang in 1933 that drew national attention to the extent to which organized crime infected St. Paul. Despite this temporary distraction, the brewery expanded both its territory and its plant until it was at one point the fifth-largest brewery in the nation. In 1949 William Figge Sr. died after 55 years of service to the company and his son William became the new brewmaster. Three years later, Figge became president of the company. The brewery ex-

panded into nearly every state and became a prominent sponsor of sporting events and broadcasts. During the 1950s Minnesota had no major league baseball or football team and only one major university, so Hamm sponsored teams at many levels of competition all over the country—the most noteworthy being the Chicago White Sox and the Chicago Cubs. Hamm purchased breweries in California, Texas, and Maryland. (Additional information about Hamm Brewing's expansion may be found in chapter 7.)

The most enduring aspect of the Hamm legacy came to life in the early 1950s, when a new advertising campaign was developed around a bumbling cartoon bear. The Hamm's Bear, originally intended for use only in cartoons, eventually became three-dimensional in manifestations ranging from a salt shaker a few inches tall to a life-sized Hamm's Bear costume. The bear was retired in the late 1960s, but returned as a result of popular demand (though in a different form). In 2005 the bear was memorialized in stone on the plaza near the Hamm Building. (For more on the Hamm's Bear, including illustrations, see the sidebar in chapter 7.)

A century of family ownership and management at Hamm's came to an end in October 1965, when the brewery was sold to Heublein Inc., a food and beverage conglomerate based in Hartford, Connecticut. The brewery fared well under the new ownership at first, but by 1971 the brewery was losing money. A group of Hamm's distributors bought the company from Heublein in 1971, but they in turn sold it to Olympia Brewing Company of Tumwater, Washington, in 1975. In 1983 Pabst purchased Olympia and its brands, but the St. Paul brewery was traded to Stroh Brewing Company of Detroit to avoid antitrust action by the federal government. The brewery continued to operate until 1997, brewing the Stroh's brands, a variety of other labels, and even Schmidt's City Club. Much of the brewery complex still stands, though some of the oldest buildings have been damaged by van-

Hamm joined many other national brewers in offering beer in 16-ounce cans. They were not as popular as the 12-ounce size, so the cans are less common today. The striking starburst design was introduced in the early 1950s. This version has a slot in the top to serve as a coin bank. FROM THE COLLECTION OF DAVE WENDL.

dals or salvage operations. (Additional aspects of this brewery's story are covered throughout the book.)

Wurm & Winker (1859?–1860?)
Location: Desnoyer Park

Wurm and Winker is the second mystery brewery from the 1860 Census of Industry. Both partners would go on to be proprietors of their own breweries: Conrad Wurm elsewhere in St. Paul and Andrew Winker in Shakopee. According to the census, the partners produced 200 barrels in the 1859–60 tax year, but nothing else is known about their brewery.

Many states required special packaging to indicate that the beer complied with all state alcohol regulations. States often tested beer and fined brewing companies if the beer was not in compliance. Despite the high number of packaging combinations, longtime bottling house workers at both Hamm and Schmidt declared that the right beer almost always went out in the right package. This crown cap is from the late 1940s. FROM THE COLLECTION OF PAT STAMBAUGH.

Drewry & Scotten (1860–1864)
Drewry & Greig (1864–1867)
L. B. Greig (1867–1870)
John Holland (1870–1872)
Jacob Gahr (1872–1875)
North Star Brewery, William Constans (1875–1884)
Constans & Schmidt (1884–1896)
North Star Brewing Co. (1896–1900)

Location: Dayton's Bluff at Commercial Street and Hudson Road

The history of the North Star brewery is one of the most complicated of any brewery in the state. Originally founded by Edward Drewry and George Scotten in 1860, this partnership lasted until the summer of 1864, when Scotten was replaced by L. B. Greig and the firm was renamed the Northwestern Brewery (sometimes spelled North Western). (An 1881 history of Ramsey County claims that this brewery was founded in 1855, but this account contains other dates that do not correlate with either the city directories or the excise records.) Both Scotten and Greig were primarily financial partners while Drewry was in charge of brewing. The sequence becomes complicated in 1867 when Drewry and Greig split up and Greig apparently retained the Dayton's Bluff brewery. Drewry's next recorded address was on Stillwater Road (see North Star Ale and Porter Brewery). Grieg kept the brewery for a couple of years (though tax records suggest it was idle during 1869), until John Holland took over in 1870. The newly renamed Holland's Brewery lasted only until 1872, when Jacob Gahr and Co. acquired the brewery and changed the name back to North Star Brewery.

Some stability returned to the firm around 1875 when William Constans, a grocer and dealer in brewery supplies, took over the brewery with William Gilger. Though Gilger left to start a brewery in Willmar in 1878, Constans would help see the brewery through its next two brewers, Reinhold Koch and Jacob Schmidt. Schmidt was made a partner in the brewery in 1884 after helping the brewery make significant increases in production. By 1890 Schmidt had brought a young bookkeeper named Adolph Bremer into the company. Bremer would eventually work his way up in the business, marry Schmidt's daughter Maria, and take over the newly incorporated

company in October 1899. The brewery suffered a fire in 1897 and burned down in 1900, but Bremer and company purchased the struggling St. Paul Brewing Co. on West Seventh St. and reformed as the Jacob Schmidt Brewing Company. The North Star bottles salvaged from the old brewery were used at the new location, and the North Star became the symbol for the new Schmidt brewery.

(For additional information on the Schmidt brewery, see the entry for Christopher Stahlmann's Cave Brewery in St. Paul.)

Leip's Chicago Ale Brewery (1861–1865)

Location: Corner of Exchange and Eagle streets

A former wholesale liquor dealer, William Leip started his Chicago Ale Brewery in 1861. His product was popular, and he took out an ad in the St. Paul city directory to advertise his Cream Ale. By mid-1864 he was in partnership with George Coffin, and the firm had more than doubled its average monthly output from about thirty barrels to more than sixty barrels. However, by the summer of 1865, the company was out of business. Coffin moved on to partner with George Oakes in another brewery, but Leip disappeared from the city directories.

Lawrence Nessel (1863?–1864)

Location: Unknown

Lawrence Nessel does not appear in any extant St. Paul city directory, but he is listed in the excise records for 1863 and 1864. He brewed lager and typically sold between ten and fifteen barrels each month. His last appearance in the excise records is in October 1864, when he paid a $2.50 tax penalty.

Conrad Wurm (1863–1877)

Johanna Wurm (1877–1889)

Location: Jefferson Avenue and Grace Street

Conrad Wurm operated a brewery in St. Paul from 1863 until his death in 1877, after which his widow, Johanna, took over the business. Existing production figures suggest that the brewery never produced much more than 300 barrels per month, which made it one of St. Paul's smaller breweries. Outside of the production figures contained in various records, very little is known about the history of Wurm's brewery.

George Fetsch (1864–1865)

Location: Unknown

Excise tax records show that George Fetsch (or Felich) had a short career as a brewer in St. Paul. He produced four and a half barrels of beer in October 1864 and more than doubled his output two months later. His final appearance in the records was in January 1865. It is possible that Fetsch took over Lawrence Nessel's brewery, but there is no surviving evidence for this other than the coincidence of closing and opening dates. Fetsch does not appear in the city directories during this period.

Kranzlein & Schmidt, White Beer Brewery (1864–1865?)

Kranzlein, Smith & Miller (1866–1867)

Location: Eagle near Third Street

It appears that for a short time John Kranzlein and his partners operated two breweries, one in St. Paul and one in Minneapolis. The St. Paul operation was first listed in the city directory in 1864 under the misspelled entry of Kranclein and Smidt as a "White Beer" brewery. In the 1866 directory, the firm is still listed among the brewers in the business section, but they are labeled in the individual listings as "dealers in wines and liquors," with no mention of brewing. The excise records do not report any beer production by the St. Paul operations of this business, though they did pay a tax for their distilling activities. It is possible that the brewing portion of the company was taxed through the Minneapolis location, where Kranzlein and Miller lived, but it is also possible that the St. Paul location sold beer brewed in Minneapolis.

Coffin & Oakes (1865–1867)

Edward Drewry, Eliza Drewry, Drewry & Sons (at various times between 1867 and 1917)

Location: Stillwater Road (Payne Avenue near Minnehaha Avenue)

George Coffin and George Oakes started their ale brewery on Stillwater Road in August 1865, after Coffin left the firm of Leip and Coffin. In October 1867, Edward Drewry Sr. took over this brewery after he and L. B. Greig dissolved their partnership. The firm was under the name of Edward Drewry until 1872, when the business was put in the name of Eliza Drewry. Under the later name of Drewry and Sons, the firm continued to brew ale and also imported ale and stout. Drewry and Sons was still in business in 1917, but soon afterward became a casualty of Prohibition.

Edward D. Neill's 1881 *History of Ramsey County* claims that this brewery was the one

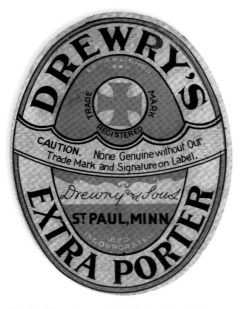

This label from Drewry's Extra Porter dates to between 1890 and 1906. BOB KAY COLLECTION

started by Putnam and Dexter in 1861, but this is not supported by contemporary sources. An analysis of the Putnam and Dexter brewery may be found under the entry for that firm.

Edward L. Drewry Jr. left St. Paul in 1875 to brew on the northern frontier, stopping first in Pembina, Dakota Territory. In 1877 he rented a run-down brewery in St. John's, Manitoba, and began to repair and expand the plant. He and his brother Frederick William later built the company into the largest brewery in Winnipeg. Drewry's survived until it was purchased by Canadian Breweries in 1953. Another brother, George, moved to Kenora, Ontario, in 1883. Later he operated the Lakewood Brewery. After Ontario's short period of prohibition, the brewery was reopened by William S. Drewry in 1927 as the Kenora Brewery, but it closed in 1929. (Additional information about Drewry and Sons, along with photographs of artifacts, can be found in chapters 2 and 3.)

Melchior Funk (1865–1893)
Melchior Funk Brewing Co. (1893–1903)
Location: Corner of Cascade and Colborne

Melchior Funk started his own brewery in 1865 after leaving the partnership with Ullrich

Schweitzer. According to Neill's 1881 *History of Ramsey County*, the brewery was powered by steam and equipped with the latest machinery. The capacity was given as 2,000 barrels, and Funk was apparently quite close to capacity since he brewed more than 1,700 barrels in 1879. After Funk died in 1893, his sons John and William operated the brewery.

Hermann Kreitz (1865–1866)
Location: Herkimer Avenue

According to the 1863 city directory, Hermann Kreitz owned a saloon on Third Street between Market Street and St. Peter Street. The next year his entry reports his occupation as distiller, and in business listings of the 1866 directory, Kreitz is included with the brewers. The excise records only include him as a distiller in St. Paul. Kreitz appears also to have owned a brewery in Minneapolis (see the Minneapolis section above).

Putnam & Dexter (1867)
Location: Near Phalen Creek

Edward Neill's *History of Ramsey County* claims that Putnam and Dexter started the brewery that later became Drewry and Sons in 1861, but includes no other details. John Putnam was listed as a brewer in the 1863 city directory, but since he was boarding (and presumably working) at Eagle and Exchange, it is unlikely that he started the brewery at Dayton's Bluff that the Drewrys later operated. Putnam was not listed in the next directory and does not reappear until 1867, when he joined Andrew J. Dexter in operating a brewery on Phalen Creek (spelled Phalin in the directory). This brewery was near Drewry's Northwestern Brewery, and it is possible that Drewry bought out his neighbors, which would explain Neill's claim. Putnam and Dexter appear in the 1867 excise records, but no production figures are given.

St. Paul Malt & Ale Co. (1868–1872)
Location: Phalen Creek

St. Paul Malt and Ale appears in the excise records from 1868 to 1872 and in the city directory from 1869 through 1871, but no details are known about the business, other than that I. van Etten was the treasurer and R. E. Gray was the secretary. It may have been a successor firm to Putnam and Dexter, but this would not square with accounts claiming that their business became part of the Drewry enterprise.

O. McFarland (1874–1875?)
A. T. Upham (1875–1877)
Frank Hornung (1877–1881)
Location: Minnehaha, east of Payne

O. McFarland appears to have started a brewery at this location, but it was taken over the next year by A. T. Upham, who was also a watchmaker, jeweler, and dentist. Upham does not appear in the city directory after 1875, but Frank Hornung is listed in 1877 at the same address as Upham's brewery. Hornung had been a brewer for Fred Emmert before taking over this brewery on his own. This brewery's high point of production seems to have been in 1874, when Schade reported that A. L. Upham [*sic*] made more than 500 barrels. By 1879 Hornung produced just 102 barrels.

Roelke Bros. (1874–1875)
Location: Unknown

The Roelke brothers are listed in *Schade's Brewers Handbook*, but no production is listed. They do not appear in the St. Paul city directories.

Minnesota Weiss Beer Brewery (1884?)
Location: Unknown

The only listing of this firm is in *American Breweries II*, so the brewery may never have been built.

Joseph Hamm & John Reimer (1885–1886)
J. H. Reimer (1886–1892)
Location: Joy Avenue near the railroad bridge

Joseph Hamm was a foreman for Bruggemann's brewery before setting out on his own. The brewery was destroyed on 12 October 1892 by a fire that also burned $2,000 in cash.

Setzer & Reichow (1885–1886?)
Herman Reichow (1886–1887)
Location: Mendota Road near the railroad bridge

According to St. Paul city directories, the short-lived Setzer and Reichow brewery appears to have been owned by Frederick O. Setzer and William Reichow and operated by their sons Frederick E. Setzer and Herman Reichow. By 1886 the firm is listed in the excise records under the name of Herman Reichow, who appears in the 1886 and 1887 excise tax records only for assessments of tax penalties.

George Schlenk (1888–1889?)
Location: 1263 Fauquier Place

George Schlenk is listed as a brewer in the business section of the 1889 city directory. He does not appear in excise records or any other

sources that would provide independent confirmation or additional information.

J. L. Bausch & Son (1895)
Location: Unknown

Little is known about this firm except for a city directory listing.

Summit Brewing Company (1986–present)
Location: 910 Montreal Circle

Mark Stutrud founded Summit Brewing Company on University Avenue in 1986 with a secondhand brewing system imported from Germany. Summit was the first microbrewery in Minnesota, offering Extra Pale Ale and Great Northern Porter on draught and in bottles. Summit gradually introduced new beers to its line, including Maibock, Winter Ale, and India Pale Ale.

By the late 1990s, Summit had outgrown its original cramped quarters. In 1997 the company broke ground for the first new brewery in St. Paul since the turn of the century. The new brewery on Montreal was built with an original capacity of 65,000 barrels per year, but theoretically has enough room to expand to 375,000 barrels.

The extra capacity allowed Summit to create new and different beers. In 2001 Summit introduced Grand Pilsner, something of a departure from the ales and specialty lagers

In this view of the Summit brewhouse, the lauter tun, in which the wort is separated from the grain, is at rear and the brew kettle is in front. COURTESY OF SUMMIT BREWING COMPANY.

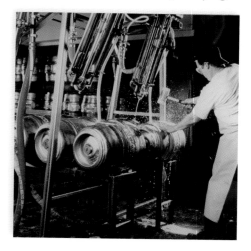

John Schroder bungs a keg of draught Summit in the racking room. COURTESY OF SUMMIT BREWING COMPANY.

that had been the brewery's trademark to that point. In 2004 the brewery began a series of draught-only offerings, starting with Oatmeal Stout.

In 2006 Summit Brewing celebrated its twentieth anniversary with a party on Harriet Island and Extra Special Bitter Anniversary Ale.

More information about Summit Brewing can be found in chapter 8.

Flat Earth Brewing Company (2007–present)
Location: 2035 Benson Avenue

Jeff Williamson started work on Flat Earth Brewing Company during 2006. The former assistant brewer at Town Hall Brewery purchased a brewing system from the Steelhead Brewery on Fisherman's Wharf in San Francisco and installed it in a converted industrial building. Williamson introduced his draught Belgian-style ale, called Flat Earth Pale Ale, at the Minnesota Craft Brewer's Guild's Winterfest Big Beer Festival in January 2007. Future beers are expected to include styles seldom found fresh locally, such as California common and Baltic porter.

St. Peter [Nicollet County]

Seeger & Engesser (1856–1858?)
Matthew Engesser (1856–1880)
Matthew Engesser & Sons (1880–1888)
Engesser Brewing Co. (1888–1942)
Location: 1202–1212 South Front Street

Matthew Engesser and William Seeger started building a brewery on land donated by St. Peter Land Company in 1856. According to some accounts, Engesser bought Seeger's share before the building was completed. But an article in the *St. Peter Free Press* in 1858 still lists Seeger as one of the proprietors. Brewing equipment was shipped in from Cincinnati, and Engesser started making beer. The 1860 Census of Industry records Engesser's production that year as 1,000 barrels. This may have included some exaggeration, since Engesser's reported

"You Pay" openers, popular during the 1930s and 1940s, doubled as spinners: the opener could be spun on the table to determine who bought the next round. This example must be from the 1930s, since not enough patrons bought enough rounds to keep Engesser Brewing Company around into the 1940s. FROM THE COLLECTION OF PAT STAMBAUGH.

One of the most visually striking labels to adorn a Minnesota beer bottle was lithographed by Hancock Epsten Company of Omaha, Nebraska. The notation that the average weight was 12 ounces net indicated continuing problems with bottle consistency. This label probably dates to the mid-1910s, after the state had begun building highways in earnest. FROM THE COLLECTION OF KEN MALZ.

figures throughout the 1870s are never more than 400 barrels per year. It appears Engesser occasionally exaggerated in the other direction as well, since he was arrested and had his brewery seized in 1866 for tax fraud.

Starting in 1880, Engesser began to bring his sons Joseph and Edward into the business. They were faced with a crisis almost immediately, when the floods of 1881 undermined the foundation of the brewery, which later collapsed. They rebuilt and expanded the brewery, eventually expanding it to a capacity of 15,000 barrels by the time of World War I.

Engesser Brewing switched to soft drinks during Prohibition and was therefore able to keep the plant going and retain some employees during the 1920s. After beer became legal again, Engesser reopened and offered brands like Famous '56, Royal Stock, and Engesser Export. However, the new president, Harry LaDue, started spending the brewery's money on a lavish rathskeller and expensive trips. This alone might not have hurt the brewery in an earlier time, but the improved roads of the 1930s made it easier for large breweries to target markets like St. Peter. Engesser tried to move into the Twin Cities market to stay profitable. Because they employed an African American driver, Engesser was able to sell beer to the African American community in the Twin Cities during the boycott of the Minneapolis and St. Paul breweries (see chapter 6).

A fire in 1939 damaged the company's financial health even more, and by 1941 the company was unable to meet its payroll. The employees bottled one final vat of beer, and the brewery closed for good.

Fred. A. Veith (1865?–1873?)
Location: Unknown

Fred Veith appears in the excise records in 1866, but the amount of beer he sold that year indicates that he had probably started somewhat earlier. Veith was one of three area brewers to be arrested for tax irregularities in 1866, and he was also part of a syndicate of St. Peter brewers who agreed to raise their prices from $8 to $9 a barrel because of the increased cost of ingredients.

Veith probably aged his beer in caves in Oshawa Township, which may account for Veith's address sometimes being given as Oshawa during this period. The date Veith left his St. Peter business to open a brewery in Le Sueur is not mentioned in contemporary records.

Two different sources say that there were four breweries operating in St. Peter into the 1880s, but no information has been found on what the fourth one would be (after Engesser, Stelzer, and Hohmann). It is possible that this number included Veith's brewery in nearby Oshawa.

Keoke & Kuhl (1866–1867)
Stelzer Bros. (1867–1870)
Jacob Stelzer (1871–1888)
George Stelzer (1888–1891)
Location: East of Front Street on the Mississippi River, between Grace and Mulberry streets

Keoke and Kuhl built their new brewery in St. Peter in the summer of 1866 at a cost of about $4,000. An article in the *St. Peter Tribune* reported that it would "be one of the cleanest breweries in the valley. Mr. Keoke is determined to avoid the too common filth in the vicinity of such establishments by giving all the refuse material an unobstructed passageway to the river."

Less than a year after opening, the firm of Keoke and Kuhl dissolved and the brewery was sold to the Stelzer brothers, Philip and Jacob. Jacob soon took the lead role and operated the brewery until 1888. Jacob's son George ran the brewery during its last few years of operation.

Hohmann & Harm (1867)
Hohmann & Co. (1868–?)
Hohmann & Young (1880–1883?)
Location: South Front, between St. Paul and Elm streets

August Hohmann first appears in the excise records in 1867 with his partner, Mr. Harm. Little is known about this brewery in the 1870s since Hohmann's production is not recorded in either Schade's or Salem's list. It is possible that the brewery may have lain idle

for several years. Hohmann is listed in Polk's 1880 *Gazetteer*. The Gresham *History of Nicollet and Le Sueur Counties* claims that four breweries were in operation in 1883, so it is likely that Hohmann was still around at that point.

St. Vincent (Kittson County)

Raywood & Co. (Raywood & Lennon) (1879–1880?)
Location: Fourth Street and Atlantic Avenue

Raywood and Lennon (spelled Lemon in Salem's list) began work on their brewery along the Red River in July 1879. According to the *Pembina* (Dakota Territory) *Pioneer*, in thirteen days they had the brewery building completed and the first batch of ale under way. The staff of four men was headed by George Raywood, a 38-year-old English native who had previously been a brewer in Winnipeg, Manitoba.

After two brief mentions in the *Pioneer*, the brewery largely disappears from the records. It is listed in the Polk 1880 *Gazetteer*, but the *Pioneer* ceased publishing in 1880 and no information about the end of the brewery is known.

Sauk Centre (Stearns County)

George Gruber (1865?–1884)
Henry Diehl (1884–1885?)
Ahrentz & Co. (1885?–1890)
Frank Minnette (1890–1891)
Location: West of Main Street on Sauk Lake

George Gruber began brewing on Sauk Lake sometime after the Civil War. The Mitchell *History of Stearns County* claims Gruber started in 1865, but he does not appear in excise records until 1867. His brewery burned in 1870, but he rebuilt. Gruber's production fluctuated wildly in the 1870s and 1880s: he reported production of nearly 500 barrels in 1875, was down to nineteen barrels in 1879, but was back up to fifty barrels a month by April 1881. Gruber was shipping some of his beer to nearby towns; the *Glenwood Leader* carried an ad in 1873 for Anderson and Jorgensen, liquor dealers, who claimed they had "Sauk Centre beer kept constantly on hand."

Little is known so far about the later years of the brewery. *American Breweries II* lists Henry Diehl as operating the brewery for four years, but excise records show Ahrentz and Co. (recorded as Albert and Co.) applying for a brewing license in October 1885. The *Sauk*

Centre Avalanche reported on 4 September 1890 that "Frank Minnette has purchased his partner's interest in the brewery at this place, and will henceforth 'go it alone.'" He operated the brewery for less than a year before it burned in 1891. Minnette went into iron mining and was elected to the state legislature in 1892 as a Democrat. A park now occupies the site of the brewery. The reference in *American Breweries II* to Antoinette I. Minette [*sic*] as proprietor of the brewery in the 1890s appears to be an error.

Sauk Rapids (Benton County)

Momberg & Jochem (1884–1888)
Sauk Rapids Brewing Co. (1888–1895)
Location: NE corner of Broadway and Gorman (now approximately Third Street and Benton Drive S.)

In January 1884 crews began blasting out frozen ground to begin the construction of Momberg and Jochem's brewery in Sauk Rapids. The building was a wood frame structure measuring 33 × 50 feet. The first batch was brewed on St. Patrick's Day that year and was first sold on April 28. The brewery had a capacity of about twenty barrels per batch and was known briefly as the Eagle Brewery. Fred Momberg retired from the business just before the brewery suffered major damage in a devastating cyclone on 14 April 1886. The Jochem family's large house was destroyed (the family was not at home). The brewery was repaired at a cost of $3,000 and continued brewing for several years. Around 1888 the name of the firm was changed to Sauk Rapids Brewing Co., and it remained in business under that name until it was destroyed by fire on 14 February 1895. Jochem's uninsured loss was between $4,000 and $5,000, and he opted not to rebuild.

Shakopee (Scott County)

Herman Strunk (1856–1859)
Joseph Niehof & Co. (1859)
Strunk & Dorre (1859–1864?)
Andrew Winker (1864–1870?)
Andrew Winker's Estate (1870?–1878)
Hubert Nyssen, Shakopee Brewery (1878–1920)
Location: West of Shakopee, near the railroad tracks

The *Shakopee Valley Herald* reported in October 1856, "We understand that the Brewery of Mr. H. H. Strunck [*sic*] will soon be in operation. Our citizens will then be able to procure a pleasant and healthy drink without much trouble." Strunk ran the brewery until December 1859, when he rented it to Joseph Niehof and Company. The new management advertised in the *Scott County Democrat* that they "intend to carry on the Brewery Business, and by strict attention to the wants of the public, they hope to merit a share of the patronage of the public. The proprietors hope to see all of the old customers of this establishment and as many new ones as may deem proper to give them a call." This arrangement only lasted a few months, and Strunk resumed operations again in partnership with Philip Dorre. Strunk and Dorre also had a distillery at their plant and advertised a variety of whiskeys in addition to lager, bock, ale, and porter.

Sometime during the Civil War, Andrew Winker purchased the brewery. He operated it until his death in 1870 at age 27. The brewery produced well over 500 barrels a year, and sometimes sold more than 100 barrels per month. The family kept the property, but it may have lain idle for part of the next few years. In 1873 Hubert Nyssen came to work in the brewery. He married Winker's widow, Mary, in 1875 and began to reinvigorate the brewery. By 1878 he had pushed production over 1,200 barrels—roughly the same amount as A. T. Husmann produced on the other side of town. Throughout this time, the property was still owned by Mary Nyssen.

In 1885 the brewery suffered a major fire during which the brewery suffered approximately $12,000 worth of damage and Hubert Nyssen fell from the roof onto a pile of stone and suffered a broken leg. Nyssen began rebuilding almost immediately and reestablished his large business.

In 1897 the brewery caught fire again, though this time the fire company got to the scene quickly and put out the fire with water from the brewery's cistern. Damage was only $500, and production was not interrupted. That same fall the *Scott County Argus* reported an incident in which the team hauling Nyssen's brewery wagon was startled by a sudden move from a toy balloon vendor. The wagon overturned and the balloon man was injured by a flying board.

Nyssen added a bottling facility to his operation and advertised that the brewery would deliver a case of quarts for $2. Another ad, this one from 1897, noted that Nyssen "Buys in Shakopee. Sells in Shakopee. Trades in Shakopee. Gets Labor in Shakopee. Pays Wages in Shakopee. Drink Shakopee Beer." Nyssen was forced to pay a lot more wages in Shakopee than he planned in 1912, when the bottling works and stables burned down, killing the brewery's three horses. Unfortunately, these were the only uninsured buildings on the property. Nyssen rebuilt and continued in business until Prohibition.

After beer became legal again in 1933, plans were made to convert a Shakopee flour mill into a brewery. John Hoerner, formerly of Brainerd Brewing, was hired to be the new brewmaster, but Shakopee Breweries, Inc., never went into production. The old Nyssen brewery was used as distillery, a winery, and a puppy mill and stands vacant today.

This delicate, barrel-shaped glass from Heller's Union Brewery was designed for the home, not for being slammed on a bar top. COURTESY OF THE MINNESOTA HISTORICAL SOCIETY.

Adolph Albachten (1857?–1867)
Albachten & Husmann (1867–1870)
J. B. Husmann (1870–1874)
A. T. Husmann (1874–1882)
J. B. Husmann (1882–1884)
Husmann Bros. (1884–1888)
H. Husmann (1888–1890)
H. H. Heller, Union Brewery (1890–1901)
J. M. Engelhorn (1901–1908)
Location: West of Shakopee along the railroad tracks, one-quarter mile east of the Strunk-Nyssen brewery

Adolph Albachten was in Shakopee and employed as a brewer by the time of the 1857 territorial census. By 1860 he had expanded production to nearly 800 barrels—nearly as large as most of the breweries in St. Paul and larger than most breweries elsewhere in the state. Like his nearby neighbor Herman Strunk, Albachten operated a distillery as well as a brewery. In 1867 Albachten took J. B. Husmann as a partner, and Husmann became sole proprietor in 1870. For the next two decades, different members of the Husmann family were listed as proprietors of the brewery. The Husmann brewery typically produced about 1,200 barrels per year during the 1870s, main-

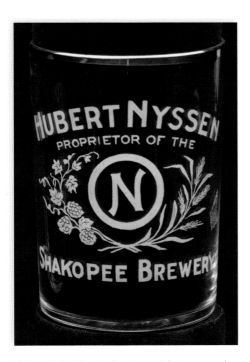

This small glass from Hubert Nyssen's brewery was decorated with gold trim around the lip and etched with hops and barley. It is typical of the glasses produced in the late 1890s. COURTESY OF THE MINNESOTA HISTORICAL SOCIETY.

taining its position as one of the largest breweries in the state outside of Minneapolis and St. Paul.

Herman H. Heller purchased the brewery in 1890 and operated it into the next century. By this time Nyssen's Shakopee Brewery had grown much bigger than Heller's Union Brewery, and there is no evidence that Heller followed his rival into the bottled beer business. J. M. Engelhorn was the proprietor of the brewery until it burned in May 1908.

Silver Lake [McLeod County]

Wenzel Chalupsky (1887?–1905)
Frank Chalupsky (1905–1913)
Silver Lake Brewing Co. (Frank A. Chalupsky,
    proprietor) (1913–1919)
Location: On Silver Lake, west of Tower Avenue

The Chalupsky family operated the Silver Lake brewery throughout its existence. Brewing industry sources give an opening date of 1888 for this brewery, but a booklet celebrating Silver Lake's centennial claims the brewery was built during 1886 and 1887. Wenzel (sometimes spelled Wencel) sold the brewery in 1905 to his brother Frank for $10,000. The brewery made occasional appearances in the excise records and brewing journals, but little information about the operations was given. The area newspapers ran few articles about the brewery, so details on the brewery's history are scarce. While licensed as a large brewer, the threshold for this was still just 500 barrels. Advertisements in the *Silver Lake Leader* seem to indicate that most of the Silver Lake brewery's beer was sold in saloons in the immediate area. One ad in 1915 provides a list of saloons that offered Silver Lake beer in eighth-barrel kegs. When Brainerd Brewing closed, John Hoerner moved to Silver Lake and became brewmaster until Prohibition.

Sleepy Eye [Brown County]

G. W. Kramer (1873–1880)
Frank Burginger (1880–1888)
Anton Steffen (1888–1912)
Steffen Brewing Co. (1912–1914)
Bernard Schueller (1915–1920)
Location: Third Avenue NE, northeast of town

According to two articles published in the *Sleepy Eye Herald-Dispatch*, the Sleepy Eye brewery was started in 1873 by George W.

This glass from the Sleepy Eye brewery probably dates from the 1890s. FROM THE COLLECTION OF PAT STAMBAUGH.

Kramer. In 1880 he sold it to a former sea captain, Frank Burginger, who brought his Chilean-born wife, Rosa, to Sleepy Eye. Burginger sold the brewery to Anton Steffen in 1888, then took his own life two days after he sold the brewery.

Anton Steffen was a brother of Balthazar (Bat) Steffen of Hastings. Steffen was proprietor for nearly two decades, but in 1893 he hired Anton Guldan to be the brewmaster. Guldan had worked for several years at the Schell and Hauenstein breweries in New Ulm. The brewery did not have a bottling works, but Guldan bottled some of the beer at his home and sold the bottles for one dollar per dozen. Steffen's ads announced that he brewed Pale, Wiener, Kulmbacher, and Lager beers.

Steffen Brewing Company was incorporated in 1912 with a capital stock of $30,000. It lasted only two years before the brewery was sold to Bernard Schueller.

Spring Grove [Houston County]

John "J. P." Myhre (1867)
Muller & Myhre (1867–1868)
J. P. Myhre (1868–1873?)
Location: The old Knudsen farm

The 1882 *History of Houston County* noted that J. P. Murray [*sic*] built a brewery on a 22-acre lot and ran it for several years until the

business collapsed. Excise records show that production did not begin until 1867 and that Myhre took on Mr. Muller as a partner for about a year. After Muller left, Myhre hired a Norwegian immigrant, Paul Elartson, to work in the brewery. The 1870 census indicates that the brewery operated for only seven of the previous twelve months and produced 308 barrels of beer, which was by no means the smallest total on the list but was still in the bottom quarter. Myhre appears in the 1873 state business directory, but not in Schade's list of breweries for 1874 or 1875.

Stillwater [Washington County]

Norbert Kimmick (1851–1857)
Susannah Kimmick (1857–1860)
Francis X. Aiple (1860–1869)
Herman Tepass (1869–1887)
Aiple & Piper (1887–1889)
Frank J. R. Aiple (1889–1896)
Location: 734–802 S. Main Street

Norbert Kimmick started the third brewery in the state in Stillwater in 1851. (More about the early years of this brewery is in chapter 1.) Kimmick died in 1857, and his widow took on active management of the brewery. In 1860 she married the brewery manager, Francis X. Aiple, and the business was carried on under his name for several years. Aiple died in 1869, and Susannah remarried again, this time to Herman Tepass, who took control of the brewery. After his death in 1887, Susannah turned management of the brewery over to her son, Frank Aiple Jr., who operated it until 1896. The original brewery was destroyed by fire in the late 1880s, but a new "model brewery" was completed in 1890. In 1896 the plant was sold to Jung Brewing Company of Milwaukee, which turned it into a malt house.

Despite the sale of the family brewery, the Aiples remained in the brewing business into the next century. They bought the former Martin Bruggemann brewery in St. Paul and operated it from 1901 to 1905.

The logo for the Aiple's St. Paul brewery (1901–05) was much simpler than the Victorian artwork on its earlier glass, most likely from the 1890s. FROM THE COLLECTION OF PAT STAMBAUGH.

Gerhard Knips (1858?–1877)

Hoerner, Muhlbrook & Maish (1877)

St. Croix Brewing Co. (1877)

Location: North of town on Highway 95, at the historic marker commemorating the Tamarack House

According to an article by Brent Peterson in the *St. Croix Valley Press* (10 February 2000), Gerhard Knips started his brewery in the part of Stillwater known as Dutchtown in either 1858 or 1859. The 1860 Census of Industry reported that Knips had produced approximately 500 barrels during the previous year. In the early 1860s Knips was selling nearly as much beer as rival Frank Aiple, but after the Civil War ended, Aiple made several improvements and expansions and far outstripped Knips's capacity. By 1865 Knips was selling just over fifty barrels in his busiest months, but Aiple was selling ninety barrels in the same time frame.

Knips made about $1,000 worth of improvements to his cellar in 1870, but his production was still far behind that of Aiple's successor, Herman Tepass, and newcomer Joseph Wolf. Knips was usually licensed as a small brewer of fewer than 500 barrels, but it is known that he exceeded this threshold,

because in May 1876 he was required to pay a penalty for having insufficient stamps. The revenue collector added a note in his report explaining that Knips did not think he should have to pay a penalty for underestimating his production. An article in the *Stillwater Lumberman* (18 May 1975) claims that Knips was the first American brewer to bottle beer. While American breweries bottled ale and porter well before Knips began business, he would have been among the first in Minnesota to bottle his own beer if he was bottling by the mid-1870s.

In 1877 Knips retired from brewing and leased the business to Joseph Hoerner, Dietrich Muhlbrook, and F. W. Maish for six years at $1,200 per year. Less than a month later, Maish left the firm, now called St. Croix Brewing Company in excise records. In August 1877, Muhlbrook announced that operations at the brewery were suspended. In addition to financial difficulties, he blamed a recent wave of temperance activity in the county, in which about 1,000 people "took the pledge" not to drink. The drop-off in business in the saloons was noticeable, and the smaller St. Croix Brewing was unable to compete with the Aiple and Wolf breweries.

Gerhard Knips considered moving to Texas and actually visited to look over the prospects, but finally settled in Nobles County. The brewery building was later converted into a board-

ing house for workers who came to Stillwater during World War I. The brewery was torn down in 1935 to allow widening of Highway 95—only the back wall remains as a retaining wall.

Martin Wolf (1869–1871)

Wolf, Tanner & Co. (1871–1875)

Joseph Wolf & Co. (1875–1879)

Joseph Wolf, Empire Brewery (1879–1896)

Joseph Wolf Co. (1896–1919)

Location: 402–414 S. Main Street

While Martin and Joseph Wolf both arrived in Stillwater in the early 1850s, neither of them entered the brewing business until nearly two decades later.

The first appearance of Martin Wolf in the excise records is in 1869. Two years later Joseph took a share in the brewery as part of Wolf, Tanner, and Co. The brewery burned in February 1872, with a loss of two men and more than $15,000. The firm built a new brewery, which was the largest of the three in Stillwater. By 1879 Joseph Wolf and Co. was the largest brewery in Minnesota outside of Minneapolis and St. Paul, and it was closing in on Gluek's with annual production of nearly 3,400 barrels. Wolf's brewery was powered by steam and employed twelve men. Sometime in the mid-1880s, Wolf added a bottling department, and he continued to add on to other parts of the brewery. Wolf continued to engage in his original business—wholesale liquor—and built a large warehouse alongside the brewery for this business.

"Jo" Wolf was often lauded for his community spirit, and the brewery sponsored everything from parade floats to a baseball team. The *Pine City Pioneer* reported in 1902 that "a couple of Pine City players went to help out in a game in Stillwater against the 'Wolf's Brewing Co.'s' team of picked players." Wolf's team won anyway, 11–2.

Wolf's brewery outlasted the two breweries in Stillwater that started earlier and was the only one to survive until Prohibition. After beer became legal again in 1933, a group of investors from St. Paul purchased the complex and prepared to make it operational again under the name Wolf's Brewery. This plan, like so many similar plans in the early 1930s, came to naught, at least at the time. The brewery buildings were maintained and in the 1990s,

Wolf's brewery in Stillwater was decorated for a celebration in 1912. PHOTOGRAPH BY JOHN RUNK; COURTESY OF THE MINNESOTA HISTORICAL SOCIETY.

Vittorio's Restaurant became a brewpub; beer was once more made in the building and stored in the cellars. (See the Vittorio's entry in the Brewpub section.) During the early 2000s, the brewery was redeveloped as a condominium, restaurant, and retail complex.

Hasse & Hermann (1875–?)
Location: South Stillwater

Hasse and Hermann is yet another mystery brewery. An exhaustive search of Stillwater newspapers yielded no information, and its year(s) of production fall during a gap in excise records. But *Schade's Brewers Handbook* indicates that it produced twenty-four barrels of beer in 1875. Since it was located in South Stillwater, it seems unlikely that Hasse and Hermann were operating Knips's brewery on the north side of town, so it is necessary to conclude, based on the evidence so far, that this is in fact a separate brewery.

Taylors Falls [Chisago County]

Schottmuller & Bro. (1856–1869)
Joseph Schottmuller (1869–1874)
Jacob Berger & Bro. (1874–1877)
J. Schottmuller (1877–1884)
George Zigner (1884–1888)
Schottmuller Bros. (1888–1890)
Location: Behind the Chisago House, at the corner of Bench and Front streets

Joseph and Frank Schottmuller built a small brewery in Taylors Falls in 1856. They enlarged the plant in 1860, but it was still a very small brewery. Seldom during the 1860s did they sell more than ten barrels of beer in a month. In 1861 they expanded their operation by adding a hall to the brewery and by extending their cellars farther into the bluff.

In 1869 Joseph became the sole proprietor, as Frank left to seek his fortune elsewhere. Frank owned a brewery in Ashland, Wisconsin, from 1872 until 1885, but eventually rejoined his brother in Taylors Falls. During Frank's absence, Joseph was arrested in 1879 for supplementing his business with an illegal distilling operation. Jacob Berger (spelled Beyer by Schade) made some improvements to the brewery during his years as proprietor, but most of the business changes passed without much comment in either the local papers or the brewing industry journals.

Tower [St. Louis County]

Michael Fink (1892–1893)
Iron Range Brewing Co. (1893–1895)
Iron Range Brewery (1895–1897)
Iron Range Brewing Association (1897–1899)
Iron Range Brewing Association, Inc. (1899–1919)
Location: S. Third and Pine streets

Michael Fink, once the owner of the brewery that became A. Fitger & Co. in Duluth, built a brewery in Tower in 1892. He fell into financial trouble almost immediately and sold the brewery to a group of investors from Duluth who formed Iron Range Brewing Co. After a few years, a group of Tower residents led by Samuel Owens, George Huner, and W. H. McQuade formed a stock company, purchased the brewery, and changed its name to Iron Range Brewing Association. Most of the recorded history of this brewery concerns the frequent ownership changes as investors struggled to find an arrangement that would make a profit.

This neck label is from Iron Range Brewing Association's Export Pilsener Style Beer. FROM THE COLLECTION OF KEN MALZ.

The brewery was equipped with a bottling house and shipped beer throughout the region. When St. Louis County went dry in 1918, Iron Range Brewing Association converted to produce near beer and hired the former brewmaster from the now-closed Virginia Brewing Co. to make "Iron Beer."

Most of the brewery still stands and today contains the Iron Ore Bar.

Traverse des Sioux [Nicollet County]

Jacob Schmahl (1852–1866)

Location: At the bend of the old stage road, near the Treaty Site History Center

Soon after the signing of the Treaty of Traverse des Sioux in 1851, a permanent settlement was added to the existing trading post to take advantage of the location at the Minnesota River crossing point. Jacob Schmahl (spelled various ways, including Small) arrived around 1852 and soon built a hotel and a brewery just north of where the city of St. Peter would soon emerge. The 1860 Census of Industry suggests Schmahl brewed as much as 1,650 barrels a year at that time, but the 1866 excise tax records have him averaging ten barrels a month, so the larger number may have referred to small kegs. Schmahl's brewery was once attacked by the local chief Red Iron, who, according to an account in Thomas Hughes's *Old Traverse des Sioux*, buried an ax in the wall of the building during an intoxicated rage. Schmahl was one of three Nicollet County brewers whose breweries were seized in September 1866 on suspicion of tax evasion. Schmahl does not appear to have reopened his brewery, and in 1870 he moved his family to Redwood Falls.

Veseli [Rice County]

Rapham & Pavek (1887?–1890)
Joseph Pavek (1890–1907)

Location: North end of Grace Street

The small farm village of Veseli (also Wesley or Wheatland), located between Northfield and New Prague, is one of the smallest municipalities in Minnesota ever to host a brewery. Joseph Pavek started brewing there sometime in the mid-1880s. *Wing's Brewers Handbook* of 1887 lists him along with his partner, Mr. Rapham. The brewery flourished and, starting in 1891, was listed as a large brewery in the excise records. The brewery experienced a fire in August 1898, but Pavek rebuilt and continued his business. Pavek's brewery sponsored a baseball team called the Veseli Brewers (logically enough). In 1905 the Brewers won 21 of the 22 games they played. The brewery closed sometime around 1907.

Virginia [St. Louis County]

Virginia Brewing Co. (1906–1918)

Location: Corner of Lake Boulevard and Ohio Avenue

The January 1905 issue of *Brewers' Journal* contained the news that P. R. Vail of Ely had decided to build a brewery on the Iron Range and was going to select between Hibbing, Virginia, and Eveleth. Two months later, the same publication announced that the choice had been made and Hibbing was the winner. For some reason the decision was reversed, and the new brewery was built in Virginia instead.

The Virginia Brewing Co. brewery was designed by Bernard Barthel of Chicago and was a showpiece for small breweries. The brewery cost $150,000 and was equipped with the latest machinery. Soon after the first brew was made, the owners announced an ambitious plan to build depots in six cities, build a new storage house, and electrify the brewery. By 1911, the company felt confident enough to propose a depot in Duluth, which already had three significant breweries. The brewery operated with few newsworthy events until St. Louis County went dry in 1918 and the brewery closed.

The brewery still stands, and the exterior maintains much of its original appearance. The building is on the National Register of Historic Places.

While not as blatant as those breweries that actually called their beer Budweiser or Bud, the labels of the Virginia Brewing Company were nearly identical to those of the famous import from St. Louis. One label expert suggested that this was simply a stock pattern offered by a label manufacturer, with no actual intent to deceive on the part of the brewer. Whatever the case, in 1908 Anheuser-Busch successfully sued Virginia Brewing Company to stop using the labels. Text in the upper banner advised consumers to check the top for the trademark, since brewers had frequent problems with independent operators refilling bottles with inferior beer. Note the use of German in the product description. FROM THE COLLECTION OF KEN MALZ.

The Virginia Brewing Co. building was featured on a souvenir spoon. This ornate item also features three barrels beneath the state seal, but they are marked XXX, so they are likely to be flour barrels. FROM THE COLLECTION OF PAT STAMBAUGH.

This postcard from around 1910 shows two of Virginia's important businesses: Virginia Brewing Company and Virginia & Rainy Lake Lumber Co. Virginia's brewing water came from a well, not from the lake, and so was not affected by the log booms. FROM THE COLLECTION OF PAT STAMBAUGH.

Wabasha [Wabasha County]

Mary and Charles Leslin (1872?–1885)
John T. Ginther (1885–1890)
Robert Anderman (1890–1894)
Wabasha Brewery, Christian Grass (1894–1919)
Location: One and a half miles west of Wabasha

While the record is confused by the brief partnership of Burkhardt and Leslin at Reads Landing in 1871–1872, it appears that Charles and Mary Leslin built their own brewery outside Wabasha. On 12 September 1873 the *Winona Daily Republican* reported a new brewery being built near Wabasha, though construction began in 1872 according to other accounts. It is very unlikely that the Leslins took over one of the Reads Landing breweries since the Leslins' Wabasha brewery and the two Reads Landing breweries all appear in Schade's brewery list of 1875 and in Salem's lists of 1878 and 1879. The business was conducted in Mary's name, even though Charles was alive and listed as a brewer in the 1880 census and Mary was listed as "keeping house." The 1884 excise records

indicate that the brewery was producing more than 500 barrels per year.

Little is known about the brewery under John T. Ginther or Robert Anderman, though Anderman had been employed at the short-lived Millville brewery in Oakwood Township. Christian Grass took over the brewery in 1894 and kept it in operation until Prohibition. Like his near neighbors, the Burkhardts, Grass operated his brewery with horse power and without electricity into the twentieth century. Sanborn fire insurance maps show no evidence of a bottling house.

Waconia [Carver County]

Merz & Zahler (1865)
Zahler & Gnau (1866–1868)
Zahler & Bro. (1868–1871)
Michael Zahler (1871–1884)
George Karcher (1886–1888?)
Location: Unknown

Michael Zahler, a former employee of Christopher Stahlmann's Cave Brewery in St. Paul and co-proprietor of the St. Michael brewery, started a brewery in Waconia. After going through a series of partners, Zahler become sole proprietor in 1871. Before 1875 Zahler typically sold just over 300 barrels per year. But the brewery burned that year, and Zahler took the opportunity to upgrade the brewery.

By the end of the decade, Zahler sold twice as much beer each year as before the fire.

Zahler enlarged the brewery again in 1882 and upgraded the machinery at the same time. In 1886 he rented the brewery to George Karcher of Chaska, who had previously rented the Peter Iltis brewery. Karcher remained in Waconia only a few years, and the brewery disappears from the records after 1890. In 1906 Peter Beyrer considered purchasing a brewery in Waconia, but purchased a brewery in Chaska instead because it was less expensive. The report in the *Waconia Patriot* does not say that Beyrer was attempting to purchase the old Zahler brewery, but this is the most likely possibility.

An 1884 photograph of the brewery can be found in chapter 2.

Wadena [Wadena County]

Carl & Roller (1881–1883?)
Peter Wermerskirchen (1883–1885)
Location: On the Northern Pacific Railway (now BNSF) tracks

While the evidence is not conclusive, it appears that there were two different breweries in Wadena. The first, started by Carl and Roller

This glass is the only known artifact of the Wadena Brewing Company at this time. FROM THE COLLECTION OF PAT STAMBAUGH.

and later owned by Peter Wermerskirchen, burned in 1885 and was not rebuilt. This may have been the predecessor of the Ebner family's Wadena Brewing Co., but local sources record that the King and Ebner brewery was built new in 1886.

King and Ebner (1886–?)
Annie E. Ebner (?–1892)
Henry Ebner (1892–1895)
Wadena Brewing Co. (1895–1916)
Location: 600 Fifth Street SE

The *Wadena County Pioneer* reported that Henry Ebner, late of Dayton, Minnesota, and William King were in a partnership to erect a brewery in Wadena. The *Pioneer* continued to report on the progress of the brewery until July, when the brewery placed the first beer brewed by Fred Eberline on sale. Despite the name changes, the ownership of the brewery changed very little over the first decade since it essentially stayed in the family. Wadena Brewing Co. suffered a fire in its first year and changed hands several times but was generally successful. It closed in 1916 because of the enforcement of the Indian treaty provisions against alcohol sales.

This barrel glass is from the Waseca Brewery during Robert Reichel's proprietorship. FROM THE COLLECTION OF PAT STAMBAUGH.

Waseca [Waseca County]

Solomon Ginsberg & Bro. (1869–1877)
Simon Kraft (1877–1880)
Location: Clear Lake

Solomon and Edwin Ginsberg, brothers of Charles Ginsberg of Mantorville, established their brewery on Clear Lake and began brewing in September 1869. Edwin was in the news when the *Waseca Leader* reported that he had had a tapeworm removed that measured about forty feet. The Ginsbergs later started a new brewery in Appleton. The Ginsbergs typically sold just over 500 barrels of beer a year, although Simon Kraft sold more than 800 barrels in 1878. (This brewery may have been the predecessor of Waseca Brewing Co.; see that brewery's history for the discussion.)

John Bierwalter (1879–1880)
Joseph Ramsdale (1880–1884)
Anthony Guyer (1884–1888)
Hermann Wenner (1888–1896)
Ingersoll Brewing Company
Robert Reichel (1897–1901)
Neverman & Hannah (1901)
Robert Reichel (1901–1902)
Adam & Reichel (1902–1905)
Waseca Brewing Company (1905–1912)
Location: Clear Lake near Fourth Avenue NE

There is some question as to whether this is a separate brewery or a continuation of the Ginsberg-Kraft concern. An 1887 history claims that the brewery then operated by Anthony Geyer was started in 1869 by Edward and Solomon Ginsberg. However, Salem's list includes both Simon Kraft and John Bierwalter, and a report in the *Winona Daily Republican* in June 1878 states that a new brewery was being constructed on the bank of Clear Lake. Little is known about the reason for the frequent ownership changes, though several of the proprietors were also involved in other Waseca enterprises.

John Bierwalter was best known in Waseca as a saloon keeper, but he rented the brewery during 1879 and 1880. He was succeeded by Joseph Ramsdale, who moved from Fairmont to take over the brewery. According to the 1887 *History of Steele and Waseca Counties*, Anthony Guyer rented the brewery in 1886 and was manufacturing twenty to twenty-five barrels per week. After succeeding Guyer, Hermann Wenner left Waseca to operate the brewery in

Northfield. The Waseca brewery burned down during Wenner's tenure in July 1894; arson was suspected.

After a long career in the paint and wallpaper business, Robert Reichel took over the brewery in 1897 and operated it for most of the next ten years. Waseca Brewing Company remained in operation until 1912, when Waseca voted dry in a close and hotly contested election. According to a series of articles in the *Waseca Herald*, the first count gave the wets an 11-vote margin out of 700 votes cast, but subsequent examinations of individual ballots for irregularities and a state supreme court decision ruled in favor of the drys.

Watertown [Carver County]

Jacob Dietz (1865–1872)
Catherine Becker (1872–1875)
Fritz Lueders (1875–1884)
Location: Unknown

Jacob Dietz began selling beer in Watertown in 1865. He appeared in the police reports in 1867 for selling beer without revenue stamps, but otherwise prospered. By 1870 he had built the business up to approximately 600 barrels per year, and all seemed to be well. But in July 1872 Dietz took his life by cutting his throat with a carving knife. The Chaska *Weekly Valley Herald* speculated that excessive drinking caused him to go insane.

Dietz's widow married John Becker (Beges in some sources) and continued the business under her new name for the next three years. The brewery sold about 300 barrels of beer during the mid-1870s. Fritz Lueders bought the brewery in 1875 and brewed for almost a decade, but had trouble competing against much larger breweries and ultimately closed in 1884.

Waverly [Wright County]

Heis Brown (1868)
Location: Unknown

Heis Brown appears in the excise tax records in February 1868. No further information about Brown or his brewery has been located.

West Albany [Wabasha County]

Andrew Hook (1870–1871)
Location: Unknown

The first mention of Andrew Hook's brewery in West Albany, a village east of Zumbro Falls, appears in the 1870 excise tax records, when he paid his license fee in December to begin production in 1871. In January he sold four barrels of beer. Hook does not appear again in the excise records and was not included in the 1871 summary published in the *St. Paul Globe* in October.

West Newton [Nicollet County]

Eckert & Feeder (1870–1871)
Location: On the riverbank, about eight miles northwest of New Ulm

Eckert and Feeder appear in the excise records in December 1870. Two local histories mention the brewery in passing, but little detailed information has been found. One account suggests that the brewery closed because of poor water quality.

Willmar [Kandiyohi County]

William Gilger (1878–1898)
Location: On Foot Lake near Tenth Street NE

William Gilger left the North Star Brewery in St. Paul to start a new brewery in Willmar in 1878. The *Western Minnesota Press* reported in 1880, "The Willmar Brewery is taking a first-rate start, furnishing beer to customers all along the line from Breckinridge to Dassel and doing a splendid business. The product is highly appreciated, where it has been introduced, and its demand is on the increase."

After this, information on Gilger's brewery is scarce. Even his obituary, which praised him as one of the great citizens of the city and mentioned his service in the French army during the Franco-Prussian War, made no mention of what he did or how he earned the money that enabled him to build the Gilger Block.

Winona [Winona County]

Brentle, Scherer & Rath, Gilmore Valley Brewery
   (1855–1858)
Beck & Rath (1858–1862)
C. C. Beck (1862–1877)
Location: Near U.S. Highway 14 and Gilmore Creek on St. Mary's University campus

In 1855 Brentle, Scherer, and Rath founded the first brewery in southeastern Minnesota

As many traditional and local symbols as possible are combined in a few square inches on the label for Bub's German Style Beer. Sugar Loaf is in the right background; the *Münchner Kindl* (child of Munich) is in the foreground, along with hops and barley. Elf or troll-like brewers sample the beer straight from the aging vats. Fakler Bros. Co. (later Winona Bottling Co.) bottled Bub's beer around the turn of the century, when this label was used. FROM THE COLLECTION OF KEN MALZ.

in the Gilmore Valley. Details about the first years of operation are scarce. In 1858 Charles C. Beck purchased the shares of Brentle and Scherer and became a partner in the company. Beck was a "practical brewer" who had worked in breweries in Germany, Philadelphia, Dubuque, and Prairie du Chien before arriving in Winona. Beck became sole proprietor in 1862.

In 1866 Beck's brewery was by far the largest in Winona and one of the largest in the state. He used the profits to expand the brewery complex, adding a new brewery saloon, a pavilion on top of the brewery, and more capacity. In 1872 he built a new brick brewery building with sufficient storage for his expanding business. Beck's brewery required 200 tons of ice each year to keep the cellars cool.

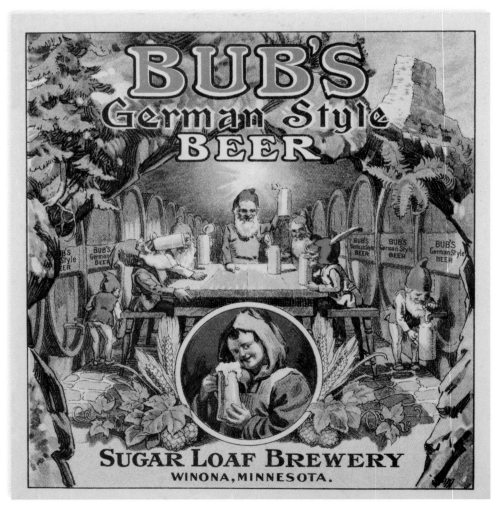

In 1875 he sold nearly 2,500 barrels of beer, one of the highest totals in the state outside of the Twin Cities. Beck owned 160 acres of land near the brewery and grew some of his own barley. Beck's beer was held in high regard, at least by the staff of the *Winona Republican*, who were frequent recipients of his generosity, especially during bock season.

In August 1877 a catastrophic fire destroyed the brewery and caused $12,000 worth of damage. Beck initially considered rebuilding, but ultimately decided to retire to farming. Traces of Beck's storage caves remained for many years near the Ek Family Village on the St. Mary's University campus. The Beck family home was eventually converted into Cotter Hall and used by the University until it was destroyed by fire in March 2006.

Jacob Weisbrod (1856–?)

Rath & Weisbrod (?–1867)

Weisbrod & Garlock (Weisbrod & Co) (1867–1871)

Bub & Burmeister (1871?–1873?)

Peter Bub, Sugar Loaf Brewery (1874?–1911)

Sugar Loaf Brewery, Peter Bub Estate (1911–1920)

Peter Bub Estate (1933–1935)

Peter Bub Brewery, Inc. (1935–1969)

Location: Sugar Loaf Road and E. Lake Boulevard

Sugar Loaf bluff is Winona's most distinctive landmark. Jacob Weisbrod established a small brewery behind the bluff in East Burns Valley. He found this spot limited his ability to expand, so he moved around to the city side of Sugar Loaf and built a new brewery. The brewery became a popular gathering place for Winona residents. In 1869 Weisbrod hired Peter Bub to be his new foreman. Bub worked at Phillip Best Brewing Company in Milwaukee for three years before coming to Winona. Weisbrod died of typhoid fever in August 1871, and Bub married his widow, Margaret, and assumed ownership of the brewery in 1872. Bub entered a partnership with local hotelier John Burmeister, but during the same period the brewery was also the subject of a suit by Weisbrod's former partner, Garlock. In December 1872, the brewery was destroyed by fire, but Bub and Burmeister immediately rebuilt. By

This bottle for Bub's German Style Beer (1937) is one of the few painted-label bottles ever produced by a Minnesota brewery. The reverse emphasizes both the local connection with the Sugar Loaf bluff and the traditional cave-aging process. FROM THE COLLECTION OF DAVE WENDL.

1874 Bub was the sole proprietor of Sugar Loaf Brewery.

Bub continued Weisbrod's practice of hosting parties at the brewery. At one of these

Even after Prohibition began, the Peter Bub Estate continued to make deliveries of its products by the barrel and by the case. The side panel of the truck advertises Sugar Loaf Brew and Bub's Root Beer. FROM THE COLLECTION OF DAVE WENDL.

Becker & Schellhas,

WINONA BREWERY,

WINONA, - MINN.

This Thanksgiving greeting card was typical of Victorian trade cards. The whimsical design did not advertise the product so much as the gratitude of the company for its clients' trade. FROM THE COLLECTION OF DAVE WENDL.

Philip Comersburgh (1860?)
Location: Unknown

Philip Comersburgh is listed as brewer in the 1860 census. Since he owned $5,000 worth of real estate, it is unlikely that he was an employee of either of the other breweries in town. It is possible that he may not have been employed as a brewer at the time of the census, but it is an intriguing possibility that there might have been another brewery in Winona in its early years.

Neuffer & Becker (1863–1866)
John S. Becker (1866–1871?)
Becker & Faehr (1871?–1873)
John S. Becker (1874–1882)
Becker & Schellhas (1882–1891)
William Schellhas (Brewing Co.) (1891–1920)
Location: Between state Highway 43 and Sugar Loaf Road

Neuffer and Becker started their brewery in 1863 a few hundred yards away from the Weisbrod Brewery at Sugar Loaf. According to the earliest available figure, in 1866 Neuffer and Becker sold much more beer than Weisbrod, and nearly as much as the much older Gilmore Valley Brewery. Neuffer sold his interest to Becker in 1866, and the latter continued the business with his father-in-law as a (sometimes silent) partner. One local account claims that business declined after the death of Becker's wife and father-in-law, but the figures show very respectable sales of nearly 1,500 barrels in 1874 and 1875 and sales in excess of 2,500 barrels in 1879—several hundred barrels more than Peter Bub's brewery. This increase came in spite of a fire that destroyed much of the brewery in 1875. The mayor refused to authorize the fire company to go outside the city limits because he feared it was a trick by arsonists to get the fire engines out of town so they could torch the city proper.

In September 1883 Becker sold half of his interest in the brewery to William Schellhas, who had been the brewer for Peter Bub. Schellhas directed an expansion of the brewery to a capacity of 15,000 barrels in 1892. The most unusual venture of the Becker and Schellhas partnership was the creation of a branch brewery in Ogden, Utah. Schellhas started the venture in 1891, but the next year they switched places, with Becker ultimately remaining in Utah.

parties, he was charged with tapping kegs of unstamped beer, but Bub demonstrated to the revenue agent how a stamp could slide off a sweaty keg. Aside from minor incidents like this, the Sugar Loaf Brewery had a long stretch without any major disaster. Throughout the 1870s Sugar Loaf Brewery sold between 2,000 and 2,500 barrels every year. Bub expanded or rebuilt parts of the brewery almost every year, and by the turn of the twentieth century, the brewery had a capacity of nearly 20,000 barrels per year. Bub sold bottled beer as well as draught (though a few accounts claim that Bub's brewery did not sell bottled beer until after Prohibition, the ads and the labels themselves show otherwise). When Peter Bub died in 1911, management of the brewery was taken by his son-in-law, William M. F. Miller, who would be faced with the crisis of Prohibition.

Bub's was the only Winona brewery to remain in production during Prohibition. Under Miller's direction, the company made a combination of soft drinks and near beer. The brewery was raided at least once during Prohibition and stocks of beer with illegal alcohol content were seized. The most important decision Miller made during the 1920s was to hire Carlus Walter as the new brewmaster in 1928. Walter would remain with the brewery for the next four decades, ultimately becoming president of the company.

Bub's was one of the nine Minnesota breweries that had 3.2 percent beer available for sale on 7 April 1933. Bub's focused on supplying the local area and built a steady business. During World War II the brewery changed the name of its German Style beer to All-American beer for patriotic reasons. Despite having a solid local market, changes in the brewing industry would eventually spell the company's doom. Bub's was able to afford some limited television advertising, but could not compete for the viewers' attention against the national brewers. Costs, taxes, and shrinking market share forced Bub's to close in September 1969, after 107 years in the same location. Playing cards with Bub's All-American logo can be seen in chapter 3, and additional information on the brewery's history is in chapters 6 and 7.

The brewery escaped destruction in 1897 when a fire started in the barrel pitching shed. This time quick work by the fire department saved the brewery from total destruction. Schellhas Brewing Co. expanded throughout southeastern Minnesota until Prohibition. The company made unfermented wort for illegal brewing during Prohibition, but was forced to stop in 1931 and closed thereafter.

Park Brewing Co. (1904–1919)

Location: Front and Walnut streets

In 1903 the directors of Park Brewing Co. hired Chicago brewery architect Richard Griesser to design their new brewery building. The first batch of beer was ready for sale in the summer of 1904. Park Brewing Co. managed to avoid the fires that plagued the other Winona breweries, though the employees had their share of industrial accidents. Park's Sunshine brand became popular, and the company did its best to be a good corporate citizen by building a new public dock on the Mississippi River and by offering the public access to the brewery's well when there was a question about the sanitation of the city's water supply.

When Prohibition arrived, Park dumped its remaining supply of beer and dissolved the company. The building was used first as an apple warehouse and then was converted for use by the Peerless Chain Company. Most of the brewery still stands. Additional information about Park Brewing Company may be found in chapters 4 and 5.

Young America
[Carver County]

George Krahnschnable (1866–1871)
August Schmasse (1871–1879?)
Location: On Young America Lake near Fifth Avenue NE

George Krahnschnable started brewing in Young America in 1866. He appears in the excise records through 1869 but is not represented for the next two years. August Schmasse (or Schnasse), a former employee of August Schell, became proprietor of the brewery in October 1871. During the 1870s Schmasse

sold an average of 300 barrels each year. One local account claims that the brewery burned in 1878, but Schmasse reported sales of 389 barrels in 1879, and it is unlikely that all of that was preserved from the fire. Schmasse is still listed as a brewer in the 1880 census, though this does not mean he was employed at the time.

The 1906 Food and Drugs Act text is not present, indicating that this Sunshine beer bottle dates from the earliest years of Park Brewing Company. FROM THE COLLECTION OF DAVE WENDL.

The bar at Barley John's features just as much handcrafting as the beer: the bar and cribbage tables are made of trees from the property of friends and family of owner John Moore, the tap handles are mouth-blown glass, and some of the beers are made with hops grown on the premises. Visible near the center of the picture is a firkin, a small keg containing cask-conditioned ale. COURTESY OF BARLEY JOHN'S BREW PUB.

Minnesota Brewpubs: Pairing Beer and Food

I N RECENT YEARS, THERE HAS BEEN A RELAXATION OF THE STRICT DISTINC-
tions in Minnesota law between commercial breweries, which package beer for
consumption somewhere other than the brewery itself, and brewpubs, which
are licensed to sell their product only at their establishment. Brewpubs should not
be confused with restaurants that have unique beers brewed for them at a commercial brewery. To be considered a brewpub, the beer must be produced on the
premises (or in a few cases, at another branch of the same chain). While lobbyists
for Minnesota's craft brewers are calling for legislation to bring the state's practices in line with those of many other states, at the moment brewpubs may not sell
beer by the keg to customers and commercial breweries are limited in their ability
to sell beer in a retail brewery store. Brewpubs may sell their beer to customers
for off-premises consumption in half-gallon jugs called growlers, provided they
comply with local ordinances. Commercial breweries may offer samples of their
products at the end of a tour or serve them at a private party at the brewery. A few
commercial breweries recently have obtained permission to sell growlers at the
brewery. Because of these distinctions, the history of Minnesota's brewpubs is best
treated in a separate section.

Writing the history of a brewpub is both easier and harder than recording
the history of a commercial brewery. For many of the brewpubs listed here, the
business still exists or the personnel were still available for interviews. In several
cases the brewpubs were or are located in historic buildings. The beers are often
distinctive and provide insight into historic brewing styles. On the other hand,
there are usually few events of note other than opening and closing dates—which
is probably fine with the proprietors, because that means they have avoided fires,
floods, and other calamities. In a few cases, the brewpub was open for a very short
time and gained little attention. A further difficulty for the historian is the temptation to evaluate the food and the beer in the course of describing the establishment, which is more appropriately the job of a critic.

Most of Minnesota's brewpubs, whether started in an existing building or a new structure built specifically for that establishment, were conceived as brewpubs from the beginning. A few, such as O'Gara's and O'Hara's, were local institutions for many years before they adding brewing capability. The nature of the restaurant business makes any attempt at creating a definitive list of brewpubs frustrating at best—during the last two years, four brewpubs closed, one converted into a commercial brewery, and three opened—and rumors of forthcoming changes are common whenever beer lovers and brewing industry employees gather. Even so, Minnesota's brewpubs should be included in this volume because of the distinctive contributions they have made to brewing and beer culture in the state. Additional illustrations and information concerning several of the brewpubs appear in chapter 8.

Albert Lea [Freeborn County]

Green Mill Brewing Co. (2003–2004)
Location: 2218 E. Main Street

The first brewery in Albert Lea in almost 120 years began brewing in June 2003. The Green Mill restaurant chain installed a seven-barrel brewing system to see if the brewpub concept would be successful at locations other than St. Paul. Brewer Ron Flett commuted between St. Paul and Albert Lea during the short time when both brewpubs were in operation. The venture was not as successful as the company had hoped, in part because the restaurant's customers generally preferred national brands. (For additional information, see the St. Paul entry below.)

Bemidji [Beltrami County]

1st City Brewery & Grill (1999–2006)
Location: 128 First Street

In 1999 the 1st City Brewery and Grill, located in a restored railroad station, served the first batch of beer brewed in Bemidji since 1915. The brewhouse was located in a rustic cellar—in stark contrast to the fancy restaurant on the main floor. Until it closed in early 2006, the brewery offered several regular beers and rotating seasonal selections. (A beer sampler placemat from 1st City is featured in chapter 8.)

Duluth [St. Louis County]

Fitger's Brewhouse (1995–present)
Location: 600 E. Superior Street

Inspired by the Colorado brewing scene, Tim Nelson and Rod Raymond opened Fitger's Brewhouse in 1995. Located inside the historic Fitger's brewery complex, Fitger's Brewhouse has built a reputation for bold and creative beers. Among its signature beers are Witchtree ESB, Starfire Pale Ale, and Ole Redbeard Barleywine. Witchtree and Big Boat Oatmeal Stout have earned gold medals at brewing competitions. Between the brewhouse and the adjoining Red Star Club, as many as sixteen beers may be available at a time. Fitger's Brewhouse occasionally presents theme weeks featuring several different versions of a particular style, perhaps four different stouts, four different bock beers, or similar ranges of other styles. One of the most unusual beers is Wildfire, which is made with several different varieties of hot peppers. (Additional information about Fitger's Brewhouse is in chapter 8.)

Eagan [Dakota County]

Granite City Food & Brewery (2005–present)
Location: 3330 Pilot Knob Road

See the St. Cloud entry below.

Eden Prairie [Hennepin County]

Water Tower Brewing (1997–2003)
Location: 12200 Singletree Lane

Water Tower Brewing was supposed to be the first in a chain of brewpubs operated by bowling giant Brunswick. The building was started in 1996 but did not open until the next year. Brewer Dave Berg offered seven different beers that had been brewed on the premises.

A coaster collected by the author at Water Tower Brewing in 1998.

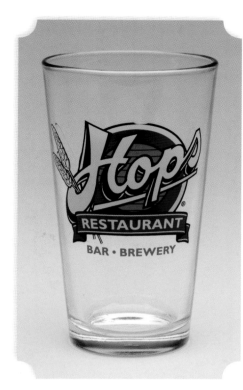

After nearly a decade in the Twin Cities, the Hops chain closed its establishments in Eden Prairie and Maple Grove as part of a corporate reorganization. FROM THE AUTHOR'S COLLECTION.

Despite the company's evaluation, the location did not attract the level of business that had been anticipated, and the operation did not succeed.

Hops Restaurant, Bar & Brewery (2001–2004)
Location: 11528 Leona Road

In 1999 the Hops chain of restaurants entered the Twin Cities market, the company's most distant venture from its headquarters in Florida. Despite the efforts of award-winning brewer Bob DuVernois, the Eden Prairie location suffered because the restaurant was very difficult to find. The Maple Grove restaurant, on the other hand, was in a highly visible location along Interstate 94. The parent company experienced financial difficulty and restaurants were closed in part because of a decision to concentrate operations in the South. Currently, a handful of restaurants are still in operation in Florida, a small reminder of what was once an extensive chain.

Lucan (Redwood County)

The BrauHaus (2004–2006)
Location: 111 Main Street

Originally a family restaurant and lounge, the BrauHaus became the first brewpub in the southwest part of the state when Dustin Brau began to offer his handcrafted beer in 2004. Among his specialties were a Scotch Ale, a Strawberry Wheat, and two Belgian-style beers. The population of Lucan is only about 220 people, which makes it one of the smallest Minnesota towns ever to host a brewery, and its two-barrel brewing system was among the smallest of any brewpub in the state. In 2006 Brau began to convert the brewpub into a small commercial brewery. Brau Brothers Brewing Co. presented its first beer at Autumn Brew Review in October 2006. (A growler from the BrauHaus is shown in chapter 8.)

Mankato (Blue Earth County)

Bandana Brewery (2003–2006)
Location: 302 N. Plainview Avenue

Brewer Dave Berg started brewing at the Bandana Brewery in 2003. Located in the former Elks club, the brewery featured beers named after local communities such as Mankato Gold, Rapidan Brown, and St. Peter Red. Berg also gained a reputation for high-alcohol seasonal specialties such as Hamburg Doppelbock and Skyline Weizenbock. However, the majority of the restaurant's clientele preferred national brands, and brewing stopped in the fall of 2006.

Maple Grove (Hennepin County)

Hops Restaurant, Bar & Brewery (1999–2005)
Location: 7855 Elm Creek Boulevard

See the Eden Prairie entry above.

Granite City Food & Brewery (2004–present)
Location: 11909 Main Street

See the St. Cloud entry below.

Minneapolis (Hennepin County)

Taps Waterfront Brewery (1989–1991)
Location: 25 Main Street SE

Tom Netolesky and Bill Grones opened Taps Waterfront Brewery and Comedy Club in the historic Brown Ryan Livery Stable near the Mississippi River in Old Saint Anthony. Taps offered both ale and lager styles. Taps did much to introduce Minnesotans to craft beer, but suffered from consistency problems and a poor location. In 1991 the state's pioneer brewpub closed. See chapter 8 for additional information.

Rock Bottom Restaurant & Brewery (1994–present)
Location: 800 LaSalle Plaza

The Rock Bottom Brewery in Minneapolis is part of a large nationwide chain of brewpubs (nearly thirty today), many of which are in downtown neighborhoods rather than suburban malls. During its first few years, the Minneapolis Rock Bottom offered a relatively unimaginative line of ales, but as the tastes of the beer-drinking public evolved, head brewer Todd Haug began to introduce different styles of beer and became more creative with the standard offerings. When Haug left to become the head brewer at Surly Brewing Co., Bryon Tonnis continued to experiment, with excellent results. Rock Bottom was one of several dozen breweries and brewpubs nationwide that celebrated Benjamin Franklin's 300th birthday in 2006 by brewing Poor Richard's Ale using a recipe designed to taste like the ales common in Franklin's day. (See chapter 8 for additional information. A Rock Bottom growler is included in a photo in that chapter. While the legend on the growler claims that the restaurant was established in 1993, it did not open until 1994.)

District Warehouse Brewing (1996–1999)
Location: 430 First Avenue N.

The District opened and began to offer handcrafted beers under the supervision of brewer Russ Lane, who had prior brewing experience with James Page and Summit. Several Twin Cities brewers or brewpub operators worked there at one point or another, including Blake Richardson of the Herkimer and John Moore of Barley John's. The District shared a dining area with Rosen's Bar and Grill, which grabbed most of the attention. At times, patrons attempting to be served at the District were directed to Rosen's instead. The District stopped brewing in 1999.

Minneapolis Town Hall Brewery (1997–present)
Location: 1430 Washington Avenue S.

Town Hall has won more medals at the Great American Beer Festival, including a Gold

Many brewpubs offer some kind of customer loyalty program—often called a pint club or a mug club—that offers discounts and special privileges to members. Some are free upon application, while others require either an initial or an annual fee. Town Hall's club offers numerous benefits, but only a limited number of spots are available each year. FROM THE AUTHOR'S COLLECTION.

Brewpubs have become an important part of the Minnesota food and drink scene. This poster for the Schwarzbier of The Herkimer Pub & Brewery emphasizes the local connections. Design by Jim Davis of MindSpark Creative. COURTESY OF THE HERKIMER PUB & BREWERY.

Medal in 2001 for Czar Jack Russian Imperial Stout, than any other Minnesota brewpub. Mike Hoops and his staff typically have five beers available, including an award-winning Scotch Ale, two or three seasonal beers, and two cask-conditioned ales. Former head brewer John Haggerty moved to Holland, Michigan, to develop creative beers at New Holland Brewing Company.

The Herkimer Pub & Brewery (1999–present)
Location: 2922 Lyndale Avenue S.

Planned by Blake Richardson, and initially conceived as the Bowery Pub and Brewery, the Herkimer opened in December 1999. The Herkimer is unusual among brewpubs for offering only German-style beers, most of which are lagers. Many brewpubs brew more ales than lagers, because ales are ready to serve sooner and take up less scarce storage space. While many brewpubs offer a handmade soda on their menu, the Herkimer is one of the very few to brew its own "energy drink," TripleCaff. The walls are decorated with retro-style art deco and pinup posters created by local artist Jim Davis. The Herkimer joined the ranks of gold medal–winning Minnesota brewpubs with its 2006 Great American Beer Festival award for brewer Dave Hartman's Kellerbier.

Cask-conditioned ales have a thinner head than other beers because they are less highly carbonated. The beer is drawn up to the taps by pulling on the handles of the beer engines instead of being pushed up by carbonation in the serving tanks. The four cask ales of Sherlock's Home in Minnetonka are shown here: Stag's Head Stout, Palace Porter, Piper's Pride, and Bishop's Bitter. COURTESY OF WILLIAM E. BURDICK.

Minnetonka [Hennepin County]

Sherlock's Home (1989–2002)
Location: 11000 Red Circle Drive

After several years of lobbying at the state Capitol to have Minnesota's laws changed to allow brewpubs to operate, William Burdick opened Sherlock's Home in Minnetonka. Sherlock's Home was the second brewpub in Minnesota, but it was the first to offer "real ale." The four hand-pulled cask ales were Stag's Head Stout, Palace Porter, Piper's Pride (Scotch Ale), and Bishop's Bitter. Sherlock's also offered three pushed beers and an occasional firkin of a seasonal such as Winter Warmer. Sherlock's hosted beer tastings, Scotch tastings, and homebrewing contests—often featuring renowned British beer writer Michael Jackson as a guest speaker or judge. Burdick closed Sherlock's in 2002 to concentrate on his Granite City ventures. (The story behind Minnesota's first brewpub is told in more detail in chapter 8.)

Moorhead [Clay County]

Trapper and Trader (1996–2001)
Location: 617 Center Avenue

Trapper and Trader was popular with college students but did not develop a reputation for distinctive beers. It was converted into a sports bar in 2001.

New Brighton [Ramsey County]

Barley John's Brew Pub (2000–present)
Location: 781 Old Highway 8

John Moore began brewing in January 2000 in a remodeled building that had previous lives as an A&W and a Chinese restaurant. His first brews were ready in time for St. Patrick's Day. The brewhouse features the smallest brewing system capable of doing German-style decoction brewing in North America. (Decoction brewing adds extra steps to the mashing process, but enhances the flavor of bocks and other German beer styles.) Moore began his career as a dietitian but attended the Siebel Institute of Technology and became a brewer. The brewpub, which Moore runs in partnership with his wife, Laura Subak, has built a reputation for unusual beers such as Wild Brunette wild rice ale and for several strong beers that are barrel-aged for added flavor. One of these, Rosie's Ale, is a barrel-aged version of Wild Brunette that goes through additional fermentation until its alcohol content approaches 20 percent, making it among the strongest beers in the world. (A photograph of a barrel of Rosie's Ale aging in the cellar is included in chapter 8, and a photo of the Barley John's bar opens this chapter.)

Rochester [Olmsted County]

Clubhaus Brewpub (1994–1999)
Location: 7 Second Street SW

The Clubhaus was Rochester's only brewpub to date. After the initial enthusiasm wore off, business started to decline. A massive road construction project cut off access to the area, which made it difficult for the Clubhaus to survive.

Roseville [Ramsey County]

Granite City Food & Brewery (2006–present)
Location: 851 Rosedale Center

See the St. Cloud entry below.

St. Cloud [Stearns County]

O'Hara's Brew Pub & Restaurant (1996–2007)
Location: 3308 Third Street N.

O'Hara's was the first brewery to set up business in St. Cloud since St. Cloud Brewing Co. closed its doors in 1939. The brewpub opened in a restaurant that had been a fixture in the neighborhood since 1945. Among the regularly available beers were Quarry Rock Red, Sid's Irish Stout, and Pantown Pale Ale, named for the part of the city where the Pan automobile was made in St. Cloud in the 1920s. (A photo of a growler from O'Hara's is included in chapter 8.) O'Hara's closed in May 2007.

Granite City Food & Brewery (1999–present)
Location: 3945 Second Street S.

The Granite City chain takes its name from the nickname of St. Cloud, the chain's original location. There are currently five locations in Minnesota and another thirteen throughout the upper Midwest, but more are planned by the parent company, Founders Food and Firkins. For all Granite City locations except St.

The short-lived Clubhaus left few artifacts to record its existence. Items such as this pint glass are scarce. FROM THE COLLECTION OF WAYNE THEUER.

Cloud, the wort is made at a central facility and shipped to the individual restaurants as part of a patented process called Fermentus Interuptus.

St. Louis Park [Hennepin County]

Granite City Food & Brewery (2006–present)
Location: 5500 Excelsior Boulevard

See the St. Cloud entry above.

St. Paul [Ramsey County]

Mill Street Brewery/Green Mill Brewing Co. (1995–present)
Location: 57 S. Hamline Avenue

Mill Street Brewery was built inside the existing Green Mill restaurant at the intersection of Hamline and Grand avenues. Brewer Ron Flett came to Mill Street after several years at James Page Brewing Company in Minneapolis. The brewery generally offers five beers plus one rotating seasonal style. The India pale ale and stout have occasionally been offered "on nitro," where the beer is pushed from the serving vessel with nitrogen instead of carbon dioxide. Among the most requested seasonal styles are the Pumpkin Ale and Grand Old Stone Beer (released in conjunction with the Grand Old Day community celebration), where hot rocks are used in the boil phase to help caramelize the wort.

Shannon Kelly's (1995–1998)
Location: 395 Wabasha Street

Founded by Jamie McGovern in 1995, Shannon Kelly's was the first brewpub in St. Paul. Blake Richardson took over as brewer soon after the restaurant opened. While credited with helping to educate local beer drinkers about the possibilities of craft beer, Shannon Kelly's was forced to close when the building in which it was located was razed to make way for the Lawson Software headquarters building.

O'Gara's Bar & Grill (1996–present)
Location: 164 Snelling Avenue N.

Jim O'Gara opened his tavern on Snelling Avenue in 1941. Under his management and that of his son Tim and grandson Dan, O'Gara's became a St. Paul institution. The

Cofounder and owner Sean O'Byrne and head brewer Bob DuVernois relax for a moment before the lunchtime rush in front of Great Waters Brewing Company. Sean has a pint of Golden Harvest Ale, and Bob is enjoying his Brown Trout Ale. COURTESY OF GREAT WATERS BREWING COMPANY.

original tavern expanded and added several more rooms. One of these was O'Gara's Brewpub, which included a seven-barrel brewing system so brewer Brian Benkstein could craft ales especially for O'Gara's.

Great Waters Brewing Co. (1997–present)

Location: 426 St. Peter Street

Founders Sean O'Byrne and Mark van Wie started Great Waters in an appropriate location—the Hamm Building. A few years later, Mark left Great Waters to operate other St. Paul restaurants that became known for their fine beer lists, even if the beer was not brewed on the premises. With four beer engines for cask-conditioned ales, Great Waters is the Minnesota brewpub most in compliance with the standards set by the Campaign for Real Ale

(CAMRA), a British organization that seeks to keep traditional brewing methods and styles alive. The brewery has had four different head brewers, each of whom adjusted the recipes of the standard offerings to suit his own tastes. Great Waters was a co-host for the dedication of the Hamm's Bear monument, which stands just a few steps away from the restaurant's patio.

Vine Park Brewing (1997–2003)

Location: 242 W. Seventh Street

David Thompson started Vine Park Brewery as a brew-on-premises operation, in which customers paid a fee to brew and bottle their own beer. By the next year, the business also included a brewpub, which became an extremely popular destination when the Minne-

sota Wild National Hockey League team began play in Xcel Energy Center. The brewpub and adjoining brewery were converted into a conventional sports bar in 2003.

The brew-on-premises part of the operation has relocated to 1254 West Seventh Street under the management of Dan Justesen.

Shakopee [Scott County]

The Brew Station (1999–2002)
Harwell's Steakhouse (2002–2003)

Location: 1128 Vierling Drive

The Brew Station was a combination homebrew shop and brewpub. In 2002 it was converted to Harwell's Steakhouse and offered beers crafted by brewer Jonathan Crist. The restaurant closed at the end of 2003.

Stillwater [Washington County]

Vittorio's (1997–2001)

Location: 402 S. Main Street

The Joseph Wolf brewing complex in Stillwater was mostly vacant after the company closed for good in 1925. In the mid-1940s, local businessman Tom Curtis purchased the building, flooded the caves, stocked the pools with trout, and offered fishing and cave tours. In 1973 Sondra Gozzi opened Vittorio's Restaurant, which became a popular destination for several decades. During the last few years of operation, Vittorio's also offered handcrafted beers, including a porter and a German ale. Most of the building remains intact, and part of it is currently used as a coffee shop.

Winona [Winona County]

Backwater Brewing Company/Wellington's Pub & Grill (1995–present)

Location: 1429 W. Service Drive

Backwater Brewing is the only brewpub in Minnesota currently sharing a building with a bowling alley. It also features one of the smallest brewing systems of any brewpub in the state.

Notes

From Barley to Bar Stool

1. This discussion of brewing history draws on several sources: Stanley Baron, *Brewed in America: A History of Beer and Ale in the United States* (Boston: Little, Brown & Co., 1962); Michael Jackson, *Michael Jackson's Beer Companion: The World's Great Beer Styles, Gastronomy, and Traditions*, 2nd ed. (Philadelphia: Running Press, 1997); Gregg Smith, *Beer in America: the Early Years—1587–1840* (Boulder, Colo.: Siris Books, 1998); Richard W. Unger, *Beer in the Middle Ages and the Renaissance* (Philadelphia: University of Pennsylvania Press, 2004); Bill Yenne, *The American Brewery* (St. Paul: Motorbooks International, 2003); *One Hundred Years of Brewing* (Supplement to the *Western Brewer*), reprint edition (New York: Arno Press, 1972).

2. For the section on brewing chemistry, several sources were consulted: Jackson, *Beer Companion*; Garrett Oliver, *The Brewmaster's Table: Discovering the Pleasures of Real Beer with Real Food* (New York: HarperCollins, 2003); Lee W. Janson, *Brew Chem 101: The Basics of Homebrewing Chemistry* (Pownal, Vt.: Storey Communications, Inc., 1996); Randy Mosher, *Radical Brewing: Recipes, Tales & World-Altering Meditations in a Glass* (Boulder, Colo.: Brewers Publications, 2004); John Palmer, *How to Brew*, 1st ed. (online edition at www.howtobrew.com); Charlie Papazian, *The Complete Joy of Home Brewing* (New York: Avon, 1984); Gordon Strong, et al., *Beer Judge Certification Program Style Guidelines for Beer, Mead and Cider* (version 2005-A), (online at www.bjcp.org); issues of the periodicals *Brew Your Own*, *Brewers Digest*, and *Zymurgy*. The contributions of members of the Minnesota Homebrewers Association and the St. Paul Homebrewers Club were also essential.

3. *Minneapolis Sunday Tribune* (5 May 1963): E1, E5; Moira F. Harris, *The Paws of Refreshment: The Story of Hamm's Beer Advertising* (St. Paul: Pogo Press, 2000), 44; *Minneapolis Star Tribune* (3 October 1997) (online archives) and (14 May 1998): B1.

4. The brewing publications of the era did not use these terms with precision, and newspaper advertisements tended to use whatever term was most familiar to the local audience. See M. L. Byrn, *The Complete Practical Brewer* (Philadelphia: Henry Carey Baird, 1852), reprint edition by Raudins Books, 2002.

1. Pioneer Brewing

1. *Minneapolis Star Tribune* (6 July 2000): T2.

2. *Red Wing Argus* (5 January 1871): 4.

3. Richard W. Unger, *Beer in the Middle Ages and the Renaissance* (Philadelphia: University of Pennsylvania Press, 2004): 11–13.

4. Virginia Brainard Kunz, *Saint Paul: The First 150 Years* (St. Paul: The Saint Paul Foundation, 1991): 11–14.

5. Judge Advocate General, Selected Courts Martial, National Archives Record Group 153, microfilm M 227, roll 2, Minnesota Historical Society.

6. *One Hundred Years of Brewing* (New York: Arno Press, 1974; reprint of the 1903 H.S. Rich & Co. edition): 228.

7. Edward D. Neill, *History of Hennepin County and the City of Minneapolis* (Minneapolis: North Star Publishing Co., 1881): 420.

8. *St. Anthony Express* (31 May 1851): 3.

9. Edward D. Neill, *History of Washington County and the St. Croix Valley* (Minneapolis: North Star Publishing Company, 1881): 523.

10. John G. Rice, "The Old-Stock Americans," in *They Chose Minnesota*, June Drenning Holmquist, ed. (St. Paul: Minnesota Historical Society Press, 1981).

11. Harriet E. Bishop, *Floral Home; or First Years of Minnesota* (New York: Sheldon, Blakeman and Company, 1857): 105, 109.

12. Territorial Archives: Petitions: Joint Committee, Box 115.I.19.12F, folders Petitions 1851 & Petitions 1853, Minnesota Historical Society. Norbert Kimmick was one of the signers of a petition from Stillwater "wets."

13. *Minneapolis Sunday Tribune* (12 May 1901): unnumbered back page.

14. *Chatfield Democrat* (29 January 1859): 3.

15. *Minnesota: Its Progress and Capabilities*. Second annual report of the Commissioner of Statistics (St. Paul: Wm. R. Marshall, 1862): 61, 74, 84.

2. Fewer Ales, More Rails

1. Richard Moe, *The Last Full Measure: The Life and Death of the First Minnesota Volunteers* (New York: Henry Holt, 1993): 24–25.

2. Stanley Baron, *Brewed in America: A History of Beer and Ale in the United States* (Boston: Little, Brown and Co., 1962): 213.

3. Some authors have written that the rates were $50 and $100, but the rate guide from 1862 and the actual amounts paid support the lower figures. The fees were doubled later in the decade.

4. Baron, *Brewed in America*, 215.

5. Timothy Holian, *Over the Barrel: The Brewing History and Beer Culture of Cincinnati, Vol. 1, 1800–Prohibition* (St. Joseph, Mo.: Sudhaus Press, 2000): 60; Bill Yenne, *The American Brewery* (St. Paul: MBI Publishing Co., 2003): 34.

6. *Minnesota Staats-Zeitung* (28 June 1862): 3.

7. *Hastings Conserver* (24 July 1866): 4.

8. *Rochester Post* (25 December 1869): 3.

9. *Superior Chronicle* [Wis.] (15 October 1864): 4.

10. Mark Peihl, "Moorhead's Brewery," *Clay County Historical Society Newsletter* (January-February 1992): 3–4.

11. *Martin County Sentinal* [sic] (various issues from 7 January 1876 through 1 July 1880).

12. Alden O. Droivold, ed., *History of Rushford: Whiskey, Wheat and Wagons* (Rushford, Minn.: Rushford Area Historical Society, 1988): 2. If Wegener really came to America in 1870, as local accounts hold, his service was brief since the war only lasted from 1870 to 1871.

13. *Alexandria Post* (various issues); *Illustrated Album of Biography of the famous Valley of the Red River* (Chicago: Alden, Ogle & Company, 1889): page number missing from copy at Douglas County Historical Society.

3. Patronize Home Industry

1. Adam Smith, *The Wealth of Nations*, Book I, Chapter II, paragraph 3 (Harvard Classics edition online at www.bartleby.com).

2. George E. Warner and Charles M. Foote, *History of Dakota County, Minnesota* (Minneapolis: North Star Publishing Co., 1881): 216.

3. *Alexandria Citizen* (14 June 1900), special edition: no page number.

4. *Freeborn County Standard* (Albert Lea, Minn.) (19 January 1871): 3.

5. *Pope County Press* (Glenwood, Minn.) (7 March 1884): 4; *Freeborn County Standard* (3 June 1885): 5.

6. *Mower County Transcript* (Austin, Minn.) (18 November 1869): 4.

7. *Rochester Post* (14 July 1899): 2; (13 May 1871): 3; (12 May 1899): 1, 2, 3; (26 May 1899): 1.

8. *Le Sueur Sentinel* (23 July 1874): 4.

9. *Detroit Record* [Minn.] (7 August 1886): 3.

10. *The Northwest on Wheels: An Illustrated Magazine of Literature, Agriculture and Western Progress* (St. Paul and Minneapolis, July 1885) available at East Otter Tail County Historical Museum, no other information available.

11. James Daly and Ludwig Fellerer, speech to Otter Tail County Historical Society, Alcohol & Chemical Use: Breweries folder, Otter Tail County Historical Society.

12. *Perham Enterprise-Bulletin* (30 October 1986): 7.

13. Ibid.

14. *Mantorville Express* (27 June 1862): 2.

15. *Winona Daily Republican* (17 August 1872): 2; (19 August 1872): 2.

16. *Rochester Record & Union* (28 July 1876): 3.

17. *Hastings Gazette* (22 December 1866): 4.

18. *Weekly Valley Herald* (Chaska, Minn.) (8 August 1878): 1.

19. *Sauk Rapids Sentinel* (21 October 1884): 4.

20. *Shakopee Argus* (1 March 1862): 3; *Shakopee Tribune* (6 August 1909): 8.

21. *Rochester City News* (27 June 1860): 2.

22. Randy Carlson, *The Breweries of Iowa* (Bemidji, Minn.: Self-published, 1985): i.

23. *Ellsworth News* (14 November 1902): 5.

4. Craft Becomes Industry

1. John E. Land, *Historical and Descriptive Review of the Industries of St. Paul, 1882–1883* (St. Paul: John E. Land, 1883): 111. Cited in Gary J. Bruggemann, "Beer Capital of the State—St. Paul's Historic Family Breweries," *Ramsey County History* 16:2 (1981): 10.

2. *Rochester Post* (4 April 1868): 3.

3. *Minneapolis Star Tribune* (17 November 2006): B3.

4. *Mower County Transcript* (17 March 1870): 4.

5. "Ice Making on Mississippi River," Breweries file, Dakota County Historical Society.

6. *Jordan Independent* (28 January 1915): 12.

7. *Rochester Post and Record* (31 March 1899): 3.

8. Stanley Baron, *Brewed in America* (Boston: Little, Brown and Company, 1962): 237.

9. *Minneapolis Journal* (28 July 1903): 7.

10. *Freeborn County Standard* (Albert Lea, Minn.) (29 April 1885): 6.

11. Clarence Johnson, *Fitger's: The Brewery and its People* (Duluth, Minn.: Fitger's Publishing, 2004): 14.

12. Contract between Chicago and Northwestern Railway Company and Park Brewing Co., Park Brewing Co. folder, Winona Historical Society.

13. *Freeborn County Standard* (19 August 1885): 2.

14. Thomas C. Cochran, *The Pabst Brewing Company: The History of an American Business* (New York: New York University Press, 1948): 173.

15. Ibid., 175.

16. *Rochester Post* (17 May 1894): 2.

17. *Rochester Post* (27 January 1893): 1.

18. The exterior of the Hamm's depot in East Grand Forks was restored in 2003. See Moira F. Harris, "Restoring the Eagles in East Grand Forks," *American Breweriana Journal* 134 (March–April): 19–21.

19. Cochran, *Pabst Brewing Company*, 180–81.

20. *Winona Daily Republican* (9 October 1890): 3; *Ogden* [Utah] *Standard* (19 April 1891): 4 and (31 March 1893): 3; *Utah History Encyclopedia*, online edition www.media.utah.edu/UHE/o/OGDEN.html

21. *Minneapolis Journal* (28 March 1901): 5; Robert Hajicek, "Glencoe Brewing Co.," *Breweriana Collector* (Winter 1993): 21. Hajicek lists the capital stock as $40,000.

22. *Minneapolis Journal* (18 April 1900): supplement p. 12.

23. Johnson, *Fitger's*, 28.

24. *Minneapolis, Minnesota; her phenomenal progress, incomparable industries, and remarkable resources . . . The Flour City, the industrial center of the Northwest* (Minneapolis: Railway Publishing Company, 1902?): 177; A. Blissenbach, *Souvenir of Mankato, Minn.* (Mankato, Minn.: Blissenbach Studios, 1900?): 29.

25. Ron Feldhaus, *The Bottles, Breweriana and Advertising Jugs of Minnesota: 1850–1920* (Minneapolis: North Star HBCA, 1986): 16.

26. Thomas Hughes, *History of Blue Earth County and Biographies of its Leading Citizens* (Chicago: Middle West Publishing Company, 1909): 337–38.

27. Moira F. Harris, ed., *Louise's Legacy: Hamm Family Stories* (St. Paul: Pogo Press, 1998): 85–114.

28. William Bell Mitchell, *History of Stearns County, Minnesota* (Chicago: H.C. Cooper, Jr. & Co., 1915): 375.

5. From Temperance to Prohibition

1. The historical background of drink and the temperance movement is primarily drawn from: Andrew Barr, *Drink: A Social History of America* (New York: Carroll & Graf, 1999) and from Mark Edward Lender and James Kirby Martin, *Drinking in America: A History. The Revised and Expanded Edition* (New York: The Free Press, 1987).

2. Lender and Martin, *Drinking in America*, 69.

3. *Houston County Journal* (Caledonia, Minn.) (22 September 1877): 1.

4. *Redwood Falls Mail* (24 December 1869): 4.

5. *Henderson Democrat* (4 February 1859): 2.

6. *Rochester Post* (14 November 1890): 2.

7. *Brainerd Tribune* (26 June 1880): 4.

8. *Hastings Gazette* (13 July 1867): 4.

9. Franklyn Curtiss-Wedge, *History of Freeborn County, Minnesota* (Chicago: H. C. Cooper, 1911): 346–47.

10. *Jackson Republic* (19 December 1874): 3.

11. *Minneapolis Journal* (25 May 1908): 1.

12. *Minneapolis Journal* (25 September 1908): 1–2; (21 November 1908): 1; (4 January 1909): 6.

13. *Minneapolis Journal* (21 November 1908): 1.

14. *Minneapolis Journal* (14 April 1912): 14.

15. Sean Dennis Cashman, *Prohibition: The Lie of the Land* (New York: The Free Press, 1981): 7.

16. *Minneapolis Journal* (4 January 1907): 7.

17. *Waseca Leader* (14 April 1877): 3.

18. *Moorhead Weekly News* (28 March 1901): 4.

19. *Bemidji Weekly Pioneer* (10 December 1914): 1; (4 March 1915): 1; (25 February 1915): 1.

20. *Yearbook of the United States Brewers Association: 1913* (New York: USBA, 1913): 37.

21. *Winona Republican-Herald* (11 March 1910): 8; (30 September 1914): 6; (6 October 1914): 5.

22. "Traveling Men's Liberty League of Minnesota," pocket binder, c. 1909, author's collection.

23. Ernest Gordon, *When the Brewer Had the Stranglehold* (New York: Alcohol Information Committee, 1930): 3.

24. Letter from Franklin D. Roosevelt to Mrs. Fred Schuster, Schuster Family folder, Olmsted County Historical Society.

25. *Winona Republican-Herald* (9 February 1920): 1.

26. *Minneapolis City Directory*, 1919 (ads in left side lines).

27. *Rochester Post & Record* (4 November 1921): 6.

28. *Little Falls Daily Transcript* (13 May 1920) and invoices, both in Kiewel Brewing Co. folder, Morrison County Historical Society, Little Falls, Minn.

29. Richard Sweet, unpublished article on Kiewel activities in Canada, Kiewel Brewing Co. and Related Businesses folder, Morrison County Historical Society; Bonnie DeBoe, interviewer, Elisabeth E. Hjermstad (Kuenzel) oral history recorded 22 July 1976, RC 0101 F, Dakota County Historical Museum.

30. *Dodge County Star* (3 April 1924) and Mantorville *Express* (2 December 1927), Mantorville Brewery folder, Dodge County Historical Society.

31. *Winona Republican-Herald* (18 October 1923): 1; (28 February 1924): 1.

32. Hjermstad Oral History, Dakota County Historical Society; Michael Hajicek, interview by author (August 2004); *Winona Daily News* (5 December 1984): 1, 7.

6. New Jobs, New Containers, New Rules

1. Stanley Baron, *Brewed in America: A History of Beer and Ale in the United States* (Boston: Little, Brown and Co., 1962): 321.

2. Baron, *Brewed in America*, 320–23. All contemporary newspaper accounts claim that nineteen states offered legal beer on this date.

3. Roland C. Amundson, "Listen to the Bottle Say 'Gluek, Gluek, Gluek,'" *Hennepin History* (Winter 1988–89): 6.

4. *Winona Republican-Herald* (6 April 1933): 1.

5. *Winona Republican-Herald* (8 April 1933): 3.

6. *Montgomery Messenger* (29 September 1933): 2.

7. *Little Falls Daily Telegraph* (31 August 1933): 1; (2 May 1934): no page number available.

8. Warren M. Persons, *Beer and Brewing in America: An Economic Study* (New York: United Brewers Industrial Foundation, 1941): 24–39.

9. *Minneapolis Tribune* (7 June 1941): 1, 3; (3 April 1946): 1. The Hamm and Bremer kidnappings are covered in detail in Paul Maccabee's *John Dillinger Slept Here: A Crooks' Tour of Crime and Corruption in St. Paul, 1920–1936* (St. Paul: Minnesota Historical Society Press, 1995). The Minneapolis Brewing Company robbery was not solved until five years later.

10. *St. Cloud Journal-Press* (21 August 1933): no page number available; *Melrose Beacon* (15 February 1934): 1.

11. *Melrose Beacon* (5 October 1933): 1; (19 October 1933): 1; *Minneapolis Star* (2 April 1972): 13B.

12. *Park Region Echo* (Alexandria, Minn.) (11 April 1935): 1; (30 May 1935): 1; (16 April 1936): 1.

13. *Park Region Echo* (13 April 1939): no page number available.

14. *Mantorville Express* (29 March 1934): no page number available.

15. *Mankato Free Press* (22 September 1933): 9.

16. Mansel Blackford, *A History of Small Business in America* (New York: Twayne Publishers, 1991): 69.

17. "History of Local 343 of the International Union of United Brewery, Flour, Cereal, Soft Drink and Distillery Workers of America" (St. Paul: Privately published, 1968): 31–42.

18. *Local Job Descriptions for Two Establishments in the Malt Liquor Manufacturing Industry*. Preliminary Job Study No. 5-113, Works Progress Administration and Minnesota Department of Education (St. Paul: United States Employment Center, 1939): 2–6.

19. *Little Falls Daily Telegraph* (15 February 1938): 1. Henry Pertler, 60, had worked at the brewery for thirty years.

20. "Historical Facts of Interest About our Union" (St. Paul: Local 343, privately published, 1968): 1–4.

21. June Drenning Holmquist, ed., *They Choose Minnesota: A Survey of the State's Ethnic Groups* (St. Paul: Minnesota Historical Society Press, 1981): 84; *Minneapolis Spokesman* (various issues of April, May, and June 1935).

22. Persons, *Beer and Brewing*, 22.

23. *The Friendly Faucet* (June 1937): 7. (*The Friendly Faucet* was the in-house newsletter of Minneapolis Brewing Company during the years after repeal.)

24. Material in this section is drawn from various pages in Baron, *Brewed in America*; Lee Nuernberg, *Beer Cans of Minnesota* (Columbia Heights, Minn.: North Star Chapter BCCA, 1982); *United States Beer Cans: The Standard Reference of Flat Tops and Cone Tops* (Fenton, Mo.: Beer Can Collectors of America, 2001).

25. Grain Belt Breweries, Inc., Company Records, Box 14, Folder 5, Minnesota Historical Society.

26. Persons, *Beer and Brewing*, 25.

27. *St. Peter Herald* (2 April 1981): 5.

28. Baron, *Brewed in America*, 332–34.

29. Andrew Barr, *Drink: A Social History of America* (New York: Carroll & Graf, 1999): 335.

30. *Alexandria Citizen News* (12 March 1942): 3; (21 May 1942): 1, 3.

31. *New York Times* (11 November 1944): 16.

32. *New York Times* (13 February 1942): 18.

33. "Notes on Estimates of Minimum Civilian Consumer Requirements," *New York Times* (21 February 1942): 24.

34. *Brewers Digest* (October 1946): 29.

35. Kihm Winship, "Three Millennia of Beer Styles," *All About Beer* 21:1 (March 2000): 31; Amundson, "Listen to the Bottle": 7; Index to Patents and Trademarks (Washington, D.C.: U.S. Patent and Trademark Office, 1943 and 1944).

36. *New York Times* (5 May 1943): 33; (12 September 1943): S11.

37. *Brewers Digest* (August 1945): 33, 41.

38. *Brewers Digest* (March 1945): 59; (April 1945): 33; (July 1945): 60.

39. *St. Paul Pioneer Press* (7 January 1945): 14; (11 January 1945): 1; (14 January 1945): 11; (21 January 1945): 12; (13 February 1945): 1.

40. *Brewers Digest* (June 1946): 32.

41. Blackford, *A History*, 74.

42. Kevin Busse, "The 'Missing Years' of Jordan Beer," *American Breweriana Journal* (July-August 2002): 21-23.

7. Sky Blue Waters, Bland Yellow Beer

1. *Brewers Digest* (February 1950): 30; *Brewers Almanac: 1952* (New York: United States Brewers Foundation, 1952): 3.

2. *Brewers Digest* (April 1952): 59-60.

3. *Brewers Digest* (September 1949): 57.

4. *Vintage TV Beer Commercials: 100 Beer Commercials of the 1950s & 60s* (VHS) (Schnitzelbank Press, 1995).

5. *Brewers Digest* (April 1953): 52-53; (September 1950): 86; (July 1953): 44-45.

6. *Brewers Digest* (August 1954): 101; (October 1948): 69.

7. *Little Falls Daily Transcript* (3 November 1913): 1.

8. *Brewers Digest* (August 1954): 76; Grain Belt Breweries, Inc., corporate records, box 8, scrapbook of 1957, unidentified clipping, Minnesota Historical Society (hereafter, Grain Belt Scrapbooks).

9. *Brewers Digest* (June 1954): 84.

10. *Brewers Digest* (October 1953): 57.

11. *Brewers Digest* (May 1948): 66; (March 1952), 72; (July 1953): 69, 74.

12. *The Grain Belt Diamond* (May 1961): 11; (October 1961): 11; *Northwest Teamster* (2 March 1961), all in Grain Belt Scrapbooks, 1959-1964. The rhythmic shouts of, "Cold beer here! Schmidt beer here!" still echo in my ears and those of many other fans decades after the demolition of Metropolitan Stadium and the takeover of beer concessions by out-of-state brands.

13. Grain Belt Scrapbooks, 1959-1964; "Grain Belt Brewery Memories Book," 2003, Pierre Bottineau Library, Minneapolis; Schmidt/Heileman employees interviewed by author (July 2004); *Brewers Digest* (December 1947): 66.

14. *Pioneers in Caring: The Projects of the Hamm Foundation* (St. Paul: Hamm Foundation, 1995): various pages; Margot Fortunato Galt, *Otto Bremer: His Life and Legacy* (St. Paul: Bremer Foundation, 1994): various pages.

15. *Brewers Digest* (April 1953): 64.

16. *Brewers Digest* (October 1948): 33.

17. *Brewers Almanac: 1957* (New York: United States Brewers Foundation, 1957): 4.

18. *Brewers Digest* (June 1946): 32; (October, 1946): 10.

19. Gerri Kustelski, brewing chemist for Hamm, Stroh's, and Summit, interview by author (18 July 2005). This claim was also supported through interviews with several brewmasters, though I will refrain from mentioning them in connection with this issue.

20. *Omaha World-Herald* (28 May 1967), Grain Belt Scrapbooks, 1964-1968.

21. *Minneapolis Tribune* (6 August 1967): 5c.

22. *Minneapolis Tribune* (16 March 1959), Grain Belt Scrapbooks, 1959-1964.

23. Moira F. Harris, *The Paws of Refreshment* (St. Paul: Pogo Press, 2000): chapter 3 inclusive; John Smallshaw, "Howard Hughes and Gulf Brewing Co." *American Breweriana Journal* (May-June 2004): 19.

24. *Minneapolis Star* (16 October 1957), Grain Belt Scrapbooks, 1957-1959.

25. Grain Belt Scrapbooks, 1957-1959, various items.

26. *Brewer's Bulletin* (6 April 1967), Grain Belt Scrapbooks, 1964-1968.

27. *Minneapolis Tribune* (6 August 1967), Grain Belt Scrapbooks, 1964-1968.

28. *Omaha World-Herald* (17 December 1967): 1; *Brewer's Bulletin* (2 May 1968): 1, Grain Belt Scrapbooks, 1964-1968.

29. Peter H. Blum, *Brewed in Detroit: Breweries and Beers Since 1830* (Detroit: Wayne State University Press, 1999): 53, 241-43.

30. Several former employees interviewed by author (various dates).

31. Pete Clure, interview by author (31 July 2005).

32. *Minneapolis Tribune* (2 May 1964): 8.

33. *Minneapolis Tribune* (10 November 1964): 7.

34. *Mankato Free Press* (19 July 1967): 15, 19.

35. Frank Bures Jr., Historical summary of Winona breweries, Breweries folder, Winona County Historical Society, Winona, Minn.; Br. H. Raphael Erler, "What Winona Makes—Makes Winona," *Chronicles* (Winona County Historical Society newsletter, Fall 1982).

36. *New York Times* (7 January 1965): 41; (20 March 1965): 31; (12 October 1965): 67; Harris, *Paws*, 28-29.

37. *Brewers Digest* (September 1972): 136; (November 1972): 86; *Minneapolis Star* (2 March 1976), Industries: Brewing: Grain Belt Brewery folder, Hennepin County Historical Society, Minneapolis; Tony Kennedy, "A Regional Brand's Boisterous Century," *Minneapolis Star Tribune* (30 August 1993): 1D.

8. The Waters Turn Dark Amber

1. Philip Van Munching, *Beer Blast: The Inside Story of the Brewing Industry's Bizarre Battles for Your Money* (New York: Random House, 1997): 117–18.

2. Anchor Brewing Company, "Gold Rush to Earthquake," http://www.anchor brewing.com/brewery/ourhistory.htm.

3. *Brewers Digest* (November 1948): 26–29.

4. John Dominick, "It's the Water," *Crossings* (Stearns County Historical Society newsletter) (October-November 1992): 6.

5. *Midwest Beer Notes* (February-March 1997): B14; Mike Kneip, interview by author (11 July 2005).

6. *Minneapolis Star Tribune* (10 March 1995): D1; (19 November 1998): D1.

7. Kneip interview.

8. Les Nuernberg, ed., *Beer Cans of Minnesota* (Columbia Heights, Minn.: North Star Chapter-BCCA, 1982): 3–64; Ted Marti, interview by author (8 July 2005).

9. *St. Paul Pioneer Press Dispatch* (27 May 1987): 1B.

10. Ted Marti, interview by author (24 July 2006).

11. *Midwest Beer Notes* (May-June 1992): 7.

12. *Midwest Beer Notes* (June-July 1993): 1–2, 8.

13. *Minneapolis Star Tribune* (30 April 1999): D1; (23 July 2002): D1; (25 March 2003), D1; Marti (8 July 2005).

14. Paul D. Koeller and David H. DeLano, *Brewed with Style: The Story of the House of Heileman* (La Crosse, Wis.: University of Wisconsin–La Crosse Foundation [R C Printing], 2004): 107–21. Koeller and DeLano make a few minor date and spelling errors in their coverage of St. Paul events.

15. *Minneapolis Star Tribune* (10 December 1991): D1; (13 June 1992): D1.

16. *Minneapolis Star Tribune* (30 August 1993): D1; (3 June 1993): D1.

17. *Minneapolis Star Tribune* (14 June 1994): D1; *Midwest Beer Notes* (October-November 1996): 29; *Midwest Beer Notes* (February-March 1996): 5; Charlie Long, interview by author (February 2005); Sig Plagens, interview by author (July 2004).

18. *Minneapolis Star Tribune* (15 August 1997): D1; (12 December 1997): D8; (20 February 1998): D1; (7 May 1999): D3; (4 August 2000): D1.

19. *Minneapolis Star Tribune* (22 February 2002): D1; (25 June 2002): A1; (14 May 2004): A1.

20. Materials provided by Minnesota Department of Revenue, Special Taxes Division; Richard Kaye, interview by author (14 March 2006).

21. Summit Brewing Company, "Summit History," http://www.summitbrewing. com/history.php; *Midwest Beer Notes* (July-August 1992): 1–2.

22. *Midwest Beer Notes* (May-June 1992): 1–2.

23. Marti interview (8 July 2005).

24. Van Munching, *Beer Blast*, 152.

25. Pete Slosberg, *Beer for Pete's Sake: The Wicked Adventures of a Brewing Maverick* (Boulder, Colo.: Siris Books, 1998): 70–73; *Midwest Beer Notes* (February-March 1997): B21.

26. *Midwest Beer Notes* (November-December 1993): 9; (December 1996-January 1997): 26; (April-May 1998): 20; *St. Paul Pioneer Press Dispatch* (27 May 1987): 2B.

27. *Great Lakes Brewing News* (February-March 1999): 22; *Duluth News Tribune* (21 April 2005): online version; John Judd and Dan Hay, interviews by author (July 2005).

28. *Midwest Beer Notes* (February-March 1996): 35; (June-July 1997): A4; (June-July 1999): 13; Tod Fyten, interview by author (various dates).

29. *Minneapolis Star Tribune* (12 September 1996): D1; (17 September 1998): D1–D2; David Johnson, interview by author (October 1996).

30. *New York Mills Herald* (19 March 1998): 1.

31. *Minneapolis Star Tribune* (22 July 1997): D1; (3 February 1998): D1; (16 December 1998): D1; (29 September 1999): D3; (16 October 1999): D3; (22 December 2000): D1; "Stevens Point Buys James Page Brands," *Modern Brewery Age*, 21 March 2005, http://www.findarticles. com/p/articles/mi_m3469/is_12_56/ ai_n13597748.

32. Omar Ansari and Todd Haug, interviews by author (various dates).

33. Bill Burdick, interview by author (July 2005).

34. *Great Lakes Brewing News* (February-March 2004): 28.

35. *Midwest Beer Notes* (February-March 1996): 25.

36. Burdick interview; *Midwest Beer Notes*, various issues.

37. The brewpub section is based on interviews with owners, managers, or brewers at each business, selected issues of *Midwest Beer Notes* and *Great Lakes Brewing News*, and conversations with Jim Lee Ellingson, Minnesota correspondent for *Great Lakes Brewing News*.

38. *Midwest Beer Notes* (February-March 1997): A21.

Index

A

ABA. *See* American Breweriana Association
Abel, Herman, 233
Aberle, Andreas, 203, 226
Aberle, Christian, 41, 203
Aberle, Fred, 41, 203
Aberle & Ahrentz, 226
Aberle Bros., 203
Adam & Reichel, 305
adjuncts, 4
advertising, xi, 65, 75, 148-55, 159-60, 178;
    bumper stickers, 169; cartoons, 153, 162;
    expenditures, 150, 160; in magazines,
    148; in newspapers, 150; outdoor signs,
    151; point of sale, 7, 150, 151-52, 157-58;
    on radio, 150, 162; relation to sales, 150,
    169, 216; restrictions on, 126; strategy,
    149-50, 153; on television, 150, 162;
    during wartime, 140-41, 149. *See also*
    Hamm's Bear; marketing; *individual
    breweries*
African Americans, 133-34, 270, 297
agents, 53, 78-79, 81-82, 271, 274. *See also*
    branch offices; depots
Ahles, John, 225
Ahrentz & Co., 298
Aiple, Francis X. (Frank), 20, 21-22, 300, 301
Aiple, Susannah. *See* Burkhard, Susannah
Aiple Brewing Company: St. Paul, 288, 300,
    301; Stillwater, 300, 301
Alaska: exports to, 143, 163, 219
Albachten, Adolph, 28, 58, 299
Albert Lea, Minnesota, 38, 49, 202, 312

alcohol consumption: historical trends,
    97-102, 159. *See also* beer
ale, 13-15, 35, 98, 215, 255-56, 260; bottle-
    conditioned, 256; definition of, 1; produc-
    tion of, 14, 35-37; sales compared with
    lager, 35-36. *See also* beer
Alexandria, Minnesota, 31, 40, 41-42, 47-48,
    129-30, 202-3
Alexandria Brewing Association, 203
Alexandria Brewing Co. (1905-1917), 70, 77,
    203
Alexandria Brewing Co. (1935-1943), viii, 55,
    129-30, 144-45, 186, 203, 278
Allen, Joe, 174
Alton, Minnesota, 203
Altoona Brewing Co. (Altoona, Pennsylvania),
    159
Alum-A-Bottle, 176-77
Amana (Amish) colony, 174, 214
Ambleside Brewing Co., 185, 186, 257
American Breweriana Association (ABA), 50,
    199
American Breweries (Bull, Friedrich, and Gotts-
    chalk), ix, 197
American Breweries II (van Wieren), 197
American Brewers Association, 139
American Can Company, 135, 137
American Federation of Labor (AFL), 143
American Indians: and alcohol, 23, 303;
    treaty enforcement, 41, 54, 110, 112, 271.
    See also Dakota War of 1862
American Society for the Promotion of Tem-
    perance, 99
Anderman, Robert, 304

Andersen, Gail, 236
Anderson, Christian, 215
Anheuser-Busch Brewing Co. (St. Louis, Missouri), 78, 81, 160, 169, 171, 227, 249; advertising, 110, 150; branch in St. Paul, 79; and Virginia Brewing Co., 303
Anneke, Percy S., 215
Anneke, Victor, 216
Anoka, Minnesota, 103
Ansari, Omar, 187, 208
anti-German sentiment. See German immigrants
Anti-Saloon League, 109. See also prohibition
anti-trust actions, 168
Appel, Susan K., 91
Appleton Brewing Co., 204
Aquatennial, Minneapolis, 155, 162
Arbes, Peter, 237–38
architecture, 90–91. See also individual breweries
Arizona Brewing Co. (Phoenix, Arizona), 145
Arlington, Minnesota, 232
armed forces: and alcohol consumption, 17, 31–32, 112, 139, 141. See also breweries (businesses): and government contracts
Arneson Distributing, 177, 269
Arnold, J. B., 291
Arnoldy, Peter, 209
art deco, xi; in advertising, 51, 122, 153
Ashland, Wisconsin, 302
Aslesen, Ole, 260
Associated Brewing Company, 165–66. See also Pfeiffer Brewing Company; Schmidt, Jacob, Brewing Company
Atlas Brewing Co. (Chicago, Illinois), 236
Aubol, G. A., 221
Austin, Minnesota, 38, 204
Autumn Brew Review, 170. See also Minnesota Craft Brewer's Guild

B

Backwater Brewing Company, 316
Balder, Frank, 285
Ballantine Brewing Co. (Newark, New Jersey), 150
ball tap knobs, 146
Baltimore, Maryland, 88; Hamm's operations in, 161
Baltimore loop seal, 71
Baltimore Orioles, 161
Bandana Brewery, 191–93, 313

Bang, Joseph, 282
Banholzer, Frederick, 288
Banholzer, William, 288
bankruptcy: of breweries. See breweries (businesses): finances
Baptists, 99
Barge, Jacob, 253
Barker-Karpis gang, 127–28
barley, 3–5; brewery purchases of, 52; cultivation in Minnesota, 3, 28, 250, 306
Barley John's Brew Pub, 192, 193, 310, 315
Barn Bluff (Red Wing, Minnesota), 278
Baron, Stanley, 32, 69, 75
barrel, measurement unit, 5. See also kegs
Barrett, Joseph, 42–43, 272
Barrett & Barrett, 255
Barthel, Bernard, 91, 303
baseball: beer sales at games, vii, 102; and breweriana, 50; sponsorship by breweries, 154–56, 161, 209, 232, 301, 303
basketball, 259
Battle, Laurie, 148
Bauer, John, 226
Bauer, Joseph, 271
Bausch, J. L., & Son, 296
Bavaria, Germany, 15, 46. See also Reinheitsgebot
Baxter, George M., 225
Bazil (brewer in Montgomery), 260
BCCA (Breweriana Collectibles Club of America), 50
Beaver, Minnesota, 204
Beaver Falls, Minnesota, 205
Beck, Charles C., 306–7
Beck, Peter, 236
Becker, Catherine, 305
Becker, Gustav L., 83
Becker, John (Beges) (brewer in Waconia), 305
Becker, John S. (brewer in Winona), 308
Becker & Faehr, 308
Becker & Schellhas, 308; in Ogden, Utah, 82–83, 308
beer: definition of, 1; health claims for, 77, 110, 126, 141, 289; home consumption, 104, 141, 148, 149, 150, 157–58; illegal production of, 118, 119–21, 285; price of, 28, 47, 58, 77, 124, 157–58, 164, 169, 172, 175, 266, 298; quality of, 125, 160, 172, 175; recipes, 144, 158–59, 216; as refreshment, 117, 147, 158–59; serving, 10; in social life, 99–100, 102, 141, 143–44, 147–48,

153; at sporting events, 102, 155; as status symbol, 153, 172–73; strength, 10, 113, 116, 123, 126, 147, 158, 193, 218; styles, 1, 4, 5, 9–10, 15, 77, 173, 178, 182–83, 189–90, 192–93; tavern consumption, 134–35, 148, 157–58; as temperance beverage, 102; 3.2 percent, 123, 126, 140, 158; during wartime, 139–44, 158; wood aged, 192, 193. See also ale; bock beer; bottled beer; draught beer; legalization of beer; malt tonic; individual breweries
beer bottles. See bottles
Beer Can Collectors of America. See Breweriana Collectibles Club of America
beer cans. See cans
beer gardens, 21, 55, 56, 77, 202, 226, 241, 262, 283, 292
Beerhalter, John S., Jr., 216
Beerhalter, John, Sr., 27, 216
Beer, Its History and Its Economic Value as a National Beverage (Salem), 197
Beer Judge Certification Program (BJCP), 9
beer kegs. See kegs
beer labels. See labels
beer signs. See signs
Behnke, Fred, 267–68, 269
Behrns, William (Claus), 246
Belle Plaine, Minnesota, 24, 205
Bemidji, Minnesota, 112, 205–6, 312
Bemidji Brewing Co., 110, 112, 205–6
Bender, Charles J., 226
Bender, Jacob, 269
Benkstein, Brian, 316
Bensberg, Jacob, 33, 263, 288
Berg, Dave, 192, 313
Berg, Gustaf, 279
Berger, Jacob, 302
Berghoff Brewing Company (Ft. Wayne, Indiana), 228
Bergland, Jacquie, 184
Bergson, Herb, 184
Berne, Minnesota, 206
Bernhard, Jacob (Bernhardt), 263, 264
Beroun Bohemian Brewing Co., 61–62, 206
Best, Phillip, Brewing Co. (Milwaukee, Wisconsin), 41, 78, 240, 273
Betz, Andreas, 25, 34, 204, 262, 267
Betz and Friton, 25, 262
Beyrer, Fred, Jr., 212
Beyrer, Fred, Sr., 211–12, 239, 304
Bierbauer, Albert, 89, 92
Bierbauer, Jacob, 89, 92, 240

Bierbauer, Louisa, 240
Bierbauer, Rudolph, 240
Bierbauer, William, 34, 240
Bierbauer, Wm., Brewing Co., 82, 240–41, 244. *See also* Mankato Brewing Company
biergartens. *See* beer gardens
Bierwalter, John, 101, 305
Bierwalter, Lizzie, 101
billboards. *See* signs: outdoor
Billy beer, 175–76, 214
Bion, Christian, 273
Bion, Louis, 273
Bion, Marie, 273
Birkhofer, Conrad, 65, 202, 253–54
Birkhofer, Conrad, Brewing Co., 65, 84, 110, 253–54, 255; saloons owned by, 85, 254. *See also* Purity Brewing Co.
Birkhofer, Hans, 202–3
Birkhofer, Sophia, 202
Bisek, Joseph, 236
Bishop, Harriet, 22–23
Black, James, 109
Blanding, Arthur, 215
Blass, John, 273
Blatt, Philip, 242
Blatz, Val., Brewing Co. (Milwaukee, Wisconsin), 78, 81, 82, 108, 274
blob top bottles. *See* bottles
Blue Earth, Minnesota, 38, 206–7
Blue Label Saloon (Ellsworth, Minnesota), 62
bock beer, viii, 83, 115, 159, 178, 183, 258, 266, 277, 280
Boeckler, R. C., 242
Boehme & Cordella, 91
Bofferding, Nicholas, 249
Bohemian immigrants, 60–62
Bombach, Henry, 279
Bombach & Koke, 210, 279
Bond, Alan, 178–79
Boppel, Arthur, 207
Boppel, Edward, 207
Borchers, Louis, 275
Boston Beer Company (Boston, Massachusetts), 183
bottle caps. *See* crown caps
bottle-conditioned beers, 256
bottled beer, 7, 69–75; early examples, 16, 69–71, 237, 257, 277; popularity of, 134–35, 144; prices of, 124; in taverns, 125. *See also* bottlers, independent; bottles; bottling lines; bottling process
bottle openers. *See* openers

bottlers, independent, 64, 69, 73–74, 223, 254, 267, 300
bottles: Alum-A-Bottle, 176–77; "big mouth," 165; "bomber" (22 oz.), 184, 186; closures, 70–71; development of, 64, 70–71; mini-bottles, 224; nonreturnable, 135, 144, 157; picnic, 134; return or retrieval of, 73, 151, 157; "steinie," 135, 307; stoneware, 70, 262; types, 71, 218, 255. *See also* bottling lines; bottling process; cases; *individual breweries*
Bottles, Breweriana, and Advertising Jugs of Minnesota, 1850–1920, vol. 1 (Feldhaus et al.), 197
bottling lines, 11, 70–72, 138, 182, 184, 186, 280–81; rate of bottling, 281
bottling process, 70–75, 280–81; government restrictions on, 72–74
Boulder Brewing Company (Boulder, Colorado), 181
Bowery Pub and Brewery. *See* Herkimer Pub & Brewery
bowling alley: part of brewery, 253, 275, 316
bowling leagues, 155
Bowman Bros. and Gerst, 49, 202
Brabender, Henry, 234
Braham, Minnesota, 207
Brainard Flouring Mills, 292
Brainerd, Minnesota, 207
Brainerd Brewing Co., 207
branch offices, 78–82. *See also* agents; depots
Brandes, Henry, 273
Brandt & Gerdes (Brandt and Sheffield), 223, 224, 225
Brau, Dustin, 193, 313
Brau Brothers Brewing Co., 193, 240
BrauHaus, 190, 193, 313
Bremer, Adolph, 128, 289, 294
Bremer, Edward, 127–28
Bremer, Karl, 183
Bremer, Maria Schmidt, 294
Bremer, Otto, 93–94, 143, 164, 289
Brennis, Peter A., 240
Brentle, Scherer & Rath. *See* Gilmore Valley Brewery
breweriana, 225; collecting of, 50–51, 162
Breweriana Collectibles Club of America (BCCA), 50
breweries (buildings): capacity of, 5, 179, 182; construction and layout of, 30, 72–73, 75, 90–91, 130, 186–87, 280, 281; conversion to other uses, 118, 129, 229, 237, 245;

dance/meeting halls at, 55–57, 58, 102, 155; equipment, 130, 187, 189, 296; location of, 38, 45–46, 188, 195–96; preservation of, 180; restarting dormant plants, 54–55, 124–25, 128–29; and technological innovation, 49, 65–75, 135–37; tours of, 10; working conditions in, 66–67, 131–33, 168, 235, 237. *See also* caves; icehouses; *individual breweries*
breweries (businesses): and civic contributions, 49, 52; compared to other businesses, 46, 106, 158, 172–73; consolidation of, 88–89; as crop buyers, 49, 52; as employers, 48–49, 127, 129, 130–34, 138–39, 175, 179, 180, 286; finances, 25, 33, 65, 84–89, 104, 117–19, 127–29, 160, 166–69, 174–76, 179, 181, 216–17; and government contracts, 140–41, 143, 144, 219; incorporation, 85–86; national rank of Minnesota, 138, 196; number in Minnesota, 138, 195–96; owned by saloon owners, 219, 285; preconditions for starting, 38–39, 40–41, 84, 182–91, 195–96; production levels, 33, 138, 182, 264; and prohibition, 104, 111, 112, 113, 115–21; and saloons ownership, 106–9; shipping costs, 160; during wartime, 139–45. *See also* advertising; brewpubs; contract brewing; delivery; marketing; microbreweries; *individual breweries*
Brewers' Best beer, 167–68, 278
Brewer's Cave beer, 66
Brewers' Journal, 27
brewers (brewmasters and proprietors): political involvement of, 92; popularity of, 47–49, 52, 89, 92–93, 285; during prohibition, 118–20; prosperity of, 89, 92–94, 233, 244; training of, 26–27. *See also individual breweries*
brewery employees, 94–95, 130–36; accidents, 66–67, 131, 133, 237, 267, 268; African Americans as, 133–34; conditions, 131–33; specialization of, 26–27, 94–95, 131–32, 271; unionization of, 95, 133, 143–44, 151; wages of, 28, 133; during wartime, 140, 142–44; women as, 71–72, 133, 142–43. *See also individual breweries*
brewing process, xviii, 1–9, 20–21, 26–27, 160, 193, 271
brewpubs, 188–93, 196, 310–16; finances, 188, 190–91; legality, 188, 190
Brew Station, 316

Brick, John, 285

Brick, Leo P., 238

Brick & Legler, 285

Brickhouse, Jack, 154–55

Brink, Louis, 34, 228, 286

Brisman, Gerhard, 210

British immigrants, 47. *See also* English immigrants

British investment in Minnesota breweries, 86–87

Brooklyn Center, Minnesota, 187, 208

Browerville, Minnesota (Hartford), 208

Brown, Charles (& Co.), 222, 226

Brown, Heis, 305

Brown, Tom, 155

Brown & Bigelow, 153

Brown Ryan Livery Stable, 313

Brownsville, Minnesota, 24, 208–9

Brownsville Bluff Brewery, 208–9

Bruggemann, Frank, 288

Bruggemann, John, 288

Bruggemann, Martin, 210, 288

Bruggemann & Schweitzer, 288

Bruggemann Brewing Co., 71, 288, 295

Brunner, Karl, 262

Brunswick Corporation, 190

Bruzek, Dan, 236

Bryan, Maurice, 176, 214

Bub, Peter (Brewing Co.), 51, 121, 124, 168, 180, 307–8

Bull, Donald, ix

Burdick, William (Bill), 188, 189–90, 191, 314–15

Burg, E. F., 219

Burginger, Frank, 300

Burke, H. S., 215

Burkhard, Susannah, 21–22, 300

Burkhardt, Gottfried, 274–75

Burkhardt, Gottlieb, 274–75

Burkhardt, Henry, 274–75

Burkhardt, Jacob, 274–75

Burkhardt, Samuel, 274–75

Burkhardt & Co., 214, 274–75

Burmeister, John, 307

Burnquist, J. A. A., 265

Burton-on-Trent (England), 2

Busch, Edward F. W. (Fred), 92–93, 230–31

Busch, J. Gottlieb, 36, 215

Busch, John Lorenz, 230–31

Buselmeier, Amalie, 273

Buselmeier, Rudolph (Busselmeyer), 45, 273, 283

C

Caldis, Sam, 130, 203

Caledonia, Minnesota, 209

California: exports to, 183. *See also individual cities*

Camahl & Busse, 217

Campaign for Real Ale (CAMRA), 171–72, 193, 316

Campbell-Mithun (advertising agency), 162

Canadian investors in Minnesota breweries, 87

Canby, Minnesota, 23, 209–10

Cannon Falls, Minnesota, 210

cans: advantages of, 135, 187; air-filled, 177; blanks, 216; commemorative, 177, 266; cone top, 135–37, 152, 176–77, 268; Crowntainer, 135, 137; with opening instructions, 137, 213; proportion of sales, 135, 144, 157; restrictions on use of, 137, 141, 144; sizes of, 187, 213, 293; styles of, 135–37

capacity, of breweries. *See* breweries (buildings): capacity of

cap lifter. *See* openers

Cappelletti, Geno, 155

Carl, George, 228

Carl, J. B. *See* Karl, Johann Baptist

Carl & Roller, 304–5

Carlsberg Brewery (Copenhagen, Denmark), 8, 75

Carlson, John A., 255

Carver, Minnesota, 210

Cascade Brewery, 282

cases: cardboard, 144, 151–52, 278; as measurement of sales, 5; wooden, 64, 144, 151, 156

cask-conditioned ales, 187, 193, 314. *See also* real ale

Cass, Lewis, 32

cassava, 142

Catholic (Roman) churches: and immigrant communities, 99–101; and prohibition, 100–101

caves, 18, 66–67, 195–96; drawbacks of, 66–67; excavation of, 223; injuries in, 66–67; lagering (storing) beer, 15; in marketing, 66; as safe storage area, 66. *See also individual breweries*

CCSI. *See* Crowncap Collectors Society International

census records. *See* United States Census

Cervecería Cuauhtémoc (Monterrey, Mexico), 119, 218

Chalupsky, Frank, 261, 300

Chalupsky, James, 258

Chalupsky, John, 258

Chalupsky, Joseph, 206

Chalupsky, Matthias, 258

Chalupsky, Wenzel, 300

Chase Valley Glass, 78

Chaska, Minnesota, 33, 57–58, 210–12

Chatfield, Minnesota, 28, 212

Chicago, 91; exports to, 151, 154–55, 169

Chicago Ale Brewery (St. Paul), 294

Chicago Cubs, 154

Chicago investors in Minnesota breweries, 87, 243

Chicago White Sox, 154

China: exports to, 179

Chisholm, Minnesota, 217

Choudek Bros. *See* Soulek Bros.

Christ, Christina. *See* Hoffman, Christina

Christ, Jacob, 24, 275–76

Christensen (brewer in Rush City), 283

Christenson, Jens, 202

Christenson, Theo., 227

Cincinnati, Ohio, 222

City Club beer, 122, 129, 289, 290, 293

Civil War, 31–35; effect on exports, 33–34

Cleary, Russell, 166

Closner, Christian, 206

Closner, David, 206

Clough, Reginald, 149

Clubhaus, 190, 315

coasters, 50, 150, 184, 216

coffee, 208

Coffin, George, 294

Coffin & Oakes, 36, 294

Cokins, Harry, 258–59

Cold Spring, Minnesota, 212–14

Cold Spring Brewing Company, 50, 174–76, 212–14; Mankato Brewing Company purchase, 168, 174, 241; products, 111, 126, 146, 174–76, 218. *See also* Gluek Brewing Company (Cold Spring)

collecting beer items. *See* breweriana: collecting of

College of St. Scholastica, 157

Collins, Thomas, 212

Colorado: exports to, 164, 183, 184, 248

Comersburgh, Philip, 307

Communication Center, The, 157

cone top cans. *See* cans: cone top

Constans, William, 294
construction: of breweries. *See* breweries (buildings): construction and layout of
Consumers Brewing Co. (Ellsworth, Minnesota), 63, 222
Continental Can Company, 135
contract brewing, 173, 183; by August Schell Brewing Company, 173, 177, 183, 186; by Cold Spring Brewing Company, 175–76; by James Page Brewing Company, 182; by Minnesota Brewing Company, 173, 179, 181, 186; by Stroh Brewing Company, 173; by Theo. Hamm Brewing Co., 292
cooperative breweries, 128, 221, 261, 262
coopers, 29, 274. *See also* kegs
Coors, Adolph, Brewing Company (Golden, Colorado), 159, 171
corks, 70–71, 256
corkscrews. *See* openers
corn, 4, 52, 142, 158
county option, 104–5, 112
Courtland, Minnesota, 214
creameries: conversion of breweries to, 118, 237, 245
Crescent Creamery, 282
crimes: at breweries, 80, 116, 127–28, 180, 224, 229, 237, 270, 275
Crist, Jonathan, 316
Crookston, Minnesota, 214
Crowncap Collectors Society International, 50
crown caps, 134, 135; development of, 70; shortages of, 141, 142, 144–45
Crown Cork and Seal Corporation, 70, 135, 137
Crowntainer. *See* cans: Crowntainer
Cullen Bill, 123
Curtis, Tom, 316
Czech immigrants, 46–47

D

Dakota Territory, exports to, 42, 53. *See also* North Dakota; South Dakota
Dakota War of 1862, 34, 87, 240, 243, 257, 262, 263
Daniels, Josephus, 112
Danish immigrants, 202
Davis, Levi, 234
Decker, Benjamin, 217
Decker, Nicholas, 215, 217
Deer Brand beer, 177

Deinhardt, Charles, 28, 38, 205, 212, 234
delivery, 17, 58–59, 69, 124, 134; to homes, 58, 81; to saloons, 69
delivery trucks, 125, 133, 134, 307
delivery wagons, 17, 19, 81, 94
depots, 46, 78, 80–82, 203. *See also* agents; *individual breweries*
Detroit Brewing Co. (Minnesota), 53, 215
Detroit Lakes, Minnesota, 53, 215
Deuss, Gerhard (Duess, Gebhard), 33, 211
Dexter, Andrew J., 295
Dick, Charles E., ix
Dick Bros., 286
Diehl, Henry, 298
Dietrich & Drischel, 279
Dietz, Jacob, 305
Dietz, John, 116
Dillesby, John, 206
displays. *See* advertising: point of sale
distilling, 98, 227; at breweries, 21, 222, 223, 278, 286, 299, 302
distributors, 175, 183, 184, 266. *See also* three-tier system
District Warehouse Brewing, 313
Dobmeier, Tac, 207
Doerr, A. V., 78
Donant, George, 207
Donndelinger (brewer in Hastings), 230
Doran, James M., 121
Dorniden, M., 76
Dorre, Philip, 299
Douglas, Robert, 227
draught beer, 182; prevalence of, 69–70; relative to packaged beer, 134–35, 144, 148
Dreher, Anton, 15, 276
Drescher, Adam, 279
Drewry, Edward, 294
Drewry, Edward L., Jr., 295
Drewry, Eliza, 294
Drewry, Frederick William, 295
Drewry, George, 295
Drewry, William S., 295
Drewry & Greig, 35, 294
Drewry & Scotten, 33, 294
Drewry & Sons, 36, 37, 50, 294–95
drunkenness. *See* alcohol consumption
dry-hopping, 7
drys. *See* temperance: advocates
Dubuque, Iowa, 17, 306
Duluth, Minnesota, 36, 47, 167, 193, 215–20, 312

Duluth Brewing & Malting Company, 118, 119, 120, 143, 169, 217–19, 220; advertising, 51, 219; depots, 81, 82, 207, 217; products, 146, 169, 216, 217–19; Sobriety Company, 216, 217–18
DuVernois, Bob, 191, 313

E

Eagan, Minnesota, 312
Eagle Brewing Co., 222
Eahtonka Brewery, 270, 271
East Coast Breweriana Association (ECBA), 50, 197
East Grand Forks, Minnesota, 81–82, 221
East Grand Forks Brewing Co., 70, 81–82, 221
Eberlein, Fred, 205, 305
Ebner, Annie E., 305
Ebner, Henry, 305
Eckert & Feeder, 306
Edelweiss Brewing Co., 257
Eden Prairie, Minnesota, 190–91, 312–13
Ehlermann, Charles, & Co., 6
Eich, J. H., 285
Eichstadt, Louis, 217
Eickmann, Frank, 228
Eickmann, Peter, 228
Eighteenth Amendment, 114–115, 121. *See also* prohibition
eighth-barrel (pony keg). *See* kegs: sizes of
Elartson, Paul, 300
Elizabeth, Minnesota, 221–22, 251
Ellinson, Conrad, 212
Ellinson, Eugene, 212
Ellsworth, Minnesota, 62–63, 222, 261
Elmira Township, Minnesota, 212
Elysian, Minnesota, 52, 222
Emmert, Frederick, 291, 295
Empire Brewery, 285
Enderle, Lorenz, 33, 284–85
Endres Bros., 64
energy drinks, 177, 314
Enes, Christian, 232
Enes, Hans, 232
Enes, John, 232
Engelhorn, J. M. (Max) (Ingelhorn), 229, 233, 300
Engelhorn, Mrs. Bina, 229
Engesser, Edward, 297
Engesser, Joseph, 297
Engesser, Matthew, 297

Engesser Brewing Co., 12, 50, 134, 138, 139, 297

English immigrants, 20, 36, 222

Erickson, John, ix, 260

Erickson, Peter, 209

Erickson & Ibach, 284

Estad, Ole, 215

Evansville, Minnesota, 222

Eveleth, Minnesota, 303

Excelsior Brewery. *See* Hamm, Theo., Brewing Co.

excise tax. *See* taxation

Export beer, 74

Extra Pale Ale beer (Summit), 11, 182, 183

F

Fackler & Landowski, 209

Faeder and Arnold, 215

Fahrenholz, Louis, 283

Fairmont, Minnesota, 36, 222

Falconer, Gilbert, 215

Falk, Franz, Brewing Co. (Milwaukee, Wisconsin), 280

Falls Breweries, 145, 227. *See also* Fergus Breweries, Inc.; Premier Brewing Co.

Fargo, Harry, 215

Faribault, Minnesota, 24, 34, 52, 222–25

Faribault Dairy Company, 223

farmers: as brewers, 14, 41, 206; as customers, 45, 59; as suppliers, 49, 52; using spent grain, 52

Farmer's Alliance, 109

Farmfest, 177, 266

Faunce, Horrace, 206

Federal Trade Commission, 141

Feigal, Rudolph, 73–74, 252

Feldhaus, Ron, 197

Fellerer, Andrew, 53–54, 273

Fellerer, Joseph, 54–55

Ferber, John, 273–74

Fergus Breweries, Inc., x, xi, 226–27

Fergus Brewing Co., 76. *See also* Falls Breweries; Fergus Falls Brewing Co.; Premier Brewing Co.

Fergus Falls, Minnesota, 104, 225–27

Fergus Falls Brewing Co., 226

fermentation, 8–9, 192

Ferris, John, 216

Fetsch, George (Felich), 294

Fetzner, Herman, 209

Fetzner, John, 66, 204, 208–9

Fetzner, Valentine, 208–9

Fey, Frank, 270

Fey, John, 270–71

Ficker & Doffing (& Donndelinger; & Kelnhofer), 230

Figge, Chris, 292

Figge, William, Jr., 293

Figge, William, Sr., 293

finances: of breweries. *See* breweries (businesses): finances

Fink, Michael, 215, 302

Finkel, Charles, 175, 178, 266

Finnegans Irish Amber, 184

fires: in breweries, 66, 90; protection against, 92, 245. *See also individual breweries*

First City Brewery & Grill, 191, 312

Fitger, A., & Co., 72–73, 86, 172, 215–16. *See also* Fitger Brewing Co.

Fitger, Arnold, 216

Fitger, August, 215–16

Fitger Brewing Co., 27, 81, 82, 124, 157, 215–17, 220; advertising, 158, 216, 219; brewery complex, 180, 184, 193, 215, 216–17; depots, 207, 216; products, 84, 119, 135, 136, 146, 149, 215, 216; and prohibition, 118, 119, 215

Fitger's Brewhouse, 51, 180, 193, 312

Fitzsimmons, James, 236

Flat Earth Brewing Co., 187, 297

flat top cans. *See* cans

Fleckenstein, Anna, 223

Fleckenstein, Edward, 123

Fleckenstein, Ernst, 222–24, 288

Fleckenstein, Gottfried, 222–23, 288

Fleckenstein, Johannis, 223

Fleckenstein, Louis, 223

Fleckenstein, Orpha, 167

Fleckenstein, Paul, 206

Fleckenstein, Theodore, 206

Fleckenstein Brewing Co., 12, 66, 167, 222, 223–25

Fleckenstein Bros. Brewery, 222

Flett, Ron, 312, 315

flooding: of breweries, 204, 275, 277, 297. *See also individual breweries*

Florida: exports to, 160, 184

foam scrapers, 12

Foell, Jacob, 271

Folliard, Kieran, 184

Forestville, Minnesota, 64, 227–28

Fort Snelling, 15, 17, 31

Founders Food and Firkins. *See* Granite City Food & Brewery

Frank, John (Frink), 205

Frank, William, 233

Franke, W., 217

Frankfort (township), Minnesota, 286

Frazee, Minnesota, 53, 228, 286

Frazee City Brewery, 228

Freeport, Illinois, 21

Frenzel, Heinrich, 262

Frey & Zahler, 286

Friedrich, Manfred, ix, 197

Frietschel, M., 237

Friton, August, 214, 262

Fritschle, Charles, 292

Fritz, Joseph, 210, 211

Froehler, John, 261

Froehler, Michael, 261

Froehler, Victoria, 261

Frontenac, Minnesota, 228

Fuermann, Charles, 272

Fuller, Cornelius, 17

Funk, Frank, 33, 285

Funk, Melchior, 295

Funk, William, 291, 295

Funk & Thiery, 285

Fyten, Tod, x, 185, 245

G

Gadbois, Leo, 184

Gaeto, Charles, 229

Gahr, Jacob, 294

Galena, Illinois, 17

Ganser, Adam, 272

Ganser, Peter, 34, 272

Gassler, William, 242

Geanopolus, John, 130, 203

Gebhardt (brewer in Carver, Minnesota), 210

Gehring, Sebastian, 235, 291

Geiger & Eberman, 270

Geil, John H., 273

Gemeinde Brau beer, 214

General Breweries (Prince Albert, Saskatchewan), 239

Gerdts, E., 242

German-American Bank of St. Paul, 94

Germania Brewing Association (Brewing Co.), 88, 253

German immigrants, xi, 16, 18, 46–47, 89, 92, 101, 113, 196; as beer drinkers, 46, 97–98; as brewery employees, 133; politics of, 32

Geyser Bottling Works, 219

Gilbride, Patrick J. (Gilbridge), 36–37, 252–53

Gilger, William, 234, 294, 306

Gilmore, C. J., 234

Gilmore Valley Brewery, 24, 66, 306

Gilson, David, 186

Ginsberg, Anna (mother), 244

Ginsberg, Anna Naegli, 244–45

Ginsberg, Charles, 28, 55–56, 204, 244–45

Ginsberg, Edwin, 204, 305

Ginsberg, Solomon, 204, 305

Ginsberg Bros., 204

Ginther, John T., 304

Gjernes & Pfaffin, 283

Gjernes & Reidy, 283

Glacial Lakes Brewing Co., 186, 270

Gladstone, Michigan, 83–84

Glander, Charles, 271

glasses (drinking): styles of, 231, 249, 272, 276, 299, 301

Gleeson, M. J., 219

Gleim, Henry, 230

Glencoe, Minnesota, 116, 228–29

Glencoe Brewing Co., 86, 116, 180, 228–29

Glenwood, Minnesota, 49, 229, 298

Gloeggler, Barnhard, 34, 251

Gluck, Fred, 208

Gluek, Alvin, 124, 250

Gluek, Arthur, 250

Gluek, Charles, 167, 249

Gluek, Eugene, 250

Gluek, Gottlieb, 249

Gluek, John, 249

Gluek, Louis, 249, 250

Gluek Brewing Company (Cold Spring), 176–77, 212, 214

Gluek Brewing Company (Minneapolis), 124, 125, 131, 247, 249–51; advertising, 150–51, 155, 250–51; brewery and construction, xviii, 25, 69, 91, 249; brewing science, 250; employees, 131; finances, 167; government contracts, 140; incorporation, 86; products, 134, 135, 136, 250; razing of brewery, 167; sales range, 151, 167; sale to G. Heileman, 167, 251; saloons, 108–9, 249–50; Stite, ix, 142, 167, 176–77, 250

Gluek's Restaurant and Bar, 250

Godfrey, Ard, 22

Golden Grain Juice Company, 116–17. See also Minneapolis Brewing Company

Goodhue County Brewing Co., 145, 146, 276, 278. See also Remmler Brewing Company

Good Templars, 103, 237

Gopher beer, viii, 130, 263

Gopher State Ethanol, 181

Gottschalk, Robert, ix

Gozzi, Sondra, 316

Graeber, Nicholas, 241, 242

Graf, John Jacob, 245

Grafmueller, Adolph, 270

grain. See farmers; World War I; World War II; individual grain varieties

Grain Belt beer, vii, 89, 146, 159, 161, 169, 171, 248–49; advertising, 2, 110, 151, 152, 153, 155; brewed by August Schell Brewing Company, 178, 249, 267; brewed by Minnesota Brewing Company, 178, 179

Grain Belt Breweries, Inc., 248–49; brewery building, ix, 249; finances, 169; growth of, 163–64; sale of, 169, 249. See also Minneapolis Brewing Company

Grain Belt Park, 2, 154, 156

Grand Meadow, Minnesota, 80

Grand Rapids, Minnesota, 81

Granger, Minnesota, 229

Granger Brewing Co., 229

Granite City Food & Brewery, 191, 312, 315

Granite Falls, Minnesota, 80

Grant, Bert, 188

Grass, Christian, 304

Grassinger, John, 232

Grauss, Wendell, 230

Gray, J. A., 226

Gray, R. E., 295

Great American Beer Festival (GABF), 178, 179, 181, 186, 192, 193, 313–14

Great Depression, 127; effects on breweries, 119, 124

Great Northern Porter beer, ix, 182

Great Waters Brewing Company, ix, 193, 316

Greek immigrants, 129–30

Green Death. See Gluek Brewing Company (Minneapolis): Stite

Green Mill Brewing Company, 312, 315

Greig, L. B., 294

Griesser, Richard, 91, 268, 281, 309

Groebner, Joseph, 262

Groetsch, John, 232

Grones, Bill, 188, 313

growler: modern, 190, 193, 311; pre-prohibition, 70, 232; "Silver Growler" can, 137

Gruber, George, 213, 298

gruit, 5

Guinness Irish Stout, 9, 37

Guldan, Anton, 300

Gulf Brewing Co. (Houston, Texas), 161

Gund Brewing Co. (La Crosse, Wisconsin), 64, 78, 82, 274

Gunther Brewery (Baltimore, Maryland), 161

Gutheil, Oscar, 202

Guyer, Anthony, 305

H

Haas, John, 231

Haas & Schmidt, 242

Haemen, Jacob, 212

Haggerty, John, 314

Hajicek, Ben, 234

Hajicek, John, 234

Hajicek, Joseph, 120, 233–34

half-barrel. See kegs: sizes of

Hall, Michigan, 210

Hall and Keller, 210

Halvorson, Kittel, 109

Hamm, Joseph, 295

Hamm, Louise, 21, 292

Hamm, Theo., Brewing Co., 2, 64, 124, 164, 292–93; advertising, vii, 150, 152–55, 162, 163; in Baltimore, 161; brewery and construction, 76, 92, 136, 180; in California, 151, 160–61; in Chicago, 154–55, 160, 169; depots or branches of, 82, 160–61, 211, 291; employees, 131, 292; finances of, 160–61, 168–69; in Florida, 160; in Houston, 161; in Iowa, 155; in Kansas City, 154, 160; ownership changes, 168–69, 293; products, 51, 126, 146, 159, 171; sports sponsorship, 152, 154–55, 161; in wartime, 142, 143, 144

Hamm, Theodore, 93, 292; residence, 92

Hamm, William, Jr., 127, 293

Hamm, William, Sr., 292

Hamm Building (St. Paul), ix, 193

Hamm Memorial Psychiatric Clinic, 157

Hammond, Earl, 162

Hammond, Winfield S., 112

Hamm's Bear, xi, 160, 161, 162, 169; monument to, xii, 51, 162, 316

Hamm's Club, xii, 51, 162

Handschuh, Joseph M., 258–59

Handsuch, Joseph, 128, 258, 259, 260

Hanover, Minnesota, 286

Hansen, Emil Christian, 8, 75

Hanson, Carl O., 219

Hardke & Karow, 257, 258

Harris, Moira F., 162, 169
Hartland & Stradcutter, 205
Hartman, Dave, 314
Hartman, John, 39, 278
Harvey, William Hope "Coin," 83
Harwell's Steakhouse, 316
Hasle, Edward, 84, 255
Hasse, Henry, 229
Hasse, Reinhart, 229
Hasse & Herman, 302
Hastings, Minnesota, 24, 36, 47, 57, 229–32
Hastings Brewing Company, 67, 119, 231–32
Hauenstein, Charles, 268
Hauenstein, Hans P., 268
Hauenstein, John, 34, 47, 267–68
Hauenstein, John, Jr., 268
Hauenstein, John (Brewing) Co., 164, 180,
    267–69
Hauenstein beer, 177, 267, 268–69
Haug, Todd, 187, 190, 208, 313
Hay Creek Brewery, 39, 278
Heatherington, John, 203
Heiland, Catherine (Kate), 67, 234–35
Heiland, Fred, 234–35, 269
Heiland, John, 235
Heileman, G., Brewing Company, 165, 166,
    169, 178–79, 218, 219, 249, 290; and
    Cold Spring Brewing Company, 174–75;
    depots, 228; employees, 210; exports to
    Minnesota, 64, 79, 168. See also Schmidt,
    Jacob, Brewing Co.
Heimberger, Joseph, 211
Hein, Henry, 251
Heinrich, Adolph, 252
Heinrich, John, 128
Heinrich, Julius, 252
Heinrich Brewing Association, 88, 251, 252
Heinsath, William, 279
Heising, Christina, 21, 276–77
Heising, William, 36, 276–77, 282
Heller, Herman H., 299, 300
Hemmisch, J. M. (Mat), 246
Hemstead, Werner, 207
Henderson, Leon, 141
Henderson, Minnesota, 77, 232–33
Hendry, Bruce, 179, 181
Henes and Keller Co., 73
Henius & Co., 284
Hennepin Brewing Co., 256; saloons, 109
Herberger, Carl, 285
Herberger, Fritz, 285
Herberger & Schmidt, 285

Herkimer Pub & Brewery, 10, 314
Herman, Jacob, 228
Hermann Monument (New Ulm, Minnesota),
    xi, 177, 268
Hermanutz, Eugene, 213
Hertz, Annie, 210
Hertz, Berthold, 210
Heublein, Inc., 168, 169
Heydrich (brewer in New Ulm), 214
Hibbing, Minnesota, 303
Hilger, John, 245, 246
Hilgers, Peter, 235–36
Hill, James J., 88, 89, 255
Hilt, Henry, 212, 213
Hirschi, John (Hirchi), 206, 244
Hirth, Charles F., 239
Hjermstad, Elizabeth Kuenzel, 67, 120
Hoch, Reiner, 217
Hochmuth (brewer in Ortonville), 271
Hoefs, Rudolph, 238
Hoerner, John, 207, 234, 238, 299, 300
Hoerner, Joseph, 301
Hofflin, Joseph, 251
Hoffman, Christina (Mrs. Philip), 21, 275–76
Hoffman, Fred, 207
Hoffman, John, 207, 240
Hoffman, Lorenz, 278
Hoffman, Mark, 186, 270
Hoffman, Nicholas, 221
Hoffman, Philip, 275
Hoffman & Grubb, 230
Hohmann, August, 298
Hohmann, John H., 244
Hokah, Minnesota, 233
Holl, August, 269
Holland, John, 294
Holz, Alfred, 227
homebrewing, 13–15, 17. See also beer: illegal
    production of
Hook, Andrew, 306
Hoops, Dave, 193
Hoops, Mike, 192, 193, 314
Hoppe, Lora Noerenberg, 252
hops, 5–7, 76; cultivation in Minnesota, 28,
    202
Hops Restaurant, Bar & Brewery, 190–91, 313
Horejs (brothers, brewers in Beroun), 206
Hornung, Frank, 295
horsepower: in breweries, 35
horses: in deliveries, 17, 235, 247, 277. See also
    individual breweries
hotels, 45, 53, 77, 285, 303

Houston, Texas, 161
Hovel, Cleo, 162
Huber Brewing Company (Monroe, Wiscon-
    sin), viii, 172, 183
Hubner, Theodore, 226
Hudson, Wisconsin, 287
Hug, Pagel & Spar, 260
Hughes Tool, 161
Huner, George, 302
Husmann, J. B., 299–300
Hutchinson, Minnesota, 233–34
Hutter stopper, 71
Huxhold, C. H. (& Wagner), 49, 66

I

Ibach, Joseph, 28, 241, 242–43, 274, 284
Ibach, Margaret, 242
IBUs (International Bitterness Units), 6
ice: harvesting for breweries, 49, 66–68;
    produced by breweries, 67–68
ice cellars, 246
icehouses: cost of construction, 67; as part of
    breweries, 30, 67
Illinois: exports to, 151, 184
Iltis, Peter, 59, 211
immigration: to Minnesota. See individual im-
    migrant groups
Imperial Brewing Co., 86, 87–88, 255–56
imported beer, 183
incorporation. See breweries (businesses):
    incorporation; individual breweries
Ingersoll Brewing Co., 305
Inquiry into the Effects of Ardent Spirits on the
    Human Mind, An (Rush), 98–99
insurance, 85. See also breweries (businesses):
    finances
International Bitterness Units (IBUs), 6
Interstate Highway 35: construction of, 169,
    216–17, 219
Inward, Charles, 237
Iowa: breweries in, 15, 16, 195, 270; exports
    to, 62; Granite City in, 191; imports from,
    16, 77; prohibition in, 97, 202, 270
Irish immigrants, 98, 99, 101, 212
Iron Ore Bar (Tower, Minnesota), 303
Iron Range Brewing Co. (Association), 302–3

J

Jackson, Michael, 190, 314
Jackson, Minnesota, 38, 104, 222, 234
Jacobs, Irwin, 169, 182, 249
Jacobs, Sheldon, 182
Jacoby, Anton, 242
James Page Brewing Company. *See* Page, James, Brewing Company
Janesville, Minnesota, 203
Japan: exports to, 183
Jefferson, Thomas, xi, 69
Jochem (brewer in Sauk Rapids), 298
Johnny's Bar (St. Paul, Minnesota), 182
Johnson, Charles J., 219
Johnson, David, 185, 257
Johnson, John T., 248
Johnson, Myron C., 174, 213
Johnson, Thomas, 252
Jordan, Minnesota, 24, 66, 234–36
Jordan Brewery. *See* Schutz & Hilgers Jordan Brewery
Jordan Brewing Association, 234, 235
Jordan Brewing Company, 234, 235
Juditsch, F. (T.), 226, 227
Jumer, Fred, 228–29
Jung Brewing Co. (Milwaukee, Wisconsin), 79, 300
Jungle, The (Sinclair), 110
Justesen, Dan, 316
Just for Openers (JFO), 50

K

Kaiser, William, 235
Kallberg, Anders (Chellberg), 207
Kansas, 97
Kansas City, Missouri, 82, 138, 239
Karcher, George, 211, 304
Karl, Johann Baptist (John Carl), 269
Karlsbrau beer, 218
Karlson and Lundgren, 255
Kaufmann, John, 245
Keffler & Borser, 230
kegged beer. *See* draught beer
kegs, 45, 72–73, 296; pitching, 235; prices of, 124, 211; retrieval by breweries, 59–60, 151; sizes of, 5, 189, 211, 278
Keller (brewer in Carver, Minnesota), 210
Keller, Andrew F., Pittsburg Brewery, 77, 292
Kelley, P. J., 254
Kelnhofer, Anthony, 230
Kennedy, D., 245

Kenora, Ontario, 119, 232, 295
Kensington, Minnesota, 236
Keoke & Kuhl, 298
Kerner, Joseph, 207
Kiene, Gustav, 217
Kiesel, L., 234
Kiewel, Ben, 238
Kiewel, Charles, 214, 238–39
Kiewel, Charles E., 214
Kiewel, Frank D., 159, 163–64, 248
Kiewel, George, 119
Kiewel, Jacob, 104, 214, 227, 238–39
Kiewel & Haas, 227
Kiewel & Miksche, 227
Kiewel Associated Products, 118, 125, 214, 239
Kiewel Brewing Co., 125, 130–31, 133, 167, 238–39; advertising, 151, 239; branch of Minneapolis Brewing Company, 239; Crookston branch, 214; products, 111, 146, 159, 238. *See also* Kiewel Associated Products
Kiichli, Louis, 217
Kimber, Emmet, 237
Kimber, Isaac, 237
Kimmick, Norbert, 21, 300, 318n1–12
Kimmick, Susannah. *See* Burkhard, Susannah
King, William, 305
Kinzel, George, 237
Kittson, Norman, 22
Klein & Kiichli, 217
Kleinmann, Charles, 233
Kleinmann, John, 233
Klenk, Philip, 209
Klinkert, Christian, 232
Knapp, August, 274
Knips, Gerhard, 301
Knoblauch, Adolph, 34, 208, 272, 273
Knutson, Harold, 129
Koch, Jim, 183
Koch, Reinhold J. (John), 238, 294
Koehnlein, John, 221, 251
Koke (brewer in Courtland, Minnesota), 214
Kokes, Thomas, 261
Korean War, 144, 145
Koschel, William, 234, 235
Kowitz, Ferdinand, 210
Kraatz, R., 209
Kraft, Simon, 305
Krahnschnable, George, 309
Kramer, George W., 300
Kramer, Peter, 33, 284
Kramer & Seberger, 284

Kranzlein, John G., 251–52, 294
Kranzlein, Smith & Miller, 294
Kranzlein & Schmidt White Beer Brewery, 294
Krauch, Ludwig, 214
Kreimer Bros., 217
Kreitz, Herman (Hermann), 252, 295
Kreitz & Bernds, 252
Krejci & Gilmore, 234
Krueger, G., Brewing Co. (Newark, New Jersey), 135
Kubesh, J., 206
Kuenzel, Adolph Gustav, 67, 119, 231–32
Kuhn & Mayer (& Hess), 246
Kumm, Roy, 160, 164, 169

L

labels, 34, 64, 152, 164, 176, 254; government requirements, 110, 126, 137–38, 248; lawsuits, 54, 303; neck labels, 250, 302; stock designs, 34, 241, 284
labor. *See* brewery employees
La Crosse, Wisconsin, 64, 77, 166, 168, 208, 210, 233
Lacy, John, 212
Lademan, F. W., 209
Ladner, John, 212
LaDue, Harry, 297
lager, 15. *See also* beer: styles
lagering, 9. *See also* caves
Lake City, Minnesota, 34, 225, 228, 236–37
Lakeside Brewing Co., 271
Lake Superior Brewing Co., 180, 184, 220
Lamm, Stephen, 242, 244
Lancer, J. F., 236
Landowski (brewer in Brownsville, Minnesota), 209
Lane, Russ, 313
Lanesboro, Minnesota, 237
Lanesburg Township, Minnesota, 237, 260
Langen (family, brewers in Hokah, Minnesota), 233
Langer, William "Wild Bill," 221
Larkin Bros., 36, 260
Larson & Nelson, 283
Latto, Rudolph, 57, 230
Laurent & Murphy, 230, 231
Lauritzen, Peter, 254, 256
Lauritzen Malt Company, 256
Lavoisier, Antoine-Laurent, 8
Le Duc, William, 22

Lee, William E., 112
legalization of beer, 123–25; effects on economy, 127, 129, 130–31, 138–39
Lehle, Louis, 253
Leiferman (& Ploog), 203
Leiferman, Clemens, 242
Leinenkugel, Jacob, Brewing Co. (Chippewa Falls, Wisconsin), viii, 183
Leip, William, 77, 294
Leip & Coffin, 36, 294
Leivermann, Augustus (Gus), 211
Leivermann, Bernard, 57–58, 210–11
Leivermann, Mrs. B. (Bertha), 210
Lemmel, Edward, 228, 271
Lenhardt, Erhardt, 238
Le Roy, Minnesota, 39, 237
Leslin, Charles, 33, 274–75, 304
Leslin, Mary, 21, 274–75, 304
Le Sueur, Minnesota, 237–38, 271–72
Lever Food and Fuel Control Act, 113
Liden, Andrew, 84, 253
Lienau, C. H. (Leman), 210
light beer, 171, 179. See also beer: styles
Lightning stopper, 71, 134
Lill & Diversey (Chicago, Illinois), 33
Lint, Jacob, 274
Litchfield Brewing Co., 234, 238
Little Falls, Minnesota, 238–39
Little Falls Brewing Co., 238
local option, 104–5, 274; elections, 305
Loe (brewer in Carver, Minnesota), 210
Lohff, Henry, 251
Lohmeier (brewer in Fergus Falls, Minnesota), 225–26
Long Prairie Brewing Co., 239–40
Los Angeles, California, 160
Lovit soft drinks, 217
Loyal Liberty Protective League, 112
Lucan, Minnesota, 190, 193, 240, 313
Luce, Sidney, 215
Lueders, Fritz, 305
Luhmann, Peter, 274
Lumpp, H. A. (Henry), 205, 207, 225

M

Maas, Philip, 226, 227
Madelia, Minnesota, 240
Maertz, Ralph, 258–59
Maes, Dominick, 270
Maes, Henry, 270, 273
magazines: advertising in, 148, 160

Maine laws, 22–23, 97–98, 101. See also prohibition
Maish, F. W., 301
Malta near beer, 118
malting, 3–4; by breweries, 4, 218, 219. See also individual breweries
malt liquor, 142, 219–20, 250. See also beer: styles; Gluek Brewing Company (Minneapolis): Stite
maltsters, 4, 6, 269
malt tonic, 64, 111, 256, 265, 281
Mankato, Minnesota, 24, 38, 87, 191–93, 240–44, 313
Mankato Brewing Company, 131, 174, 240, 241; finances of, 145, 167–68, 241; Jordan brewery, 66, 145, 236, 241; products, 136, 137, 141, 146, 168, 241. See also Bierbauer, William, Brewing Co.; Cold Spring Brewing Company
Mannheim, John, 212, 272
Mantorville, Minnesota, 28, 55–56, 120, 244–45
Mantorville Brewing Company (1937–1939), 128, 244, 245
Mantorville Brewing Company (1996–present), 184–85, 245
Maple Grove, Minnesota, 191
Mapleton, Minnesota, 82
marching bands, 156, 232, 266
Marin & Medved, 238
Marine-on-Saint Croix (Marine), Minnesota, 24, 245
Marion, Minnesota, 245
Maritzen, August, 91, 92, 247
Marke, Samuel, 237
marketing, 151–54, 157–60, 163–64
Marquette, Michigan, 217
Marshalltown, Iowa, 202
Marti, Alfred, 266
Marti, Emma Schell, 264, 266
Marti, George, 264, 266
Marti, Ted, 117, 232, 266
Marti, Warren, 266
Martin, Billy, 155
Martin, Gerald R., 241
mashing, 4–5. See also brewing process
Massolt, William, Bottling Co., 88, 255, 256
Mathes, Frank E., 143, 159, 248
Matson, Andrew, 255
Maurin Bros., 286
May, Charles, 211
Mayo, W. W., 280

Maytag, Fritz, 174
Mazeppa, Minnesota, 245–46
McAuliffe, Jack, 181
McCarthy, L. F., 227
McFarland, O., 295
McGovern, Jamie, 315
McInerny, John, 221
McNeil, Alexander, 206–7
McQuade, W. H., 302
McQuaid, Phyllis, 188
mead, 96
Mead, H. W., 257
Medved, Peter, 238
Meeske, Carl, 218
Meeske, Charles, 217–18
Meighen, Felix, 227
Meighen, Thomas, 64
Meiner, John, 239
Melander, John, 278–79
Mellin, Carl G., 210
Melrose, Minnesota, 128–29, 246
Melrose Brewing Co., 246
Memphis, Tennessee: exports to, 33–34
Menars, Albert (Menaks), 261
Menominee, Wisconsin, 274
mergers. See breweries (businesses): consolidation of
Merz, C. L., 258
Merz, Caroline, 284, 285
Merz, Wendelin, 284, 285
Merz & Zahler, 304
Mesenbrink (brewery owner in Jordan), 234, 235
Methodists, 99
Metropolitan Stadium (Bloomington, Minnesota), 155
Metzler, Dan, 276
Meyer, Albert, 274
Meyer, Anton, 226
Meyer, Gerald, 248–49
Meyer, John, 279
Michel, C. & J. Brewing Co. (La Crosse, Wisconsin), 64, 78–79, 244
Michigan: exports to, 83–84, 247–48, state regulations, 83
Mickus, Charles, 71, 261
Mickus, Joseph, 130, 261, 278
microbreweries, 181–87; definitions of, 181–82
Midwest Brewing Co. See Red Wing Brewing Co.
Miksch (brewer in New Munich), 261

Miksch Bros., 49, 229
military. *See* armed forces
Miller, John B. *See* Mueller, John B.
Miller, William M. F., 123
Miller & Ackerman, 212
Miller & Heinrich, 80. *See also* Heinrich
    Brewing Association; Mueller, John B.
Miller Brewing Co. (Milwaukee, Wisconsin),
    181; employees, 209; exports to Minne-
    sota, 64, 79, 82, 166, 171, 193, 207, 249
Mill Street Brewery, 315
Millville, Minnesota, 246
Milton Township, Minnesota, 206
Milwaukee, Wisconsin, 232
Milwaukee beer: as generic style, 20, 77
Milwaukee Bottling Co. (Minneapolis, Min-
    nesota), 78
Milwaukee Road railroad, 38
Minars, Albert, 208
mineral water, 174–75, 213–14
Miner & Barrett, 272
Minges, John, 228, 236–37
Minneapolis, Minnesota, 34, 65, 84, 246–57,
    313–14; agencies or branches in, 78–79;
    saloons in, 74, 106–9
Minneapolis Brewing & Malting Co. *See* Min-
    neapolis Brewing Company
Minneapolis Brewing Company, 52, 116–17,
    125, 246–49; acquisitions by, 164, 167,
    269; advertising, 150–53, 155, 163–64; in
    Alaska, 163; brewery and construction,
    69, 71, 88, 89, 155, 180, 247; delivery
    wagons and vehicles, 81, 247; depots,
    80–81, 228; employees, 71–72, 95, 131,
    155; finances, 127, 159, 163–64; formation
    of, 88–89; as Grain Belt Breweries, Inc.,
    163–64, 248; labels, 137–38, 152; produc-
    tion, 163–64; products, 36, 135, 136,
    164; robbery at, 128, 320n9; sales range,
    80–81, 161, 163–64, 247–48; saloons
    owned by, 107–9, 116; in wartime, 142. *See
    also* Golden Grain Juice Company; Grain
    Belt beer; Grain Belt Breweries, Inc.;
    Grain Belt Park
Minneiska, Minnesota, 257
Minnesota Brewers Association, 140–41
Minnesota Brewing Co. (Hastings), 230, 231
Minnesota Brewing Company (St. Paul),
    178–81; contract brewing by, 173, 182;
    products, 66, 178–79
Minnesota Central railroad, 38
Minnesota City, Minnesota, 258

Minnesota Commission of Public Safety, 113
Minnesota Craft Brewer's Guild, 170, 208
Minnesota North Stars, vii, 166
Minnesota State Capitol, 113, 114
Minnesota State Fair, 77
Minnesota Supreme Court, 23
Minnesota Territory, 13, 24
Minnesota Twins, vii, 155
Minnesota Vikings, vii, 155
Minnesota Weiss Beer Brewery, 295
Minnetonka, Minnesota, 189, 314
Minnette, Frank, 298
Missouri: breweries in, 195. *See also* Anheuser-
    Busch Brewing Co.
Mitsch, George, 289
Moerlein & Windisch (Cincinnati, Ohio), 33
Molitor, Anton, 246
Molson Breweries (Montreal, Quebec), vii,
    168
Momberg, Fred, 298
Momberg & Jochem, 58, 298
Monahan Bottling Co., 253
Montana: exports to, 248
Montgomery, Minnesota, 61, 258–60
Montgomery Brewing Co., 61, 128, 145, 258
Moore, John, 193, 310, 313, 315
Moorhead, Minnesota, ix, 36, 260, 315
Moose beer, 119, 217
More & Carlson, 255
Mueller, A. W., and Co., 225
Mueller, F. W. (Miller), 284
Mueller, John B., 251–52, 253
Mueller and Heinrich, 246, 251, 252
Muhlbrook, Dietrich, 301
Mundigel, Zingel & Co., 221
Murphy, J. L., 258
Murphy's Irish Stout, 37
Murrow, Edward R., 154
museums of breweriana, 51
Myhre, John P. (Murray), 300

N

NABA. *See* National Association Brewery
    Advertising
Naegli, Henry, 244–45
Naegli, John, 242
Nagel, August, 203
Nagel, Henry, 203
Nagel, Otto, 211
National Association Brewery Advertising
    (NABA), 50

National Brewery Museum, 51, 199
National Prohibition Act. *See* Volstead Act
National Recovery Administration (NRA), 131
National Register of Historic Places, xii, 180,
    303
near beer, 54, 116–19, 225, 272, 289
Nebraska: exports to, 248; Granite City in,
    191; prohibition in, 97. *See also* Storz
    Brewing Company
needle beer, 117
Negaunee, Michigan, 217
Neiman (brewer in Belle Plaine), 205
Nelson, Tim, 312
neon signs. *See* signs: neon
Nessel, Lawrence, 294
Netolesky, Tom, 188, 313
Neuffer, J. F., 282
Neuffer & Becker, 34, 308
Neusuess & Troost, 282, 283
Neverman & Hannah, 305
New Albion Brewery (Sonoma, California),
    181
New Brighton, Minnesota, 193, 315
New Holland Brewing Co. (Holland, Michi-
    gan), 314
Newman, Cecil, 133–34
New Munich, Minnesota, 94, 118, 128, 261
New Prague, Minnesota, 61, 261
New Prague Brewing Co., 67, 261
newspapers: advertisements, 150, 151; cover-
    age of breweries, 47–49, 52, 53, 62–63,
    128–30, 199; and temperance, 101–4
New Ulm, Minnesota, 25, 34, 46, 57, 214,
    262–70
New Ulm Bottling Works, 267
New Ulm Brewing & Malting Co., 262
New Ulm Brewing Co., 269
New York Mills, Minnesota, 186, 270
Nicolin, Frank, 234, 235
Nicolin, J. H., 285–86
Nicolin Beverage Co. 285–86
Nicollet Island, 151
Niedermair, Joseph, 239
Niehof, Joseph & Co., 298, 299
1919 Root Beer, 266
Nininger, Minnesota, 230
Noerenberg, A. J. (August), 74, 113
Noerenberg, Frederich D., 74, 87, 88, 252
no license. *See* saloons: licenses
Nordlager beer, 136, 216
Nordlagers (BCCA chapter), 50
Norrish, Samuel (Murisch), 231

North, Ann Loomis, 97
North Central Commercial Club, 102
North Coast Limited (train), 53
North Dakota: exports to, 53, 84, 217, 221, 272; Granite City in, 191; prohibition in, 84, 97, 221; special beers for, 84, 217. *See also* Dakota Territory
Northern Pacific Brewing Co., 53–55, 273
Northern Pacific Railway Company, 40, 53
Northfield, Minnesota, 212, 270, 305
North Mississippi Brewery, 288
North Star Brewery/North Star Brewing Co., 294
North Star Chapter, BCCA, 50
Northwest Airlines, 181
Northwestern Brewery (Alexandria), 48
Northwestern Brewery (St. Paul), 294, 295
Norwegian immigrants, 14, 300
Nyssen, Hubert, 58–59, 298, 299
Nyssen, Mary. *See* Winker, Mary

Oakes, George, 294
Oak Township, Minnesota, 261
Oakwood Township, Minnesota, 246
oats, 142, 222
O'Brien, James, 226
O'Byrne, Sean, 316
O'Connell, Michael, 212
Odell, Reuben, 227
Oechsle & Gjernes, 283
Oechsle & Schaupp, 49, 283
Oehlschlager, Peter, 194, 225–26
O'Gara's Bar & Grill, 315–16
Ogden, Utah, 82–83
Oglethorpe, James, 98
O'Hara's Brew Pub & Restaurant, 190, 315
Oklahoma: exports to, 164, 293
Olde English "600" ("800") malt liquor, 166, 219–20
Old Heidelberg beer, 286
Oleson, Erick, 284
Oleson & Ackerman, 284
Oliva, J. F., 276
Olson, Floyd B., 123
Olson, William, 252
Olson & Anderson, 255
Olympia Brewing Company (Tumwater, Washington), 159, 168
Omaha, Nebraska, 164
One Hundred Years of Brewing, 17, 197

one-way bottles. *See* bottles: nonreturnable
Onsgard, Lewis K., 121
openers: corkscrews, 70, 256; "flat figural" style, 50; utility, 256, 281; wooden, 236
opening instruction cans. *See* cans: with opening instructions
Orinoco, Minnesota, 107
Orion township, Minnesota, 212
Ort, C., 252
Ort, Peter, 102, 207
Orth, Alfred, 246
Orth, Edward, 246
Orth, John, xi, 18–21, 246
Orth, John, Brewing Company, 28, 29, 33, 36, 88, 246; brewery, 19, 90. *See also* Minneapolis Brewing Co.
Orth, John W., 246
Orth, Mary, 18
Ortonville, Minnesota, 228, 270–71
Oshawa, Minnesota, 271–72, 298
Oster, John, 212, 213
Osterfeldt, B., 205
Otter Tail City, Minnesota, 42–43, 53, 272
Otto Bremer Foundation, 157
Otto's Brewery, Inc., 124–25, 126, 130, 139, 245
Owatonna, Minnesota, 34, 208, 272–73
Owens, Evan, 104, 234
Owens, Samuel, 302

Pabst, Frederick, 73
Pabst Brewing Co. (Milwaukee, Wisconsin), 64, 78–80, 81, 150, 160, 162, 166, 168–69
Page, James, 182, 257
Page, James, Brewing Company, 182–83, 184, 186, 257; products, ix, 177, 181, 182; stock offering, 186
Paier, Frank, 235
Painter, William S., 70
Paquin, Felix, 223
Paquin, Norbert, 34, 223, 225
Park Brewing Company, 73, 91, 116, 180, 309
Parker, William, 257
Parrant, Pierre "Pigs Eye," xii, 15, 179
Pasteur, Louis, 8, 75
pasteurization, 75
Pavek, Joseph, 61, 303
Paws of Refreshment: The Story of Hamm's Beer Advertising (Harris), 162, 169
Peddler Grove, 203

Penn, William, xi, 14
Peoples Brewing Co. (Duluth, Minnesota), xiii, 110, 134, 140, 146, 150, 219–20
Pepin Lake Brewing Co. (or Brewery) (Montgomery), 258, 260
Perchal & Bazil, 260
Perham, Minnesota, 53–55, 273
Peschak, Joe, 234
Peter Schroeder Brewing Co. *See* Northern Pacific Brewing Co.; Schroeder, Peter
Peters, Ferdinand, 212, 213
Petersen, Nic, 73–74, 243
Peterson, J. O., 255
Peterson, P. L., 203
Pete's Wicked beers, 173, 175, 179, 183
Pexa, Frank, 258, 259
Pfaudler Vacuum Fermentation Company, 9
Pfeffer, Joseph, 233
Pfeiffer, Jacob, 283, 284
Pfeiffer, John, 283–84
Pfeiffer Brewing Company (Detroit, Michigan), 164–65, 290. *See also* Associated Brewing Company; Schmidt, Jacob, Brewing Co.
Pfister & Waller, 284
Philadelphia, Pennsylvania, 15
Phillips, John C., 257
Piemeisel, John, 235, 261, 269
Pierre Bottineau Community Library, 249
Pig's Eye beer, xii, 178, 179
Pilsen (Plzeň), Czech Republic, 2, 15
pilsner (pilsener), 15, 178
Pine City, Minnesota, 45, 273
Pine Island, Minnesota, 206, 245, 273–74
Pint, Matt, Jr., 62
pint clubs, 314
Pittsburg Brewery. *See* Hamm, Theo., Brewing Co.
Pittsburgh, Pennsylvania, 17, 88
Pitzl, Anna, 128, 261
Pitzl, Mathias, 50, 94, 120, 261
Pitzl, Norberg, 120
Plagens, Sig, 179
Plaisted, Edward, 203
Plaisted, W. B., 203
playing cards: from breweries, 51, 162
Plotzer, Michael, 233
Polish immigrants, 202
pony keg. *See* kegs: sizes of
porter, 9, 36, 69, 295
postcards, 83, 243
potatoes, 142, 158

Potosi, Wisconsin, 51
Prairie du Chien, Wisconsin, 306
Prairie Street Brewery (Milwaukee, Wisconsin), 232
Preiser and Codletz, 212
Preiss & Eickmann, 274
Preiss & Wimmer (Brewing Co.), 228, 285
Premier Brewing Co., 50, 226–27
Presbyterians, 99
Preston, Minnesota, 28, 180, 274
Preston Bottling Co., 64
Priestly, Joseph, 8
Prince Albert, Saskatchewan, 239
Princeton, Minnesota, 274
Pritchard, W. W., 227
prohibition, 109–21; brewers' responses to, 110, 112, 115–21, 139; enforcement, 24, 120–21, 207, 221; exceptions, 121; legislation, 112, 115; in Minnesota, 115–21; regional variations in, 104–5; repeal of, 121; violations of, 119–20, 244, 261, 274. *See also* temperance; *individual breweries*
Prohibition Party, 109
Puerto Rico: exports to, 143
Pulkrabek, Charles, 204
pure food and drug laws, 109–110
Purity Brewing Co., 110, 253–54; saloons, 108, 254
Putnam, John, 295
Putnam & Dexter, 295

Q

Quakers, 99
quarter-barrel. *See* kegs: sizes of

R

radio program sponsorships, 150, 152, 174, 187
Radly, Frank, 237, 261
Rahr, William, 4
Rahr Malting Co., 3–4
rail cars, refrigerated, 78, 143
railroads, 60, 196; effect on breweries, 37–40, 42–43, 233; shipments on, 45–46, 142, 143
Rainier Brewing Company (San Francisco, California), 160
Ramsdale, Joseph, 305
Ramsey, Alexander, 31
Ramsey, O. P., 204

Rank, John, 249
Rapham & Pavek, 303
Rappold, Chris, 283
rathskellers, 58, 113, 114
Rausch, Charles, 288
Raymond, Rod, 312
Raywood & Lennon, 298
Reads Landing, 28, 33, 42, 43, 236, 274–75
real ale, 8, 171–72, 189. *See also* beer: styles; cask-conditioned ales
Red Lake Falls, Minnesota, 214, 275
Red Lake Falls Brewing Co., 275
Red Wing, Minnesota, 14, 24, 36, 39, 81, 210, 275–79
Red Wing Brewing Co., 14, 24, 118, 133, 139, 275–76
Red Wing (Food) Products Co., 118, 276
Redwood Falls, Minnesota, 23, 209, 279; temperance in, 101
refrigeration, mechanical (artificial), 66–69; advantages of, 67–68; in breweries, 67–68, 84; in homes, 134, 148; use of anhydrous ammonia in, 68, 268
Regal Supreme beer, 140, 219, 220, 241
Reichel, Robert, 305
Reichow, Herman, 295
Reichow, William, 295
Reidinger, Charles, 236
Reimer, John H., 295
Reinheitsgebot (Beer Purity Law), 1–2, 4, 182
religion: and temperance, 98–100
Remelly & Thiery, 285
Remmler, Adolph, 276, 277–78
Remmler, Otto, 278
Remmler Brewing Co., 6, 8, 115, 210, 276, 277–78
Renz, F. A., 288
repeal of prohibition. *See* prohibition: repeal of
Rex beer, 119, 217
Rheingold Brewing Co. (Los Angeles, California), 160
Rice Lake, Wisconsin, 230, 239
Richardson, Blake, 313, 314, 315
Richmond, Minnesota, 279
Richter, August, 260
Richter, Ben, 260
Richter, Edward, 258–59, 260
Richter, George, 260
Richter Bros. & Hug, 260
Richter-Washa Brewing Co., 260
Riedel, George, 274

Rifakes, Carol, 192
Rifakes, Pete, 192
Ritter, Joseph, 232
Rochester, Minnesota, 24, 36, 49, 56–57, 80–81, 279–83, 315
Rock Bottom Brewery, 190, 313
Roelke, Bros., 295
Roemer, Frank, 222, 261
Roemer, Jim, 222
Roemer, John, 62, 222
Rohner, Gebhardt, 239
Rolette, Joseph, 22
Rollingstone, Minnesota (city), 258
Rollingstone, Minnesota (township), 257, 258
Roos, George, 274
Roos, Jacob, 274
Roosevelt, Franklin Delano, 113, 121, 123, 128, 131, 143
Root River Brewery, 233
Rosen's Bar and Grill, 313
Roseville, Minnesota, 315
Rosie's Ale beer, 192, 193, 315
Rother and Manske, 245, 246
Rouch (brewer in Chaska, Minnesota), 211
Rowe (proprietor, North Mississippi Brewery), 288
Royal Bohemian/Royal 58 beer, 218–19
RSP Architects, 180, 249
Ruckhaber, Benjamin, 275
Rush, Benjamin, 98–99
Rush City, Minnesota, 283
Rush City Brewing Co., 59, 283
Rushford, Minnesota, 38, 49, 283–84
Rybak, Mathias, 261
rye, 142

S

saccharometers, 26
Saile, Charles, 33, 229, 230, 275
St. Anthony, Minnesota, 13, 18–20, 28, 97, 246–51
St. Boniface, Manitoba, 119, 214, 239
St. Charles, Minnesota, 284
St. Cloud, Minnesota, 33, 191, 211, 284–86, 315
St. Cloud Brewing Co., 139, 285, 286
St. Croix Brewing Company (1877), 301
St. Croix Brewing Company (1994–present), 183, 184, 245
St. John's, Manitoba, 295
St. Joseph, Minnesota, 34, 286

St. Louis, Missouri, 20, 34, 49, 88, 244. *See also* Anheuser-Busch Brewing Co.

St. Louis Park, Minnesota, 315

St. Mary's University (Winona, Minnesota), 307

St. Michael, Minnesota, 286

St. Paul, Minnesota, 13, 15, 17–18, 34, 164; breweries in, 285–96, 315–16; brewing industry conditions in, 28, 84, 143; temperance and prohibition in, 98, 112

St. Paul Brewing Co., 289

St. Paul Malt & Ale Co., 295

St. Peter, Minnesota, 23, 24, 297–98

St. Vincent, Minnesota, 298

sake, 1

Salem, Frederick W., 197

Saloon Brewing Co., 184

saloons: bottling beer, 74; as brewery customers, 45; brewery ownership of, 106–9, 160; furnishings and interiors, 105–7; licenses, 104, 107–9, 112; location, 107, 108–9; as part of brewery, 104, 106, 234, 269, 279; as social center, xi, 70, 105–6; and social ills, 43, 103–6, 107, 108–9, 148

Samuel Adams beers, 183

Sanborn fire insurance maps, 67

Sand Creek, Minnesota. *See* Jordan, Minnesota

Sandstedt, F. G., 219

Sandstone, Minnesota, 87–88, 255–56

Sandusky, Ohio, 238

San Francisco, California, 151

Sargl, Michael, 212–13

Saudi Arabia: exports to, 291

Sauk Centre, Minnesota, 298

Sauk Rapids, Minnesota, 298

Sauk Rapids Brewing Co., 298

Scandia Bottling, 219

Scandinavian immigrants, 97

Schade's Brewers Handbook, 197

Schaefer, George, 284

Schaller, Jacob, 229

Schaller, Michael, 229

Schatz-Brau Brewery Co., 128–29, 246

Scheibel, Jim, 179

Schell, Adolph, 264

Schell, August, xi, 263–64; residence, 93, 264

Schell, August, Brewing Company, viii, 12, 44, 60, 67, 105, 177–78, 232, 263–67; brewery, 9, 30, 34, 35, 180; contract brewing, 173, 182, 183, 266–67; craft beers, 178, 183, 266–67; employees, 27, 132, 264; museum, 51, 267; products, 96, 111, 117, 135, 178; sponsorships, 156. *See also* Grain Belt beer

Schell, Otto, 111, 264

Schell, Theresa, 264

Schellhas, William, 83

Schellhas, William (Brewing Co.), 34, 70, 308–9; depots of, 82; in Utah, 82–83. *See also* Becker & Schellhas

Schell's Border Batch (BCCA chapter), 50

Schell's Hobo Band, 266

Schell's Park, 264

Schewing, George, 212

Schiek's Restaurant, 106

Schillinsky (drum major at Fort Snelling), 17

Schindler, M., 284, 285

Schlenk, George, 295–96

Schlitz, Joseph, Brewing Company (Milwaukee, Wisconsin), 9, 53–54, 78, 150, 160, 169, 215, 216, 266

Schmahl, Jacob (Schmall), xi, 23–24, 28, 209–10, 279, 303

Schmahl, Julius, 24

Schmasse, August, 264, 309

Schmid, Henry, 26, 119, 218

Schmidt, Jacob, 289, 292, 294

Schmidt, Jacob, Brewing Co., 2–3, 289–91; advertising, 118, 122, 150, 166; brewery and construction, 51, 58, 91, 180; employees, 131, 143, 155, 165; finances, 164–66; marching band, 156; marketing, 159; packages, 71, 122, 149, 289; products, vii, 51, 118, 122, 129, 146, 159, 165–66, 171; during Prohibition, 118, 120; sales range, 129; scenic cans, vii, 165; during wartime, 142, 143. *See also* City Club Beer; Heileman, G., Brewing Company; Minnesota Brewing Company (St. Paul); Pfeiffer Brewing Company; Stahlmann, Christopher, Brewing Co.

Schmidt, John C., 236, 237

Schmidt, John E., 237

Schmidt, Nicholas, 261

Schmitt, Christian, 205

Schmitt, Mathias, 205

Schmucker, Joseph, 57, 262

Schmucker, Joseph, Brewing Co., 262, 263

Schnagl, Anna, 245

Schnagl, Ferdinand, 214, 245, 283

Schnagl, John George, 245

Schnitz, John P., 246

Schoepf, Christopher, 229

Schon & Schnitzius City Cooperage, 29

Schorn, James, 241

Schottmuller, Frank, 302

Schottmuller, Joseph, 302

Schroeder, Louis, 283

Schroeder, Peter, 53–54, 215, 239, 273

Schueller, Bernard, 300

Schulz, William, 238

Schulz & Kaiser, 261

Schumann, Otto, 245

Schumann, William, 120, 245

Schuster, Frederick W., 280–81

Schuster, Henry, Jr., 280–81

Schuster, Henry, Sr., 56, 92, 279–80

Schuster, Mrs. Henry, 113

Schuster, Josephine, 279

Schuster & Joest, 66, 279

Schuster Brewing Co., 59, 75, 81, 83, 116–17, 279–82; depots, 80, 82; exports of, 82; malt tonic, 64, 82, 83; purchases by, 49; saloons, 107

Schutz, Peter, 235–36

Schutz & Hilgers Jordan Brewery, 12, 180, 235–36; closing, 145, 236; as Schutz & Kaiser, 67, 235. *See also* Mankato Brewing Company

Schwartz, Albertina, 222

Schwartz, John, 222

Schwartz, Peter, 222

Schwartzhoff, Adolf (Schwarzhoff), 208

Schwebach, Philip, 209

Schweitzer, Ullrich, 291

Scotten, George, 294

Seabiscuit, 250

Seberger, Peter, 284

Sedlmayr, Gabriel, 15

Seeger, William, 297

Setzer, Frederick E., 295

Setzer, Frederick O., 295

Shakopee, Minnesota, 4, 24, 28, 58–59, 298–300, 316

Shannon Kelly's, 190, 315

Sheehy, John, 258

Sheeran and Filler, 223

Sheffield, S. A., 225

Shelley's Wood Roast, 182

Sherlock's Home, ix, 189–90, 314

Shimek, Joseph, 206

Sibley, Henry, 14

Siebel Institute of Technology (Brewing Academy), 27, 258, 315

Sierra Nevada Brewing Company (Chico, California) 181

signs: indoor, 2, 51, 138, 163, 224, 286; neon, 153, 218, 225; outdoor, 44, 118, 151
Silver Lake, Minnesota, 229, 300
Silver Lake Brewing Co., 300
Silver Spray beverage, 119, 216
Sinclair, Upton, 110
Sinderman, August, 209
Sioux Uprising. *See* Dakota War of 1862
six-pack: introduction of, 149; styles of, 149, 172, 175, 185
Skreypek, Theodore, 207
Slaby, Joseph, 239
Slappi, Joseph, 287
Sleepy Eye, Minnesota, 180, 300
Slosberg, Pete, 183
Slow Food Movement, 173
Smales, Gideon Smales, 36, 222
small beer, 5, 215. *See also* beer: styles
Smith (brewer in Preston), 274
Smith, Adam: *The Wealth of Nations*, 47
Smith, John H., 53, 209, 215
Smith, Martin, 219
Smith, Peter, 230
Smith, R., & Bro., 282
Smraker, John, 228
Sobriety Company, 118, 119, 120, 217–18
soft drinks: as alternative to beer, 117, 159; bottled by breweries, 219, 224, 225, 265, 266, 293, 307, 308
Somers & Lint, 274
Sommer, Franz, 276
Sommers & Ibach, 28, 274
Sons of Temperance, 103
Soulek Bros., 260
South Dakota: exports to, 62, 270–71; Granite City in, 191; imports from, 62; label requirements in, 138; prohibition in, 97
Spier, Christian, 215
Spring Grove, Minnesota, 300
spring water. *See* water
Stag beer, 179, 219, 241
Stahlmann, Christopher, 33–34, 252, 289
Stahlmann, Christopher, Brewing Co., 16, 33–34, 66, 71, 289; bottled beer, 277; products, production, 28, 33, 35. *See also* Schmidt, Jacob, Brewing Co.
Standard Brewing Co. (Mankato, Minnesota), 87, 243–44
Stanley and Albert, 151. *See also* Minneapolis Brewing Company: advertising
steam beer, 75, 174
steamboats, 14, 58

steam brewing. *See* pasteurization
steam power, 54, 75. *See also individual breweries*
Steffen, Anton, 231, 300
Steffen, Balthazar, 231, 232
Steffen Brewing Co., 300
Stein, Bill, 51
Stelzer, George, 298
Stelzer, Jacob, 298
Stelzer, Philip, 298
Stenger, Adam, 26, 36, 56–57, 283
Stevens Point Brewery (Stevens Point, Wisconsin), viii, 183, 186, 257
Stillwater, Minnesota, 13, 21, 300–302, 316
Stite. *See* Gluek Brewing Company (Minneapolis): Stite
stock: sales of, 54, 186
Storz Brewing Company (Omaha, Nebraska), 164
stout, 37, 187, 222. *See also* beer: styles
Stradcutter, Bernard, 205
Strauch, Adolph, 204
Strauch & Ginsberg, 204
Striegel, John, 233
strikes, 71–72, 143–44, 159
Stroh Brewing Co. (Detroit, Michigan), 168; St. Paul plant, 168–69. *See also* Hamm, Theo., Brewing Co.
Strunk, Herman H., 298–99
Stumpp, Frank, 207
Stutrud, Mark, 182, 296–97
Stuttgart, Germany, 212
styles, of beer. *See* beer: styles
Subak, Laura, 193, 315
Sugar Loaf Brewery, 307–8
Summit Brewing Company, 7, 11, 90, 182, 183, 186–87, 296–97
Sundbeck, Arvid, 253
Surly Brewing Co., 187, 208
Swanson, J. A., 255
Swede Hollow (St. Paul), 92
Swedish immigrants, 234, 278
Swedish Movement Cure Institute, 256
Sweeney's Saloon, 173, 177, 184
Swift, Howard, 162
Swingler, Anton, 205
Swiss immigrants, 206
Swistowisz, Walter, 245

T
Taft, William Howard, 271
tap handles, 146
Taps Waterfront Brewery, ix, 188, 313
taverns, 127, 134–35, 148. *See also* saloons
taxation, 32–33, 72–73, 127, 139, 140–41, 159; effect on profits, 32–33, 139; enforcement, 23, 32, 72–73, 194, 297, 301; of microbreweries, 181–82; rates, 32, 127, 139, 145; records, 197–98; stamps, 32, 194, 198, 308; by states, 160, 293; tax-paid withdrawals, 5. *See also individual breweries*
Taylor's Falls, Minnesota, 302
television, 150, 308
temperance, 97–104; advocates (drys), 23, 97, 121, 207, 305; and anti-ethnic opinion, 22; campaigns, 22–23, 234, 301; circumvention of laws, 56; legislation, 22–23; in Minnesota, 22–23, 60, 97–98; opponents (wets), 23, 305, 318n1–12; during World War II, 139. *See also* prohibition
Tepass, Herman, 22, 300
Tepass, Susannah. *See* Burkhard, Susannah
Terry & Walter, 275
Texas: exports to, 154
Theimer, Emil, 52, 222
Thompson, David, 316
Thompson, George, 229
Thompson, S., 283
Thoreson, John, 202
3.2 percent beer. *See* beer: 3.2 percent
three-tier system, 124. *See also* distributors
Thune, Dave, 179
tied house saloons. *See* saloons: brewery ownership of
Tivoli (New Ulm, Minnesota), 57, 262
Tjerneld, John, 257
Toberer, John C., 267
Tobin, Daniel, 143
Tolliver, Charles, 206–7
Tolliver, Westwood, 206
Tonnis, Bryon, 313
Torah, Minnesota. *See* Richmond, Minnesota
Tower, Minnesota, 302–3
Towgood, Kathleen A., 203
Towgood, Walter A., 203
Town Hall Brewery, 9, 192, 193, 313–14
Townsend, Edward C., 205
Trader & Trapper, 315
Trausch, Joseph, 245–46
Traveling Men's Liberty League, 112, 113
Traverse des Sioux, Minnesota, 23–24, 303

trays, serving, 91, 232
Treasure Cave, Inc., 223
Troost, Fred, 59, 282
Troost, Henry, 283
Trout, Conrad, 242
Troyer, Dominick, 291
Tschirgi, Mathew, 17
Turners, 257
Tyranena Brewing Company (Lake Mills, Wisconsin), 185, 257

U

Udermann, Valentine, 284, 285
Ulmer, George, 33, 49, 52, 210
Ulmer, M. (Michael), 229–30, 275
Ulmer beer, 177
Unden, Charles, 217
Unger, Richard, 14–15
unions. *See* brewery employees: unionization of
United Brewers Industrial Foundation (UBIF), 139
United Brewery Workmen of America, 95, 116
United States Brewers Association (USBA), 32, 112, 139
United States Brewers Foundation (USBF), 148
United States Census, 24–25, 28, 198
Upham, A. T., 295

V

Vail, P. R., 303
van Etten, I., 295
Van Munching, Philip, 172
van Wie, Mark, x, 316
Van Wieren, Dale, 197
Veith, A. F. (Fred), 237, 271–72, 297–98
Veith, Fritz, 271
Veseli (Wesley), Minnesota, 61, 303
Vesterheim Norwegian-American Museum, 14
Vietor, Gustav, Jr., 283
Vietor, Gustav, Sr., 283
Vill, Oswald, 258
Vill, Otto, 34, 257–58
Vine Park Brewing, 316
Virginia Brewing Co., 91, 303, 304
Vitrolite corner signs, 118
Vittorio's, 316
Voelke, J., 275
Volk, Carl, 40, 41, 202

Volkert, George, 241
Vollbrecht, Emil, 238
Volstead, Andrew, 115
Volstead Act, 115, 120, 123. *See also* prohibition

W

Wabasha, Minnesota, 275, 304
Wachsmuth, Fred, 260
Waconia, Minnesota, 33, 34, 212, 304
Wadena, Minnesota, 213, 304–5
Wadena Brewing Co. 305
Wagenheim, Steve, 191
Wagner (brewer in Austin, Minnesota), 204
Wagner, John, 15
Wagner, Philip, 209
wagons. *See* delivery wagons
Wahl & Henius American Brewing Academy, 8, 26–27
Waldon, Sandy, 186, 270
Walker, Ryan, 191
Wally the Beerman, 178
Walter, August, 214, 275
Walter, Carlus, 121, 168
Walter, Julia, 214
Waltham, John, 284
Walty, Gottlieb, 275
Walz, A., 261
Walz, Alphonse, 259
War Food Administration (WFA), 139–40, 142
War Labor Board (WLB), 143
War Production Board (WPB), 141
wartime restrictions. *See* Korean War; World War I; World War II
Waseca, Minnesota, 38, 305; and temperance, 101, 305
Waseca Brewing Co., 305
Washa, John, 260
Washington, George, xi, 14
water, 1–3, 160; public taps at breweries, 2–3; spring water, 212
Water Tower Brewing Company, 190, 312–13
Watertown, Minnesota, 305
Waukesha Springs Imperial Brewing Co. (Waukesha, Wisconsin), 78, 79
Waverly, Minnesota, 305
WCTU (Woman's Christian Temperance Union), 103, 115
Weber, Claudius, 213, 279
Weber, Nick, 285
Wegener, Rudolph, 41, 202, 318n2–12
Wegener, Rudolph, Brewing Co., 202–3

Weid, Nicholas, 283
Weihenstephan Brewery (Bavaria, Germany), 26
Weile, Rudolph, 202
Weinand, Frank, 204
Weisbrod, Jacob, 307
Weisel, Jacob, 204
Weisner and Wrede, 246
Weiss, Ernst, 286
Weiss, George, 286
Weiss, John, 279
weiss beer (weisse, weizen), 178, 252. *See also* beer: styles
Welch, Peter, 241–42
Wellington's Pub & Grill. *See* Backwater Brewing Company
Wells, Fargo & Company Express, 38
Wenner, Herman, 270
Wermerskirchen, Peter, 304, 305
West Albany, Minnesota, 306
West End Malt Ale Co., 219
Western Brewer (journal), 27, 197
West Newton, Minnesota, 306
Westphal, Herman A., 253
wets. *See* temperance: opponents
Wetzig, Robert, 233
Whale Brand ales and soft drinks, 88, 255, 256
wheat, 4, 52, 142, 252
wheat beer. *See* weiss beer
Wheeler, Wayne B., 109, 115
whiskey, 98
White, Thomas, 221
White & Jarvis, 221
Whitman, Albert, 162
Wichman, John, 245
Wichman and Gartner, 245
Wiedemann, George, 262
wild rice, 182, 192, 257
Wilhelm, G. W., 257
Wilkommen (Noerenberg residence), 252
Williamson, Jeff, 297
Willmar, Minnesota, 306
Wilson, Woodrow, 113
Windolph, Anton, 211
Winker, Andrew, 293, 298, 299
Winker, Mary, 234, 299
Winona, Minnesota, 34, 68, 120–21, 124, 306–9, 316
Winter Carnival, St. Paul, 162
Winters, H. & Co., 272

Wisconsin: breweries in, 195; exports to, 151, 209, 277; imports from, viii, 20, 54, 64, 77–82; temperance in, 97. *See also individual Wisconsin breweries*

Wisconsin Glass Co., 78

Wise, Charles, 236

Wise, Edward, 225, 236

Wolf, Fred, 91

Wolf, George, 241, 242

Wolf, Joseph, Co. 86, 241, 301, 302

Wolf, Martin, 301

Wolf, Tanner & Co., 301

Wolf & Lehle, 264

Woman's Christian Temperance Union, 103, 115

women: and beer, 148, 158, 238–39, 246, 259; as brewers or brewery owners, 21, 118, 244–45; as brewery employees, 71–72, 133, 142–43; and temperance, 22–23, 103. *See also individual breweries*

Wood, Lawson, 153

World War I, 113, 265

World War II: contributions by breweries, 139–41; conservation, 236; effects on breweries, 51, 137, 142–45, 147, 158, 259; government requirements, 139–40, 145

wort, 5, 250, 309, 315. *See also* brewing process

Worthington, Minnesota, 234

Wurm, Conrad, 293, 294

Wurm, Johanna, 294

Wurm & Winker, 293

Wykowski, Herman, 267

Y

Yaeger, Charles, 230

Yaeger & Borser, 229, 230

Yager, Fred, 274

Yakima Brewing and Malting Co. (Yakima, Washington), 188

Yarusso, Frank, 66

yeast, 1, 8, 9, 13, 75

Yoerg, Anthony, xi, 17–19, 287

Yoerg, Louis, 287

Yoerg Brewing Co., 28, 66, 287–88; employees, 131, 143, 287; finances, 144, 288; origins, 17–19; production, 35; products, 137

Yoerg Milk Company, 287

Young, Henry, 211

Young America, Minnesota, 309

Youngstrom Bros., 257

Z

Zadro, Attilio, 130

Zahler, Anton, 252

Zahler, Joseph, 286

Zahler, Michael, 33, 286, 304

Zaiser, John, 207, 225

Zertler, Fred, 285

Zimmerman & Featherston, 275, 276

Zumalweiss beer, 119

DOUG HOVERSON is a history teacher at Saint Thomas Academy in Mendota Heights, Minnesota. He is the associate editor of *American Breweriana Journal,* a bimonthly periodical of brewery history and advertising. He is an award-winning homebrewer and a certified beer judge.